LABORATORY ANIMAL HANDBOOKS 8

ANIMAL ANAESTHESIA

By

C. J. GREEN, Ph.D., B.Vet.Med., M.R.C.V.S.

1979

LONDON

LABORATORY ANIMALS LTD

Published by
LABORATORY ANIMALS LTD
LONDON

Printed in Great Britain by Spottiswoode Ballantyne Ltd.
Colchester and London

CONTENTS

PREFACE

The Laboratory Animal Science Association has long recognized the need for a handbook on the anaesthesia of animals used in biomedical research. Originally, it was intended to deal only with the few species commonly described as 'laboratory animals' but it was soon realized that this would leave out whole classes of animal in which investigations are made. It was decided that even field studies requiring chemical restraint and immobilization could properly come within the scope of this text. Notes—many necessarily brief—are therefore included on the restraint of a wide range of species, including zoo and exotic animals, so that the reader can at least be directed toward the key literature on the subject.

The text has been written with the needs of both the biological investigator and the veterinarian in mind. The first eight chapters are intended to provide guidance on the principles of anaesthetic management, laying particular emphasis on the way normal physiology is modified by the administration of drugs acting on the nervous system. Some readers—perhaps the majority—need only a superficial introduction to general principles, and for them the first chapter will be enough. Others require information about management during really sophisticated investigations in which the physiological status is continuously monitored—hence, in Chapter 8 an attempt is made to introduce the reader to electrocardiography and other monitoring techniques.

No attempt has been made to describe all the drugs which have been used for animal anaesthesia in the past—apart from anything else, many have been withdrawn for commercial reasons, and it is likely that the range of agents available for animal use will soon contract still further as these become uneconomic to supply to such a limited market. Others have such severe disadvantages that they were considered unworthy of inclusion—however, where agents are known to be in common use in laboratories in spite of their poor performance, they have been described in detail and their unwanted side-effects highlighted. The pharmacology of the remainder is described in a set pattern for easy reference and to emphasize the need to consider the effects if any on the cardiopulmonary and other systems.

The second half is intended as a straightforward recipe book. The literature relevant to each group of animal is reviewed, and from this information and experience in our own laboratory, I have attempted to distil a guide to the best ways of restraining and anaesthetizing the animals in order of personal preference. Although this approach may appear dogmatic, it was considered more helpful than offering a bewildering choice of agents or techniques without stating the advantages and disadvantages of each. Many with experience will disagree with my choice but at least newcomers to the problems will have been given a starting point from which to make their own assessment. A glossary of commonly used terms, abbreviations and symbols is included to help those unfamiliar with anaesthetic jargon. Finally, in such a short text, I have made no attempt to rival existing textbooks on veterinary anaesthesia, but hope by including a large and up-to-date bibliography to inform readers of recent developments and to stimulate an interest in the comparative aspects of anaesthesia.

C. J. Green
Division of Comparative Medicine
MRC Clinical Research Centre
Northwick Park
Middlesex

ACKNOWLEDGEMENTS

Too many people have contributed to the genesis of this text to name all of them individually. Of my colleagues at the Clinical Research Centre, I am particularly grateful to Dr C. R. Coid for continuous encouragement; to Mr J. Cooper for many discussions about the anaesthesia of birds and reptiles; to Dr M. Halsey for advice about the pharmacology of drugs and mechanisms of anaesthetic action; to Dr M. Cross for providing helpful notes on electronic monitoring equipment; to my assistants, Mrs S. Precious and Mrs A. Palmer, who carried out many of the anaesthetic trials in different animals; to Miss M. Smith who has typed the script; and to Miss Jenny Wade and her colleagues in the Library who traced and checked nearly 1500 references. Many of the illustrations were done by students of the Middlesex Polytechnic whilst working in the Department of Medical Illustration.

Dr P. Lees, Reader in Pharmacology at the Royal Veterinary College, London, went to endless trouble to suggest improvements in the factual content, and allowed me to quote his notes on the classification of drugs acting on the central nervous system. Mr J. M. Hime and Mr D. Jones, veterinarians to the Zoological Society of London, have both provided valuable suggestions on the chemical restraint of exotic species, and their written contributions to new developments in this field have provided much of the source material in this text. Mr R. Medd of the Huntingdon Research Centre was helpful in describing many techniques for anaesthetizing primates and rodents during experimental surgery. Not least I am indebted to Mr P. N. O'Donoghue, who has edited the text and offered literary and factual criticism which has always been most helpful.

Finally, I wish to acknowledge my debt to the excellent textbooks of Hall (1971), Lumb & Jones (1973) and Eger (1974). From the number of references made to these works it will become clear that they have provided the framework for this handbook. Similarly, I have used much of the biological data collected together by Altman & Dittmer (1961; 1964; 1974), and freely adapted that information in the light of recent evidence and experience in our own laboratory to produce simplified data tables. Wherever possible due reference to original sources has been made and any omissions are unintentional.

GENERAL PRINCIPLES

WELFARE OF THE ANIMAL AND SAFETY OF PERSONNEL

The anaesthetic management of experimental animals presents a number of special problems. Perhaps the greatest difficulty is encountered in selecting agents which cause minimal interference to the experiment and interpretation of data, yet provide humane restraint and suppress perception of noxious stimuli. The nature of the surgical procedure and the duration of anaesthesia anticipated will also be important considerations. For example, it may be necessary to anaesthetize a number of small animals simultaneously for a short period of time knowing that the procedure can be completed quickly under light surgical anaesthesia. At the opposite extreme, it may be necessary to maintain stable anaesthesia for long periods up to 24 hours and expect the animals to survive at the end.

These difficulties will be discussed in detail later in this text but it is necessary to stress at the outset that the humane treatment of the experimental animal and the safety of personnel take precedence over all other considerations when selecting the anaesthetic protocol. Most important must be the provision of adequate analgesia with drugs which decrease or suppress the perception of painful stimuli. Secondly, humane restraint should be applied. Environmental adaptation, gentle handling and the use of modern sedative drugs are important in minimizing apprehension and stress, as well as protecting animals from involuntary excitement and possible injury during anaesthetic induction and recovery. Finally, when exposing personnel to potential risks, we should consider the best ways of avoiding injury from bites, scratches or kicks; the possible toxicity of volatile agents in poorly ventilated laboratories; and the risk of accidental or deliberate self-injection with potentially lethal agents or dangerous drugs of addiction.

AVAILABLE TECHNIQUES

Full surgical anaesthesia involves analgesia, decreased perception of other external stimuli, suppression of reflex activity and loss of skeletal muscle tone. These may be accompanied by varying degrees of central depression of the central nervous system (CNS). For example, during general anaesthesia, the animal is rendered unconscious, and analgesia and muscular relaxation develop as CNS depression becomes more profound—depending on the agent used. However, surgical conditions can be obtained in other ways, for example by merely sedating the animal to depress central sensory and motor activity, and interfering with pain transmission at a local level by injecting drugs adjacent to the surgical site. Clearly, there is no point in attempting to satisfy all the above criteria for full surgical anaesthesia if a safer technique is satisfactory. As a general proposition analgesia is always necessary, humane restraint (physical or chemical) is usually needed, but muscular relaxation is often not essential. The aim should be to maintain the lightest level of CNS depression possible.

Many drugs act synergistically or additively on the CNS so that the dose rate of each agent can often be reduced thus decreasing the risk of toxicity. This concept of administering a combination or succession of agents with the object of maintaining the lightest degree of CNS depression and, at the same time, ensuring low mortality and minimal stress—*balanced anaesthesia*—is of obvious value to the experimentalist.

A range of agents is available to satisfy these requirements, and can be used singly or in combination.

Local analgesics (local anaesthetics)
Surface application by spray, drops or ointments.

Infiltration by injection around a lesion or discrete area, or by injection around a whole field taking account of the fan-like spread of nerve fibres.

Regional nerve block, where the drug is injected immediately around a specific nerve trunk.

Spinal nerve block, where the drug is deposited into the vertebral canal to block post-thoracic areas of the animal.

Centrally acting analgesics
These drugs are given parenterally, and are potent suppressors of central pain perception.

General central depressants
Sedatives, tranquillizers (ataractics) and hypnotics which, in safe doses, do not usually produce profound depression of the CNS.

These agents may be used alone, in combination with any of the above techniques, or as adjuncts to general anaesthesia.

General anaesthetics
These can involve inhalation of gas or volatile liquid vapour; parenteral administration by the oral, rectal, intravenous, intraperitoneal, or sub-cutaneous routes of non-volatile agents; or a combination of inhalation and parenterally administered agents.

Muscle relaxants
These must always be used with extreme care in conjunction with analgesics or general anaesthetics.

Whichever technique is selected, it will inevitably interact with several biological systems. The anaesthetist can only minimize the resultant physiological deviations by exercise of his skill and by an appreciation of the interaction between drug and animal. An attempt will be made in this text to describe the principal pharmacological actions of commonly used agents, particularly their effects on cardiovascular, respiratory, renal and hepatic functions. The metabolic effects of anaesthetic agents have been reviewed by Ngai & Papper (1962) and Strobel & Wollman (1969), whilst more recently Eger (1974) and Dundee & Wyant (1974) reviewed the uptake and actions of inhalational and intravenous anaesthetic agents respectively. General considerations in the anaesthetic management of experimental animals have also been extensively discussed (Miller *et al.*, 1969; Short, 1970*a*; Short, 1970*b*; McIntyre, 1971; Purdie, 1972; Holland, 1973).

BIOLOGICAL VARIATIONS
Animals may vary in their qualitative response to a drug (for example, they may be stimulated rather than depressed) or they may show quantitative variation in dose response. A number of factors may account for such variations, including weight, age, species, strain, sex, health and nutritional status, prior exposure and adaptation, body temperature, pulmonary and cardiovascular function, and endocrinological variations associated with seasonal or circadian rhythms. As a general rule, they are related to metabolic rate, and the uptake, distribution and elimination of the drugs.

Species
Most instances of species variation are related to differences in the ratio of basal metabolic rate (BMR) to body surface area. Small mammals such as mice having a high ratio, need relatively large doses of anaesthetic. The variation in BMR is further accentuated when considering avian species or poikilothermic vertebrates. Reptiles and amphibians vary metabolic rate with environmental temperature, and are relatively resistant to hypoxia; in fact, low ambient temperature may be used as an aid to restraint since these animals are sluggish and relatively tractable during hypothermia, and

reduced metabolic rate will significantly reduce the drug dosage required to produce anaesthesia.

Birds, on the other hand, have a higher BMR than mammals of comparable mass and this is reflected in their higher body temperature (41–45°C) and rapid heart rate. Birds are particularly likely to develop cardiac arrhythmias, to become exhausted in response to stress, and to suffer from hypothermia if the integrity of the feathered integument is impaired.

Animals whose evolutionary role has been to flee from predators often show more variation in response to some anaesthetic agents than hunting species. For example, rabbits are far more difficult to anaesthetize with pentobarbitone than cats, dogs or ferrets and, in our experience, are more susceptible to cardiac arrhythmias and to acute cardiovascular failure ('shock'). This is probably associated with the release of catecholamines into the circulation in response to fear. Yet other anomalies may be related to the relatively high concentrations of hydrolysing enzymes in some species which make it impossible to present an effective anaesthetic concentration to the cells in the CNS. For example, while the potent morphine analogue fentanyl is a highly effective sedative and analgesic in rabbits, reaching its full effect within 5 min of intramuscular injection, it has very little sedative effect in guinea-pigs at comparable doses, and analgesia takes at least 15 min to develop (Green, 1975). Why morphine-like drugs should act as potent CNS depressants in rats and rabbits yet, at equianalgesic doses, produce tremors and convulsions in mice has not been satisfactorily explained. Similarly, it is difficult to explain why the dissociative anaesthetic ketamine, a valuable agent in sedating primates, birds and reptiles if given by intramuscular injection, should prove such a poor central depressant and analgesic in rats and guinea-pigs when administered by the same route.

Strain

Marked variation in dose response to anaesthetics as a result of genetic variance has been reported (Kalow, 1962; Mackintosh, 1962). The latter author showed that hybrids between two inbred strains of mice gave a more consistent response to pentobarbitone administration than did the inbred parents. Similarly, a strain sensitivity to nitrous oxide has been reported in rats (Green, 1968). Greyhounds, whippets and dalmatians are well-known to respond more to short-acting barbiturates than do many other breeds of dog; narcosis may be more profound than expected at the computed dose, and recovery may be delayed for periods up to 48 h. Some breeds of pigs are susceptible to malignant hyperthermia triggered by muscle relaxants and volatile anaesthetics (Jones et al., 1972). Strain differences probably reflect liver and plasma enzyme differences; for example, some strains of rabbit are able to break down atropine more rapidly than others because of higher plasma atropinesterase levels (Stormont & Suzuki, 1970). Genetic influence in abnormal drug responses has been discussed by Motulsky (1965).

Age and weight

Differences in response (Mann, 1965) are mainly related to changes in liver enzyme activity with age (Kato & Takanaka, 1968) and the laying down of extensive fat depots in older animals. The former influences the rate of degradation of anaesthetic agents and assumes particular importance during continuous or repeated administration of barbiturates over extended periods. Body fat, on the other hand, may take up high concentrations of thiobarbiturates only to release them again as plasma levels fall, thus presenting a potentially serious threat during the post-operative recovery period. During periods of rapid growth, changes in enzyme activity in relation to organ weight and function are also likely to influence the response to anaesthetics (Brody, 1945; Adolph, 1957). Two groups have demonstrated the limited ability of young rats and guinea-pigs to metabolize drugs to glucuronides (Lathe & Walker, 1957; Brown & Zuelzer, 1958), whilst Fouts & Adamson (1959) observed that the liver of adult rabbits was more efficient at handling hexobarbitone and chlorpromazine than that of the very young animal. Young rats and rabbits were also shown to be more sensitive than adults to pentobarbitone and ether by Weatherall (1960). A similar finding has been reported in dogs; very young animals and older adults were most sensitive to barbiturates, whilst those in the 3- to 12-month range recovered most rapidly (De Boer, 1947). Experience in this laboratory has confirmed that all rodents and rabbits are more sensitive to barbiturates and other central depressants during the first 3 weeks of life.

It can be concluded that the BMR will be lower in the young, the aged and the obese. As the basal rate falls so will the rate of detoxification, and less anaesthetic agent will be required.

Sex differences

According to Quinn et al. (1958), sex differences in dose response do not occur in rats or mice before the age of 4 weeks but they then develop quickly. Several groups have reported that female rats are more sensitive to hexobarbitone and pentobarbitone than males (Moir, 1937; Crevier et al., 1950), and this was confirmed in 2 strains of rat by

Collins & Lott (1965). Pregnant female rats were shown (Nicholas & Barron, 1932) to be more susceptible to amylobarbitone than non-pregnant females, whereas males were less susceptible than both and this was explained by a 7% higher measured BMR in the males than in the non-pregnant females. Female rats are also much more sensitive to the neuromuscular blocking activity of d-tubocurarine than males of similar age (Wolf *et al.*, 1964). Conversely, male mice were more sensitive to pentobarbitone than females according to Brown (1959) and, although Kennedy (1934) could demonstrate no sex variation in dose requirement for hexobarbitone in mice, narcosis lasted about 25% longer in males than in females in many, but not all, strains in other studies with that drug (Noordhoek & Rümke, 1969; Rümke & Noordhoek, 1969).

Health

However good the technique, anaesthesia must be recognized as a disturbance from the normal physiological state, and biological systems which are already subject to pathological change may be particularly affected. Although it is frequently taken for granted that experimental animals are healthy subjects, it cannot be stressed too strongly that this is often a false assumption based on a failure to recognize disease. Indeed, most conventionally reared animals are suffering from low-grade or sub-clinical infections. The resulting cardiopulmonary, hepatic or renal dysfunction can profoundly affect the uptake and elimination of anaesthetics.

Respiratory disease is endemic in most conventional colonies of rats, guinea-pigs, mice and rabbits, especially in older animals, The insidious onset of symptoms is difficult to detect, and gross pathological changes in the lung have usually occurred before any overt signs of disease become apparent. Similar chronic lung lesions are commonly found in pigs, sheep and calves, whilst in primates the picture is often further complicated by the presence of lung-mites and occasionally by tuberculosis. Since efficient gas exchange across the alveolar membrane is of prime importance in the anaesthetized animal, it must be clear that catarrhal exudates which obstruct the airways or lung lesions interfering with gaseous exchange will present a major danger to successful anaesthesia. The increased anaesthetic risk presented by chronic respiratory disease in rodents was emphasized by Stevenson (1964), while Paterson & Rowe (1972) obtained a significantly lower mortality during pentobarbitone anaesthesia in rats if they were obtained from a specified pathogen free (SPF) colony.

Examples of hepatic and renal insufficiency are commonly encountered. They may be associated with gross parasitism such as fascioliasis in sheep and calves, and with hepatic coccidiosis in rabbits; with bacterial and viral infections in mice, dogs and primates; with depressed ascorbic acid levels in guinea-pigs; and with fatty degeneration of the liver in small primates such as marmosets. Toxaemia and low liver glycogen reserves will depress the rate of detoxification of drugs so that much lower dosages will be required, whilst 'normal' doses may prove lethal.

Cardiovascular disease is less likely to be encountered but a combination of events may lead to failure of this system—collectively known as acute cardiovascular failure (CVF) or *shock*. The development of acute CVF during an operation has a profound and potentially lethal influence on anaesthetic administration. Not only will the metabolic rate be depressed, but poor circulation will lead to limited uptake and distribution of the drugs.

The solution to these problems is self-evident. The animals should be carefully selected before including them in an experiment. Large experimental animals must be given a thorough clinical examination. Pigs should be selected from minimal disease herds known to be free of enzootic pneumonia. Primates should be quarantined for at least 6 weeks, tested for tuberculosis, given a chest x-ray where possible and observed for any clinical symptoms developing during the quarantine period. Rats and mice should be obtained from hysterectomy-derived, barrier-maintained stock of known disease-free status. It is also important to use minimal-disease rabbits and guinea-pigs when possible, although it is often difficult to procure such animals. When the use of conventionally reared stock is unavoidable, it must be remembered that older animals almost invariably suffer from chronic respiratory disease, thus increasing the need for care at all stages of anaesthesia, not least during the post-operative recovery period.

Nutrition and diet

Both nutritional composition and the quantity of the diet fed to the animals may affect drug responses. For example, rats fed an inadequate diet developed a relative resistance to pentobarbitone administered intraperitoneally (Peters & Boyd, 1965), whilst sleeping-time was significantly extended following hexobarbitone administration if mice were previously deprived of food for 24 h (Conney & Burns, 1962). A deficiency of ascorbic acid in the diet has been said to increase the sensitivity of guinea-pigs to pentobarbitone (Beyer *et al.*, 1944). Modern husbandry practices are unlikely to produce such deficiencies—in fact, the reverse may occur. Experience in this laboratory, where rabbits and guinea-pigs are allowed continual access to a pelleted diet, has shown that animals commonly become overweight with intra-abdominal fat and are then significantly more difficult to anaesthetize in a predictable way.

The nutritional status of the animal should be considered when deciding whether or not to withhold food for 12–24 h prior to anaesthesia. An empty stomach is undoubtedly helpful to the surgeon and may be important to the experiment in other respects, but it must be remembered that low plasma glucose, mobilized liver glycogen stores and possibly altered circulating fatty acid levels may alter drug detoxification rates and hence the successful outcome of anaesthesia. This may be particularly significant in herbivores but less important in carnivores, since the metabolic rate of dogs has been shown to increase by up to 90% after a meal—the *specific dynamic effect*—and take up to 18 h to return to the BMR (Dukes, 1947). It is even more important in birds since their high BMR necessitates a high intake and turnover of food—starvation is rapidly lethal and 6 h without food prior to anaesthesia may render a small bird hypoglycaemic and dangerously sensitive to depressant drugs (Arnall, 1964).

Previous experience and adaptation

It has been shown that drug action may be potentiated in rats by earlier handling and injection (Beaton & Gilbert, 1968). It is our experience that gentle handling and adaptation to the laboratory environment reduce extremes in response to drug administration in rodents and rabbits. For example, significantly higher dosages of barbiturates and morphine analogues are needed if the animals have been startled, and this is probably because pituitary-adrenal-thyroid endocrine mechanisms have been aroused (including sympatho-adrenal stimulation) and the metabolic rate elevated.

Many groups have demonstrated that repeated administration of barbiturates, phenothiazines and sedative-analgesics leads to a non-specific tolerance (Burns et al., 1965) which may last for up to 14 days. This is due to accelerated degradation of the agents as a result of increased enzyme activity in hepatocytes, and produces a significant reduction in sleeping time; for example, the sleeping time of mice was reduced by 50% after 6 daily injections of thiopentone (Hubbard & Goldbaum, 1949).

Biological rhythms

Circadian and seasonal rhythms associated with endocrine activity controlled by the pituitary,

adrenals and gonads may explain some variation in anaesthetic drug response, particularly when laboratory schedules of husbandry have been superficially imposed on long-established internal biological 'clocks'. Cyclical rises and fall in BMR may be associated with diurnal, hibernatory or seasonal sexual behaviour. Even in laboratory mice which are adapted by selection to their artificial environment, circadian rhythms are well established. It has been shown that mice are most sensitive to pentobarbitone at about 0700 and significantly less so at mid-day (Lindsay & Kullman, 1966). Brain and pineal concentrations of 5-hydroxytryptamine have been shown to vary in a circadian manner (Snyder et al., 1967) and this may, in turn, affect neurotransmitters in the CNS. Sable-Amplis et al. (1974) have demonstrated a seasonal response to morphine administration in rabbits; in the first 3 months of the year this results in markedly depressed plasma cortisol levels, whilst in midsummer morphine increases plasma levels above normal. Circadian rhythms have even been shown to alter the minimum alveolar concentrations (MAC) of halothane and cyclopropane in rats by 5–10% (Munson et al., 1970).

ENVIRONMENTAL FACTORS

The physical conditions surrounding the animal have important implications for management before, during and after anaesthesia.

Management practices

Abnormal temperature, humidity, light and noise can each induce neuro-endocrinological disturbances which may seriously diminish the ability of the animal to cope with the additional stress of anaesthesia and surgery. The outcome may depend on which stage of the 'general adaptation syndrome' (Selye, 1950) has been reached. If the animal is anaesthetized during the alarm or adaptation stages, the investigator must be prepared to allow for changes in response to standard drug dosages, whilst if the stage of exhaustion has been approached, the anaesthetist may well provide the lethal touch.

Experience in this laboratory indicates that rodents are less stressed by low than by high environmental temperatures. Rats and rabbits exposed to high ambient temperatures (28–32°C) for several weeks have proved particularly difficult to maintain under anaesthesia for more than 2 h.

The harmful effects of noise on rodents has been extensively reviewed recently (Pfaff, 1974). Sound-induced convulsions were observed in random as well as in-bred mice (Iturrian & Fink, 1968), whilst deliberate noise administration to mice markedly increased the toxicity of sympathomimetic amines (Chance, 1947).

Changes in the social hierarchy or isolation of an animal from its peers may also produce significant physiological changes (Baer, 1971).

All animals should be allowed time for conditioning in their quarters before use in experiments. Stable environmental conditions are essential, whilst repeated gentle handling by personnel will further lessen the stress and fear when eventually anaesthesia is induced.

Management during anaesthesia

In many experiments, the investigator will wish to maintain the anaesthetized animal in as near a normal physiological state as possible. At the very least it should be a reproducible preparation. The maintenance of homeostasis (involving thermal, fluid and electrolyte balance) will have to be ensured by artificial means.

Temperature

Differences between ambient and body temperature must be minimized, since the hypothalamic heat-regulating mechanism is depressed during anaesthesia and the animal is no longer able to shiver. As rodents, small primates and small birds have extensive surface areas to their body mass, heat losses will be correspondingly greater than in bigger animals. This heat loss will be accentuated by removal of hair or feathers, and by washing prior to surgery.

Loss of heat from the respiratory tract is also important and this is not surprising if it is appreciated that the alveolar surface area is about 20 times that of the body surface; again, it is relatively greater in small animals. According to Vale (1973), heat loss via the respiratory tract in patients breathing dry gases at ambient temperature or lower is 50 kJ/hour, and Sulyok et al. (1973) showed that respiratory heat loss decreased 4-fold when the relative humidity of the environment rose from 20 to 80%.

At ambient temperatures of 22°C, we have measured rectal temperatures in mice as low as 30°C within 10 min of inducing halothane anaesthesia, and as low as 32°C within 20 min of induction in rats. Low body temperature has profound effects in modifying drug activity (Munson, 1970). For instance, pentobarbitone was more depressant and its distribution in body tissues was significantly altered, when rats and dogs were anaesthetized at an ambient temperature of 15 rather than 30°C (Setnikar & Temelcou, 1962). In rats, pentobarbitone and chlorpromazine each had a lower LD_{50} at 8 and 36°C than a 26°C, thus illustrating that hyperthermia as well as hypo-thermia enhances the toxicity of central depressant drugs (Keplinger et al., 1959).

It is concluded that a heat source should be supplied even for short anaesthetic periods. Body temperature should be monitored and maintained within the normal range. However, heated pads should be thermostatically controlled and the animal should be moved at frequent intervals to avoid the risk of thermal burns (skin lesions caused by a combination of heat and pressure at points of contact).

Fluid balance

Fluid loss is almost invariably high during anaesthesia partly because of continuous evaporation from the operation site and skin, and partly because of evaporative loss from the respiratory system where exhaled gases are often being continuously displaced by dry gases. A 3 kg rabbit can lose 100–150 g bodyweight during the course of a laparotomy operation lasting 1·5 h, even in the absence of haemorrhage. Clearly, this evaporative loss will be intimately related to heat loss. It is therefore important to supply measured volumes of fluid by iv infusion to maintain total body fluid volume, and it is preferable to humidify inspired anaesthetic gases.

Electrolyte and acid-base balance

This will be fully discussed later in the text since it is a neglected area in anaesthesia of laboratory animals. It should be noted here that fluid loss giving rise to reduced circulating volume and cardiac output, and hence decreased capillary perfusion, may in turn cause body tissues to change to anaerobic respiration with a consequent fall in plasma pH. If, at the same time, plasma oxygen tension (PaO_2) falls and carbon dioxide tension ($PaCO_2$) increases as a result of poor gas exchange in the lungs, carbonic acid is formed to excess (respiratory acidosis) and plasma pH may fall to toxic levels. A vicious circle may then be established which is difficult to reverse.

Respiratory acidosis can be avoided by adequate lung ventilation and by maintaining a flow of gases to the trachea sufficient to flush away expired CO_2. Metabolic acidosis can be prevented by maintaining total body fluid volume at normal levels and avoiding hypoxia, so that tissues are adequately perfused with blood and O_2.

Postanaesthetic management

All too often there is an exponential fall in the attention devoted to the animal as soon as the experimental procedure is completed—just when it is most at risk. The partially recovered animal may be unable to cope with its environment and can die

14

from hypothermia, respiratory obstruction, cardiovascular failure, self-inflicted injury, or from mutilation by its peers if returned to a box of conscious animals. It cannot be emphasized too strongly that skilled nursing must be maintained until the animal is fully conscious. A warm recovery box is the first essential and this must be prepared before the animal is anaesthetized. The optimum ambient temperature will vary with species but as a general guide, birds need 38°C; mice, hamsters and small primates 35°C; rats, guinea-pigs, rabbits and pigs 33°C; cats, dogs and similar carnivores recover well at 25–30°C (experience in this laboratory). This, of course, assumes that body (core) temperature is normal at the time of anaesthetic withdrawal. If the animal is allowed to become hypothermic, the metabolic rate will be correspondingly depressed and recovery may be delayed by slow detoxification of the anaesthetic agent.

Respiratory obstruction is a further hazard during the recovery period. We have observed mice, rats and primates struggle toward the corner of a cage and press their face against any available solid surface with obvious embarrassment to breathing. Winter & Flataker (1962) reported a higher mortality in rats after anaesthesia with pentobarbitone if they were allowed to recover in solid cages as compared with mesh cages, and this was attributed to airway obstruction. In addition, obstruction may be caused by relaxation of pharyngeal and tongue muscles and loss of swallowing reflexes—food may then be regurgitated and aspirated into the respiratory tract. Similarly, excessive bronchial secretions may occlude the airway. This is especially important in guinea-pigs and chinchillas which produce copious secretions, and in mice or small birds in which a single drop of mucus may block the airway. A patent airway is the primary responsibility of the anaesthetist during recovery. Attention should be paid to the position of the head and neck, and suction apparatus should be available to aspirate unwanted accumulations in the pharynx.

Most important of all, an endotracheal tube should be retained in place until chewing and swallowing reflexes have fully recovered—this serves to isolate the respiratory tract from the oesophagus and allows artificial ventilation to the instituted if necessary. Animals which have been artificially ventilated whilst under the influence of muscle-relaxant agents, barbiturates or morphine analogues need special care. Under no circumstances should intermittent positive pressure ventilation (IPPV) be withdrawn until the anaesthetist is convinced that the depressant effects of the drugs have worn off, or have been successfully reversed with specific antagonist drugs.

Most of the hazards of cardiovascular failure can be avoided if an indwelling intravenous catheter is retained in place during recovery, and if circulating blood volume is maintained by continuous infusion of fluids and plasma expanders. In the absence of monitoring equipment, an assessment should be made on clinical criteria such as quality of pulse, colour of membranes and extremities, and auscultation of the heart. When it is impracticable to infuse fluids iv as in mice and small birds, they should be administered ip or sc in carefully calculated volumes.

THE EXPERIMENTAL PROTOCOL

The requirements of the particular experiment must now be considered by the investigator. Clearly, the type and extent of surgical interference will bear significantly on the choice of anaesthetic method. Many procedures performed on rodents are brief, but management is often complicated by the need to work with groups of animals. It may be more convenient to induce anaesthesia in several animals together before starting surgery. This, and the common requirement to work without assistance, accounts for the popularity of injectable agents for use in mice and rats. Furthermore, such drugs are usually inexpensive, there is no need for special apparatus for administration, and the absence of masks allows better access to any part of the animal's head.

The requirement for drugs that do not significantly modify the normal physiology or interfere with responses of particular interest to the experiment makes an understanding of the complex drug interactions essential. Acute preparations in which the animal is anaesthetized for a long period present perhaps the greatest challenge to our skill. They are frequently needed for measuring pharmacological responses so it is particularly important that relative homeostasis is maintained.

The experimental protocol may include procedures and concurrent drug administration which interfere with metabolic rate, with the uptake and distribution of drugs, or with their mode of action by competing for receptors. For example, hyperthyroidism will increase the metabolic rate, whilst conversely, totally thyroidectomized animals will require markedly reduced doses of anaesthetic. Several antibiotics have been reported to interfere with degradation of anaesthetics; pentobarbitone narcosis was shown to be markedly prolonged by small residues of chloramphenicol (Teske & Carter, 1971), and the risks of concurrent administration of several anaesthetics with a number of different antibacterials (including polymyxin B, sulphonamides, neomycin, tetracyclines and streptomycin) have been described (Adams, 1970).

Adrenalectomy severely compromises the ability of animals to handle anaesthetic and surgical stress, so that replacement therapy with steroids is essential prior to the experiment. Several aberrant reactions have been reported as a result of ionizing radiation (Nair, 1969; Saksonov & Kozlov, 1968), although admittedly very high irradiation doses were used.

Many superficial operations can be humanely performed with adequate analgesia and chemical restraint (*neuroleptanalgesia*) without the risks of full surgical anaesthesia. If a general anaesthetic is necessary, it is preferable to administer it by inhalation or by intravenous injection so that the depth of anaesthesia can be assessed during the induction. As stated earlier, our aim must be not only to maintain the lightest degree of CNS depression during the operation, but also to restore the animal to full consciousness as rapidly as possible at the end. The judicious use of short-acting barbiturates and anaesthetic steroids is of particular value in this context, as are the specific antagonists nalorphine and levallorphan to reverse narcosis induced with morphine-like drugs.

SUMMARY OF RECOMMENDATIONS

(i) Whenever possible, assay the anaesthetic method in a limited trial before depending on it for the surgical procedures involved in the experiment.

(ii) Pay particular attention to the health of the animal before using it in an experiment.

(iii) Take as a base-line for drug selection the minimum degree of CNS depression necessary for the procedure compatible with the animals' welfare.

(iv) Consider if and to what extent the anaesthetic drugs or techniques will affect the validity of experimental results, and how they may interact with other drugs being used.

(v) Even in the absence of sophisticated equipment, make some attempt to have certain basic items available to ensure adequate pulmonary ventilation. A regulated source of O_2 should be supplied to animals, whether they are anaesthetized with inhalational or with injectable agents. An endotracheal tube should be passed whenever the occasion and size of animal allow, and aspiration suction should always be available.

(vi) Regard the conservation of heat as an integral part of anaesthetic management in all species but particularly in small mammals and birds. Operate with the animal on a thermostatically controlled surface and monitor body temperature continuously.

(vii) Administer warm, balanced salt solutions by continuous iv infusion whenever practicable and keep plasma expanders available in case of extensive haemorrhage.

(viii) Pay particular attention to post-anaesthetic nursing. Allow animals to recover in an environment approaching the normal body temperature of the species, maintain iv fluid infusions and leave an endotracheal tube in place until the swallowing reflex is fully recovered.

(ix) Consider the implications for laboratory safety.

CHAPTER TWO

PHYSIOLOGICAL CONSIDERATIONS

INTRODUCTION

The transport of oxygen, carbon dioxide and anaesthetic agents within the body, and the maintenance of homeostasis during anaesthesia will depend on the effectiveness of respiratory, cardiovascular, hepatic and renal functions. It is therefore important that the investigator should understand the interactions between these systems and how they may be modified by anaesthetic drugs. The ideal would be anaesthesia with minimal disturbance to the systems and hence also to the fluid and metabolic environment of tissues. In pursuing this ideal, it follows that fluids, acid-base and electrolyte balance should be maintained within normal limits, and that gaseous exchange and transport across cellular membranes between the cell and its external environment should proceed at approximately normal levels.

The notes on the four main systems outlined below are particularly relevant to mammals. Differences will, of course, be considerable when comparing amphibians, reptiles and birds, and these are described in notes on individual species elsewhere.

RESPIRATORY SYSTEM

Mechanical aspects

The first requirement of breathing is to supply body tissues with sufficient oxygen (O_2) for metabolism and to remove carbon dioxide (CO_2). Efficient gas exchange occurs by diffusion down a gradient from a high to a low partial pressure across the alveolar membrane of the lung only if pulmonary ventilation, perfusion of alveolar capillaries and the physical condition of the membrane are each operating within physiological limits.

Pulmonary ventilation is the physical presentation to the alveolar membrane of a suitable volume of gas containing at least 20% oxygen and is accomplished by the rhythmic expansion and contraction of the lungs. The efficiency of the process will depend on unimpeded gas flow along patent airways and on the distension of a sufficient number of alveoli. Under normal circumstances, gases first traverse the upper respiratory tract, the trachea and bronchi in which no gas exchange takes place—*anatomical dead space*—but sufficient CO_2 is exhaled to prevent rebreathing and a consequent build-up in plasma CO_2 tension. However, if the respiratory excursions are shallow, insufficient fresh gas will be inspired to dilute that portion of the previously exhaled gases still trapped in the dead space. Conversely, an animal may 'over-respire' with fast and deep excursions in which case CO_2 may be cleared too quickly, with adverse effects on acid–base balance and the cardiovascular system. In other words, it is the rate at which alveolar air is replaced by atmospheric air which is important.

In the anaesthetized animal, dead space may be increased by a constricted or flexed larynx, by the presence of excess saliva or regurgitated ingesta in the pharynx, and by excess tracheobronchial secretions. Each will diminish the laminar gas flow along the airway. In addition, old age, disease, depressed respiratory centres and bad positioning of the animal may all contribute to increasing total dead space, by decreasing the quantity of lung tissue which can usefully expand and inflate. Clearance of CO_2 may be further impeded by mechanical connections between the respiratory tract and anaesthetic equipment—*equipment dead space*—and by resistance to expiration. Continuous rebreathing of CO_2 has serious repercussions which are discussed later.

Assuming that the lungs are well ventilated with sufficient concentrations of O_2, inadequate gas exchange may still result from increased *alveolar dead space*. Poor capillary blood flow over the alveoli (pulmonary perfusion) associated with low blood pressure and cardiac output, lung collapse, haemorrhagic shock or arterio–venous shunting, will seriously impair the rate of exchange. Similarly, the alveolar membrane may be rendered inefficient by chronic fibrosis or by catarrhal exudates impeding the passage of gases and anaesthetic vapours.

It follows that minimizing equipment dead space during inhalational anaesthesia, and minimizing resistance to expiration at all times, should be considered by the anaesthetist in planning the protocol. A patent airway should be established by passing an endotracheal tube or performing a tracheotomy whenever practicable, and adequate gas flows with high O_2 concentrations should be supplied. If spontaneous respiration is inadequate, intermittent positive pressure ventilation (IPPV) should be employed at carefully calculated rates and tidal volume after considering the respiratory characteristics of the animal (Kleinman & Radford, 1964; Stahl, 1967).

The same basic principles apply to birds and reptiles, although the anatomical differences from mammals are important in managing ventilation. In birds, gas exchange takes place in capillaries within the walls of parabronchi ('lungs'), which open into the bronchial system at both ends. The gas composition in parabronchi will therefore alter considerably as it passes from the inspiratory to

expiratory end of the tract. There are then 4 pairs and a single air sac through which gases may flow during inspiration and expiration (Piiper & Scheid, 1973). The lungs of reptiles are characterized by the presence of non-respiratory regions and large interconnections believed by Hughes (1973) to allow equalization of gas distribution. Snakes typically have only one functional lung which consists of a long hollow tube ending in a blind air sac. Birds and snakes can be intubated with ease but the nature of the blind sacs and of gas exchange have implications for the anaesthetist which will be explored later.

Control of respiration

The complex system controlling frequency and depth of respiration has been fully described by Comroe (1965). Central respiratory centres situated in the brain stem respond to various stimuli which have been transmitted from central and peripheral chemo-, baro- or stretch-receptors. Peripheral chemoreceptors are stimulated by depressed O_2 tensions in circulating blood (hypoxic hypoxia), while central chemoreceptors respond to alterations in hydrogen ion concentration. The latter may be mediated by respiratory (e.g. hypo- or hypercapnia) or metabolic (e.g. the production of lactic acid from anaerobic glycolysis) changes.

Most agents which depress the CNS are respiratory depressants. The central chemoreceptors are particularly sensitive to depression by morphine analogues, barbiturates and general anaesthetics such as halothane.

Table 2.1. Respiratory measurements in common species

Species	Bodyweight (kg)	Tidal volume (ml)	Minute volume (l/min)	Frequency (breaths/min)	O_2 consumption (cc/g/h)
Baboons	5·0	48·0	1·6	35	
Cats	2·0–3·0	12–18	0·3–0·4	26 (20–30)	700
Dogs	30–40	350–450	5·0–7·0	15–18	600
	10–15	200–280	3·5–4·5	20–25	
Domestic fowl	1·0–1·5	35	0·7	15–35	500
Guinea-pigs	0·5	1·0–4·0	0·1–0·4	80–110	800
Hamsters	0·10	0·8	0·06	80 (30–140)	2900
Horse	700	9 (8·5–9·5) × 10³	100–110	8–12	250
Mice	0·02	0·15	0·024	180 (100–250)	3500
Macaca spp.	2·5–3·0	39	1·4	38 (30–50)	
Oxen	400–500	3·0–4·5 × 10³	80–100	25–30	390
Pigs	200	3·8 × 10³	36	12 (8–18)	220
	25	420	6·0	14 (12–18)	
Rabbits	3·0–3·5	20 (19–25)	1·10	50 (35–60)	640–850
Rats	0·25	1·6 (1·5–1·8)	0·22	90 (70–150)	2000
Sheep (and goats)	45	280–330	5–6	20 (12–30)	220

These values are given as very rough guides. They are adapted from Clarkson (1956), Crossfill & Widdicombe (1961), Altman & Dittmer (1964), Gleystein & Stroud (1971) and Binns *et al.* (1972), and results in our laboratory (CRC).

Pulmonary inflation–deflation reflexes (Hering-Brauer), and other reflexes responding to mechanical movements of the thorax further modify respiration. These, too, are sensitive to all anaesthetic agents but particularly to ether and trichloroethylene.

The consequences of poor gas exchange

Insufficient ventilation results in decreased O_2 availability to the tissues (*hypoxia*) and retention of CO_2 in the blood (*hypercapnia*). Hypoxia interferes with membrane integrity and cellular metabolism in a complex sequence of events which will eventually lead to cellular swelling and cell death. Essential organs, particularly the CNS and liver, may be severely damaged by relatively brief periods of O_2 deprivation. Capillary endothelium is also damaged by hypoxia, particularly at the intercellular junctions, allowing fluid and plasma proteins to leak into the surrounding interstitium to produce the classical sequence of oedema, rising vascular resistance, sludging of erythrocytes, capillary shunting, inadequate cell perfusion and reduced circulating blood volume (*hypovolaemia*). The clinical symptoms are falling blood pressure, pulse rate and cardiac output after initial rises in each, accompanied by increased respiratory rate. Although cyanosis of membranes and extremities associated with rising concentrations of reduced haemoglobin in the blood is a helpful but by no means infallible symptom of hypoxia, colour changes may never be detected in very anaemic or heavily pigmented animals (Lumb & Jones, 1973).

Hypercapnia with carbonic acid excess gives rise to a *respiratory acidosis*. Since the main buffer for regulating body acid–base balance (bicarbonate : carbonic acid) exists in relative molar concentrations of 20 : 1 in the extracellular compartment, it will be apparent that quite small accumulations of carbonic acid have a marked effect on pH. This fall in pH may be compounded by a bicarbonate deficit resulting from metabolic disturbance and lactic acid production from anaerobic metabolism. As plasma pH falls from a physiological 7·4 to 7·0, cardiac output may also decrease so that pulmonary perfusion becomes increasingly inefficient. Another vicious cycle is set up in which dependent lobes of the lung develop interstitial oedema, thus further decreasing perfusion and gas exchange. Effectively, dead space is increasing. The animal will die if plasma pH falls to 6·8.

Our solution to this problem is to slightly hyperventilate all animals subject to prolonged surgery, monitor acid–base balance at 30 min intervals, and administer bicarbonate as required (see Chapter 8 for details).

CARDIOVASCULAR SYSTEM

All anaesthetic agents may depress cardiac rate, rhythm and output by direct effects on the myocardium. Furthermore, they act upon vasomotor, cardio-accelerator and cardio-inhibitor centres in the CNS, and produce other cardiovascular changes indirectly by their depressant effect on respiration. The centrally mediated cardiovascular reflexes are variously depressed by different agents according to Price (1961) who described an ascending scale of potency starting at the lower end with α-chloralose as the least depressive, followed by thiopentone-nitrous oxide,

Table 2.2. **Cardiovascular measurements in common species**

Species	Heart rate (beats/min)		Arterial blood pressure (mmHg)		Blood volume (ml/kg bodywt)	Complete circulation time (s)
	mean	range	mean systolic	mean diastolic		
Cats	150	110–240	120	75	75	10·0
Dogs	80	70–100	112	56	90	10·5
Domestic fowl	300	180–460	130	85	60	
Guinea-pigs	280	260–400	120	90	75	
Hamsters	350	250–425	150	110	78	
Horses	40	35–50	90	60	75	
Mice	570	500–600	113	81	80	
Macaca spp.	192	165–240	160	127	75	
Oxen	62	60–70	130	90	60	
Pigs	75	60–85	170	108	65	
Rabbits	220	205–235	110	80	70	10·5
Rats	350	260–450	116	90	50	
Sheep (and goats)	76	70–80	120	80	60	

These values are given as rough guides. They are adapted from Altman & Dittmer (1964, 1974) and Archer (1965) in conjunction with results in this laboratory (CRC).

cyclopropane, oxybarbiturates, ether, halothane and chloroform.

There are many additional factors influencing cardiovascular function during surgery which are indirectly mediated by the anaesthetic agents. The effects of poor pulmonary ventilation, hypoxia and hypercapnia have already been outlined, and these are the most important. Hypoxia will depress myocardial function, whilst hypercapnia may cause arrhythmic deviations in contractility and hence cardiac output.

Apart from myocardial contractility, cardiac output is a function of venous return to the heart and total circulating volume. Posture may profoundly influence venous return, especially in prolonged experiments, and it is particularly important to avoid positioning heavily pregnant or obese animals on their backs. Similarly, animals with complex stomachs are at risk. Rumenal tympany may very easily exert pressure on the vena cava and lymphatics, and seriously interfere with venous circulation; the venous system may then dilate to collect blood and increase its capacity from the normal 70–80% up to 90% or more of the total circulation (Lumb & Jones, 1973). The negative pressure in the thorax during inspiration which normally assists venous return is relatively ineffective if respiration is slowed during anaesthesia. It will be abolished during open chest surgery. It must also be remembered that venous return will be limited during positive-pressure ventilation of closed-chest subjects. In all cases, the necessary precautions should be taken.

Total reduction in circulating volume must also be considered in estimating cardiac output. Again this may escape the attention of the anaesthetist during prolonged surgery, when insensible fluid loss from the operative site, skin and respiratory tract may be considerable yet undetected in the absence of haemorrhage.

Management of cardiovascular function will be discussed in more detail elsewhere (p. 88), but attention is here drawn to the emphasis that should be placed on cardiac output and its implications for pulmonary and tissue perfusion. Provided due attention is paid to output and effective ventilation (hence plasma pH, O_2 and CO_2 tensions), serious problems with cardiac arrhythmias are unlikely to be encountered. Cardiac slowing—*bradycardia*—may be caused indirectly by vagal stimulation, or directly by the depressant effects of some anaesthetic agents on myocardium, whilst cardiac acceleration—*tachycardia*—may be caused by increased sympathetic nervous system activity or suppression of vagal activity. In addition, some agents (e.g. chloroform and cyclopropane) are said to sensitize the myocardium to the arrhythmogenic actions of catecholamines.

For readers seeking further information, the implications of drug interaction with cardiovascular function are discussed in detail by Price (1961), Prescott (1969), Grogono & Lee (1970) and Lumb & Jones (1973), whilst the effects of individual agents on this system in man are comprehensively catalogued by Wood-Smith *et al.* (1973).

RENAL SYSTEM

Extracellular fluid is continually reprocessed by the kidneys to ensure that its volume, osmolality, pH, electrolyte and other solute concentrations are maintained within physiological limits. A volume equivalent to the total extracellular fluid of the organism (or 20% of the bodyweight) is filtered and modified every 2 h in the normal mammal (Deetjen *et al.*, 1975). Fine regulation of salt and water balance is effected by circulating hormones produced by the pituitary and adrenal glands, as well as by the kidney itself, and released in response to central and peripheral receptor activation. It follows that deviations in cardiovascular function, acid-base and fluid balance, and central nervous function resulting from anaesthesia and surgery will have profound effects on renal function. The kidneys will attempt to maintain homeostasis but may be defeated by one or more of several factors such as hypoxia, acidosis, hypovolaemia and low blood perfusion pressure. If this is prolonged beyond 2 h, tubular cells may be irreversibly damaged, and excretion of drug metabolites will be reduced.

Consider first the maintenance of acid–base balance. The pH of blood is held constant by extra- and intra-cellular buffers, by respiratory control of CO_2 and by kidneys. As indicated above, most pathological shifts in metabolism and respiratory function result in acidosis due to bicarbonate deficit (metabolic) and carbonic acid excess (respiratory). The body compensates in two ways: first, respiratory activity is increased in an attempt to remove excess CO_2 from the blood; and second, the kidneys endeavour to conserve bicarbonate ions and excrete buffered hydrogen ions. In the event of an alkalosis developing during anaesthesia, exactly the reverse occurs—the kidneys excrete bicarbonate and selectively withhold hydrogen ions, and respiration is depressed. Respiratory compensation is by far the most important to the anaesthetist since adjustment in acid–base balance can be made in minutes (or even seconds) by altering ventilation, while renal compensation may take hours to reach maximal effect.

No consistent direct effect of anaesthesia on renal function has been detected but oliguria is commonly experienced in the post-anaesthetic period due to release of antidiuretic hormone from the posterior pituitary gland (Bastron & Deutsch, 1976). However, three factors can influence renal function during anaesthesia. Activation of the renal nerves can stimulate renin release and hence lead indirectly to increased aldosterone secretion; more profound simulation can lead to vasoconstriction and hence reduction in renal plasma flow (RPF) and glomerular filtration rate (GFR). This may account for the oliguria sometimes encountered during anaesthesia with ether and cyclopropane both of which activate the sympathetic nervous system. Again, although autoregulation of intra-renal vessels minimizes the effect of changes in mean arterial pressure within the range of 80–180 mmHg to produce only small changes in RPF and GFR, there will nevertheless be alterations in water and electrolyte excretion. Moreover, if mean arterial blood pressure falls below about 65mmHg, glomerular filtration ceases and results in anuria—a distinct possibility if hypotensive agents such as halothane or methoxyflurane are used for anaesthesia. Finally, certain anaesthetics and other CNS depressants (ether, barbiturates and morphine-like drugs) act centrally to stimulate the release of ADH from the posterior pituitary and reduce the production of urine.

Diminished urine output may be dangerous when injectable agents such as barbiturates, some of which are excreted via the kidneys, have been used. Of the commonly used inhalational anaesthetics, chloroform may cause permanent renal damage, whilst ether reduces RPF and GFR during administration. Methoxyflurane has been shown to cause impaired renal function in man due to the effects of fluoride ions in the distal tubules (Jones, 1972), and this may be an important consideration in experimental work where renal function is crucial to the interpretation of results. In such cases, simple tests for kidney function could well be included in the clinical examination prior to anaesthesia. This should be done, for example, in dogs which are destined for use in renal transplantation experiments so that animals suffering from chronic nephritis can be avoided. It is also worth emphasizing that drinking water should be available until shortly before the induction of anaesthesia unless there are compelling reasons for earlier withdrawal. Pigs in particular are susceptible to water deprivation, and young weaned pigs may develop nervous symptoms of high plasma salt concentrations after only a few hours if housed at high environmental temperatures. Further damage to the kidneys during anaesthesia and surgery will be less likely if the animal is well hydrated. It is our practice to insert an indwelling intravenous catheter and commence fluid therapy with balanced salt (Hartmann's) and dextrose–saline solutions right from the outset of any major interferences.

HEPATIC SYSTEM

Although the enzymes responsible for drug metabolism are found in many tissues of the body, the liver is much the most important locus of activity. These enzymes are present in the cytoplasm and mitochondria of hepatic cells, with the most versatile groups concentrated in the microsomes. As diffusion through the lipid membrane of the microsome is the deciding factor in determining which drugs are metabolized by microsomal enzymes, only those drugs which are highly lipid soluble (e.g. anaesthetic agents) will be affected.

In general, metabolic biotransformation increases the water solubility and hence the rate of excretion of the metabolites. There are four principal pathways of drug metabolism: first, *oxidations*, including hydroxylation of aromatic ring and alkyl side chains, oxidative deamination and dealkylation, and the formation of sulphoxides; second, *reductions*, e.g. conversion of nitro- and azo-groups to amines; third, *cleavages*, by hydrolysis of esters and amides; and fourth, *conjugations* in which drugs or their metabolic products combine with endogenous substrates, e.g. methionine, acetylcoenzyme A and glucuronyl residues. Some drugs are metabolized by a single process, but the majority undergo transformation through a sequence of at least 2, usually initially through oxidation, reduction or hydrolysis, followed by conjugation of the metabolite to produce a pharmacologically inactive and water soluble product. Some drugs are metabolized by more than one route even within the individual animal, while different species may deal with a drug in quite different ways, e.g. the rabbit deaminates amphetamine but the dog hydroxylates it (Bowman *et al.*, 1968).

Oxidations are particularly important in the biotransformation of injectable anaesthetic and other agents acting on the CNS. Primary alcohols are oxidized first to aldehydes, thence to the carboxylic acid and finally to H_2O and C_2O. Barbiturates are oxidized primarily at position 5 of the barbituric acid ring to form keto, hydroxy or carboxybarbituric acids, e.g. pentobarbitone is partly oxidized to 5-ethyl-5-(3-hydroxy-1-methylbutyl) barbituric acid. Steroids also undergo aromatic hydroxylation.

Side chains can be removed by oxidative dealkylation or deamination, e.g. hexobarbitone is both demethylated and oxidized, whilst amphetamine is an example of a drug in which an amino group ($-NH_2$) is removed to form benzyl methyl ketone and ammonia.

Thio-ethers such as phenothiazines undergo sulphoxidation to form sulphoxides, e.g. chlorpromazine is converted to chlorpromazine sulphoxide. Desulphorization of thiopentone converts this barbiturate to pentobarbitone.

Reduction is a less common form of drug transformation but there are two examples which are particularly relevant to anaesthesia. Chloral hydrate is reduced to trichlorethanol which then combines with glucuronic acid and is excreted by the kidneys in this conjugated form. Halothane is part metabolized in the liver by reductive dehalogenization in which chlorine and bromine radicals are removed.

Hydrolysis is important in the detoxification of esters and amides. Acetylcholine and similar compounds such as suxamethonium are hydrolysed by pseudocholinesterase to acetic (or succinic) acid and choline; other esterases are responsible for transforming esters such as atropine, many of the local analgesics in common use (e.g. procaine), as well as the morphine-like analgesic pethidine.

Conjugation (or synthesis) plays a particularly important role in the transformation of many products of normal metabolism, e.g. the glucuronic conjugation of steroid hormones and bile salts, and the methylation of catecholamines. Drugs or their metabolic products combine with endogenous substrates which in turn are mainly the products of carbohydrate or amino-acid metabolism.

The methyl radicle is donated by methionine during the methylation of phenols and amines to render them pharmacologically inactive. The acetyl radicle is donated by acetylcoenzyme A during acetylation reactions. Acetylcoenzyme A is also involved in amino-acid conjugations, e.g. glycine and glutamine combinations with acid molecules such as salicyclic acid. Perhaps the most versatile reaction involves the formation of glucuronides from the conjugation of uridine diphosphate glucuronic acid with an acceptor molecule, e.g. morphine. Glucuronic acid conjugates are usually secreted into the small intestine via the bile duct.

The rate of drug metabolism by the microsomal enzymes can alter markedly and activity may be increased or decreased. Enzyme activity is stimulated by many agents including barbiturates, phenothiazines, analgesics, tricyclic antidepressants and inhalational anaesthetics. Increased activity is related to an increase in the quantity of enzymes present in the microsomes in response to circulating drug, a process termed *enzyme induction*. Clearly, this increase in activity will tend to reduce the degree and duration of action of a drug. Drugs which increase microsomal enzyme activity will enhance their own rate of metabolism—*self induction*—and this accounts for the tolerance which develops in response to repeated administration of barbiturates.

Microsomal activity is low in the normal neonate but the administration of an activating drug leads to a rapid acceleration in their rate of appearance. Similarly when enzyme levels are low in adults, e.g. during starvation, hepatic disease, diabetes and other disease states, increased production of microsomal enzymes may again be activated by drug administration.

Conversely, inhibition of microsomal enzyme activity may result from drug administration. This phenomenon probably accounts for the sex differences in response to some barbiturates as androgens stimulate and oestrogens and progesterone inhibit enzyme activity.

The biliary system has an important part to play in excreting drugs and their metabolites. Apart from normal body constituents such as bile acids and bilirubin, drugs of high molecular weight may be transported as conjugates with glucuronic acid into the intestine. There they may be eliminated in the faeces or, alternatively, hydrolysed by β-glucuronidase and the released drug may then be reabsorbed and carried to the liver in the portal vein to be reconjugated—*the entero-hepatic shunt*—e.g. chloramphenicol and some analgesics such as etorphine.

CHAPTER THREE

PHARMACOLOGY OF DRUGS ACTING ON THE CNS

INTRODUCTION

The pharmacology of drugs acting on the CNS has important implications for the interpretation of experimental results which should be appreciated. The agents modify nerve function in the CNS, but they also affect other systems within the body *indirectly* via the somatic (involving skeletal muscle) and the autonomic divisions (controlling vital functions such as respiration and cardiac performance) of the nervous system, and *directly*, for example by their direct actions on the heart and smooth muscle.

During normal consciousness, the CNS exists in a constant state of flux, with the cerebral cortex and brain stem operating in a synchronous fashion to receive and interpret input signals. The brain stem reticular activating system (RAS) can be compared to an amplifier which provides 'gain'—continuous interaction between neuronal loops in the RAS allows responses to positive and negative feedback to be processed thence to inhibit or facilitate signals to the cerebral cortex. The complexity of such a system can perhaps only be grasped by appreciating that the human brain probably contains 15 to 20 000 million neurones, any one of which may interconnect with 10 000 others. This dynamic state should be borne in mind when considering the pharmacology of drugs acting on the CNS. Drugs will modify CNS activity in a similarly dynamic manner and there can never be a true 'steady state' (unless the animal dies). For example, some CNS depressants may stimulate in certain concentrations and depress in others; hence there can be no simple classification system which applies in all circumstances.

It would be useful to the investigator about to establish an experimental protocol to know the nature of drug action, i.e. whether it produces analgesia, sedation, ataraxy or muscle relaxation, and to have precise information regarding its effects on vital centres controlling respiratory and cardiovascular function. In addition, the site and mode of action at cellular and molecular levels should be considered. However, in our present state of knowledge, it is only possible to classify *depressant* drugs by the nature of their peak activity at safe dosages (although a little more is known about sites of action of CNS *stimulants* and a great deal of information has been accumulated about agents modifying the peripheral nervous system).

The drugs may be classified broadly as CNS stimulants, non-selective CNS depressants or narcotics, and partially selective depressants. A classification is shown in Table 3.1 (Lees, 1977) and a list of definitions is given later in this chapter. The reader is urged to appreciate the dynamic of the system, and consider the continuum of pharmacological activity—from convulsions at one end by deepening narcosis through sedation, sleep and anaesthesia, to coma and death at the other—which is characteristic of many CNS depressants (e.g. barbiturates) but not of others (e.g. ataractics, dissociative anaesthetics).

NATURE OF ACTION

The division into stimulants or depressants holds true in general but it must be remembered that some depressants may provoke symptoms of stimulation. For example, morphine-like drugs are depressant in rats, dogs, hamsters and other species, but produce tremors and convulsions at equinalgesic doses in mice and cats. Similarly, if given rapidly by intravenous injection they may stimulate the CNS in those species which are normally sedated. These drugs may also have depressant effects on the vasomotor, cough and respiratory centres in the medulla, yet stimulate the vagal centre and the chemoreceptor trigger zone (CTZ) which in turn stimulates the emetic centre. Variable effects have also been experienced with barbiturates. Several short-acting barbiturates including methohexitone are normally depressant yet may produce symptoms of CNS stimulation characterized by twitching, tremors, limb paddling movements and even convulsions at the time of induction and during the recovery period. Similarly, although they produce some degree of analgesia during anaesthesia, barbiturates may enhance the awareness of pain during recovery or when administered in sub-anaesthetic doses. These findings reflect the imbalance between central facilitatory and inhibitory pathways as these are differentially modified by the drugs, by behavioural adaptations or by release from those constraints.

A similar phenomenon is encountered when using CNS stimulants. Initial excitation is often followed by depression, and the stronger the first phase, the more profound will be the depression——in fact it may result in death through respiratory failure.

Awareness of these variable responses is important to the experimentalist. Species differences must obviously be considered as well. Excitatory behaviour may suggest that the animal is too 'light' during anaesthesia and it may then be given further increments of drug with fatal results. Conversely, stimulants such as bemegride should be used in emergency with great care since depression may be compounded in the second phase of their action.

SITES AND MODE OF ACTION

All anaesthetic agents modify the transmission of impulses along neurones in the CNS. It will be recalled that transmission consists of *transduction*, or initiation of a sensory impulse by conversion of energy into electrical signals (nerve action potentials or NAP), *axonal conduction* involving electrotonic or cable transmission sustained by relay stations, and *transmission at synaptic junctions* dependent on chemical rather than electrical excitation. The release of chemical transmitter (noradrenaline, acetylcholine, dopamine, 5-hydroxytryptamine, gamma-amino-butyric acid and others unknown) is triggered by the arrival of the NAP at the nerve terminal. The chemical transmitter increases permeability to sodium and potassium ions with consequent depolarization of the adjacent cell membrane. The summation of several such depolarizations triggers the firing of a NAP in the secondary neurone. Input impulses are then interpreted and a motor response generated.

The drugs presumably act at one or more of these points (Eger, 1974). Local analgesics (local anaesthetics) are thought to interrupt either the transduction from sensation to electrical NAP, or the transmission centrally along the axon. Inhaled anaesthetics, barbiturates, central analgesics and hypnotics may inhibit transmission or central interpretation. Neuromuscular blocking agents act specifically on the skeletal neuromuscular junction in the response arc.

It is useful to consider the sites of action of drugs at three levels: the macroscopic anatomical loci within the CNS; the cellular or microscopic level; and the molecular level.

Anatomical loci

It is impossible to identify one primary site of action in the CNS for individual drugs; some evidence suggests that one anaesthetic may have a dominant effect at one site whilst another may exercise its effect at a different locus (Halsey, 1974). Peripheral nerves are generally thought to conduct normally during surgical anaesthesia and it has been demonstrated experimentally that anaesthetic concentrations block synaptic transmission but not axonal conduction (Larrabee & Posternak, 1952). Synaptic transmission within the spinal cord has also been demonstrably inhibited by anaesthetic agents independently of inhibition by higher CNS centres (Galindo, 1969; Freund et al., 1969). The cerebral cortex may also be directly depressed by ether and halothane (Darbinjan et al., 1971), whilst cyclohexylamine derivatives such as ketamine are thought to exercise their main effects on the frontal (dissociative) cortex (Miyasaka & Domino, 1968). The brain stem reticular activating system (RAS) has long been considered the most important site of action of anaesthetics. Excitation of the RAS through a series of polysynaptic pathways, interacting via neuronal loops responsive to both positive and negative feedback, is necessary for arousal of the cortex. Inhibition of activity produces insensibility and anaesthesia. Several anaesthetics have been shown primarily to decrease RAS activity (Davis et al., 1957). However, it must be admitted that precise loci are difficult to map. Few drugs act directly at only one site and, even if they do, modification at that site is likely to produce indirect modifications at others. Consequently, the result is inevitably a rather non-selective type of action for many drugs.

Cellular sites of activity

Most available evidence suggests that narcotic drugs inhibit synaptic transmission at anaesthetic dosages, and that much higher concentrations are needed to interfere with axonal transmission (Larrabee & Posternak, 1952). Blockade at excitatory synapses is probably the main locus involved when inhalational agents are used (Schmidt, 1963). Several modes of action have been proposed: the drugs may directly mimic or antagonize transmitter action, prolong the time for which the transmitter acts, promote transmitter release from presynaptic stores, deplete the stores of transmitter, or prevent the release of transmitter by NAP (Eger, 1974). A small reduction in terminal NAP (Løyning et al., 1964) and in the sensitivity of the sub-synaptic membrane has been attributed to barbiturates (Crawford & Curtis, 1966; Bloom et al., 1965). In a review of the subject, Halsey (1974) concluded that there was no firm evidence to confirm the nerve terminal and quantal release or, alternatively, the subsynaptic membrane as exclusive cellular loci of action; however, it was suggested that the postsynaptic membranes were those most probably involved.

Sites of molecular activity

The correlation between lipid solubility and anaesthetic potency suggests that the molecular site of action has hydrophobic properties; lipid regions within the neuronal cell membrane or hydrophobic areas within proteins or enzymes seem the most likely loci of anaesthetic activity.

Various theoretical models and hypotheses have been proposed to account for the action of anaesthetic agents at the molecular level. The microtubule theory (Allison & Nunn, 1968) and hydrate theory (Pauling, 1961; Miller, 1961) are now considered to be improbable. A more convincing case has been argued for some modification in ionic channels or 'pores' (Mullins, 1972). These pores may be directly blocked by drug molecules, or closed by lateral expansion of the rest of the membrane (Clements & Wilson, 1962). Alternatively, by their affinity for the hydrophobic loci of proteins, it is possible that anaesthetic agents prevent protein mobility or aggregates forming, thereby preventing transmitter molecules from activating the subsynaptic membrane (Allison, 1972).

DEFINITIONS AND BASIC PROPERTIES
(AFTER LEES, 1977)

Spinal stimulants (e.g. strychnine) enhance spinal reflexes by suppressing spinal inhibitory mechanisms.

Medullary stimulants or analeptics (e.g. bemegride) stimulate certain medullary centres—in particular the respiratory centre. The term analeptic is also used by some authors to describe any respiratory stimulant, irrespective of the site of action, and by others to describe *any* drug which lessens narcosis.

Classical cortical stimulants (e.g. cocaine, amphetamine and caffeine) produce symptoms of hyperexcitability such as increased mental awareness and motor activity and prevention of sleep. At high dose levels convulsions may occur.

Psychotomimetics (e.g. lysergic acid diethylamide, mescaline, harmine, bufotenine and marijuana) produce effects which resemble certain psychotic states. These drugs are presumed to exert stimulant actions on the higher centres of the brain but in fact little is known of their action. They differ from the classical cortical stimulants in that there are no signs of marked hyperexcitability. Hallucinations and delusions occur in response to these drugs. Psychotomimetics have some value in human psychotherapy but they have not been used in the treatment of animals.

Antidepressants or thymoleptics (e.g. imipramine, isoniazid) are also difficult to classify in the present scheme. These drugs produce a mild stimulation of higher centres but do not cause symptoms of marked hyperexcitability even at high dose levels. They are thus aptly called antidepressants rather than stimulants—they elevate the mood. Thymoleptics are used in man to treat psychotic depressions but they are not currently employed in animals.

Narcotic is a general term which is usually used to describe any kind of general CNS depressant drug, i.e. sedatives, hypnotics and anaesthetics. They may, however, depress in some doses yet stimulate in others, and may produce different effects in different species.

Sedatives (e.g. chloral hydrate at low doses) are drugs which depress the CNS sufficiently to cause lethargy, drowsiness, indifference to the surroundings and decreased motor activity. They allay fear and apprehension but the animal remains conscious.

Hypnotics (e.g. thiopentone, chloral hydrate) are literally drugs which induce hypnosis or sleep. The word is usually used in slightly different ways in human and animal anaesthesia. In man, hypnotic is commonly used to describe a drug which induces or maintains sleep—a small dose of a depressant drug is used to produce what is essentially a state of 'real' sleep. In animal work, a hypnotic is a drug which induces deep sleep from which the animal can be aroused with difficulty, covering a part of the spectrum variously described as basal narcosis or light general anaesthesia. They may have some analgesic properties but by no means all do.

General anaesthetics (e.g. ether, halothane, methoxyflurane and pentobarbitone) cause a reversible general depression of the CNS, the state of

Table 3.1. Classification of drugs acting on the CNS (after Lees, 1977)

(1) *CNS stimulants*—divided into groups according to the *main site of action*
  (i) *Spinal*—strychnine, brucine
  (ii) *Medullary*—bemegride, nikethamide, leptazol, picrotoxin, doxapram
  (iii) *Cortical*—sub-divided according to the *nature of the final response, i.e. the type of action*
    (a) Classical cortical stimulants—cocaine, the amphetamine group (amphetamine, dexamphetamine, ephedrine) and the xanthines (caffeine, theophylline, theobromine)
    (b) Psychotomimetics—lysergic acid diethylamide, harmine, bufotenine, marihuana
    (c) Antidepressants—imipramine, isoniazid

(2) *Non-selective CNS depressants*—divided into groups according to the *nature of the final response*
  (i) *Sedatives*—bromide, some barbiturates, chloral hydrate, paraldehyde, ethyl alcohol, sedative-analgesics of the morphine type, xylazine
  (ii) *Hypnotics*—short-acting barbiturates (thiopentone, methohexitone, thiamylal, hexobarbitone), propanidid, chloral hydrate, alphaxolone-alphadolone, etomidate, metomidate.
  (iii) *General anaesthetics*—sub-divided according to the *physical state:*
    (a) Gases—nitrous oxide, cyclopropane
    (b) Volatile liquids—diethyl ether, methoxyflurane, trichloroethylene, halothane, chloroform, enflurane, isoflurane
    (c) Solids: (water soluble)—some barbiturates (pentobarbitone), tricaine (MS 222), metomidate, etomidate
    Solids: (water insoluble)—propanidid, alphaxolone-alphadolone

(3) *Partially selective CNS depressants*
  (i) *Tranquillizers (ataractics)*—sub-divided according to the *intensity of action, i.e. potency*
    (a) Major tranquillizers (neuroleptics)—phenothiazine derivatives (chlorpromazine, acepromazine), butyrophenone derivatives (azaperone, haloperidol, droperidol, fluanisone), rauwolfia alkaloids (reserpine)
    (b) Minor tranquillizers—weaker phenothiazine derivatives (promazine, promethazine), propanediol derivatives (meprobamate), diphenylmethane derivatives (benectyzine), benzodiazepine derivatives (chlordiazepoxide, diazepam)
  (ii) *Centrally acting muscle relaxants*—mephenesin, guaicol-glycerol-ether
  (iii) *Anticonvulsants*—phenobarbitone, trimethadione, phenytoin
  (iv) *Analgesics*—sub-divided according to *chemical structure* and *pharmacological activity*
    (a) Narcotic- or sedative-analgesics—morphine, codeine, pethidine, heroin, etorphine, fentanyl, pentazocine, buprenorphine, fentathienyl
    (b) Antipyretic-analgesics—acetylsalicylic acid, phenacetin, paracetamol
  (v) *Dissociative anaesthetics*—phencyclidine, ketamine, tiletamine
  (vi) *Neuroleptanalgesics*—combinations such as fentanyl-droperidol, fentanyl-fluanisone, etorphine-acepromazine, etorphine-methotrimeprazine

general anaesthesia involving hypnosis, analgesia, relaxation of voluntary muscles and suppression of reflex activity. In combination, these four components permit extensive surgical operations to be undertaken without the animal being aware of the fact or feeling pain and hence without moving, i.e. sensory perception and motor activity are both diminished.

Tranquillizers or ataractics (e.g. acepromazine, azaperone) exert a quietening effect, lessening anxiety and calming naturally vicious animals. They may be used to facilitate the handling of animals and as preanaesthetic treatments. Ataractics thus have similar uses to and some properties in common with sedatives. There are, however, important differences. For example, most tranquillizers do not make animals exceedingly drowsy, and at high dose levels they do not produce hypnosis or general anaesthesia—rather they produce a state of *catalepsy*, in which the animal, though conscious, remains motionless and part of the body may be 'moulded' or placed in unusual positions. Moreover, a sudden sensory stimulus may provoke an essentially normal arousal response in a tranquillized animal, whereas the response would generally be more sluggish in a sedated animal. They do not possess analgesic properties when used by themselves. Ataractics are usually divided into two groups, major tranquillizers (or neuroleptics) and minor tranquillizers, on the bases of degree of effect attainable in man. Both groups are used in man, the former to treat psychoses and the latter in the treatment of neuroses, but the major tranquillizers are employed most frequently in animals.

Centrally acting muscle relaxants (e.g. mephenesin, guaicol-glycerol-ether) produce relaxation of skeletal muscles by their action on the spinal cord.

Anticonvulsants (e.g. phenytoin) are CNS depressants, whose primary action is an ability to suppress convulsions arising from CNS stimulation.

Analgesics are CNS depressants, whose primary

action is to diminish the perception of pain. They are divided into two major groups on the basis of their chemical structures and pharmacological activities: (a) the narcotic- or sedative-analgesics (e.g. morphine), and (b) the antipyretic-analgesics (e.g. acetylsalicylic acid).

Variation in chemical structure amongst the sedative-analgesics has led to the introduction of some interesting compounds. Small changes in structure may lead to a marked alteration of analgesic potency (e.g. fentanyl and etorphine); greater specificity—apomorphine, for example, is a centrally acting emetic; and antagonistic or partial agonistic as opposed to agonistic activity—e.g. nalorphine and diprenorphine are competitive antagonists to morphine-like compounds.

Neuroleptanalgesics produce a state of depression of the CNS by the combined administration of a neuroleptic and a sedative-analgesic of the morphine type. It is probably correct to regard it as being equivalent to, although by no means the same as, a light plane of general anaesthesia in most species without the skeletal muscle relaxant component.

Dissociative anaesthetics (e.g. phencyclidine, tiletamine and ketamine) produce a state of CNS depression that is characterized in man by a feeling of dissociation from the surroundings, unconsciousness, catalepsy, vivid dreams and analgesia, but with little or no muscular relaxation. In many respects dissociative anaesthetics seem to produce a similar state to that of neuroleptanalgesia.

CHAPTER FOUR

PREANAESTHETIC MEDICATION AND CHEMICAL RESTRAINT

INTRODUCTION

Preanaesthetic medication may fulfil many requirements, particularly when used as part of a balanced anaesthetic technique. The main aims are to: reduce or abolish pain perception; reduce apprehension in a frightened subject; permit quiet recovery, ideally eliminating struggling and hence danger to the animal and the anaesthetist; reduce the amount of general anaesthetic needed and hence its potential toxicity; reduce secretions of salivary and bronchial glands; reduce gastric and intestinal mobility; and lastly, block vago-vagal reflexes thus preventing cardiac slowing or arrest.

The introduction of potent sedative-analgesics, dissociative anaesthetics, new tranquillizers (ataractics) and anaesthetic steroids during the last 10–15 years has revolutionized chemical restraint of wild or dangerous species, and these agents are valuable in many laboratory situations. The advances in this field owe much to the fact that the agents are rapidly absorbed from intramuscular sites with the obvious advantage that they can be administered simply and quickly and, where necessary, from a distance by projectile syringe. It is only possible to describe a few of the more commonly employed agents here, but key references to use under experimental conditions and in exotic species are included. Chemical restraint of wild and zoo animals has already been comprehensively reviewed (Bauditz, 1972; Jones, 1973, 1977a; Young, 1973; Alford et al., 1974; Harthoorn, 1975).

The specialist projectile equipment required for injecting drugs for the chemical restraint and immobilization of wild or dangerous mammals has also been reviewed (Jones, 1976). The 'Cap-Chur Pistol' is useful in laboratories where large numbers of primates are held, enabling escaped animals to be recaptured with a minimum of risk to attendant personnel. Alternatively two blowpipe systems are useful; both the 'Miniject' and the 'Telinject' blowpipes (Wentges, 1975) propel plastic disposable syringes of up to 2 ml capacity for a maximum effective range of 6 m. A list of manufacturers of these and other weapons suitable for field work involving capture of larger mammals is detailed later (Appendix A).

DRUGS AVAILABLE

These notes should be used in conjunction with Table 3.1. and the definitions in Chapter 3. Only anticholinergics and the central depressants including tranquillizers, hypnotics, sedative-analgesics, anaesthetic steroids and dissociative drugs are included here, and the barbiturates are dealt with in Chapter 7. Recommendations and contraindications are either derived from other authors or they are based on experience in this laboratory and are suffixed (CRC).

Anticholinergics

Atropine sulphate

This is the only agent commonly used.

Pharmacology
Atropine blocks the action of acetylcholine at post-

29

ganglionic termini of cholinergic autonomic fibres and therefore exerts a general parasympatholytic action in the body.

CNS. Cerebral and medullary centres may be stimulated and subsequently depressed by high dosage, but normal doses exert no significant actions.

Autonomic nervous system (ANS). The muscarinic actions of acetylcholine are inhibited—hence atropine depresses secretory activity, most smooth muscle and vagal reflexes on the heart.

Cardiovascular system. Atropine increases heart rate by peripheral inhibition of the cardiac vagus but blood pressure is usually unchanged.

Respiratory system. Bronchial muscles are relaxed, secretions are reduced and minute volume is slightly increased, but there is an overall increase in physiological dead space (Nunn & Bergman, 1964).

Uptake and fate in the body. Atropine is rapidly absorbed, quickly disappears from the circulation and is distributed throughout the tissues. It is broken down by plasma esterases, and its half-life will vary with species, e.g. it is rapidly transformed in some strains of rabbit which have high concentrations of atropinesterase. Atropine crosses the placenta.

Indications
Atropine is used to diminish salivary and bronchial secretions, to protect the heart from vagal inhibition and to prevent the muscarinic action of anticholinesterases, e.g. neostigmine when they are given to reverse non-depolarizing muscle relaxants (see Chapter 6).

It should be given routinely to primates, pigs, guinea-pigs and chinchillas since these species are particularly susceptible to airway occlusion by excess secretions, especially if irritant volatile or gaseous agents (e.g. ether or cyclopropane) are chosen for anaesthesia. Its effects in rabbits are variable due to the enzyme differences already outlined (CRC).

Contraindications
It should be avoided in all cases where a marked tachycardia is already established. Opinion varies concerning its use in ruminants since secretions, though reduced, are not abolished and become more viscid (Hall, 1971). It has been used in goats and sheep at this centre without problems being encountered (CRC).

Dosage and administration
Atropine may be given by the sc or im routes 30–40 min, or iv immediately, before anaesthesia is scheduled. In treating hypotension associated with

bradycardia, or neutralizing the side effects of neostigmine, it should be given iv.

The following species dosages (im, sc or iv) are recommended:

	Dosage (mg/kg)	Time to effect (min)	Duration of effect (min)†
Horse	0·02	30–40*	60
Sheep	0·3	30–40*	20
Goats	0·3	30–40*	20
Pigs	0·1	30–40*	60
Primates	0·05	30–40*	60
Dogs	0·05	30–40*	20
Cats	0·1	30–40*	20
Rabbits	0·2	20	15
Guinea-pigs	0·05	10	15
Rats	0·05	10	15
Mice	0·05	10	25

* Effects produced in 2–3 min after slow iv injection.
† These times are *very* approximate.

Tranquillizers (ataractics and neuroleptics)

The most commonly used agents in laboratory animals are the phenothiazine derivatives (promazine, chlorpromazine, acepromazine and methotrimeprazine), the butyrophenones (droperidol, fluanisone and azaperone), and the benzodiazepine, diazepam.

Neurolepsis was originally described as a drug-induced behavioural state in which awareness to surroundings was markedly depressed yet drowsiness was not a feature (Delay, 1959). Although some agents, e.g. promethazine do cause drowsiness, the subjects are usually easily aroused. Another general feature of these agents is that they depress the chemoreceptor trigger zone (CTZ) and so indirectly suppress the emetic centre.

Phenothiazine derivatives

Promazine hydrochloride ('Sparine')

Pharmacology
Promazine has similar properties to chlorpromazine but is less potent, and the absence of a chlorine atom may account for its lack of side effects and toxicity. In contrast to chlorpromazine, it is unlikely to cause hypotension in any species.

Indications
Promazine is a useful premedicant for dogs, cats, ruminants and horses, and synergism allows a reduction of 40% in barbiturate dosage. The duration of action lasts for 4–6 h. If given with pethidine, analgesia is enhanced, and this combination is excellent for post-operative nursing of laboratory animals which might otherwise suffer

pain. We consider that promazine is the phenothiazine of choice for ensuring smooth emergence from anaesthesia since side effects are less likely to occur. It is also valuable in reducing stress in physically restrained primates (CRC).

Dosage and administration (im or slow iv)

Species	Dosage (mg/kg)	Time to effect (min)	Duration of effect (h)
Large*	1–2	40–60 (im) 5 (iv)	4–6
Primates	2–6		
Dogs	2–6	20–40 (im)	3–4
Cats	2–6	5 (iv)	

* Horse, cow, sheep, goat, pig.

Chlorpromazine hydrochloride ('Largactil')

Pharmacology
The structure is identical to promazine except that a chlorine atom is substituted for a hydrogen atom in the molecule. Chlorpromazine generally potentiates the action of anaesthetics, hypnotics and analgesics but has very wide pharmacological properties.

CNS. Chlorpromazine depresses the CNS, particularly the RAS and hypothalamus, and has marked anti-emetic action. The temperature regulating centre is also depressed.

Cardiovascular system. Chlorpromazine may produce a significant degree of hypotension by several mechanisms. Depression of vasomotor tone by a central action and a peripheral α-adrenoceptor blocking effect are probably the major causes. The fall in pressure is thus caused by decreased peripheral resistance, while cardiac output may be increased because of a reflex-mediated effect on the heart.

Respiratory system. This may be depressed or stimulated, although the drug seems to antagonize respiratory depression associated with sedative-

peripheral vasodilation and depression of the thermal regulatory mechanisms. Hypothermia may be marked in small mammals such as mice.

Other effects. The drug has mild local analgesic and antihistaminic activity. Liver dysfunction may also result, particularly from prolonged administration. Other side-effects include ganglion blocking, atropine-like, anti-5HT and quinidine-like actions.

Indications
Provided its wide pharmacological activity is borne in mind, chlorpromazine is a valuable aid to the anaesthetist in providing a stress-free subject for induction of anaesthesia, in assisting smooth emergence from anaesthesia, and in enhancing the actions of anaesthetics and analgesics (e.g. up to 50% less pentobarbitone may be given). It is also particularly effective in suppressing the CTZ—hence the emetic centre—and in deliberately depressing the thermoregulatory centre during controlled hypothermia (see Chapter 7, p. 83). It may counter to a limited extent the respiratory depression associated with barbiturates and sedative-analgesics. Chlorpromazine has also been claimed to prevent shock if given prior to anaesthesia since α-blockade inhibits sympathetic vascular responses (but conversely, it must never be given to the already deeply anaesthetized subject, and it is vitally important that fluids should be administered to ensure that hypovolaemia does not occur—otherwise the α-blocking effect of the drug may lower arterial pressure to a point where perfusion of the heart and brain becomes inadequate).

Contraindications and precautions
Chlorpromazine should not be used in ruminants as the recovery period is unduly prolonged. It seems to provoke excitement in some horses when given iv injection, probably because of muscular weakness as well as hypotension.

Dosage and administration of chlorpromazine hydrochloride

Species	Dosage (mg/kg)	Route	Time to effect (min)	Duration of effect (h)
Horse	1·0–3·0	im (or very slow iv)	45 (5)	4–6
Dog	2·0	im (or iv)	45 (5)	4–6
Cat	2·0	im	45	3–5
Rabbit	3·0	im (or iv)	30 (3)	3–4

analgesics. Respiration is usually stimulated in rabbits (CRC). Bronchial secretions are suppressed.

Metabolism. There is little effect on metabolic rate but body temperature may fall rapidly due to

Acepromazine maleate ('Acetylpromazine')

Pharmacology
The structure is identical to promazine except that 1 hydrogen is substituted by $COCH_3$. Potency is

very similar to chlorpromazine, but the agent is much less toxic and less likely to produce untoward reactions in ruminants and horses. However, there is less detailed information available about its side effects.

Indications
As the agent is rapidly absorbed from im sites and reaches peak effect in 15–30 min, this is the preferred phenothiazine derivative in this laboratory (CRC) where it has been found effective in horses, pigs, goats, sheep, calves and dogs. We were unable to detect significant cardiac disturbance attributable to acepromazine in many carefully monitored beagles which were subject to thoracotomy and cardiovascular surgery (c.f. chlorpromazine and xylazine (see p. 37)).

Dosage and administration
See under sedative-analgesics.

Butyrophenones
Each agent in this group is a strong anti-emetic. They are thought to inhibit the limbic-hippo-campal system rather than the RAS. Effects on the respiratory and cardiovascular system are said to be minimal (Edmonds-Seal & Prys-Roberts, 1970).

Droperidol ('Droleptan')

Pharmacology
Droperidol (dehydrobenzperidol) is a neuroleptic producing mental calm and indifference. Large doses may cause extra-pyramidal effects. It is the most potent anti-emetic so far produced. When given by im injection there is virtually no effect on

Dosage and administration of acepromazine maleate

Species	Dosage (mg/kg)	Route	Time to effect (min)	Duration of effect (h)
Ruminants and horses	0·1	im (or slow iv)	10–30 (2–4)	4–6
Pigs	0·2	im (or slow iv)	10–15 (1–2)	3–5
Dogs	0·5	im (or slow iv)	10–15 (1–2)	3–5
Cats	0·5	im (or slow iv)	5–10 (1–2)	3–5

Methotrimeprazine hydrochloride ('Levoprome')

Pharmacology
The structure differs from promazine at 2 loci—at one hydrogen is substituted by OCH_3 and at the other an isobutane group is included. The drug has very similar effects to chlorpromazine but the hypotension produced is even greater. However, its big advantage is that it has a strong non-addictive analgesic component of its own (comparable to morphine) which is further amplified if combined with other analgesics (Lumb & Jones, 1973). It potentiates barbiturates by 40–60%.

Indications
It has been used in combination with the potent sedative-analgesic etorphine to produce a state of neuroleptanalgesia in dogs and other mammals. This combination has been used for many years in rats and rabbits (Medd, 1975), although in trials at this centre we found that it produced more respiratory depression, extrapyramidal effects and hypotension than other neuroleptanalgesic combinations (CRC).

Contraindications and precautions
This drug is contraindicated in old animals and when the experimental procedure is likely to involve cardiovascular changes, since there is a real risk of hypotension developing. It is extremely painful at the im injection site.

cardiovascular or respiratory functions. It is claimed to possess 400 times the potency of chlorpromazine (Marsboom & Mortelmans, 1964) but in view of the relative doses since reported in different species, it is more likely to be about 10 times as potent.

Indications
The drug has been used in pigs and proved satisfactory by im injection at 0·1 to 0·4 mg/kg (Mitchell, 1966; Lamberth, 1968). Combined with the sedative-analgesic fentanyl, it has been used extensively in the USA in dogs (Hamlin et al., 1968), rabbits (Strack & Kaplan, 1968), guinea-pigs (Rubright & Thayer, 1970) and in rats and mice (Lewis & Jennings, 1972), apparently with good results.

Dosage and administration.
See under sedative-analgesics.

Fluanisone ('Haloanisone')

Pharmacology
Fluanisone has similar properties to droperidol and has few side effects. Its potent anti-emetic activity completely suppresses vomiting when given together with fentanyl, and it potentiates the analgesic activity and limits any cardiovascular or respiratory depression caused by fentanyl. It is also claimed to depress muscle tone to some extent.

Indications

Fluanisone has proved a valuable neuroleptic in combination with fentanyl. Its use in pigs (Mitchell, 1966), dogs (Marsboom et al., 1964), primates (Marsboom et al., 1964a), and rabbits, rats and hamsters (Green, 1975) has established it as a particularly useful agent in experimental work.

Dosage and administration

See under sedative-analgesics.

Azaperone ('Suicalm')

Pharmacology

Substitution of a nitrogen atom on the pyridyl ring has produced another butyrophenone which is particularly useful in pigs. Barbiturates and sedative-analgesics are potentiated and their dosage reduced by up to 60%. Azaperone is broken down by simple oxidation to non-toxic metabolites which are rapidly excreted in urine and faeces (Heykants et al., 1971).

Indications

Azaperone has been used extensively in clinical practice for reducing stress and aggression in pigs, and as a premedicant for anaesthesia in these animals (Marsboom & Symoens, 1968). Experience at this centre (CRC) indicates that it is an excellent preanaesthetic agent for pigs up to 50 kg, but that results are rather erratic in larger subjects, in which phencyclidine or ketamine with diazepam are preferred. Following premedication with azaperone, pigs have been successfully anaesthetized with methohexitone, thiopentone or metomidate, as well as with nitrous oxide and halothane (CRC). Azaperone has also been used successfully in horses either alone as an ataractic (Aitken & Sanford, 1972) or together with metomidate to produce anaesthesia (Hillidge et al., 1973).

Contraindications and precautions. Pigs must be kept quiet after administration since they are highly sensitive to auditory stimuli, particularly metallic noises (CRC). Hypothermia can also be a problem—in this laboratory, rectal temperature fell rapidly to 33°C within 15 min of im administration of azaperone to pigs held in an ambient temperature of 22°C. Repeated administration results in a marked tachyphylaxis, and atropine should be given concurrently to counter the profuse salivation provoked.

Dosage and administration

Species	Dosage (mg/kg)	Route	Time to effect (min)	Duration of effect (h)
Pigs (<50 kg)	2·0–4·0	im	15–20	1–2
Horses	0·5–1·0	iv	20–50	2–5

Benzodiazepines

This is another group of ataractics whose activity is principally on the amygdala of the limbic system. Their main advantage over other types of tranquillizer is their freedom from side effects and their therapeutic ratio which is even wider than the phenothiazine and butyrophenones groups. Only one of the group, diazepam, has been used to any extent in animal work, although another, zolazepam, has recently been reported as valuable in combination with the dissociative anaesthetic, tiletamine.

Diazepam ('Valium')

Pharmacology

Diazepam is insoluble in water and is presented in a mixture of organic solvents comprising propylene glycol, ethyl alcohol and sodium benzoate in benzoic acid.

CNS. It exerts potent tranquillizing, muscle relaxant and anti-convulsant actions in animals and potentiates barbiturates, analgesics and inhalation anaesthetics (e.g. the inspired concentration of halothane can be reduced by 35%). It has no anti-emetic effect and lacks the autonomic blocking actions of phenothiazine derivatives.

Respiratory system. There is some respiratory depression, and arterial pCO_2 may rise when large doses are given.

Cardiovascular system. Cardiac output and blood pressure are usually unchanged although a slight tachycardia may occur after iv injection (Healy et al., 1970).

Indications

Diazepam has been little used in animal anaesthesia, possibly because it is not water soluble. However, the marked muscle relaxant and anti-convulsant properties make it an ideal agent to combine with morphine-like drugs in those species such as mice which are otherwise stimulated (Green, 1975) and it is useful combined with short-acting barbiturates such as methohexitone in small rodents. Similarly, it has proved an excellent adjunct to dissociative anaesthetics such as phencyclidine and ketamine in primates, pigs, rabbits, guinea-pigs, rats, mice and birds (CRC). It has been recommended for use in dogs suffering from 'shock' and where prolonged tranquillization is required in this species (Hall, 1976b). We have used it iv in conjunction with fentanyl-fluanisone in dogs to allow intubation followed by maintenance of surgical anaesthesia with $N_2O:O_2$ (1:1) but have encountered CNS stimulation in greyhounds when it has been administered iv.

Dosage and administration

Diazepam is best administered by ip injection in rodents, and im or iv in dogs, pigs and primates.

Species	Dosage (mg/kg)	Route	Time to effect (min)	Duration of effect (h)
Pigs	1·0–2·0	im (or iv)	2–10 (2)	4–6
Dogs	1·0	im (or iv)	10–15 (2)	6–8
Primates	1·0	im (or iv)	10–15 (1)	4–6
Rabbits	1·0	im (iv)	5–10 (1)	1–2
Guinea-pigs	2·5	ip (im)	2–5 (5)	1–2
Rats	2·5	ip	2–3	1–2
Hamsters	5·0	ip	2–3	1–2
Mice	5·0	ip	1–2	1–2

Zolazepam

This is a diazepam analogue with similar ataractic activity. It is still undergoing investigation, and has been evaluated in combination with the dissociative anaesthetic tiletamine for use in exotic species (Beck, 1972; Gray *et al.*, 1974), in primates (Kaufman & Hahnenberger, 1975), dogs (Bree *et al.*, 1972), sheep (Conner *et al.*, 1974), large cats (Seidensticker *et al.*, 1974), chinchillas (Schulz & Fowler, 1974), as well as laboratory animals (Ward *et al.*, 1974). As this is likely to produce similar results to ketamine and diazepam given concurrently but in separate injections (as described above), this may well prove a useful mixture if it becomes commercially available.

Hypnotics

Four hypnotic agents other than barbiturates are important in laboratory animal work—metomidate, propanidid, a mixture of two steroids alphaxalone and alphadolone, and xylazine. Each produces a state of hypnosis depending on dose and route of administration, but the degree of analgesia is very variable with species. For example, im injection of the steroid combination safely produces deep sedation in cats, rats and primates but, in rabbits and guinea-pigs, it has little effect in the volumes which can be realistically injected im (CRC).

Metomidate hydrochloride ('Hypnodil')

Pharmacology

Metomidate produces sleep for variable periods in mammals, birds, reptiles and fish. It has strong central muscle relaxant but no analgesic properties. However, in combination with some neuroleptics, e.g. azaperone, or with sedative-analgesics such as fentanyl, it produces a state resembling general anaesthesia in several species.

Cardiovascular system. Cardiac rate, output, and ECG are remarkably stable after iv injection. During the sleeping period, cardiac rate slows down.

Respiratory system. During sleep, the respiratory rate falls but amplitude increases and the minute volume remains stable.

Indications

In combination with the neuroleptic azaperone, this agent gives excellent results in pigs up to 80 kg. The mixture has been used to produce general anaesthesia suitable for many operations. It is convenient to use since premedication and induction of anaesthesia can be performed in the holding pens; the pigs can then be transferred to inhalation anaesthesia with $N_2O:O_2$ after they have been prepared for surgery and positioned on the operating table. Pigs are well maintained for up to 6 h on a 50:50 mixture of N_2O and O_2 with occasional incremental iv doses of metomidate or fentanyl (CRC).

The agent is also valuable for the restraint of a variety of species of bird (Houston & Cooper, 1973; Cooper, 1974*a*). It has been used in poultry at this centre for several years—the degree of narcosis obtained has varied from sedation to light surgical anaesthesia but was not apparently related to dosage.

Metomidate has been recommended by the manufacturers for neuroleptanalgesia in mice when combined with fentanyl, but in the particular strains of mice assessed in trials at this centre, we did not find it satisfactory (c.f. fentanyl with diazepam). Although the animals appeared well sedated, they exhibited exaggerated leaping and running movements as soon as they were touched or stimulated by noise (CRC).

The combination of metomidate and azaperone has also been used successfully in the anaesthesia of horses (Hillidge *et al.*, 1973), and this appears to be a useful alternative to thiopentone induction.

An analogue called etomidate has been used in man in recent years (Kay, 1976) and this may prove valuable in animals in future.

Contraindications and precautions

Since salivation is often profuse in pigs, atropine should be given prior to azaperone premedication. Heat loss is very noticeable during anaesthesia with these agents unless precautions are taken. It is also worth noting that recovery excitement, including muscle tremors and involuntary movements, can be fairly marked. Furthermore, intravascular haemolysis occurs in the horse (Hillidge *et al.*, 1973) and in mice (Lees, 1977).

Dosage and administration of metomidate hydrochloride

Species	Dosage (mg/kg)	Route	Time to effect (min)	Duration of effect (min)
Birds	10–15	im	1–4	10–50 (mean 30)*
Pigs				
(<15 kg)	10†	ip	10–15	25–40
(>15 kg)	4‡	iv	3–5	20–30
Horses	3·5	iv	1–2	5–10§

* The peak effect varies greatly with species, e.g. it has very little effect in Ciconiiformes (storks, etc.).
† Given simultaneously with azaperone (2 mg/kg im).
‡ Given 5–10 min after azaperone (2 mg/kg im).
§ Light surgical anaesthesia develops rapidly—full recovery takes up to 2 h.

Propanidid ('Epontol')

Pharmacology

Propanidid is insoluble in water and is dissolved in Cremophor EL. A eugenol derivative, propanidid produces unconsciousness of extremely short duration when given iv. It is rapidly broken down by liver and plasma esterases, 90% being eliminated within 2h via the urine. Respiratory rate is increased for 15–30 s after induction but is then depressed. There is almost invariably a fall in blood pressure. This is very marked in dogs and may be an anaphylactic reaction to the drug vehicle, Cremophor EL. A review of the pharmacology and value of propanidid is given by Conway & Ellis (1970).

Indications

Propanidid has had limited application in animal anaesthesia (Clarke & Dundee, 1966). We have used it for induction of anaesthesia in rabbits and rats by iv injection because the animal recovers within minutes of induction and the investigator can be relatively confident that metabolites will not interfere with other areas of experimental interest—it may therefore have a place in establishing acute preparations to be maintained for long periods, e.g. with α-chloralose. Furthermore, it is ideal for minor procedures as the animals recover rapidly and completely, e.g. rabbits regain consciousness within 5 min of induction, and normal behaviour and appetite return in 10 min.

Dosage and administration

Species	Dosage (mg/kg)	Route	Duration of effect (min)	Time to full recovery (min)
Rabbit	8–10	iv	2–3	5–10
Rat	8–10	iv	2–3	5–10

Alphaxolone-alphadolone acetate ('Saffan')

Pharmacology

The commercial preparation consists of alphaxolone 9 mg/ml and alphadolone acetate 3 mg/ml dissolved in Cremophor EL. The combination, hereafter refered to as alphaxolone-alphadolone, produces a state of sedation and hyponosis if given by im injection, and surgical anaesthesia in several species if given by rapid iv injection (Hall, 1972a; Eales, 1976). The therapeutic index ($LD_{50}:ED_{50}$) is approximately 4 times that of injectable barbiturates in mice. The pharmacology has been reviewed by Child et al. (1971).

CNS. Unconsciousness is accompanied by good muscle relaxation in most animals, but the degree of analgesia depends on species and route of administration, e.g. it is good in primates, domestic cats, rats and mice but only moderate in rabbits (CRC). Recovery of consciousness after a single injection is rapid and the animal is quickly restored to normal appetite and behaviour. We have used alphaxolone-alphadolone by continuous infusion or repeated injections for periods up to 10 h without tachyphylaxis, tolerance or cumulation developing in rats or mice (Green et al., 1978).

Cardiovascular system. Following iv injection in man, there is a fall of 10–20% in central venous and arterial blood pressure, but cardiac output is maintained. Heart rate increases by up to 20%. However, in cats there is an initial fall in arterial blood pressure of 20–30% within 1·5 min of iv injection followed by an increase to a mean of 10% above normal 5 min later. The heart rate increases by 20–40% (Child et al., 1971). In rhesus monkeys a similar transient fall of 20–30% in arterial blood pressure was observed to return to normal in 3–4 min (Box & Ellis, 1973).

Respiratory system. After iv injection, there is usually some depression of ventilation and even brief apnoea followed by shallow, rapid respiration.

In cats, primates, rats and mice, respiratory depression is not a problem at dosages sufficient to produce light surgical anaesthesia, but in rabbits we found that alphaxolone-alphadolone frequently depressed respiratory rate until the animals were hypoxic before surgical analgesia had developed (Green, 1975).

Fate in the body. Narcosis is terminated by hepatic metabolism, the breakdown products being excreted mainly in bile. Hence, in contrast to thiopentone, the drug is non-cumulative.

Indications

Alphaxolone-alphadolone is the injectable agent of choice in cats; im it is a useful hypnotic and basal narcotic, and it is an excellent short-acting anaesthetic iv. Hence, it is useful for minor

since the Cremophor solvent causes release of histamine. Unexpected deaths have been encountered in red-tailed hawks (*Buteo jamaicensis*) by Cooper & Redig (1975) and Frank & Cooper (1974). In another communication, Cribb & Haigh (1977) reported unusual responses after slow iv injection of alphaxolone-alphadolone in red-tailed hawks, mallards (*Anas phatyrhynchos*) and Canada geese (*Branta canadensis*), and showed from ECG measurements that they were associated with complete sinus arrest, followed by escape beats and a tachycardia. Less serious cardiac arrhythmias were encountered in all cases. It must be concluded that these steroids should be used with caution in *all* birds. Cats may occasionally exhibit transient flushing and oedema of limb and ear extremities.

Dosage and administration of alphaxolone-alphadolone acetate

Species	Dosage (mg/kg)	Route	Time to effect (min)	Duration of effect (min)*	Time to full recovery (min)
Primates	6–9	iv	rapid	10	40
	12–18	im	7	10–12	45
Cats	9	iv	rapid	10	30–90
	12	im†	7–8	15	60–90
Pigs	2	iv	rapid	10	15–30
	5	im	3–6	10–20	20–40
Rabbits	6–9	iv	rapid	3–7	15
Guinea-pigs	10–20	iv	rapid	4–8	15
Rats	10–20	iv	rapid	4–6	10
Mice	10–20	iv	rapid	4–6	10
	90	ip	3	15–20	30
Birds	12–14	iv	rapid	8–15	15–30

* Light surgical anaesthesia in most species after iv administration. May be continued for many hours by incremental or continuous infusion in *all* these species.
† By deep im injection into *anterior* thigh muscles.

procedures or for induction of anaesthesia prior to intubation and maintenance with inhalational agents. It is also valuable im in primate sedation, and is particularly safe in marmosets (CRC). Provided it is given iv, alphaxolone-alphadolone is a good short-acting anaesthetic in rabbits, rats and mice, and is suitable for continuous iv infusion in these species for maintenance of anaesthesia up to 10 h (Green *et al.*, 1978). Its value in bird restraint and anaesthesia has also been reported by Cooper & Frank (1973), who concluded that it was reliable only if administered iv. The efficacy of alphaxolone-alphadolone in cats has been reported by several authors (Evans *et al.*, 1972; Hall, 1972*b*; Stock, 1973; Dodds & Twissell, 1973), in primates (Box & Ellis, 1973; Phillips & Grist, 1975) and in pigs (Cox *et al.*, 1975; Baker & Reitter, 1976).

Contra-indications and precautions

Alphaxolone-alphadolone must not be used in dogs

Xylazine hydrochloride ('Rompun')

Pharmacology

CNS. Xylazine is a potent hypnotic, with central muscle relaxant and possibly analgesic properties (depending on dosage and species). Excitement has not been observed during induction or recovery. The depth of narcosis is dose dependent in each species but varies from a sleep-like state to deep basal narcosis. Xylazine potentiates barbiturates by up to 50% and has a wide margin of safety (therapeutic index 10).

Cardiovascular system. The heart rate is reduced, and after iv administration there may be a transient increase in pressure followed by a slight decrease. Partial atrio-ventricular (A-V) block may occur in horses after iv injection of large doses, but this may be prevented by iv administration of atropine (0·01 mg/kg). Bradycardia with partial A-V block has also been observed in dogs and cats—in fact in our experience, cardiac arrythmias occurred in the majority of a series of beagles after preanaesthetic medication with xylazine (CRC).

Respiratory system. Although the respiratory rate is depressed, depth increases and arterial blood gas tensions are unchanged. This pattern is common to horses, cattle, dogs and cats.

Miscellaneous. Horses, dogs and cats often respond to loud, metallic noises while apparently deeply sedated with xylazine. Horses may appear startled and raise their head, but they rarely move their limbs or struggle, while dogs and cats may even sit up suddenly—however, all 3 species soon settle down quietly again (CRC). Emesis is usually caused in cats and occasionally in dogs after administration of xylazine (CRC).

Indications

Xylazine is the sedative of choice in horses and cattle in which it can be given by im or iv injection, and it is also of value in dogs, cats and primates. Horses are deeply sedated for 15–30 min. Excitement is not provoked by external stimuli and the animal is reluctant to move; however, it does not become recumbent in spite of the muscle relaxation

foetal circulation to sheep (CRC). Goats are extremely sensitive to xylazine and in our experience the therapeutic index is narrow.

We have assessed xylazine in combination with ketamine at different dose rates in rabbits, rats, guinea-pigs and mice. The overall results were fair but not as good as those obtained with sedative-analgesic and neuroleptic combinations in these species. Good surgical conditions were obtained in rabbits when both agents were given iv, however (CRC).

Xylazine is itself a valuable agent for the chemical restraint and immobilization of wild and zoo species such as Camelidae and Cervidae (Hime & Jones, 1970). Furthermore, it can be used either alone or in combination with other drugs such as dissociative agents and the potent sedative-analgesics for many other exotic animals (Jones, 1973).

Contraindications and precautions

The investigator should be aware of the possible cardiac arrhythmias which may interfere with several aspects of the experiment.

Dosage and administration of xylazine

Species	Dosage (mg/kg)	Route	Time to effect (min)	Duration of effect (min)
Horse	0·5–1·0	iv	rapid	20–30
	2·0–3·0	im	5	20–90
Cattle	0·1	im	5–15	60–180*
Sheep†	1·0	im	5–10	40–60
Goats	0·05	im	5–10	40–60
Primates	1·0–2·0	im	5–10	30–60
Dogs	1·0–2·0	im	3–10	30–90
Cats†	1·0–2·0	im	3–5	20–60
Rabbits†	3·0	iv	rapid	20–60

* May persist for many h if given iv at higher doses.
† Surgical conditions are provided if given concurrently with ketamine (10 mg/kg im).

produced. Cattle are sensitive to very low doses, and deep basal narcosis with some analgesia, muscle relaxation and recumbancy may be produced by iv injection of higher doses. We have used xylazine premedication in dogs for several years but would not now recommend it for thoracic or cardiac surgery where halothane was included in the anaesthetic regime, as we have encountered cardiac arrhythmias in a high proportion of cases. Similarly, we have used the drug in cats to supplement ketamine anaesthesia with the intention of decreasing muscle tone. Although we now prefer alphaxolone-alphadolone in most cases, xylazine-ketamine is a useful combinations for intractable individuals and for immobilizing wild and zoo cats. Xylazine was found to be an essential adjunct to ketamine anaesthesia during experiments involving

Sedative-analgesics

Several sedative-analgesics are valuable in the anaesthetic management of experimental animals and in the chemical restraint of wild species. Pethidine, fentanyl, thiambutene and etorphine are the agents most commonly used, and each possesses morphine-like properties. They were introduced in an attempt to avoid the unwanted side effects of morphine or because of their greater analgesic potency. They can be specifically antagonized with opiate-receptor antagonists such as nalorphine, diprenorphine, levallorphan and naloxone. A non-addictive benzomorphan compound, pentazocine, is also useful in laboratory animals. Analgesic potency is not easy to determine and the figures quoted below should be regarded as approximate.

Pethidine hydrochloride ('Demerol')

Pharmacology

CNS. Pethidine is structurally similar to atropine, and has mild CNS depressant but potent analgesic activity (approximately 1/10 that of morphine). It is rapidly absorbed following im or sc injection to develop peak activity in 15–20 min; plasma levels then fall rapidly until the drug is no longer detectable after 4 h.

Cardiovascular system. Pethidine depresses the vasomotor centre at high dose levels only. It possesses some anti-arrhythmic properties and ventricular dysrhythmias may be prevented. Blood pressure usually remains constant at therapeutic doses.

Respiratory system. Pethidine is less depressive of the medullary respiratory centre than morphine at equianalgesic dose levels. The main effect is on respiratory rate which is markedly slowed. Bronchial secretions are slightly reduced. Pethidine crosses the placental barrier and depresses foetal and neonatal respiration.

Indications

Pethidine is a particularly useful drug in the anaesthetic management of dogs. It can be used to provide mild sedation and central analgesia both when operating under local analgesia and general anaesthesia, and to enhance the weak analgesic effects of hypnotics such as xylazine. Perhaps it is most useful in providing post-operative analgesia during recovery—but it is essential to ensure that spontaneous respiration is adequate before administration.

Contraindications and precautions

Rapid iv injections should be avoided since respiratory failure and cardiovascular collapse may be precipitated. The drug is particularly dangerous during post-operative care of animals with liver disease or liver dysfunction following transplantation of that organ.

Dosage and administration

Species	Dosage (mg/kg)	Route	Time to effect (min)	Duration of effect (h)
Dogs	10	sc, im	15–20	1–2
Cats	3–5	sc, im	15–20	1–15

Fentanyl citrate ('Sublimaze')

Pharmacology

Fentanyl is a potent analgesic (up to 100 times more potent than morphine). It is chemically related to pethidine but possesses a half-life of only 7 min and a duration of action of approximately 30 min. It is rapidly absorbed from im injection sites, and analgesia, sedation and respiratory depression develop in 3–8 min depending on species.

CNS. Central depression, ataxia and exaggerated response to loud noises are seen in most species.

Cardiovascular system. Iv or im administration of fentanyl produces bradycardia in dogs and rabbits due to increased vagal tone, but this seems to have little effect on cardiac output or blood pressure at normal dose levels. However, hypotension may develop when high doses are administered or if fentanyl is given iv to supplement barbiturate anaesthesia. Vagal inhibition of the heart can be prevented by prior administration of atropine.

Respiratory system. The effects are rather unpredictable although most commonly fentanyl depresses both rate and depth of respiration, particularly when used with another respiratory depressant such as pentobarbitone.

Indications

Fentanyl is a useful agent in laboratory animal anaesthesia. It may be used as an analgesic supplement to nitrous oxide:oxygen ($N_2O:O_2$) anaesthesia in dogs, pigs, primates and rabbits, with or without muscle relaxants. It is most commonly combined with a neuroleptic such as droperidol or fluanisone, and used to produce the state of neuroleptanalgesia. Similarly, it may be employed to supplement other central depressants, such as xylazine, metomidate or short-acting barbiturates. In addition to reports from this laboratory (Green, 1975) where fentanyl-fluanisone has been extensively employed in rabbits, rats, pigs, primates, dogs, mice, hamsters and guinea-pigs, the neuroleptanalgesic combinations have been employed elsewhere in dogs (Marsboom *et al.*, 1964); rats, guinea-pigs, mice and rabbits (Lewis & Jennings, 1972); guinea-pigs (Rubright & Thayer, 1970); rabbits (Strack & Kaplan, 1968) and primates (Field *et al.*, 1966). Fentanyl-droperidol has been used in rats together with a reduced pentobarbitone dose rate of 15 mg/kg (Garcia *et al.*, 1975); these authors reported lower mortality than with pentobarbitone alone at higher doses, but noted sex differences and circadian variations in sensitivity to the agents. Fentanyl has also been used with some success in the chemical restraint of wild and zoo animals (Pienaar, 1968; Jones, 1973).

Contraindications and precautions

Great care should be exercised in giving fentanyl or fentanyl-fluanisone iv, particularly when animals are already anaesthetized with barbiturates, since bradycardia, hypotension and respiratory depression may occur, and the changes may be difficult to reverse. Although emesis does not occur, animals usually defaecate soon after administration, and may pass loose stools for 2–3 days afterwards (observed in dogs, rats and rabbits—CRC).

Dosage and administration

It is more convenient to express the dosage of the fentanyl-fluanisone (or fentanyl-droperidol) combinations in ml/kg bodyweight. The commercial solutions contain 0·2 mg/ml of fentanyl base and 10 mg/ml of fluanisone, and 0·4 mg/ml fentanyl and 20 mg/ml of droperidol respectively.

can be rapidly reversed by injecting nalorphine (1–2 mg/kg sc).

Indications

Thiambutene is useful as a longer acting sedative-analgesic than fentanyl for use in dogs, primates, rabbits, guinea-pigs and rats. It can be used as an analgesic supplement to other central depressants such as barbiturates, xylazine and diazepam. Thiambutene-diazepam is a particularly useful combination which can be given iv to these animals to produce neuroleptanalgesia very rapidly (CRC). Low doses are valuable for post-surgical analgesia.

Dosage and administration of fentanyl citrate

Species	Dosage (ml/kg)	Route	Time to effect (min)	Duration of effect (min)
Dogs	0·1–0·4	im	10	20–40
Primates	0·2	im	10	20–40
Rabbits	0·3	im	6–10	20–30
Rats	0·3–0·4	im, ip	8, 3	15–30
Guinea-pigs*	1·3	im, ip	15, 5	20–40
Hamsters } Mice† }	0·1 of 1/10 dilution solution	ip	2	15–20

* In guinea-pigs, neurolepsis does not develop with this combination but analgesia does. For neuroleptanalgesia it is necessary to use fentanyl-fluanisone (0·5 ml/kg ip) concurrently with diazepam (2·5 mg/kg ip).
† In mice and hamsters, it is necessary to inject diazepam (5 mg/kg ip) beforehand.

Fentanyl-induced respiratory depression can be rapidly reversed by giving nalorphine iv or im, but it must be remembered that the drug's analgesic effect will also be counteracted.

Thiambutene hydrochloride or diethylthiambutene hydrochloride ('Themalon')

Pharmacology

CNS. Thiambutene is a strong sedative-analgesic approximately equipotent with morphine. The response is related to dosage and route of administration. Injection iv produces a deep but shorter lasting effect than either im or sc administration.

Cardiovascular system. Thiambutene depresses the vasomotor centre at high iv dosages and there may be an immediate fall in arterial blood pressure.

Respiratory system. Although the respiratory centre is generally depressed, this is only significant if high dosages have been given. Respiratory rate is then markedly slowed. However, at therapeutic doses respiratory rate may increase or decrease.

Gastrointestinal tract. Vomiting does not usually occur after administration of thiambutene, but defaecation may occur during recovery. Salivation is usually excessive but can be prevented by giving atropine.

Uterus. This agent crosses the placenta and depresses foetal respiration. However, the effect

Contraindications and precautions

Overdosage results in respiratory depression, hypotension and convulsions, particularly if the drug is administered rapidly iv. Occasionally, idiosyncrasy occurs in individual dogs and normal doses provoke hysteria, vocalization and convulsions, but we have not encountered problems if the animals have already been given diazepam iv or im. This agent must not be used in cats.

Dosages and administration

Thiambutene is supplied in 50 mg tablets which are crushed and dissolved in sterile water. Solutions up to 100 mg/ml (i.e. 10%) may be used without provoking irritation at the injection site. The times quoted below are dependent on the dosage used:

Species	Dosage (mg/kg)	Route	Time to effect (min)	Duration of effect (h)
Dogs	1·0–2·0	iv	2–3	0·5–3
	2·0–10·0	im	5–20	1–4
	5·0–20·0	sc	20–30	2–8
Primates	0·5–1·0	iv	2–3	0·5–2
	2·0–5·0	im	5–15	1–3
	5·0–10·0	sc	10–20	2–4
Rabbits	1·0–2·0	iv	1–2	0·5–2
	2·0–5·0	im	5–10	0·5–1·5
Guinea-pigs	5·0–10·0	im	5–10	0·5–1·5
	2·0–3·0	ip	2–5	0·5–1·5
Rats	5·0	im	5–10	0·5–1·0
	2·0	ip	2–5	0·5–1·0

Etorphine hydrochloride (M. 99)

Pharmacology
Etorphine is a thebaine derivative chemically related to morphine but with between 200 (man) and 80 000 (hippopotamus) times the narcotic and analgesic potency of the latter drug.

CNS. Etorphine is a powerful central depressant analgesic in most species, although it causes excitement in mice and cats. Reflex response to pain is abolished without loss of consciousness and the respiratory and cough centres are depressed.

Cardiovascular system. Etorphine produces tachycardia and hypertension in ungulates, although in rats, dogs and monkeys it usually causes a bradycardia and hypotension.

Respiratory system. Respiration is depressed in all species.

Indications
Etorphine has been used extensively for the immobilization of wild and zoo animals both alone and in combination with tranquillizers such as methotrimeprazine or acepromazine. Its potency enables large species such as elephant, rhinoceros, hippopotamus and bear to be immobilized with small volumes which are easily injected from projectile syringes and, as the agent has a relatively wide therapeutic index, accurate estimation of weight is not so vital (although occasional deaths have been reported even with 'safe' doses). Animals become catatonic but usually remain standing. The use of etorphine has been widely reported by Harthoorn & Bligh (1965), Harthoorn (1965, 1966; 1975), King & Klingel (1965) and Jones (1973).

The etorphine-acepromazine combination, has become widely accepted for the chemical restraint of horses and many species of wild and zoo animal, but the etorphine-methotrimeprazine mixture designed for small animal use has had more limited appeal. We have used the latter in primates, dogs, pigs, calves, rats, guinea-pigs, rabbits and mice, but in all species cardiac arrhythmias and respiratory depression were more pronounced than with equi-analgesic doses of fentanyl-fluanisone.

Etorphine-acepromazine has been used extensively in equine sedation and anaesthesia, but it produces several side effects which should be noted. It increases cardiac rate and arterial blood pressure initially but the latter usually returns to normal probably because the acepromazine, by virtue of its α-blocking actions, offsets the vasoconstriction caused by etorphine. It also markedly reduces arterial blood O_2 tension.

Contraindications and precautions
The potency and addictive properties of etorphine render it a dangerous drug to handle under laboratory conditions. Despite its undoubted value in the field of game and equine immobilization, we feel that the use of etorphine-acepromazine is not warranted in densely populated laboratories where inexperienced personnel may gain access to it without realizing its potency. The diluted etorphine with methotrimeprazine is less reliable than fentanyl-fluanisone—at least in our hands—so we no longer use it in small species. It must not be used in cats. Relapse several hours after remobilization with diprenorphine has been encountered in donkeys (Dobbs & Ling, 1972; Van Laun, 1977).

Dosage and administration
Etorphine is commercially available in large and small animal presentations. The former contains 2·45 mg etorphine and 10mg acepromazine in each ml, whilst the small animal preparation contains 0·074 mg etorphine and 18 mg methotrimeprazine per ml. Reversal with the specific antagonist diprenorphine is recommended in each case at 0·272 mg/kg by slow iv injection.

Species	Dosage (ml/50 kg)	Route	Time to effect (min)	Time to walk* (min)
Horses†	0·5	im, iv	3–4 (im)	1–4
Pigs†	0·5	im, iv	3–5 (im)	1–10
Dogs‡	0·12 ml/kg	im	2–10	1–30
	0·06 ml/kg	iv		

* After iv injection of antagonist.
† 'Immobilon LA'.
‡ 'Immobilon SA'.

Pentazocine lactate ('Talwin')

Pharmacology
CNS. Pentazocine has strong analgesic with weak sedative properties. The analgesic potency in man is about 30% that of morphine. It is supposedly nonaddictive in man, and is a weak antagonist to other morphine-like drugs. It may stimulate the CTZ and hence the emetic centre in the brain stem to produce nausea and vomiting.

Cardiovascular system. This agent causes minimal disturbance to the cardiovascular system at therapeutic doses.

Respiratory system. Pentazocine is a mild respiratory depressant.

Fate in the body. About 80% of a total dose of 1 mg/kg is excreted in 24 h—mostly eliminated in urine and faeces.

Indications
The absence of addictive properties makes pentazocine an attractive alternative to morphine-derivatives for use in laboratory animals. It is valuable whenever analgesia is required with minimal side effects, e.g. as an alternative to pethidine during post-surgical nursing. We have

used it in horses, dogs, pigs, primates, rabbits and rats (CRC).

Contraindications and precautions
Respiratory depression may be induced in some individuals—but this can be antagonized by naloxone.

Dosage and administration

Species	Dosage (mg/kg)	Route	Time to effect (min)	Duration of effect (min)
Horses	0·5–3·0	iv	2–3	15–30
	0·5–6·0	im	10–15	5–150
Pigs	2·0	im	10–15	30–120
Dogs	2·0	im	10–15	30–120

Dissociative anaesthetics

Three cyclohexylamine analogues—phencyclidine, ketamine and tiletamine—have been used in many species of animal to produce an anaesthetic state termed 'dissociative anaesthesia'. Their main site of action is thought to be on the frontal ('dissociative') cortex and the effects on the RAS are considered less important (Corssen *et al.*, 1968). In man, they produce a cataleptoid state involving loss of consciousness, intense somatix analgesia and limited or no muscle relaxation. Pharyngeal and laryngeal reflexes are usually retained but may be abolished when high doses of drug are used. Cardiovascular centres are stimulated and respiration is generally well maintained. In man, hallucinations and emergence delirium have limited their clinical use but it is not known whether similar phenomena are manifested in animals.

Phencyclidine hydrochloride ('Sernylan')

Pharmacology
CNS. In animals, phencyclidine stimulates or depresses the CNS depending on species and dose, stimulation sometimes occurring with high dose rates. Rats and mice exhibit excitement and ataxia whilst hamsters, cats, dogs, primates, birds, reptiles, frogs and fish are depressed. A cataleptoid state is produced progressing to surgical anaesthesia if supplemented with sedative-analgesics or neuroleptics. Muscle relaxation is poor in all species and muscle tone may even increase. The thermoregulating centres are always depressed and body temperature usually falls rapidly unless artificially maintained. Recovery is slow in cats and the cataleptic state may persist for 24h.
Cardiovascular system. Blood pressure may be slightly elevated if high doses are given by im injection, but bradycardia and arrhythmias may occur if given by the iv route.
Respiratory system. Respiration remains stable after im injection of cataleptic doses, but transient apnoea may occur after rapid iv injection.

Indications
Phencyclidine is compatible with many other narcotics and neuroleptics, which are potentiated to a marked degree. It has been used extensively for the chemical restraint of wild animals (Jones, 1973), although the slow rate of recovery is often a disadvantage when the operator wishes to release the animal again safely. Immobilizing doses may produce tremors or convulsions unless administered with ataractics or neuroleptics.
In laboratory practice, phencyclidine has been most used in the sedation for safe handling of experimental primates. Although we still use it when primates must be sedated for long periods, the short-acting analogue ketamine is preferred for most procedures (CRC). Phencyclidine still retains a place in the sedation of large pigs either alone or supplemented with azaperone, acepromazine or fentanyl—sharing as it does with these agents the advantage that a small volume can be quickly injected im into an intractable animal (CRC).

Contraindications and precautions
Since salivation is always profuse in primates and pigs, atropine should be administered. Body temperature invariably falls dramatically in both species.

Dosages and administration
Phencyclidine is rapidly absorbed after oral or parenteral administration. In laboratory animals it is preferably given im.

Dosage and administration of phencycladine

Species	Dosage (mg/kg)	Route	Time to effect (min)	Duration of effect (min)	Time to full recovery (h)
Primates*	2–5	im	10	120–240	6
Pigs†	2	im	3–10	60–120	4
Rabbits	4	im	5–10	20–60	2
Hamsters ‡	4	im	5–10	20–60	2
Guinea-pigs	3	im	5–10	20–60	2

* Cataleptic sedation and good analgesia.
† Deep sedation, some analgesia and recumbency in some cases.
‡ Variable sedation.

41

At these dose levels, a cataleptoid state is produced and, in our experience, necessitates supplementation with other injectable narcotics or inhalation of $N_2O:O_2$ to produce surgical anaesthesia (CRC).

Ketamine hydrochloride ('Vetalar', 'Ketalar')

Pharmacology

CNS. The effects are similar to phencyclidine except that in all species ketamine has a much shorter duration of action. In man, intense analgesia develops even in the absence of sleep, and the subject is cataleptic. In cats and primates it produces profound analgesia and catalepsis without muscle relaxation; during recovery, tonic-clonic spasms may occur even in the absence of sensory stimuli. Salivation is always increased and atropine should be given—although laryngeal reflexes are usually retained, excess fluid does accumulate and can block the airway.

Cardiovascular system. Probably as a result of central sympathetic stimulation, blood pressure and heart rate increase soon after im administration in most animals; cardiac output is unchanged or slightly increased.

Respiratory system. There may be a mild depression of respiration although, in our experience, rabbits and rats usually exhibit an increase in respiratory rate. Although laryngeal reflexes are preserved (except when high dosages have been given) it is still necessary for the anaes-

narcosis is only moderately increased but the 10–30 mg/kg; at the higher dose rates, depth of duration of effect is prolonged. Its use has also been reported in dogs (Dawson *et al.*, 1971), pigs (Roberts, 1971), rats at 60 mg/kg in combination with pentobarbitone 20 mg/kg (Youth *et al.*, 1973), birds at 60 mg/kg im (Bree & Gross, 1969; Kittle, 1971; Cooper, 1975), laboratory rabbits and rodents (Weisbroth & Fudens, 1972), sheep (Thurman *et al.*, 1973) and reptiles (Glenn *et al.*, 1972).

However, our experience has not always agreed with reports in the literature. We believe it to be the drug of choice for handling primates, birds, reptiles and large wild cats, but it is not used by us in dogs, pigs, sheep or domestic cats unless they have previously been given ataractics or sedatives such as acepromazine (dogs), diazepam (mice, rats, guinea-pigs), azaperone or diazepam (pigs), or xylazine (sheep, rabbits and cats). Supplementation with these agents is required to enhance analgesia, reduce muscle tone and prevent tonic-clonic convulsions during recovery.

Dosage and administration

Ketamine produces deep cataleptic sedation with low doses (1–2 mg/kg) in most species if given by the iv route. However, the advantage of this agent is that it has a wide therapeutic index and can be given im by the inexperienced anaesthetist or to dangerous species for restraint. The dosages below all refer to im administration of ketamine without other agents.

Dosage and administration of ketamine hydrochloride

Species	Dosage (mg/kg)	Route	Time to effect (min)	Duration of action (min)	Time to full recovery (min)
Cats	10–30	im	1–5	30–40	100–150
Primates	15–30	im	3–5	30–45	100–150
Pigs*	10–15	im	2–4	30–45	60–90
Birds	40–100†	im	1–3	20–30	40–50
Reptiles	40–80	im	30+	60–120	up to 96 h

* To provide peaceful sedation, diazepam (1 mg/kg im) should also be given.
† To prevent emergence struggling, metomidate (10 mg/kg im) should be given concurrently.

thetist to pay close attention to airway patency (Sears, 1971).

Fate in the body. Ketamine is metabolized in the liver by N-demethylation and hydroxylation of the cyclohexanone ring to form water-soluble conjugates which are excreted by the kidneys.

Indications

Ketamine has such a wide therapeutic index (it is 5 times greater than pentobarbitone in dogs) that it can be safely given iv or im in most species. However, there is considerable variation in species sensitivity. Primates and cats require im doses of

Tiletamine hydrochloride (CI-634)

Pharmacology

Tiletamine is chemically related to ketamine and has a very similar spectrum of activity. Onset of catalepsy is rapid after im injection, and lasts for 30–50 min depending on species and dosage. Most reports are of clinical trials with tiletamine in combination with the diazepam analogue, zolazepam (combination called CI-744).

Cardiovascular system. Tiletamine alone produces a bradycardia in cats (Calderwood *et al.*,

42

1971). Using the combination tiletamine-zolazepam, Ward *et al.* (1974) observed tachycardia with slight rises in blood pressure and cardiac output in dogs, and concluded that these effects were all small in comparison with similar dosages of ketamine.

Respiratory system. In dogs, respiration is first stimulated and then depressed, but a significant respiratory acidosis does not develop (Ward *et al.*, 1974).

Indications

Tiletamine-zolazepam has been recommended for use in dogs, cats, sheep, rats (Ward *et al.*, 1974), primates (Bree, 1972; Kaufman & Hahnenberger, 1975) and a wide variety of exotic species (Gray *et al.*, 1974). It seems likely that this will be a useful combination if it becomes available commercially, since our findings with similar mixtures (e.g. ketamine-diazepam or ketamine-xylazine) have been encouraging in many different species (CRC).

LOCAL AND REGIONAL ANALGESIA

INTRODUCTION

Local analgesic techniques offer many advantages over general anaesthesia, and should always be considered as a possible alternative. Perhaps their greatest advantages in experimental work are that they cause minimal disturbance to the animal's biochemical and physiological processes and, since they exert little or no effect on placental and foetal circulation, are particularly valuable in uterine and foetal surgery. Furthermore, they allow many procedures to be carried out in ruminants with the animal standing, thus causing minimal disturbance to rumenal function, and they permit surgery on aged, obese and other poor-risk subjects which might otherwise be impossible.

Full accounts of the clinical applications of local and regional analgesia in animals have been given by Hall (1971) and Lumb & Jones (1973), and there have been no recent developments in drugs or techniques available to merit repetition in this chapter. Only those techniques which are commonly used in experimental situations will be described.

GENERAL PROPERTIES

Most local analgesics are tertiary amino esters or amides of aromatic acids prepared as water soluble salts (usually hydrochlorides or carbonate bases). Although the highly lipid-soluble free base has long been considered responsible for the activity of local analgesics, it is possible that the salt may be the active moiety. The drugs are thought to prevent the migration of ions across the neurone membrane, probably by competing for calcium ions at receptors controlling permeability. They thus prevent axon depolarization during transmission of nerve action potentials (NAP). Small diameter fibres are preferentially blocked, so pain, temperature, touch and motor functions are lost in that order.

All the commonly used local analgesics are destroyed mainly in the liver—hence liver dysfunction may result in increased drug toxicity —while some, e.g. procaine are also metabolized in the circulating blood plasma.

INDIVIDUAL AGENTS

Only lignocaine and amethocaine have received wide acceptance in laboratory animal work. Lignocaine is used as a general purpose local analgesic and amethocaine as a surface analgesic for topical use.

Lignocaine hydrochloride ('Xylocaine')

Pharmacology

Lignocaine has superseded other agents because it is chemically stable, possesses a high therapeutic ratio, is non-irritant and possesses a rapid onset of action which is maintained for a convenient period. Its ability to diffuse rapidly through tissues makes it an ideal agent for infiltration and nerve blocks. However, since this property also means that it will be absorbed into the systemic circulation at a relatively rapid rate, adrenaline (1 or 2 : 100 000) is often included in the solution, e.g. when it is to be injected into the epidural space. The rate of absorption is then approximately halved.

If lignocaine is absorbed in toxic concentrations, the symptoms are usually those of initial depression of the CNS progressing to muscle twitching, convulsions and marked hypotension. The total quantity of agent administered should therefore be kept to a minimum and as dilute a solution should be used as practicable. This is particularly important in small mammals and birds. The latter have long been considered highly sensitive to local analgesics, but it is more likely that mortalities encountered in the past resulted from excessive dosage using 2% solutions without first diluting them. For instance, it has been estimated that ligno-caine has a toxicity some 1·5 times that of procaine; since the sc LD_{50} of procaine has been reported as 430 mg/kg in guinea-pigs, 460 in rabbits, 450 in cats and 250 in dogs (Booth, 1965), it is evident that a mere 0·3 ml of a 2% lignocaine solution will be close to the LD_{50} in a small bird weighing 20–30 g. Solutions should always therefore be diluted to 0·25–0·5% to reduce the risk.

Indications and dosages

Adrenaline 1 : 100 000 is included in all suggested solutions unless otherwise specified.

Infiltration analgesia. A 0·5% solution of ligno-caine is commonly employed, although in infiltrat-ing extensive areas it is preferable to dilute the solution to 0·25% with normal saline.

Nerve block. A 1% solution is used.

Epidural and caudal block. A 1% solution is used in most species.

Spinal block. A 2% solution is generally used.

Surface analgesia. A 2% solution is used on the cornea, and the mouth, pharynx, larynx and trachea may be sprayed with 2 or 4% solutions.

Amethocaine hydrochloride('Pontocaine')

Pharmacology

Amethocaine is a local analgesic of the procaine group with a slower onset (5 min) but longer duration (2–3 h) of action than lignocaine. It is about 10 times as potent as procaine but is highly toxic if absorbed too rapidly—the symptoms of toxicity are an initial stimulant and secondary depressant action on the CNS, hypotension due to peripheral vasodilatation, and possibly cardiac failure with ventricular fibrillation. It is particularly effective in the desensitization of mucous mem-branes (10 times the potency of cocaine).

Indications

This drug should only be used for surface anal-gesia, and is the drug of choice for instillation into the eye for corneal analgesia. Concentrations of 0·25–0·5% are adequate for this purpose and have little effect in delaying corneal healing. A 0·5% solution is adequate for desensitizing other mu-cous membranes, e.g. the mouth, vagina or urethra.

ANALGESIC TECHNIQUES

Surface or topical analgesia, infiltration or field blocks, nerve block (conduction analgesia), and spinal blocks will be briefly described here and then discussed in more detail in later sections in relation to individual species.

Surface or topical analgesia

This is used principally for experimental eye surgery. For this purpose, a few drops of 0·25% amethocaine can be given to render the cornea and conjunctiva insensitive to pain. As a general rule, many local analgesics are well absorbed through all mucous membranes but are ineffective in most areas of intact skin except the bovine teat. Intact skin can be temporarily desensitized for a few seconds by spraying a fine jet of ethyl chloride on to a small localized area, when rapid evaporation and the consequent fall in temperature interfere with pain transduction.

A

tissue to be excised

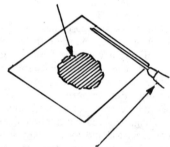

needle advanced at shallow angle and injection made into sub-cutaneous tissue at 5mm intervals

B

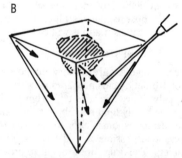

needle advanced at various angles into muscle layers and injection made until area to be excised is surrounded by inverted cone of analgesic

Fig. 5.1 Infiltration or field block—the 'cone' pattern

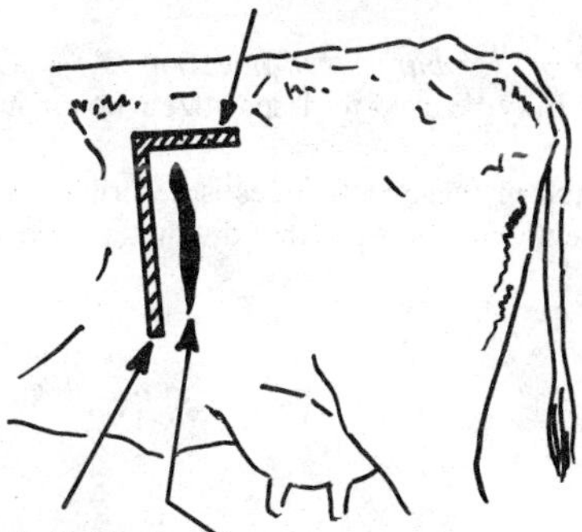

horizontal line of infiltration
below lumbar vertebrae

vertical line
just posterior   flank incision
to final rib

Fig. 5.2 Infiltration or field block—'inverted-L' pattern

Infiltration or field block

Lignocaine is injected around the lesion or area to be desensitized, first incorporating only the superficial layers but then injecting deeper subcutaneous tissues to take account of the fan-like spread of nerves from central to peripheral structures. The most useful blocks are:

Cone block. 0·25–0·5% lignocaine solution is first injected in a superficial ring or diamond pattern, and then a cone is formed in the deeper tissues (Fig. 5.1). This is the most commonly employed pattern in small mammals, birds and reptiles, where local analgesia is used as an adjunct to basal narcosis with drugs such as ketamine, xylazine or an inhalation mixture of $N_2O:O_2$.

Ring block. 0·25–0·5% lignocaine is infiltrated around a tail or limb to render distal structures insensitive.

Inverted-L block. Superficial lines are infiltrated first, and the deeper muscle layers progressively desensitized (Fig. 5.2).

Each of these blocks allows an area to be desensitized without actually infiltrating solution into tissue to be incised. The techniques are simple and effective provided care is taken not to leave isolated sensitive areas. This is particularly important in preparing the bovine flank for laparotomy incisions, as it is difficult to include the sensitive peritoneum in the infiltration. It is now common to block such areas using spinal or conduction analgesia but, in our experience, infiltration blocks in sheep, goats and cattle give more consistent results.

Nerve blocks

A 0·5–1% solution is injected either close to individual nerves serving a specific anatomical area, or around several nerves and their branches. Three of these are used in experimental procedures:

Infraorbital nerve block in which the innervation of the upper jaw is blocked—a useful technique in dogs.

Mandibular nerve block in which the innervation of the lower jaw is blocked—also useful in dogs.

Conduction analgesia of the trunk by *paravertebral analgesia* in which spinal nerves are blocked as they emerge from intervertebral foramina—this is particularly useful in surgery of the bovine flank and is described on p. 173.

Spinal blocks

For all practical purposes, the techniques are limited to epidural analgesia in animal work; lignocaine (with adrenaline 1:200 000) is injected into the spinal canal outside the dura mater. Solutions then pass along this space at a rate and for a distance depending on the volume injected, the strength of the solution and on the posture of the animal. Great care must be taken in placing the needle, since venous sinuses run longitudinally in the floor of the vertebral canal and accidental puncture may allow rapid absorption of lignocaine into the general circulation. The site of injection depends upon the type of block desired. A simple descriptive classification is based on the distance forward that the analgesic solution extends.

Posterior block. Sensory perception of the tail, anal and vulval regions is lost, but motor control of the hind limbs is retained.

Anterior block. Sensory blockade may extend forward to thoracic level. Clearly this will become more dangerous if it is allowed to develop further forward when autonomic nervous control over the respiratory and cardiovascular systems may be affected. Coordination of the hind limbs is usually lost and great care must be exercised in preventing injuries to the animals as they fall and struggle to stand again.

The most usual anatomical sites of injection are:

Caudal. Injection is made between the 1st and 2nd coccygeal vertebrae. This site is distal to the termination of the spinal cord and its meninges. Spinal block at this level is valuable in cattle, sheep and dogs.

Lumbosacral foramina. Epidural injection at this level allows a much bigger flank area to be desensitized and it is useful in sheep, pigs, dogs and guinea-pigs.

Anterior lumbar sites. Injection of 1–2% lignocaine may be used to desensitize whole zones of the flank in cattle and goats.

Each of these techniques is described in detail in the sections dealing with individual species.

MUSCLE RELAXANTS

INTRODUCTION

Muscle tone is thought to be maintained by continuous nerve action potentials (NAP) transmitted from anterior horn cells in the spinal cord. Muscle relaxation can be deliberately induced either *centrally* by blocking NAP generation by deep general anaesthesia or with drugs that block spinal interneurones—the centrally acting group of muscle relaxants—or *peripherally* by blocking nerves with local analgesics, and by specifically blocking neuromuscular transmission with certain drugs which act at the myoneural junction —peripherally acting muscle relaxant drugs. In addition, muscle tone can be reduced by drugs such as diazepam and xylazine acting on synapses in the spinal cord.

The neuromuscular junction can be blocked in 4 ways: by *deficiency block*, either by interference with transmitter synthesis or with its release—many agencies such as calcium ion deficiency, and concurrent administration of neomycin, kanomycin and streptomycin (the aminoglycoside group of antibiotics) diminish quantal release of acetylcholine and may significantly prolong the paralysis produced by muscle relaxants; by *depolarizing block*, when agents such as suxamethonium compete with acetylcholine for motor end-plate receptors and cause a persistent depolarization which, in turn, prevents the generation of further action potentials in the muscle; by *non-depolarizing* or *competitive block* in which agents such as gallamine or pancuronium compete with acetylcholine for end-plate receptors but do not depolarize the end-plate once attached—the end-plate potential will then fail to reach the triggering threshold; and by *dual block* (*desensitization block*) when in certain circumstances a non-depolarizing block may be caused by a depolarizing drug.

Muscle relaxants have been employed routinely in human anaesthetic practice for more than 20 years, but they have had more limited use in animals. Animal applications have included the chemical immobilization of wild game and horses (a technique which is now little used) and the facilitation of endotracheal intubation in dogs, cats and pigs (Lumb, 1972). Nevertheless, the balanced combination of preanaesthetic medication with analgesics, maintenance of light anaesthesia with a $N_2O:O_2$ gas mixture, and of muscle relaxation together with assisted or intermittent positive pressure ventilation (IPPV) is considered by many to provide the best surgical conditions for clinical use in man. The objective is to obtain complete relaxation of skeletal muscle without recourse to dangerously deep levels of surgical anaesthesia.

Muscle relaxants have no analgesic effects but they do prevent the animal from responding to a painful stimulus. Once skeletal muscles are paralysed, the only indicators to perception of pain are rapid eye movements and increased heart rate—and even these are unreliable guides. Hence, the anaesthetist must exercise great care in their use. Furthermore, there is a statutory legal requirement to obtain special permission for use in experimental work: it should be clearly understood that UK Home Office approval will only be given after careful consideration of the expertise available and the necessity for use in a particular experiment.

When contemplating a given surgical procedure using muscle relaxation, it is first necessary to establish the degree of analgesia which would be needed for that particular procedure and, using this as a minimal standard, superimpose muscle relaxation on the protocol. The combination must be assayed for suitability of both dosage and duration of effect.

The practice of attempting to achieve a near-physiological preparation in animals by inhalation of $N_2O:O_2$ by IPPV, after muscle relaxants but no analgesics have been given, is wholly unacceptable and should never be used. Although $N_2O:O_2$ (1:1) is valuable in providing background narcosis to many balanced anaesthetic regimes, it confers insufficient analgesia for *any* surgical procedure in animals, and morphine-like drugs should be given. Pethidine is valuable in providing good analgesia for up to 2 h duration; when more profound analgesia is required, fentanyl is highly effective but lasts only about 20 min.

Whichever muscle relaxant is used, spontaneous respiration is usually abolished since the thoracic skeletal muscles and the diaphragm are paralysed. Hence, some form of IPPV is essential. When short-acting agents such as suxamethonium have been used, the animals can be ventilated via an endotracheal tube connected to a source of gas with an intervening rebreathing bag which can be compressed manually at regular intervals by the anaesthetist. For long periods of relaxation, it is more convenient to connect the animal to a mechanical respirator.

INDIVIDUAL AGENTS

Depolarizing drugs

Suxamethonium bromide ('Brevedil M')

Pharmacology
Suxamethonium (succinylcholine) is a short-acting depolarizing agent which produces relaxation within 10–15 s of iv injection for a duration of about 5 min depending on species.

CNS. It has no effect on the CNS.

Cardiovascular and autonomic nervous systems. The ganglion-stimulant action may lead to vagal stimulation and this may produce bradycardia and hypotension, especially if repeated doses are given iv. However, this can be prevented by the previous administration of atropine. Suxamethonium does not reach the foetal circulation.

Respiratory system. Respiratory muscles are paralysed and there may be some increase in bronchial secretions.

Muscular system. All skeletal muscle is rapidly paralysed; suxamethonium mimics release of acetylcholine at the neuromuscular junction and depolarizes the motor end-plate. As a result of depolarization, muscular relaxation is preceded by initial stimulation which takes the form of muscle fasciculations. This activity cannot be reversed by neostigmine but is short-lived anyway since suxamethonium is broken down rapidly by plasma pseudocholinesterase. Species variation in duration of effect is related to plasma concentrations of this enzyme—in fact, after a period, a dual non-depolarizing block may develop.

Indications
Suxamethonium is indicated whenever profound muscle relaxation of short duration is required. It is, therefore, the drug of choice in animals in which passing an endotracheal tube is commonly made difficult by laryngeal spasm, e.g. rabbits, pigs and cats.

Contraindications and precautions
Premedication with atropine should always be given in animals to prevent excessive bronchial secretions and vagal inhibition of the heart. The drug should not be used in cases of severe liver disease and is probably contraindicated in liver transplant surgery. Suxamethonium is one drug which precipitates the familial hyperpyrexial syndrome (p. 189) in some breeds of pigs (Landrace, Pietrain and others)—if this does occur it can be treated with procaine (Harrison, 1971) and IPPV (CRC).

Dosage and administration

	Dosage (mg/kg iv)	Time to effect (s)	Duration of effect (min)
Dog	0·3	10–15	5–10
Pig	2·0	10–15	2–3
Cat	1·0	10–15	2–3
Rabbit	0·5	10–15	5–10
Ruminants	0·02	10–15	6–8

Non-depolarizing drugs

Gallamine triethiodide ('Flaxedil')

Pharmacology
Gallamine is a non-depolarizing muscle relaxant which competes with acetylcholine to prevent combination at motor end-plate receptor sites. It can, therefore, be reversed by an anticholinesterase such as neostigmine. This prevents breakdown of acetylcholine released from synaptic vesicles in the nerve terminal adjacent to the synaptic cleft, and allows acetylcholine to accumulate, displace the relaxant from end-plate receptors and thus reverse the block. The action commences 1–2 min after iv administration and in man persists for 20–40 min.

CNS. There is no effect on the CNS at normal doses.

Cardiovascular and autonomic nervous systems Vagal nerve supply to the heart is inhibited by an atropine-like action to produce a tachycardia in all species. The increased heart rate is occasionally accompanied by irregularity associated with electrical conduction disturbances, but there is no direct effect on the myocardium. Occasionally, hypotension develops in cats and pigs.

Respiratory system. There is no effect other than paralysis of respiratory muscles.

Muscular system. All skeletal muscles are rapidly paralysed.

Placental barrier. Appreciable quantities of gallamine cross the placenta without significant effect on the foetus.

Fate in the body. Gallamine is not detoxified in the body and is excreted unchanged in the urine—hence, negligible amounts of the agent will be excreted in the absence of renal function (Feldman *et al.*, 1969).

Indications

Gallamine is indicated in major abdominal and thoracic surgery where complete muscular relaxation or artificial control of respiration is required. It can be used in foetal and intrauterine surgery to allow relaxation without increasing the depth of general surgical anaesthesia, thus avoiding depression of foetal respiration. Unlike d-tubocurarine, it does not cause histamine release and so can be used with safety in any species.

Contraindications and precautions

Gallamine should not be used in experiments involving damaged or transplanted kidneys since excretion will be delayed in the presence of renal failure. It is also best avoided during cardiac surgery because of the vagal inhibitory action. Anesthetics with a curare-like action, particularly ether, potentiate the muscle relaxation, and the dosage of gallamine should then be halved.

Dosage and administration

The dosages and times given below assume that full muscle relaxation is required, so that the animal will be supported with O_2 and IPPV during the inevitable period of respiratory arrest.

	Dosage (mg/kg iv)	Time to effect (min)	Duration of effect (min)
Dog	1·0	1–2	15–20
Cat	1·0	1–2	10–20
Pig	2·0–4·0	1–2	10–20
Lamb	0·4	1–2	10–240
Calf	0·4	1–2	10–240
Cow	0·5	1–2	20

Supplementary doses can be given to extend the period of effect.

Paralysis can be reversed by administering neostigmine (0·01–0·02 mg/kg iv) always administered after atropine (0·04–0·1 mg/kg iv depending on species) to prevent the muscarinic effects of acetylcholine on smooth muscle and cardiac function. If reversal is incomplete, further neostigmine (0·025 mg/kg iv) should be given after

10 min without giving more atropine. It is essential to continue with IPPV until spontaneous respiration is fully established and maintaining arterial blood plasma PaO_2 and $PaCO_2$ tensions within normal limits.

Pancuronium bromide ('Pavulon')

Pharmacology

Pancuronium is a synthetic amino-steroid with similar non-depolarizing activity to gallamine. After iv injection it takes from 2–3 min to act and has a duration of effect lasting 45–100 min depending on species. It can be reversed completely with neostigmine and atropine.

CNS. Pancuronium does not cross the blood-brain barrier and, unlike d-tubocurarine, it appears to be devoid of ganglionic blocking and histamine releasing activity.

Cardiovascular system. In man, there is a moderate rise in cardiac rate of some 20%, and a rise in arterial blood pressure of 10–20% without an increase in cardiac output. This is due to the mild vagolytic activity of pancuronium, and can be prevented by prior administration of atropine.

Respiratory system. Respiratory muscles are paralysed.

Placental barrier. Pancuronium can be detected in foetal blood but apparently exerts no harmful effects.

Fate in the body. Much of the drug is metabolized in the liver and excreted in bile, but some is excreted unchanged in urine. It is probably therefore the relaxant of choice where renal failure is a problem, as in a kidney transplantation (Slawson, 1972).

Indications

It is probably the relaxant of choice in most situations as it can be easily reversed with neostigmine, it is longer-acting than gallamine and is more readily eliminated than the latter in poor-risk cases.

Contraindications and precautions

Malignant hyperpyrexia in pigs has been reported after administration of pancuronium (Chalstrey & Edwards, 1972), but it has not been encountered at this centre (CRC).

Dosage and administration

According to Monks (1972), pancuronium is about 6 times as potent as d-tubocurarine, and doses as low as 0·02–0·08 mg/kg are recommended for man, with initial doses not to exceed 0·1 mg/kg. Limited experience in pigs suggests that iv doses of

0·05 mg/kg are adequate for paralysis and the effects last 40–80 min (CRC).

CONCLUSIONS

Muscle relaxants are useful agents in the hands of experienced anaesthetists. The short-acting drug suxamethonium is useful to facilitate the intubation of pigs, rabbits and cats, whilst pancuronium or gallamine should be used for longer procedures, particularly when thoracic surgery necessitates the abolition of spontaneous respiration.

CHAPTER SEVEN

GENERAL AND BALANCED ANAESTHESIA

INTRODUCTION

Classification of general anaesthetic and related techniques

General anaesthesia is a state of general depression of the CNS involving hypnosis, analgesia, suppression of reflex activity and relaxation of voluntary muscle. Anaesthetic agents have a spectrum of narcotic activity which may be both dose- and time-related, extending from sedation through hypnosis, basal narcosis, light surgical and medium surgical anaesthesia to deep surgical anaesthesia, coma and death. However, there are related techniques available which do not readily fit into this general continuum concept yet provide conditions to satisfy most surgical requirements e.g. dissociative anaesthesia is adequate for quite traumatic surgery in primates.

The techniques which are most useful in providing surgical conditions can be classified under 4 main headings. In addition, electronarcosis is included in case it becomes more widely accepted in the future. Some of the drugs administered parenterally e.g. dissociative anaesthetics, propanidid and anaesthetic steroids have been described elsewhere since they are commonly used in attaining moderate levels of narcosis or chemical restraint as aids to induction, but they will be further described in this chapter when it is felt that they are particularly valuable as anaesthetics in their own right. The techniques comprise:

(i) Inhalation of:
  (a) Volatilized liquids such as ether, enflurane, methoxyflurane or halothane
  (b) Gaseous agents such as cylcopropane, nitrous oxide (N_2O), or carbon dioxide (CO_2)
(ii) Parenteral administration of:
  (a) Short-acting water-soluble barbiturates
  (b) Steroids
  (c) Dissociative anaesthetic agents
  (d) Neuroleptanalgesic combinations
  (e) Miscellaneous agents
(iii) Hypothermia
(iv) Combinations of any of these with muscle relaxant drugs
(v) Electronarcosis

Signs and stages of anaesthesia

There can be no simple description of the animal's responses to anaesthetic administration. The stages and planes of surgical anaesthesia proposed by Guedel (1951) were an attempt to divide the state of anaesthesia into neat packages each correlating with a given set of reflexes. However, they were based on observations in man inhaling ether without premedication. Reflex behaviour varies so much with the drugs used and the species of animal that the description has become increasingly irrelevant and unhelpful, and should now be abandoned. For example, voluntary and involuntary excitement stages during induction and recovery have no place in modern anaesthetic management and are almost always avoidable; furthermore, many of the eye responses seen in man are quite different in other animals and when other agents are administered. Whatever other observations are made, the most valuable criteria of anaesthetic depth must be the animal's response to stimuli. The aim must be to prevent the perception of painful stimuli without undue depression of physiological functions. A few simple tests will be described.

As long as excitement and motor activity during induction are suppressed by suitable pre-anaesthetic medication, the course of narcosis deepening to complete surgical anaesthesia follows a fairly standard pattern. Initially, the animal is able to walk but becomes progressively ataxic; then it lies down but is able to turn or lift its head without support. As narcosis deepens, the *righting*

reflex is lost and the animal makes no attempt to turn over to the prone position when placed on its back. The whole body relaxes—although slight tremors may still be present, limb movements may still be provoked by painful stimuli and the *swallowing reflex* may be evoked on separating the jaws and pulling the tongue. When surgical levels of anaesthesia are approached, the *palpebral reflex* (blink when the inner canthus of the eye is touched) is lost, and deliberate dilatation of the anal sphincter fails to produce an increased rate of breathing (*respiratory reflex*). When the animal fails to react to *any* external stimuli, a state of surgical anaesthesia has been reached.

Recovery may differ in its time course but it follows a similar pattern. The palpebral reflex and the respiratory response to anal sphincter dilation return in that order. Some degree of muscle trembling will now often become apparent, the animal will attempt to right itself and it will lift its head in response to noise or other sensory stimuli. Most animals will then pass into a state of sleep from which they can be aroused and they are capable of walking if awakened. Complete recovery may take anything from minutes to days depending on species and the drugs used, e.g. 2–10 min for rabbits anaesthetized with propanidid, and up to 48 h for greyhounds with pentobarbitone.

The most important indications of depth of narcosis will now be considered in more detail.

Responses to painful stimuli. As CNS depression increases, the reflex withdrawal and flexion of a hind limb which has been extended and then had the interdigital skin pinched (*the pedal reflex*) weakens and slows until it disappears when light to medium levels of surgical anaesthesia have been attained. This is a useful test in dogs, cats, rats and mice. The disappearance of head shaking in response to an ear pinch is a surer guide to attainment of surgical levels of analgesia in rabbits and guinea-pigs, whilst a failure to respond to tail pinching is a good indication in rats, mice and snakes. In birds, the comb, wattles, cloaca or digits may be pinched or stretched to test for analgesia.

Skeletal muscle relaxation. As narcosis deepens, the jaws can be opened progressively more easily (a most useful test in dogs and cats), the limbs can be extended without reflex withdrawal, and abdominal muscle feels 'floppy' when picked up and allowed to drop.

Eye and palpebral responses vary with species and, to a lesser extent, with the drugs employed—nevertheless they yield valuable information:

(a) The loss of voluntary movements is important—the eyeball may be fixed centrally or ventrally, or it may go through rapid horizontal or vertical oscillatory movements (*nystagmus*) before surgical anaesthesia is reached.

(b) Response to gently tapping the inner canthus of the eyelids (the *blink* or *palpebral reflex*) is lost as light to medium surgical anaesthesia is attained.

(c) The conjunctival membranes should be observed at frequent intervals to detect colour alterations. The anaesthetist should be able to discern gross changes such as the pallor associated with surgical shock or haemorrhage, or the cyanosis which develops when the animal is poorly ventilated and tissues are starved of oxygen.

Colour changes are best observed in the conjunctiva, gums, palate and tongue of horses, cattle, sheep, goats, dogs and cats; the feet, ears and muzzles of rodents; the reflected colour of a light directed into the eye of rats and rabbits; the tongue and buccal cavity of primates; the comb and wattles of birds; and the snout of pigs. Cyanosis or extreme pallor indicate profound disturbance of physiological functions, but it should be remembered that accumulation of CO_2 in the blood will not be indicated by colour changes, unless it is accompanied by low PaO_2.

Respiratory pattern. The most useful information is obtained from close observation of respiratory movements. The rate and quality are both important, as are violent alterations evoked by surgical stimuli.

(a) During induction, or as the animal lightens in recovery, breathing may range from rapid irregular movements to temporary cessation (*apnoea*). For example, a rabbit may hold its breath for 60 s or more if induction is attempted with inhalational agents such as halothane without premedication.

(b) When a state of medium surgical anaesthesia is reached, breathing is generally slow and regular, and marked thoracic excursions should not be evoked by surgical stimuli.

(c) If narcotic depression progresses to deep surgical anaesthesia, the thoracic movements may exhibit an obvious pause between inspiration and expiration (*delayed thoracic respiration*). Any further depression results in laboured inspiratory movements involving obvious physical efforts of the abdomen and diaphragm without contribution from the thoracic muscles. No animal can be expected to survive for long at this depth of anaesthesia without assisted respiration.

Terminology

The times taken to reach or recover from various levels of central depression are necessarily rather subjective as there are no well-defined end-points. However, the following terms are used throughout this chapter and are based on the signs just described:

Time to onset of effect is the time elapsing between *initial* administration of the agent and the first signs of drowsiness and ataxia.

Time to peak effect is the time between initial administration and the development of the maximum effect expected of that drug at the stated dose.

Duration of effect is the length of time at which that peak effect can be expected to last e.g. the period allowed for surgery from a single administration of an injectable anaesthetic.

Time to recovery is the length of time between initial administration and the moment that the animal can be aroused from sleep and is capable of standing unaided or walking without falling.

Time to full recovery is the interval between initial administration of a single dose and the time when the animal is eating and behaving normally.

It should be noted that many authors use the term 'sleep time' rather loosely. Whenever it is used in this text in quoting other sources it is taken to mean the total time from establishing hypnosis to the moment that the animal can be aroused and will stand unaided.

INHALATION ANAESTHESIA: MEANS OF ADMINISTRATION

Methods of administration: principles

The essential requirements of all inhalational methods are the provision of sufficient O_2 to the alveolar membranes, adequate clearance of CO_2 from the lungs and from the environment immediately adjacent to the animal's face, and presentation of anaesthetic gases or vapour at adequate partial pressure to the alveolar membrane. Alveolar ventilation is the principal factor in satisfying these 3 requirements but in other respects each should be considered as a separate problem by the anaesthetist. For example, an asphyxiated animal, dying principally from O_2 deprivation, may be saved by rapid administration of high O_2 concentrations but this alone will not prevent alveolar CO_2 partial pressure from continuing to rise unless ventilation is adequate—attention must be devoted to correcting both sources of failure.

The tension of anaesthetic agent in the CNS (and hence the depth of anaesthesia) is directly related to the alveolar tension of the agent. It is important both to reach and to sustain adequate alveolar partial pressures to achieve a stable state. The presentation of anaesthetic agent to the alveoli provides its own problems, especially during the induction phase. Initially, the circuit itself may retard the development of effective anaesthetic partial pressure in the alveoli because the volume of gas already in the circuit has to be replaced and because most agents, but particularly methoxyflurane, have a high affinity for rubber and for soda lime. Hence, it is necessary to provide a high gas flow rate and high anaesthetic concentration during the initial stages if rapid anaesthetic induction is required.

Once the agents gain access to the animal's respiratory system, the rate of increase in alveolar concentration will be governed by both ventilatory and circulatory factors. Increases in ventilation *without* concomitant changes in cardiac output will increase the rate of alveolar rise—and this will be most pronounced when using the more soluble anaesthetics—whereas *parallel* increases in ventilation and circulation will initially exert opposing effects on anaesthetic uptake. However, as increased tissue perfusion results in increased rate of equilibration, there will eventually be an overall improvement in uptake of the agent (Eger, 1974).

Conversely, during recovery, ventilation rapidly lowers alveolar anaesthetic concentration, and the agent diffuses down concentration gradients from blood and tissues. This rate of reverse output will again depend on cardiac output and anaesthetic solubility. The animal faces two main hazards during recovery as a result. In the poorly ventilated subject, a sudden output of anaesthetic gas e.g. N_2O from the blood may raise alveolar concentration and dilute alveolar O_2—the so-called *concentration effect*—endangering the animal by producing *diffusion hypoxia*. In addition, if the animal continues to breathe from the anaesthetic apparatus, it may inhale anaesthetic previously absorbed in rubber components even though the main source of agent has been shut off. This is why it is so important to retain endotracheal tubes in place until the animal has regained swallowing reflexes and why it should be maintained on O_2 for 2–3 min after the N_2O has been turned off.

Methods of administration: essential components of apparatus

The only pieces of equipment which are essential and common to all controlled methods no matter what inhalational technique is adopted are a source of O_2 (cylinder + reducing valve + flowmeter calibrated for low as well as high flow rates to cope with a wide range of species), a system for vaporizing volatile drugs, and some means of presenting gases to the animal's respiratory system. In addition, a means of warming and humidifying inspired gases is highly desirable. In a recent review of anaesthetic management of neonate and poor-risk infants, Inkster (1975) emphasized the need to heat and moisturize inflowing anaesthetic gases, and described a suitable heating coil for this pur-

pose. The outer surface to bodyweight ratio and its significance for temperature regulation in small animals was emphasized early in this text; a similarly high ratio is true of lung surface to bodyweight, with the additional hazard that cold, dry gases magnify heat loss still further by latent heat of evaporation. In an attempt to overcome this problem, we have introduced a second vaporizer into our rodent circuits in which the anaesthetic gases pass over water at approximately 45°C.

The apparatus can be as simple or sophisticated as economy and the animals involved dictate. In small rodents, for example, anaesthesia can be induced in a clear plastic box connected to the O_2 and vaporizer, and several animals can be maintained simultaneously by connecting them to multiple outlet manifolds constructed of glass. Effective but inexpensive circuits can be built using readily available plastic, rubber and glass components. For larger animals such as dogs, on the other hand, it is more convenient to purchase anaesthetic apparatus which is commercially available.

In the absence of mechanical aids to ventilation, efficient breathing depends on minimum impedance to inspiratory and expiratory flow—a requirement best satisfied by wide-bore, straight-line tubes—and minimum dead space so that exhaled alveolar gases are either expelled into the atmosphere, or recycled through a soda-lime canister for CO_2 extraction.

Methods of administration: types of circuit

Various systems have been designed to satisfy the requirements described above and these are classified according to differing criteria. Perhaps the simplest classification involves two considerations only: (a) the presence or absence of a reservoir incorporated in the circuit to satisfy peak inspiratory flow, and (b) whether rebreathing of exhaled gases is permitted after CO_2 has been absorbed in soda-lime (Eger, 1974). In open systems, O_2 is obtained from the atmosphere or supplied at a sufficient rate to flush away exhaled CO_2, and neither feature is incorporated. In semi-open systems, rebreathing of exhaled gases is not allowed and a reservoir is included in the circuit. In closed systems, rebreathing is allowed after CO_2 has been absorbed in soda-lime and a rebreathing bag is included. Closed are converted to semi-closed systems by opening one or more expiratory valves in the circuit. This classification is adopted here, although it is not widely used in veterinary anaesthesia in the UK.

Open systems

Open methods are widely used in laboratory animal anaesthesia because they are simple and inexpensive. They also have the advantage that they offer a very low impedance to spontaneous breathing. However, they are wasteful of anaesthetic agents, and high concentrations of volatile agents such as halothane or ether may be released into the immediate environment. Furthermore, there is always a tendency for anaesthetic gases to become diluted with ambient air during the inspiratory phase so that the depth of anaesthesia is unstable, and weak agents such as N_2O may be diluted below effective levels. Finally, except when using the Ayre's T-piece (Ayre, 1956) there is no possibility of controlling or assisting ventilation. In the case of the T-piece it is possible to inflate the lungs by occlusion of the open end—taking care to avoid over-inflation.

Open drop

In this technique, a volatile anaesthetic e.g. ether, halothane or methoxyflurane is dripped onto a piece of absorbent gauze within a mask. The mask is then applied loosely to the face of the animal so that a stream of air or O_2 passed through the gauze will vaporize the liquid for inhalation and, furthermore, will wash away exhaled gases so that rebreathing should be avoided. The technique is cheap and simple, but carries the danger that excessively high concentrations of anaesthetic may be inhaled by the animal.

Conversely, ambient air will be drawn in during inspiration to dilute anaesthetic concentrations. The anaesthetist must therefore expect very variable depths of anaesthesia. Nevertheless, it is a useful technique for inducing anaesthesia in small laboratory mammals and birds if sufficient O_2 is administered to prevent hypoxia with a high enough total gas flow to prevent rebreathing of CO_2.

A simple apparatus made for a few pence from laboratory plastic ware is shown in Fig. 7.1. A disposable plastic syringe holder ('Brunswick' 30, 20 or 10 ml depending on the size of animal) serves as an open mask and is attached to a rubber gas line by means of a connector secured at one end by epoxy-resin adhesive. Volatile anaesthetic is released to the gauze through a plastic cannula in measured volumes from a syringe. A gas flow of approximately twice the minute volume (tidal volume × respiratory rate/min) is sufficient to prevent rebreathing. Flows of 300 ml/min for guinea-pigs, 200 ml/min for rats, 100 ml/min for mice and 100–500 ml/min for different size birds up to adult fowl are suggested (CRC).

Insufflation

This term, strictly speaking, refers to the release of anaesthetic agents with O_2 or air within the trachea by means of a small catheter passed either through the mouth and larynx or via a tracheostomy. Some commentators, however, include the mask technique described above and others include delivery by a catheter opening into the oral cavity. In this text, insufflation refers to delivery of gases into the trachea *or* the oral cavity by a catheter which is small enough in diameter to allow alveolar gases to pass outside the catheter to the environment during expiration. The gas flow should be approximately twice the minute volume of the animal to prevent rebreathing, and inhaled gases will include room air during inspiration. As exhalation occurs around it, it follows that the tube should be as small as possible to prevent airway restriction. The technique is useful for maintenance of anaesthesia in rodents and birds. It is simple, safe, and above all in small animals, presents minimal dead space and resistance to expiration. The disadvantages are similar to those described for the open-drop method. In addition, drying and cooling of the airway assume rather more significance as this is a primary cause of heat loss in small mammals and birds.

Ayre's T-piece

The T-piece consists of a length of tubing with a small side inlet (the upright limb of the T) into which the anaesthetic gases are passed (Fig. 7.2.). One end of the tubing is attached to an endotracheal tube (close fitting or cuffed) and the other is open to the atmosphere. When the capacity of the reservoir tube equals one-third of the tidal volume, the total gas flow into the system to prevent dilution with room air should be about twice the respiratory minute volume (Ayre, 1956). Hence, gas flows of 12–15 litre/min for an adult

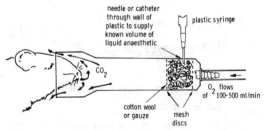

Fig. 7.1. Simple 'open drop' vaporizer and nose cone suitable for small rodents and birds.

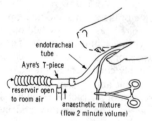

Fig. 7.2. Ayre's T-piece connected to an endotracheal tube. Reservoir of corrugated rubber tubing.

beagle or weaner pig of 15–20 kg, and 1·5–2.0 litre/min for cats and rabbits weighing 3 kg should be supplied. Such flows should virtually eliminate rebreathing, and airway resistance is minimal. The system has the advantage over open-drop and insufflation methods that ventilation can be assisted by intermittent brief occlusion of the open reservoir limb. This is useful either for emergency resuscitation or during thoracic surgery when ventilation must be supported artificially for brief periods.

Semi-open systems

These by definition have a reservoir but do not allow rebreathing. The reservoir serves to provide a volume of gas which will satisfy the peak inflow at inspiration. Two systems are particularly valuable in the management of laboratory animals: the Jackson Rees modified T-piece (Rees, 1950) which is useful for many small animals including rabbits, cats, primates (up to 10 kg), neonatal pigs, puppies, and poultry, and has been used successfully for the maintenance of anaesthesia for periods up to 6 h in this laboratory (CRC); and the Magill system which also has a reservoir and minimizes rebreathing by voiding exhaled gases through an overflow valve close to the face of the animal—this system is valuable in dogs, pigs, cats, primates and rabbits for relatively short anaesthetic periods of up to 2 h duration (CRC). Both systems have advantages over the open methods. Observation of the reservoir bag allows assessment of respiration to be made; the bag may be compressed to control and assist respiration; a more stable anaesthetic state is obtained since inspired gases cannot be diluted by ambient air and, conversely, decreased ventilation will not raise the inspired concentration; and finally, N_2O is not diluted and can be used effectively. However, the inflow rate must be adequate to prevent rebreathing and the non-return valve in the Magill system is not efficient at low flow rates. In addition, heat and evaporative losses from the respiratory tract must be avoided as described earlier.

Rees' modified Ayres T-piece

The modification consists of a tube and rebreathing bag to serve as a reservoir added to the open limb of the T. An inflow rate of 2·2 times the minute volume of the animal should be provided to ensure that expired gases are washed out efficiently and not drawn back into the lungs. The reservoir volume (expiratory limb and rebreathing bag) should be roughly equivalent to the tidal volume of the animal so that ambient air is not sucked back into the respiratory tract to dilute incoming anaesthetic gases. The expiratory and inspiratory sequence, and design of the T-piece is shown in Fig. 7.3 (after Rees, 1965; Eger, 1974).

Magill attachment

This is the most commonly used system in animal anaesthesia in the UK. Essentially, it consists of a non-return expiratory valve located as close to the animal as possible, corrugated tubing of sufficient length and volume to ensure that exhaled alveolar gases do not return to the reservoir bag, and a reservoir bag having a capacity at least 8 times the tidal volume of the animal with the anaesthetic gas supply flowing either through or over the reservoir bag (Fig. 7.4).

The Magill system permits a lower inflow rate than the T-piece while ensuring no rebreathing by preferentially exhausting alveolar gas through the overflow valve when pressure rises to a maximum during the last phase of exhalation, and by conserving inflowing and equipment dead space gases, i.e. fresh gases. Efficiency depends on the overflow valve lifting at low pressures and it is important that it is checked before use. In theory, rebreathing is completely prevented by a gas inflow equal to the animal's minute volume (Kain & Nunn, 1967) but we always allow a 10% safety margin (CRC).

The Magill system is adequate for anaesthesia of relatively short duration when attached to a close fitting mask (up to 2 h), and we have used it in pigs, dogs, cats and rabbits for periods up to 4 h with an

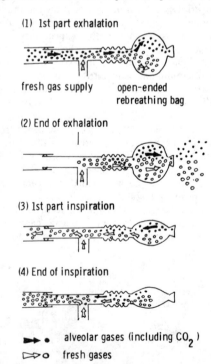

(1) 1st part exhalation

fresh gas supply   open-ended rebreathing bag

(2) End of exhalation

(3) 1st part inspiration

(4) End of inspiration

➤● alveolar gases (including CO_2)

▷○ fresh gases

Fig. 7.3 Rees' modified T-piece showing sequence and movement of alveolar (including CO_2) and fresh gases (adapted from Eger, 1974).

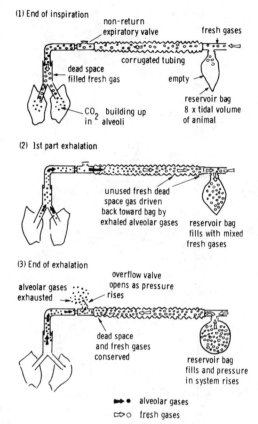

(1) End of inspiration

non-return expiratory valve fresh gases

corrugated tubing

dead space filled fresh gas

empty

CO_2 building up in alveoli

reservoir bag 8 x tidal volume of animal

(2) 1st part exhalation

unused fresh dead space gas driven back toward bag by exhaled alveolar gases

reservoir bag fills with mixed fresh gases

(3) End of exhalation

overflow valve opens as pressure rises

alveolar gases exhausted

dead space and fresh gases conserved

reservoir bag fills and pressure in system rises

➡• alveolar gases
⇨o fresh gases

Fig. 7.4. Magill attachment: design and sequence of gas movements (adapted from Eger, 1974).

endotracheal tube. However, we have experienced failures when valves have not functioned properly (CRC).

Approximate flow rates which are suitable with this system:

	Weight (kg)	Flow (litre/min)
Dog	15	4
	25	6
Cat	2–3	0·5·1·0
Rabbit	2–4	0·5–2·0
Guinea-pig	0·5–1·0	0·5–1·0

In the smaller species, these figures are higher than theoretically necessary, but the use of lower flows is limited by the relative inefficiency and difficulty in calibrating most vaporizers for low flow rates. Hence, it is not possible to operate the system at the actual minute volume of small animals.

Closed and semi-closed systems
The two essential features of a closed system are that rebreathing of exhaled gases is permitted after CO_2 has been absorbed in soda-lime, and a reservoir bag is included. Closed are modified to

semi-closed systems by opening one or more expiratory valves in the circuit.

The absorption of CO_2 from exhaled gases by passage through soda-lime granules should theoretically allow rebreathing without significant elevation of inspired CO_2. Furthermore, if there are no leaks in the system (i.e. it is perfectly closed), and once the anaesthetic has equilibrated in blood and alveoli, then a given volume of anaesthetic agent should shuttle between alveoli and the absorber without diminishing appreciably. If this were so, the only input into the system would need to be small volumes of O_2 to replenish that utilized by body metabolism. For example, a 25 kg dog would need an input of approximately 100–150 ml of O_2 per minute. In practice, however, there will always be leaks in the system, and soluble agents such as halothane and methoxyflurane will be taken up in tubber tubing. The input of gas will have to be established by trial and error to keep the volume of gases in the reservoir bag approximately constant, and occasional additions of anaesthetic agent may be needed to prevent progressive lightening of anaesthesia. In addition, soda-lime is never 100% efficient, and it is good practice to flush the system with fresh gases every 30 min or so to avoid CO_2 concentrations building up.

Closed and semi-closed systems are of most value when anaesthetizing larger animals weighing 15 kg or more, when economy of anaesthetic agent becomes significant and where contamination of the operating environment has to be minimized. The main advantage to the animal is that body heat and moisture are not being continuously removed by fast flowing gases. They also present several potential dangers, however. Resistance to expiration is always higher in circuits incorporating soda-lime absorbers and this assumes greater significance during prolonged anaesthesia and when small animals are being anaesthetized. In addition, equipment dead space increases with time as soda-lime becomes exhausted, hence CO_2 tensions in inspired gases may rise steadily. Finally, the generation of heat in the soda-lime–CO_2 reaction may cause hyperpyrexia. It is concluded that closed systems should not be used for long periods of anaesthesia (over 3 h) and particular care must be exercised when anaesthetizing small animals weighing less than 15 kg. The dangers can generally be avoided by partially opening the expiratory valve and running the circuits semi-closed.

The importance of using semi-closed systems to make the best use of N_2O should be emphasized at this stage. The animal should be saturated with N_2O, and the gas must not be diluted with nitrogen or with more O_2 than is needed to satisfy metabolic requirements. This is affected most quickly and

59

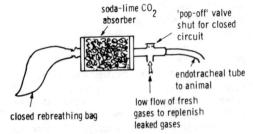

Fig. 7.5. Water's to-and-fro system: can be used closed or semi-closed by employing expiratory valve shut or open.

economically in semi-closed systems. However, it is dangerous to use N_2O in completely closed systems as it is difficult to maintain adequate O_2 tensions in the alveoli even though apparently satisfactory $O_2:N_2O$ ratios (e.g. 1:1) are supplied to the apparatus.

Two types of system are commonly used in the UK—the Water's to-and-fro system, and circle absorption systems.

Water's to-and-fro system
This is similar to the Rees T-piece system described earlier except that a soda-lime absorber is interposed between the inflow port and the reservoir bag (Fig. 7.5.). It can be used as a closed or semi-closed system by virtue of an expiratory 'pop-off' valve close to the animal's face. However, the to-and-fro system can be criticized on several grounds: first, exhaustion of the proximal soda-lime will permit rebreathing of CO_2 as the last fraction of exhaled alveolar gas will fail to be treated; the soda lime offers considerable resistance to expiration and since the alveolar gases are the last to leave the lungs, they will be the first gases rebreathed, and the inspired anaesthetic concentrations of a soluble agent may be significantly reduced—whereas a poorly soluble gas e.g. cyclopropane will maintain relatively stable concentrations. Nevertheless, to-and-fro systems are popular with some workers as they are relatively inexpensive to buy or construct and are sparing of anaesthetic agent. For example, they have been used with halothane–O_2 to anaesthetize rhesus monkeys for periods of 2 h without elevating $PaCO_2$ (Medd, 1974), and with cyclopropane–O_2 to anaesthetize the domestic fowl (Hill & Noakes, 1964).

The circle absorption system
Circle systems are the most widely accepted in modern anaesthetic practice and are better than to-and-fro types because they are more efficient at removing CO_2, and they are relatively efficient at maintaining inspired anaesthetic concentrations.

Again, by employing overflow 'pop-off' valves open or shut, these circuits can be used as semi-closed or closed systems respectively and allow re-

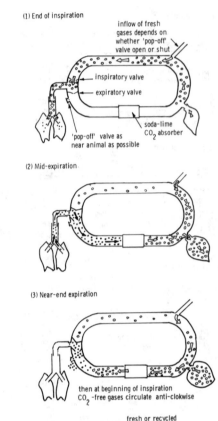

Fig. 7.6. Circle absorption system: ideal arrangement of valves and sequence of gas movement (after Eger, 1974).

breathing of exhaled gases after removal of CO_2. When purchasing or making up a circuit, four elementary rules should be observed to avoid any possibility of rebreathing exhaled CO_2: first, valves must be interposed between the reservoir bag and the animal on both the inspiratory and expiratory sides of the circuit; second, inflow of fresh gases must not enter the system between the expiratory valve and the patient; third, the overflow valve must not be placed between the animal and the inspiratory valve; and last, the 'pop-off' valve should be near the animal (Eger, 1974).

The arrangement and sequence of gas flow is shown in Fig. 7.6. The effects of inflow, overflow and valve placement on the economy of the circle system have been investigated and discussed by Eger & Ethans (1968).

Methods of administration: artificial respiration (intermittent positive pressure ventilation or IPPV)

Artificial ventilation is essential during intra-thoracic surgery when air is allowed into the chest cage, when muscle relaxant drugs are being used, and in emergency failure of spontaneous respiration, e.g. when barbiturate overdosage has depressed the respiratory centre. Furthermore, it is often necessary in the management of experimental animals which are being maintained for long periods of anaesthesia.

During spontaneous respiration, expansion of the rib cage creates a negative pressure within the pleural cavity, and alveolar tissue of the lung expands as atmospheric pressure transmitted from the oro-pharynx and along the trachea and bronchial tree exerts a distending force within the lung tissue. Distension is opposed by the elasticity of lung tissue. Artificial positive pressure ventilation is fundamentally different from natural breathing since it is achieved by raising pressure above atmospheric pressure at the mouth and forcing gas into the lung before lowering it again to allow the lungs to contract. When the chest is closed, this positive pressure will present several potential hazards. It may interfere with venous return to the thorax in the great veins, the heart may be compressed during the inspiratory phase so that cardiac output falls, and by raising the intra-alveolar pressure above atmospheric pressure, the perfusion of lung capillaries will be reduced and arterio-venous shunting may occur.

These potentially harmful effects will each be accentuated if a very high positive pressure is employed and is maintained for a long part of the cycle. At its simplest, it follows that any form of ventilator should aim to expand the lungs rapidly at a relatively high gas flow (inspiratory phase) and immediately allow expiration over a longer period against the lowest possible expiratory resistance. However, there are other considerations which complicate the picture. Considerable interest has been shown in alterations to this basic cycle for use in paediatric anaesthesia and intensive care, and these may well prove valuable in small animal work. In particular, the maintenance of residual pressure during the expiratory phase (positive-end-expiratory pressure or PEEP) has been advocated for maintaining alveolar distension and preventing pulmonary oedema (Becker & Koppe, 1969; McIntyre et al., 1969), for use after open-heart surgery (Stewart et al., 1973) and for lungs of low compliance (Hatch et al., 1973). The simplest way of achieving slight positive relative to atmospheric pressure without expiratory resistance to flow is by submerging the outflow tube in an appropriate depth of water (Kolf et al., 1972). Alternatively, a T-piece occluder-ventilator with a PEEP valve included may be used (Mattila & Suutarinan, 1971; Inkster, 1973). It has also been suggested that deterioration in lung compliance can be prevented by holding a pressure plateau at peak inspiration

and this, too, may become an essential feature of design (Herzog & Norlander, 1968).

Controlled respiration can be achieved by rhythmic compression of a reservoir bag or by a mechanical ventilator. In the former circumstance, a higher respiratory rate than normal should be used, the bag should be compressed rapidly and released quickly at the peak of inspiration, and then a period should be allowed for normal emptying of the lungs. Mechanical ventilators may be either flow or pressure generators. In the former, flow is controlled by the ventilator setting, and pressure will depend on airway resistance and lung compliance. Conversely, in pressure generators the pressure is pre-set, and the flow and volume delivered will then vary with lung characteristics.

It is theoretically best to ventilate at a level which keeps $PaCO_2$ normal—but in practice, it is usual to hyperventilate to counteract other tendencies toward an acidosis. The rate should be set at the normal respiration rate and the tidal volume adjusted either on known criteria or by observing thoracic excursions.

Artificial ventilation of the lungs has been extensively reviewed by Mushin et al. (1969), Hall & Massey (1969) and Inkster (1975).

Equipment available

Inhalational apparatus

The different types of equipment available commercially have been well reviewed by Hall (1971) and Lumb & Jones (1973), who described suitable apparatus for administering inhalational agents to species ranging from cats to large horses. It would be out of place in this text to reproduce what they have described. An attempt will be made instead to suggest how laboratories can adapt existing commercial models in the light of the principles outlined earlier in this chapter.

For dogs, pigs, cats, nonhuman primates, calves, sheep, goats, rabbits and guinea-pigs, the basic requirements are supplied in such equipment as the Airmed 'Universal', the Penlon 'SAM', the Cyprane Small Animal Unit or the MIE 'Casualty and Out-Patients Anaesthetic Unit'. These provide the facility for giving N_2O and O_2 separately through different flowmeters, and flushing the circuit with O_2 if required. The flowmeters are calibrated for low as well as high flows so that they can be adapted for use with separate rodent vaporizers to be described. They can be fitted with vaporizers for ether, methoxyflurane and halothane. The mixed gases can then be supplied to a Magill system, a Jackson Rees modified Ayres T-piece or a Waters to-and-fro circuit; alternatively, they can be taken to multiple outlet manifolds or to clear plastic induction boxes for anaesthetizing numbers of rodents at one time. This type of apparatus is reasonably adaptable and less than half the cost of Boyle-type trolleys fitted with circle absorption rebreathing circuits.

Alternatively, a simple trolley can be fashioned from box section steel frame and wheels ('Speedframe') and fitted with the appropriate cylinder yokes, flexible flowmeters (e.g. 'Platon Flowbits') calibrated for each gas to be used, halothane vaporizer and suitable connecting tubing.

Whatever the type of apparatus, it is essential to calibrate the vaporizers by measuring the inhalational concentration actually delivered to the animal. This should be done over a range of total gas flow rates and a range of possible vaporizer temperatures, time having been allowed for anaesthetic saturation of the rubber components in the circuit. Under no circumstances should the charts provided by manufacturers be regarded as anything but guides. Calibration is most accurately achieved by a 'Hook and Tucker Halothane Meter'.

When supplying inhalational agents to rats, hamsters, mice and other small animals, low gas flows of 500–750 ml/min are adequate and higher volumes will simply overflow into the laboratory. If accurate concentrations of anaesthetic are to be delivered to the animal, small vaporizers which are efficient at such flow rates must be specially constructed (Reese & Nunn, 1961; Payne & Chammings, 1964; Stevenson, 1964; Parbrook, 1966; Jacobs, 1967; Simmons & Smith, 1968; Sebesteny, 1971; Duke *et al.*, 1971; Mulder & Brown, 1972; Smith *et al.*, 1973; Mulder, 1973; Mauderley, 1975; Guthy, 1975; Carvell & Stoward, 1975). These vary from relatively sophisticated devices incorporating, for example, specially blown glass vaporizers, to very simple units constructed entirely of standard laboratory glassware and silicone rubber connections.

The set designed by Sebesteny (1971) can be strongly recommended, although the high quality flowmeters it incorporates render the unit rather expensive, and the control valves are very easily damaged. Nevertheless, it certainly provides fine control of halothane, enflurane or methoxyflurane concentrations at low gas-flow rates of 500–750 ml/min. The gas mixture can pass via a 3-way tap to a mask (glass or plastic) or endotracheal tube and modified Ayres T-piece, or it may be directed to an induction box constructed of clear plastic. In each case, the overflow gases are led along polyethylene tubing to exhaust direct into ventilation extracts thus minimizing pollution of the operating area.

The unit described by Carvell & Stoward (1975) was specially constructed from glass as a modification of the design by Parbrook (1966), and this too is a highly effective miniature vaporizer. However, as low cost is frequently an important consideration in laboratory work, we favour simpler modifications of Parbrook's original equipment which can be constructed from stock glassware. Although properly designed valves (e.g. Wade "All Plastic' Needle Valves) give finer control of gas flow in the circuit, adequate substitutes can be fashioned out of gate clamps placed across short lengths of silicone rubber tubing. The anaesthetic gas mixture is humidified by passing it over warm water in a second test tube or in a glass manifold and can then be directed via 3-way taps and silicone rubber tubing to a face mask as described earlier. This vaporizer can be calibrated accurately even though it is of such simple design.

Gas mixtures can be delivered to small animals by mask or catheter tubing. We construct masks from plastic syringe containers or from suitable size plastic beakers. Inlet and outlet ports are constructed from tube connectors ('Portex') glued to the mask, and a diaphragm is constructed from the fingers of latex rubber gloves with an aperture cut to allow a tight fit around the animal's head. Alternatively, tapered plastic catheters ('Medicut') can be passed into the mouth of the rodent to insufflate the respiratory system, or passed under direct vision as an endotracheal tube once anaesthesia has been induced by mask. Intubation of rats and guinea-pigs is a simple operation provided a suitable light source is used to illuminate the larynx (Medd & Heywood, 1970; Jaffe & Free, 1973).

Mechanical ventilators

3 types of pump have been used in this laboratory for a range of animals from mice to young cattle and can be recommended—the range of Harvard Animal Ventilators, the Palmer Animal Ventilator, and the Air-Shields 10000 Respirator.

Harvard Animal Ventilators are all constant volume, piston pumps producing positive pressure for inspiration and relying on lung compliance (elasticity) for expiration. Valve ports are fitted for introducing respiratory gases and for the collection of exhaled gases along separate pathways to reduce mixing and to minimise dead space. Expired air is passively discharged into the environment through a valve port or may be recycled as required. The pump draws air or non-explosive gases into the cylinder during the first $\frac{1}{2}$ cycle and delivers this to the animals in the second $\frac{1}{2}$ of the cycle.

2 types of motor control are available—variable speed motors produce a continuously variable pumping speed at a fixed inspiratory:expiratory ratio (50:50), and variable phase models which can, in addition, be adjusted to deliver a continuously variable ratio of inspiration:expiration (from 35:65). The variable speed models are

suitable for routine animal ventilation whilst the variable phase models are intended for experimental work in which it is important to mimic normal or abnormal respiratory patterns.

The Model 621 Variable Speed Bovine Ventilator is designed for sheep, goats, large pigs, cattle and other large species. The stroke volume is adjustable from 100–200 ml per stroke and, with a continuously variable rate of 6 to 45 strokes/min, the minute volume can be adjusted from 600–9000 ml/min. Hence, it is capable of ventilating adult cattle and small horses or ponies up to about 450 kg in weight, but not larger subjects.

The Model 607 Variable Speed Dog Ventilator is useful for many laboratory species including dogs, cats, rabbits, pigs, sheep and goats. The volume is adjustable from 30–750 ml/stroke and, at the continuously variable rate of 7 to 50 strokes/min, the ventilator can provide a minute volume of 210–37,500 ml. There are two variable phase adaptations of this model: the Model 613 Variable Phase Dog Ventilator allows adjustment of both the phase ratio and stroke rate—the inspiratory ratio can be changed from 35 to 65% of a single stroke cycle and speed can be adjusted from 5 to 40 strokes/min; and the Model 614 Quantitative Dog Ventilator (Rush Pump) which has a similar specification but in addition is designed to prevent leakage and allow accurate measurements of gas flows.

The Series 660 Intermediate Ventilators are designed for laboratory animals of 0·2–15 kg such as cats, monkeys, rabbits and birds. Thus it covers many of the animals which could be ventilated on the Model 607 but it provides in addition finely calibrated volume control to within 1% of actual output as well as capacity for ventilating small animals below 1 kg.

The two Rodent Ventilators (Series 680) differ only in the respiratory frequency and tidal volumes which can be supplied. The Model 680 produces 30–200 strokes/min and tidal volumes from 0·2–10 ml/stroke. Model 681 produces 15–100 strokes/min and tidal volumes from 0·5–30 ml/stroke. Both ventilators are suitable for guinea-pigs, rats, mice and small birds.

Overall verdict: these pumps are difficult to fault for everyday use. They are all reliable, simple in design and robust.

The C.F. Palmer Animal Ventilator Model 5255 is designed for use in animals ranging from mice to sheep, goats and calves, and incorporates a combined centrifugal air pump which generates air pressure and electronic control unit which generates the pulse wave, and a solenoid valve unit which is the ventilating head and is sited close to the animal to minimize dead space.

The ventilator can be used in either an open or closed circuit system, and a facility is provided for introducing gaseous anaesthetics or O_2 directly into the valve unit. The respiration rate can be varied from 9 to 160/min, the maximum pressure generated is 50–55 cm H_2O, the inspire ratio is variable from 20–50% and there is facility for expiratory pause which can be varied up to a 30% maximum.

Overall verdict: this pump has the advantage that it can ventilate most of the animals commonly used in experimental work. It is not so simple to service as the Harvard pumps but now that problems encountered with the early specimens of this model have been overcome, it appears to be reliable.

The Air-Shields Respirator 1000 is designed for clinical use in man and is able to ventilate paediatric and adult cases. We have used it to ventilate animals up to 300 kg in weight and found it an excellent machine. It operates within a preset tidal volume i.e. it will deliver essentially the same volume of air or gases in the face of changes in resistance and compliance. The cycle can be repeated at a minimum rate of 5/min up to a maximum of 60/min. Inspired air or gases are humidified by means of a high speed spinning disc to provide effective hydration of the respiratory tract. A maximum tidal volume of 2·5 litres can be supplied and inspiratory flow capacity ranges from 1 to 120 litres/min.

Overall verdict: although not designed for animal use, it is suitable for ventilating dogs, pigs, sheep, goats, young cattle and small ponies. It is expensive but has an efficient humidifier and can be fitted with a PEEP valve.

INHALATIONAL ANAESTHESIA: AGENTS AVAILABLE

Introduction

The relative merits of inhalational compared with injectable agents have to be carefully weighed when selecting a method for a particular experiment.

The main advantages of inhalational agents are that the depth of anaesthesia can be altered rapidly, the animals recover from anaesthesia quickly and the agents are either exhaled unchanged or only relatively small proportions are metabolized by the liver and are therefore less likely to interfere with experimental results (for example, N_2O is thought to be totally eliminated via the respiratory system, halothane and ether 80%, and methoxyflurane about 50% eliminated unchanged).

There are several disadvantages. Although ether is frequently used in simple open methods of administration, other inhalational agents require more sophisticated apparatus and, in experiments where the laboratory worker is performing short and simple procedures on large numbers of animals, e.g. skin grafting of mice, inhalation anaesthesia is inconvenient and time-consuming. Furthermore, some inhalational agents (particularly ether) are irritant to mucous membranes and are unpleasant for the animals during introduction and recovery. Finally, these agents are potentially dangerous in a confined laboratory space.

Ether forms explosive mixtures with air, O_2 and N_2O, and its flammability presents a fire hazard at all times. It must never be used with thermo-cautery, microcoagulation or electronic equipment. In addition, care must be taken to ensure that bunsen burners are not used in adjoining laboratories, and animals which have been killed under ether anaesthesia must not be stored in refrigerator cabinets where electrical connections may spark an explosion.

Trichloroethylene cannot be used with soda-lime in closed circuits since it reacts with the alkali to liberate dichloracetylene, phosgene and carbon monoxide. All the other anaesthetics which are described in this chapter can be used safely in closed circuits.

Pollution of the environment with inhalational anaesthetics must be considered a hazard to personnel until proved otherwise especially since many laboratories are poorly ventilated and large numbers of animals may be anaesthetized with open methods of administration. Measurable quantities of anaesthetic vapour in the operating theatre have been shown to correlate well with blood levels in staff (Hallen et al., 1970), and statistical evidence suggests that anaesthetists have an increased incidence of malignant disease (Bruce et al., 1968) and a higher rate of spontaneous abortion (Askrog & Harvard, 1970). It is possible that repeated exposure to halothane causes hepatic and to methoxyflurane renal damage, whilst N_2O may depress haemopoietic centres. The evidence to date is somewhat equivocal but it seems sensible to work in well-ventilated areas, and to direct waste anaesthetic gases away from the operating area to the floor (McInnes & Goldwater, 1972), to a window or ventilation extract, or to a specially designed absorber containing activated charcoal (Vaughan et al., 1973).

Anaesthetic potency

The potency of an agent is difficult to define and the term has given rise to considerable confusion in the literature. It is not difficult to see why this should be. Some workers have compared potency on the basis of inspired concentrations needed to produce a given degree of CNS depression (i.e. the lower the concentration required, the more potent the agent), whilst others have compared the rapidity with which the 'end-point' is reached. Another basis for comparison derives from the ability to produce light, medium or deep surgical anaesthesia (i.e. a potent anaesthetic must be capable of depressing the CNS to Stage IV of the Guedal classification) regardless of the time taken to reach that level. Since the speed of induction depends on so many factors in which intrinsic characteristics of the agent (e.g. its solubility in blood) play an important but partial role, and since there can be no well-defined end-point during anaesthesia, the term potency has been loosely applied until recently.

In 1965, Eger and his colleagues introduced the important concept of 'minimal alveolar anaesthetic concentration' or MAC, as a way of comparing the potency of different anaesthetic agents. This they defined as the alveolar concentration of an agent at 1 atmosphere pressure which will prevent response to specified stimuli in 50% of subjects. The alveolar concentrations can be measured quite simply and it is assumed that, given sufficient time for equilibration, the partial pressure at the site of action in the CNS equals the partial pressure in arterial blood which in turn equals the alveolar partial pressure. MAC is determined by anaesthetizing the animal with the agent, measuring the alveolar concentration and holding it steady at a predetermined level for at least 15 min to ensure equilibration between alveoli and the CNS. The animal is then stimulated (e.g. by tail clamp or electrical pulse) and observed for movement or lack of movement, an all-or-none response. This is repeated at different alveolar concentrations until the MAC is measured (Eger et al., 1965).

The variability of MAC within a species is small, and is also remarkably low between species and even classes of animal. For example, MAC for halothane in dogs is 0·87, in cats 0·82, rats and mice 0·95–1·1, goldfish 0·76 and in toads 0·67 (Eger, 1974). This is true of other inhalational agents (Table 7.1). Furthermore, MAC values are reproducible if repeated in the same animal at different time intervals.

Thus MAC provides a means of quantifying the relative potencies of different agents in different species of animal. It can then be used to evaluate factors which influence anaesthetic requirement e.g. the depression of MAC which occurs when the animals are premedicated with central depressants. Similarly, it may be used during experiments involving other pharmacological agents which may interact with the anaesthetics. By providing a standard expression of anaesthetic dose, MAC

Table 7.1. MAC values for inhalational anaesthetics in different species

Agent	Dog	Cat	Rat or mouse	Goldfish	Toad
Methoxyflurane	0·23	0·23	0·22	0·13	0·22
Halothane	0·87	0·82	0·95	0·76	0·67
Enflurane	2·2	1·2	—	—	—
Ether	3·04	2·1	3·2	2·2	1·63
Cyclopropane	17·5	19·7	17·0	—	9·0
Nitrous oxide	188·0	—	150·0	—	81·5
Trichlorethylene	—	—	0·6 (0·75)*	—	—

Note the low variability of MAC from species to species. Values were obtained after applying a tail clamp or 40 V electrical pulse (adapted from Eger, 1974).
* Mouse = 0·75.

may be useful in defining clinical signs of anaesthetic depth in different species.

Uptake and distribution of inhalational agents

The rate of uptake of inhalational agents into any body tissue depends on the rate of entry into the circulation, the blood supply to that tissue, the blood:tissue partition coefficient, and the concentration gradient existing between blood and the tissue concerned. The CNS is in constant competition with other tissues for the available volume of anaesthetic agent in the circulation. During induction the anaesthetic is taken up into body tissues until equilibrium is reached between inspired tension and tissues—hence, for maintenance there should theoretically be no net uptake of an anaesthetic which is not excreted or metabolized. During recovery, no further agent will be presented to the lungs, inspired tension will fall, and tissues will release agent into the circulation and thence to the alveoli across reverse tension gradients.

Induction

Several factors determine the rate of uptake and hence the rate of induction. For practical purposes, the major difference during induction is between alveolar and inspired anaesthetic tensions. The solubility of the agent in blood, inspired tension, alveolar ventilation, cardiac output (hence lung perfusion) and mixed venous anaesthetic levels each affect alveolar anaesthetic tension.

Alveolar ventilation

The rate and efficiency of ventilation has the biggest initial effect on the rise of alveolar anaesthetic partial pressure and hence several respiratory factors will profoundly influence the rate of rise.

The high respiratory rate in small rodents (e.g. 180/min in mice) accounts for the rapid induction and recovery which is associated with inhalational anaesthesia in these animals. In contrast, the slow respiratory rate in large mammals such as the horse (9–12/min) accounts for the far slower uptake of agent and the difficulty in achieving high enough concentrations of some agents (e.g. ether) to induce anaesthesia. The respiratory differences between reptiles and mammals exert an even greater influence on inhalational anaesthesia in the former, e.g. tortoises may ventilate only once an hour in the presence of anaesthetic vapour, and induction without premedication may be unsuccessful. The highly specialized respiration of birds allows rapid induction with inhalational anaesthetics but the possibility of high concentrations of agent accumulating in dependent air sacs and then suddenly passing to the lungs is a danger, particularly in small or young birds. Lastly, anything which alters the respiratory rate, e.g. voluntary breath-holding when first exposed to an irritant inhalational agent such as ether will significantly alter the rate of induction.

Uptake from lungs

The rate of uptake from the lungs into the circulation also affects the speed of induction. It is directly related to:

(i) The difference between partial pressure of anaesthetic on one side of the alveolar membrane and the venous blood perfusing it.

(ii) The perfusion of alveoli, the overall rate of perfusion being directly related to cardiac output. Thus uptake will be limited from underperfused alveoli even if they are well ventilated just as uptake will be restricted in the presence of adequate alveolar perfusion if they are underventilated.

(iii) Solubility of the agent in blood. Highly soluble agents (e.g. ether) are rapidly taken up by pulmonary blood and the alveolar partial pressure of the agent falls quickly—hence, since *arterial* blood and brain tensions equilibrate with alveolar tension, *induction will be slow*. On the other hand, with insoluble gases such as N_2O or cyclopropane, alveolar tension rises quickly and induction is rapid. The induction phase with soluble agents may be shortened by increasing the inspired anaesthetic tension.

(iv) An inverse, but non-linear relationship, existing between the rate of transfer of the agent and pathologic changes in the lung (e.g. fibrosis, thickening and catarrhal exudate).

(v) Abnormalities in the balance of ventilation to perfusion, which may be produced in animals by:

    (a) poor perfusion of some areas of lung if the animal is placed in an unusual position e.g. large animals in the supine position;

    (b) atelectasis and pneumonic changes producing right-to-left circulatory shunts;

    (c) emphysema which may alter the normal flow and distribution of gases.

(vi) The concentration and 2nd gas effects: as anaesthetic agent is taken up from the lungs, alveolar volume is potentially reduced and more gas is inspired to maintain intrapulmonary pressure—the higher the inspired anaesthetic concentration which can be supplied, the more will inspiratory flow be accelerated. If a primary gas such as N_2O is supplied in higher concentrations (70%), the uptake will effectively increase the fractional concentration of a 2nd gas e.g. halothane, and increase inspiratory ventilation. Hence, the rate of rise in alveolar tension of halothane (or other volatile agent) will be markedly accelerated during the first 10 min of induction by the simultaneous administration of large volumes of N_2O.

Tissue uptake from circulation

The rate of uptake of anaesthetic by body tissues from the circulation is directly related to blood flow to the individual tissue, the difference between partial pressure of the agent in arterial blood and the tissue, and the solubility of the agent in that tissue relative to its solubility in blood (partition coefficient tissue : blood).

The brain receives a high proportion (for its weight) of the output from the left ventricle, hence all inhalational agents are rapidly taken up by the CNS. The partition coefficient (tissue : blood) of most inhalational agents is close to unity, but halothane induces anaesthesia significantly quicker since its brain : blood partition coefficient is 2·6. Equilibration with other tissues, particularly the poorly vascularized fat depots, may take several hours.

Maintenance

If an animal is allowed to breathe spontaneously, the relationship between alveolar partial pressure, ventilation and circulatory pressures will be subjected to various feed-back mechanisms following the immediate induction phase. First, depression of the respiratory centre will lead to decreases in respiratory rate and tidal volume so that the input of anaesthetic into the lungs will be depressed. Secondly, depression of cardiac output (e.g. by halothane) will in turn depress lung perfusion and allow a rapid increase in anaesthetic partial pressure in alveoli.

The practical consequences are important because if ventilation is artificially maintained by IPPV or if animals are hyperventilating for some other reason whilst cardic output is reduced, dangerously high blood concentrations of anaesthetic may build up particularly with highly soluble agents such as ether or methoxyflurane.

Recovery

When the inspired partial pressure of anaesthetic agent is lowered almost to zero at the end of anaesthesia, the alveolar tension would likewise rapidly decrease provided good ventilation was maintained; however, the reverse output from tissues to blood and thence to alveoli will prevent this happening for some time. The rate of recovery will be dependent on similar factors to those controlling the rate of induction, e.g. blood solubility, cardiac output and venous to alveolar anaesthetic concentration gradients. Since brain concentrations of agent approximate the alveolar tension at any given time, it follows that depression of the CNS will persist so long as alveolar tension remains high.

Two opposite effects from those noted during induction may be dangerous to the animal during recovery. First, the outpouring of high concentrations of N_2O may dilute alveolar O_2 and thereby produce 'diffusion hypoxia', and secondly, if the animal continues to breathe from anaesthetic apparatus, recovery may be delayed due to inhalation of anaesthetic agent absorbed in rubber components. In addition, recovery may be protracted in obese animals since the poorly vascularized fat depots will continue to release anaesthetic into the circulation for several hours, and this will be most marked when highly lipid-soluble agents (e.g. methoxyflurane) have been used.

Summary

For rapid and smooth induction it is best to:

    (a) Ensure good alveolar ventilation.

    (b) Flush the apparatus briefly with anaesthetic agents to allow for absorption by rubber components before introducing it to the animal.

    (c) Avoid administering high concentrations of irritant agents such as ether since this is likely to induce breath-holding and delay uptake of agent from the alveoli.

    (d) Induce with spontaneous respiration and allow a steady state to develop before switching over to IPPV if this to be used during maintenance.

(e) Use N_2O with O_2 in a ratio of 70:30 with low concentrations of volatile agent e.g. halothane for the first 5–10 min induction, and then reduce the N_2O to 50% during maintenance.

(f) Use insoluble agents such as N_2O as the main anaesthetic for animals in a shocked condition, e.g. during deliberately induced haemorrhagic shock experiments.

During the recovery phase, it is important to flush out absorbed agents from the rubber components of equipment and ensure good ventilation with adequate O_2 until excretion of most of the anaesthetic from blood and tissues has occurred. This is particularly important when N_2O has been used for long periods if the diffusion hypoxia described above is to be avoided.

Individual inhalational agents

Volatile liquids

Ether (*diethyl ether*)

Physical properties
Ether is highly soluble in water and blood (water:gas partition coefficient 13·1) and hence both induction and recovery are slow (induction 5–10 min—recovery to the point where the animal can stand unaided 10–20 min depending on the duration of anaesthesia). When used without other inhalational agents, an induction concentration of 10–20% of ether is necessary and a 4–5% concentration is needed for maintenance.

Ether is highly inflammable and forms explosive mixtures with O_2, air and N_2O. The low boiling point (37°C) and easy vaporization allows it to be used in open-drop systems or in simple vaporizers in closed and semi-closed systems.

Pharmacology
Nervous system. The respiratory centre is paralysed well before the vasomotor centre if anaesthesia is deepened to dangerous levels. The sympathetic system is stimulated with consequent elevated levels of circulating catecholamines. Ether is a potent depressant of the CNS (MAC is 3·2% in rats) although induction is slow because of the high blood solubility and is often prolonged further by breath-holding. It is a very good analgesic.

Respiratory system. Ether is extremely irritant to the mucosal lining of the mouth and respiratory tract, and may induce laryngospasm in cats and rabbits. Bronchial and salivary secretions are stimulated in all species and are particularly dangerous in guinea-pigs and chinchillas unless the animals have been premedicated with atropine. Not only do these secretions increase the dead space of

Table 7.2. Main physical properties of inhalational anaesthetics described in this text

Drug	Molecular formula	Molecular weight	Boiling point °C at 760 mmHg	Saturation vapour pressure at 20°C	Partition coefficients at 37°C blood/gas	oil/gas	brain*/blood	fat/blood	Partition coefficient at 23°C rubber/gas	MAC %v/v (dog)†
Cyclopropane	C_3H_6	42·08	−32·86	4800	0·457	11·8	0·76	12·9	6·6	17·5
Diethyl ether	$(C_2H_5)_2O$	74·12	34·6	442	12·1	65	1·03	3·7	58	3·04
Enflurane	$CHFClCF_2$–O–CF_2H	184·50	56·5	184	1·78	98	1·45	36·2	74	2·2
Halothane	$CF_3CHClBr$	197·39	50·2	243	2·3	224	2·30	60·0	120	0·87
Methoxyflurane	$CHCl_2CF_2$–O–CH_3	164·97	104·8	23	12·0	970	1·70	48·8	630	0·23
Nitrous oxide	N_2O	44·02	−88·5	38760	0·474	1·4	1·06	2·3	1·2	188·0
Trichloroethylene	C_2HCl_3	131·40	86·7	64·5	9·15	714	1·67	67·0	830	0·6‡

* Brain—grey matter.
† Measured in response to tail clamping or electrical stimulus of 40 V.
‡ Rat.

67

the lungs during anaesthesia, but they also pre-dispose to respiratory infections and exacerbate any chronic respiratory disease already existent in the animals.

If induction is carried out with ether alone, rabbits, cats and guinea-pigs often hold their breath for long periods, but once past this stage, the respiratory rate is stimulated whilst the tidal volume is virtually unchanged; hence volume is augmented until medium surgical anaesthetic levels are reached. Respiration is not stimulated following treatment with preanaesthetic agents which are themselves respiratory depressants and ether may, in this circumstance, contribute to a progressive decline in pulmonary ventilation.

Conclusion. Induction of anaesthesia with ether is extremely unpleasant in all animals. However, its immediate effect on the respiratory system is only dangerous in guinea-pigs and chinchillas, and death is only likely to occur in other species from paralysis of central respiratory centres when very high concentrations of ether are administered. A greater danger is presented in the post-operative period, when respiratory infections may develop.

Cardiovascular system. During light levels of ether-induced anaesthesia, sympathetic simulation ensures that blood pressure, cardiac output and peripheral resistance remain remarkably stable. However, this is effectively masking a strong direct myocardial depressant effect exerted by ether; during deep surgical anaesthesia the myocardial depression becomes evident, and paralysis of the vasomotor cardioexcitatory centres may result in falling cardiac output and progressive failure of the cardiovascular system. Ether does not sensitize the heart to the arrhythmogenic effect of catecholamines.

Conclusion. Ether is as well tolerated by the cardiovascular system as any other inhalational general anaesthetic.

Alimentary system. Salivary and gastric secretions are significantly increased. Vomiting may be a problem in dogs, cats and primates during recovery. The reduction in gut tone and motility which generally occurs during ether anaesthesia is usually rapidly reversed in the recovery phase.

Neuromuscular system. Probably resulting from a dual effect in which neuromuscular junction transmission is depressed in curare-like manner, and transmission in spinal cord motorneurones is also depressed, skeletal muscle tone is markedly reduced—in fact ether produces greater muscular relaxation than any other inhalational agent.

Metabolic change. Alterations in carbohydrate metabolism are mediated by sympatho-adrenal stimulation, and an associated metabolic acidosis may occur. Hepatic function may be depressed for several days following anaesthesia, but the effects are readily reversible and are probably caused indirectly by associated changes such as acidosis and altered hepatic circulation. Renal function may be depressed during anaesthesia as a result of increased rates of secretion of antidiuretic hormone and sympathetically mediated constriction of the renal vascular bed, and this may result in oliguria or even anuria. Transient depression of tubular function may persist for some hours after anaesthesia and this may be accompanied by oliguria and the appearance of albumin and cellular casts in the urine.

Uterus and placenta. Ether rapidly crosses the placenta and may depress foetal respiration.

Fate in the body. Approximately 80% is exhaled unaltered by the lungs, and the remainder is metabolized or excreted over 24 h.

Overall verdict
Ether is still the safest agent in the hands of inexperienced anaesthetists. If it were not for its unpleasant effects during induction and recovery, and the fire and explosion hazard it presents, it would be near to an ideal as well as being an inexpensive agent for experimental animal anaesthesia. It undoubtedly still has a place—indeed it may again become the most popular inhalational agent if the fears concerning the potential toxicity of other anaesthetics are confirmed.

Halothane ('Fluothane')

Physical properties
Halothane boils at 50°C and is fairly soluble in blood (blood:gas partition coefficient = 3·6) so that alveolar and arterial concentrations equilibrate much quicker than ether, but slower than N_2O which is relatively insoluble in blood. Induction and recovery (to unaided standing) with halothane are therefore fairly rapid (1–3 and 5–10 min respectively). A concentration of 4% is required for induction in most species if it is used without preanaesthetic agents or other inhalant anaesthetics, but this must be reduced as soon as the animal loses reflex responses to painful stimuli. Maintenance is achieved with 0·5–2% concentrations depending on the depth of anaesthesia required and the use of other agents. Halothane is neither explosive nor inflammable so it can be used safely when diathermy or thermocautery are being used. Its high affinity for rubber results in far lower concentrations being delivered to the animal than indicated by the vaporizer during the initial stages of anaesthesia (2–5 min). Its potency makes the use of a properly designed vaporizer mandatory. Halothane is compatible with soda-lime so it can be used in rebreathing systems. The vapour is generally described as pleasant to inhale but is strongly resented by rabbits during induction.

68

Pharmacology

Nervous system. Halothane is a potent CNS depressant (MAC of about 1·0% in rats), the depression it produces following a similar pattern to ether except that excitatory phases during induction or recovery are rarely encountered. The vital medullary centres are paralysed in a similar sequence but paralysis of the vasometer centre occurs much more quickly after paralysis of the respiratory centre than with ether. Cerebral blood flow is increased. The balance between sympathetic and parasympathetic tone is altered slightly in favour of the latter. Analgesia is moderate during induction and only approaches ether in this respect at high concentrations in medium to deep surgical anaesthesia.

Respiratory system. Halothane is not irritant to respiratory mucosa and does not stimulate salivary or bronchial secretions. In general, respiratory frequency and amplitude are both depressed, and alveolar ventilation is reduced in direct proportion to anaesthetic depth, the $PaCO_2$ rises and, unless corrective steps are taken, a respiratory acidosis develops. Hence for long procedures involving medium or deep surgical anaesthesia, assisted ventilation (IPPV) is preferred; furthermore, the concentration of halothane should be reduced to 0·5–1%, and supplemented with N_2O in the inspired gases and the iv administration of analgesics and muscle relaxants as required.

Conclusion. Halothane is less likely to produce respiratory problems than ether.

Cardiovascular system. The most marked effect of halothane is a progressive fall in blood pressure which is proportional to the depth of anaesthesia. This is due to direct myocardial depression (which may even cause asystole in the presence of very high concentrations) and peripheral vasodilation which is not compensated by increased sympathetic tone as it is with ether. The vasodilator action of halothane has been variously ascribed to central depression of vasomotor tone, partial blockade of sympathetic ganglia, reduced vascular sensitivity to noradrenaline, and a direct spasmolytic action on arteriolar smooth muscle. Relatively increased parasympathetic tone allows vagal inhibition and cardiac slowing (bradycardia) to develop; this can be blocked by premedication with or reversed by iv administration of atropine. Halothane sensitizes the heart to the arrhythmogenic effects of circulating catecholamines, so that alterations in rhythm are commonly encountered during light levels of anaesthesia, particularly in cats. Hence the administration of adrenaline or naradrenaline is contraindicated during halothane anaesthesia, and circumstances causing their endogenous release (e.g. struggling during induction, surgical stimulation during very light anaesthesia

and the accumulation of blood CO_2 at deeper levels of anaesthesia) should be avoided.

Conclusion. Halothane is safe only at low concentrations (0·5–1%), and the higher concentrations needed for induction should be reduced as soon as practicable. It is dangerous in the hands of inexperienced personnel attempting to maintain anaesthesia with open-drop methods and is a poor agent for long periods of maintenance anaesthesia whenever near-physiological cardiovascular dynamics are required for the experiment.

Neuromuscular system. Halothane does not have the same intensity of myoneural effect as ether and hence muscle relaxation is not so good at light levels of anaesthesia. No attempt should be made to improve relaxation by administering higher concentrations but it should instead be supplemented with muscle relaxants such as gallamine or pancuronium.

Metabolic changes. Renal function is depressed and oliguria occurs during halothane anaesthesia, but this is probably related to cardiovascular disturbances and is not significantly worse than with other agents. The BMR is depressed and this, combined with peripheral vasodilation, may lead to lowered body temperature and accidental hypothermia. As with other anaesthetic agents, a transient depression of hepatic function may occur with halothane. A more specific direct hepatotoxic action has been reported in a small number of human patients (Moult & Sherlock, 1975), although attempts to explain the mechanisms of damage in animal models have not been successful (Reves & McCracken, 1976).

Uterus and placenta. Halothane crosses the placenta and depresses the foetus. Uterine muscle tone is depressed and its contractility inhibited as a direct result of the potent spasmolytic activity of halothane.

Fate in the body. Approximately 80% of halothane administered is exhaled unchanged and the remainder is metabolized and excreted.

Overall verdict

Halothane is a potent agent which is excellent for most experimental procedures. However, several rules should be followed to use it to maximum advantage. A calibrated vaporizer capable of a delivering low concentrations is essential, and halothane should be used at low concentrations in conjunction with $N_2O:O_2$ (1:1) together with small doses of muscle relaxants and analgesics in a balanced regimen (CRC). Because halothane is relatively expensive, it is best used in rebreathing systems with sodalime absorption of CO_2. This is also to be recommended since its toxicity to man is not established one way or the other (Simpson *et al.*, 1971) and as further precaution, it should be used in well-ventilated conditions with exhaled gases ducted away from the operating environment.

Methoxyflurane ('Penthrane')

Physical properties

Methoxyflurane is highly soluble in blood which, together with its marked affinity for body fat depots, results in a slow rate of induction and a very slow recovery (10–20 and 30–60 min respectively). Its boiling point is so high (105°C) that it is virtually impossible to achieve a concentration higher than 3·5% at room temperature even with high gas flow rates and, as that is the safe induction concentration, it is not easy to administer an overdose no matter how badly the agent is administered. Furthermore, its high affinity for the rubber components in equipment makes it even more difficult to actually administer a 3·5% concentration to the animal. Concentrations of 0·4–1·0% are sufficient for anaesthetic maintenance. Methoxyflurane concentrations below 4% are non-explosive and non-flammable at normal temperatures.

Pharmacology

Nervous system. Methoxyflurane is a potent agent with a MAC of about 0·22% in rats. Once anaesthetic concentrations have been attained in the CNS, depression follows the general pattern. The respiratory and vasomotor centres are directly depressed particularly at deeper levels of anaesthesia. There appears to be no alteration in the balance of sympathetic: parasympathetic tone Methoxyflurane is the most potent analgesic of any of the inhalational agents, and analgesia persists well into the post-operative period.

Respiratory system. Methoxyflurane is not irritant to the respiratory tract. During induction, the respiratory rate usually increases to compensate for a decrease in tidal volume but, as anaesthesia deepens, both the rate and amplitude are depressed, and $PaCO_2$ is elevated to levels similar to those obtained with halothane. This becomes important if medium to deep levels of surgical anaesthesia are maintained for more than 60 min when IPPV should be provided. Lower concentrations of methoxyflurane can then be used to maintain anaesthesia at a steady level once respiration is controlled.

Conclusion. Respiratory depression and moderate levels of acidosis are only likely to develop after long periods of administration with high concentrations. Methoxyflurane should be used at 0·4–1% maintenance concentration together with $N_2O:O_2$ (1:1).

Cardiovascular system. Methoxyflurane tends to depress the myocardium and cardiac output in proportion to the depth of anaesthesia. However, provided blood volume is well maintained, this is not accompanied by marked hypotension since peripheral vasoconstriction compensates, but at deep surgical levels or after prolonged periods of administration significant hypotension may develop. Methoxyflurane is less likely than halothane or cyclopropane to sensitize the heart to the arrhythmogenic effects of catecholamines and it does not increase the level of circulating catecholamines.

Conclusion. This agent is safer than halothane at equivalent concentrations.

Neuromuscular system. Although it is not thought to act directly on the myoneural junction, methoxyflurane provides good skeletal muscle relaxation even during light surgical anaesthetic levels with low (0·4–1%) concentrations. This can be potentiated if necessary with gallamine or pancuronium provided controlled ventilation is available.

Metabolic changes. A specific hepatotoxic effect has not been demonstrated. Unfortunately, kidney function is usually severely impaired, probably due to the effect of fluoride ions released from metabolites rendering the distal convoluted tubule unresponsive to anti-diuretic hormone—hence the animal produces a high output of dilute urine.

Fate in the body. Some 50% of methoxyflurane is exhaled unaltered by the lungs and the remainder is metabolized by dechlorination and cleavage of carbon-fluoride bonds. The slow release of the agent into blood from fat depots may take many hours so that complete recovery may be delayed for up to 24 h.

Overall verdict

Methoxyflurane at low concentrations of 0·25–0·5% and in combination with $N_2O:O_2$ (1:1) and a muscle relaxant is an excellent agent for maintenance of anaesthesia after induction with a rapid-acting injectable agent. The prolonged post-operative analgesia is often a valuable contribution to the animal's welfare, but may interfere with the experimental protocol. The slow recovery period usually proceeds quietly and with little or no excitement. We believe that it should not be used for kidney transplantation experiments in any animal. However, it is extremely safe for inhalational anaesthesia of small species including guinea-pigs, rats, mice, hamsters and small birds—in fact it is the agent of choice (CRC). Particular care should be taken in minimizing exposure of personnel to methoxyflurane by ensuring that waste gases are vented direct to ventilation extracts. Since it is very expensive, it is best administered in rebreathing circuits with soda-lime absorption when anaesthetizing larger species—however, the agent is suitable for open-drop methods of administration to small species.

Enflurane ('Ethrane')

Physical properties
Enflurane is a halogenated ether, a volatile non-flammable and non-explosive liquid with a boiling point of 56·5°C. It resembles halothane in many respects. Because of its low blood:gas partition coefficient (1·8), induction of anaesthesia is rapid (100–180 s), depth of anaesthesia can be readily altered, and prompt recovery usually follows withdrawal (2–4 min). The oil:gas partition coefficient is 98. It is relatively insoluble in rubber (rubber:gas partition coefficient at room temperature of 23°C is 74).

Pharmacology
Nervous system. Enflurane is a potent anaesthetic with a MAC of 2·2% in dogs. Anaesthesia is rapidly induced and is maintained with concentrations of 0·5–1·5%. In man, it has marked stimulant effects on the CNS, and EEG activity is increased in proportion to depth of anaesthesia. Convulsions have been reported to occur in some patients (Linde *et al.*, 1970).

Respiratory system. The minute volume of spontaneous respiration is maintained and respiratory rate increased unless deep levels of anaesthesia are attained, when both are depressed.

Cardiovascular system. Cardiovascular dynamics are usually remarkably stable although there may be a slight fall in blood pressure. Enflurane sensitizes the myocardium to the arrhythmogenic effects of catecholamines to a similar extent to halothane. Cardiac output remains sensitive to changes in $PaCO_2$.

Neuromuscular system. Good muscle relaxation is obtained with enflurane.

Other effects. Enflurane does not produce nausea or vomiting in man during recovery, and adverse hepatic and renal effects have not been reported.

Fate in the body. Relatively little biotransformation occurs in the body and only traces of metabolites have been found in the urine (hence any renal damage should be minimal).

Overall verdict
Enflurane may well prove to be a good inhalational agent for use in animals, although the stimulant effect on the CNS will probably limit its use in man. Its lack of flammability, low MAC, lack of effects on vital functions, and rapid excretion unchanged from the lungs when anaesthesia is terminated suggest that it may be an excellent alternative to halothane.

Trichloroethylene ('Trilene')

Physical properties
Trichloroethylene is a colourless liquid with a smell similar to chloroform. The high boiling point of 86·7°C makes vaporization difficult at room temperature. The vapour is not flammable in air but will ignite in the presence of pure O_2 in concentrations above 10% at temperatures above 20°C. It is decomposed by alkalis and heat and breaks down to form dichloroacetylene—which is explosive—and phosgene and carbon monoxide—which are highly toxic—*it must not therefore be used with soda-lime in closed circuits*. The blood:gas and oil:gas partition coefficient at 37°C are 9·2 and 960 respectively, and the rubber:gas partition coefficient at 23°C is 830 (i.e. it is readily taken up by rubber components in apparatus). It is decomposed by light in the presence of moisture.

Pharmacology
Nervous system. Trichloroethylene exerts a similar depressant effect on the CNS as other inhalational agents. It is a very potent analgesic but is commonly described as a relatively weak anaesthetic and only suitable for producing light levels of anaesthesia. However, this is not strictly true as it has MAC of 0·6% in rats—it is only 'weak' because of its high solubility in blood, fat and rubber which hinder uptake by the CNS. Paralysis of the respiratory and vasomotor centres is rare with the concentrations normally used for anaesthesia (0·3–1·5%) but centrally-mediated respiratory deviations are commonly encountered (see below). There is usually some increase in vagal tone. Induction is slow (2–5 min in dogs) and recovery takes about 30 min.

Respiratory system. Trichloroethylene is not irritant to the upper respiratory tract and this, together with its lack of objectionable odour, allows excitement-free induction in most animals. This agent produces marked and unique effects on the respiratory system—respiratory rate and depth both increase during induction of anaesthesia in dogs and cats, and tachypnoea is common. Rapid, deep respirations therefore indicate that deep anaesthesia has been obtained.

Cardiovascular system. Depression of myocardium is minimal and blood pressure is usually unchanged even though cardiac rate is decreased. Cardiac arrhythmias are often encountered, e.g. atrial fibrillation and ectopic ventricular systoles (Johnson *et al.*, 1958), and the myocardium is sensitized to the arrhythmogenic effects of catecholamines and hence to high $PaCO_2$ during spontaneous respiration.

Alimentary system. There is no significant alteration in gut tone or salivary secretions. Nausea and vomiting are often encountered after prolonged administration.

Neuromuscular system. Trichloroethylene provides poor muscle relaxation in all species, and overdosage occurs if attempts are made to achieve good surgical conditions. Struggling may occur during recovery period.

Metabolic changes. There is apparently little effect on normal metabolic processes but a respiratory acidosis may occur. Hepatic and renal function are less impaired at the time of anaesthesia than with chloroform or ether. Cloudy swelling and necrosis of hepatocytes can be found after prolonged or repeated anaesthesia with trichloroethylene.

Uterus and placenta. Uterine muscle is depressed during anaesthesia. The agent rapidly crosses the placenta into foetal circulation.

Fate in the body. Approximately 80% of inhaled trichloroethylene is excreted unchanged by the lungs. The remainder is transformed to chloral hydrate, thence to trichloroethanol and trichloroacetic acid and these are excreted in the conjugated form in urine. Maximum urinary excretion occurs at about 48 h after administration, but may continue for up to 7 days.

Overall verdict

Trichloroethylene has little to commend its use in experimental animals other than its potent analgesic activity and low cost. These are outweighed by its disadvantages, namely poor muscle relaxant properties and its effect on the respiratory and cardiovascular systems if attempts are made to achieve surgical anaesthesia. If it is used, it should be administered in low (0·5–1·0%) concentrations together with $N_2O:O_2$ (1:1) and a muscle relaxant.

Gaseous agents

Nitrous oxide (N_2O)

Physical properties

Nitrous oxide is supplied in cylinders in liquid form under a pressure of 46 atmospheres (46 kg/cm^2). It is neither flammable nor explosive. As it is relatively insoluble in blood and body fluids, induction and recovery are rapid. The gas has a true but weak narcotic action (MAC is approximately 150% in rats) and concentrations above 80% (with 20% O_2) are needed to induce very light levels of anaesthesia. However, since 15–20% O_2 should be presented to the alveolar membrane,

some 25–30% O_2 must be present in inspired gases to ensure that dilution effects and dead space accumulation of CO_2 do not allow hypoxia to develop. In practice, therefore, concentrations of 60:40 or 50:50 $N_2O:O_2$ are used most commonly in animal work as an adjunct to other more potent agents. In man, the addition of 70% N_2O to inspired gases reduces the MAC of halothane and methoxyflurane by about 60%. It can be used in partial rebreathing systems but should not be used in completely closed systems since CO_2 may rise and O_2 fall within the circuit.

Pharmacology

Nervous system. The nature of CNS depression is similar to that caused by other inhalational agents but it is only possible to achieve a moderate degree of depression (basal narcosis) at safe practical concentrations. Paralysis of the vital centres does not occur unless concurrent hypoxia develops. Analgesia is weak at 50% inspired concentrations. At this concentration, N_2O does not appear to alter autonomic balance.

Respiratory system. N_2O is not irritant to respiratory mucosa, and respiration is usually regular and slightly enhanced during induction. Violent movements indicate that hypoxia is developing.

Conclusion: N_2O is extremely safe if adequate oxygenation and a patent airway are maintained both during the anaesthetic period and for at least 10 min after withdrawal of the gas.

Cardiovascular system. There are virtually no detectable changes in myocardial contractility, venous return or arterial pressure except those associated with mild fear and raised catecholamine levels when for example, rabbits are introduced to a mask. Any changes which do occur rapidly disappear once a state of sleep is attained.

Conclusion. N_2O is very safe and appears to cause as little cardiovascular disturbance as any known agent. However, it must be appreciated that this is accompanied by low potency and it is probably not true to say that it is inherently safer than other agents. For example, the MAC of N_2O is approximately 150% in rats, whereas the MAC of halothane is only about 1·0%. It follows that an inspired concentration of 80% N_2O is equivalent to about 0·5% halothane in this species, and at these relative concentrations the latter also has minimal cardiovascular effects.

Neuromuscular system. Relaxation is very poor and muscle relaxants are not potentiated.

Metabolic effects. No significant effects on renal or hepatic function have been demonstrated.

Uterus and placenta. N_2O crosses the placental barrier but without apparently depressing the foetus.

Fate in the body. Metabolic transformation does not occur and N_2O is rapidly excreted by the lungs.

Overall verdict

Higher concentrations than 50% N_2O with O_2 should not be administered by inexperienced anaesthetists. It is therefore too weak an anaesthetic to use alone, but is an extremely valuable adjunct to more potent agents either with or without muscle relaxants and analgesics. The possibility of toxicity and environmental pollution cannot be discounted even though problems which were at one time encountered with contamination of N_2O cylinders by toxic higher oxides of nitrogen have now been overcome.

Cyclopropane

Physical properties

This is supplied as a liquid in cylinders under pressure ($4\cdot4$ kg/cm^2). It is poorly soluble in blood (blood : air partition coefficient $0\cdot47$) so that induction and recovery are rapid (1–3 and 15 min respectively) and its anaesthetic properties are derived from its high lipid solubility. It is a more potent agent than N_2O having a MAC of about 17% in rats. As a rough guide, anaesthesia may be induced rapidly with 20–25% cyclopropane with O_2, and can be maintained to suit the surgical requirement with approximately 10% for light and 20% for medium surgical anaesthesia. Concentrations above 25% should not be used. Since cyclopropane is explosive when mixed with air or O_2, a closed rebreathing system is mandatory.

Pharmacology

Nervous system. The CNS is depressed as described for other agents, and good analgesia develops. The respiratory centre is easily paralysed, but control from the vasomotor centre is usually well maintained for some time after respiration has ceased. The autonomic system is affected in a complex fashion, although vagal tone usually predominates. Unlike most other anaesthetics, which often alter the balance between sympathetic and parasympathetic nervous systems, cyclopropane tends to increase the activity of both branches of the ANS. Manifestations of parasympathetic stimulation may include bradycardia, laryngospasm and increased gut motility, while sympathomimetic responses may involve tachycardia, increased myocardial contractility, raised peripheral resistance, decreased renal blood flow, and metabolic changes such as raised glucose and lactate levels in the circulation and a state of metabolic acidosis.

Respiratory system. Cyclopropane does not irritate mucous membranes at anaesthetic concentrations and respiration is not reflexly stimulated. Direct depression of the respiratory centres causes a progressive depression of tidal volume and respiratory rate which often limits the achievement of adequate depths of surgical anaesthesia unless IPPV is provided.

Conclusion. Maintenance with spontaneous respiration is too difficult for inexperienced anaesthetists since the anaesthetic depth oscillates rapidly with alterations in minute volume. Even with IPPV the input of cyclopropane has to be adjusted frequently.

Cardiovascular system. Hypertension is invariably produced during the early phases of cyclopropane anaesthesia in association with increased cardiac rate and output arising from sympathoadrenal stimulation. Hypotension may develop after long periods of administration and may be severe if cyclopropane administration is terminated abruptly. Haemorrhage and capillary oozing may be difficult to stop at operative sites.

Cardiac arrhythmias are commonly encountered and are related both to high arterial concentrations of anaesthetic and of CO_2. The occurrence of arrhythmias in the presence of increased PaCO$_2$ probably reflects the stimulation of central sympathetic mechanisms which the latter causes. Atropine should not be administered under these circumstances but ventilation should be assisted and cyclopropane administration temporarily suspended.

Conclusion. Cyclopropane is safe only in experienced hands. The early hypertensive effects may be useful in maintaining blood pressure in near-physiological preparations.

Neuromuscular function. Muscle relaxation is fairly good.

Metabolic effects. Renal function and urine output is depressed by increased ADH secretion and renal vasoconstriction during cyclopropane anaesthesia. As a result of sympathetic stimulation, liver glycogenolysis is increased and the conversion of glucose to lactate in voluntary muscle is increased. Cyclopropane is not thought to be hepatotoxic.

Uterus and placenta. Cyclopropane passes the placental barrier and depresses foetal respiration.

Fate in the body. Biotransformation of cyclopropane has not been demonstrated and it is probably wholly excreted by the lungs, hence recovery from anaesthesia is rapid.

Overall verdict

The explosive hazard limits the widespread use of cycloprane. However, provided that good rebreathing closed-circuit systems and experienced staff are available, cyclopropane is a good agent for the anaesthesia of sheep and goats.

Carbon dioxide (C_2O)

Although a mixture of 40% CO_2 in air is fatal to most animals, a mixture of $50:50$ $CO_2:O_2$ has been used by several workers for induction of anaesthesia in mice, rats and guinea-pigs (Payne & Chamings, 1964). These authors claimed that mice would tolerate up to 10 min of such exposure.

However, our own experience has been less happy. Hypertension, with increased venous return, and an initial increase in respiratory rate and amplitude commonly occurs. As might be expected, this may lead to capillary bleeding. Results from this laboratory (CRC) indicate that CO_2 anaesthesia is suitable for very short procedures such as cardiac puncture, but that exposure beyond 3 min results in petechial haemorrhages in the bronchial tree and lung parenchyma, and this may well be lethal in animals with existing chronic respiratory disease.

Overall verdict

The rapid induction and recovery (45 s each) make $50:50$ $CO_2:O_2$ a useful mixture for very short procedures, but the period of administration should not exceed 2 min.

ANAESTHESIA WITH INJECTABLE AGENTS

Equipment

It will be evident that a suitable hypodermic needle and syringe are all that are essential for parenteral administration of these drugs, but additional items are particularly valuable when continuous or sequential administration of agents may be necessary.

The butterfly infusion set is simply a needle attached to a length of plastic tubing terminating in a Luer fitting. This has the advantage that once taped in position the animal can move without dislodging the needle and further anaesthetic may be administered as required.

The 'Medicut' intravenous cannula consists of a plastic cannula with a metal needle in the lumen, the needle being slightly longer than the cannula. After percutaneous placement in the vessel, the needle can be withdrawn and the plastic tube retained. This has the advantage that movement will not result in damage to the vein by a metal needle point nor is the cannula likely to be dislodged from the vein.

The 'Bardic I-Catheter' consists of a plastic cannula passing through the lumen of a metal needle. After placement, the cannula is passed for a safe distance along the vessel to ensure retention and the needle is withdrawn.

The 'Buretrol' burette infusion set, which is a disposable plastic set suitable for infusion of blood and fluids by gravity feed allows measured volumes of fluids to be delivered.

Injectable agents

Soluble short-acting barbiturates

General pharmacology and chemistry
The barbiturates in clinical use are all sodium salts of barbituric acid or its thio-derivative, whose chemical structure has been modified to increase lipid solubility and hence potency. Pentobarbitone, thiopentone and methohexitone are each important in animal anaesthesia.

Nervous system. Barbiturates depress the CNS through the narcotic spectrum from sedation, hypnosis, basal narcosis to general anaesthesia and coma. They are now thought to depress conduction within the whole CNS with no particular dominant site of activity although the RAS was at one time considered to be most depressed (Wyke, 1957). Presynaptic nerve terminals appear to be depressed by the lowest plasma concentrations of barbiturate so it is probable that this is the most important microscopic site rather than any interference with axonal transmission. Activity is directly related to the concentration of undissociated molecules which, in turn, will be increased by a fall in plasma pH and by decreased binding with plasma proteins when given with other drugs which may compete for binding receptors. The barbiturates have little or no analgesic action, and at low concentration may even enhance the perception of pain.

Respiratory system. All barbiturates are respiratory depressants in direct proportion to the dose administered. The sensitivity of the respiratory centre to CO_2 is reduced.

Cardiovascular system. At hypnotic doses barbiturates have little overall effect on the cardiovascular system, but at anaesthetic doses there is a fall in blood pressure following direct depression of the vasomotor centre and possibly some direct depressant actions on the arteriolar musculature and myocardium.

Metabolic effects. There is little effect on the BMR during barbiturate-induced hypnosis but O_2 uptake and BMR are markedly depressed when anaesthetic doses are given. Renal function is little altered except that antidiuretic hormone (ADH) secretion is increased and urine output depressed. There may be transient depression of hepatic function and phenobarbitone significantly increases the production of liver microsomal enzymes. Guinea-pigs, rabbits, hamsters, birds and, to a lesser extent, dogs are susceptible to sudden deepening of anaesthesia if they are given dextrose–saline, sodium lactate or adrenaline during recovery from barbiturates—the so-called *glucose effect*—and recovery time may be extended by 40–50%.

Neuromuscular system. Although there is some experimental evidence that thiopentone produces a neuromuscular block, most barbiturates produce poor relaxation unless high doses are used.

Uterus and placenta. All barbiturates cross the placenta and depress foetal respiration.

Fate in the body. After absorption, barbiturates are distributed in all tissues and fluids in the body (i.e. they readily penetrate cell walls). They are then metabolized by the liver and the products eliminated by renal excretion. Re-distribution and metabolism of barbiturates are important in determining the duration of their effect, e.g. thio-barbiturates are rapidly taken up by fat depots and this accounts in part for their short duration of effect.

Pentobarbitone sodium ('*Sagatal*')

Pharmacology
In the general description above, the oxybarbiturate pentobarbitone was taken as the 'type' barbiturate.

Anaesthetic indications and precautions
Attempts to obtain surgical levels of anaesthesia with pentobarbitone alone are hazardous in most species. Respiration is depressed, particularly in the early stages of anaesthesia, and recovers only slowly. $PaCO_2$ is invariable elevated. The cardiovascular system is also affected—the mean systemic arterial systolic and central venous pressure are both markedly depressed even though the heart rate and peripheral resistance may be elevated. The BMR and hence body temperature falls. Lastly, analgesia is always poor until deep levels of anaesthesia are obtained when vital medullary centres will likewise be depressed.

Body (core) temperature must be maintained by operating on a heated pad, and allowing animals (particularly small rodents) to recover in high ambient temperatures (e.g. dogs and cats 25°C, mice and rats 35°C). A patent airway should be ensured by aspirating fluid accumulations and intubating the animal whenever practicable, and high O_2 concentrations should be supplied to maintain normal PaO_2. For long periods of anaesthesia and whenever spontaneous breathing is significantly depressed, IPPV should be considered.

The deficiencies of pentobarbitone can be partially offset by concurrent administration or pre-medication with low doses of analgesics and tranquillizers, thus decreasing the required pentobarbitone dosage by up to 60%.

Dosages and administration
Pentobarbitone can be given iv, ip, im or even sc, but whenever possible it should be given slowly iv to effect with small incremental doses, allowing at least 60 s between each increment for tissue equilibration and observation of the CNS depression produced. In smaller laboratory species it can be given ip as a single computed dose having weighed the individual.

Dosages up to 30 mg/kg can be given iv in dogs, cats, sheep, goats, calves, rabbits and ferrets. We use a 3 or 6% solution depending on species, injecting $\frac{1}{2}$ the computed dose rapidly and the remainder to effect over a period of at least 5 min to allow time for the agent to cross the blood–brain barrier. Peak activity (light surgical anaesthesia) will then be maintained for approximately 30 min in dogs, cats and ferrets, although there is very wide variation from breed to breed and among individuals. Pentobarbitone is more rapidly metabolized in goats, sheep and rabbits, and peak activity is maintained for 15–20 min only. Higher doses (30–60 mg/kg) are given to rodents ip but there is much more variation in response. Very young animals need much smaller doses. If it is necessary to extend the period of narcosis, small increments may be given to effect at a maximum rate of 5 mg/kg but great care must be taken to ensure that the animal does not suddenly become too deeply anaesthetized.

Recovery is always relatively slow but varies in duration in different species. For example, mice may be completely ambulatory in 45–120 min whilst some greyhounds may take up to 48 h, and cats can take up to 72 h to recover fully. In the latter cases, intravenous fluid therapy should be instituted (not with glucose or lactated preparations) and constant nursing is needed. Convulsive movements, involuntary paddling of limbs and crying may occur. Such excitatory behaviour is suppressed if tranquillizers or analgesics are given concurrently, but complete recovery will then be further delayed.

Overall verdict
Pentobarbitone is still the most widely used injectable anaesthetic in experimental work despite its disadvantages. It is a valuable agent provided its potential toxicity is understood and appropriate measures are taken.

Thiopentone sodium ('*Intraval sodium*', '*Pentothal*')

Pharmacology
Thiopentone has a shorter duration of activity partly due to its high affinity for fat (particularly blood fat) and partly because it is metabolized in

the liver quite rapidly during the early stages of anaesthesia (Dundee & Wyant, 1974).

Nervous system. Unlike pentobarbitone, thiopentone rapidly diffuses into the brain after iv administration and peak activity is achieved within 30 s. Although it is a potent hypnotic, thiopentone is a poor analgesic, and in humans it has been shown that in small doses (less than 2 mg/kg) it actually lowers the pain threshold (Clutton Brock, 1960). As with other thiobarbiturates, acute tolerance develops (Dundee, 1956). The respiratory centre is readily depressed but the autonomic nervous system is little affected by small doses of thiopentone, and vagal tone is usually normal.

Respiratory system. Respiration is always markedly depressed. Following rapid administration, there is usually an increase in depth of respiration followed by a short period of apnoea. When breathing is resumed there is usually a reduction in tidal volume and respiratory rate. If thiopentone is given slowly to effect, respiration is depressed in ratio to depth of anaesthesia. The sensitivity of central chemoreceptors to variations in hydrogen ion concentration—and hence of the respiratory centre to plasma CO_2—is markedly depressed.

Cardiovascular system. As thiopentone depresses the myocardium, and cardiac output falls in proportion to plasma concentrations, fatalities may occur if the drug is given too rapidly to poor-risk subject. Although thiopentone is not thought to affect cardiac irritability directly, cardiac arrhythmias are exhibited in dogs and man, and are probably associated with high $PaCO_2$ or with hypoxia. Severe hypotension may occur if large doses of thiopentone are given rapidly, resulting both from peripheral vasodilation following depression of the vasomotor centre and decreased cardiac output. However, if thiopentone is given to effect, hypotension is usually mild and transient as sympathetic tone to arterioles is raised in response to baroreceptor feed-back mechanisms, i.e. a compensatory increase in peripheral vascular resistance occurs. Following these reflex adjustments, arterial pressure and cardiac output both return to normal.

Neuromuscular system. Skeletal muscle tone is markedly reduced. This is probably due to central depression, although there is some evidence that high doses of thiopentone produce a curare-like effect at the myoneural junction.

Metabolic effects. Hepatic and renal functions are depressed by large doses but the effects are generally transient.

Uterus and placenta. Thiopentone rapidly crosses the placental barrier, but concentrations in foetal blood are usually significantly lower than in maternal blood (Levy & Owen, 1964).

Fate in the body. Plasma concentrations rise rapidly after iv administration and thiopentone exerts its effects in the CNS almost immediately. Thiopentone then diffuses more slowly into other tissues and is mainly retained in poorly vascularized fat depots and in skeletal muscle. Hence, the plasma level falls and thiopentone is redistributed from nervous tissue down concentration gradients into plasma, and consciousness returns. Thiopentone is slowly metabolized in the liver, and breakdown products are excreted by the kidneys. Nearly 50% of the original dose may still be present in the body after 24 h, so that subsequent doses of thiopentone will accumulate, particularly when adipose tissue has become saturated with the drug, and anaesthesia may then be very prolonged.

Anaesthetic indications and precautions

Thiopentone is an alkaline solution (pH 11) and is thus extremely irritant to body tissues. It is essential to use the most dilute solution commensurate with suitable volumes and to take particular care to ensure that the solution is injected iv. A 1·0% solution is used in cats and rabbits, and a 2·5% solution in all other species except horses and adult cattle when a 10% solution is used (CRC). It may be given rapidly iv or more slowly to effect. Rapid administration of 6–8 mg/kg induces deep narcosis within 15–30 s unaccompanied by excitement, and allows sufficient time to pass an endotracheal tube and transfer the animal to an inhalational technique. However, it is safer to compute a dose of 20–30 mg/kg, give ⅓ rapidly and then the remainder to effect over a period of 60–90 s, in which case peak narcosis will last from 10–15 min and full recovery will take 60–90 min. The anaesthetic period can be extended by giving small incremental doses, but the accumulation of unmetabolized thiopentone will saturate tissues, and the recovery period will be so prolonged that it will obviate any advantage gained by using a short-acting drug. Moreover, the cumulative depression of myocardial function suggests that sequential injections of thiopentone should not be used at all.

Thiopentone should not be used in neonates as they are deficient in liver enzymes capable of degrading the drug. As a general rule, it should not be given to any animal under 8 weeks of age.

Dosages and administration

Horse. Rapid iv injection of a 10% solution at 10 mg/kg produces light surgical anaesthesia in a single vein to brain circulation time and the peak effect lasts 3–4 min. Recovery is usually accompanied by excitement unless a suitable ataractic is given. It is essential to avoid intra-arterial injection.

Cattle. Rapid iv injection of a 10% solution at 10 mg/kg induces light surgical anaesthesia in one

76

circulation time. The animal starts to recover in 4–6 min but does not struggle. Hypocalcaemia may occur in recently calved cows.

Sheep and goat. A 2·5% solution of thiopentone may be given rapidly iv at 6–8 mg/kg or more slowly to effect at 25 mg/kg iv.

Pig. A 2·5% solution should be given after pre-medication (diazepam, ketamine, acepromazine or azaperone) at a dose of 6–10 mg/kg iv slowly to effect taking particular care to avoid perivascular injection.

Dog and cat. Dilute solutions (1–2·5% depending on size) should be given iv either rapidly at 6 mg/kg to induce anaesthesia lasting 3–6 min or at 20–30 mg/kg slowly to effect to produce 10–15 min of anaesthesia.

Rabbit. Slow iv injection of a 1·25% solution at 30 mg/kg affects light surgical anaesthesia lasting 10–20 min.

Overall verdict

Thiopentone is an extremely valuable agent for providing smooth induction of narcosis which is to be followed by endotracheal intubation and maintenance with inhalational agents. It is the agent of choice for horses, most breeds of dog and small ruminants. It is also the best agent for anaesthetizing animals during deliberate hypothermia (see p. 83).

Methohexitone sodium ('Brevane', 'Brietal Sodium')

Pharmacology

Methohexitone is a rapidly acting oxybarbiturate which is more potent than thiopentone and more rapidly metabolized. Its short period of peak activity is attributable partly to rapid degradation in the liver and partly to redistribution in body tissues.

Nervous system. After rapid iv injection of methohexitone, consciousness is lost in a single vein-to-brain circulation time and regained in 2–5 min (i.e. less time than with equivalent doses of thiopentone).

Respiratory system. A transient period of apnoea lasting 30–60 s is commonly encountered and produces a moderate rise in $PaCO_2$. Respiration can be restarted easily by manual compression of the thorax.

Cardiovascular system. A single injection usually results in a fall in cardiac output, vasodilation of skin vessels and a modest but transient fall in blood pressure.

Anaesthetic indications and precautions

Light surgical anaesthesia is induced almost immediately after iv injection and lasts for 2–5 min depending on dosage and species. It is used as a 1% solution in small and 2·5% solution in large animals. Methohexitone is not irritant to tissues and presents little danger of thrombosis. Induction is sometimes associated with involuntary muscle movements and coughing; the incidence of such excitatory phenomena is sometimes increased if antanalgesic drugs such as promethazine are given (Dundee & Wyant, 1974) but diminished following pretreatment with sedative-analgesics. The duration of anaesthesia may be prolonged by sequential incremental administration or by continuous iv infusion. The time to full clinical recovery varies with species, but most dogs are ambulatory within 30 min and rabbits recover even more quickly—usually within 15–20 min. Recovery is often accompanied by twitching of the head and neck muscles, and muscle tremors along the trunk and limbs, especially if there are noises or sudden changes in light intensity.

Methohexitone is a valuable agent for inducing a light plane of anaesthesia prior to maintenance with an inhalational technique. It is especially useful to the experimentalist in combination with sedative-analgesics and $N_2O : O_2$ in all species, in setting up acute near-physiological preparations, and in the chemical restraint of primates when administered by the im route.

Dosage and administration

Dogs, cats and rabbits	4–10 mg/kg iv
Calves	6 mg/kg iv
Primates	15 mg/kg im

Overall verdict

Methohexitone is an excellent agent for induction and for brief periods of anaesthesia in dogs, cats, ruminants, rabbits and rats, combining safety during induction and rapid recovery which may, however, be accompanied by some excitement.

Dissociative anaesthetics

The three commonly used cyclohexylamine analogues, phencyclidine, ketamine and tiletamine have been described in detail in Chapter 4. A few additional notes are warranted on the use of these agents to produce surgical anaesthesia.

Phencyclidine hydrochloride ('Sernylan')

Anaesthetic indications and precautions

Phencyclidine has been used to produce light surgical anaesthesia in *Macaca mulatta* and *M. iris* monkeys for periods up to 24 h (CRC). It was given repeatedly im as required and the animals were well maintained so long as heat and fluid loss were prevented. However, tolerance did develop in some individuals to the extent that at the end of

24 h, doses of up to 10 mg/kg were needed to obtain the same effect as was initially produced with 1–2 mg/kg im. In our experience, the response in marmosets (*Callothrix jacchus*) is erratic and it is difficult to achieve surgical anaesthesia at safe dosages (1·5–2·0 mg/kg im). Whenever surgical anaesthesia is required, we intubate all primates after sedation with phencyclidine before administering $N_2O:O_2$ (1:1). Very small doses of pentobarbitone (5 mg/kg iv) and pethidine (1 mg/kg iv) are then given as required.

Large boars and sows have been sedated with 2 mg/kg of phencyclidine, followed by intubation, administration of $N_2O:O_2$ (1:1) and intermittent iv injections of methohexitone (3 mg/kg) or pentobarbitone (5 mg/kg) as required (CRC).

Ketamine hydrochloride ('Vetalar')

Anaesthetic indications and precautions
Ketamine is the agent of choice for all primates with the possible exception of marmosets in which alphaxolone–alphadolone im and iv is preferred. In other species, although there are many reports of successful anaesthesia with this agent used alone, ketamine has proved less consistent in the degree of anaesthesia produced when assessed in this laboratory (CRC).

Ketamine is particularly valuable in managing intractable cats of all sizes, since it is effective im and has a wide safety margin. A narcotic state approaching surgical anaesthesia can be obtained by the concurrent administration of xylazine. Alternatively, anaesthesia can be deepened by inhalational techniques or iv administration of small doses of alphaxolone–alphadolone.

There have been reports of satisfactory anaesthesia with ketamine as the sole agent in pregnant sheep (Taylor *et al.*, 1972) but our experience has been less encouraging. However, following sedation with xylazine im, ketamine iv provides reasonably satisfactory conditions for minor surgery in this species and is a useful combination in the absence of inhalational anaesthesia.

In pigs, we have used ketamine (10 mg/kg im) injected 2 min after diazepam (1 mg/kg im) to produce light surgical anaesthesia suitable for many procedures (CRC).

Reptiles are well sedated for restraint after im administration of ketamine, and we believe it to be the drug of choice in snakes, turtles, tortoises and terrapins. Surgical conditions can be achieved using infiltration with local analgesics or inhalation of $N_2O:O_2$ (1:1) together with very low concentrations of methoxyflurane (0·2–0·4%) following induction with high doses of ketamine.

Birds are also effectively and relatively safely immobilized with ketamine im, and it is particularly valuable in large exotic species which are difficult to handle. Surgical conditions can then be obtained with inhalational agents, infiltration with local anaesthetics, or iv administration of barbiturates.

Dosage and administration
Ketamine hydrochloride is supplied for veterinary use as a 100 mg/ml solution.

Cats. 44 mg/kg im (with a maximum total of 50 mg/kg for extended periods of narcosis).

Primates. 20–25 mg/kg im (a maximum total dose of 40 mg/kg should not be exceeded).

Sheep. 2 mg/kg by iv injection.

Pigs. 5 mg/kg im produces mild sedation within 2 min and this lasts for about 30 min. Full recovery takes 1·5–2 h. 20 mg/kg im produces deep cataleptic sedation within 60 s and this lasts for about 45 min. Full recovery takes 2–3 h.

Snakes and terrapins. Up to 50 mg/kg im may be needed for deep sedation but a very protracted recovery period extending for up to 96 h is likely if larger doses are used.

Birds.

Small species	50 mg/kg im
Large species	20–40 mg/kg im

In most species the peak effect develops within 6–8 min and lasts for 30–40 min. Complete recovery usually takes 5–8 h.

Neuroleptanalgesic combinations

Neuroleptanalgesia has been described as a narcotic state resembling in some respects light surgical anaesthesia but without loss of consciousness. It is true that superficial surgical procedures can often be carried out under neuroleptanalgesia. However, whenever ideal operating conditions including skeletal muscle relaxation are required, low dosages of volatile inhalational agents together with N_2O and O_2 (1:1) can be superimposed. Alternatively, muscle relaxants, barbiturates, or tranquillizers such as diazepam can be given concurrently at very low dosages.

The combinations of fentanyl–fluanisone, etorphine–methotrimeprazine and etorphine–acepromazine are available commercially, and thiambutene–acepromazine, or pethidine–acepromazine can be given separately but simultaneously to achieve less profound effects. The ability to reverse the narcosis with antagonists such as nalorphine, diprenorphine or naloxone is of great benefit, both in emergency management and in allowing early recovery at the end of surgery.

The indications for laboratory species have been outlined earlier in Chapter 4. Etorphine–acepromazine is also an excellent combination for many exotic species, but particularly bears, hyenas, zebras, elephants, rhinoceros, antelopes and kangaroos.

Anaesthetic steroids (alphaxolone–alphadolone)

The combination containing alphaxalone and alphadolone acetate produces light surgical anaesthesia in several species if given by rapid iv injection. In cats, rats, mice, primates and birds, anaesthesia can be extended with a wide margin of safety by giving small increments to effect. It is also compatible with inhalational techniques. In each case it is usually safer than the equivalent narcosis with barbiturates. In experiments with rats we have found that alphaxolone–alphadolone can be given continuously iv for periods up to 10 h without tolerance or cumulation developing (cf barbiturates and dissociative agents).

Miscellaneous agents

Tribromoethanol ('Avertin')

Pharmacology

Tribromoethanol is a white crystalline powder which is only slightly soluble in water and is therefore dissolved in amylene hydrate to form a stock 100% w/w solution. This is diluted (usually to 2·5%) in distilled water at 40°C immediately prior to administration. Solutions are easily decomposed by light and temperatures above 40°C to produce hydrobromic acid and dibromoacetaldehyde and these are both highly irritant to body tissues.

Nervous system. Tribromoethanol produces a generalized depression of the CNS with a marked action on the medulla, both the respiratory and cardiovascular centres being depressed.

Metabolic effects. Tribromoethanol is conjugated with glucuronic acid in the liver and excreted in the urine as tribromoethanol glycuronate. Amylene hydrate is eliminated unchanged in urine and from the lungs.

Anaesthetic indications and precautions

This drug is of historical interest in human and veterinary anaesthesia, but is still used by some investigators in laboratory dogs, cats, rats and mice. In dogs and cats it is given by rectal infusion (dogs 400–600 mg/kg and cats 300 mg/kg) and is rapidly absorbed, the onset of narcosis developing in 2–3 min, reaching a peak in 15 min and the effect lasting for 2 h. In rodents a 2·5% solution is given ip at a dosage of 125–350 mg/kg. This produces excellent anaesthesia at the time but postoperative fatalities associated with fibrous adhesions around abdominal viscera and gut dysfunction are often encountered.

Overall verdict

The variable results reported from different laboratories using tribromoethanol in rodents may be due to strain differences or simply to stock solutions which contain products of decomposition. Experience in this laboratory confirms that a 2·5% solution is very irritant in rats and, although some strains of mice will tolerate a single dose of tribromoethanol ip, a high mortality is experienced if they are anaesthetized a second time whatever the time interval (CRC).

Chloral hydrate

Pharmacology

Chloral hydrate comes as colourless, translucent crystals which are freely soluble in water. Solutions may be sterilized by boiling for a few minutes without decomposition.

Nervous system. Chloral hydrate is a good hypnotic, depressing the cerebrum with loss of reflex excitability, and producing deep sleep which lasts for several hours. In hypnotic doses it has a very weak analgesic action and the medullary centres are only slightly affected. Because it is such a poor analgesic, large doses have to be given to induce medium surgical anaesthesia and the vasomotor and respiratory centres are then severely depressed to produce hypotension and depressed respiration. In all animals, chloral hydrate crosses the blood–brain barrier slowly and it is difficult to assess the depth of anaesthesia because narcosis will continue to deepen for several minutes after injection has finished. The parasympathetic branch of the ANS is stimulated and vagal activity is potentiated to produce primary bradycardia and occasional A–V block.

Respiratory system. Hypnotic doses depress respiration only mildly, but anaesthetic doses exert a marked depressant effect via the respiratory centre. Overdosage causes a progressive depression of the centre to the point of respiratory failure and death.

Cardiovascular system. Anaesthetic doses of chloral hydrate severely depress the vasomotor centre and this, together with marked myocardial depression and bradycardia, produces significant hypotension. Vagal activity is potentiated and induced atrial fibrillation is sustained for much longer in animals under chloral hydrate anaesthesia than normal subjects. The carotid sinus reflex is markedly enhanced.

Metabolic effects. Large doses given repeatedly over a long period may cause fatty degeneration of the liver, heart and kidney. Liver microsomal enzyme activity is slightly depressed.

Uterus and placenta. Chloral hydrate crosses the placental barrier but does not significantly depress foetal respiration.

Fate in the body. Chloral hydrate is rapidly absorbed from the gastro-intestinal tract and the onset of effect is observed in 5–10 min after oral administration. It is rapidly reduced in the blood to trichloroethanol, which is taken up by the CNS and exerts its hypnotic effect. Trichloroethanol is in turn conjugated with glycuronic acid to form uro-chloralic acid which is excreted by the kidneys. A small quantity of chloral hydrate is normally excreted unchanged in urine but larger quantities may be found in animals with liver damage.

Anaesthetic indications and precautions

Chloral hydrate, administered iv or orally by stomach tube or drench, has been used extensively in horses and cattle until quite recently when it was superseded by more convenient agents. However, respiratory depression renders it an unsatisfactory anaesthetic in dogs and other small animals. In addition, solutions are irritant to gastric mucosa and should not be used in concentrations greater than 5%. For the same reason, it is particularly important to avoid perivascular infiltration during iv injection since it may cause extensive necrosis of the vessel wall and surrounding tissue. In spite of its limitations, it is still used occasionally in horses, and is often used in laboratory rats, guinea-pigs and hamsters, either alone ip or in combination with pentobarbitone and magnesium sulphate ('Equithesin'). This combination has also been used extensively as an im injection in birds.

Dosages and administration

Horse. Oral administration by drench or stomach tube of a 5% solution at a dosage of 120 to 150 mg/kg produces basal narcosis. The onset of narcosis is seen in 5–10 min and the maximum effect develops in 15–20 min.

Slow iv injection (over 4–5 min) of a 10% solution at a dosage of 120 mg/kg (i.e. 500–800 ml volumes may be necessary using gravity infusion apparatus and a suitable iv catheter) induces basal narcosis within 5–7 min. Further increments may be given to effect if chloral hydrate is the sole general anaesthetic agent.

Recovery will take 45–60 min for initial injection depending on the depth of narcosis attained, and the animals should be restrained with hobbles until they are able to rise. Excitement and struggling during recovery can be minimized by the use of tranquillizers.

Rats, guinea-pigs and hamsters. After ip injection of a 10% solution at 200–300 mg/kg the onset of narcosis is seen in 3–5 min and the peak effect is maintained for 60–120 min.

Overall verdict

Chloral hydrate is a poor analgesic and severely depresses the respiratory system at anaesthetic doses. It is not, therefore, recommended for use as a general anaesthetic but may be used as a hypnotic to attain basal narcosis and a fair degree of muscle relaxation.

Chloral hydrate–magnesium sulphate–pentobarbitone sodium ('Equithesin')

Anaesthetic indications and precautions

Various combinations of these agents have been recommended (Millenbruck & Wallinga, 1946; Jones, 1949) with the intention of avoiding excitement during induction and recovery, and improving safety in attaining surgical anaesthesia as compared with chloral hydrate alone. The mixture now most commonly used consists of 21·3 g chloral hydrate, 4·8 g pentobarbitone and 10·6 g magnesium sulphate in 500 ml of an aqueous solution containing propylene glycol and 9·5% alcohol ('Equithesin').

This was recommended for use in healthy birds at a dosage of 2·5 ml/kg im (injected into the pectoral muscles) but at a reduced rate of 2·0 ml/kg im in poor risk cases (Gandal, 1956). It was assessed for iv injection in rabbits after premedication with diazepam at 10 mg/kg or with 0·3 mg/kg paraldehyde (Hodesson *et al.*, 1965) but some deaths were encountered.

Dosages and administration

Birds. 2·5 ml/kg im—the maximum effect (light surgical anaesthesia) is attained in 5–15 min and lasts 30–60 min.

Overall verdict

There seems little merit in using this mixture in any species of animal.

Paraldehyde

Pharmacology

Paraldehyde is a colourless liquid polymer of acetaldehyde which solidifies at temperatures below 11°C.

Nervous system. Paraldehyde is a central depressant with potent sedative and hypnotic properties. It has a wide margin of safety as it depresses cerebral function without markedly depressing vital medullary centres (the LD_{50} in dogs is 3·5 g/kg).

Respiratory system. Respiration is unaffected by low hypnotic doses but is moderately depressed by the higher dosages needed to produce basal narcosis or light surgical anaesthesia.

Cardiovascular system. Little effect is observed unless high doses are used.

Uterus and placenta. Paraldehyde crosses the placental barrier but has little effect on foetal metabolism.

Fate in the body. Paraldehyde is quickly absorbed but its subsequent fate is not definitely known. About 80% is probably broken down in the liver and the remainder excreted by the lungs.

Anaesthetic indications and precautions
Paraldehyde has been used in dogs, rabbits, baboons, porpoises and amphibians to produce a state of hypnosis which could be supplemented with other more potent central depressants or with inhalational agents. However, im injection is very painful and, as the taste is unpleasant, oral dosing is not recommended. It should not be given to subjects with liver disease as they become comatose.

Dosage and administration
Rabbits. Doses of 1 ml/kg im or ip produces anaesthesia in 20–30 min (Pandeya & Lemon, 1965).

Frogs. 4·2 ml/kg injected into the ventral lymph sac produces narcosis in 15 min (Blume & Sroka, 1943).

Overall verdict
Better drugs are now available.

α-Chloralose

Pharmacology
Chloralose is prepared by heating equal quantities of anhydrous glucose and anhydrous chloral (trichloracetaldehyde) to yield α- and β-isomers. Only α-chloralose has narcotic properties. A 1% concentration in 0·9% v/v isotonic saline solution should be freshly prepared immediately before use by heating to 50–60°C and then should be used at 40°C before the α-chloralose has time to precipitate out of solution. Alternatively, it can be mixed in a warm (60°C) solution of 10% polyethylene glycol in water when it will remain in solution on cooling.

Nervous system. Chloralose exerts similar but longer-lasting depressant effects on the CNS as chloral hydrate. Loss of consciousness is induced by iv doses of 80–100 mg/kg but is often accompanied by muscle twitching and spike activity on EEG recordings similar to those produced by CNS stimulants. The activity of the autonomic nervous system is believed to be unaffected, and vasomotor tone is well maintained throughout the 10 h period of anaesthesia. The peak narcotic activity is not reached until about 15 min after iv injection so it is usually more practicable to induce anaesthesia initially with an inhalational agent or a short-acting agent such as methohexitone or alphaxolone–alphadolone.

Respiratory system. Respiration is not depressed until very high dosages are administered. Reflex activity and medullary control are well maintained.

Cardiovascular system. Blood pressure is well maintained or is elevated, and cardiac rate is often markedly increased.

Metabolic effects. Liver microsomal enzyme activity is slightly depressed.

Fate in the body. Chloralose is broken down to chloral and glucose.

Anaesthetic indications and precautions
Chloralose is used extensively in physiological and pharmacological experiments, and is particularly valuable for long non-survival preparations requiring minimal physiological disturbance and little surgical interference. Its low solubility and hence the need to inject large volumes, and the long period required for peak activity to be attained, produce difficulties at induction which are best overcome by iv injection of a short-acting drug (methohexitone, alphaxolone–alphadolone or propanidid, depending on species) followed by intubation and administration of $N_2O:O_2$ (1:1). Basal narcosis to light surgical anaesthesia is maintained for 8–10 h, but recovery is accompanied by struggling unless $N_2O:O_2$ is administered to completion. Urethane has been administred concurrently in the past at 500–800 mg/kg iv (with chloralose at 50–80 mg/kg iv) in order to suppress spontaneous muscle activity in dogs, cats and rabbits (Linzell, 1964), but in view of the risks associated with urethane (see below) we believe that $N_2O:O_2$ should be used instead, preferably with IPPV.

Dosage and administration
Dogs. 80–110 mg/kg iv of a 1% solution—the peak effect is attained in 15 min and maintained for about 10 h.

Cats. 80–90 mg/kg iv of a 1% solution.

Rabbits. 80–100 mg/kg iv of a 1% solution.

Overall verdict
Chloralose is still an extremely valuable drug for maintenance of basal narcosis for long periods in non-survival experiments. It should be supplemented with $N_2O:O_2$ (1:1) administered by IPPV.

Urethane (ethyl carbamate)

Pharmacology
Urethane is the ethyl ester of carbaminic acid. It is readily soluble in water (1 g in 0·5 ml) and the solution is neutral. It is usually given iv as a 10–20% solution.

Nervous system. Urethane produces long periods of central nervous depression in mammals, fish and amphibians. It is thus similar to chloralose but does

81

not have CNS stimulant properties. Urethane has been shown to cause hyperpolarization of isolated nerve cell membranes. It also possesses some anticholinesterase activity.

Respiratory and cardiovascular systems. Urethane has been considered to produce minimal effects on both systems and has been used for experimental animal work for this reason. However, significant disturbance to the cardiovascular system has been demonstrated in rabbits, and severe damage shown to occur in blood components and endothelial cells (Bree & Cohen, 1965).

Metabolic effects. Urethane stimulates the adrenal medulla and cortex and liver microsomal enzyme activity. Cell division in bone marrow and lymphoid tissue is depressed.

Anaesthetic indications and precautions
Urethane has traditionally been used for producing long periods of narcosis in non-survival experiments, usually in combination with chloralose. Doses up to 500 mg/kg iv produce hypnosis lasting 8–10 h in dogs, cats and rabbits, and basal narcosis is achieved with 500–1000 mg/kg iv. Urethane suppresses the muscle activity associated with chloralose.

However, urethane is mutagenic and carcinogenic, and mice, rats and rabbits develop a high incidence of lung tumours after administration of this drug (Wood, 1956; Auerbach, 1967). In our opinion, urethane presents an unjustifiable risk to laboratory personnel and its use is banned at this centre (CRC).

Overall verdict
Urethane should not be used.

Propoxate hydrochloride (R7464)

Pharmacology
Propoxate hydrochloride is a member of a series of 1-substituted imidazole-5-carboxylic acid esters which have hypnotic activity in a variety of animal species (e.g. metomidate in pigs). Propoxate has been developed for the safe anaesthesia of cold-blooded vertebrates, particularly fish. It is a potent, polyvalent and safe anaesthetic which is very soluble in fresh and salt water (Thienpont & Niemegeers, 1965). It is about 100 times as potent as tricaine (see below).

Dosage and administration
Concentrations ranging from 0·5–10 ppm have been used to obtain varying depth of CNS depression in lower vertebrates.

Fish. Immersion in a solution containing 0·25 ppm of propoxate produces long-lasting tranquillization for periods up to 16 h. The onset of effect is observed in 5 min and peak effect is reached in 25–35 min.

Immersion in a concentration of 4 ppm produces light surgical anaesthesia which develops in about 60 s. Fish can then be removed from the solution for several hours without harmful effect provided they are kept moist, and will remain anaesthetized until they are again immersed in untreated water.

Frogs. Immersion in a solution containing 16 ppm of propoxate produces loss of righting reflex within 10 min.

Overall verdict
Propoxate is difficult to obtain but is an excellent anaesthetic for fish.

Benzocaine

Pharmacology
Benzocaine is the ethyl ester of para-aminobenzoic acid. It is very insoluble (0·04%) in water but the dry powder has local analgesic properties. The addition of benzocaine to distilled water has little effect on pH. To produce a suitable solution for anaesthetizing fish it is dissolved in acetone at a rate of 40 mg/ml and this is stable for storage up to 3 months if protected from light in a dark bottle. The stock solution is then added to fresh and salt water as required

Dosage and administration
Benzocaine in an immersion solution is an excellent anaesthetic for fish (Laird & Oswald, 1975). It is recommended at a concentration of 20–30 ppm (5 ml of stock solution in 8 litres water) for producing sufficient anaesthesia for tagging, marking and measuring fish, and 50 ppm for surgical anaesthesia. Fish are not apparently stressed by immersion in benzocaine solutions (in contrast with tricaine).

Overall verdict
Benzocaine is likely to become the agent of choice for fish. It is effective, readily available, inexpensive, and almost certainly completely safe for personnel handling it.

Tricaine methanesulphonate (MS 222)

Pharmacology
Tricaine is an isomer of benzocaine with a methanesulphonate group attached to ethyl *m*-aminobenzoate. It is a fine white crystalline powder with a molecular weight of 261·3 which is readily (11%) soluble in water. At working concentrations suitable for anaesthetizing fish (30 ppm) it forms acid solutions (pH 3·8).

Dosage and administration

Tricaine is used as a solution in which fish or amphibia are immersed, or it can be sprayed onto the gills of large fish e.g. sharks or rays. Concentrations of 1:30 000 up to 1:1000 have been recommended depending on the depths of CNS depression required.

Fish. Depending on water temperature and species, a working concentration of 30 ppm is generally used for sedation (marking, tagging and measurements). Surgical anaesthesia may require 50–100 ppm.

Frogs. Immersion in a solution of 1000 ppm produces anaesthesia within 6 min and the duration of effect varies with the length of immersion time.

Overall verdict

Tricaine has been by far the most widely used fish anaesthetic for many years as it is effective, soluble and is thought to be safe for handling by personnel. However, fish are stressed by the low pH (Wedemeyer, 1970), and it is 25 times more expensive than benzocaine. It may now be replaced by benzocaine.

DELIBERATELY INDUCED HYPOTHERMIA

Although accidental hypothermia presents one of the main problems in anaesthetic management and may be lethal, deliberate depression of body temperature may paradoxically be utilized in anaesthesia. As body temperature falls, metabolism is reduced and tissue requirement for oxygen diminishes. This fact has been put to effective use in protecting organs whilst the blood supply is temporarily suspended.

Whole-body hypothermia is particularly valuable in protecting the CNS at both brain and spinal cord level from ischaemic damage whilst the circulation is temporarily arrested for cardiac surgery or when major vessels are clamped.

Whole-body cooling can be achieved in two ways, either by *surface cooling*, in which the animal is immersed in a bath containing an ice-water slush, or by *extracorporeal cooling* in which blood is passed from a cannulated artery through a heat exchanger and returned to the venous circulation.

Although there are species differences in technique, a few basic rules should be observed when inducing hypothermia.

Surface cooling

(a) Premedication with chlorpromazine at 1 mg/kg by iv injection assists in overcoming the animal's thermoregulatory system.

(b) Thiopentone should be used for induction of anaesthesia and an endotracheal tube must be passed.

(c) A muscle relaxant is essential to prevent shivering, and IPPV should be instituted.

(d) Hartmann's solution should be administered by slow iv infusion. Further thiopentone can be added to this solution as required.

(e) Maintenance of anaesthesia is best achieved with $N_2O:O_2$ (1:1).

(f) The animal should be laid on its back in the container of ice slush, with feet and head above the water level.

(g) Careful monitoring of core temperature (rectal or oesophageal probe) and an ECG are essential because cardiac arrhythmias may develop at any time in the cooling periods. A slightly raised plasma pH is useful in counteracting the tendency to atrial and ventricular fibrillation, and this can be achieved by hyperventilation.

(h) The risk of fibrillation is greatly increased when temperatures fall below 28°C. The animal should be removed from the cold slush when its core temperature is still only 32°C, dried and placed on a heated blanket for the duration of the operative period since the temperature will still fall to 29–30°C whilst anaesthesia is maintained. Body temperature will rise rapidly once anaesthesia is discontinued and shivering recommences. At a temperature of 28°C the maximum safe period of circulatory arrest is 8 min. Longer periods result in hypoxic brain damage.

Extracorporeal cooling

Most of the comments regarding anaesthetic management during surface cooling apply also when hypothermia is achieved by extracorporeal methods. The carotid or femoral artery is cannulated, and polyethylene tubing used to convey blood to the heat exchanger. A pump is needed to force the blood through this system and back to the venous circulation by the jugular or other suitable vein.

The main advantage of extracorporeal cooling is that carefully controlled depression of temperature can be achieved and the animal can be readily rewarmed. However, contact between blood and artificial surfaces often causes serious problems—haemolysis and interference with blood coagulation mechanisms increases the clotting time while, conversely, thrombosis can be a danger unless heparin is used to prevent it.

An extension of the extracorporeal circulation method is used when longer periods of cardiac interference are required—*the cardiopulmonary bypass technique* using a heart–lung machine. The combination of hypothermia and extracorporeal circulation allows the surgeon access to a bloodless non-beating heart for periods up to 60 min. Heart-lung machines consist essentially of an oxygenator, a pump, and a heat exchanger for cooling and rewarming blood. Access to venous blood is obtained by cannulating the anterior and posterior vena cavae through a thorocotomy. The blood circulates through the by-pass circuit and is returned to the arterial circulation via the femoral artery.

MUSCLE RELAXANTS AND BALANCED ANAESTHESIA

The dangers of using muscle relaxants have already been emphasized but it must be stated again that provision of adequate analgesia must be the prime concern of the anaesthetist. Nevertheless, we believe that their judicious use in combination with sedative-analgesics, IPPV and low concentrations of inhalational agents provide the safest means of obtaining good surgical conditions together with minimal physiological disturbance to the organism (CRC). Perhaps the three most useful combinations are as follows:

(a) Anticholinergic—atropine
  Neuroleptanalgesia—fentanyl–fluanisone, fentanyl–droperidol, pethidine–acepromazine or thiambutene–diazepam
  Muscle relaxant—pancuronium or gallamine
  IPPV—O_2 or air
(b) As above but IPPV with $N_2O:O_2$ (1:1)
(c) As above but IPPV with $N_2O:O_2$ (1:1) supplemented with 0.1–0.5% methoxyflurane or 0.25–0.5% halothane as required.

These techniques can be used for long periods of anaesthetic maintenance provided the anaesthetist pays attention to fluid and heat balance.

ELECTRONARCOSIS

Although this technique is of little practical value to the experimental surgeon, the reader should be aware of its potential place in anaesthesia. The subject has been extensively reviewed (Short, 1964; Michwitz & Reinhard, 1966; Herin, 1969; Dallman et al., 1970; Lumb & Jones, 1973).

ANAESTHETIC MANAGEMENT

MONITORING

Introduction

As the laboratory worker often has to act as both anaesthetist and surgeon, he must form the habit of continuously assessing respiratory and cardiovascular function. While this can be done by specialized monitoring equipment, there is no substitute for observation of the respiratory rate and pattern, the colour of visible mucous membranes, pulsation of blood vessels and the vascular tone of visible organs in the operative field by the worker himself. Nevertheless, there are valid reasons for making objective measurements—the most obvious ones being the evaluation of particular aspects of the subject's condition that are relevant to the surgery or experiment, and the maintenance of a stable physiological state during anaesthesia.

Measurements of respiratory function

Respiratory pattern

This pattern is usually evaluated by counting the breaths/min and, at the same time, observing the quality of breathing—whether it is shallow or deep, regular or irregular, whether there is a distinct pause during or at the end of inspiration and so on. Alternatively, the excursions of the reservoir rebreathing bag can be counted. Electronic recordings are based on fluctuations of temperature measured by a thermistor in the airway. Respiratory depression during spontaneous breathing usually becomes irreversible when it falls to about one third of the normal rate.

Tidal and minute volumes

These can be measured directly on ventimeters (Lumb & Jones, 1973), rotor or inferential meters (Byles, 1960; Lee & Atkinson, 1968; Cooper, 1969), or the pneumotachograph (Lumb & Jones, 1973).

The normal ventilation requirements of some common laboratory animals were assembled by Galla (1969) and the normal tidal volumes in ml can be estimated by multiplying the total weight of the animal in g by 0·0062 (Adolph, 1949).

Respiratory standards for artificial ventilation (Kleinman & Radford, 1964) have been calculated (rough values given in Table 2:1).

Respiratory and anaesthetic gases

Gas analysers working on infra-red absorption respond quickly to changes in the airway and are accurate. The animal's exhaled breath either passes directly through a sampling cell, or alternatively samples are aspirated from the trachea or top of the endotracheal tube and then analysed (Burton, 1969). Oxygen concentrations of inhaled or exhaled gases can be measured polarographically by a modified Clarke electrode (Burton, 1969).

The end-tidal partial pressure of CO_2 is used in assessing adequacy of ventilation by making 2 assumptions. Firstly, end-tidal air is assumed to be in equilibrium with alveolar air and although this is true during mechanical ventilation, it is only roughly so during shallow spontaneous respiration. Secondly, air in the alveoli is assumed to be in equilibrium with arterial blood in pulmonary capillaries. The technique is simple. The last part of an expirate is aspirated by needle inserted through the endotracheal tube. A plateau reading is obtained when the aspirated gas is drawn through an infra cell and the % of CO_2 read directly from the instrument. The normal value is 3·5–4·5%, giving corrected $PaCO_2$ values of 30–40 mmHg. If higher values are obtained, then the CO_2 content of arterial blood is too high and ventilation should be increased.

Arterial blood gases

Oxygen(O_2)

Hypoxia is detected clinically by observation of visible skin and mucous membranes in the intact animal, and colour change in blood vessels and organs of animals which are open on the operating table. However, it must be remembered that cyanosis may not become apparent in anaemic animals until arterial O_2 saturation has fallen to 55% (Lumb & Jones, 1973).

Arterial pO_2 (PaO_2) is measured to assess the adequacy of oxygenation during anaesthesia and whilst on artificial respirators, and to determine the alveolar to arterial pO_2 gradient as an index of venous mixing. Blood for analysis is drawn anaerobically into a heparinized glass syringe from a catheterized artery (femoral, carotid, coccygeal or mandibular as convenient). The syringe must be sealed and care taken that no bubbles of air remain on the syringe wall. PaO_2 is then measured with a modified Clark electrode (Smith & Hahn, 1969) as soon as possible after collection. If the sample cannot be tested at once, it should be placed on ice or refrigerated at 4°C. Interpretation of the measurements and the significance to be attached to them is described by Brewis (1969). Measurements on toenail blood taken from dogs was described by Sharpe et al. (1969), and on blood collected from the aorta of cats by Woldring et al. (1966).

The normal values of O_2 partial pressure in mmHg are:

Inspired air = 160
Alveolar air = 100
Arterial blood = 90–100
Venous blood = 40
Interstitial fluid = 30
Intracellular fluid = 10 (variable)

Carbon dioxide (CO_2)
Arterial pCO_2 ($PaCO_2$) is measured to determine the efficiency of ventilation and to calculate the dead space to expired tidal volume ratio ($V_D : V_T$). The CO_2 electrode is basically a pH electrode (Smith & Hahn, 1969).

The normal resting values of CO_2 partial pressures (mmHg) vary with species but are approximately:

Tissues = 50
Venous blood = 46
Arterial blood = 40
Alveolar air = 40
Expired air = 32
Atmospheric air = 0·3

A few points are worth recalling regarding pCO_2 in arterial blood. Carbon dioxide is transported from tissue to alveoli as dissolved CO_2 in plasma and erythrocytes (carbonic acid), as carbamino compounds with haemoglobin (and other proteins) in erythrocytes, and as bicarbonate (HCO_3^-) ions in plasma and erythrocytes in the following proportions:

Plasma	% Transport
Dissolved CO_2	5
HCO_3^-	57
Cells	
Dissolved CO_2	3
Carbamino Hb	27
HCO_3^-	8

The plasma carries a high proportion of the CO_2 as HCO_3^- ions in normal circumstances. However, if this buffered system becomes unbalanced e.g. by an excess of CO_2 in plasma or by a loss of HCO_3^- ions, the pH will fall and an acidosis is established. Secondly, the CO_2 dissociation curve is virtually linear so that doubling the ventilation halves the alveolar (and hence arterial) pCO_2 and vice versa. Finally, it must be remembered that high $PaCO_2$ will not be indicated clinically by cyanosis unless accompanied by hypoxia.

Acid-base balance
Measurement of plasma pH is achieved with a glass microelectrode in blood samples collected as above. The acid–base status is determined by plotting pH against $\log pCO_2$ and reference to nomagram, or by the Micro-Astrup equilibration technique (Adams et al., 1968; Smith & Hahn, 1969). The CO_2–HCO_3^- diagram (Lee & Atkinson, 1968) is a further useful aid in evaluating the status of the animals.

Acid–base balance is perhaps the most meaningful biochemical measurements which can be made by the anaesthetist. Marked deviations from the normal blood pH of 7·4 indicate that anaesthetic management is at fault. If the pH rises above 7·45 then an alkalosis is established, and below pH of 7·35 an acidosis. Assuming that the animal was healthy at the start of surgery, and the system has not suddenly been overloaded with hydrogen ions (H^+), for example from a transplanted liver or a released limb tourniquet, then the failure is likely to be due to poor ventilation.

Why should this be so? Consider first the deviations induced by metabolic disturbances. The pH of blood is continuously buffered to take up the excess H^+ resulting from normal metabolism (lactic, sulphuric and carbonic acids). This is achieved by respiratory exchange, by both intra- and extracellular buffers and by the kidneys. Carbonic acid and HCO_3^- together constitute the most important buffering mechanism and are normally present in extracellular fluid in a ratio of 1:20. Metabolic disturbances affect the relative HCO_3^- concentration so that a deficit (below 24 mEq/l) will result in acidosis, whilst an excess results in an alkalosis.

Metabolic acidosis may be caused by loss of sodium bicarbonate via the faeces in diseases involving diarrhoea, diminished renal excretion of acid (important immediately after experimental nephrectomy and renal transplantation), accumulation of ketonic acids in the body (important after hepatic failure and liver transplantation), administration of acidic drugs, release of acidic products such as lactic acid into the circulation from tissues subjected to ischaemia (e.g. replantation of organs or extremities which have been rendered ischaemic by tourniquet), by therapy with some diuretics and finally, by the administration of some anaesthetics e.g. ether and cyclopropane. The body attempts to compensate for bicarbonate ion (HCO_3^-) deficit initially by increased respiratory activity to excrete CO_2 from the alveoli and secondly by excretion of buffered H^+ and conservation of HCO_3^- in the kidneys. Metabolic alkalosis may result from excess loss of acid through vomiting, or by excessive loss of potassium ions (K^+) via the kidneys due e.g. to overdosage with adrenal corticosteroids. The animal attempts to correct the imbalance with slow, shallow respiration, and renal retention of H^+ and excretion of HCO_3^+. However, such gross metabolic changes are unlikely to be encountered in experiments other than those suggested above.

In contrast, deviations in respiratory function resulting in rapid alterations in CO_2 elimination—hence alterations in blood concentrations of carbonic acid (H_2CO_3)—are commonly encountered, and exert profound effects on the experimental animal. An excess of H_2CO_3 (above $1 \cdot 2$ mmol/l) results in respiratory acidosis whilst a deficit results in respiratory alkalosis. Poor lung ventilation results in retention of CO_2, raised $PaCO_2$ (hypercapnia), whilst hyperventilation (only of importance with IPPV) results in a respiratory alkalosis. Although the kidney attempts to compensate by differential excretion of HCO_3^- or H^+ as appropriate, this is a relatively slow process and cannot compete with the rapid alterations associated with cardiopulmonary dysfunction.

To summarize, the most important points to remember are:

(a) Pathological changes nearly always result in acidosis.

(b) Respiratory acidosis is generally the more significant danger in anaesthesia of experimental animals.

(c) Since H_2CO_3 is in equilibrium with HCO_3^- in a ratio of $1:20$, it follows that small deviations in the former exert a profound effect on pH, and attempts at correcting an acidosis require high doses of HCO_3^-.

(d) Death will ensue if pH falls below $6 \cdot 8$ or rises above $7 \cdot 8$.

Cardiovascular measurements

The role of the kidneys in osmoregulation must necessarily be diminished by the artificial conditions occurring during surgery, and the extent to which autoregulatory and antidiuretic feedback mechanisms can influence fluid balance becomes limited. Since there is a continual tendency to lose water by several routes and hence develop hypovolaemia during surgery, it follows that the anaesthetist must make good this loss. He has to consider fluid balance in the intracellular and extracellular compartments, but for practical purposes, cardiovascular measurements will give him a fair indication of *total* body fluid balance.

Fluid loss may result from haemorrhage during major surgery, evaporative loss from the lungs particularly when ventilating with dry gases, insensible loss from the skin, transudative loss of water and plasma proteins from exposed serosa, particularly the peritoneum, and loss of fluids into the gut. These losses will be reflected in decreased blood volume which can be estimated from a number of direct or indirect measurements (Table 8.1).

Simple monitoring consists not only of close observation of colour, pulse and vascular tone of internal and external tissues, but an assessment of blood loss by direct means, by collecting and weighing all swabs, and by measuring the volume of blood in the suction container, thus providing a guide to the need for whole blood replacement.

The rate and strength of the pulse are traditional indicators of cardiovascular function. The pulse can be palpated or monitored with special equipment (Prys-Roberts, 1969) in a convenient artery (mandibular, carotid, radial, femoral or coccygeal). In general, a full, bounding and regular pulse indicates good function, whilst a fast, weak, thready pulse may herald impending cardiovascular collapse.

The heart should be auscultated by stethoscope, preferably an oesophageal version, to monitor the rate and nature of contractions. Dysrhythmias may be associated with the drugs in use, anaesthetic sensitization with catecholamine release, or with surgical manipulation.

Objective measurements are particularly valuable during experimentally induced and accidental cardiac or fluid insufficiency; in major surgery likely to be attended by haemorrhage; during surgery involving cardiopulmonary by-pass and induced hypothermia; during transplantation of major organs; and when unusual postures accompanied by muscle relaxants and vasodilators are necessary for the procedure (e.g. neurosurgery).

The most valuable cardiovascular measurements are: the central venous pressure (CVP) which provides a good index of cardiac loading and circulating volume, and hence a guide to the fluid replacement needed; the pulmonary wedge pressure; arterial blood pressure as a measure of cardiac function and peripheral resistance; an electrocardiogram (ECG) to indicate cardiac rhythm.

Table 8.1. Sources of abnormal deviations in cardiovascular function and methods of measurement (after Cross, 1977)

Parameter	Measurement	Possible cause of abnormal deviation
Blood volume	1. Direct measurement by indicator dilution methods 2. Assessment of loss (wt. of swabs and volume in suction apparatus)	Hypovolaemia due to: 1. Surgical blood loss 2. Pooling in capillary beds 3. Fluid loss into interstitial space 4. Transudative loss (particularly from exposed intestines) 5. Evaporative loss from skin and respiratory tract

Venous return	Central venous pressure:
	1. By water manometer
	2. Electromanometer
	3. Aneroid manometer
		Depressed due to:
		1. Hypovolaemia
		2. Impaired venous return because:
		  (a) Vena cava has been clamped or occluded
		  (b) Surgeon is leaning on chest or abdomen

Cardiac filling		(c) Anaesthetist has too high a pressure in circuit particularly with IPPV (d) During thoracotomy negative pressure effect is lost
Cardiac function	Mechanical—simple assessment based on auscultation with stethoscope or observation if chest open	Depressed myocardium due to: 1. Anaesthetic agent used 2. Hypoxia 3. Hypercapnia 4. Hypothermia 5. Diseased myocardium

	Electrical: 1. Pulse rhythm
	          2. ECG
	          3. Arterial pressure pulse
		Cardiac hyperexcitability due to:
		1. Catecholamines
		2. Hypoxia
		3. Anaesthetic and other agents

Cardiac output	1. Direct by dye indicator or thermal dilution
	2. Indirect by arterial blood pressure:
	  (a) Electromanometer
	  (b) Aneroid system
	  (c) Ultrasonic techniques
		
		Arterial hypotension due to:
		1. All above reasons
		2. Fall in peripheral resistance

Tissue perfusion	Renal—urine production Skin—core to skin temperature differential	Poor tissue perfusion due: 1. All above reasons 2. α-adrenoreceptor stimulating drugs

Central venous pressure (CVP)

The heart takes blood from a low pressure venous reservoir or capacitance system and pumps it into a high resistance arterial circuit. Blood then drains back into the reservoir. Under normal circumstances the venous side of the circulation contains 70–80% of the total blood volume, but in acute cardiovascular failure (CVF) the vessels may dilate to pool up to 20 times the blood in the arterial system (Wiedeman, 1963).

Central venous pressure is commonly measured with a water manometer attached to an intravenous catheter. The measurement must be *central* and *venous*, so it is essential to ensure that the catheter tip lies within the thoracic cavity but outside the right ventricular cavity or the pulmonary artery. In practice, the simplest method is to cannulate the jugular or cephalic vein, and advance the tip until it enters the anterior vena cava or the right atrium. Cannulation may be achieved percutaneously through a wide bore needle or, more safely, via a short plastic introducer ('Intramedicut'). When it has been introduced to the appropriate level, the catheter is connected to a conventional infusion set by a 3-way tap. A tube attached to the side arm of the tap acts as the water manometer. To make a measurement, the catheter is first flushed to ensure patency, and the manometer tube is filled with 0·9% saline solution to a level at least 20 cm above the animal's chest level.

The 3-way tap should be below the level of the operating table. The tap is then turned so that the full manometer tube is in connection with the venous catheter, and the drip is turned off. The saline level in the manometer tube will fall slowly with characteristic oscillations in time with respiratory movements (respiratory swing). The column comes to rest when the hydrostatic pressure in the tube is balancing the pressure in the great veins. A standard reference zero position is chosen to nullify animal and operating table movements. The mid-point of the right atrium is usually taken as zero, and is measured at the mid-point of the chest at the fourth intercostal space. Some workers prefer the table top and some the sternal angle as alternative reference points. Whichever is selected, it is essential to define it for the duration of the experiment and ensure that all measurements are taken from the same place. The normal value of CVP is 4–7 cm of saline solution with reference to the mid-right atrium.

The anaesthetist has to interpret the measurements remembering that CVP reflects the degree of venous filling and the cardiac output. Hence a high CVP is associated with either overtransfusion or reduced cardiac output whilst, conversely, a low CVP reflects either low blood volume or a high cardiac output. As cardiac output is too difficult to measure routinely, the information will have to be interpreted in the light of known fluid losses and measurements of arterial blood pressure.

Central venous pressure is the most important single measurement. It informs the anaesthetist of the ability of the right heart to tolerate and eject a fluid load and provides a guide to occult bleeding (Sykes, 1963; Northfield & Smith, 1970; Irvin et al., 1972). However, it does not indicate the functional efficiency of the left side of the heart, which may fail independently of the right. Strictly speaking CVP does not indicate the circulating blood volume, but within limits the pressure of blood in the reservoir provides some idea. Certainly it is true that if the CVP is kept at, or slightly above normal levels, blood volume is adequate and there is no need to transfuse to supplement it.

Observations of changes in CVP at 10 min intervals after fluid challenge with about 4 ml/kg of plasma expanders (e.g. dextran 70 solution) provide valuable information on the management of acute cardiovascular failure (CVF).

Pulmonary wedge pressure
This measurement provides a good index of functional competence of the left side of the heart (Swan et al., 1970; Forrester et al., 1971; Rosenbaum et al., 1973), but it is not a good index of cardiac output (Azzoli et al., 1972). After percutaneous cannulation of the subclavian vein, a fluid load is injected (as with CVP) and the responses are interpreted in the same way (Gilbertson, 1974). It has been shown that pulmonary oedema can be prevented if the left atrial pressure, as indicated by the pulmonary wedge pressure, is kept below 10–12 mmHg.

Arterial blood pressure
The pressure in the arterial tree is a product of cardiac output and total peripheral resistance, expressed in the equation:

Mean arterial pressure = mean cardiac output
× total peripheral resistance.

The cardiac output itself is the product of heart rate (measurable) and stroke volume (unknown) expressed as:

Cardiac output = stroke volume × heart rate

It will be readily appreciated that the absence of constants in these expressions diminishes the usefulness of the data. Low arterial pressure may be related to a low output or to a low resistance and vice versa. However, it is possible to make an educated guess as to the origin of the pressure wave by the nature of that wave. In the high output, low resistance state, the pulse pressure (difference between systolic and diastolic pressures) is high at the same time as the mean arterial pressure is low.

Arterial pressure may be measured by invasive (direct) or non-invasive (indirect) methods. In the former case a catheter is inserted directly into a suitable artery, either percutaneously or through a small surgical incision. Direct methods are more accurate and permit continuous measurements to be made. On the other hand, indirect methods avoid surgical risk and can be accomplished quickly with less complex equipment. In experimental preparations, invasive methods are more useful since an arterial line also permits frequent sampling of arterial blood for gas and acid–base estimations, and a venous line must be established anyway both for infusions of fluid and for measurements of CVP.

Several arteries are suitable for catheterization. The saphenous artery is conveniently catheterized in most species once it is separated from other components of the neurovascular bundle where this traverses the medial aspect of the tarso-metatarsal joint. Alternatively, the femoral artery can be catheterized in smaller mammals (e.g. 4 kg and below). In horses, the mandibular, carotid or digital arteries can be used, and the coccygeal artery is often the most convenient in cattle. The radial artery is the most readily available in primates. During intrathoracic surgery in which the chest has been opened by sternal section, the internal mammary artery may be used.

Once the artery is cannulated, the catheter should be filled with heparinized saline solution (500 units heparin/ml). It is then connected to a standard pressure transducer via a length of manometer connecting tube, or the transducer may itself be conveniently strapped to the animal's leg. Alternatively the line can be connected to an aneroid manometer via a 3-way tap which can be used frequently to flush the line.

The classical non-invasive technique for measuring arterial pressure has been to place an inflatable sphygmomanometer cuff around a limb or tail base, pump this up until arterial flow is just occluded and then deflate it until flow recommences. The pressure is measured when Korotkoff arterial sounds become audible by stethoscope placed over an artery distal to the cuff. However, partly because of differences in artery size and limb geometry, the soft low-pitched Korotkoff sounds transmitted from many animals, including the dog, laboratory rat and the horse, are beyond the range of the human ear. Reliable arterial pressures may then be difficult to achieve by this method (Garner, 1973). One way of overcoming this problem is to use a displacement condenser microphone taped over the artery to amplify the sounds and pulse waves (Weinreb et al., 1960). The moment at which blood begins to flow past the cuff as it is slowly deflated is taken as the systolic pressure.

Several additional ways of determining the moment that the systolic peak is reached are based on quick-response plethysmographs which record changes in flow distal to the cuff. The type most commonly used employs a small photoelectric transducer which transmits a beam of light into the tail vascular bed and measures fluctuations in reflected light (varying with pulse) by a sensitive photocell. The signals are translated into audible sounds or charted simultaneously for permanent records of systolic pressure. Clearly, any plethysmographic technique which is designed to measure changes in blood *flow* in a suitable appendage, can be adapted to measure blood *pressure* if combined with an inflatable cuff.

The introduction of ultrasonic (Doppler shift) sphygmomanometers for indirect transcutaneous measurement of arterial blood pressure has improved the accuracy to within 9% of direct arterial catheter measurements. Apart from man, they have been used for measurements in dogs (Freundlich et al., 1972; Strömberg & Story, 1972; McGrath et al., 1974), cats (McLeish, 1977), horses (Garner et al., 1972; Hahn et al., 1973) and rats (Newman & Looker, 1972). Ultrasonic energy at a repetition rate of about 10^6 pulses/s is transmitted from a battery-driven quartz crystal and is reflected back to a receiving crystal from flowing blood cells or from the arterial wall. The signal is then reconverted via an amplifier to audible sound. Hence, the probe can be programmed to sense either flow velocity within a vessel by reflecting signals from the cell membranes, or to sense movements in the arterial wall. In combination with an inflatable cuff, the probe can then be used to measure systolic and diastolic pressure reasonably accurately.

Electrocardiogram (ECG)

An electrocardiogram supplies useful information about electrical activity in the heart but none about mechanical events, providing immediate information about cardiac rate and rhythm, but nothing about cardiac output.

The normal sequence of events in myocardial stimulation may be altered by anaesthetic or other drugs, as well as by hypoxia, hypercapnia, toxins, temperature deviations, behavioural responses, cardiac lesions and electrolyte imbalance (particularly of potassium, magnesium, sodium and calcium ions).

Electrical changes in the heart can be measured from several points or leads on the body surface. The simplest is a bipolar lead between right forelimb and left hindlimb (Lumb & Jones, 1973), but Hamlin (1976) recommended leads attached to all 4 limbs and to 2 positions on the thorax monitored separately. The animal should be insulated from the operating table by a rubber mat, and care exercised in preparing the lead sites; 70% ethyl alcohol should be applied to wet the hair, followed by a proprietary electrode paste, so that good contact is established between skin and plate. The latter should then be strapped in position to ensure good contact without impeding venous return to the area. While Hamlin (1976) does not recommend alligator clips applied externally or hypodermic needles inserted subcutaneously because artefacts in the trace are likely to occur, they are the only practicable way of obtaining traces in small laboratory species.

Interpretation of the ECG trace and the common arrhythmias likely to occur in experimental animals are described briefly in this chapter (p. 106).

Other measurements

Temperature

Body temperature should always be monitored during anaesthesia, since the development of hypothermia is a common problem. Conversely hyperthermia may be precipitated by excitement and stress during induction of anaesthesia; by high ambient temperatures and failure to lose heat from the respiratory tract; and by increased metabolism in response to certain agents such as halothane and suxamethonium. Pigs and cats are particularly susceptible and it is highly likely that it occurs in small rodents without being recognized and reported. A conventional rectal thermometer is adequate provided it is positioned in contact with mucosa and is not insulated by faeces. However, a more accurate measure of core temperature is obtained from a thermistor thermometer placed in the oesophagus.

Renal function
A simple measure of renal function can be obtained by catheterizing the bladder via the urethra and measuring urine output.

Electroencephalograph (EEG)
Changes in electrical potentials in the brain tend to be suppressed by anaesthetic agents (French *et al.*, 1953) and use may be made of this phenomenon to monitor depth of anaesthesia (Courtin *et al.*, 1950; Martin *et al.*, 1959). Characteristic changes associated with individual anaesthetic agents were described by Faulconer & Bickford (1960). Further reference should be made to contributions by Klemm (1968, 1969, 1976), Hamlin *et al.* (1965) and Hatch *et al.* (1970).

THERAPEUTIC SUBSTANCES

The circumstances in which these therapeutic substances would be used are given in detail in other sections in this chapter.

Volume expanders

Whole blood
Blood should be collected aseptically into a solution of citric acid, sodium citrate and dextrose (ACD solution) and stored at 4–6°C. The ACD prevents aggregation of erythrocytes and minimizes haemolysis and consequent leakage of intracellular potassium ions into the plasma. The blood can be stored for up to 21 days at 4–6°C (70–80% of transfused erythrocytes can then survive at least 5 days in the recipient circulation).

The anaesthetist should be aware of several dangers inherent in transfusion. The sodium citrate in ACD can cause cardiac failure during transfusion and this is a real danger in cases of shock (CVF), cardiac disease, severe anaemia or liver damage. This toxicity can be avoided by simultaneous administration in a different vein of calcium gluconate at 70 mg/kg and procaine at 5 mg/kg. In addition, the pH of stored blood is often as low as 6·8, potassium ion concentrations are usually high, there is no ionized calcium available, and incompatibility reactions are possible although unlikely unless the recipient has been sensitized with previous transfusions. Hence, if large volumes

of blood are to be given it is wise to inject iv prophylactic doses of calcium chloride, procaine, sodium bicarbonate and corticosteroids such as dexamethasone. In emergency, where it is essential to transfuse rapidly, blood can be pumped into the arterial system to maintain arterial pressure. Whole blood should be warmed to near 37°C immediately before transfusion. The volumes of blood transfused should be given to effect (e.g. the response in CVP) but the following values give some idea of the amounts required.

Dog (20 kg)   80–100 ml
Calf (100 kg)   400–450 ml
Large animals 2–3 litres

Plasma
Plasma may be obtained by centrifuging ACD blood or decanting the plasma after sedimentation. As it is often obtained from outdated stored blood, the precautions regarding low pH and high potassium ion concentrations in blood transfusions should also be noted. Of a total plasma protein concentration of 6–7%, 60% is albumin and this, because of its molecular weight (70 000), is responsible for about 90% of the total colloid osmotic pressure exerted by blood. 1 g of albumin will retain 18 ml of water within the circulation (Lumb & Jones, 1973). Liquid plasma can be stored at room temperature for up to 6 months if it is sterile but it is simpler to keep it frozen at a low temperature (−15 to −80°C) and then thaw and filter it just before use.

A rough estimate of the volume necessary to dilute circulating blood and restore a normal haematocrit (e.g. to counteract endotoxic shock haemoconcentration) is to give 1·45 ml/kg for each unit the haematocrit reading exceeds 45 (Lumb & Jones, 1973).

Despecified bovine serum albumin
Bovine serum albumin (mean mw 70 000) is a valuable natural blood product with several advantages. It can be given in small volumes iv at the same time as non-colloidal electrolyte solutions are given orally or injected subcutaneously (absorbed as required by the body); it will keep almost indefinitely; and it rarely produces allergic or anaphylactic responses.

Dosage: solutions (20%) should be given iv at a rate of 1·25 ml/kg initially, followed by 0·75 ml/kg at 2–3 h intervals up to a maximum of 5 ml/kg (1000 mg/kg).

Dextran 40 ('Rheomacrodex')
This contains a water-soluble, high molecular weight polysaccharide (mw 40 000), most of which is excreted via the kidneys within 6 h, and has a

mild diuretic effect. It has a transient effect in expanding blood volume and is used primarily for improving microcirculation, disaggregating erythrocytes and reducing blood viscosity. Dextran 40 is particularly valuable in preventing blood sludging, and maintaining circulatory volume and flow during hypothermic cardiac bypass. It is often used as part of the priming fluid for pump oxygenation equipment.

Dextran 40 is available as a 10% solution with 0.9% saline (NaCl) or with 5% dextrose in water. It is given at a dosage of 10–15 ml/kg/24 h during the first day of treatment, but volumes should not exceed 10 ml/kg/24 h on subsequent days.

Dextran 70 ('Macrodex')
Dextran 70 has a mean molecular weight of 70 000. It exerts a considerable osmotic pressure in the circulation to withdraw fluid from the tissues into the blood vessels and so increases circulating plasma volume. It is therefore used as a synthetic plasma expander and is effective for 4–8 h after injection. A basic priming dose of 6 ml/kg is injected iv and the remainder slowly up to 10–15 ml/kg/24 h. Dextran 70 should never be the sole agent used for replacement of volume deficits but should be given together with lactated Ringer's solution and plasma or other substitutes.

Gelatin polypeptides ('Haemaccel')
Gelatin is a protein obtained from collagen which, when modified to a non-gelling form is a useful colloid (mean molecular weight 33 000) for inclusion in synthetic plasma substitutes. It has been used for many years as a 6% solution, having the advantages of low cost, low toxicity, no demonstrable antigenicity, and ease of storage. However, the colloidal effect is relatively short-lived since about 60% of the gelatin is excreted unchanged via the kidneys within 6 h and some 80% is removed in 24 h. This may, in turn, load the kidneys and may be damaging during renal insufficiency (Lumb & Jones, 1973).

Dosage: solutions should be given iv by slow infusion at a rate not exceeding 2 ml/kg/min and up to a total of 5 ml/kg.

Lactated Ringer's solution
This solution contains 0·6% NaCl, 0·03% KCl, 0·22% CaCl and 0·03% Na lactate. The lactate is metabolized by the liver to yield excess bicarbonate and hence avoid the risk of metabolic acidosis, and the pH of the solution can be buffered to 8·2 by adding 45 ml of 8·43% sodium bicarbonate solution to 1000 ml to further reduce this risk.

Lactated Ringer's solution has been recommended for priming pumps in cardiopulmonary bypass (De Boer, 1969), for blood replacement

during surgery (Rush et al., 1969) and in experimental haemorrhagic cardiovascular failure (Moss, 1969). Whenever haemoconcentration is likely to occur, dilution to a haematocrit of about 30%, depending on species, is helpful in lowering viscosity and maintaining tissue perfusion. Oxygen transport is maintained by increased cardiac output but, since the total peripheral resistance falls with lowered viscosity, there will be no significant increase in cardiac work load. The saline solution rapidly equilibrates between the intravascular and extravascular compartments, thus increasing the total extracellular fluid volume. Hence, blood volume and pressure are maintained.

Dosage: as an approximate guide, a maximum single dose of 7 ml/kg can be given, and the daily volume should not exceed 6% of the total body-weight (e.g. 3500 ml to a 50 kg animal).

Sodium chloride injection (B Vet C)
This solution is commonly referred to as 'normal saline' and consists of an isotonic concentration of 0·9% w/v NaCl in water.

Compound injection of sodium chloride (B Vet C)
This is commonly known as Ringer's solution and consists of 0·86% NaCl, 0·03% KCl and 0·04% hydrated $CaCl_2$.

Dextrose-saline
This consists of 5% dextrose in isotonic saline solution. It is valuable for iv injection during anaesthesia and during the recovery period for maintaining blood volume and pressure, and for producing a mild diuresis. It must never be given ip or sc as it attracts water from the vascular system, and thus further diminishes total plasma volume and venous return to potentially fatal levels (Webb et al., 1950).

Dextrose
This is used as a 5% solution in water. It is then isotonic with blood but contains no electrolytes and is rapidly metabolized to release water. Dextrose solution must not be given ip or sc as it attracts water and electrolytes from the intravascular compartment (10–20% in 3 h after injection) and may cause a fatal plasma hypovolaemia.

Diuretics
It is important that the kidneys are given every opportunity to maintain adequate function during surgery and anaesthesia so that anaesthetic agents and their metabolites are eliminated quickly without coming out of solution in the kidney tubules; the dynamic equilibrium between fluid, electrolyte and acid–base balance is maintained within vital

limits; and toxic breakdown products resulting from surgery and trauma are eliminated.

Adequate renal arterial pressure and a fluid load are the best insurance against renal failure, but 2 specific diuretic agents, mannitol and frusemide are useful adjuncts.

Mannitol (10% solution)
Mannitol is a sugar which is not utilized by the body, and the entire administered dose is filtered through the glomerulae with no tubular reabsorption (i.e. it is an osmotic diuretic). It must be given iv as a 10% solution. It has long been thought completely safe but recently it was suggested that where renal cellular damage is already present, mannitol may induce tubular necrosis (McDowall, 1976).

Dosage: 500–1000 mg/kg iv.

Frusemide ('Lasix')
This is a powerful diuretic with relatively short-lived activity. Its effect develops within minutes of iv injection, and urine excretion is enhanced for up to 2 h.

Dosage: 2–4 mg/kg iv.

Alkalinizing agents
Acid-base balance can usually be maintained in the mechanically ventilated, anaesthetized animal by slight respiratory hyperventilation (p. 99). However, when blood buffers are overloaded it may be necessary to inject an alkalinizing agent and sodium bicarbonate ($NaHCO_3$) is recommended.

It is conveniently supplied as an 8·4% solution so that 1 ml contains 1 mEq of $NaHCO_3$, and has a pH 7·5–8·0. It should be diluted with sterile water to a 1·4% (isotonic) solution for injection.

Injected sodium bicarbonate supplies HCO_3^- to supplement the endogenous alkali reserve of plasma, lymph and intracellular buffering mechanisms. It is indicated in all cases of acidosis except those losing chloride from the alimentary tract, those with a developed low plasma potassium ion concentration and, since it enhances sodium ion retention, in cases of congestive heart failure and oedema.

The dosage is calculated on the basis of plasma pH indicated by plasma CO_2 deficit. The CO_2 deficit is the difference between the normal plasma CO_2 concentration (27 mEq/l) and the actual measured value. The $NaHCO_3$ needed to make up the base deficit is then calculated from the formula:

0·6 × bodyweight (kg) × CO_2 deficit (mEq)
$$= NaHCO_3 \text{ (mEq)}$$

This assumes that 60% of bodyweight represents the fluid volume in which bicarbonate ions are distributed. For example, if a 60 kg animal has a measured plasma CO_2 of 17 mEq/l, the CO_2 deficit is (27 − 17 = 10) hence:

$$0·6 × 60 \text{ kg} × −10 = −360 \text{ mEq of } NaHCO_3.$$

To convert plasma CO_2 from vol % into mEq/l the former measurement is divided by 2·24 e.g. 60 vol % $CO_2 = 60/2·24 = 27$ mEq/l.

However, if no facilities for acid–base or blood gas determinations are available, an empirical dosage of 5·0 mEq/kg (420 mg/kg) $NaHCO_3$ can be given safely to subjects where an acidosis is considered likely on clinical grounds. To buffer the low pH of ACD blood during transfusion the animal should be injected with 50 mEq of $NaHCO_3$ for every 1000 ml of ACD blood administered. Sodium bicarbonate overloading may produce a severe alkalosis with low plasma potassium and sodium retention.

Drugs acting on the respiratory system
A few drugs are of value in management of respiratory emergencies but are of only secondary importance compared with the physical and mechanical measures recommended (p. 102).

Respiratory analeptics
These are drugs which stimulate the respiratory centre and thereby promote improved respiratory function. They should be used with care since they stimulate the CNS and animals are partially restored to consciousness for a short period. The CNS, including the respiratory centre, may then be profoundly depressed after the brief arousal, sometimes to a deeper level than before as secondary depression is added to that already existing. Nevertheless, analeptics are often useful in saving an animal near death, giving the anaesthetist time to institute full resuscitative procedures.

Doxapram hydrochloride ('Dopram')
This agent provides a marked and sustained stimulus to the respiratory centre, producing hyperventilation with increased tidal volume and respiratory rate. Doxapram is better than other agents in dogs (Klemm, 1966) and in cats (Polak & Plum, 1964), with a wide safety margin between the convulsive dose and respiratory stimulatory dose. More useful information is contained in contributions by Jensen & Klemm (1967), Soma & Kenny (1967) and Short et al. (1970).

Doxapram simultaneously has marked effects on the cardiovascular system. It stimulates the brain stem vasomotor areas to provoke a sympathoadrenal mediated rise in systolic and diastolic blood pressure. Cardiac output and cardiac rate are raised, and tissue perfusion and renal blood flow are therefore enhanced. It is the most valuable single agent in treating anaesthetic emergencies.

Dosage: dog—1 mg/kg iv (stimulus dose-related up to about 5 mg/kg iv)
cat—2 mg/kg iv
rat—1 mg/kg iv (and other routes)
horse—0·5 mg/kg iv

Intravenous injection will produce a response in 10–30 s.

Methetharimide ('Megimide', 'Bemegride')
This drug produces an increased rate and depth of respiration, raised pulse rate and blood pressure, and partial arousal to consciousness. It should be given by slow iv injection to effect at an estimated rate equivalent to the barbiturate dose at 20–30 mg/kg. Its effect is enhanced if given at the same time as amphetamine when treating barbiturate depression (Cairy et al., 1961). Relapse into deeper narcosis is commonly encountered with this agent after an initial arousal, so it must be used with care.

Amphetamine sulphate ('Benzadrine') and methamphetamine hydrochloride ('Methedrine')
Both drugs have α and β-adrenergic stimulant activity as well as a potent stimulant action on the medullary respiratory centre, and they raise blood pressure, relax bronchial and intestinal muscles, and markedly increase the rate and depth of respiration. The optimum dose for emergency treatment of dogs in 4·0–4·5 mg/kg iv, but as low as 0·2–0·7 mg/kg iv in large animals.

Sedative-analgesic antagonists
These drugs reverse the narcotic effects of morphine-like drugs, possibly by competitive inhibition. They are therefore valuable in reversing respiratory depression in emergency if sedative-analgesics have been included in the anaesthetic protocol, as well as in terminating CNS depression as required routinely at the end of the experimental procedure. However, in reversing CNS and respiratory depression it should be remembered that they also reverse analgesia.

Nalorphine hydrochloride ('Lethidrone')
Nalorphine is antagonistic to morphine-like drugs including codeine, morphine, fentanyl, thiambutene, pethidine, heroin and methadone. It has no effect on respiratory depression caused by other CNS depressants.

The dose is 1 mg of nalorphine for every 10 mg of morphine or 20 mg of pethidine used originally. A total dosage of 2 mg/kg should not be exceeded. Respiratory depression in newborn animals after the dams have been given morphine-like drugs can be reversed by injecting nalorphine into the umbilical cord. Reversal should be apparent in 20–60 s after iv injection.

Levallorphan tartrate ('Lorfan')
This is very similar to nalorphine except that it is more potent. 1 mg will antagonize about 50 mg of morphine and 100 mg of pethidine. A total dose of 0·5 mg/kg should not be exceeded.

Naloxone hydrochloride ('Narcan')
Naloxone is a derivative of oxymorphine and antagonizes that agent, as well as other morphine-like drugs. It is 13× more potent than nalorphine and 3× more potent than levallorphan in counteracting respiratory depression in rabbits and rats. It is claimed that naloxone given with oxymorphine (0·03 : 1·5) eliminates the respiratory depression but not the analgesia in cats and dogs (Palminteri, 1966). Naloxone can be injected into the umbilical vein of neonates at 0·4 mg/kg to reverse respiratory depression induced by morphine-like drugs. It is a specific antagonist for pentazocine (Kallos & Smith, 1968).

Diprenorphine hydrochloride ('Revivon')
This drug has a similar antagonistic action to nalorphine but is 35 times more potent and has a duration 2–3 times as long. It is used as antagonist to the potent sedative-analgesic etorphine, at 4 times the dose of etorphine (Alford & Wozniak, 1970).

Bronchodilators
Atropine, adrenaline, isoprenaline, theophylline and aminophylline have bronchodilatory activity, but these effects are of secondary importance in anaesthetic management.

Symptomatic treatments
There is considerable disagreement whether or not corticosteroids improve the resolution of pulmonary oedema and aspiration pneumonitis—some have claimed positive benefit (Bannister et al., 1961; Lawson et al., 1966; Wilson, 1972) while others disagreed (Chapman et al., 1974; Dudley & Marshall, 1974).

In view of the equivocal evidence we administer methylprednisolone (30 mg/kg) or dexamethosone (1·0 mg/kg) in addition to ensuring good ventilation with IPPV, and restoring blood volume and cardiac output.

Vasoactive substances
These drugs act on α and β-receptors in the vascular system (Ahlquist's classification) and either stimulate or inhibit muscle tone in the vessels.

Alpha-adrenoreceptor stimulating (α-mimetic) agents

These increase peripheral resistance by vaso-constriction and are effective in raising arterial blood pressure at the expense of increased cardiac work and decreased tissue perfusion (except in the heart and brain). Hence, their use is contra-indicated in most circumstances, and β-mimetic or α-lytic agents are more often used along with other forms of therapy. One drug only is in common use.

Methoxamine hydrochloride ('Vasoxyl')

Methoxamine produces an immediate vasopressor response after iv injection and this persists for about 60 min. It suppresses cardiac arrhythmias provoked by anaesthetic agents such as cyclopropane.

Dosage: 0·4–0·8 mg/kg iv is effective in restoring and maintaining blood pressure in hypo-tensive animals. Tachyphylaxis develops rapidly and as a second dose may produce aberrant responses, methoxamine is best used once only in an emergency.

Beta-adrenoreceptor stimulating (β-mimetic) agents

Isoprenaline hydrochloride ('Isuprel')

This drug stimulates β-receptors (and α-receptors to a slight degree) and thereby induces vaso-dilation in some regions, bronchodilatation and increased cardiac output. Hence it can be used as a cardiac stimulant in the treatment of CVF and in treatment of bronchospasm. It has also been shown to enhance lung compliance (Halmagyi et al., 1964). The beneficial effect demonstrated in endotoxin-shocked dogs (Starzecki et al., 1968) was attributed to increased cardiac output with decreased peripheral and renal resistance and hence improved tissue perfusion. Isoprenaline can be used at a dosage of 0·001 mg/kg iv in cardiac arrest and for the treatment of bronchospasm.

Mephentermine sulphate ('Wyamine')

Mephentermine has β-mimetic with inotropic (increase in the force of cardiac contraction) and chronotropic (increase in the heart rate) effects due to release of endogenous noradrenaline in the heart—cardiac output and heart rate are therefore both increased. It is used at 0·3 mg/kg iv to produce an effect lasting 30–50 min.

Mixed alpha and beta-adrenoreceptor stimulants

Levarteranol bitartrate (L-noradrenaline)

Although levarteranol may stimulate α and β-receptors, the α-effects usually predominate. The drug has been used extensively in the past for treating hypotension during surgery as it has marked vasopressor activity. The heart rate is reflexly slowed and there is little or no increase in cardiac output. The dosage recommended is up to 10 μg/kg im or iv infusion at 2 ml/min of an 8 μg/ml solution.

Adrenaline acid tartrate (B Vet C)

Adrenaline is a potent vasopressor, and a rapid rise in systolic and diastolic blood pressure after iv injection is caused mainly by arteriolar constric-tion, augmented by increased cardiac rate and increased myocardial contraction. This effect per-sists for a few minutes only after a single injection because adrenaline is rapidly taken up and metabolized.

Adrenaline has been used in the past to stimulate the myocardium during threatened or actual cardiac arrest. It is injected iv (not intracardiac) at a rate of 0·2 ml/kg of a 1 : 10 000 solution, at the same time as cardiac massage and artificial res-piration are instituted. Adrenaline is definitely contra-indicated during anaesthesia with cyclo-propane and halogenated compounds as irrever-sible cardiac fibrillation is likely to be induced, and this danger must always be borne in mind if adrenaline is injected whatever anaesthetic agent is in use.

Amphetamine sulphate ('Benzadrine')

Amphetamine has marked effects as a CNS and cardio-respiratory stimulant, an antispasmodic and as a metabolic stimulant. The peripheral vaso-constriction and direct myocardial stimulation caused by amphetamine results in a slow rise in systolic and diastolic pressure which may persist for several hours. The respiratory system is stimu-lated via the cortex and the brain stem (par-ticularly the medullary respiratory centre) to pro-duce a marked increase in rate and depth of respiration.

Dosage: amphetamine is supplied as a 5% solution. A dose of 4–4·5 mg/kg iv is recom-mended for dogs and cats, but the dose for large farm species is smaller at 0·7 mg/kg iv.

Methylamphetamine hydrochloride ('Methedrine')

Methylamphetamine is a more potent CNS stimu-lant than amphetamine and produces slightly less effect on the cardiovascular system.

Dosage: the commercial solution contains 40 mg/ml and is given at 4 mg/kg iv.

Metaraminol bitartrate ('Aramine')

Metaraminol is a potent vasopressor with pro-longed duration of action (relatively resistant to degradation by monoamine oxidase). Its actions are virtually identical with noradrenaline. There is a rapid rise in blood pressure due to peripheral vaso-constriction and increased myocardial contractility. The CNS is not stimulated, and barbiturate narcosis may be slightly prolonged.

Dosage: the solution contains 10 mg/ml. The dose is 0·1 mg/kg iv and its effect is produced in 60 s.

Alpha-adrenoreceptor blocking (α-lytic) agents

Phentolamine mesylate ('Regitine')
Phentolamine is a potent α-lytic agent, lowering peripheral vascular resistance and arterial blood pressure, whilst increasing venous return. Its use in dogs and other laboratory species has been reported by Meier *et al.* (1949) and Bradley (1965). It can be administered im, but if injected iv it must be given very slowly. Fluid supportive therapy is essential with this drug as it will cause profound hypotension if the animal is hypovolaemic.

Dosage: 0·2 mg/kg im or iv.

Phenoxybenzamine hydrochloride('Dibenzyline')
Phenoxybenzamine blocks α-receptors, lowers peripheral vascular resistance and arterial blood pressure, and increases venous return. It may be used in the treatment of CVF to relieve arterial vasoconstriction and increase organ perfusion. It is given slowly by iv injection, and fluid therapy is necessary to ensure that the circulating volume is maintained. The onset of action takes 30 min and the effect persists for up to 24 h.

Dosage: 0·25–2 mg/kg iv.

Beta-adrenoreceptor blocking (β-lytic) agents

Propranolol hydrochloride ('Inderal')
Propranolol is a β-adrenergic blocking agent which reduces the inotropic and chronotropic actions of sympathetic stimulation on the heart. It is particularly effective for treating cardiac arrhythmias during anaesthesia, accompanied by a decreased heart-rate and reduction in cardiac work.

It should be administered to effect at a rate not exceeding 1 mg/min up to a dosage of 0·2 mg/kg, and its effect lasts up to 4 h.

Cardiac arrest and fibrillation

Calcium chloride (or gluconate)
Calcium ions enhance myocardial tone and contractility. Hence, calcium chloride is useful during cardiac arrest when the heart is dilated and flaccid. It should be injected iv and cardiac massage continued to distribute the calcium ions throughout the heart.

Dosage: 15 mg/kg iv as a 10% solution.

Potassium chloride
The potassium ions produce myocardial relaxation and inhibition, and the salt is a useful adjunct to

electrical defibrillation in reversing ventricular fibrillation.

Dosage: 50 mg/kg of a 5% solution by iv or intraventricular injection.

Adrenaline acid tartrate (B Vet C)
Adrenaline is still commonly used during cardiac arrest as described on p. 109.

Theophylline ('Aminophylline')
Theophylline has a direct action on myocardium as well as stimulatory effects on the vasomotor and vagal centres in the CNS. The overall effect is usually to increase myocardial contractility without increase in cardiac rate to produce an increase in ventricular output. Coronary vessels are dilated, thus allowing increased blood supply and oxygenation to the heart.

This drug has been used in cases of cardiac failure, injected iv or intracardiac, but the marked peripheral vasodilation which occurs should be counteracted if necessary. Probably as a result of improved cardiac output and peripheral dilatation, a marked but short-lived diuresis is produced.

Dosage: cats—20 mg/kg iv (using dilute
　　　　　solution 35 mg/ml)
　　　　dogs—20 mg/kg iv
　　　　horses and cattle—2 mg/kg

The injection should be given slowly and can be repeated if necessary.

The anaesthetist is routinely concerned with maintaining respiratory and cardiovascular dynamics as near normal as possible, and these have been described in detail elsewhere (p. 55). It is proposed to deal here with fluid, electrolyte and acid–base balance, and temperature management in rather more detail. These notes are written particularly for those who are setting up experiments involving long periods of anaesthesia or traumatic surgery, where such management may be crucial to success.

Fluid and electrolyte management

The management of imbalance in fluids and electrolytes during the anaesthesia of infants has been reviewed by Bennett *et al.* (1970), Herbert *et al.* (1971), Harris (1972) and Young (1973), and these descriptions are particularly valuable in suggesting improvements for animal management.

Fluid

The most important consideration in fluid balance is the extracellular fluid volume, since dehydration and hypovolaemia are the commonest abnormalities encountered.

The size and age of the animal are especially significant in the maintenance of extracellular fluid volume. In small or very young animals the surface area (which is directly related to BMR) is high relative to body mass and this, in turn, is directly related to the extracellular water 'reserve'; hence small animals are particularly susceptible to deviations in fluid balance.

The kidneys will attempt to maintain fluid and electrolyte balance in the face of fluid loss due to haemorrhage, transudative and evaporative losses. If the animal has acute renal failure, the urine osmolality will be close to that of plasma (Fine & Eliahou, 1969), and the sodium concentration will be greater than 50 mM/l (Platts, 1966). Renal failure has several implications for management of which 3 are particularly important. Firstly, the body will be unable to tolerate a fluid load. Pulmonary interstitial oedema may then develop as a result of overload (Zimmerman, 1971) or raised capillary permeability (Crosbie et al., 1972). Secondly, several agents used in anaesthetic management (particularly the muscle relaxant gallamine) which are themselves excreted via the kidneys, will be retained in the body and hence their effects will be much prolonged. Finally, accumulation of electrolytes and toxic metabolites may present problems during anaesthesia and in the recovery period.

Electrolyte

The single most important cation in extracellular fluid (ECF) is sodium (Na^+). Together with the anion chloride (Cl^-), it is responsible for 93% of ECF osmolality, and any deviation must be regarded as potentially dangerous (Danowski et al., 1955; Boyd et al., 1970; Flear & Singh, 1973). The balance is achieved by glomerular filtration followed by 70–85% reabsorption in the renal tubules under the control of aldosterone, cortisol, cortisone and, perhaps a specific natriuretic hormone (Blythe et al., 1971).

The most frequent cause of hyponatraemia is haemodilution, associated with excess oral or iv intake of low Na^+ fluids accompanied by delayed renal excretion of water. Haemorrhage and excess withdrawal of fluid from the gastrointestinal tract into the intravascular compartment will further deplete the Na^+ concentration in the ECF. In addition, if cell membrane integrity is lost, Na^+ may move into the intracellular fluid (ICF) and, at the same time, K^+ and solutes such as adenosine, creatine, hexose and triosephosphates which are normally non-diffusible can pass out into the ECF. This can be identified by the discrepancy between Na^+ concentration in ECF and in ECF osmolality;

if Na^+ concentration falls yet the osmolality remains normal, then clearly other electrolytes and solutes must be maintaining it. This condition has been described as the sick cell syndrome (Flear & Singh, 1973), and will be most damaging to myocardial cells in aggravating cardiac failure (Flear & Greener, 1970). The sick cell syndrome may be associated with hypoxia, acidosis, septicaemia, malnutrition, malperfusion and ischaemic damage to isolated organs (e.g. storage followed by transplantation). A rational approach to treatment is complicated by the need to reverse hypovolaemia without causing pulmonary oedema but several regimens have been proposed recently (Sodi-Pallares et al., 1962; Coran, 1973). In brief, it is suggested that blood volume should be maintained by iv infusion of plasma expanders (e.g. gelatin polypeptides) hence improving tissue perfusion, and cellular metabolic processes should be stimulated with glucose, K^+ and insulin administered iv.

Conversely, fluid and Na^+ retention may be encountered during trauma and surgery (Moore, 1959), although Flear & Clark (1955) showed that Na^+ retention did not occur if the subject received an adequate blood transfusion. It is thought that the kidney is unable to excrete more than 200 mM of Na^+ in 24 h, so care must be taken not to overtransfuse with large volumes of salt solutions, as this will dilute the oncotic pressure exerted by plasma proteins, and possibly promote pulmonary oedema (Mills et al., 1967). This condition ('wet lung') associated with accumulation of fluid and Na^+ in lung, may be confused with cardiovascular failure and then treated incorrectly.

Blood gas and H^+ concentration regulation

Anaesthesia and surgery may produce changes in pH which result from metabolic (non-respiratory) deviations as well as those associated with blood gas fluctuations. Pre-operative fasting has been shown to produce a metabolic acidosis and hypoglycaemia in infant humans by Bevan & Burn (1973) who recommended that a 5% dextrose solution should be infused iv routinely. Major trauma may produce an acidosis or alkalosis, although the former resulting from excess lactic and carbonic acid in ischaemic, hypoxic or poorly perfused tissues is the more likely to occur (Root et al., 1947; Huckabee, 1961; Weil et al., 1964; Arbon & Theye, 1972). Metabolic acidosis may also be due to renal insufficiency and failure of H^+ excretion or to excess loss of bicarbonate (HCO_3^-) from the lower gastro-intestinal tract.

A metabolic alkalosis, although less likely to occur, can also result from trauma or disease. It has also been reported after massive blood transfusion with ACD blood since citrate is converted to HCO_3^- which may not then be excreted (Carmalt & Whitehead, 1966). Raised pH and HCO_3^- results in a shift to the left in the haemoglobin dissociation curve, and less O_2 will be delivered to tissues. In certain circumstances (e.g. pharmacological experiments), it may be necessary to treat the animal with arginine hydrochloride or ammonium chloride to increase the availability of H^+, or acetazolamide to hasten renal excretion of HCO_3^-. Respiratory alkalosis is unlikely to occur in experimental animals unless the animals are significantly hyperventilated during IPPV—respiratory acidosis is the most common problem in management.

The simplest means of maintaining the acid–base balance within normal limits is by slight hyperventilation with $N_2O:O_2$ (Inkster, 1975). The effectiveness of this procedure was demonstrated in human infants by Nightingdale et al. (1965) who also emphasized the need to avoid a sudden fall in pH when IPPV was stopped, and recommended prophylactic infusion with sodium bicarbonate.

Temperature maintenance

Temperature management of anaesthetized animals is of primary importance in maintaining a stable experimental preparation for long periods. Hypothermia may affect the nature and duration of drug responses, it predisposes the heart to arrhythmias and it is an additional stressor to the pituitary-adrenal system.

There are several important sources of heat loss in the anaesthetized animal. The large surface to body mass ratio in small animals and birds, particularly in neonates and immature young, encourages heat loss to the environment. This loss is further facilitated by the peripheral vasodilation produced by some anaesthetics. In addition, heat loss from the respiratory tract is highly significant (Vale, 1973) and is enhanced by high flows of dry, cold gases in non-rebreathing anaesthetic systems. Humidification of gas within the tracheobronchial tree requires latent heat of vaporization to raise the temperature e.g. from 22 to 37°C but this can be avoided if incoming gases are warmed and humidified (Forbes, 1974). Since the alveolar area of lungs is about 20× the body skin area, and the minute volume to body surface area ratio is higher in young animals than adults (2× in man), it follows that heat exchange with the environment is extensive and should be counteracted by heating and humidifying inspired gases particularly in small or young animals (Rashad & Benson, 1967). The advantages and disadvantages of humidifying inspired gases have been reviewed by Boyes & Howells (1972) who concluded that it was worthwhile in all cases. Inkster (1975) has

described a method of humidifying incoming gases to a T-piece to near 100% relative humidity at temperatures approaching 40°C for paediatric anaesthesia. Further latent heat of evaporation is lost from surgical exposure of tissues and from skin which has been clipped and prepared for surgery. Finally, temperature may be further depressed by the iv administration of cold fluids.

Central thermoregulation is severely depressed during anaesthesia and after administration of many ataractic and sedative drugs. The animal is then unable to shiver or to control heat loss by peripheral vasoconstriction or by insulation by erecting hair or feathers. The anaesthetist must therefore take over this role.

Management of temperature must be considered from the moment the first preanaesthetic drug is administered to the time the animal is ambulatory and fully recovered. Several precautions may be taken to conserve heat. As little of the animal's natural insulation as possible should be removed during preparation for surgery, and the operating environment should be free of draughts and maintained at about 22–24°C. All intravenous infusions should be warmed to 38°C, and it is desirable to humidify and warm inspired gases to 90–95% relative humidity and 38–40°C. Larger animals such as dogs, pigs and monkeys should be covered with blankets (reflective 'alpine' blankets are particularly valuable), whilst small mammals and birds should be wrapped in cotton-wool and aluminium foil. In addition, external sources of heat, including heated pads (electrical or circulating water) under the animal, and local radiant heat from infra-red lamps or electric light bulbs overhead, should be supplied with care. Core and skin temperature should be monitored throughout the operation, and care taken to ensure that neither hyperpyrexia or local burns develop as a result of over-enthusiastic heating. If the core temperature rises more than 2°C above skin temperature, steps should be taken to prevent core hyperpyrexia. It is also essential to ensure that fluid therapy is maintained whenever additional heat is being supplied, since heat applied directly to a hypovolaemic subject may precipitate cardiovascular failure.

Liver transplantation

The surgical technique involves clamping the posterior vena cava and the portal vein so that the venous return to the heart is greatly reduced. Profound changes in acid-base balance are commonly encountered, and there is bound to be an abnormal degree of haemorrhage.

Halothane has been widely accepted as the most

Table 8.2. Rectal temperature of common species*

Species	Mean Temperature (°C)	Mean Temperature (°F)
Baboons	39·0 (38·2–39·7)	102·4 (102·0–103·4)
Cats	38·6 (38·0–39·2)	101·5 (101·0–102·0)
Dogs	38·3 (38·1–38·9)	101·2 (100·5–102·2)
Domestic fowl	41·7 (40·0–42·4)	107·0 (104–108)
Ferrets	38·8 (37·7–40·1)	101·9 (100·0–104·0)
Gerbils	37·4 (35·8–39·0)	99·3 (96·3–102·8)
Goats	39·4 (38·5–40·0)	103·0 (102·0–104·0)
Guinea-pigs	38·8 (37·2–39·5)	101·5 (99·2–103·0)
Hamsters	37·4 (36·1–38·9)	99·3 (97·0–102·3)
Horses	38·1 (37·5–38·6)	100·5 (100·0–101·0)
Marmosets	37·5 (34·0–39·8)	99·4 (93·2–103·6)
Mice	37·4 (35·5–39·0)	99·3 (95·0–102·2)
Monkeys (*Macaca* spp)	38·9 (38·4–39·6)	102·1 (100·5–103·0)
Oxen	38·5 (38·0–39·0)	101·5 (100·5–102·5)
Pigs	39·0 (38·6–39·5)	102·4 (102·0–103·0)
Rabbits	38·3 (37·0–39·4)	101·1 (99·1–102·9)
Rats	38·0 (36·0–39·5)	100·7 (96·8–103·0)
Sheep	39·4 (38·2–40·0)	103·0 (102·0–104·0)

* These values are a very rough guide. Temperatures will be raised after exercise, in response to fear, in young animals, in lactating females, in sheep in full fleece and in high ambient temperature. They will usually be lowered during anaesthesia.

suitable anaesthetic for pig liver transplants, but the possibility of hepatotoxicity should be borne in mind (Sharpstone et al., 1971). Methoxyflurane is also likely to be hepatotoxic if the animal is exposed for long periods (Coultas et al., 1969). All agents will decrease the splanchnic and hence hepatic blood flow, and this reduction will be magnified by hypoxia, hypercapnia, vaso-constriction and hypotension. A balanced technique combining N_2O, muscle relaxant and analgesic was recommended by Farman et al. (1974). A similar technique was suggested by Aldrete et al. (1969); they pretreated recipients with diazepam and atropine, and then intubated them under suxamethonium or pancuronium; maintenance was continued with $N_2O:O_2$ supplied by IPPV hyperventilating to produce a deliberate respiratory alkalosis ($PaCO_2$ about 30 mmHg); muscle relaxation was obtained with pancuronium, and analgesia with phenoperidine. Pancuronium was considered to be the muscle relaxant of choice by this group (Aldrete et al., 1969), but since pancuronium is metabolized in the liver before excretion, this conclusion must be viewed with some suspicion. Gallamine was recommended by Biver et al. (1975) for pig liver transplantation, and this would be logical as it is excreted unchanged via the kidneys; this group also found azaperone and metomidate useful for induction, followed by intubation and maintenance with $N_2O:O_2$ (2:1) by IPPV supplemented with low doses of metomidate.

Control of acid-base and plasma electrolyte deviations is particularly complex during liver transplantation for several reasons. Transfusion of ACD blood which may have a pH of 6·8 can lead to a rapid fall in plasma HCO_3^- and subsequent citric and lactic acid intoxication accompanied by hyperkalaemia. Indeed it may be preferable to use only heparinized blood (Czajkowski et al., 1976). In addition, the transplanted liver may have a pH of 6·8 and base deficit of 25 mM/l so that, when the haemostat clamps are removed, blood is released systemically with pH 6·8. This initial acidosis should be corrected by injecting 10 mM of sodium bicarbonate with each 500 ml of whole blood. Excess K^+ is usually released systemically when the liver is revascularized to produce an initial hyperkalaemia. However, once the liver resumes function then a rapid metabolic alkalosis may be produced, this in turn enhancing uptake of K^+ by cells, so that plasma K^+ may be lowered below normal and persist for several hours. It is therefore best to delay correction of plasma K^+ deviations until the post-surgical period.

Other supportive measures which are of value include administration of dextrose solution in the later stage of the operation and post-surgical period to prevent hypoglycaemia, and the maintenance of IPPV for as long as possible after the operation (i.e. until swallowing and biting reflexes are regained and the righting reflex is restored).

Kidney transplantation

The main requirements in management during renal transplantation experiments are the maintenance of a fluid load and diuresis before kidneys are removed from the donor, and stimulation of diuresis as soon as possible after revascularization without overloading an organ with depressed initial function.

Halothane in low concentrations (0·5%) is valuable in anaesthetic maintenance but methoxyflurane is definitely contra-indicated because of its nephrotoxicity due to release of free fluoride ions. Pancuronium is considered to be the muscle relaxant of choice as it is metabolized in the liver and excreted in bile, it can be safely reversed with atropine and neostigmine, and in addition, will not jeopardize oxygen flux (Kelman & Kennedy, 1971). Gallamine is contra-indicated as it is entirely excreted by the kidneys. Fentanyl, thiambutene, phenoperidine or pentazocine may be used as analgesic supplement to muscle relaxation, but pethidine may lower cardiac output and hence renal perfusion (Mostert et al., 1970). Postoperative analgesics should be given in small doses at frequent intervals.

Anaesthesia of baboons during renal allotransplantation was described by Foster et al. (1968).

Cardiac surgery

Anaesthetic management for experimental thoracotomy has been described in calves (Donawick et al., 1969), in dogs and cats (Mitchell, 1968) and in rats (Kluge & Tveten, 1968). The requirements for cardiac surgery in calves were outlined by Short et al. (1969).

Ventilation is particularly important in these cases. The application of positive-end-expiratory-pressure (PEEP) in which residual pressure is maintained during the expiratory phase to maintain alveolar distension and prevent pulmonary oedema (Becker & Koppe, 1969; McIntyre et al., 1969) is of particular value in open-heart surgery (Stewart et al., 1973).

Intracardiac surgery necessitates the use of an extracorporeal heart-lung machine for cardiopulmonary bypass. Combined with deliberate hypothermia, it allows the surgeon up to 60 min to work in a flaccid and bloodless field (Sealy et al., 1961). Equipment has been compared and reviewed by Trinkle et al. (1969). The technique is now fairly standard. Briefly, the animal is anaesthetized, intubated and mechanically ventilated (preferably with PEEP as above). Pancuronium is the muscle relaxant of choice as it has minimal depressant effect on arterial blood pressure. After thoracotomy has been performed, the animal is heparinized with 1·5 mg/kg. The oxygenator and tubing are primed with dextrose-saline solution (Cooley et al., 1962). Catheters are inserted in the anterior and posterior venae cavae, and blood is withdrawn to pass through the machine before being pumped back into the femoral artery. In dogs, the flow rates should seldom exceed 75 ml/kg/min (Lumb & Jones, 1973).

The aorta is clamped to prevent retrograde flow, and the heart is arrested by injecting a solution of potassium citrate (0·8%), magnesium sulphate (2·4%) and prostigmine (0·001%) proximal to the clamp so that it enters the coronary arteries by retrograde perfusion. With this technique and moderate hypothermia (28°C), the heart will withstand 30–60 min of ischaemia. In comparison, the dog heart will only tolerate up to 20 min ischaemia at 37°C (Wesolowski et al., 1952). It should also be noted that potassium citrate is toxic under normothermic conditions.

Calcium chloride is injected to treat hypotension after restoring the normal circulation and removing the bypass (Sabawala & Keats, 1972), and protamine (1% solution) is given iv at 2 mg/kg to neutralize the heparin. The management of humans on prolonged cardiopulmonary bypass has been described recently (White et al., 1971; Rea et al., 1973) and these reports are well worth studying by anybody about to embark on experimental surgery involving bypass in animals.

Neurosurgery

Since neural cells are so sensitive to normothermic ischaemia and hypoxia, the anaesthetic management of subjects for neurosurgery often combines deliberate hypothermia with postural or drug-induced hypotension. The object of induced hypotension is to reduce bleeding but maintain tissue perfusion.

The operative site is elevated above the CVP level mark so that veins in elevated sites will collapse and hence less bleeding will ensue. However, there are several precautions which need to be taken. There is a danger of rebound bleeding when a normal posture is resumed and there is then little reserve capacity to sustain any sudden loss of fluid that may occur; hence it is essential to have a pump already connected to a wide bore iv cannula prepared to inject fluid rapidly. Furthermore, there is a tendency for low PaO_2 values to develop, so it is important to supply high O_2 concentrations (at least 50%) and hyperventilate on IPPV.

Hypotension can then be deliberately increased by administering selected drugs. Phentolamine can be given to produce blockade of sympathetic outflow, pooling of blood in the dependent venous system, and accompanying blockade of the reflex arterial vasoconstriction mechanism. Alternatively, high epidural blockade or deep halothane anaesthesia may be used with similar effects.

Control of cerebral oedema is also a factor in the management of these cases. Dexamethasone has been used in human work for this purpose and it is claimed to be effective (Galicich & French, 1961; Maxwell *et al.*, 1972; Beks *et al.*, 1972). Diuresis is induced by injecting mannitol at 500–1000 mg/kg every 4–6 h and is claimed to be safe (Lewis, 1970). However, if mannitol is not excreted properly e.g. where renal function is poor, mannitol may induce tubular necrosis (McDowall, 1976).

MANAGEMENT: EMERGENCIES

Respiratory failure

Respiratory failure implies inability to maintain arterial blood gases within normal limits. As soon as failure is suspected, immediate action directed to the respiratory tract should take precedence over all other emergency care. Failure is most likely to be caused either by inadequate ventilation resulting in insufficient movement of gases in and out of the lungs, or to poor gas exchange across the alveolar-blood barrier in spite of adequate ventilation. Of these 2 main alternatives, poor ventilation presents by far the most commonly encountered hazard.

Inadequate ventilation is usually caused by depression of respiratory centres resulting from hypoxia or narcotic overdosage; upper airway obstruction, either by paralysis of anatomical soft structures or by excess saliva, bronchial secretions, blood or regurgitated ingesta; and by a decrease in thoracic or lung expansion associated with paralysis by muscle relaxants, fluid in lungs or thorax, pneumothorax, or pressure exerted by distended abdominal viscera (particularly in ruminants).

Diagnosis depends on close attention to respiratory rate, the nature of thoracic movements, audible symptoms of airway obstruction, and colour of visible membranes. The warning signals of impending failure have been well described by Lumb & Jones (1973), and may consist of respiratory arrest (*apnoea*), hypoventilation (*hypopnoea*), jerky respiration (*tracheal tug*), apneustic and gasping respiration, irregular and slow breathing, hyperventilation (*hyperpnoea*) and accelerated respiratory rate (*tachypnoea*).

Temporary respiratory arrest often occurs after rapid iv thiopentone or methohexitone administration and requires no immediate action unless it becomes prolonged. The anaesthetist should keep a close watch on the animal and attempt to stimulate spontaneous breathing by rhythmically applied pressure on the sternum. However, if apnoea is observed at any other time during anaesthesia, immediate emergency action is demanded, particularly if the subject is a bird or small mammal. Staff should be trained to activate a fixed procedure in a strict sequence to avoid panic measures. Firstly, anaesthetic administration must be stopped and the anaesthetic equipment flushed with a high flow of O_2; the airway should be checked to ensure patency and any obstructions removed; artificial respiration with O_2 should be initiated by squeezing the rebreathing bag or pressing on the sternum rhythmically to encourage movement of gas in the lungs; if the animal is not already intubated, a tube should be passed where possible, but when this is too difficult (e.g. in a small rodent) a polyethylene tube passed into the mouth can be used for mouth-to-mouth resuscitation; the heart should be checked frequently during this procedure to ensure that arrest has not already occurred; finally, suitable drugs should be given iv using narcotic antagonists where indicated, or respiratory analeptics such as bemegride at 20 mg/kg iv.

Hypopnoea, irregular, shallow or slow breathing usually indicate poor ventilation and this is potentially dangerous even in the presence of high O_2 gas flows, since CO_2 elimination will be inefficient. Endotracheal intubation and artificial ventilation with high concentrations of O_2 is indicated. These respiratory deviations usually result from profound CNS depression and overdosage, but may simply be caused by rapid induction with barbiturates.

An increase in the rate and depth of breathing may result from surgical stimulation, and from the effects of hypercapnia or hypoxia on peripheral chemoreceptors as the medullary centres attempt to compensate. Similar precautions should be taken and, where rebreathing circuits are being used, the soda-lime absorbent should be checked.

Airway obstruction is indicated by increased diaphragmatic and abdominal movements accompanied by reduced excursions of the reservoir bag. Partial obstruction may be signalled by noisy breathing, snoring in dogs and 'rattling' or 'bubbling' in rodents and birds. This may result from laryngospasm and bronchospasm, aspiration of irritant rumenal or gastric ingesta, kinking of endotracheal tubes, occlusion by tongue or soft palate associated with bad positioning of the head and neck, or simply overproduction of mucoid secretions in the mouth and throat. Corrective measures include checking each of these possibilities and aspirating any accumulated fluids by suction.

Laryngeal and bronchial spasm may be induced by inhalation of irritant anaesthetic agents (e.g. ether) or regurgitated fluids, or provoked by premature attempts to pass an endotracheal tube. The symptoms are coughing and a high-pitched inspiratory sound. Cyanosis may develop and, if spasm is not relieved, complete respiratory failure may result. Cats, rabbits and guinea-pigs are particularly prone to spasm and, in emergency, it may be necessary to perform a tracheostomy and pass a catheter into the trachea. In most cases, adequate relief is obtained by administering O_2 via a mask or oral tube, spraying the larynx with 4% lignocaine and injecting suxamethonium at 0·3 mg/kg iv after ensuring that the cause has been removed.

Miscellaneous abnormal breathing patterns may also be observed. Jerky inspiration (tracheal tug) associated with paralysis of respiratory muscles may develop with deep ether anaesthesia or after muscle relaxants have been given. Apneustic breathing, in which a series of slow, deep inspirations are then held until exhalation occurs by elastic recoil, may be encountered during deep barbiturate anaesthesia and with dissociative anaesthetics. Gasping respirations occur as an animal dies of cardiac arrest.

Poor gas exchange may result from: uneven perfusion of lungs due to gravity e.g. an animal lying on its back for long periods (Hall *et al.*, 1968; Littlejohn & Mitchell, 1972); hypoventilation of dependent portions of lung; atalectasis in dependent lobes of lung; hypovolaemia and decreased cardiac output; pulmonary oedema and shunting of pulmonary capillary blood through unventilated areas of alveolar collapse; catarrhal exudates and fibrous thickening of the alveolar wall associated with disease; aspiration and accumulation of blood, mucous or stomach content; pneumothorax and pulmonary embolism.

Treatment consists principally of removing the causal defect where possible, changing the position of the animal on the operating table, increased inflation of the lungs, protecting the airway from further insult (e.g. aspiration of rumenal content), and ensuring that venous return to the heart is not impeded by intra-abdominal pressure by passing a stomach tube and relieving gas in the stomach.

These respiratory problems will be largely avoided if the animal is properly ventilated and an endotracheal tube is passed early on in the anaesthetic programme. Furthermore, where practicable to do so, a stomach tube should be passed to further protect the airway and to prevent gas building up and exerting pressure on the diaphragm and major vessels. In addition, the animal should not be retained in one position for extended periods, should be well hydrated with balanced salt solutions and plasma volume expanders when necessary, and great care must be taken when closing the chest after intrathoracic surgery to ensure that all air is evacuated by suction cannula and hyperinflation of the lungs as the final sutures are tied.

Cardiovascular failure (CVF) or 'shock'

Acute cardiovascular failure (CVF) is primarily a failure of blood flow resulting in inadequate tissue perfusion and hence cellular hypoxia. The main precipitating factors are:

(a) Haemorrhage leading to hypovolaemia and hypotension.

(b) Septic conditions, particularly where Gram-negative organisms are releasing high concentration of endotoxin into the circulation.

(c) Depressed cardiac function.

(d) Neurogenic factors such as severe damage to the spinal cord or paralysis resulting from anterior epidural analgesia.

In most cases, the body compensates spontaneously and eventually recovers. Where it is unable to do so, a vicious cycle of events is set up which may be irreversible if therapy is not instituted as an emergency procedure. Some of the important factors which contribute to failure are shown schematically (Fig. 8.1). To summarize that information, it can be seen that CVF leads to tissue hypoxia and the development of a fatal acidosis. The cycle will be irreversible once the CNS has been damaged by hypoxia and once pH falls below 6·8.

The compensatory mechanisms which are entrained are shown in Fig. 8.1, and clearly, it is important for the anaesthetist to ensure that therapy is aimed at assisting them. The ability of the animal to compensate depends very largely on the continued integrity of the pituitary-adrenal system. If the stressing factor is not removed, then stage 3 of the general adaptation syndrome (Selye, 1937) is reached and the adrenal system becomes exhausted.

The most important reasons for shock developing during surgery are haemorrhage (blood loss of 40–50% is sufficient to induce severe shock in dogs), rough handling or occlusion of the blood supply to abdominal viscera, hypothermia or abnormal reactions to anaesthetic agents.

The anaesthetist must be able to recognize the clinical symptoms. Skin and mucous membranes become pale due to peripheral vasoconstriction, and the abdominal viscera usually become cyanotic as hypoxia develops. The pulse is weak and rapid due to decreased circulating blood volume, and mean arterial blood pressure falls to below 90 mmHg. An initial tachycardia is usually encountered as the heart attempts to compensate for low cardiac output but, as hypoxia develops, the myocardium is depressed and a bradycardia may develop. Respiration is usually rapid and shallow, and body temperature falls.

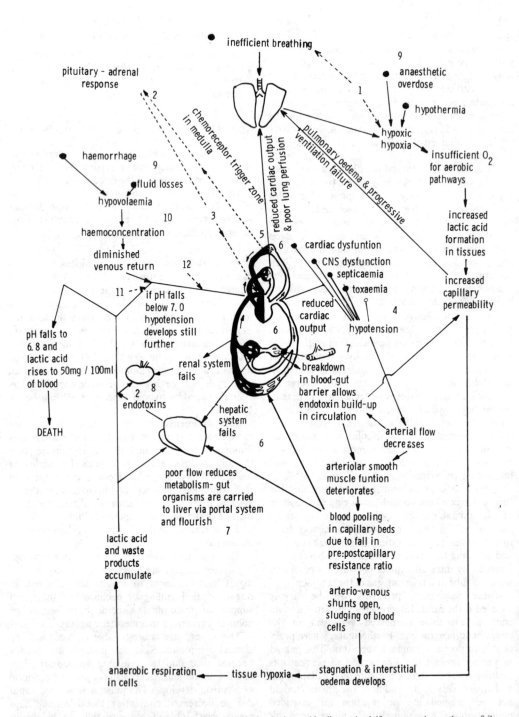

Fig. 8.1. Scheme of acute cardiovascular failure (shock) cycle developing and leading to death if compensation or therapy fails. Key: ● = precipitating factors; n = compensation or therapy; → = progressive failure; ⇢ = compensating factors. ① increased breathing rate, artificial ventilation and analeptics; ② release endogenous ACTH, aldosterone, catecholamines, ADH and renin-angiotensin; ③ sympathetic response—cardiac acceleration; ④ sympathetic response—peripheral vasoconstriction to raise arterial blood pressure; ⑤ warning signals to pituitary-adrenal system in response to plasma alterations; ⑥ natural attempt to redistribute blood to vital organs; ⑦ therapy with broad spectrum antibiotics useful; ⑧ therapy to stimulate diuresis once hypovolaemia is corrected; ⑨ remove precipitating factor; ⑩ therapy with whole blood, plasma substitutes and dextrans; ⑪ sodium bicarbonate therapy to correct acidosis; ⑫ therapy to improve venous return and correct postural deficiencies.

Emergency treatment consists of the following measures in order of priority:

(a) The precipitating factor and anaesthetic agents must be removed.

(b) Good lung ventilation and adequate O_2 and CO_2 exchange must be ensured—so endotracheal intubation is essential in these cases and artificial respiration should be started as soon as possible.

(c) The circulating blood volume should be expanded as rapidly as possible with buffered Ringer's lactated Hartmann's solution to improve cardiac output.

(d) Diluted whole blood or, if this is not possible, plasma expanders containing a suitable colloid such as gelatin polypeptides, low sodium albumin or dextran 70 should be transfused to prevent interstitial oedema developing (particularly in the lung). Whatever agent is used, it is essential to maintain adequate oncotic pressure within the vascular compartment yet keep blood viscosity to a minimum. Haemodilution to a 30% haematocrit confers positive benefit since there is less likelihood of sludging and microemboli forming in capillary beds, peripheral blood flow is enhanced and more O_2 is delivered to tissues. However, this clearly can only to be taken to a level within the residual O_2-carrying capacity of the circulation, otherwise the heart will have to do more work to increase cardiac output.

Measurements of central venous pressure (CVP) give a fair indication of the need to transfuse. Fluids or blood should be given until it measures about 4–7 cm water.

(e) Cardiac failure is indicated by a high CVP without clinical improvement in the animal. Heart rate and cardiac output can be effectively increased with isoprenaline injected as a continuous iv infusion (1 part isoprenaline in 5000 parts of 5% dextrose solution given at 1 ml/min for up to 10 min at a time).

(f) Supportive therapy is indicated as follows:

(i) Sodium bicarbonate ($NaHCO_3$) should be given iv to combat the inevitable acidosis. Vials are supplied as an 8.4% solution so that 1 ml contains 1 mEq and the volume to be given can be estimated from two simple formulae:

Dose of $NaHCO_3$ in ml (mEq) =

$0.6 \times$ bodywt (kg) $\times$ base deficit

(e.g. $0.6 \times 60 \times -10 = 360$ ml)

$$\text{Dose of } NaHCO_3 = \frac{\text{weight in kg}}{0.5}$$

$$\times \frac{\text{duration of respiratory arrest}}{2}$$

After the initial injection, it should be given at a rate of 1.0 mEq/kg over a 10 min period.

(ii) Steroid therapy with betamethasone (0.10 mg/kg) or dexamethasone (0.05 mg/kg) iv is indicated to supplement possibly exhausted adrenal output, although there is some doubt whether this is valuable in cases where CVF is already established (Wilson, 1972; Hassan, 1973; Kursajimia et al., 1974). Large doses are considered to be helpful if given before shock is produced or fully established since steroids probably stabilize lysosomal membranes and prevent release of enzymes and vasoactive substances (Lefer et al., 1969; Glenn & Lefer, 1970; Spath et al., 1973). Pretreatment with steroids reduces acid phosphatase levels in serum compared with shocked untreated animals (Rammazzotto et al., 1973).

(iii) Broad-spectrum antibiotic therapy is indicated to prevent proliferation of liver saprophytes and invasion of the gut wall with enterobacteria.

(iv) The subject should be insulated against further heat loss, but should not be exposed to heat sources such as radiant heat or heated blankets, as these will cause cutaneous vasodilation and a possibly critical fall in blood pressure. However, if the skin temperature remains static whilst the core temperature rises, it is possible to produce core hyperthermia. If the difference between the two temperatures becomes greater than 2°C, it is then advisable to promote peripheral vasodilation with an active source of heat under a space blanket (Lewis & Mackenzie, 1972) as well as infusion of fluids and α-adrenergic blocking agents.

(v) α-adrenoreceptor blocking agents have been proposed as useful in treating CVF (Nickerson, 1963). Phenoxybenzamine blocks peripheral α-receptors and has positive inotropic and chronotropic actions (Moran & Perkins, 1961; Willey, 1962). It has been shown experimentally that treatment with phenoxybenzamine improved survival of monkeys with endotoxic CVP, when enhanced renal function was thought to be the main benefit (Vick, 1964). It has since been used clinically (Wilson et al., 1964; Shoemaker & Brown, 1971; Pearson, 1972). It may also confer benefit by increasing cerebral blood flow thus expediting restoration of central control of peripheral vessels (Kovach, 1972). Phenoxybenzamine is given as an initial bolus of 0.5 mg/kg iv followed by infusion over 4 h of a further 0.5 mg/kg. The effects appear within 20 min and last for 8–12 h.

The α-adrenergic blocking agents thymoxamine and phentolamine are also useful as vasodilators, the former administered as a bolus of 1 mg/kg iv repeated after 60 min if necessary and phentolamine at 0.3 mg/kg iv repeated after 10 min. The object of giving these drugs is to increase peripheral circulation, improve organ perfusion, and reduce cardiac work but they must be used *only* when the CVP is high. If blood volume is thought to be low, peripheral dilation may produce hypotension and reduced cardiac arterial blood flow. Hence, they must be given in conjunction with blood volume expanders.

(vi) Adenosine triphosphate (ATP) depletion, particularly in the liver and kidneys, is thought to be responsible for cellular collapse in CVF (McShay et al., 1945; Rosenbaum et al., 1957). When ATP was administered to experimental animals with induced haemorrhagic CVF, survival was greatly improved compared with untreated controls, but it was relatively ineffective in treating endotoxin-induced CVF (Talaat et al., 1964; Massion, 1965). More recently it was suggested that as ATP is a chelating agent for calcium ions, unwanted haemodynamic effects might result from administration of ATP alone and that it should be given with magnesium chloride to give the best results (Chaudrey et al., 1974).

(vii) As a last resort, when blood pressure is still falling in spite of a high CVP and adequate circulating volume, vasopressor agents may be used. It must be emphasized that all vaso-constrictors increase cardiac work and myocardial O_2 consumption (Waldhausen et al., 1965); they also reduce visceral and tissue perfusion, leading to stagnation in ionic transport within the fluid compartments and to general inhibition of cell activity (Lillehei et al., 1963; Hermreck & Thal, 1968). In addition, the flow to renal cortex and medulla is reduced (Grängsjö & Persson, 1971).

Nevertheless, Mueller et al. (1970) believe that noradrenaline has a place in improving diastolic pressure and coronary perfusion, but emphasize that it must be used over a very short period. It has been pointed out that cardiac performance can be maintained if coronary perfusion pressure is adequate in septic CVF (Elkins et al., 1973). Nor-adrenaline was used to increase cardiac output together with α-adrenergic blocking agents in experimental animals (Thal et al., 1971).

Isoprenaline either alone or in combination with α-blocking drugs has also been recommended in treating CVF (Goldberg, 1968; Pearson, 1972). A dose rate of 2–4 mg in 500 ml of dextrose–saline solution is said to improve both cardiac output and tissue perfusion in man (Fowler & Holmes, 1969). It should be used for a short time (10 min) only to avoid cardiac fatigue and an O_2 debt developing.

Methoxamine at 0·8 mg/kg iv has been the agent of choice in the past but has probably been supplanted by doxapram. Doxapram raises cardiac output without increasing cardiac work, enhances tissue perfusion and increases renal blood flow and urine output (MacDonald et al., 1964; MacCannell

et al., 1966; Loeb et al., 1971; Rosenblum et al., 1972).

(viii) Miscellaneous agents which have been recommended include digitalis glycosides to increase myocardial contractility, glycogen to stimulate the heart and dilate some vessels, dopamine to dilate renal vessels, and pheno-thiazine ataractics e.g. chlorpromazine for their effects in blocking peripheral α-receptors and stabilizing lysosomal membranes. These agents are little used in modern intensive care management.

Cardiac arrhythmias and arrest

Arrhythmias usually precede complete arrest of the heart and the aetiology of each is closely related. Deviations in reflex sympathetic and parasympa-thetic stimulatory and inhibitory arcs are probably those most frequently encountered—if relative parasympathetic tone increases, the heart slows (bradycardia) and hypotension may result, whereas when sympathetic tone gains the ascen-dancy, the reverse is true. These alterations are often associated with drug administration e.g. bradycardia often occurs when morphine-like drugs are given. Similarly, poor anaesthetic tech-nique, for example when administering excess concentrations of cyclopropane, halothane or methoxyflurance to apprehensive subjects with raised catecholamine levels may also produce arrythmias. Raised $PaCO_2$ and hypoxia resulting from poor ventilation predispose to atrial and ventricular fibrillation, whilst ventricular fibril-lation and death may result from electrolyte imbalance, particularly with high concentrations of serum potassium.

Arrhythmias and the electrocardiogram (ECG)

Reference should be made to other sources for a full description of ECG interpretation in animals (Buchanan, 1965; Rubin, 1968; Hamlin, 1976; Hilwig, 1976) and it is only possible to indicate here the circumstances in which arrhythmias may arise.

A heart rate of 60–180 beats/min in resting dogs is considered normal regardless of the animal's size (Hamlin, 1976). In the horse, the range is 22–45 beats/min (Hilwig, 1976), although this frequently increases during examination to 35–45 beats/min. If the rate falls below the lower limit, it is termed *bradycardia* while rates above the upper end of the range represent *tachycardia*.

The normal rhythm, however, is markedly irregular, accelerating during inspiration and slow-ing down during expiration (probably due to variation in vagal efferent activity in line with ventilation). This is termed *respiratory sinus arrhythmia* even though it is a normal sequence.

Sinus arrhythmia is abolished by vagolytic agents such as atropine, by the administration of general anaesthetic agents, and during fever, excitement, pain or disease states.

The nature of the contractile wave which controls the synchrony of the heart chambers depends largely on the dominant site of electrical discharge. The pacemaker which triggers the sequence of contractions is usually sited at the sino-atrial (SA) node. However, it often lies in other sites or foci, which are then regarded as misplaced or *ectopic*. Rhythms (and arrhythmias) are then classified by the dominant site of initial discharge. If the pacemaker foci are sited above the ventricles, e.g. the SA node or in the atrial myocardium, then the associated rhythms are classified as *supraventricular*. Alternatively, they may reside within the ventricles, sometimes in ventricular myocardium, but more commonly, in the main bundle of His, the left or right bundles of His or in the Purkinje fibres, and are classified as *ventricular*.

The origin of the contractile wave may be identified by analysis of the ECG, particularly from the sequencing of the P-wave and the QRS complex (Fig. 8.2).

Supraventricular rhythms and arrhythmias

The normal or *sinus rhythm* when the pacemaker is sited in the SA node is shown on the ECG trace (Fig. 8.2). It has a distinct positive P-wave of normal contour occurring at regular intervals and preceding the QRS complex by a short time interval. If this is slower than normal it is termed a *sinus bradycardia*, while a faster rate is termed *sinus tachycardia*. An ectopic atrial beat is identified by the P-wave, which may be positive (pacemaker in the right atrium) or negative (pacemaker in the left atrium), and which precedes the QRS complex by a greater time interval (2nd trace Fig. 8.2).

Ectopic beats originating in the atrioventricular (AV) node or junction produce a normal QRS trace without a P-wave, and hence the Q–Q interval is compressed.

Atrial fibrillation is characterized by the absence of discrete P-waves, by irregular undulations in the base line, and by a rapid and irregular sequence of QRS complexes (50–120 beats/min in the horse). The P-waves are replaced by fibrillation waves (f-waves) having a frequency between 200–500/min in the horse (Fig. 8.2). Atrial fibrillation is usually associated with cardiac disease and should not present a problem in healthy experimental animals.

Atrioventricular conduction disturbances

The atrioventricular (AV) conduction time is the interval between the onset of atrial activation and

(1) Normal sinus rhythm

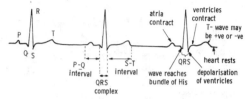

(2) Atrial ectopic beats

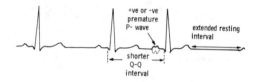

(3) Atrial fibrillation

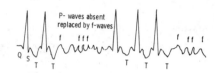

(4) Ventricular fibrillation

Fig. 8.2. The normal ECG trace and some arrhythmias.

the onset of ventricular activation. This is represented by the PQ interval in the ECG trace. The normal PQ interval in dogs ranges from 70–140 ms, whilst in horses it is 250–400 ms.

Disturbances in this conduction may simply prolong or shorten its duration, or they may produce complete or partial block. As an approximate guide, AV conduction may be prolonged or blocked by parasympathetic efferent activity, depressed sympathetic efferent activity, parasympathomimetic drugs, sympatholytic drugs, digitalis glycosides and inflammatory disease of the AV node. Conversely, parasympathetic withdrawal, enhanced sympathetic efferent activity, parasympatholytic drugs, sympathomimetic drugs, or the presence of accessory pathways which circumvent the slow conducting portions of the AV node each tend to accelerate AV conduction and shorten the PQ interval.

In *1st degree AV block*, each QRS is preceded by a P-wave, the PQ interval is extended (Fig. 8.3). This disturbance is usually caused by enhanced vagal tone e.g. after the administration of

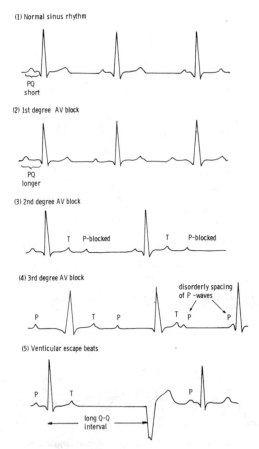

(1) Normal sinus rhythm

PQ short

(2) 1st degree AV block

PQ longer

(3) 2nd degree AV block

T   P-blocked   T   P-blocked

(4) 3rd degree AV block

disorderly spacing of P -waves

P   T   P   T P   P

(5) Ventricular escape beats

P   T   P

long Q-Q interval

Fig. 8.3. Atrioventricular blocks and ectopic ventricular escape beats.

morphine-like drugs or digitalis glycosides. It has little clinical significance.

2nd degree AV block is characterized by a normal or prolonged PQ interval, but occasional P-waves occur without being followed by a QRS trace (Fig. 8.3). Again, this block may be caused by morphine-like drugs or digitalis glycosides and is not considered dangerous.

3rd degree AV block is characterized by loss of synchrony between the P-wave and QRS complex, indicating loss of coordination of atrial and ventricular activity (i.e. there is a complete block in conduction along normal pathways). This type of block should not be encountered during experimental anaesthesia as it is probably caused by severe disease of the AV node.

Ventricular rhythms and arrhythmias
Ventricular ectopic beats usually produce a QRS complex of high amplitude, long duration and unusual configuration, followed by a T wave of high amplitude and opposite polarity to that of the

QRS. The QRS deflection is dominantly positive when the ectopic beat originates from the right ventricle and negative if originating from the left.

Ectopic beats or rhythms deviating from sinus rhythms may occur *singly*, in clusters of up to 3 short bursts (*paroxysmal*), rapid beats over an extended period (*tachycardia*), at an exceptionally rapid rate (*flutter* or *fibrillation*), at a rate within the normal range of sinus nodal discharge (*ectopic rhythm*) and ectopic beats alternating with single normal beats (*bigeminal*).

Single ectopic beats may arise earlier than the normal sinus beat (termed *ventricular premature beats*) or conversely after considerable delay (*escape beats*). Premature ectopic ventricular beats are usually associated with raised excitability and discharge from ventricular foci which are normally subservient to the dominant supraventricular pacemaker. Escape beats, on the other hand, occur when the dominant pacemaker is depressed and fails to discharge at a normal rate, allowing a latent ventricular focus to become dominant after a period of diastole (Fig. 8.3). Premature beats may occur between two normally spaced conduction beats (true '*extrasystole*') or may be followed by a compensatory pause with little change in the overall heart rate. In the resting horse this is considered indicative of myocardial disease (Detweiler & Patterson, 1972) but it is also commonly encountered in dogs with raised vagal tone e.g. after the administration of morphine-like drugs.

Bigeminal ectopic beats are frequently encountered after the iv administration of short-acting barbiturates, particularly thiopentone, thiamylal and methohexitone, and are not considered dangerous.

Ventricular tachycardia or ventricular paroxysmal tachycardia is a dangerous omen in all species, and predisposes to ventricular fibrillation and death. Electrolyte imbalance (particularly high serum K^+ concentrations), hypercapnia and hypoxia, especially when these accompany extensive abdominal surgery and inhalational anaesthesia, are frequent causes of these ventricular arrhythmias.

Electrolyte imbalance deserves special attention, in addition to the predisposing factors already discussed. Hypokalaemia may cause supraventricular and ventricular ectopic beats or rhythms, ST depression and decreased amplitude of the T wave. Conversely, hyperkalaemia may cause sinus bradycardia, A-V block, asystole, ventricular tachycardia and fibrillation (Katz & Bigger, 1970). The effects of K^+ are in general opposed by Ca^{++} which causes increased contractility, prolongation of systole, shortening of diastole and eventual systolic arrest (Lee & Atkinson, 1968).

In summary it can be concluded that slow supra-ventricular arrhythmias (atrial, A-V junctional or wandering pacemaker) are relatively benign and easily corrected by attention to ventilation, fluid and thermal homeostasis, and alteration of the anaesthetic regime as required. Conversely, ventricular arrhythmias should always be regarded as serious. Vigorous corrective measures should be taken to restore normal PaO_2, $PaCO_2$, K^+ concentrations, fluid and thermal balance. Anaesthetic administration should be stopped.

Cardiac arrest

Ventricular fibrillation is a terminal event, and is characterized by irregular oscillations of varying frequency and amplitude.

Diagnosis of cardiac arrest is based on dilation of the pupils, absence of pulse, cyanotic mucous membranes and loss of heart sounds on auscultation of the chest. Cardiac arrest is almost invariably preceded by respiratory arrest, and vigorous artificial ventilation will often prevent ventricular fibrillation.

It must be remembered that emergency therapy must be successful in restoring circulation to brain tissue within 3 min. The following measures should be instituted in order of priority:

(a) Airway patency should be established first and any obstructions removed. If an endotracheal tube is already in place, it should be checked to ensure that it is not twisted, kinked or so far down the trachea that it is ventilating one bronchial tree only. The animal should then be artificially ventilated by rebreathing bag or positive pressure ventilator.

(b) The chest should be compressed manually by pushing down hard on the sternum at a rate of 70–80 times/min with the animal lying on its back (external cardiac massage).

(c) The myocardium may be stimulated to recommence beating by injection of 1·0 ml of 1 : 10 000 solution of adrenaline diluted in 9 ml of water, but this should not be used if the animal is anaesthetized with cyclopropane or halogenated hydrocarbons.

(d) In emergency, time will be too short to calculate the correct dosages of sodium bicarbonate, so an empirical dose of 1·0 mEq/kg (1·0 ml/kg of the 8·4% solution) should be injected iv.

(e) Calcium chloride should be injected iv at about 10 mg/kg of a 10% solution to enhance contractility of a dilated and flaccid heart.

(f) Ventricular fibrillation can be reversed by an electrical defibrillator, or (much less effectively) by iv injection of 5 mg/kg potassium chloride (5% solution) or 0·5 mg/kg of 1% lignocaine.

(g) As a last resort and if internal cardiac massage is unwarranted, the animal should be seized by its hind legs, lifted from the operating table and swung back and forth head down. Alternatively, if no heartbeat is detected within 2 min, the thorax should be opened at the fifth intercostal space, calcium gluconate injected directly into a ventricle and gentle massage applied to the heart.

Regurgitation and vomiting

Dogs, cats and primates frequently vomit under anaesthesia and should be fasted beforehand. However, it must be appreciated that blood sugar levels and fluid balance will be adversely affected by fasting and it is essential to institute iv therapy with a dextrose–saline infusion as soon as practicable. Ruminants regurgitate regardless of pre-anaesthetic fasting. The routine use of a cuffed endotracheal tube will eliminate the hazard of aspiration pneumonia, and a stomach tube should be passed in cattle, sheep, goats and pigs to allow escape of accumulated gastric gas.

If a small animal is observed to vomit during induction of anaesthesia, it should be held up by its hind legs and vomitus should be cleared from the mouth with swabs and with suction. Anaesthesia should be delayed or postponed and the lungs hyperventilated with O_2 alone by positive pressure ventilation.

Where gastric juices are aspirated in any quantity, the low pH (1–2) provokes a severe reaction in lung tissue, and violent coughing and bronchospasm is diagnostic. The only drug therapy likely to assist the patient is intratracheal irrigation as well as parenteral therapy with hydrocortisone solution. Antibiotic therapy is thought to be of limited value, but broad-spectrum antibiotic cover seems logical to prevent infective complications. What is proven is the benefit conferred by positive pressure ventilation with high O_2 concentrations.

Anomalous anaesthetic responses

Although aberrant reactions to drugs are often used as an excuse for the failure of the anaesthetist, occasional hypersensitive and idiosyncratic responses do occur. Most emergencies however, are due to overdosage. This situation can be rapidly reversed when inhalation techniques are in use, but may be lethal where barbiturates and neurolept-analgesics have been injected.

Reversal of respiratory depression and respiratory acidosis are central to the problem of management in these cases. Treatment consists of a few common sense rules:

(a) Ensure a patent airway, hyperventilate if possible and introduce high O_2 concentrations to the animals, e.g. overdosed mice should breathe 100% O_2 until the danger period is adjudged to be over.

(b) Give warm 0·9% saline solution iv or ip at approximately 10 ml/kg/h and sodium bicarbonate iv at 1·0 mEq/kg to all species where possible.

(c) Retain animals in an artificially warm environment until they have recovered, and turn them frequently to prevent hypostatic congestion of the lungs.

(d) Where morphine-like agents have been used, they should be reversed with specific narcotic antagonists, e.g. nalorphine, diprenorphine, levallorphan or naloxone.

(e) Encourage renal function and diuresis with mannitol at 350 mg/kg iv and frusemide at 4 mg/kg iv.

Recovery and aftercare

Having described the emergencies which might occur during anaesthesia, it must be said that more experimental animals succumb during the post-operative than during the surgical period. These notes are, therefore, included under the broad heading of emergency management to emphasize that the animal will almost certainly face another set of stress factors during recovery to which it will need to adapt—in other words it will pass through another 'crisis'. Yet this is frequently ignored and the animal left to fend for itself.

Respiratory failure in the post-operative period (24–48 h) has been described as a well-defined syndrome in infants (post-surgical 'shock lung') and this seems likely to be important in animals as well. The aetiology is thought to be multifactorial, associated with exposure to high concentrations of O_2 during anaesthesia, decreased pulmonary surfactant and pulmonary oedema. The subject shows symptoms of hyperventilation and alkalosis, progressing to hypoxia and alkalaemia and, thence to acidosis ending in death (Dowd & Jenkins, 1972). The x-ray picture of opaque lung fields and 'white out' suggest disseminated intravascular coagulation (DIC) as described by Hardaway et al. (1956) and Hardaway (1961). This in turn has been ascribed to renal failure (Haahen et al., 1971) and respiratory failure (Hardaway, 1973).

Two other factors predispose to DIC, and these are very likely to cause trouble after experimental surgery in animals. Endotoxins are known to be released into the circulation as a result of sepsis or extensive tissue trauma (Caridis et al., 1972; Fine, 1973) and have been shown to raise capillary permeability with resultant DIC (Riordan & Walters, 1968). It was also recently shown that endotoxinaemia leads to posttraumatic respiratory insufficiency and the autopsy findings of DIC (Stoddart & Wardle, 1974). There is, then, strong circumstantial evidence for a causal link between the symptoms, autopsy findings and endotoxins.

Similarly, early failures with cardiac bypass were ascribed to release of serotonin and other vasoactive substances from damaged platelets which resulted in pulmonary and systemic vasospasm, increased capillary permeability and pulmonary oedema (Ricketts, 1973). Such substances are likely to be released from revascularised tissues and may account for the sudden death of apparently recovered animals.

Emergency treatment consists of IPPV to maintain PaO_2 above 60 mmHg, whilst diuretics should be administered iv together with low Na^+ albumin to promote renal function (Dowd & Jenkins, 1972). A decision whether to heparinize the animal will depend on the circumstances but has been suggested as a postoperative prophylactic measure to prevent DIC developing (Colman et al., 1972).

Even in the absence of such emergencies, the animal should receive particular care and attention.

(a) Recovery should take place in special boxes, incubators or pens which can be temperature-controlled as follows:

dogs over 10 kg bodyweight	25°C
cats	25°C
primates	30°C
pigs—post-weaning	28°C
neonates	35°C
mice and rats	35°C
rabbits	25°C

Heated pads, infrared lamps and guarded electric light bulbs can all be used as sources of heat depending on the size of the animal.

(b) An endotracheal tube should be left in place until swallowing and chewing reflexes return.

(c) No containers should be left in the pen, but water should be offered to the animal when it is reasonably aware of surroundings.

(d) Pigs, rats, mice and dogs will often attack a semiconscious animal if it is returned to share a pen or box—hence animals must always be allowed to recover by themselves or with others who are at a similar stage of recovery.

(e) As soon as any danger of respiratory depression has passed, post-surgical cases should be given small doses of analgesics such as pethidine. This will have the dual purpose of easing pain and quietening the animal so that it is less likely to bite dressings or fresh wounds.

(f) Where recovery takes a long time (e.g. over 2 h) animals should be turned every 10 min to prevent postural hypostatic lung congestion.

(g) Ruminants should be propped up on their sternum supported by bales of straw or hay, and carefully observed for signs of impending tympany.

The tender care of interested personnel is most important at this time.

CHAPTER NINE

CLASSES AMPHIBIA, REPTILIA AND AVES

CLASS AMPHIBIA

Order Anura (frogs, toads)

Gases and anaesthetic agents in solution are rapidly transferred across the skin of amphibians to diffuse into the circulation, thus providing a simple route for anaesthetic administration. Inhalational and water-soluble agents have been administered by sitting the amphibian in a moist atmosphere into which an anaesthetic mixture is passed, by immersing the animal in an anaesthetic solution, or by wrapping it in a cloth moistened with the agent. Alternatively, administration may be by intravascular or intraperitoneal injection. The simplest route for intravascular injection is through the paired dorsal lymph sacs sited one on each side of the last vertebra, and usually easily identified by their rhythmic beating. Volumes of up to 3 ml may be injected into the animal at any one time.

Ether has been used in a bell jar to anaesthetize leopard frogs, Rana pipiens (Lumb & Jones, 1973), although recovery was prolonged and respiration deeply depressed. Similarly, methoxyflurane was assessed in R. pipiens by Wass & Kaplan (1974), who observed that, after an initial excitatory phase lasting 60 s, deep anaesthesia was induced within 2 min; if the frogs were retained in the jar for a further 3 min, sufficient drug was taken up to ensure adequate anaesthetic duration for any surgical interference. Complete recovery took up to 7 h, but there were no deaths in 30 animals.

Ethanol, chlorobutanol, tricaine and propoxate have each been reported as effective water-soluble agents for anaesthetizing amphibians by immersion.

Ethanol (10%) is readily absorbed through intact skin to induce surgical anaesthesia within approximately 10 min (Fankhauser, 1945; Kaplan & Kaplan, 1961). Duration of anaesthesia varies with the ambient temperature, but deep levels may last for 20 min after removal from the alcohol and rinsing in tap water, whilst complete recovery may take up to 40 min. Fatalities were observed if higher concentrations of alcohol or longer periods of exposure were attempted.

According to Lumb & Jones (1973), frogs may be immersed in 0.2% chlorobutanol to induce anaesthesia in 4–8 min, and maintenance may be achieved by wrapping the animals in cotton wool soaked in the agent. Recovery takes 3–6 h after withdrawal from the anaesthetic. Witschi (1927) used 0.03% chlorobutanol in tadpoles of Rana temporaria but the mortality was high in comparison with tricaine.

There are many reports indicating the value of tricaine for anaesthetizing frogs of several species. Adult leopard frogs (R. pipiens) were anaesthetized by immersion in a 0.1% solution by Yankow (1962) and, since the LD_{50} was reported (Sandoz Bulletin, 1959) to be a 6.2% solution, there is clearly a wide safety margin. Common frogs (R. temporaria) were immersed in 0.1% solutions by Strzyzowski (1920), who reported that anaesthesia was induced in 5–6 min, while recovery took up to 42 min. However, if frogs were immersed for 1 h, recovery took 3.5 h, and immersion for longer than 6 h at this concentration was usually lethal. McGovern & Rugh (1944) recommended a 0.03% solution for tadpoles and adult R. pipiens. They concluded that tricaine had no effect on the fertility of frog spermatozoa and was satisfactory for amphibian embryos at all stages of development. A concentration of 0·03–0·05% was recommended by Stefanova et al. (1964) for anaesthetizing *R. temporaria*; they found that mortality was minimal in larvae and non-existent in adults. In a study comparing the anaesthetic actions of ether, ethyl carbamate (urethane) and tricaine on the clawed toad (*Xenopus laevis*), Hobson & Townsend (1964) concluded that tricaine was the best agent for anaesthetizing toads and that it could be administered by intravascular injection or simple immersion. Anaesthesia was induced in 5–17 min after immersion in a 0·15% solution, and recovery was complete within 70 min. Recovery was significantly accelerated by maintaining the animals at 26°C while partially immersed in fresh water but with their nostrils above water. *Xenopus* spp tadpoles were safely anaesthetized with a 0·03% solution of tricaine.

Propoxate was assessed in edible frogs (*Rana esculenta*) by Thienpont & Niemegeers (1965) who reported that a concentration of 16 ppm produced loss of righting reflex within 10 min. Unfortunately, they did not specify the degree of analgesia obtained at this concentration.

Several agents have been given parenterally. In a paper describing the effects of barbiturates in frogs, Kaplan et al. (1962) emphasized the wide differences in response observed. For *R. pipiens* they recommended hexobarbitone (120 mg/kg) injected into the dorsal lymph sacs which induced anaesthesia in about 20 min and lasted for some 9 h, and pentobarbitone (60 mg/kg ip) where induction averaged 18 min and deep anaesthesia persisted for 9·5 h. According to Hobson & Townsend (1964), tricaine can also be injected iv into the dorsal lymph sac at 13 mg/kg. Deep anaesthesia is induced in 3–5 min and recovery is complete in 30 min if no further doses are given for maintenance. Etorphine at 0·25 mg per animal has been given by ip injection to *R. pipiens* to produce narcosis with excellent analgesia lasting 6–12 h (Wallach & Hoessle, 1970). In bull frogs (*R. catesbeiana*), volumes of 0·4–0·6 ml of 5% procaine were injected intracranially just caudal to a midpoint between the eyes. Induction took 3–5 min and anaesthesia persisted for about 60 min (Kisch, 1947).

Spinal anaesthesia in *R. pipiens* was described by Bieter et al. (1932). They injected procaine (210 mg/kg) at the urostyle with a 0·45 mm (26 gauge) needle to produce 90–120 min of regional anaesthesia.

Recommended anaesthetic techniques
Although the oesophagus occasionally prolapses into the buccal cavity during anaesthesia, vomiting is not a problem in frogs, so they can be fed freely

Fig. 9.1. Technique for handling adult frogs.

until anaesthetized. No pre-anaesthetic treatments are warranted. In fact prior administration of chlorpromazine was held to be highly toxic to frogs (Kaplan et al., 1962). They should be acclimatized to a water temperature of 20–22°C for 2 days prior to anaesthesia. The correct technique for handling frogs and toads is shown (Fig. 9.1.). Depth of anaesthesia is easily assessed by the withdrawal reflex when digits are pinched, and by the response to pin pricks.

Frogs must not be immersed in water during the recovery period or they may drown. However, the entire body surface must be kept moist throughout anaesthesia and recovery. Since metabolic rate and hence recovery are enhanced by higher temperatures, particularly in the case of ectotherms, frogs should be allowed to recover quietly in an ambient temperature of 24°–26°.

Adult frogs are anaesthetized most easily by simple inhalational or immersion techniques. The methods of choice are described in order of preference.

Inhalation of *methoxyflurane* is the simplest and safest method. Suitable containers of glass or clear rigid plastic are prepared for induction by placing a wad of cotton wool in the bottom and spraying methoxyflurane onto it. A total of 0·5–1 ml is sufficient to produce an induction concentration of vapour (3%) in a 1 litre container. The container should then be left for 20–30 min with the lid closed to allow the volatile liquid to vaporize adequately. Deep anaesthesia is induced within 2 min of the frogs being placed in the container and is maintained for a further 40 min after they are taken out. Frogs should be allowed to recover in a separate container on moist cotton wool after being washed in warm (24°C) tap water. Full recovery takes about 7 h. The method is safe and analgesia is excellent.

Immersion in a 0·1% tricaine solution at a temperature of 21°C is also effective. Anaesthesia develops in 5–20 min and can then be maintained during operations by wrapping the subject in cotton wool moistened with the solution. At the end of the procedure, the subject should be washed in warm tap water and allowed to recover on moist cotton wool in a fresh container. Complete recovery depends on the ambient temperature but it is likely to take 25–70 min. Muscular relaxation and analgesia are both very good.

If rapid recovery is essential to the experiment, a solution of tricaine can be injected into the dorsal lymph sacs at 13 mg/kg. Induction takes 3–5 min and recovery is complete within 30 min.

If no other agents are available, ether can be used as an inhalational agent in the same way as described for methoxyflurane, using 1–2 ml in a 1 litre container. Alternatively, it can be used as a 4% solution in water. Induction takes 3–4 min and the recovery time is 30–40 min (i.e. both are relatively short). However, ether is highly irritant to frog skin and the animals are stressed when first introduced to it.

Tadpoles are safely anaesthetized in a 1:3000 aqueous solution of tricaine, induction taking only 60 s. Recovery is complete in 3 min if the tadpoles are washed in warm tap water and returned to their resident aquarium.

Table 9.1. Frog (*R. pipiens*): physiological data

Measurement	Values
Mean heart rate (beats/min)	50 (36–60)
Arterial blood pressure (mmHg)	31/21
Haematocrit (%)	14
Haemoglobin (g/100 ml)	8
Erythrocytes (10^6/mm³)	0·44
Total blood volume (ml/kg bodyweight)	80

Order Urodela (newts, salamanders, mudpuppies)

In a study comparing immersion in solutions of CNS depressants using the larvae of spotted salamanders (*Amblystoma punctatum*) as subjects, Koppanyi & Karczmar (1948) concluded that tricaine was the safest agent to use, and that induction time varied directly with larval length. At a concentration of 1:7500, the induction time increased from 1 to 10 min as larval body length grew from 12 to 33 mm. Copenhaver (1939) used tricaine in concentrations of 1:3000 in experiments on embryos, larvae and adults of *Amblystoma punctatum* and recorded well-maintained cardiovascular function in anaesthetized subjects.

Propoxate (R7464) was used by Thienpont & Niemegeers (1965) to anaesthetise adult salamanders *Triturus vulgaris*, *T. helveticus* and *T.*

cristatus without mortality. After immersion in a 1:250 000 (4 ppm) solution, the subjects lost their righting reflex in 5–20 min and recovered in 3–6 h when returned to an empty aquarium.

Recommendations
The general management described for frogs and toads applies to urodeles. Immersion in an aqueous solution of tricaine at a concentration of 1:2000 is the simplest method for adults, whilst a 1:3000–1:5000 concentration is sufficient for larval stages.

CLASS REPTILIA

Order Squamata: Suborder Serpentes (snakes)
Snakes pose particular anaesthetic problems. Since their basal metabolic rate (BMR) is low and directly related to environmental temperature, the rate of anaesthetic induction and time for recovery are very variable. In addition, snakes are relatively resistant to hypoxia and can hold their breath for several minutes to further delay induction with inhalational agents. Anatomical features are also important. The absence of an epiglottis and the anterior position of the glottis enable non-venomous snakes to be intubated under physical restraint alone and they may then be respired artificially to initiate anaesthesia. Most snakes have only one functional lung which comprises a thin-walled, hollow tube terminating in an air sac extending to cloacal level, the trachea is open along one side lying within the lung, and there is no diaphragm. These features have been suggested as predisposing to respiratory arrest (Calderwood, 1971), and they influence the use of closed-circuit anaesthesia and artificial ventilation (Jackson, 1970). The danger to the handler from venomous snakes imposes its own discipline, and it must be rembered that even non-venomous species can inflict bite wounds.

The inhalational agents, ether, nitrous oxide, halothane and methoxyflurane have each been reported as useful for anaesthetizing snakes. Induction is usually achieved in a container in which gauze soaked in one of the volatile agents (5–10 ml depending on the size of the container) can be taped to one side clear of contact with the snake (Gandal, 1968). Alternatively, the snake may be placed in a plastic bag or bin, and a suitable anaesthetic mixture piped in (Hime, 1972). Anaesthesia should be induced at an ambient temperature of 20–22°C and, although it has been suggested that recovery from some anaesthetics is accelerated by deliberate warming (Betz, 1962), the weight of evidence indicates that recovery should also take place within this temperature range.

Ether-induced anaesthesia in about 3 min when

113

snakes were exposed to high concentrations (10–15%) in a closed jar, and produced about 15 min surgical anaesthesia before further administration was necessary (Lumb & Jones, 1973). These authors reported a wide safety margin and claimed that a snake would survive up to 60 min in a closed jar containing ether vapour. Muscle relaxation was poor.

Halothane was reported to produce rapid induction and recovery by Hackenbrock & Finster (1963), who sprayed 5 ml onto gauze in an induction chamber. Light anaesthesia was obtained in 10 min and the effect of a 10 min exposure to the halothane vapour lasted up to 20 min. Kraner et al. (1965) piped a gaseous mixture of 4% halothane 72% N_2O and 24% O_2 into a plastic bag to induce anaesthesia in snakes within 20–30 min; once relaxed, the snakes were intubated and maintained on 3% halothane in $N_2O:O_2$ (1:1). The excellence of halothane both by itself and with $N_2O:O_2$ has been confirmed by Jackson (1970), Calderwood (1971), Cooper (1974b; 1976) and Hime (1972), the latter author recommending a very high induction concentration of 7% halothane in $N_2O:O_2$.

Methoxyflurane induced anaesthesia in 15–25 min when the ambient temperature was 26°C (Lumb & Jones, 1973), and it was considered the agent of choice for safe induction by Gandal (1968). However, it may be that some species of snake are particularly susceptible to methoxyflurane since anaesthetic deaths were observed in cobras (Naja naja and Ophiophagus hannah) by Burke & Wall (1970). Moreover, hypoxia has been observed after apparent recovery from methoxyflurane or ether anaesthesia although this may have been associated with deliberate attempts to accelerate recovery by warming the subject (Stunkard & Miller, 1974).

A number of agents have been administered parenterally to snakes and these have been discussed by Wallach (1969). Tribromoethanol was given orally by syringe to induce anaesthesia in 3–5 min, the time to recovery being about 6 h (Mosby and Cantner, 1955). 7 snakes of 80–180 cm in length were given 2–15 mg etorphine into the pleuroperitoneal cavity by Wallach et al. (1967) to produce loss of righting reflex and sufficient analgesia for superficial surgery. Thiopentone (16–25 mg/kg) and pentobarbitone (15–50 mg/kg) were also injected i/p to produce light surgical anaesthesia (Karkstrom & Cook, 1955; Betz, 1962). In contrast, Kraner et al. (1965) reported that thiopentone and thiamylal were both dangerous even at the low dose levels of 2–6 mg/kg; recovery was always slow (48–72 h) and there was an unacceptably high mortality rate. Cooper (1974b) also reported fatalities when using pentobarbitone,

phencyclidine or metomidate separately in snakes. Barbiturate dosages and routes of administration in a number of species have been tabulated by Calderwood (1971).

Tricaine given im to snakes at 180–270 mg/kg has been reported to produce a light plane of anaesthesia and good muscle relaxation (Karkstrom & Cook, 1955; Green, 1978a) and a 10% solution brushed over the mucous membranes of the mouth sedated rattle snakes (Bothrops atrox) within 4 min (Leloup, 1970).

Lignocaine (2% solution) is a useful agent for local infiltration analgesia (Cooper, 1974b). Procaine (10% solution) was recommended at a dose of 470 mg/kg ip for humane euthanasia of snakes with 5–15 min of injection (Livezey, 1957).

Ketamine was first reported as a valuable agent in snake anaesthesia by Glenn et al. (1972), and this has been confirmed by others (Frye & Dutra, 1973; Cooper, 1974b; Stunkard & Miller, 1974; Harding, 1977; Jones, 1977b). From these reports it is clear that there is wide individual as well as species variation in susceptibility to the drug. Doses of less than 50 mg/kg im were sufficient to tranquillize most snakes safely, whereas higher dose rates produced prolonged recovery of some 48–72 h; doses in excess of 100 mg/kg im were best accompanied by intubation and artificial ventilation to ensure adequate oxygenation. The peak effect was reached about 30 min after administration. Cooper (1974b) concluded that it was the drug of choice for snakes, but that great care was needed with subjects in poor condition. Further drawbacks were that muscle relaxation was poor in the absence of any additional anaesthetic agent, and serpentine movements often interfered with surgery.

More recently, the related dissociative agent tiletamine (with zolazepam) has been used in several species of snakes at dose rates of 15–210 mg/kg but, again, whenever sufficient agent was given to allow surgical interference, recovery was always prolonged (Gray et al., 1974).

Evidence for the value of muscle relaxants in snakes is equivocal although it is difficult to obtain complete relaxation with anaesthetic agents alone. Cooper (1974b) prefers to rely on anaesthesia without relaxants, taping the snake to a board. Calderwood (1971) reported that suxamethonium had been used successfully as a muscle relaxant, but drew attention to the resistance of venomous snakes such as Naja naja atros and some Australian elapids whose venom may contain curare-like substances (Millichamp, 1974). Conversely, after experiencing 3 fatalities in mambas (Dendroaspis spp) given low doses of gallamine, Cooper (1976) suggested that some species may be particularly sensitive to muscle relaxants.

Recommended anaesthetic techniques

Preanaesthetic management
Small snakes should be fasted for 24 h while large species such as constrictors should where possible be deprived of food for 7 days. They should be weighed and the respiratory rate at ambient temperature determined just before anaesthesia.

Physical restraint and handling
Snakes are extremely sensitive to painful stimuli and strike or contract violently when a needle is inserted for injection. It is therefore essential to ensure adequate physical restraint before attempting induction, particularly when dealing with venomous species. A simple aid to handling is a deliberate reduction in environmental temperature, since the poikilotherm becomes very sluggish at temperatures below 10°C. Various aids to safe handling have been described (Ball, 1974) including metal 'grabsticks', squeeze cages in which a wire mesh lid can be moved down on to the snake, clear plastic tubes of suitable dimension (Fowler, 1974; McDonald, 1976) and a plastic 'shield' which can be pressed down over the snake while it is contained within a cotton 'snake bag' (Harding, 1977).

Chemical restraint and surgical anaesthesia
Injectable techniques. The lightest level of narcosis compatible with safety in handling should be employed and as much of the surgery as possible should be performed under infiltration analgesia with 2% lignocaine. Of the injectable central depressants, only ketamine and tricaine can be recommended. Dosages will depend on the type of surgery to be performed, the state of the animal and other considerations such as the requirement for rapid or for prolonged recovery times. Intraperitoneal injections are given in the ventral midline—just anterior to the cloaca to avoid the pericardial cavity and liver. Intramuscular injections are easily made into the dorsal muscles of large snakes but large volumes should be given in divided doses at several sites. In smaller species it is often simpler to give injections sc and most drugs are well absorbed by this route. Similarly, when fluid therapy is required, solutions should be given sc at multiple sites.

Ketamine. Chemical restraint to light surgical anaesthesia can be achieved with ketamine given im or sc. At initial dosages up to 50 mg/kg im, snakes are moderately sedated and easily handled, and this is particularly valuable for venomous species. Single doses of the order of 50 mg/kg produce sedation for 48–72 h and are useful for example for transportation with minimal stress. An initial dose of 50–80 mg/kg usually produces a state of surgical anaesthesia suitable for most procedures but muscle relaxation is poor and serpentine movements are commonly encountered. When necessary, ketamine anaesthesia can be supplemented with infiltration of the surgical site with 2% lignocaine. The onset of peak activity occurs after about 30 min and recovery may take from 24–96 h. Where a total dose of 120 mg/kg or more has been used, recovery may take as long as 6 days.

Surgical anaesthesia can be more conveniently obtained by intubation and inhalation of $N_2O:O_2$ (1:1) with 3% halothane after a sedative dose of ketamine has been allowed 30 min to take effect.

Tricaine (180–240 mg/kg im) produces light surgical anaesthesia in 10–20 min. This is maintained for 1–2 h and complete recovery may take up to 12 h. The degree of muscle relaxation attained is better than ketamine but occasional fatalities may be experienced.

Inhalational techniques. When it is considered preferable to avoid prolonged recovery, inhalational anaesthetic agents can be used instead. Induction of anaesthesia is best achieved in a clear plastic box, fibreglass water storage tank, plastic bin, or plastic bag into which a gas mixture of 7% halothane $N_2O:O_2$ (60:40) is piped, but even at this high halothane concentration, induction may take as long as 15 min. It is important that anaesthetics in liquid state should not come into direct contact with the subject since they may induce premature skin shedding, and the oral cavity may be rendered more susceptible to infectious agents (Cooper, 1976). Anaesthesia should be induced at an ambient temperature of 20–24°C and no attempt should be made to hasten induction by deliberately warming the snakes. This method has the advantage that dangerous snakes can be anaesthetized with a minimum of handling, but care must be taken since agents such as halothane are heavier than air and may settle at the bottom of the container in dangerously high concentrations. Conversely, it is possible for snakes to raise their heads above the anaesthetic layer and thus delay the onset of anaesthesia (Hackenbrock & Finster, 1963).

Alternatively, non-venomous snakes can be held by hand, and inhalational agents may be administered by placing a mask directly over the head (Wallach 1969; Jackson, 1970), or they may be intubated directly (Lumb & Jones, 1973).

The changes occurring during induction of anaesthesia have been described by Betz (1962) and Jackson (1970). Snakes usually exhibit a short period of agitation when first exposed to the anaesthetics, then gradually quieten until respiration becomes slow but regular. It is not always easy to determine anaesthetic depth using simple reflexes as indicators, but the first indication that the snake can be safely removed from the container is complete loss of the righting reflex. Thereafter, depth of anaesthesia may be estimated by three signs. First, squeezing or pricking the tail is a particularly effective stimulant to snakes, and loss of response ('pressure response' or 'tail withdrawal reflex') indicates that surgical anaesthesia has been produced. Second, when the tip of the tongue is grasped gently with forceps and withdrawn from its sheath, it remains extruded during surgical anaesthesia, but at lighter levels there is always marked resistance to withdrawal. Finally, during surgical anaesthesia with all agents, the pupils are usually widely dilated.

As soon as the snake is sufficiently sedated (i.e. after loss of the righting reflex) it is intubated and the endotracheal tube is secured with adhesive tape around the lower jaw. Maintenance concentrations of anaesthetics (e.g. 3% halothane with $N_2O:O_2$ (1:1) are then preferably supplied via a Rees modified T-piece (p. 58), which will allow artificial inflation of the lung when required, or by IPPV set at low pressure and at a respiratory rate previously measured in the conscious animal. The depth of anaesthesia can thus be easily adjusted. This is important since the expiratory movement of the single lung is too weak to expel gases through a conventional closed system.

An ambient temperature of 20–24°C is probably most satisfactory during maintenance, and fluid balance should be maintained by frequent sc injections of isotonic saline solution, particularly if the snakes are in poor condition or if haemorrhage has occurred.

Recovery and post-surgical therapy
Recovery is assessed by return of the righting reflex and the ability to move normally. The time taken varies with the anaesthetic used and health of the animal. No attempt should be made to accelerate recovery by deliberately warming the subjects, because high concentrations of anaesthetic which have accumulated in fat depots may be released into the circulation and deepen anaesthesia at the same time that O_2 requirement increases. This may lead to serious hypoxia. After inhalational anaesthesia, recovery may be hastened by supplying O_2 through the T-piece, alternately inflating the lung and then gently evacuating it by stroking the snake's ventral surface from the cloaca forward. Alternatively, O_2 may be supplied by IPPV to accelerate recovery.

Recovery following anaesthesia with ketamine or pentobarbitone may extend from a few hours up to 6 days, depending on the total dose given. In fact, Glenn et al. (1972) concluded that this was a useful property of ketamine as artificial respiration was not required and the immobility of the snakes allowed surgical healing to proceed quickly. Nevertheless, it is difficult to keep snakes under observation for such long periods, and it is wise to maintain subjects which have received more than 120 mg/kg of ketamine on IPPV with O_2 until they show signs of recovery.

Order Chelonia (tortoises, terrapins, turtles)

Anaesthetic problems are posed by the anatomy and physiology of the chelonian respiratory system, the very low BMR which varies with environmental temperature, the ability to retract the head and limbs into the protective shell, and the adaptation in some cases to aquatic or semi-aquatic habits.

The lungs are well developed, and in some species lie closely connected to the dorsal carapace. Ventilation results from changes in volume of the pervisceral cavity produced by inward movements of the limbs and skeletal girdles (Hughes, 1973) which in turn impose pressure changes on the lungs. Although muscular sheets close to the lungs have been described as diaphragms, they exercise relatively little effect compared with the mammalian diaphragm, and exhalation probably results passively from the return of viscera to the resting position. The relatively large spaces within the lungs suggest that concentrations of O_2 and CO_2 equalize by diffusion (Hughes, 1973). The implications for the anaesthetist are that, as in snakes, the expiratory pressure will be too weak to move gases within a closed circuit, and that the ability to withstand hypoxia (particularly among the aquatic species) and survive on a single ventilatory movement per hour can make induction with inhalational agents a frustrating experience.

Hunt (1964) concluded that ether induction was contra-indicated in the tortoise (Testudo graeca) since this species was often only lightly anaesthetized after exposure to the vapour in a chamber for 3 h. Administration of high concentrations by a face mask was rarely successful because the animal retracted its head. However, Lumb & Jones (1973) claimed that ether could be administered to turtles with a 'nose cone', induction taking some 37 min and recovery up to 10 h. Muscle relaxation was achieved in a high percentage of cases, but rectal temperature and pulse rate were significantly depressed after several hours of anaesthesia. Ether has also been used to induce anaesthesia in leopard tortoises (Geochelone pardalis) by Cooper (1976). This author suggests that turning the creature on its back for a short period will stimulate leg movements and therefore increase respiration to accelerate induction.

Soifer (1968) anaesthetized a large Galapagos tortoise (*Testudo vicina*) with methoxyflurane delivered by mask. The same author is quoted by Lumb & Jones (1973) as recommending methoxyflurane as the drug of choice in turtles. He stated that anaesthesia can be induced in small species in a similar chamber to the one used for snakes, with cotton gauze soaked in the agent taped to one side of the box. Once the turtles are relaxed, anaesthesia may be maintained with masks on conventional circuits.

Stunkard & Miller (1974) suggested that anaesthesia could be induced very quickly with halothane in turtles but, as with other inhalational agents, this will clearly depend on how long the animal holds its breath. These authors also found that induction with methoxyflurane may be difficult since turtles can switch to anaerobic respiration. They suggested that induction can be accelerated either by adding 5–10% CO_2 to the inspired gases or placing the subject in a completely sealed jar to allow accumulation of CO_2; the turtle will eventually be forced to hyperventilate and thus inhale the anaesthetic.

Alternatively, drugs may be administered by mouth, by instillation into the rectum, or by im, ip, iv or intracardiac injection. Turtles were given urethane orally (2·73 g/kg), iv (2·38 g/kg), and by intracardiac injection (1.72 g/kg) in a series reported by Kaplan & Taylor (1957). The animal-to-animal variation in response suggests that urethane anaesthesia is too erratic for use in turtles, quite apart from the contraindication to this agent already considered (p. 82).

Pentobarbitone (10 mg/kg) has been given by intracardiac injection to turtles after im administration of chlorpromazine at 10 mg/kg (Young & Kaplan, 1960) with significantly better results than pentobarbitone alone. Induction took only 15 min (compared with 65 min when pentobarbitone alone was given ip at 16 mg/kg) and surgical anaesthesia was maintained for about 3 h. A dose of 18 mg/kg pentobarbitone given ip (Hunt, 1964) induced basal narcosis in tortoises within 30 min and deep anaesthesia within 80 min. This was maintained for 4 h and recovery was prolonged. More recently, Vos-Maas & Zwart (1976) reported an unpredictable response to pentobarbitone (50 mg/kg) when given to red-eared turtles (*Pseudemys scripta elegans*) im or by mouth, but found that chloral hydrate–pentobarbitone–magnesium sulphate (p. 80) (2·5 ml/kg im) produced satisfactory muscle relaxation and algesia within 45 min. This lasted for a further 30–45 min and recovery varied from 1–8 h at a temperature of 22–23°C.

For tortoises suffering from respiratory disease, Hunt (1964) suggested that tribromoethanol was a safer agent than pentobarbitone, since it was less likely to depress respiration, but in other respects the latter was more reliable. When tribromoethanol was given in combination with amylene hydrate (250 mg/kg : 125 mg/kg ip), anaesthesia was induced in 40–70 min and lasted 1–2 h. When given by rectal instillation, induction took 1–2 h and anaesthesia was maintained for a further 60–100 min.

Etorphine was used in red-eared turtles at a total dosage of 0·5–5 mg im per animal to produce ataxia, analgesia and narcosis, while 2 large Galapagos tortoises were given 10 and 15 mg im respectively, and sufficient analgesia developed for superficial surgery (Wallach *et al.*, 1967).

Ketamine and tiletamine–zolazepam have recently been used in these reptiles and have been suggested as the agents of choice. Ketamine was recommended at 60–80 mg/kg im as a safe and reliable anaesthetic (Cooper, 1976) and this has also been our experience (CRC). Tiletamine–zolazepam was assessed in 3 species of turtle at doses ranging from 3·5–14·0 mg/kg im, and a satisfactory level of CNS depression was claimed (Gray *et al.*, 1974). For the present, ketamine appears to be the most acceptable agent for chelonians, even though muscle relaxation is always poor. The subjects are usually sufficiently sedated even with low doses of ketamine (40–60 mg/kg im) to allow application of a nose cone and induction of surgical anaesthesia with an inhalational mixture of $N_2O:O_2$ (1:1) and 3% halothane (CRC).

Recommended anaesthetic techniques

Preanaesthetic management
It is not necessary to fast chelonians prior to surgery but they should be weighed and a clinical examination made for signs of ill-health whenever practicable. Depending on species and the state of health, the effective bodyweight may only be 0·3–0·5 of the observed total (body + shell). It is therefore safest to give injectable drugs at low computed dose levels and administer further increments as required.

Physical restraint and handling
Terrestrial tortoises, aquatic terrapins and hard-shelled turtles are easy to handle, but soft-shelled aquatic turtles move quickly and can bite and scratch. They should be handled with tongs and roped to firm supports (Kaplan, 1969). For some aggressive fresh-water species, it is easier to tranquillize the animals by adding tricaine (1:1000) to their aquarium water prior to handling.

Chemical restraint and surgical anaesthesia

Since induction of anaesthesia with inhalational agents is so unpredictable, it is suggested that parenteral administration of a suitable agent is the preferred method. Induction should be carried out within a temperature range of 15–18°C, under subdued lighting and with the subject standing on a warm absorbent material. Aquatic species should be kept damp throughout the anaesthetic period.

Because the skin is thick, elastic and mobile it is essential to use a sharp 0·63 mm needle (21 gauge) for all injections. Intramuscular injections are best made into the gluteal muscles of the hind limbs. Intravascular injections involve injection either into the heart or into the ventral abdominal vein (Kaplan, 1969). Intracardiac injection is technically rather perilous and achieved by directing a long needle caudo-medially after penetration of the skin between neck and forelimb. To expose the ventral vein, a suitable 'window' has to be drilled in the plastron. A simpler approach is to make a small incision to expose the jugular vein under narcosis and analgesia with etorphine (0·5 mg/kg im) or ketamine (60 mg/kg im). The vein can then be cannulated readily under direct vision (Vos-Maas & Zwart, 1976). Intraperitoneal injection can be made either by a cervical approach between neck and fore-limb or by a caudal approach into the soft tissue between tail and hind limb.

Estimation of the depth of CNS depression is not easy in chelonians. Respiration is best observed by an alternating concavity and convexity in the soft tissue between hind limbs and tail. If narcosis becomes too deep, the limb muscles controlling ventilatory movements may be paralysed and artificial ventilation may then be necessary. However, the animal may simply be holding its breath as described earlier. The eyes give no indication of depth since pupillary responses vary with the drug utilized, and the corneal blink reflex is often present even during deep anaesthesia. Loss of muscle tone in the head, neck and limbs provides the best indication of narcosis, and the withdrawal of limbs to a pin prick is a good guide to analgesia.

Ketamine (60 mg/kg im) injected into the gluteal muscles is the drug of choice. Most species are lightly anaesthetized within 30 min, the peak effect lasts for some 60 min, and full recovery may take up to 24 h. Anaesthesia can be deepened with $N_2O:O_2$ (1:1) and 3% halothane or 2% methoxyflurane supplied by mask or insufflation catheter.

Pentobarbitone (10 mg/kg ip) administered 30 min after injecting chlorpromazine (10 mg/kg im) is a useful alternative to ketamine. Induction takes 15–30 min and time to full recovery may be 6–12 h. If pentobarbitone is used alone ip, a dose of 16–18 mg/kg induces surgical anaesthesia with adequate muscle relaxation in 60–90 min and recovery takes 3–4 h.

Recovery and post-surgical therapy

Following anaesthesia, the terrestrial species should be allowed to recover in an ambient temperature of 18–20°C and high humidity (50–60%), preferably in a box with warm rough bedding such as straw. Aquatic forms should be maintained at 16–18°C with the body wrapped in damp towels.

Suborder Sauria (lizards) and Order Crocodilia (alligators, crocodiles)

Little data is available on the anaesthesia or the physiological alterations following administration of CNS depressants to these reptiles. In addition to ectothermic characteristics shared with other members of the Class Reptilia, lizards and crocodilians have slightly different respiratory and metabolic characteristics which should be noted. Lizards are regarded as the 'type' reptile by physiologists but work on their respiration has been limited. Ventilation is dependent on triphasic movements of costal muscles producing biphasic lung movements (Boelaert, 1941), while the lungs remain partially inflated during periods of apnoea separating periods of breathing. The lungs are well developed but are characterized by non-respiratory regions and large interconnections allowing equalization of gas distribution (Hughes, 1973). In crocodiles, both inspiration and expiration are actively controlled with abdominal and thoracic movements synchronized in the same direction (in contrast to lizards), and a muscular diaphragm assists lung filling during inspiration (Boelaert, 1942). Crocodiles and alligators detoxify drugs very slowly and, as a result, recovery from anaesthesia or chemical immobilization is always prolonged. In contrast, lizards recover more rapidly than snakes at comparable ambient temperatures (Cooper, 1974b).

According to Hackenbrock & Finster (1963), lizards and other small reptiles may be anaesthetized rapidly in a container in which high concentrations of halothane (5–10%) have been generated from 5 ml of the agent placed on cotton wool. Light anaesthesia was obtained in 10 min and the effect of a single exposure lasted for up to 20 min. The value of halothane has been confirmed by Cooper (1974b) both when used alone for induction and for maintenance after injection with barbiturates or ketamine. Anaesthesia was well maintained in a Nile Monitor (*Varanus niloticus*) and rhinoceros iguana (*Cyclura cornuta*) with 2% halothane in O_2.

The dissociative agents, ketamine and tiletamine, have attracted attention in recent years for use in lizards. Cooper (1974b) concluded that ketamine was effective in lizards at lower dose rates than snakes (25–30 mg/kg was sufficient to abolish the righting reflex) and recovery was also quicker than in snakes (less than 12 h in all cases). Tiletamine–zolazepam was effective at 10 mg/kg in the common green iguana (*Iguana iguana*) according to Gray *et al.* (1974), but further details were not given.

Electronarcosis was employed by Northway (1969) to achieve surgical anaesthesia in the common green iguana using a Hewlett-Packard electro-anaesthesia unit at 2000 c.p.s. and 15 mA. Recovery was immediate on removal of the electrical current.

Several injectable agents have been used in crocodiles and alligators. Pentobarbitone (45 mg/kg orally) induced deep anaesthesia in small alligators within a few hours (Pleuger, 1950). American alligators (*Alligator mississippiensis*) weighing 2–5 kg were given pentobarbitone at 8 mg/kg im (injected at the base of the tail) and recovery took 2–3 h (Brisbin, 1966). The same author used tricaine (80–100 mg/kg im) and achieved immobilization within 10 min and recovery in 9–10 h. Phencyclidine (12–24 mg/kg) immobilized alligators within 60 min of im injection and recovery took 6–7 h. Suxamethonium (3–9 mg/kg im) gave complete muscle relaxation within 4 min and recovery took 7–9 h (Brisbin, 1966).

Etorphine was used as a sedative and immobilizing agent for crocodiles at a rate of about 0·3 mg/kg im (Wallach *et al.*, 1967).

Ketamine has been used at low doses for crocodiles and alligators by Cooper (1976), who recommends a dose level of 12–25 mg/kg im for partial immobilization prior to maintenance of anaesthesia with $N_2O:O_2$ (1:1) and 2% halothane to effect.

Recommended anaesthetic techniques

General notes
Although whole-body hypothermia undoubtedly helps in the safe handling of these species, and lower doses are needed to produce the equivalent degree of narcosis if lower ambient temperatures prevail (Cooper, 1974*b*), anaesthesia is probably best carried out at an ambient temperature of 22–24°C. On balance, it is generally considered less stressful to the animal if the whole procedure is carried out within this temperature range when possible.

Fasting prior to anaesthesia is not necessary, but the animal should be carefully observed for signs of disease or inanition. If there is any doubt concerning the anaesthetic risk, very low dosages of ketamine should be given initially and the effect observed before attempting to deepen narcosis. Reptiles in poor health should be given a quarter of the estimated normal dose.

Isotonic saline solution should be injected sc at multiple sites at an approximate rate of 5 ml/kg/h. The depth of anaesthesia attained is best judged by loss of the righting reflex, loss of sensation assessed by withdrawal on pinching or pricking the feet, and by the frequency of respiration.

Injectable techniques
Ketamine is the drug of choice. Depending on the state of the animal, an initial dose of 10–25 mg/kg should be given im at the base of the tail, and the effect assessed. Onset of action may take up to 50 min and the effect may last for 4–7 h in crocodiles and alligators, and 2–6 h in lizards depending on size and age. Central depression can then be increased by giving further increments to effect, or preferably by transfer to inhalation of $N_2O:O_2$ (1:1) with 1–2% halothane or methoxyflurane.

Tricaine (80 mg/kg im) is a valuable agent for alligators and crocodiles. After im injection of a freshly prepared solution, the subjects are well relaxed within 10 min. Recovery takes up to 10 h.

Inhalational techniques
Anaesthesia may be induced in smaller species of lizard with halothane (5–10%) or methoxyflurane (3%) in a jar or box (5 ml on cotton gauze taped to the inside of the container well clear of the reptile). Induction takes 10 min with halothane and 20–30 min with methoxyflurane, and recovery takes about 20 and 60 min respectively. Maintenance is best achieved by inhalation of $N_2O:O_2$ (1:1) with 1–2% halothane or methoxyflurane delivered through a nose cone, mask or oral catheter.

Recovery and post-surgical therapy
Low temperatures will depress metabolism and hinder recovery, while high temperatures will accelerate metabolism but may produce a fatal hypoxia. It is therefore unwise to deliberately warm the subjects to accelerate recovery. They should therefore be allowed to recover at a temperature of 22–24°C on a non-slip surface and under subdued lighting.

CLASS AVES

Birds

The domestic fowl (*Gallus domesticus*) has long been regarded as an inexpensive and useful experimental animal but the range of birds investigated in laboratories is now more extensive. It is therefore proposed to discuss domestic fowl as the 'type' bird in this section, and then detail any special anaesthetic requirements in other species.

Several aspects of bird behaviour, anatomy and physiology are relevant in the selection of an anaesthetic method. These include the lower degree of pain apparently experienced during surgical interference as compared with mammals; the very high basal metabolic rate (BMR) particularly in small species; the nature of the integument and the thermo-regulatory mechanisms of birds; cardiovascular defects related to abnormal posture during surgery; the nature of the musculo-skeletal adaptations to flight and the care needed to prevent damage to wings, limbs and neck during restraint; the rapid progression to exhaustion in response to stress factors (general adaptation syndrome); and the complex nature of the respiratory tract.

Several commentators have suggested that birds do not experience pain to the same degree as mammals (Sykes, 1964). Furthermore, the state of apparent hypnosis induced in fowl if they are laid on their back has tempted some workers to conclude that chemical anaesthesia is unnecessary for many surgical procedures. However, the law regarding experimental procedures on all vertebrates specifically states that surgery must be accompanied by anaesthesia. Experience at this centre (CRC) indicates that surgical incisions and needle pricks do indeed evoke less response in the domestic fowl than mammals, but this is not so in raptors and other species. The comb, wattles, head, cloaca and digits are sensitive to painful stimuli in all birds who respond more vigorously to pinching (pressure) or stretch than to incision of tissues.

The higher BMR of birds compared with mammals of similar age and size is reflected in their high body temperature (40–44°C). The main implications for the anaesthetist are threefold. The high BMR is accompanied by high food conversion, which in turn accounts for the poor anaesthetic risk presented by small birds or chicks deprived of food and the associated hypoglycaemia (Arnall, 1964). Secondly, the rapid heart rate is subject to profound alteration in response to fear or physical exertion. Finally, the difference between ambient or inhalational gas temperature and the high body temperature increases the gradient down which heat will be lost.

Thermoregulation is both less efficient and less adaptable in birds than mammals, and the potential for heat loss is further increased during anaesthesia and in young chicks (Arnall, 1964). According to Van Tyne & Berger (1959), it takes 2 weeks for some species to acquire the ability to maintain body temperature when environmental temperature changes. Prevention of heat loss is therefore particularly important in birds, especially if they are small or young. Excessive cooling is likely if thermal insulation is decreased; if heat is lost by evaporation as cool air currents flow over damp surfaces; and as latent heat of evaporation is lost from the respiratory tract if respiratory rate increases and when anaesthetic gases are supplied at high flow rates. It follows that plumage should remain intact if possible and the minimum area possible should be prepared for surgery with water

or alcohol based solutions. A source of heat is essential however short the procedure.

Birds should not be maintained on their backs for long periods since hypotension resulting from decreased venous return is likely to develop. Acute cardiovascular failure (shock) may result from overextending and taping the outstretched wings and legs during surgery, possibly as a result of damage to the brachial and lumbo-sacral plexuses (Graham-Jones, 1960). Similar damage from violent struggling may account for cases of shock and death commonly encountered when handling small birds. Hypotension may also develop as a result of sudden alterations in posture during anaesthesia. Hence, all movements should be made very slowly and gently, taking care to avoid damage to the neck, wings and legs (Klide, 1973). The simplest way to avoid such trauma is to secure the wings to the back and position the legs together with adhesive tape. Prior tranquillization with agents administered in the food should also be considered.

The stress factors which induce the so-called general adaptation syndrome (Selye, 1950) in birds have been described by Freeman (1976). Adrenaline (Cannon, 1929), noradrenaline (Taggart et al., 1973) and glucagon (Freeman & Manning, 1976) are released into the circulation during the first (alarm) stage, and the adrenal cortex is stimulated via the hypothalamus and anterior pituitary (ACTH). This hormonal loop may be rapidly exhausted in birds before the process of adaptation has time to operate.

Acute cardiovascular failure may therefore result from one or more of the factors outlined above, particularly in small birds. Firstly, the alarm response may trigger marked fluctuations in heart rate. In addition, 'neural shock' resulting from stretched nervous plexuses, poor venous return arising from abnormal posture, and exhaustion of the adrenal-pituitary system can each make the task of the anaesthetist more difficult.

The respiratory system is adapted for respiration during level flight, soaring and diving at speed, and this has particular implications for inhalational anaesthesia. The anatomy has been well described (Zeuthen, 1942; Duncker, 1972; Piiper & Scheid, 1973). The trachea divides into two main bronchi termed mesobronchi, which in turn give rise to secondary bronchi. A proximal group, the ventrobronchi, lie on the ventro-medial surface of the lungs, and communicate with the cranial air sacs (the paired cervical and prethoracic sacs, and the single interclavicular sac). A more distal group of secondary bronchi, the dorso- and laterobronchi, arise from each mesobronchus before these terminate in paired caudal air sacs, the post-thoracic and abdominal sacs. The dorso- and ventrobronchi are joined by narrow tubes of uniform diameter, the parabronchi, which are invested by a capillary network. The parabronchi are arranged in parallel anastomosing rows on each side. This complex forms the analogue of mammalian lungs and has been termed the paleopulmo (Duncker, 1971). Another parabronchial network, the neopulmo, is sometimes formed between secondary bronchi and air sacs (e.g. none in primitive birds such as penguins, but up to 20% of the total lung area in gallinaceous and passerine birds).

The parabronchial lung of birds is a relatively rigid, constant volume structure, and ventilatory movements producing pressure changes within the body cavity are mainly transmitted to the air sacs (Hughes, 1973). Expiration is always active, whilst inspiration is thought to be passive during quiet breathing but active when the respiratory rate is stimulated (Fedde et al., 1961). Air passing through the parabronchial lung moves in one direction only (caudo-cranial from dorsobronchi via parabronchi to ventrobronchi) during both inspiration and expiration (Hazelhoff, 1951). Passage of air through the parabronchi during inspiration results mainly from the aspiratory action of the cranial air sacs, whilst the posterior sacs are active in forcing air forward through the parabronchi during expiration (Brackenbury, 1972). Differential pressures between air sacs is probably associated with resistances in different airways.

Various models for gas exchange in avian lungs have been proposed, but the elegant studies of Scheid & Piiper (1972) strongly support the idea that blood flows across the direction of gas flow in birds. Gas transfer takes place through the walls of the parabronchi. The gas composition must change from the inspiratory to the expiratory ends of the parabronchi, so it follows that capillary blood must be equilibrating with parabronchial gases of widely differing pCO_2 and pO_2 (Piiper & Scheid, 1973). The physiological significance of the combined unidirectional gas flow and cross-current gas–blood flow is that gas exchange is taking place during both inspiration and expiration. This system is highly efficient at minimizing variations in gas exchange associated with alterations in respiratory rate, particularly during panting respiration, but is dependent on an uninterrupted air flow through the lungs. Even short periods of apnoea result in severe hypoxia and this is particularly significant to the anaesthetist. Furthermore, anaesthetic gases will be rapidly absorbed into the bloodstream and this, in turn, results in rapid induction of and recovery from inhalational anaesthesia. Since the speed of induction is also inversely proportional to the solubility of the agent in blood, and the solubility in birds is lower than in mammals (Klide, 1973), it follows that potent agents such as halothane will build up plasma concentration very rapidly. It is not difficult to see, therefore, why anaesthesia in birds has proved so hazardous in the past (Gandal, 1956; Church, 1957).

The air sacs are also potential sources of anaesthetic failure. Although they may be opened to air without risk of lung collapse, the introduction of fluids and solids will interfere with ventilation. Great care must therefore be taken when giving intraperitoneal injections and in avoiding haemorrhage into the sacs during surgery. The midline approach should be made in abdominal surgery to avoid the laterally placed paired caudal sacs. Care must be exercised during artificial ventilation to avoid overinflation and possible rupture of the sacs. Aspiration of exudates or solids is also a danger in all types of bird since patency of the airway is easily lost and the air sacs are subject to aspiration pneumonitis. Finally, dangerous concentrations of inhalational agents may build up in dependent and poorly ventilated areas of the air sacs and may then be released into the circulation. It is important that the respiratory system of birds should be flushed with air or O_2 at 5 min intervals to wash out such accumulations, particularly during prolonged anaesthesia.

Early attempts at inhalational anaesthesia in poultry and small cage birds reflect the difficulties encountered as a result of the anatomical and physiological factors (Lee, 1953; Gandal, 1956; Church, 1957; Jordan et al., 1960). Agents described as the most reliable were ether (Bachrach, 1954; Friedburg, 1961, 1962; Donovan & Boone, 1965), ethyl chloride (Friedburg, 1961, 1962; Grono, 1961), halothane (Grono, 1961; Whittow & Ossorio, 1961; Marley & Payne, 1962, 1964; Jones, 1966; Graham-Jones, 1966; Myers & Stettner, 1969; Sanford, 1971), methoxyflurane (Leininger, 1965; Bennett, 1968) and cyclopropane (Hill & Noakes, 1964).

In discussing the use of ether as an agent for birds, Gandal (1956) directed attention to the danger of overconcentration within the air sacs, and recommended that volatile agents should be given intermittently, halting administration for brief periods during induction and maintenance. It is hardly surprising that difficulties were encountered with ether and ethyl chloride when they were sprayed directly into the nares of small cage birds by Friedburg (1961); it was concluded that ethyl chloride had a wider safety margin. Ethyl chloride was also recommended as a volatile agent for parakeets by Ferguson (1961) who administered it 30 min after sc injection of morphine and atropine.

Marley & Payne (1962) anaesthetized chicks by administering 0·8–1·6% halothane by insufflation either intra-orally or directly via a loose fitting endotracheal tube. They emphasized the need to use catheters which were small enough for excess gas to escape around the outside to avoid over-distension of the air sacs, and the tube was taped in position around the maxilla to ensure overflow through the mouth. Excess gas in the anaesthetic line was leaked through a side-arm under water. Although apnoea was commonly encountered, they claimed that this was not dangerous if halothane was withdrawn whilst continuing the administration of O_2, and they emphasized the need to maintain O_2 flow during recovery. They concluded that halothane is a safe anaesthetic for young and adult domestic fowl, whether healthy or sick. Other commentators have intubated poultry under direct vision without preanaesthetic agents (Anderson, 1967; Bennett, 1968), and induced and maintained anaesthesia on a closed system.

Halothane, 2–4% in O_2 at 1–2 litres/min, was used to anaesthetize turkeys by Jones (1966). The birds were not fasted or given preanaesthetic drugs but were simply induced using a face mask to deliver the gas mixture. The agent was used repeatedly in a North American bald eagle (*Haliaetus leucocephalus*) by Mapletoft & Futter (1969), without ill effect.

Gas mixtures containing halothane have also been administered directly into air sacs with the dual purpose of anaesthetizing and ventilating the birds (Burger & Lorenz, 1960; Whittow & Ossorio, 1970). In the earlier method, air or O_2 was administered into the posterior thoracic air sac and was primarily concerned with effective ventilation. In the technique of Whittow & Ossorio (1970), a 50×1.65 mm (16 gauge) needle was inserted into the intraclavicular air sac at 40° to the horizontal. After penetration of the air sac, a polyethylene catheter was passed through the lumen of the needle, and the needle was withdrawn. Halothane with O_2 proved to be the best agent for induction, but methoxyflurane was considered safer for maintenance of anaesthesia. The technique was considered suitable for birds over 50 g with the advantage that anaesthesia could be rapidly reversed in emergency.

Halothane has been recommended for small cage birds (Grono, 1961; Graham-Jones, 1966) and for avian anaesthesia in general (Myers & Stettner, 1969; Klide, 1973). The latter author suggested that up to 2% halothane in O_2 could be used safely in small birds (50 g or less) but warned that induction could be very rapid, whilst larger healthy birds needed 2.5–3% for induction, and 1–1.5% for maintenance. The mixture was delivered to small birds through a semi-open system, but a circle system was successful in large species. He further emphasized the necessity to intubate all birds over 100 g using cut-down versions of standard endotracheal tubes to reduce dead space.

Methoxyflurane is more soluble than halothane in blood (blood:gas partition coefficient in mammals is 12.0, compared with the 2.3 of halothane). Consequently, induction and recovery are slower, and fluctuations in depth are less violent. The drug is generally thought to be the safest volatile agent for use in birds (Gandal, 1967, 1969; Bennett, 1968). Small birds can be anaesthetized in suitable containers of glass or plastic; 0.1–0.2 ml of methoxyflurane on cotton–wool in a 1 litre jar should induce anaesthesia in 30–60 s and this will last from 5–10 min after the bird is removed from the jar. The same size of jar can be used as a face mask for large birds; 0.2–0.4 ml methoxyflurane is sufficient to induce anaesthesia prior to intubation and maintenance on a methoxyflurane–gas mixture administered via a semi-open or closed circuit (Gandal, 1969). Methoxyflurane was administered for maintenance by Whittow & Ossorio (1970) by the air–sac technique described above.

Cyclopropane with O_2 was administered to adult domestic fowl by Hill & Noakes (1964), and was considered an excellent anaesthetic for periods ranging from 30 min to 3 h. The birds were intubated and the gas mixture was delivered by a T-piece, connected at the expiratory end to a to-and-fro soda-lime absorption system fitted with a poly-thene rebreathing bag. It is significant that ventilation was well maintained for such long periods without CO_2 accumulating and without over-distension of the air sacs. Recovery was rapid once the cyclopropane was eliminated from the gas mixture.

A number of agents have been given parenter-ally to achieve levels of narcosis ranging from sedation to surgical anaesthesia, but the danger of overdosage, particularly in small cage birds, and the difficulty experienced with iv injections, has persuaded many workers to prefer inhalational agents (Klide, 1973). Chloral hydrate (Barger *et al.*, 1958), tribromoethanol (Mosby & Cantner, 1955), pentobarbitone (Leonard, 1960), reserpine (Hewitt, 1959; Wilgus, 1960), methohexitone (Martin, 1967), metomidate (Williams, 1967) and α-chloralose (Crider & McDaniel, 1967), have all been given orally with variable degrees of success claimed. The relative merits of different injectable drugs are difficult to analyse from the literature, since the assessment of narcosis is subjective and sources vary in their surgical requirements. Amylo-barbitone (Fretz, 1932; Biester & Schwarte, 1962), pentobarbitone (Bailey, 1953; Durant 1953; Fried-burg, 1961, 1962; Biester & Schwarte, 1962; Delius, 1966), chloral hydrate (Biester & Schwarte, 1962), phencyclidine (Kroll, 1962), tribromo-ethanol (Cline & Greenwood, 1972), and the combinations, 'Equithesin' (Gandal, 1956) and 'Combuthal' (Church, 1957) were amongst the earliest injectable anaesthetics assessed. More recently, metomidate (Marsboom, *et al.*, 1965; Williams, 1965; Cooper, 1970, 1974*a*; Callear, 1971; Manton & Jones, 1972; Ryder-Davis, 1973; Jones, 1977*b*), the cyclohexylamines, ketamine (Bree & Gross, 1969; Gerlach, 1969; Kittle, 1971; Mandelker, 1971, 1972, 1973; Borzio, 1973; Boever & Wright, 1975) and tiletamine (Gray *et al.*, 1974), xylazine (Levinger et al., 1973), and finally the steroid combination alphaxolone–alphadolone (Cooper & Frank, 1973) have excited favourable comment.

The choice of injection site is important. Intraperitoneal injection is best made in the mid-line halfway between cloaca and the sternum with the needle directed anteriorly just under the abdominal wall to avoid the air sacs (Graham-Jones, 1966). Intramuscular injections may be made into the pectoral or leg muscles using 0·40 mm (27 gauge) needles to minimize trauma. Projectile syringes may be used to inject sedative drugs into ostriches (Struthionidae) thus avoiding physical restraint and handling (Jones, 1977*b*). It was suggested by Seidenstricker & Reynolds (1969) that the pectoral muscles should not be used in falcons in case these muscles which are so important during flying were damaged; however, it could be argued that the leg muscles are more vulnerable and the pectoral muscles are the lesser risk (Cooper, 1977). The brachial (median) vein as it crosses the ventral surface of the humero-radial joint is usually the chosen site for iv injection and is best seen with the bird in a supine position with one wing held extended (Gandal 1969; Cooper, 1973). A 0·5–0·45 mm (25–26 gauge) needle should be used and care taken to prevent haemorrhage on withdrawal. In most penguins (Sphenisciformes), injection can be made into a vein on the postero-medial aspect of the flippers (Dilbone, 1965); however, in others, it is easier to inject into the vein as it courses over the medial aspect of the metatarso-phalangeal joint. The jugular veins have been used, but in some small birds, especially in budgerigars (*Melopsittacus undulatus*) only the right jugular is present (Kerlin, 1964). In small species, the vein walls are so fragile that injection is difficult and may be rendered impossible by sudden movements (Gandal, 1956).

Pentobarbitone alone has been used with variable results in different species of bird. At doses of 30–60 mg/kg iv, the depth and duration of anaesthesia were inconsistent in domestic ducks (*Anas platyrhynchos*) according to Desforges & Scott (1971), whereas domestic pigeons (*Columba livia*) were successfully anaesthetized for 45–60 min with 30–40 mg/kg iv by Graham-Jones (1966). This barbiturate has been given im to several species with limited success. Arnall (1964) used dilute

solutions in small birds at 40 mg/kg im and observed variation in the time of onset and duration of effect. In herring and lesser blackbacked gulls (*Larus* spp.), doses of approximately 80 mg/kg im induced anaesthesia in 10–20 min and this lasted for 45–95 min (Delius, 1966). Thiobarbiturates and methohexitone have not been successful when used alone im, although Spellerburg (1969) successfully immobilized McCormick skuas (*Catharacta skua mccormicki*) with a mixture of pentobarbitone and thiopentone. Barbiturates are also included in the 2 commercially available combinations which have been used in birds. 'Equithesin' consists of pentobarbitone, chloral hydrate, magnesium sulphate, propylene glycol and ethanol in aqueous solution (p. 80). The other combination, 'Combuthal', is composed of equal parts of thiopentone and pentobarbitone in water. Gandal (1956; 1969) recommended 'Equithesin' as the anaesthetic of choice in birds. In subjects ranging from 0·018 to 5·1 kg in weight, a dosage of 2·5 ml/kg im was effective in healthy birds, whereas 3·0 ml/kg im resulted in some deaths; lower doses (2·0 ml/kg im) were recommended for weak debilitated birds. Narcosis developed in 7–30 min, satisfactory anaesthesia lasted 25–90 min and recovery was complete within 180 min of the initial injection. The combination has since been used extensively. Friedberg (1961) concluded that it was safer than pentobarbitone (45 mg/kg im) used alone in small cage birds. Sanger & Smith (1957) compared the value of 'Equithesin' and 'Combuthal' in domestic fowl and turkeys (*Meleagris gallapavo*). 'Equithesin' was effective in fowl at 2·5 ml/kg im but turkeys required a significantly higher dose of 2·85 ml/kg. 'Combuthal' induced good surgical anaesthesia in fowl at an approximate dose of 60 mg/kg total barbiturate im, whilst turkeys required up to 3 times this dose for equivalent narcosis. 'Equithesin' was also successful in inducing surgical anaesthesia safely in falcons (Seidenstricker & Reynolds, 1969). They gave it im into both legs at a rate ranging from 1·5–1·9 ml/kg and claimed that local trauma at the injection site was insignificant.

Since the first reports appeared on the use of the hypnotic agent, metomidate (Marsboom *et al.*, 1965; Williams, 1965), the agent has been extensively assessed in a number of avian species (Jones, 1973; Ryder-Davies, 1973). A dose of 10–15 mg/kg im produces a state of hypnosis with good muscle relaxation, but minimal analgesia. Induction to peak effect takes 3–5 min and hypnosis usually lasts for 5–15 min. The domestic pigeon, penguins and some ducks (Anatidae) may require higher doses (Jones, 1973). Conversely, lower doses (2·5–4·5 mg/kg im) were found to be effective in Old World vultures (Houston & Cooper, 1973). Three levels of CNS depression were described. Initially, slight sedation, apathy and ptosis were observed, followed by head drooping and a period in which the bird might struggle and was easily aroused. Finally, good sedation, with muscular relaxation and no response to sound or tactile stimuli developed but analgesia was usually poor. Jones (1973) recommended the use of local analgesics in addition to metomidate for surgery. Metomidate has also proved valuable in handling birds of prey (Cooper, 1970, 1974a). This author recommended that raptors should be starved for 6 h before injection and reported that problems were not encountered after injecting metomidate into the pectoral muscles. Induction of hypnosis was always achieved rapidly (1–6 min) while doses of 5–15 mg/kg im produced a state of deep surgical anaesthesia in some individuals. Some families of bird, particularly Ciconiiformes (storks and cranes), show marked excitement during recovery (Jones, 1977b).

Phenothiazine derivatives have proved ineffective as tranquillizers in birds (Cooper, 1968), although Stunkard & Miller (1974) recommended administering acepromazine with ketamine to avoid any excitatory phase during recovery from dissociative anaesthesia.

Xylazine varies in its effects in different species (Levinger et al., 1973). Birds are usually easier to handle after injection with 25–60 mg/kg im but relaxation is always poor and some species have severe convulsions (Jones, 1977b).

The dissociative drugs phencyclidine, ketamine and tiletamine have each been used in birds with varying degrees of success. Phencyclidine was used in birds by Kroll (1962), but according to Houston (1970)—quoted by Cooper (1970)—its onset of action was very slow in the sedation of African vultures (Aegypiinae). Zebras killed with 4 g phencyclidine iv were used as bait to catch wild vultures (Ebedes, 1973). Ketamine has been widely recommended for many avian species. Mandelker (1973) used ketamine in parakeets and other small species and concluded that it was particularly safe since doses of 50–100 mg/kg im provided adequate anaesthesia, whilst the minimum lethal dose was 500 mg/kg im. Surgical anaesthesia with a good degree of muscle relaxation was induced within 45 s of im injection. Dosages ranging from 30–250 mg/kg im have been reported (Kittle, 1971), and Klide (1973) concluded that the lower dosage should be used and supplemented with inhalational anaesthesia. Bree & Gross (1969) anaesthetized pigeons with pentobarbitone (20 mg/kg im) followed 10–15 min later by ketamine (32–64 mg/kg im), and claimed that induction and recovery were achieved without excitement.

Mattingly (1972) used ketamine for raptors ranging in size from kestrels (Falco tinnunculus) to golden eagles (Aquila chrysaëtos) at a preliminary low dosage of 25 mg/kg im followed by increments to effect, while Smith & Hill (1972) commented on the low doses (45 mg/kg im) needed to achieve surgical anaesthesia with adequate muscle relaxation in a North American gold eagle (Aquila chrysaëtos canadensis). Borzio (1973) found that 18 mg/kg im was sufficient to immobilize a series of wildfowl in 1–5 min. He also used ketamine in raptors at 18 mg/kg im but commented on the long recovery time in some individuals. Stunkard & Miller (1974) recommended ketamine for avian anaesthesia but suggested that acepromazine should be injected simultaneously to avoid struggling during recovery. Ketamine was recommended for ratites by Robinson & Fairfield (1974); a dose of 20 mg/kg im was considered useful for restraint although an ostrich was still liable to strike out with legs or wings when handled. The authors claimed that it was possible to sedate this bird sufficiently with ketamine to allow endotracheal intubation followed by inhalation anaesthesia with halothane in O_2 but this is, in fact, virtually impossible even at high dose rates of 200 mg/kg im (Jones, 1978). The tiletamine–zolazepam combination has been assessed in several avian species (Gray et al., 1974) including ratites at 4–22 mg/kg im, raptors at 16–33 mg/kg im, wildfowl at 22–35 mg/kg im and parrots at 10 mg/kg im.

Tribromoethanol was considered to be particularly suitable for captive and wild mallard ducks (Anas platyrhynchos) by Cline & Greenwood (1972). Doses ranging from 100–158 mg/kg were given im to immobilize ducks for 9–20 min.

The steroid combination alphaxolone–alphadolone was assessed by Cooper & Frank (1973) for use in domestic fowl and several species of raptor. It was concluded that this was an excellent agent for achieving short periods of anaesthesia when given iv. At a dose rate of 10 mg/kg iv, surgical anaesthesia was achieved within seconds, but im and ip administration were unsatisfactory. However, caution was later expressed (Frank & Cooper, 1974; Cooper & Redig, 1975) after using it in red-tailed hawks (Buteo jamaicensis) and encountering some fatalities. Unusual responses have also been encountered in mallards and Canada geese (Branta canadensis), serious cardiac arrhythmias appearing even though the steroids were injected very slowly iv (Cribb & Haigh, 1977). Small caged birds have been given doses of up to 60 mg/kg ip to achieve short periods of anaesthesia at this centre (CRC), but this method was considered less satisfactory than inhalational anaesthesia with methoxyflurane.

Muscle relaxants have been little used in birds. The non-depolarizing agent gallamine was used at a dose rate of 2–5 mg/kg im to immobilize pigeons by Desmedt & Delwaide (1966), who commented that depolarizing drugs caused contractions of avian muscle and were therefore ineffective.

There are many reports in the literature indicating the dangers involved in using local analgesic agents in birds, particularly with procaine in small species such as budgerigars and canaries (*Serinus canarius*) (Grono, 1961; Friedburg, 1962; Graham-Jones, 1966; Sanford, 1971). However, Klide (1973) questioned whether the LD_{50} of procaine given sc to parakeets indicated any greater sensitivity than in mammals, and suggested that the poor experience previously reported was probably attributable to the use of a 2% solution of procaine. He pointed out that only 0·5 ml of a 2% solution injected into a parakeet weighing 30 g would approximately equal the LD_{50}. In his experience, procaine diluted to 0·2% was effective in achieving local analgesia and was valuable for surgery in poor-risk cases. Local analgesics have been used in larger birds without difficulties. Young (1948) employed a 2% solution of procaine in several species, and it was also infiltrated for abdominal surgery in domestic fowl and quail (*Coturnix coturnix*) by Hollingsworth & Howes (1965). Tetracaine incorporated in a spray was considered better than ethyl chloride for topical application in birds (Friedberg, 1962). A 2% lignocaine solution gave excellent results in raptors (Cooper, 1973), and it is frequently employed at this centre (CRC) in adult and young fowl as a dilute (0·5–1%) solution.

Several drugs have been used for tranquillization and immobilization when given by the oral route. Wild or intractable subjects may be tamed after tranquillization and the altered behaviour may then be established for life. Reserpine has been the drug most commonly used. Wilgus (1960) reported that geese (Anseridae) are particularly sensitive to this drug, a dose level of 0·0625 g/ton of feed being sufficient for tranquillization. It has also been used for handling wild pheasants at a rate of 8 g/15 kg of food (Hewitt, 1959), and for taming and training falcons (Dodge, 1963). Tribromoethanol in turkeys (Mosby & Cantner, 1955), metomidate powder in mourning doves (*Zenaidura macroura*) (Martin, 1967) and wild turkeys (Williams, 1965, 1967), and α-chloralose in wild geese (Crider & McDaniel, 1967) and wild turkeys (Williams *et al.*, 1966), have each proved fairly safe when used to treat bait. However, uptake of these agents into the circulation is dependent on so many factors that oral medication is generally unsatisfactory.

Recommended anaesthetic techniques

Preanaesthetic management
Large birds are probably best starved of food 6–12 h to prevent regurgitation from the crop, but the period should be limited to 2 h in the case of small cage-birds.

Physical restraint and handling
Physical restraint should be kept to a minimum. Small birds, particularly canaries, are prone to handling shock. Poultry should be grasped from above to hold the wings into the thorax (Fig. 9.2), turned over gently onto their back and quietened by gently stroking the abdomen from the sternum caudally. Small birds should be cradled in the palm of the hand taking great care not to apply pressure accidentally to the neck, but if it is impossible to restrain them quickly by hand, they can be caught in soft nets. Raptors may be tranquillized by giving reserpine or metomidate orally in meat, but

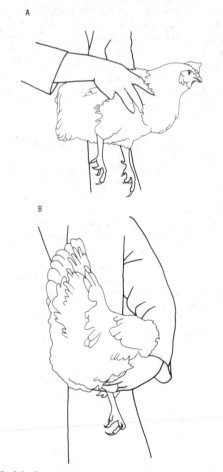

Fig. 9.2. Correct way to pick up and carry domestic fowl.

125

commonly stand for injection after being hooded. The bird may then be injected with immobilizing doses of drugs or placed in an induction chamber with inhalational anaesthetics. Larger birds such as parrots should be removed from a restraining box or cage by gripping them around the neck and wings with a hand well protected in towelling.

Intramuscular injections are made into the pectoral muscles on either side of the cariniform sternum or into the thigh muscles of large species. Particular care must be taken to ensure that blood vessels have not been accidentally penetrated. Small volumes of metomidate or ketamine solution cause no problems when injected into the pectoral muscles of raptors.

The intraperitoneal route is useful in small birds. The site for injection is in the midline halfway between the cloaca and sternum. A 10 × 0·5 mm (25 gauge) needle is suitable for small species and is inserted at a shallow angle directed cranially so that it lies almost parallel to the abdominal wall.

Intravenous injection in small species is often difficult since accessible vessels are very small and fragile. In poultry and larger birds, the brachial vein is accessible where it passes over the ventral aspect of the humero-radial joint (Fig. 9.3). The bird should be laid on its back, the wing held outstretched and venepuncture achieved with a 10 × 0·5 or 0·4 mm (25 or 27 gauge) needle. The femoral and jugular veins are also readily accessible in raptors. In penguins a vein on the posteriomedial aspect of the flippers is suitable for iv injection.

Whenever possible, birds should be weighed prior to injection, restraining them in a suitable container such as a cardboard or plastic box before placing them on the scales. However, this involves additional handling and is less important now that agents such as metomidate and ketamine with a wide therapeutic index are available. We prefer to inject a low dose on an estimated weight basis and then give further increments if required after weighing the tranquillizer subject (CRC). The bird

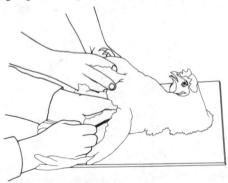

Fig. 9.3. Intravenous injection in the brachial vein of fowl.

should be returned to a suitable container and left quietly in the dark until the drug takes effect. Conservation of heat should be considered from the outset and an external source supplied accordingly.

Chemical restraint and preanaesthetic treatment
Capture of wild birds. Reserpine taken by mouth in prepared bait can be used for tranquillizing some species for long periods. However, the prolonged duration of effect may be a severe disadvantage since the birds will not eat for several days. It is valuable in taming raptors and is given at a dose of 2–4 mg/kg in meat. The 5–6 day tranquillization period entails force feeding of the subject. It is also useful for tranquillizing game birds for handling at a dosage of 8 g/15 kg of feed.

Methohexitone has some value in sedating birds if given on bait. 1·0 g of the dry salt is mixed thoroughly with 30 g of mixed crushed oats and flaked maize. Some birds take the bait readily and are then usually sedated in 10–25 min.

Metomidate may be used similarly at a rate of 2 g/30 g of grain. A solution of metomidate is prepared and thoroughly mixed with the bait, which is then allowed to dry. Some species will eat the grain whilst others avoid it. If they do take it, they are usually sedated in about 10 min.

In general, these methods are unreliable since the amount of bait taken is uncontrolled and the rate of uptake of the drug from the alimentary tract is extremely variable.

Preanaesthesia and tranquillization. Several agents are useful but their efficiency varies considerably with species.

Metomidate is a valuable injectable agent for immobilizing several species of bird but is not very effective in others, particularly Ciconiiformes. It produces CNS depression varying from hypnosis to light surgical anaesthesia depending on the species and drug dosage.

For birds weighing more than 1 kg, a dose of 10–20 mg/kg im into leg or pectoral muscles using a 5% solution is effective. In birds weighing 100 g–1 kg, a 1% solution at a dose rate of 10–20 mg/kg im should be injected into the pectoral muscles, whilst a 0·1% solution should be injected with a microlitre tuberculin syringe into the pectoral muscles of small caged varieties. Hypnosis develops rapidly in 1–6 min; the duration of peak effect varies with species, but ranges from 10–30 min in adult fowl. The very high therapeutic index makes it by far the safest injectable agent in birds even in small caged species.

Dissociative anaesthetics, particularly ketamine and tiletamine (with zolazepam) are valuable in immobilizing birds ranging from parakeets to large ratites. For canaries, budgerigars, small parakeets and other small caged birds (weight 30–60 g), 0·1 ml of the standard commercial solution of ketamine (100 mg/ml) is diluted in 0·9 ml of distilled water in a tuberculin syringe (i.e. 0·1 ml of the dilute solution will then contain 1 mg of ketamine). At 1 mg/bird injected im into the pectoral muscles, sedation will be induced in 3–4 min and the birds will recover within 20 min; at 2 mg/bird im, light surgical anaesthesia develops within 3 min, lasts for 5–12 min, and the birds recover fully in 20–30 min; at 3 mg/bird im light surgical anaesthesia develops within 2 min, but the duration of peak effect and time to full recovery are extended to 20 min and 40–80 min respectively.

Tiletamine–zolazepam is used at doses ranging from 10–20 mg/kg im to give similar results in small birds.

Poultry, wildfowl and similar species: at an initial dosage of 15–20 mg/kg of ketamine im, the birds are invariably immobilized and, in some cases, light surgical anaesthesia is achieved. This may be supplemented with further increments of 5 mg/kg at 5 min intervals if the birds are healthy. The initial effect develops in 1–5 min and may be maintained for 30 min to 6 h.

Tiletamine–zolazepam at doses ranging from 20–35 mg/kg im produces similar levels of narcosis.

Raptors: at an initial dosage of 16–18 mg/kg im, ketamine produces varying levels of narcosis within 5–7 min. The peak effect is maintained for 10–15 min and can be further supplemented at 5 min intervals up to a total of 50 mg/kg im.

Tiletamine–zolazepam is used at 16–35 mg/kg im.

Ratites: at an initial dosage of 20–80 mg/kg im, the effect of ketamine is extremely unpredictable, although a measure of immobilization and analgesia is sometimes achieved. Ostriches are still liable to strike out with legs and wings and may be dangerous to handle. Unfortunately, there is still no suitable agent which can be recommended for this group.

'Equithesin' (pentobarbitone 9·6 g, chloral hydrate 42·6 g and magnesium sulphate 21·2 g with propylene glycol and ethanol in 1 litre of water). This combination has a reasonable safety margin when given by im injection into the pectoral muscles. It is suitable for small birds, poultry and raptors at a dose of 2·5 ml/kg in healthy subjects and 2·0 ml/kg in debilitated birds.

Alphaxolone–alphadolone. Unfortunately, the steroid mixture is too inconsistent in effect when given by im injection, but it can be recommended for iv administration to poultry and most raptors. At a dosage of 5–10 mg/kg iv, a state of hypnosis is induced immediately and this lasts for 5–10 min.

At 10–14 mg/kg iv, light surgical anaesthesia with some analgesia and muscle relaxation, is achieved lasting 5–7 min. In small birds, ip injection of 55 mg/kg sedates the subject, but less consistently than metomidate or ketamine, and with no advantages over those agents.

Atropine is useful in reducing secretions in the respiratory tract if injected 5–10 min before induction at a dosage of 0·05 mg/kg im. This is best injected into caged birds using a microlitre tuberculin syringe.

Surgical anaesthesia
General notes. Body heat must be conserved and this is particularly important in small or young birds. Several precautions should therefore be taken:

(a) Inflowing gases should be warmed and moisturized.

(b) The plumage should be left intact as far as possible, and only the immediate surgical site prepared with antiseptic solutions.

(c) A source of heat should be supplied under and above the bird. A simple heated pad or circulating-warm-water blanket under and a suitably angled lamp above the bird are ideal.

(d) Whenever possible the bird should be wrapped in aluminium foil during long periods of anaesthesia.

(e) Rectal temperature should be monitored.

However, sources of heat should be supplied judiciously to prevent overheating and burns.

Although birds are thought to be more efficient than mammals in compensating for haemorrhage by rapidly restoring blood volume (Djojosugito *et al.*, 1968), hypovolaemia and dehydration may still be a problem. Care must be taken to maintain haemostasis during surgery, and diathermy or microcoagulation is a valuable aid. As Klide (1973) pointed out, if a small bird has a blood volume of 100 ml per kg bodyweight, then a canary of 20 g has a blood volume of about 2 ml. A loss of 5 drops of blood would represent about 15% of the total—enough to produce decreased venous return, severe hypotension and cardiac arrest. We routinely inject small birds with isotonic saline sc using a microlitre syringe, and dextrose–saline is injected iv in poultry and raptors at an approximate rate of 5 ml/kg/h.

The position of the bird during anaesthesia is also important. Extreme abduction of the legs and wings must be avoided. Birds should not be retained on their backs for more than 20 min without being re-positioned. Perhaps because of the combined effects of abnormal posture, lowered respiratory muscle activity and poor venous return during anaesthesia, hypotension may develop quite rapidly, particularly in small species. However, birds must be moved carefully when anaesthetized and the neck given adequate support whilst they are turned. Similarly, it is important to avoid sudden alterations in intra-abdominal pressure to avoid visceral pooling and inadequate venous return to the heart. Airway patency must be checked frequently, and fluid accumulations in the lumen removed by suction. Airway obstruction is indicated by exaggerated abdominal and thoracic movements and by tail movements during inspiration especially if the bird is lying on its back. Squeaking sounds may also be heard. This may easily be confused with a lightening of anaesthesia. Small birds are unable to survive even short periods of apnoea, and as soon as this becomes apparent emergency action should be taken. Oxygen should be directed into the mouth, and thoracic massage instituted to assist ventilation. Delay will almost invariably be fatal.

The depth of narcosis must be continuously monitored during induction, especially in young birds, since anaesthesia will develop within seconds of intubation and delivery of potent agents such as halothane. The depth is assessed by response to pinching of the comb, wattles, pericloacal skin or toes. The corneal reflex and movement of the nictitating membrane ('third eyelid') persists throughout anaesthesia, although the eyelids often droop or close completely. The respiratory status of the bird is indicated clinically by colour changes of the comb and wattle. When the respiratory rate is depressed and the animal is hypoxic, the colour changes from bright red to deep purple. In adult birds, the heart rate can be determined by palpation of the carotid vessels in the neck.

Injectable anaesthetic techniques. Anaesthesia may be induced rapidly by iv administration of pentobarbitone, methohexitone or alphaxolone–alphadolone before intubation and transfer to maintenance with inhalational anaesthesia.

Pentobarbitone should be given iv very slowly to effect, since its safety margin is low. The dose required to achieve basal narcosis may range from 15 to 60 mg/kg. The depth of anaesthesia is best monitored by pinching the comb, and administration should be discontinued when the response is weak but still present. Light surgical anaesthesia of 10–15 min duration is usually achieved.

Methohexitone can be given by rapid iv injection at a dose of 4–8 mg/kg to produce 4–5 min of light anaesthesia.

Alphaxolone–alphadolone is safer than the barbiturates in most species of bird (not, e.g. in red-tailed hawks) and, after iv injection of 10–14 mg/kg, light surgical anaesthesia will last 5–7 min.

Inhalational anaesthetic techniques. Anaesthesia may be induced by mask inhalation of $N_2O:O_2$ (1:1) and 2–4% halothane supplied at a high flow rate to wash expired gases from the face. Once the bird is relaxed, it can be intubated and maintained on $N_2O:O_2$ (1:1) with 0·5–1% halothane or methoxyflurane. Similar gas mixtures are supplied if the intraclavicular sac is catheterized directly.

Small caged species are conveniently anaesthetized in 1 litre containers into which 0·2 ml of halothane or methoxyflurane has been sprayed onto cotton gauze taped to the side of the chamber. The bird must be observed closely since induction will occur within 30–45 s. As soon as the righting reflex is lost, the bird should be transferred to an open face mask or an insufflation technique with low concentrations of anaesthetic. Any bird above 100 g in weight, particularly psittacine species, should be intubated since the airways are easily obstructed. In very small birds, a plastic tube placed in the oesophagus will draw up fluid by capillary action and prevent its aspiration via the glottis. As Klide (1973) pointed out, a single drop of fluid may totally occlude the trachea of a 30 g parakeet. He also suggested that the tongue should be held forward by means of a small hook simply constructed from a paper clip to prevent airway obstruction. The trachea may be obstructed by airway secretions whether the bird is intubated or not, and the anaesthetist should ensure that gentle suction is available to remove accumulated fluid.

Domestic fowl more than 2 weeks of age are easily intubated without preanaesthetic agents, although the anaesthetist may prefer to intubate after injecting them with metomidate or after induction with anaesthetic gas mixtures delivered by mask. In adult cockerels, the larynx should be pushed anteriorly to counter the pressure exerted on it by the tip of the tube, whilst in hens the glottis is clearly visible behind the tongue if the beak is held open. Suitable endotracheal tubes can be constructed from silicone rubber or polyvinyl tubing. A rubber infant tube of 4 mm outside diameter may be used in adult hens. The tube should be long enough to reach as far as the syrinx but kept as short as possible to minimize dead space. The end bevel should be cut at an acute angle to facilitate passage into the trachea, and a rubber covered stiffener retained until the tube is in position. On no account should a cuff be inflated. The tube should be held in place with adhesive tape around the mandible.

Alternatively, anaesthetic gases may be delivered direct to the intraclavicular air sac by the method of Whittow & Ossorio (1970) already described. The catheter is inserted without preanaesthetic treatment and anaesthesia is induced directly by this route. This provides a simple method of artificially ventilating a bird in emergency but it must be pointed out that the trachea is unguarded, and regurgitated material can still be aspirated.

We prefer to sedate all birds with injectable agents, and then achieve the desired level of anaesthesia with inhalational agents. The bird is injected with 15 mg/kg of metomidate or 15 mg/kg of ketamine and then intubated as described earlier, connected to a Rees-modified T-piece system and supplied with $N_2O:O_2$ (1:1) and 0·5–1% halothane or methoxyflurane. The gas flow must be high to ensure efficient clearance of expired gases.

Once the bird is intubated and anaesthesia has been induced, the depth of anaesthesia has to be monitored continuously throughout the surgical period. We favour emptying the system of anaesthetics at 5 min intervals and flushing the air sacs by alternatively closing and opening the expiratory tail of the reservoir bag. Overdistension of the air sacs is prevented by escape of gas around the loose-fitting endotracheal tube. Gas flows should be about 3 times the respiratory minute volume of the bird. As a guide, an adult domestic fowl of 2·5 kg has a minute volume of about 770 ml, a 300 g pigeon a volume of 250 ml, and a small cage bird of 30 g a volume of 25 ml (Klide, 1973).

Recovery and post-surgical therapy

Recovery from inhalational anaesthesia is accelerated by administering air and O_2 directly to the respiratory tract of the bird until it has regained its righting reflex. Unless this simple precaution is taken, the high concentrations of anaesthetic agent which are released into the air sacs from the circulation may not be cleared by a poorly ventilated bird, and rapid uptake by the parabronchial capillaries may result in a fatal overdose.

Following anaesthesia with injectable agents, the bird should be allowed to recover in a draught-free, well-ventilated box. This should be heated to 35°C for large birds and to 40°C for small caged species or young chicks.

Most birds pass through an excitatory phase during recovery and may damage their wings whilst struggling. We wrap small birds and chicks in aluminium foil until they are completely recovered. The wings of poultry may be fixed over the back with adhesive tape, whilst raptors are best wrapped in a towel or body stocking. All stimuli, but particularly noise and bright lights, must be avoided.

Table 9.2. Domestic fowl: physiological data

Measurement	Values
Respiratory frequency (breaths/min)	15–35
Tidal volume (ml)	35
Minute volume (1/min)	0·7
Mean heart rate (beats/min)	300
Arterial blood pressure (mmHg)	138/85
Arterial blood pH	7·54
Pa O_2 (mmHg)	85
Pa CO_2 (mmHg)	29
Haematocrit (%)	35 (25–45)
Haemoglobin (g/100 ml)	10 (7–13)
Erythrocytes (10^6/mm³)	3 (2–4)
* Blood volumes (ml/kg bodyweight)	
Total	60
Expected terminal exsanguination	40
Safe maximum single sample	9
Mean temperature (°C)	40·0

* Archer (1965).

CHAPTER TEN

ORDERS LAGOMORPHA, RODENTIA, INSECTIVORA AND CHIROPTERA

ORDER LAGOMORPHA

Domestic rabbit (*Oryctolagus cuniculi*)

Croft (1964) emphasized the danger of vertebral fractures if the rabbit struggled or if they were restrained by their head or neck. Hence, an important requirement in rabbit anaesthesia is the availability of agents which can be given im or sc, preferably in the animal's cage to minimize handling and apprehension (Green, 1975).

Rabbits are difficult to anaesthetize with injectable agents. Indeed, Field (1957) considered albino rabbits such poor subjects for pentobarbitone anaesthesia that he proposed they should only be used in acute experiments. The animal-to-animal variability in response to barbiturates was also stressed by Dolowy & Hesse (1959), who considered pentobarbitone alone unsuitable for surgical anaesthesia, and recommended chlorpromazine (25–100 mg/kg im) followed by reduced doses of pentobarbitone (20 mg/kg iv). Croft (1964) found that chlorpromazine (15 mg/kg im) definitely potentiated pentobarbitone to prolong its duration of effect. Bree *et al.* (1971) recommended that chlorpromazine should be administered only

by the iv route (7·5 mg/kg iv) since high doses (25–100 mg/kg) given im cause necrotic lesions in the muscle. McCormick & Ashworth (1971) recommended that rabbits should be given acepromazine (1·0 mg/kg im) prior to methoxyflurane anaesthesia.

Nevertheless barbiturates, including pentobarbitone, thiopentone, thiamylal and methohexitone, have all been widely used in rabbits. Cottontail rabbits (*Sylvilagus floridamus*) were satisfactorily anaesthetized with iv pentobarbitone at doses of 30–50 mg/kg (Casteel & Edwards, 1965). We have used doses as high as 60 mg/kg iv slowly to effect before achieving true surgical anaesthesia in New Zealand White rabbits, and artificial respiration with O_2 was then virtually essential to prevent deaths. Thiopentone at 50 mg/kg of a 2·5 solution was recommended for induction by Lumb & Jones (1973), whilst thiamylal (1% solution) at 31 mg/kg given slowly iv to effect was considered preferable by Gardner (1964) and produced anaesthesia lasting 5–10 min with recovery occurring in 5–15 min. Methohexitone (10 mg/kg) given rapidly iv has proved to be a valuable agent for induction and endotracheal intubation of rabbits, and at 3 mg/kg iv as an adjunct to fentanyl–fluanisone neuroleptanalgesia (Green, 1975).

Paraldehyde was compared favourably with pentobarbitone by Pandeya & Lemon (1965), although they supplemented both these drugs with inhalation of ether for abdominal surgery. Paraldehyde im or ip induced narcosis in 20–30 min. In their hands, pentobarbitone at 30mg/kg iv resulted in a 20% mortality.

Hodesson et al. (1965) assessed various combinations of injectable CNS depressants including diazepam, propiopromazine and paraldehyde, followed by iv 'Equithesin' (p. 80), and still encountered variability and some mortality. They concluded that diazepam at 5–10 mg/kg im was a valuable adjunct to other CNS depressants, and this agrees with findings in our laboratory. We have used it at 5 mg/kg ip at the same time as fentanyl–fluanisone (0·3 ml/kg im) and obtained surgical conditions for 30–50 min. Although respiration is always depressed by this combination of agents, we have been impressed by the safety and ease with which anaesthesia can be induced.

Neuroleptanalgesia using fentanyl–droperidol at 0·22 ml/kg was recommended for rabbits by Strack & Kaplan (1968), either as the sole agent or supplemented with inhalational agents. The fentanyl–fluanisone combination has been used extensively in our laboratory at doses of 0·3–0·5 ml/kg, both as the sole agent for superficial surgery and for sedation to be followed by inhalation with $N_2O:O_2$ and halothane or methoxyflurane (Green, 1975). Sedation is accompanied by profound analgesia, although respiration is always depressed and significant bradycardia is usually encountered.

Dissociative anaesthetic agents have been assessed in rabbits with rather equivocal results. Phencyclidine and tiletamine produce catalepsy, but neither produce sufficient analgesia for surgical procedures (Chen & Bohner, 1968). However, it was claimed that if tiletamine administration (20 mg/kg im) was followed by chloral hydrate, injected slowly iv some 2–5 min after catalepsy developed, anaesthesia lasting an average of 1·5 h was produced with little change in respiration (Chen & Bohner, 1968). The combination of tiletamine and zolazepam was recently assessed in several laboratory species; it was interesting to note that the degree of CNS depression obtained was often unsatisfactory in rabbits, and surgical anaesthesia was not achieved (Ward et al., 1974). Ketamine, on the other hand, was claimed (Weisbroth & Fudens, 1972) to produce good surgical conditions for 15–20 min at 44 mg/kg im, induction taking 8–10 min and recovery generally being complete 30–45 min afer injection. Intramuscular injections of 22 mg/kg provided sufficient chemical restraint for superficial procedures. Lind-

quist (1972) recommended ketamine for intubation before maintainance of anaesthesia with methoxyflurane. However, from experience of ketamine gained in this laboratory (CRC) when dosages of 10–60 mg/kg im were assessed in rabbits, we concluded that this agent has very limited application in this species. The animals were sedated at the higher doses but analgesia and muscle relaxation were poor, and certainly not adequate for major surgery (Green, 1975). Subsequent work suggested that ketamine was only capable of providing surgical conditions if given iv to rabbits already sedated with xylazine (3 mg/kg iv) or diazepam (5 mg/kg administered ip or im).

The steroids alphaxolone–alphadolone were recommended for induction and short periods of anaesthesia in rabbits at 6–9 mg/kg iv (Green, 1978). The safety margin is far narrower in our experience than in cats, and respiratory depression is common. Nevertheless, we consider it to be a good agent for induction of anaesthesia and for endotracheal intubation, one half of a computed dose being injected rapidly iv and the remainder given to effect. The degree of sedation resulting from im injection is unpredictable and administration by this route cannot be recommended.

Atropine is given at the high dose rate of 2–3 mg/kg im (Betteridge, 1973), as it is rapidly degraded by the rabbit liver (Godeaux & Tonnesen, 1949; Stormont & Suzuki, 1970). The duration of anticholinergic effects varies greatly from strain to strain of rabbit.

Croft (1964) pointed out that the responses of rabbits to muscle relaxants are also different from most other terrestrial mammals. Suxamethonium and gallamine both produce spastic paralysis and fasciculation rather than relaxation. Suxamethonium may also give rise to an irreversible bradycardia with fatal results. Consequently, Croft (1964) recommended the centrally acting relaxant mephenesin for rabbits, and claimed that it was effective if given with pentobarbitone. Doses of 30 mg/kg of a 1% solution produce a flaccid paralysis lasting 5–10 min without altering respiration or cardiovascular dynamics.

A few miscellaneous injectable agents have been suggested for anaesthetizing these animals. Magnesium sulphate supposedly produced anaesthesia of 45–90 min duration at a dose of 100 mg/kg iv according to Lumb & Jones (1973), and this could be reversed instantly with neostigmine (0·35–0·63 mg/kg iv) together with pentylenetetrazol (10 mg/kg). Urethane (ethyl carbamate) at 1–1·6 g/kg ip as a 25–35% solution was recommended for acute non-recovery experiments (Croft, 1964; Lumb & Jones, 1973). However, the damaging effects on the rabbit cardiovascular system (blood components and blood vessels) reported by Bree &

Cohen (1965), quite apart from its known carcinogenic properties, indicate that this should not be used. Croft (1964) also commended tribromoethanol at 250 mg/kg in a 3% solution to produce variable degrees of narcosis within 5 min of ip injection. The same author suggested that α-chloralose was unsuitable for use in rabbits since very large volumes are needed and violent convulsive responses are often encountered. We agree that it is a poor narcotic when used alone, but when given to rabbits at 60–80 mg/kg iv after induction with methohexitone, followed by endotracheal intubation and IPPV with $N_2O:O_2$ (1:1), it still has a place in 'physiological' non-recovery preparations (CRC). Linzell (1964) recommended a combination of urethane at 500–800 mg/kg in a 30% solution with 50–80 mg/kg α-chloralose iv for physiological experiments in rabbits.

Rapson & Jones (1964) claimed that rabbits could be hypnotized if laid on their back and talked to in a rhythmic monotonous voice, whilst at the same time repeatedly stroking their abdomen. They alleged that the animals were then sufficiently unaware of stimuli to allow cardiac puncture and surgical exposure of the femoral vein for catheterization. There is some truth in this claim but nevertheless we commend chemical restraint and analgesia for all surgical interference (CRC).

Inhalational techniques have been widely reported. Wright (1957) described anaesthesia with ether vaporized in a semi-closed system. Others have commented adversely on induction with this agent due to the violent struggling, prolonged breath-holding, excess salivation and laryngospasm it provokes (Stevenson, 1964; Lumb & Jones, 1973).

Halothane with O_2 or with $N_2O:O_2$ gas mixtures has been described by several authors (Sherrard, 1966; Watson & Cowie, 1966; Wyler & Weisser, 1972; Steward et al., 1972; Wyler et al., 1972; Betteridge, 1973; Steward, 1973). In the technique described by Sherrard (1966), rabbits were placed in a clear rigid plastic box 40 × 25 × 20 cm and induced with $N_2O:O_2$ (2·5:1) followed by halothane at 1% concentration until the rabbit could be transferred to a mask and semiclosed circuit. Steward (1973) emphasized the need to maintain rabbits on halothane concentrations of 0·5–1% after induction at 3%, after Betteridge (1973) suggested that rabbits could tolerate up to 10% concentrations.

Methoxyflurane provides good relaxation and analgesia (Hoge et al., 1969), and can be supplied by face mask or endotracheal tube, or by mask containing a sponge on to which methoxyflurane is sprayed from a syringe (Sawyer, 1965). Many other communications confirm the value of methoxyflurane for rabbits (Freeman & Barley,

1965; Hoge et al., 1969; Murdock, 1969; McCormick & Ashworth, 1971; Freeman et al., 1972; Wass et al., 1974). Anaesthesia with $N_2O:O_2$ and methoxyflurane was commended by Kent (1971).

The difficulties of endotracheal intubation were emphasized by Murdock (1969) and many workers have performed a tracheostomy instead. Nevertheless, Schaffer (1965) intubated small rabbits with the aid of a Moore premature infant laryngoscope blade, whilst a larger paediatric blade with the terminal end slightly bent was used for 2–3 kg rabbits. A special mouth speculum was described by Hoge et al. (1969). Rabbits were intubated in the prone position some 30 min after sedation with acepromazine and paraldehyde by Freeman & Barley (1965). The technique consisted of passing a tapered plastic Cole endotracheal tube through a hole in a wooden dowelling 'gag' and into the trachea. More recently, Davis & Malinin (1974) described a reliable technique in which the animals were first deeply anaesthetized with halothane in O_2 via a face mask, and a 3–3·5 mm soft rubber endotracheal tube was then passed under direct vision with the aid of a neonatal laryngoscope blade. We use 3–3·5 mm outside diameter endotracheal tubes, passed under direct vision with a paediatric blade, after first inducing anaesthesia with 15 mg/kg of alphaxolone–alphadolone iv or 15 mg/kg of propanidid iv and spraying the larynx with 2% lignocaine.

Anaesthesia lasting 45–60 s can be induced with a $CO_2:O_2$ (1:1) gas mixture supplied either to a face mask or into an induction chamber. Alternatively, dry ice can be broken up and placed in the bottom of the chamber to liberate enough CO_2 to anaesthetize the rabbit in 15–20 s; the animal must be removed promptly at this stage to allow time for inoculation or cardiac puncture before it recovers (Hyde, 1962). Inhalation of agents supplied via a Magill system and Hall-type dog mask was described by Stevenson (1964), whilst Davis & Malinin (1974) used an endotracheal tube attached to a modified Ayres T-piece and a reservoir bag fitted with an excess pressure valve at its tail. A simple closed-circuit system for administration of cyclopropane or halothane to intubated rabbits was constructed from standard laboratory glassware by Watson & Cowie (1966). An even simpler unit was described by Betteridge (1973) constructed from plastic beakers and a 750 ml thin polyethylene bag, allowing rebreathing and soda-lime absorption. An alternative to these home-made units is described by Skartvedt & Lyon (1972).

Recommended anaesthetic techniques

Preanaesthetic management
Any animals which are sneezing and have lachrymal discharge from eye and nose, matted

hair on the inside of the fore paws, diarrhoea, or mucoid faeces, should be discarded from consideration. Such subjects immediately pose anaesthetic problems quite apart from the likelihood of diseases interfering with experimental findings. The animals should be housed in a well ventilated, ammonia- and draught-free environment at an ambient temperature of 14–16°C.

Rabbits can be fasted for up to 6 h but should be allowed free access to water prior to anaesthesia.

Physical restraint and handling

Most rabbits are timid and docile, but the occasional animal may box, bite, scratch and kick personnel who come within distance. There are 2 main dangers to the rabbit during handling. Firstly, high levels of catecholamines released into the circulation make it more susceptible to cardiac arrhythmias and subsequent anaesthetic failure. Secondly, it may kick backward with both hind legs, damaging its vertebral column so that it is left with an irreparable posterior paralysis.

The animal should be approached quietly in its cage, stroked gently over head and ears and spoken to in a quiet, monotonous voice before any attempt is made to lift it out or inject it for chemical restraint. It should then be grasped by the loose skin over the shoulders with one hand, whilst the other is stroked along its back, and slid under its hindquarters, until both hands can be used to lift slowly from the cage. It should then be held close in to the body and stroked whilst it is carried to work surface or induction box (Fig. 10.1).

Rabbits panic on a slippery surface, so they should always be placed on a rubber mat and held gently by an assistant for an injection. Alternatively, they should be placed directly into a restraining box or wrapped in a towel if they are being anaesthetized without assistance.

Chemical restraint and preanaesthetic therapy

Intramuscular injection should be given deep into the anterior or posterior muscle groups of the hindlimb (quadriceps and gastrocneumius muscles respectively), or into the triceps humori muscle of the forelimb using a 16 × 0·65 mm (23 gauge) needle.

Atropine at 1–3 mg/kg im or sc is advisable some 30 min before other agents are given.

The following selection of agents is chosen on

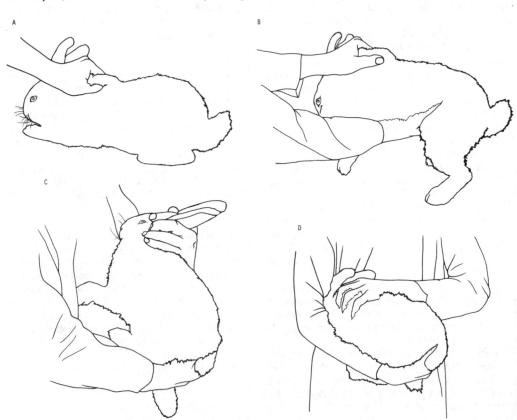

Fig. 10.1. Correct way to pick up and carry rabbits.

the basis of simplicity of im administration as well as desirability of effect, and is given in order of preference.

Fentanyl–fluanisone (or fentanyl–droperidol), 0·1–0·5 ml/kg im, produces sedation and analgesia of dose-dependant intensity and duration. At the mean dose of 0·3 ml/kg, the peak effect is reached in 5–7 min, and deep sedation accompanied by profound analgesia is maintained for 20–35 min. Respiratory depression is encountered at the high dose levels and bradycardia lasting 5–10 min develops about 7–10 min after im administration. The heart is partially protected from vagal inhibition by prior administration of atropine. In emergency, respiratory depression can be rapidly reversed with nalorphine at 1 mg/kg iv, and a supply of O_2 (2 litre/min) administered by mask or filter funnel placed loosely over the face will restore PaO_2 within minutes. This combination has been used in the anaesthetic management of several thousand rabbits over a period of 8 years in this laboratory (CRC) with a mortality of 0·2%.

Diazepam at 5–10 mg/kg im or ip provides good tranquillization and muscle relaxation but no analgesia. The time to effect is 3–5 min and the duration of effect is 2–6 h, although return to feeding may be delayed for up to 12 h.

Acepromazine at 1·0 mg/kg im tranquillizes rabbits in 5–10 min for a duration of 1–2 h.

Thiambutene and diazepam injected separately at 5 mg/kg and 1·0 mg/kg im respectively produce a state of deep sedation with good analgesia and adequate muscle relaxation in 5–10 min and lasting 1–2 h. Respiratory depression is readily reversed by nalorphine at 1 mg/kg iv.

Diazepam and ketamine injected separately at 5 mg/kg and 25 mg/kg im respectively produces a state of deep sedation accompanied by a moderate degree of analgesia.

Surgical anaesthesia

General notes. As respiratory depression is frequently encountered in rabbits, particularly if they are suffering from subclinical respiratory disease, it is important to have available a source of O_2 and a cone or mask supplying it to the face. Inhalational anaesthesia or neuroleptanalgesia techniques which are readily reversed with specific antagonists are indicated, and there are obvious advantages in ensuring a patent airway by endotracheal intubation.

Assessment of anaesthetic depth depends on the agent used. When barbiturates, alphaxolone–alphadolone or propanadid are injected to induce anaesthesia, the pedal reflex or response to pinching the heel is lost as light surgical anaesthesia is induced. Medium surgical anaesthesia has been attained when the palpebral reflex is lost, the rabbit fails to react when the ears are pinched, and when the pupils are moderately dilated and fail to react to light. Loss of the corneal reflex is a sign of dangerously deep anaesthesia in rabbits. Respirations should remain regular, even though they may be slow and of increased amplitude. Once the pupil is wide open and the eye assumes a pale mauve 'fish eye' appearance, the animal will be nearly dead (or dead) and emergency action with artificial respiration and O_2 is required. The loss of reflexes is slightly altered when inhalational agents are used, and they disappear in the order palpebral, pupillary ('light reflex' or 'photomotor reflex'), leg retraction, and reaction to ear pinch. Note that the best indicator of analgesia for surgical incision is the 'ear pinch reaction'.

When muscle relaxants are included in the anaesthetic protocol, the only reflex which indicates the loss of sensory perception is the response to light. Once the photomotor reflex is lost, it is reasonable to assume that the animal is unconscious, but analgesics will still be needed.

Injectable anaesthetic techniques. The marginal ear vein is much the simplest blood vessel to use and, provided it is dilated properly before injection is attempted (Fig. 10.2), can be punctured repeatedly. The hair should first be carefully shaved for 2–3 cm over the length of vein. The vessel can then be dilated by an assistant compressing it at the base of the ear, by massaging the whole ear, by heating it under a lamp or by rubbing the ear tip with a drop of xylene. Injection is made as distally as possible so that subsequent injections can be made more proximally into a patent vessel. A 25 × 0·65 mm (23 gauge) needle or 0·8 mm (21 gauge) butterfly needle are inserted, and the latter can be taped in place for sequential injection or continuous iv infusions. The cephalic and recurrent tarsal veins are convenient alternatives and are entered with 16 × 0·65 mm (23 gauge) needles.

The choice of injectable agent for induction and short periods of anaesthesia depends on the

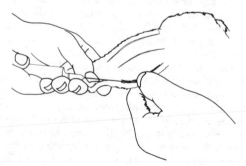

Fig. 10.2. Intravenous injection into marginal ear vein of rabbits.

experimental procedure. The following recommendations are made in order of personal preference.

Alphaxolone–alphadolone at 6–9 mg/kg iv, half given rapidly and the remainder slowly to effect, induces light surgical anaesthesia within 60 s, and this lasts for 5–7 min. Muscular relaxation is well developed at this dosage, and conditions are ideal for endotracheal intubation and maintenance with inhalational agents. Further increments of the agent at 4–6 mg/kg iv can be given to extend the anaesthetic period without cumulation developing. Respiration may be depressed but cardiovascular dynamics are relatively undisturbed. The induction and recovery periods are smooth and excitement-free, and the rabbits are fully recovered 30 min after a single injection.

Methohexitone (1% solution) at 10 mg/kg given rapidly iv produces a short period (2–5 min) of light surgical anaesthesia within 10 s. Full recovery takes up to 40 min and may be accompanied by muscle tremors and head shaking. The moderate degree of analgesia produced is similar to alphaxolone–alphadolone, but muscle relaxation is not as marked. Further increments of 4–6 mg/kg iv can be given to effect but a mild cumulative effect is observed if methohexitone is used for more than 30 min of maintenance.

Propanidid at 10–20 mg/kg by rapid iv injection produces an even shorter period of anaesthesia (1–2 min) accompanied by good analgesia and muscular relaxation. The rabbits recover quietly and are eating normally within 10 min of injection. This agent is ideal for rapid induction with minimal danger of subsequent physiological disturbance. We believe it is the agent of choice for endotracheal intubation for near-physiological preparations in rabbits.

Thiopentone (1·25% solution) at 30 mg/kg, half given rapidly iv and the remainder slowly to effect over 60 s produces light surgical anaesthesia within 60 s, and this lasts for 10–20 min. Induction is smooth but recovery may be accompanied by excitatory behaviour unless ataractics are used concurrently. We have no experience of thiamylal in rabbits but reports in the literature suggest that this too would be valuable at a 1% solution at about 30 mg/kg given slowly to effect.

Pentobarbitone (preferably as a freshly prepared 3% solution) still has a limited place for induction of basal narcosis or light surgical anaesthesia in this species if used with great care. It is rapidly detoxified in rabbits and the peak effect of a single dose will usually last only 10–20 min, although the time to full recovery and return of appetite is much more prolonged (1–4 h). A low dose of 15 mg/kg can be given rapidly iv to produce sufficient narcosis to lay the rabbit on its back for cardiac

puncture and exsanguination. If no other agent is available for maintenance of anaesthesia, freshly mixed pentobarbitone (3% solution) should be given very slowly to effect after the initial bolus of 15 mg/kg up to a total dosage of 45 mg/kg. An indwelling butterfly needle taped to the ear enables pentobarbitone to be given to effect relatively safely. Respiratory depression should be countered by supplying O_2 to the face of the rabbit.

In general, these injectable agents are unsuitable for maintaining anaesthesia in rabbits for long periods unless combined with inhalational techniques in a balanced regimen.

Inhalational anaesthetic techniques. Anaesthesia can be induced in rabbits using inhalational techniques alone. A gas mixture of $N_2O:O_2$ (3:2) administered through a Hall-type rubber cat mask and Magill system at a total flow of 2 litres/min is well tolerated by these animals. This mixture should be administered alone for 2–3 min before supplying halothane, enflurane or methoxyflurane in gradually increasing concentrations until induction concentrations of 2–3% have been reached (e.g. 1% increases allowing 2 min for equilibration of each). This slow stepwise technique avoids the panic struggling which occurs in rabbits when they are presented initially with inhalational agents at induction concentrations. Ether always provokes voluntary excitement in rabbits and, unlike cats or dogs, this species usually resents inhalation of high concentrations of halothane. Methoxyflurane is well tolerated but induction takes too long for convenience. The presence of N_2O enhances the peaceful acceptance of volatile agents and induction is accelerated (by the 2nd-gas effect described on p. 66).

Maintenance of surgical anaesthesia for periods up to 4 h can be achieved by inhalation of $N_2O:O_2$ (1:1) and 0·5–1·5% halothane, enflurane or methoxyflurane. However, these agents have a direct depressant effect on myocardium, and hypotension may be significant even when low concentrations are used. This, in turn, may be contra-indicated in an experiment where good perfusion and maintenance of microcirculation in organs is essential. Mask administration is satisfactory for periods of 30–45 min, but endotracheal intubation and administration via a Rees-modified T-piece is strongly recommended for longer periods of inhalational anaesthesia. The animal should be retained on a heated pad, and dextrose–saline or Hartmann's (Ringer's lactate) solutions administered at a rate of 10–20 ml/kg/h by continuous iv infusion.

If the experiment allows the use of injectable drugs, we prefer a balanced combination of injectable and inhalational agents, with the former chosen for reversibility (e.g. fentanyl) or for speed of response to administration (e.g. methohexitone). A sedative dose of fentanyl–fluanisone (0·3 mg/kg im) is administered before removal of the animal from its cage. 5 min later, it is transferred to the laboratory for clipping and preparation for surgery. A 0·8 mm (21 gauge) butterfly needle is taped in position in the marginal ear vein and a slow infusion of warm Hartmann's solution is started. Relaxation for endotracheal intubation is obtained by giving low doses of alphaxolone–alphadolone, propanidid, barbiturates, or the relaxant mephenesin as follows:

alphaxolone–alphadolone (4 mg/kg) by slow iv injection to effect.
propanidid (8 mg/kg) by slow iv injection to effect.
methohexitone (4 mg/kg) by slow iv injection to effect.
thiopentone (6 mg/kg) by slow iv injection to effect.
mephenesin (20 mg/kg) by slow iv injection.

Alternatively, $N_2O:O_2$ (1:1) (and 0·5% halothane if necessary) can be supplied by mask and Magill system to deepen anaesthesia for intubation. The larynx is sprayed with 2% lignocaine, and a 3–3·5 mm uncuffed endotracheal tube is passed under direct vision either with a paediatric blade and laryngoscope or with fibre-optic illumination. Insertion of the tube is performed during inspiration when the vocal cords are open, and counter traction on the laryngeal box is helpful as the tube tip is pushed between them. Complete relaxation is essential to success even if this entails transient respiratory depression. The animal can be ventilated with O_2 to reverse hypoxia very quickly once intubated. If intubation fails and the rabbit becomes hypoxic, O_2 should be supplied to the face by mask, and spontaneous breathing stimulated by gentle manual compression of the thorax or sternum. No further attempt should be made to intubate the animal until it has clearly recovered. It is worth noting here that when all other resuscitive measures have failed during respiratory emergency, the rabbit can be picked up by the hindquarters and swung backward and forward head down like a pendulum. This will often stimulate enough respiratory and cardiac activity to save the animal.

The rabbit can be maintained for long periods with a similar balanced regimen. The initial neuroleptanalgesic dose of fentanyl–fluanisone is supplemented by $N_2O:O_2$ (1:1) at a flow rate of 2 litres/min in a Rees-modified T-piece system (or Magill system for periods up to 1·5 h) to provide excellent surgical conditions. Small doses of fentanyl–fluanisone are given im at 0·15 mg/kg

every 30 min. If, during the procedure, it is found that particularly strong surgical stimuli such as clamping the aorta or rib retraction during thoracotomy elicit movement of the animal, then methohexitone at 3 mg/kg injected iv is instantly effective in deepening anaesthesia for about 10 min. This technique has the advantage that recovery is rapid even after 3–4 h of surgery. The rabbits will sit up within 30 min and appear normal in 1–1·5 h. If prolonged surgery is anticipated, pentobarbitone at 5 mg/kg is given iv instead of methohexitone and each injection will deepen anaesthesia for 30–40 min.

Acute non-recovery preparations may be required in pharmacological investigations. The anaesthetist should maintain these at as light a level of narcosis as possible, since deviation from normal physiological conditions will affect interpretation of test results. Several combinations have been assessed in this laboratory (CRC), and are recommended in order of preference. In each method, the rabbits are intubated and supplied with $N_2O:O_2$ (1:1) by IPPV.

(i) After induction with propanidid at 10 mg/kg iv, intubation and administration of $N_2:O_2$ (1:1), the rabbit is given 60–80 mg/kg of α-chloralose iv. The effect of propanidid is no longer apparent after a few min, and thereafter a state of basal narcosis–light surgical anaesthesia is maintained by the combined effect of α-chloralose (lasting 6–8 h) and N_2O. Fluid therapy and heat conservation are essential features of anaesthetic management for such prolonged periods.

(ii) After induction with fentanyl–fluanisone at 0·3 ml/kg im and inhalation of $N_2O:O_2$ (1:1) with halothane to deepen anaesthesia for intubation, the rabbit is ventilated with $N_2O:O_2$ (1:1) by IPPV. Fentanyl–fluanisone at 0·15 ml/kg is given im at 30–40 min intervals, and pentobarbitone at 3–5 mg/kg iv administered at 45–60 min intervals as required.

(iii) After induction with alphaxolone–alphadolone at 8 mg/kg iv, intubation and IPPV with $N_2O:O_2$ (1:1), further doses of steroid anaesthetic are given by continuous iv infusion at a rate of 6 mg/kg/h, commencing the 'drip' about 15 min after the initial induction dose.

Recovery and post-surgical therapy
Where applicable, the fentanyl–fluanisone mixture should be reversed with nalorphine unless it is considered preferable to maintain analgesia for a period. The rabbit should be laid prone to recover on a heated pad, and the endotracheal tube should be retained until laryngeal reflexes have been recovered. Antibiotics should not be administered until recovery is complete.

137

Table 10.1. Rabbit: physiological data

Measurement	Values
Respiratory frequency (breaths/min)	50 (35–60)
Tidal volume (ml)	20 (19–25)
Minute volume (l/min)	1·1 (0·8–1·2)
Mean heart rate (beats/min)	222 (205–235)
Arterial blood pressure (mmHg)	110/80
Arterial blood pH	7·35
Pa O_2 (mmHg)	—
Pa CO_2 (mmHg)	40
Haematocrit (%)	40 (30–50)
Haemoglobin (g/100 ml)	12 (8–15)
Erythrocytes (10^6/mm³)	6 (4–7)
*Blood volumes (ml/kg bodyweight)	
Total	70
Expected terminal exsanguination	35
Safe maximum single sample	7
Mean rectal temperature (°C)	38·3 (37·0–39·4)

* Archer (1965).

ORDER RODENTIA

Guinea-pig (*Cavia porcellus*)

Although the easiest of animals to handle physically, guinea-pigs are difficult to anaesthetize efficiently for reasons which have been reviewed (Hoar, 1969; Cannell, 1972; del Pozo & Armas, 1973; Thomasson et al., 1974; Green, 1975). There are several problems. Visible veins are fragile and difficult to puncture, and hence injectable agents are often given by the im, sc or ip routes at calculated dosages. Responses to injectable agents vary markedly with age, weight and dietary status (e.g. in the presence of ascorbic acid deficiency or low blood–glucose levels, detoxification may be prolonged). Computing accurate dosages on a bodyweight basis is difficult since the gastro-intestinal tract may contribute as much as 30–40% of the total weight if full of ingesta or as little as 18% if the animal is deliberately fasted. Adequate analgesia is difficult to achieve without deep anaesthesia unless potent sedative-analgesics are used. In addition, efficient gas exchange and lung ventilation are easily compromised for a number of reasons. The rapid respiratory rate of the normal guinea-pig (90–120/min in 800 g adults at rest) ensures rapid gas exchange but it also follows that any abnormality in the gas supply is soon translated to abnormal plasma concentrations (e.g. low O_2 in the inhaled gases will very quickly produce low PaO_2). The long airway (a total of 8 cm from nares to bronchial bifurcation in an adult) represents an extensive dead space to bodyweight ratio. The narrow airway imposes its own resistance to laminar gas flow, and this may be further constricted by the direct action of drugs.

Furthermore, it may be obstructed by viscid mucous secretions which are provoked by un-humidified, irritant anaesthetic gases (e.g. ether) in an already partially dehydrated animal (Cannell, 1973).

Atropine at dose levels of approximately 0·3 mg/kg and injected sc some 30 min prior to anaesthesia with ether was recommended by Lumb & Jones (1973), while the far lower dose rate of 0·04 mg/kg was given prior to ketamine by Weisbroth & Fudens (1972). However, atropine increases blood pressure in guinea-pigs according to Valenstein (1961), and has been associated with fatalities when used with ether and barbiturates (Cannell, 1972, 1973).

Reports on the value of ataractic, sedative or dissociative anaesthetic agents are also somewhat contradictory. Propiopromazine (20 mg/kg sc) was used by Tan & Snow (1968) as an ataractic adjunct for spinal analgesia, whilst Hopcroft (1966) recommended chlorpromazine (20 mg/kg sc) for the same purpose. Diazepam (5 mg/kg ip) produced sedation and relaxation but no analgesia in trials reported from this laboratory (Green, 1975). Neuroleptanalgesia with fentanyl–droperidol was reportedly effective in guinea-pigs (Rubright & Thayer, 1970), but Leash et al. (1973) observed self-mutilation in guinea-pigs within 7 days of im imjection of this combination. Our experience with fentanyl–fluanisone alone was unsatisfactory (Green, 1975). Analgesia took at least 15 min to develop to adequate levels, whilst muscle relaxation was poor and the animals retained a righting reflex even at very high doses (4 × the dose rate effective in rats or rabbits). However, when fentanyl–fluanisone was administered at the dose rate of 1·0 ml/kg im with diazepam (2·5 mg/kg ip), full surgical anaesthesia lasting about 60 min developed within 15 min and there were no mortalities attributable to anaesthetic failure in a large series of animals.

Thiambutene (5 mg/kg im or ip) and diazepam (2·5 mg/kg ip) have since been used with good results, the duration of surgical anaesthesia lasting up to 2 h. In each case, narcosis may be quickly reversed by nalorphine at 1–2 mg/kg ip (CRC). Pethidine has been given (2 mg/kg im) to supplement pentobarbitone anaesthesia and was considered useful (Maykut, 1958).

Ketamine was effective at 44 mg/kg im in producing light surgical anaesthesia for 15–25 min (Weisbroth & Fudens, 1972) but McCarthy et al. (1965) concluded that doses of 128–256 mg/kg im were needed for surgical anaesthesia of guinea-pigs when they were conducting some of the trials in the development of ketamine. Experience in this laboratory was different (Green, 1975). At dosages ranging from 10–200 mg/kg im, we were unable to

138

demonstrate surgical levels of analgesia or muscle relaxation, even though the righting reflex was lost. Nor were we able to achieve really satisfactory conditions if diazepam was given concurrently. Similarly, the tiletamine–zolazepam combination was unsuccessful in achieving surgical anaesthesia in guinea-pigs or rabbits, whereas it proved highly effective in other species (Ward et al., 1974).

Although amylobarbitone (50 mg/kg) and quinalbarbitone (20 mg/kg) have both been administered iv (Swanson & Fry, 1937), other workers have given barbiturates by the more convenient ip route in guinea-pigs (Carmichael & Posey, 1937; Croft, 1960; Schaffer, 1965; Hoar, 1969; Cannell, 1972, 1973). Various dosages of pentobarbitone have been suggested as effective and the extremes probably reflect the different criteria adopted for determination of 'satisfactory' anaesthesia. Mortality averaging 15% has been commonly experienced. Carmichael & Posey (1937) stated that a dose of 20–30 mg/kg ip was required for anaesthesia up to 120 min, but 15·6 mg/kg ip gave a 'sleeping time' of 35–190 min. Cannell (1972) was careful to weigh the animals accurately and used a dilute (1·5%) solution of freshly prepared pentobarbitone for good peritoneal absorption. He concluded that 37·5 mg/kg provided safe light surgical anaesthesia in animals between 200–750 g bodyweight, but 40 mg/kg was needed for deeper surgical anaesthesia. Kinsey (1940) could not detect sex-linked variability in response to pentobarbitone in guinea-pigs but noted that some tolerance developed after repeated administration. According to Croft (1960) the fatal dose is 56 mg/kg ip. Bemegride is an unhelpful antidote in this species, and Cannell (1973) recommends that manual assistance of respiration at 70–100 light presses/min over the sternum, and provision of O_2 to the oropharynx, is more likely to lead to successful resuscitation in the event of anaesthetic emergency. The curious squirming movements of guinea-pigs immediately after induction with barbiturates were noted by Croft (1960) who warned against interpreting this as a return to consciousness and hence for administration of further increments of drug. Becker et al. (1958) warned against the ip injection of pentobarbitone in pregnant females for foetal surgery, as this had an immediate adverse effect on the offspring. Similarly, the intrathoracic route was considered hazardous for the survival of the mothers when assessed by Thomasson et al. (1974). Pentobarbitone was found to act synergistically with local analgesics such as procaine to further depress cardiopulmonary function (Maykut & Kalow, 1955) but, with choral hydrate at 170–180 mg/kg ip, successful surgical anaesthesia was achieved by Valenstein (1961).

Thiopentone is not recommended for routine use in this species by Cannell (1973). At doses of 37·5 mg/kg ip he found that light surgical anaesthesia took 12 min to develop and lasted for about 38 min. The 'sleep time' was unduly prolonged to more than 6 h as compared with 2–3·5 h after pentobarbitone anaesthesia using 37·5 mg/kg ip. The same author found the depth and duration of CNS depression also varied after ip injection of methohexitone, but concluded that light surgical anaesthesia lasting about 6 min usually develops some 7 min after ip injection of 31·0 mg/kg. Fasciculations are sometimes seen during induction but disappear as anaesthesia deepens.

Inhalational anaesthesia with ether, halothane, methoxyflurane and N_2O has also been described (Hoar, 1964; Stevenson, 1964). Methoxyflurane was considered to be the inhalational agent of choice by Hoar (1964) since it did not provoke salivation or excess secretions in the respiratory tract (cf. ether), and administration by mask, chamber or closed circuit equipment was described. Induction took about 6 min, and the average recovery time was 35 min after 1–2 h of anaesthesia. A simple device for prolonged anaesthesia in guinea-pigs was recently described (Guthy, 1975). We use 0·5–2% halothane, enflurane or methoxyflurane in $N_2O:O_2$ (1:1) flowing at 2 litres/min and supplied to a face mask and Magill system or to an induction chamber (CRC).

Ether with air is often used for induction of anaesthesia in guinea-pigs in a jar or chamber, or by breathing air and vapour from cotton wool within a simple nose cone. Recovery takes about 5 min from withdrawal of the agent, but the animals do not regain full activity for 5–6 h. It is limited in application to short procedures up to 30 min and in our opinion, it should be avoided in this species because of its many disadvantages. Vomiting is easily induced; the irritant gas increases secretions and causes broncho-spasm with the attendant loss of airway patency; the animals may hold their breath for long periods to the extent that induction is prolonged and difficult; monitoring of anaesthetic depth is difficult and the animal may appear light at one moment and then suddenly in deep surgical anaesthesia; and, finally, irritation of the respiratory endothelium predisposes to respiratory infections, particularly after repeated administration.

Hyde (1962) described induction of anaesthesia in guinea-pigs with CO_2 liberated from dry ice in the bottom of a metal container. The animals were placed in the box on a wire grid to breathe in the high concentration of CO_2, and were anaesthetized in 10–15 s. Anaesthesia suitable for inoculation or cardiac puncture lasted 45 s and recovery took a further 60 s. We have piped $CO_2 : O_2$ $(1:1)$ into an induction chamber followed by mask administration for guinea-pigs, but do not recommend it for periods beyond 2 min actual administration (CRC).

Spinal analgesia has been described for abdominal, uterine and foetal surgery (Hopcroft, 1966; Tan & Snow, 1968; Thomasson et al.; 1974) and a method drawn from their collective experience is recommended on p. 141.

Recommended anaesthetic techniques
Preanaesthetic management
Guinea-pigs should be examined for their health status, and any animals with discharge from the nose or eyes or with diarrhoea should be eliminated from the experiment. Penicillin during and after surgical procedures is thought to cause delayed deaths during the post-operative period (Medd, 1977).

The animal should be fasted for 6 h prior to induction of anaesthesia since guinea-pigs are liable to vomit early during sedation and induction. When barbiturates are selected for anaesthesia, the guinea-pigs should be weighed after fasting for 12 h. Only then can an accurate dosage of injectable agent be calculated, remembering that the gut and contents may contribute about 40% of total bodyweight after a feed and only 18% after deprivation. However, it is important to remember that the subject may be dehydrated and hypoglycaemic after fasting for this length of time and replacement therapy with dextrose and fluids should be instituted early.

Physical restraint and handling
Guinea-pigs are docile animals which are easily held around the thorax and supported with the free hand (Fig. 10.3). Pregnant animals must be handled with great care.

Intramuscular injections are made with a 16 × 0·5 mm (25 gauge) needle deep into the anterior or posterior muscles of the hindlimb (quadriceps and gastrocnemius respectively). Intraperitoneal injection is the route chosen for many agents and can be given without assistance. The animal is held on its back, head down and to one side, and a 16 × 0·5 mm (25 gauge) needle inserted just laterally to the umbilicus, thus minimizing the risk of puncturing abdominal viscera (Fig. 10.4).

Chemical restraint and preanaesthetic therapy
Atropine. Although there is some doubt about the value of giving atropine to guinea-pigs, we recommend that they should be given 0·05 mg/kg sc about 30 min before other agents, particularly if ether is used for anaesthesia.

Diazepam at 5 mg/kg ip produces complete

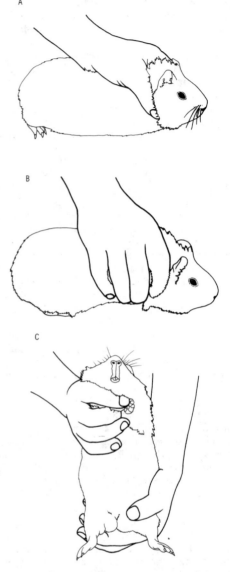

Fig. 10.3A. Correct way to grasp guinea-pigs around thorax.

Fig. 10.3B–C. Correct way to grasp guinea-pigs around thorax, and support if pregnant.

tranquillity and relaxation but no analgesia in guinea-pigs. It is particularly valuable for restraint when spinal analgesia is employed for abdominal surgery, as the guinea-pig can be taped out in position on a heated operating pad with strips of adhesive tape.

Thiambutene and diazepam at 5 mg/kg and 2·5 mg/kg respectively (ip or im) produces a state of neuroleptanalgesia with good muscle relaxation lasting about 2 h. The maximum effect is reached in 5–10 min after ip injection. Narcosis can be rapidly

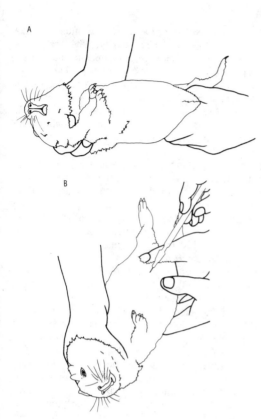

Fig. 10.4. Intraperitoneal injection in the guinea-pig.

reversed by administration of nalorphine at 2 mg/kg ip or im.

Fentanyl–fluanisone at 1 ml/kg im with *diazepam* at 2·5 mg/kg ip also provides deep neuroleptanalgesia within 10 min of injection. The peak effect is maintained for about 60 min. Narcosis is reversed by injection of nalorphine (2 mg/kg ip or im).

Alphaxolone–alphadolone at 40 mg/kg im (injected at separate sites because of the high volume) produces deep sedation with analgesia for 30–50 min, whilst the total 'sleep time' may last up to 90 min. However, probably because the drugs may be poorly absorbed from the injection site, the desired response is not always achieved.

Local analgesia
Local infiltration with 0·5–1% solutions of lignocaine may be used for surgery in conjunction with chemical restraint as above.

Spinal epidural analgesia is a valuable technique for all abdominal surgery in guinea-pigs, but particularly for caesarian section, for intrauterine and for foetal surgery. It is safe for the animal, the pups and the operator. The operation is facilitated by tranquillization with diazepam given 15–20 min

beforehand. An area over the lumbosacral space should be carefully shaved, the site of injection marked and the skin prepared aseptically. The animal is then laid on its side and the back arched. A 16 × 0·5 mm (25 gauge) needle attached to a 1 ml disposable syringe should be introduced into the lumbosacral space at a 30–40° angle and directed either caudoventrally or anteroventrally until it strikes the floor of the vertebral canal (about 1 mm from the skin surface). After ensuring that no blood or cerebrospinal fluid can be withdrawn into the syringe, 0·2 ml of warm 1% lignocaine solution should be slowly injected into the epidural space. Successful injection results in twitching of the hind limbs, followed by loss of active movements and relaxation and analgesia of the posterior half of the animal lasting up to 45 min. This can be extended if required by further injections of small doses of 1% lignocaine.

Surgical anaesthesia
General notes. Conservation of body heat is important from the moment the first agent is administered, and the animal should be draped with light cloths or aluminium foil and maintained on a heated pad. Ambient temperature in the immediate vicinity should be held at 37°C by judicious use of a 40 W light bulb directed over the animal.

Maintenance of a patent airway with minimum resistance and respiratory dead space is the prime concern in anaesthetic management of guinea-pigs, since nasal and oropharyngeal secretions become very viscid during anaesthesia and are liable to cause obstruction. The risks are minimized by frequent aspiration of secretions from the oropharynx using fine rubber catheters attached to suction and by lying the animals on their side to allow secretions to flow out. The neck should be extended to align the oral and nasal airways with the laryngeal inlet thus reducing physiological dead space. In addition, a soft polyethylene (2·5 mm) endotracheal catheter should be passed whenever possible and O_2 should be supplied to it. If this is not practicable, O_2 should be supplied by insufflation with a catheter directed into the oropharynx.

Assessment of anaesthetic depth is based on similar criteria to those described for rabbits. When barbiturates are used ip for induction, the pedal reflex is lost when light surgical anaesthesia develops. Attainment of medium surgical anaesthesia is indicated by loss of the palpebral reflex and when the guinea-pig fails to respond if the ear is pinched hard. We take the ear pinch reflex as the final guide before making a surgical incision. The anaesthetist can easily be confused by the characteristic squirming movements which are commonly seen in guinea-pigs soon after induction of anaesthesia with ip pentobarbitone. These are usually

141

manifested by hyperextension of one hindlimb, followed by flexion and contraction, in turn followed by a twisting movement of the whole body until a forelimb is extended. This may be repeated once or twice. It must not be interpreted as an indication of lightening narcosis.

The difficulty of giving injectable agents to effect by the iv route weighs heavily against the use of barbiturates, propanidid, or alphaxolone–alphadolone for surgery, since ip administration yields inconstant analgesia. We strongly favour maintenance with inhalational techniques or with neuroleptanalgesic techniques using diazepam and potent sedative–analgesics in combination (CRC).

Injectable anaesthetic techniques. Venepuncture with a 10×0.40 mm (27 gauge) needle attached to 1–2 ml disposable syringes is possible at 5 sites. The marginal ear veins may be dilated by rubbing between finger and thumb or by applying a little xylene to the ear-tip, and are then easier to enter. In male guinea-pigs, the pudic vein lying along the dorsolateral border of the extruded penis is a useful vessel for injections but can only be used after suitable analgesia has been provided. The lingual vein on the ventral surface of the tongue, the dorsal metatarsal and the anterior cephalic vein are useful alternatives, and injections in each are facilitated by good illumination and magnification.

Surgical exposure of the foreleg cephalic vein for indwelling iv catheters was recommended by Cannell (1973). A vertical incision of the lateral surface of the upper limb to a point about 5 mm distal to the cubital fossa is made. Gentle dissection of the forked aponeurosis of fascia attaching skin to underlying muscle exposes the junction with its valve dividing the basilic and cephalic systems. Closure of the skin wound is performed in one layer with 4/0 catgut or braided silk. This can be achieved under diazepam tranquillization and local infiltration with lignocaine (0·5% solution).

For those who master the technique of venepuncture in this species, methohexitone (10 mg/kg) given rapidly iv or alphaxolone–alphadolone (12 mg/kg) given slowly iv to effect can be used for both induction and short periods of anaesthesia. The steroids can then be given by 4 mg/kg increments at 10 min intervals to maintain anaesthesia for several hours without cumulation developing. Pentobarbitone can be given at a computed dose of 30 mg/kg, half rapidly and the remainder slowly to effect to produce light surgical anaesthesia lasting 15–30 min.

However, as most workers prefer a simpler approach, the following recommendations are made in order of preference.

Fentanyl–fluanisone (1·0 ml/kg im) with diazepam (2·5 mg/kg ip) provides good surgical conditions with excellent analgesia, muscle relaxation and loss of reflex activity. The peak effect develops in 5–10 min, is maintained for 60 min and complete recovery takes about 6 h. The respiratory rate is depressed but we have not encountered deaths either during the surgical and immediate postoperative period, nor in succeeding weeks. We have performed intrathoracic and intra-abdominal surgery in guinea-pigs anaesthetized with this combination.

Pentobarbitone can be administered ip to produce narcosis or light surgical anaesthesia. Dilute solutions (1%) should be freshly prepared and the dosage computed at 37 mg/kg after carefully weighing the fasted subjects. Peak effect takes 5–7 min to develop, light surgical anaesthesia usually lasts about 120 min or longer, while full recovery may take 12–20 h. However, the response is very unreliable in young and in old, obese, guinea-pigs (Cannell, 1973). Respiration is always depressed by pentobarbitone and it is virtually impossible to achieve sufficient depth of anaesthesia for intra-abdominal or intrathoracic surgery. According to Cannell (1973), the critical respiratory rate is about 25/min, below which anoxia and acidosis become irreversible. Constant aspiration of the oropharynx by suction, and a supply of O_2 by insufflation, are necessary if the animal is to recover. Nevertheless, Cannell (1972) commended pentobarbitone at 37 mg/kg ip for procedures requiring long periods of basal narcosis.

Methohexitone at 31 mg/kg ip produces basal narcosis within 4 min and this lasts for 18 min. In some individuals, light surgical anaesthesia is achieved in about 7 min from injection and then lasts about 6 min, but many animals appear to be resistant to methohexitone (Cannell, 1973).

Inhalational anaesthetic techniques. Inhalational anaesthesia can be induced directly by face mask (Hall's cat mask) and Magill system. Alternatively, anaesthetic gases can be delivered to an induction chamber equipped with an inlet connection, and with expiratory vents to allow exhaled CO_2 to escape. If neither piece of equipment is available, a face cone containing cotton gauze in which the anaesthetic vaporizes (p. 57) can be used. However, the animals should be intubated either by the oral route or by tracheostomy, whenever prolonged surgical anaesthesia is necessary. If this proves impracticable, then insufflation with fine catheters (1·0 mm) allows O_2 to be delivered directly to the trachea (although it does nothing to assist removal of CO_2). Endotracheal intubation is achieved under direct vision from an illuminated speculum ('Twinlite') or fibre-optic lighting. Suitable catheters can be constructed from soft polyethylene tubing (2 mm) and should be 4·5–5 cm in length.

The choice of agent depends on the duration of anaesthesia required and the availability of equipment in the laboratory. For induction and short periods of anaesthesia the following are recommended.

Carbon dioxide: O_2 (1:1) piped to a face mask or induction chamber, induces anaesthesia within 15 s, but it is only safe for periods up to 2 min (CRC). This allows time for simple procedures, e.g. subcutaneous implants, painless and careful placement of footpad injections, and for withdrawal of blood from the heart.

Alternatively, the method of Hoar (1962) can be used in which dry ice chips in the bottom of the intubation chamber produce gaseous CO_2 by evaporation. Guinea-pigs are unconscious within 10–15 s of breathing in the air:CO_2 mixture and must be removed at once for the surgical manipulation. They are anaesthetized for 45–60 s and then recover completely within another 60 s.

Methoxyflurane in N_2O:O_2. For direct induction of anaesthesia, we supply N_2O:O_2 (1:1) to an induction chamber or to a face mask at 1–2 litres/min and then add methoxyflurane by gradually increasing concentrations up to 2%. Induction is achieved smoothly in 4–7 min with this mixture. Anaesthesia can then be maintained with N_2O:O_2 (1:1) and 0·5–1·0% methoxyflurane administered by mask and Magill circuit (for 30–45 min) or by endotracheal tube and modified Ayres T-piece for prolonged anaesthesia. Low concentrations of methoxyflurane provoke neither respiratory secretions nor excess salivation but the agent does cause hypotension by direct myocardial depression, and the time to full recovery may be prolonged up to 10 h. At the present time, we believe methoxyflurane to be the inhalational agent of choice in guinea-pigs.

Halothane may be substituted for methoxyflurane and the same techniques employed as above. Induction is quicker (2–3 min) but considerably more care must be exercised by the anaesthetist in its administration. Cardiac arrhythmias may be induced by halothane in a frightened subject, and particular care must be exercised during intrathoracic surgery (Cannell, 1973). Maintenance concentrations of 0·5–1·5% are required with N_2O:O_2 (1:1). Full recovery is usually achieved in 15–30 min.

Recovery and post-surgical therapy
Where applicable, neuroleptanalgesia should be reversed with nalorphine unless post-surgical analgesia is required. The animal should be laid prone to recover in an ambient temperature of 30°C. The induction chamber can be heated by means of a 40 W bulb, and supplied with humidified O_2 to convert it into a recovery incubator.

Emergency treatment may be called for as a result of poor ventilation or drug overdosage. The first signs of danger are diaphragmatic breathing with exaggerated abdominal excursions. As depression progresses, spasms of the whole body are observed. A fall in respiratory rate to about 25/min necessitates immediate resuscitative treatment as the animal will otherwise soon die. Bemegride is unhelpful in stimulating the CNS of guinea-pigs during barbiturate overdosage (Cannell, 1973). Light intermittent digital pressure on the manubrium at a rate of 70–100/min encourages cardiac output and respiratory exchange, and has been used by Cannell (1973) to artificially ventilate guinea-pigs in respiratory failure with eventual full recovery. In final emergencies, respiration can sometimes be stimulated by swinging the animal gently through an arc head down.

Penicillin should not be given to guinea-pigs during the post-surgical period. We have administered oxytetracycline in the drinking water at 80 μg/ml and encountered no problems (CRC).

Table 10.2. Guinea-pig: physiological data (resting values)

Measurement	Values
Respiratory frequency (breaths/min)	90–150
Tidal volume (ml)	1·0–4·0
Minute volume (l/min)	0·1–0·4
Mean heart rate (beats/min)	155 (130–190)
Arterial blood pressure (mmHg)	90/56
Arterial blood pH	7·35
Pa O_2 (mmHg)	—
Pa CO_2 (mmHg)	40
Haematocrit (%)	40 (35–42)
Haemoglobin (g/100 ml)	14 (11–17)
Erythrocytes (10^6/mm³)	6 (4–7)
*Blood volumes (ml/kg bodyweight)	
Total	75
Expected terminal exsanguination	35
Safe maximum single sample	7
Mean rectal temperature (°C)	38·6 (37·2–39·5)

*Archer (1965).

Chinchilla (*Chinchilla villidera*)

Chinchillas are very susceptible to disease of the respiratory tract and, although ether has been used extensively for inhalational anaesthesia of these animals, it is contraindicated because of the slow recovery and post-operative pulmonary complications commonly encountered (Lumb & Jones, 1973).

143

Local analgesia with 1% hexylcaine solution infiltrated along the proposed incision line, following sedation with pethidine (15 mg/animal injected 30 min prior to operation), has been recommended for caesarian section (Hayes, 1955). Rapid recovery, the ability of the young to nurse within minutes, and the rapid return of appetite in the mother were cited as particular advantages of the technique. Epidural analgesia was used for caesarian section by Riddell (1952), entry to the spinal canal being achieved via the large lumbrosacral fossa just anterior to the iliac crests.

Thiopentone in dilute solution was injeected iv to effect for dental procedures (Boothe, 1953).

Tiletamine–zolazepam produced cataleptic sedation and surgical analgesia in chinchillas (Schulz & Fowler, 1974). They found that doses of 22–44 mg/kg im induced cataleptic sedation within 3 min, with recovery in 5–8 h depending on the dose level used.

Recommendations

Inhalational anaesthesia. Induction of anaesthesia in a chamber or by face mask using 2% methoxyflurane with $N_2O:O_2$ (1:1) is the safest means of anaesthetizing chinchillas. Maintenance by inhalation of $N_2O:O_2$ with a reduced concentration of methoxyflurane (0·5–1%) is achieved by face mask and Magill circuit or endotracheal tube and Ayres T-piece (as for guinea-pigs).

Neuroleptanalgesia with fentanyl–fluanisone (0·2 ml/kg im) and diazepam (2·5 mg/kg ip) is suitable for most surgical procedures and is accompanied by good analgesia, muscle relaxation and loss of reflex activity.

Ataraxy with diazepam (5 mg/kg ip) followed 20 min later by epidural spinal analgesia with 0·5–1% lignocaine, provides ideal conditions for caesarian section and intra-abdominal surgery.

Diazepam (5 mg/kg) and ketamine (20 mg/kg) injected separately im or ip provide deep sedation with analgesia and relaxation lasting 1–2 h.

Alphaxolone–alphadolone (20–30 mg/kg im–0·75 ml of commercial solution given in divided doses) produces deep sedation–surgical anaesthesia lasting 10–15 min with a time to full recovery of 60 min.

Coypu (*Myocaster coypus*)

The coypu has gained increasingly in popularity as an experimental animal, usually as an economic replacement for cats in certain experiments (Illman,

1961; Butterworth *et al.*, 1962). Information on the general management and husbandry of laboratory coypus is contained in articles by Flack (1964), Capel-Edwards (1967) and Davis & Shillito (1967). The aggressive nature of newly-trapped imports was emphasized by each of these authors, and a method of separating them from the group using a broom handle before grasping them by the tail about a third of its length from the base was described. Illman (1961) induced anaesthesia in coypu in 2–15 min by putting them into an airtight box containing a cotton-wool pad soaked with ether. Capel-Edwards (1967) restrained coypus by raising the tails by hand and gripping the animals between her rubber-booted feet before placing a mask containing a cotton-wool pad sprinkled with halothane over their face. Cambridge (1962) evaluated several anaesthetics in the coypu and concluded that ether is unsatisfactory for long periods of anaesthesia since pulmonary oedema develops, whilst halothane and cyclopropane are suitable. Halothane produces hypotension which can, it was claimed, be maintained at 50 mmHg for experiments lasting 6–8 h. Endotracheal intubation with tubes (3 mm) stiffened by a curved stylet can be performed by palpating the larynx, although apnoea usually occurs immediately after insertion (Lumb & Jones, 1973).

Pentobarbitone (40 mg/kg ip) was insufficient for surgical anaesthesia. α-chloralose (80 mg/kg ip) produced sedation but no anaesthesia, but a mixture of 50 mg/kg chloralose (50 mg/kg) and 500 mg-kg ethyl carbamate (urethane) was satisfactory, and a stable blood pressure of 70 mmHg or above was maintained in non-recovery preparations. Suxamethonium (2 mg-kg im) caused profound relaxation for up to 15 min without apnoea (Lumb & Jones, 1973).

Recommendations

We have no experience of anaesthetizing coypu in this laboratory. The method of handling by lifting the hindquarters off the ground by the tail and care in avoiding the sharp teeth and claws is clearly indicated by the reports quoted.

Inhalational anaesthesia with halothane or methoxyflurane with $N_2:O_2$ or O_2 is effective, but ether should be avoided. It is suggested that mask induction should be followed by endotracheal intubation (tube 3–3·5 mm) and supply by Ayres T-piece of gases at 1·5–2 litres/min (coypu 3–5 kg bodyweight).

Neuroleptanalgesia with fentanyl–fluanisone (0·2 ml/kg im) and diazepam (2·5 mg/kg ip) is tentatively suggested as a likely injectable technique for surgical interference.

144

Marmots (*Marmota caligata* and *Marmota monax*)

Marmots were recently selected for experiments on periodontal mechanics during long periods of inactivity such as hibernation (Noyes & Siekierski, 1975). These authors compared pentobarbitone, ketamine, and fentanyl–droperidol as injectable agents. They concluded that the neuroleptanalgesic combination gave superior results to the others and that the dosage should be related to nutritional status as well as absolute bodyweight. Young, well-fed specimens under 2 kg bodyweight needed 0·4 ml/kg of fentanyl–droperidol to produce surgical conditions lasting 30–60 min, whilst a lower dose computed at 0·3 ml/kg was adequate for adults and any undernourished marmot such as one just emerged from hibernation.

Recommendations
Inhalation of 2–3% methoxyflurane and O_2 or $N_2O:O_2$ (1:1) in an induction chamber followed by maintenance with 1% methoxyflurane and $N_2O:O_2$ (1:1) supplied to nose cone, endotracheal catheter or oral catheter, is the anaesthetic method of choice.

Injection of fentanyl–fluanisone (0·2 ml/kg im) and diazepam (2·5 mg/kg ip) provides satisfactory surgical conditions.

Squirrel (*Sciurus carolmiensis*)

Ether was reported as suitable for squirrels by Heuschele (1960). High doses of phencyclidine and promazine (5–10 mg/kg of each) did not provide surgical conditions in trials conducted by Seal & Erickson (1969). Tiletamine–zolazepam was considered useful in examining Formosan tree squirrels (*Callosciurus erythraeus*) at 8·3–17·0 mg/kg im (Gray *et al.*, 1974). Tribromoethanol was given orally to squirrels in doses of 0·12–0·16 mg/kg by Mosby & Cantner (1955). According to Stunkard & Miller (1974), fentanyl–droperidol is contraindicated in ground squirrels (*Citellus ungulatus*).

Recommendations
(i) Inhalation of methoxyflurane or halothane with O_2 or $N_2O:O_2$ (1:1).

(ii) Pentobarbitone at 40 mg/kg ip using a freshly-prepared 0·6% solution.

Prairie dog (*Cynomys ludovicianus*)

According to Lechleitner (1969), adult prairie dogs became cataleptoid in 2–5 min after injection of phencyclidine (8 mg-kg im). They were then maintained with ether administered by face mask.

Recommendations
(i) Inhalation of methoxyflurane with O_2 or $N_2O:O_2$ (1:1).

(ii) Neuroleptanalgesia with fentanyl–fluanisone (0·2 ml/kg im) and diazepam (2·5 mg/kg ip) is suggested as worthy of investigation.

Gerbils (Subfamily Gerbillidae)

Pentobarbitone was recommended by Marston & Chang (1965) at a dosage of 60 mg/kg sc in the loose skin at the back of the neck. Satisfactory anaesthesia lasting 2–3 h was obtained using standard 6% stock solution. Their reported mortality (2%) might indicate that pentobarbitone is safer for use in gerbils than in mice. The same authors considered ether an unsuitable agent for gerbils.

Ketamine injected im at 44 mg/kg followed 5 min later by face cone (open drop) inhalation of methoxyflurane was successful in Mongolian gerbils (*Meriones unguiculatus*). Rectal temperature fell by 1·5°C unless heat loss was prevented. Analgesia developed within 1·5 min and deep surgical anaesthesia in about 12 min after the gerbils were introduced to methoxyflurane. Induction was smooth and recovery took 40–100 min (Smith & Kaplan, 1974).

According to Petter (1967), gerbils should be handled with gloves to avoid severe bites, and the fragile tail should never be used to pick them up. However, Lumb & Jones (1973) recommend that they are grasped by the base of the tail and the scruff of the neck for restraint, as with mice.

Recommendations
Gerbils are so agile and adept at escape that we do not recommend gloves for handling. They should be grasped at the base of the tail, transferred to a grid so that they attempt to pull away, and then gripped by the scruff of the neck to present them for ip injection (see p. 151).

The simplest technique is to transfer them directly to an induction chamber and administer $CO_2:O_2$ (1:1) or $N_2O:O_2$ (1:1) before continuing with face cone or oral catheter administration of methoxyflurane (0·5–1%) and O_2 flowing at 200 ml/min. Alternatively, a combination of inhalational and injectable techniques can be used. We have deepened anaesthesia to effect with methoxyflurane and $N_2O:O_2$ after pentobarbitone (0·6% solution) at 30–40 mg/kg ip, ketamine at 40 mg/kg im, or diazepam at 10 mg/kg ip.

Hamsters (*Mesocricetus auratus* and *Cricetulus griseus*)

The need for constant handling of golden hamsters (*Mesocricetus auratus*) to prevent them becoming vicious was emphasized by Magalhaes (1967), while the techniques for handling the tamer Chinese hamsters (*Cricetulus griseus*) was described in detail by Yerganian (1967).

Pentobarbitone was evaluated for anaesthesia in golden hamsters by Orland & Orland (1946), who suggested a range of 50–90 mg/kg ip for 15–75 min of surgical anaesthesia. Similar doses of a pentobarbitone (up to 90 mg/kg) were recommended by Handler (1968) and Whitney (1963). Doses of about 60 mg/kg ip were recommended for the Chinese hamster by Yerganian (1967) using a 10×0.40 mm (27 gauge) needle and 0.25 ml tuberculin syringe for injection. Anaesthesia was induced in 3–5 min and was maintained for 0.5–3 h.

Ketamine was injected im into golden hamsters prior to maintenance with methoxyflurane to produce deep surgical anaesthesia (Strittmatter, 1972).

Neuroleptanalgesia was assessed in the golden hamster at this centre (Green, 1975). Fentanyl-fluanisone (1 ml/kg ip) produced analgesia and some sedation, but muscle tone and the righting reflex were retained. However, no excitatory behaviour was observed (cf. mice). When diazepam (5 mg/kg) was given ip concurrently, full surgical anaesthesia lasting about 60 min developed within 6 min. The respiratory rate was depressed from a normal 130 to a minimum of 75/min (i.e. well above the dangerous minimum of 40/min). We considered neuroleptanalgesia to be much superior to pentobarbitone or ketamine in hamsters. Conversely, Lewis & Jennings (1972) found fentanyl–droperidol to be unsuitable for hamsters, since the response was so unpredictable. They also noted

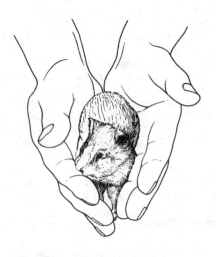

Fig. 10.5. Picking up hamsters in open hand.

that the LD_{50} was 7 ml/kg (i.e. 7 × the dose of fentanyl which we employed).

Carvell & Stoward (1975) recently described their experience with normal and dystrophic hamsters using halothane with $N_2O:O_2$. Induction in a plastic box with 3.5% (v/v) halothane in $N_2O:O_2$ (70:30) was quiet and rapid, and recovery occurred within minutes. A concentration of 2% halothane in the $N_2O:O_2$ mixture was sufficient for maintenance anaesthesia.

A detailed description of cardiac puncture for withdrawal of blood was provided by Turbyfill *et al.* (1962), whilst repeated sampling from the orbital sinus was described by Pansky *et al.* (1961) and from the tail by Bernard (1961).

Recommended techniques
Preanaesthetic management
Hamsters should not be treated with penicillin or streptomycin during or immediately after surgery as a high mortality is encountered. We have not found it necessary to deprive hamsters of food or water before anaesthesia and surgery.

Physical restraint and handling
Golden hamsters often resent handling and can inflict severe bites. Aggressive behaviour is more likely in older animals and those which have not been handled frequently. Chinese hamsters are generally more docile and are rapidly tamed by frequent handling. They may be picked up in the open hand for general examination (Fig. 10.5) and will remain docile as long as the animal's eyes are covered. Restraint for injections is best achieved by placing the hamster on the bench and gently pressing down on it with the palm of the hand. It is then grasped by the scruff of the neck between forefinger and thumb before being turned on its back for ip injection (Fig. 10.6).

Intraperitoneal injection is made with a 10×0.40 mm (27 gauge) needle about 3 mm lateral to the umbilicus. Intravenous injection is not difficult in the sedated animal and is made into the anterior cephalic vein with a 10×0.40 mm (27 gauge) needle. The vessel can be seen after careful shaving and swabbing of the anterior aspect of a forelimb. Venepuncture is considerably simplified by magnification and good illumination.

Chemical restraint and surgical anaesthesia
Carbon dioxide:O_2 (1:1) piped into an induction chamber is useful for rapid narcosis and anaesthesia of up to 2 min duration.

Ether on cotton wool in a suitable container can be used for anaesthesia of short duration without undue risk of post-operative respiratory compli-

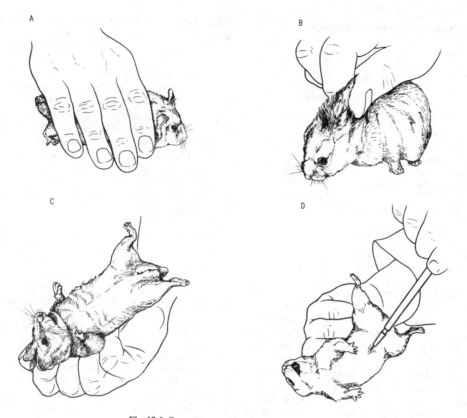

Fig. 10.6. Correct way to grasp hamsters for ip injection.

cations. As stressed earlier, it is important that small volumes of agent (1–2 ml) are sprayed onto the cotton wool and that the animal is separated from it by some form of grid or platform. The hamster can be removed to the bench for surgery, and anaesthesia maintained by a simple face cone.

Inhalation of halothane or methoxyflurane with O_2 *or* $N_2:O_2$ (1:1) can be supplied direct via a close-fitting face mask. Anaesthesia can be maintained with low concentrations (0·5–1·5%) of volatile agent and gas flow rates of 200–500 ml/min to face mask or oral catheter.

After sedation with ketamine (40 mg/kg im) or fentanyl–fluanisone (0·5 ml/kg ip) anaesthesia can be maintained with $N_2O:O_2$ (1:1) supplied to a close-fitting face mask at a flow of 500 ml/min. This is generally sufficient for abdominal surgery but can be supplemented with very low concentrations of halothane or methoxyflurane (0·5%) as required.

In the absence of inhalational apparatus or where free access to the oropharynx is required in the experiment, it may be necessary to use injectable agents only. Neuroleptanalgesia with fentanyl–fluanisone (1 ml/kg ip) and *diazepam* (5 mg/kg ip) is safe and effective in hamsters. The maximum effect develops in 5–8 min, is maintained for about 60 min, and the total sleeping time is about 120 min. Depression can be reversed by im or sc administration of nalorphine (1 mg/kg). Alternatively, *pentobarbitone* in a freshly prepared dilute solution (6 mg/ml) can be given at 36 mg/kg ip to produce 20–50 min of light surgical anaesthesia. *Chloral hydrate* may also be used (p. 80). *Alphaxolone–alphadolone* at 150 mg/kg ip (1·25 ml of commercial solution) produces deep sedation with analgesia for varying periods (20–60 min) while the time to full recovery may take 120 min.

Mouse (*Mus musculus*)

Although they must be the most frequently anaesthetized animal in laboratory work, mice are still the most difficult in which to achieve true surgical anaesthesia without some mortalities. Apart from anaesthetic overdosage, perhaps the most common causes of anaesthetic failure are excessive heat loss and hypothermia (related to the high surface:mass ratio), and rapid alterations in gas exchange (related to high metabolic and respiratory rate). In addition, the narrow airway is easily obstructed by excessive secretions or pharyngeal accumulations

Table 10.3. Hamster: physiological data

Measurement	Values
Respiratory frequency (breaths/min)	80 (30–140)
Tidal volume (ml)	0·8 (0·4–1·2)
Minute volume (l/min)	0·06
Mean heart rate (beats/min)	350
Arterial blood pressure (mmHg)	150/110
Arterial blood pH	7·39
PaO_2 (mmHg)	—
$PaCO_2$ (mmHg)	59
Haematocrit (%)	49 (39–59)
Haemoglobin (g/100 ml)	16 (2–30)
Erythrocytes ($10^6/mm^3$)	7 (4–10)
Blood volumes (ml/kg bodyweight)	
Total	78
Expected terminal exsanguination	30
Safe maximum single sample	5
Mean rectal temperature (°C)	37·4 (36·1–38·9)

of saliva. Other problems arise because of the small size of these animals. Because visible veins are fragile and difficult to enter, many workers avoid injecting agents to effect but give a single computed dose ip, and this is clearly a less controlled technique. The marked variation in responses to drugs associated with sex, strain, age, weight and nutritional status increases the risk of overdosage. Finally, anaesthesia is often required for groups of animals allowing the surgeon some 10–20 min for each procedure yet enabling him to move from mouse to mouse without delay. It is then inevitable that each animal will have less individual attention than ideal. The general aspects of anaesthesia in small rodents was outlined by Stevenson (1964) but there is surprisingly little detailed information on the anaesthesia of mice available in the literature. Early reports (Dolowy *et al.*, 1960; Jones & Krohn, 1960; Buchsbaum & Buchsbaum, 1962; Hagen & Hagen, 1964; Payne & Chamings, 1964; Brown & Dinsley, 1967) discuss the merits and drawbacks of a limited range of agents, but all agree that there is no single ideal anaesthetic method.

Preanaesthetic agents have received scant coverage. Tarin & Sturdee (1972) injected mice with atropine (0·04 mg/kg sc) and found that it reduced, but did not eliminate, the copious secretions associated with ether anaesthesia. Chlorpromazine (25–50 mg/kg im) was claimed to improve the chances of survival in mice if given together with pentobarbitone (40–60 mg/kg ip) compared with mice anaesthetized with pentobarbitone alone (90 mg/kg ip) (Dolowy *et al.*, 1960). It increased the duration of surgical anaesthesia, but it is difficult to draw significant conclusions from their paper since there was marked variation between groups. After assessing

metomidate, xylazine, acepromazine, ketamine and diazepam either alone or in combination with sedative-analgesics we concluded that diazepam (5 mg/kg ip) was much superior to other preanaesthetic agents (Green, 1975).

Lewis & Jennings (1972) reported that doses of 0·2–0·5 ml/kg im of fentanyl–droperidol were necessary to produce satisfactory neuroleptanalgesia in mice. However, in our trials, fentanyl–fluanisone alone produced hyperaesthesia in mice at all dose levels assessed. Analgesia was well developed but the animals would suddenly leap vertically in the air and run around their box if disturbed. Only when diazepam was administered concurrently at 5 mg/kg ip were surgical conditions obtained (Green, 1975).

Pentobarbitone (90 mg/kg ip) administered by 0·55 mm (24 gauge) needle and tuberculin syringe, produced surgical anaesthesia in some mice but there was wide variation and 20% mortality in results reported by Dolowy *et al.* (1960). Similarly, Tarin & Sturdee (1972) had such poor experience with pentobarbitone that they eliminated it from consideration in their search for an agent capable of producing well-controlled deep surgical anaesthesia. Variation in responses have been recounted by several authors. Diurnal periodicity and an influence of sociopsychological conditions on the responses of mice to pentobarbitone was described by Davis (1962), who found that the duration of anaesthesia was maximal between 1400 and 1600. Strain variation was noted by Payne & Chamings (1964) and Kalow (1962), while MacKintosh (1962) showed that hybrids of 2 inbred strains of mice responded more consistently to pentobarbitone than the individual inbred strains themselves. Brown (1959) found that male mice of several strains had a longer sleeping time than females using equivalent dose for weight but, according to Quinn *et al.* (1958), this sex difference only develops after the 1st month of life. A similar phenomenon was reported in mice after iv administration of hexobarbitone by Rümke & Noordhoek (1969) who noted a 25% longer sleep time in males compared with females of the same strain; 2 weeks after castration no such difference was detectable. The same authors (Noordhoek & Rümke, 1969) observed that these changes correlated well with liver content of microsomal cytochrome P-450. However, much of the evidence is conflicting (Jay, 1955; McLaren & Michie, 1956). Marked prolongation in sleeping time was noted in starved mice after administration of barbiturates (Conney & Burns, 1962), whilst the influence of chronic respiratory disease in increasing anaesthetic risk was emphasized by Stevenson (1964). Doubt has been cast (Bree & Gross, 1969; Stunkard & Miller, 1974) on the actual concentrations of pentobarbitone in commercial solutions and this, too, may account for some of the variability reported. We have certainly obtained more consistent responses using freshly mixed solutions without preservatives and accepting a short shelf life (CRC). Detailed information on the uptake, distribution and anaesthetic effect of C_{14}-labelled pentobarbitone after iv injection in mice was recently supplied in a valuable contribution by Saubermann et al. (1974).

Tribromoethanol at 125 mg/kg ip was recommended by Payne & Chamings (1964), who suggested that a 0.25% solution was not irritant to viscera and produced very good anaesthesia, whereas a 2.5% solution caused fibrous adhesions between stomach, liver and spleen. Martin (1959) diluted stock solution with ethanol to a 2.5% solution and gave 0.2 ml to each mouse, but when this was repeated by Jeffries & Price (1964) the mortality rate was high; 10% of the mice died within 6 h of injection and a further 20% regained consciousness but died within the next 5 days. Tarin & Sturdee (1972) assessed this agent at 370 mg/kg ip and, although anaesthesia was satisfactory, the mortality at 3 months was 35–40%. Autopsy examination revealed fluid distension of the stomach and intestine, and it was concluded that intestinal ileus was the cause of death. We found that this drug produced excellent surgical anaesthesia in mice at 125 mg/kg ip, but some batches and some strains of animal died of intestinal complications whilst others did not. It is now no longer used in this laboratory (CRC). However, tribromoethanol has only been evaluated in solution with amylene hydrate, and it is possible that the latter could be responsible for the intestinal lesions.

Ketamine was recommended at 44 mg/kg im for mice by Weisbroth & Fudens (1972)—who claimed that surgical anaesthesia was obtained and animals recovered in 15–30 min—and by Stunkard & Millar (1974), who also gave atropine (0.04 mg/kg im). However, we have been unable to attain satisfactory anaesthesia with this drug in mice at doses ranging from 20–300 mg/kg im or ip, even when given with xylazine or diazepam (CRC). Unless there is very marked variation in response to ketamine in mice, it is difficult to understand this disparity in results.

Steroid anaesthesia with alphaxolone–alphadolone was evaluated in trials by Child et al. (1971). Injections were made into the tail veins of mice to produce a mean 'sleep time' of 11 min at a dose of 24 mg/kg with no fatalities. As judged by loss of righting reflex (AD), the therapeutic index $(LD_{50}:AD_{50})$ was approximately 30 as compared with 7 for thiopentone, 7 for methohexitone, 8 for propanidid and 8.5 for ketamine. However, since the dose required for a useful sleep time was 24 mg/kg, and the LD_{50} was 48 mg/kg, the margin for error is probably only about 2:1. We have used alphaxolone–alphadolone for periods up to 4 h in mice giving 6 mg/kg iv at 15 min intervals after an initial dose of 20 mg/kg iv, and have found it an ideal injectable agent by that route. The absence of tolerance or of cumulative effects developing is particularly valuable (Green et al., 1978).

Ether has traditionally been used for inhalational anaesthesia in mice, usually administered by simple open-drop methods (e.g. on cotton wool in a jar followed by maintenance with a simple face cone). This has the obvious merit of low cost and simplicity. However, the disadvantages of respiratory tract reaction to such an irritant agent, and provocation of excessive mucous secretions, pulmonary oedema and airway obstruction have been emphasized (Payne & Chamings, 1964; Tarin & Sturdee, 1972). These authors considered this agent to be 'highly unsuitable' for mice since, in addition, it was so difficult to maintain a consistent level of surgical anaesthesia.

Halothane has also been used in mice but with mixed success. Tarin & Sturdee (1972) found that the margin of safety was too narrow for simple methods of administration and felt that, in the absence of an assistant, precise control would not be possible even with more sophisticated equipment. We have recently used enflurane to anaesthetize mice, and found it to be very similar to halothane (CRC). Most commentators agree that methoxyflurane is the safest agent to use whether by simple open-drop methods or with sophisticated apparatus (Hagen & Hagen, 1964; Pindak & Kendrick, 1969; Tarin & Sturdee, 1972). Several advantages have been cited. Surgical anaesthesia is easily maintained and it is difficult, even deliberately, to kill the mouse. The post-operative survival rate is 100% with no lesions evident at autopsy. Furthermore, it does not require the presence of an assistant to act as anaesthetist. The long recovery time of 10–20 min can be an advantage because surgery about the head and neck can be performed without the encumbrance of masks or tubes after administration is terminated. In addition, it can be used in cheap, compact apparatus and up to 3 mice may be induced as a batch. Finally, methoxyflurane is non-explosive and is relatively safe for man (McCaffrey & Mate, 1963; Corssen et al., 1966).

Short periods of anaesthesia have been achieved by inhalation of CO_2 in air (Hyde, 1962), whilst Payne & Chamings (1964) recommended a $CO_2:O_2$ (1:1) mixture for up to 10 min anaesthesia, emphasizing the desirability of this method for cardiac puncture since respiration and venous return to the heart are both stimulated. We do not agree that this is safe for 10 min and would not advise administration for more than 2 min (CRC).

Various circuits and pieces of apparatus for inhalation anaesthesia of mice have been described. Low cost, simplicity, ability to achieve anaesthetic concentrations of volatile agent at low gas flows, and the need to anaesthetize groups of mice simultaneously, have been the most desirable requirements of such sets. Induction chambers have been described using everyday laboratory ware e.g. bell jars (Hagen & Hagen, 1964), coffee jars (Hoge, 1966; Gandal, 1967) or desiccators (Tuffery, 1967). A more sophisticated chamber was designed by Mulder & Brown (1972) in which CO_2 was absorbed with soda-lime, and air was circulated by a fan so that the whole unit could be kept closed. The features of an induction chamber which we consider essential are a perforated platform or grid between the animal and volatile agent to prevent skin or mucous membrane contact burns, an inlet to allow piped O_2, $CO_2:O_2$ (1:1), $N_2O:O_2$ or other anaesthetic gas mixtures to be supplied if required, and an escape exit for exhaled air to prevent build up of CO_2 around the animal.

The simple apparatus incorporating flowing gases described by Hagen & Hagen (1964), was modified by Tarin & Sturdee (1972) to allow overflow gases to be used to induce a 2nd or 3rd mouse whilst the 1st was under surgery. Payne & Chamings (1964) organized an operating surface such that ether, CO_2 or trichlorethylene could be supplied to several face masks at the same time for batch anaesthesia, whilst Smith et al. (1973) described a more complicated apparatus involving a mechanical respirator supplying an inlet manifold from which several animals could be anaesthetized with halothane at the same time. A version of the 'copper kettle' vaporizer was designed to supply known concentrations of volatile agent to rodents but it required cooling (Reese & Nunn, 1961). Attention was drawn by Sebesteny (1971) to the inefficiency of converted human or veterinary anaesthetic apparatus run on open circuit as described by Marley & Payne (1962) and Cook & Dorman (1969), even when provided with mouthpieces suitable for mice (Warren, 1964; Jacobs, 1967). Sebesteny (1971) designed a halothane vaporizer based on principles outlined by Luschei & Mehaffey (1967). A rather simpler calibrated halothane vaporizer was designed by Parbrook (1966) in which a standard 500 ml/min flow of O_2 was held constant and halothane concentrations were calibrated for a temperature of 20°C using a Hook & Tucker halothane meter. This set was later modified by Parbrook and its use was recently described by Carvell & Stoward (1975). Other designs have been described, some very simple (Mauderly, 1975), others more sophisticated (Simmons & Smith, 1968; Krahwinkel & Evans, 1972; Mulder, 1973; Smith, 1973), while Boutelle & Rich (1969) designed a unit suitable for anaesthesia during irradiation. We have used the unit designed by Sebesteny (1971), modified only by passing the gas mixture over a test tube of warm water for humidification, and can recommend it on the basis of 6 years' experience. The only disadvantages are the expense of the flowmeters and the easily damaged valves incorporated in them (CRC). Similarly, we have modified the Parbrook vaporizer unit (Parbrook, 1966) to incorporate gate clamps as valves and a 2nd test tube of water for humidification of gases, and found it effective (CRC). This is constructed very cheaply from existing laboratory glassware and plastic tubing.

A few reports on monitoring cardiovascular parameters in mice exist in the literature. Weeks & Jones (1960) describe a technique for making direct blood pressure measurements by connecting a chronic indwelling catheter from an abdominal artery to a pressure transducer. Indirect methods have involved measurements of the arterial pulse in the tail (Van Proosdij-Hartzema, 1954; Dowd & Jones, 1968). A microphone was used to detect systolic endpoint by Friedman & Freed (1949). An electronic technique based on a beam of light transmitted through the tail has been used in mice to measure flow varying with application of cuff pressure (sphygmomamometer) (Van Nimwegan et al., 1973).

Recommended anaesthetic techniques
Preanaesthetic management
The importance of using mice from barrier-maintained colonies free of chronic respiratory disease (CRD) cannot be overemphasized. Having obtained such mice, it is also worth maintaining them behind a simple barrier system as suggested from this laboratory by Cooper et al. (1977) while they are on experiment. Treatment with antibiotics is contra-indicated during anaesthesia and surgery, although there may be value in adding tetracyclines to drinking water at 55 μg/ml after surgery as suggested by Tarin & Sturdee (1972).

Physical restraint and handling
Mice should be lifted from their box by the base of the tail held between thumb and forefinger and immediately transferred to the grid cage top or a cloth surface, e.g. the coat of the handler. As it attempts to escape, the mouse is grasped by the loose scruff of the neck between thumb and forefinger, the tail is gripped between the 4th and 5th fingers, and it is presented for ip injection belly uppermost (Fig. 10.7). Mice are liable to climb up

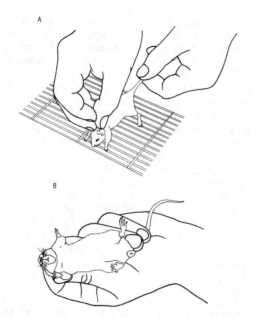

Fig. 10.7. Correct way to grasp and hold mice for ip injection.

their own tail if this is gripped tightly at the tip, and then bite the handler.

Various methods of restraint have been devised to allow easy access to tail veins for injection (Taber & Irwin, 1969; Stevenson, 1964) or for long periods of immobilization with minimal stress to the animal (Danscher, 1972). We favour a small clear plastic cylindrical holder, fitted with a plunger to adjust for length of animal at one end, and a notched window at the other for access to the tail (Fig. 10.8).

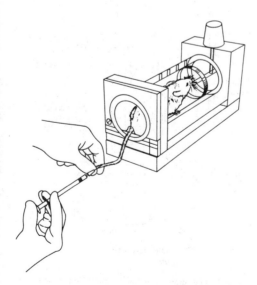

Fig. 10.8. Restraining device for mice and rats.

Intraperitoneal injections are made 2–3 mm lateral to the umbilicus using a 10 × 0·40 mm (27 gauge) needle, with the mouse lying on its back and slightly head down. Intravenous injection is achieved via a lateral tail vein or by the dorsal metatarsal vein using 10 × 0·40 or 0·35 mm (27–28 gauge) needles. Puncture of the tail vein is simplified by adequate restraint, warming the whole mouse under a lamp, and dipping the tail in warm water (40–50°C) for 1–2 min before making the first attempt. Needles can then be taped in place with adhesive tape around the tail. When it is important to ensure that accurate volumes of liquid are infused wholly iv, the needles can be inserted after surgical exposure of the vein under magnification and tied in place with ligatures. Sequential injections can then be given over many hours. The dorsal metatarsal vein can be clearly seen if the hair is clipped and swabbed with alcohol, and entry is facilitated if performed under magnification.

Chemical restraint and preanaesthetic treatment

Atropine at 0·04 mg/kg should be given sc into the loose scruff of the neck about 30 min before other agents.

Neuroleptanalgesia is effective in mice if the commercial fentanyl–fluanisone solution is diluted 1/10 in normal saline and given at 0·1 ml/30 g ip after injecting diazepam at 5 mg/kg ip. Maximum effect is reached in 2–3 min and is maintained for 60–90 min. Sleep time varies from 70–120 min, while the time to complete clinical recovery with return of appetite may take up to 12 h. Respiratory rate is depressed, but not dangerously so in our experience. Mortality is very low provided due attention is paid to body temperature and hydration.

Alphaxolone–alphadolone given ip at 60–90 mg/ kg (i.e. 5 mg per 20–30 g mouse or 0·6 ml of commercial solution) produces varying degrees of narcosis from sedation to light surgical anaesthesia. The wide therapeutic index in mice would suggest this to be an excellent agent for mice, but poor uptake im or ip and the relatively large volumes for injection limit its usefulness.

Surgical anaesthesia

General notes. Strict attention must be paid to conservation of body heat in so small an animal. This can be achieved by placing a heated pad under the animal and warm lamps overhead, taking care not to overheat the animal. Heat loss can be minimized by supplying gases already warmed and humidified to minimize latent heat of evaporation losses from the respiratory tract, by wrapping exposed surfaces in cotton gauze drapes or aluminium foil, and by keeping areas shaved and swabbed for surgery to a minimum.

Maintenance of a patent airway and good

oxygenation is the next prime concern of the anaesthetist. This is achieved by giving atropine at 0·04 mg/kg sc, pharyngeal aspiration with fine polyethylene catheters attached to suction, insufflation by oral catheter with a high concentration of O_2 and a supply of O_2 to induction and recovery chambers, and by lying the mice on their side with neck extended to provide minimum expiratory resistance to laminar flow.

Assessment of anaesthetic depth is based on the respiratory rate, and corneal, tail-pinch and pedal reflexes. The last observation is the most reliable indication of the development of surgical anaesthesia in mice.

Injectable anaesthetic techniques. Once the anaesthetist has mastered the art of venepuncture in mice (lateral tail vein or dorsal metatarsal vein) there are several options for induction of anaesthesia, depending on the period of anaesthesia required. We prefer them in the following order.

Alphaxolone–alphadolone (20 mg/kg iv) by slow injection (0·3 ml of a 1/10 dilution of the commercial preparation) produces deep anaesthesia with analgesia and good relaxation within 10 s. The maximum effect is maintained for 5–8 min, sleep time averages 10 min and the time to full recovery is 20–30 min. Further increments (6 mg/kg iv) can be given at 15 min intervals via an indwelling needle in the tail vein or via the catheterized jugular vein for long periods of stable anaesthesia. So far we have only attempted to maintain anaesthesia in mice for periods up to 4 h and we have observed no cumulative effects or tolerance in this time.

Propanidid (20 mg/kg iv) by slow injection produces deep surgical anaesthesia for 2–3 min and the mice recover completely within 10 min.

Methohexitone at 6 mg/kg by slow iv injection induces anaesthesia within 10 s. This lasts 3–4 min and full recovery occurs in about 50 min. Some accumulation is apparent if sequential injections are given to extend the anaesthetic period.

Thiopentone (30–40 mg/kg iv) by slow injection produces light surgical anaesthesia in 10–15 s and this lasts for 10–12 min. Accumulation is very marked with this agent and incremental doses should not be used for prolonging anaesthesia.

The alternatives if the operator chooses to inject by other routes are more limited.

Neuroleptanalgesia with fentanyl–fluanisone and diazepam provides good surgical conditions as described earlier. The drugs can be given ip or sc but the full effect develops more slowly by the latter route. Fentanyl–droperidol is equally effective.

Pentobarbitone should be freshly prepared from powder at 5 mg/ml in warm saline to obtain maximum consistency in response (alternatively,

stock commercial 60 mg/ml solution should be diluted 1/10). Dosage varies with so many factors that a trial group should be anaesthetized before each experiment if this is feasible. In toxicological tests involving administration of an agent to anaesthetized mice, a control group should receive the same dose of pentobarbitone as the groups under assessment. About 40 mg/kg ip should produce basal narcosis, but surgical anaesthesia may require doses from 50–90 mg/kg ip. Narcosis develops in 5–7 min and a plateau maximum effect is maintained for 20–40 min; the sleep time is approximately 120 min, whilst the time to full recovery may be 6–24 h. The need to prevent heat loss is particularly important when pentobarbitone is used, and O_2 supplied either locally to the individual, or to a recovery incubator in the case of groups, is mandatory if the mice have been deeply anaesthetized.

Mephenesin (100 mg/kg ip) produces approximately 10 min of profound central muscle relaxation without apnoea in mice. This should be administered after fentanyl–fluanisone (0·05 ml of 1/10 diluted solution ip) pentazocine (2 mg/kg ip) or with a low dose of pentobarbitone (20 mg/kg ip) to provide surgical conditions for a short period.

Inhalational anaesthetic techniques. Volatile agents and gases can be supplied to mice in induction chambers, or else by nose cones connected to flowing gases with the volatile agent actually within the cone (Fig. 7.1) or by insufflation catheters carrying mixtures to the pharynx or to a tracheostomy. Where possible, a properly

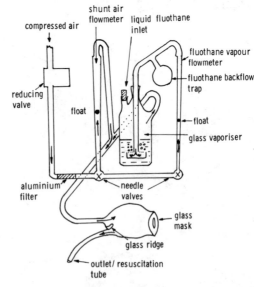

Fig. 10.9. Line drawing of home-made halothane anaesthetic apparatus (Sebesteny, 1971).

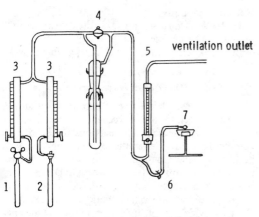

ventilation outlet

Fig. 10.10. Anaesthetic circuit specially designed to operate at low flow rates. 1 oxygen; 2 nitrous oxide; 3 flowrators; 4 vaporizer; 5 G.A.P. meter; 6 gate clamp; 7 mask on operating table (Carvell & Stoward, 1975).

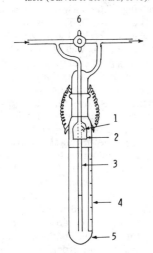

Fig. 10.11. The all-glass vaporizer. 1 spout; 2 glass cowling; 3 central column; 4 scale of halothane concentrations %; 5 reservoir; 6 2-way tap. The arrows indicate the direction of gas flow (Carvell & Stoward, 1975).

designed vaporizer should be used, and a rodent respirator (IPPV) should be considered for prolonged anaesthesia. Details of the construction of the Sebesteny apparatus are given in Fig. 10.9. Alternatively, the Parbrook halothane vaporizer is cheaper to construct and is simple to use. Laboratories serviced by glassblowers are recommended to construct the modification described by Carvell & Stoward (1975) shown in Fig. 10.10 and 10.11. Any of these units can be used to vaporize halothane, enflurane or methoxyflurane, but need calibrating for each agent.

Premixed $CO_2:O_2$ (1:1) is useful for rapid anaesthetic induction within seconds in a chamber, and is suitable for inoculations or cardiac puncture.

Maintenance should not be attempted for longer than 2 min.

Methoxyflurane with O_2 or air is the volatile agent of choice for inhalation by whatever delivery system. Induction is smooth and rapid (1–3 min) if mice are introduced to a chamber in which methoxyflurane on gauze (0·5–1·0 ml in 1 litre chamber) has been allowed time (say, 10 min at room temperature) to evaporate, and they can then be transferred to the delivery system of choice for surgery. Provided body temperature is maintained, there is little danger of killing mice with this agent even during prolonged periods of anaesthesia. Recovery is smooth, but the period to full recovery may be very prolonged (up to 24 h), depending on the duration of administration. Gas flows of 100–500 ml/min and concentrations of 0·5–2% methoxyflurane are necessary for anaesthesia.

Halothane with O_2 requires more care on the part of the anaesthetist, and it is unsafe to induce a group of mice together. However, the rapid smooth induction within 1–2 min, the excellent surgical conditions obtained and the rapid recovery (2–3 min) make it a valuable agent if it is vaporized in properly designed equipment.

Ether retains a useful place in mouse anaesthesia in spite of the disadvantages already outlined. It is inexpensive and can be used in the simplest of containers in the absence of other preferred methods. It is likely to remain a favourite amongst zoologists and others working under field conditions for its very simplicity. However, to avoid unnecessarily high concentrations of ether being used, measured volumes (2–4 ml) should be sprayed onto gauze in the container.

Table 10.4. Mouse: physiological data

Measurement	Values
Respiratory frequency (breaths/min)	180 (100–250)
Tidal volume (ml)	0·15
Minute volume (l/min)	0·024 (0·011–0·036)
Mean heart rate (beats/min)	570 (500–600)
Arterial blood pressure (mmHg)	113/81
Arterial blood pH	7·4
PaO_2 (mmHg)	—
$PaCO_2$ (mmHg)	50
Haematocrit (%)	40 (35–45)
Haemoglobin (g/100 ml)	15 (10–20)
Erythrocytes (10^6/mm^3)	9 (7–11)
*Blood volumes (ml/kg bodyweight)	
Total	80
Expected terminal exsanguination	35
Safe maximum single sample	7
Mean rectal temperature (°C)	37·4 (35·5–39·0)

*Archer (1965).

153

Under no circumstances must chloroform be used in laboratories or animal houses for rodent anaesthesia or euthanasia. Not only is this agent hepatotoxic, but minute traces in the environment have been shown to interfere seriously with the breeding performance of male mice (Tuffery, 1967).

Hypothermia. Neonates may be cooled in an ice–water slush at 1–2°C for 20–30 min, and retained with elastic bands on a piece of sponge soaked in ice cold water for the duration of the operation. This technique is commonly used for thymectomy of 1–2 day old pups. On completion of the operation, the pups should be dried on paper tissue, warmed to 37°C in an incubator, and returned to their original cage as a group to join a single unoperated littermate. They should be rubbed in the original bedding to ensure that they acquire the dam's scent, thus minimizing the risk of cannibalism when she is eventually returned to them some 15 min later.

Recovery and post-surgical therapy
The animals should be dried and allowed to recover in a warm environment at an ambient temperature of about 35°C. A suitable incubator can be constructed from clear rigid plastic provided with a facility for piped O_2 or 95% O_2:5% CO_2 to be supplied through a simple humidifier. In the absence of inflowing O_2, it is important to ensure that air circulates within the chamber to ensure that dangerous pockets of CO_2 do not build up locally.

Tetracyclines (55 μg/ml) may be given in drinking water after recovery is complete. Mice usually drink straightaway when awake, but may need tempting to eat with crushed oats, flaked maize or other palatable mixtures.

Voles (*Microtus* and *Clethrionomys* spp)

Short-tailed field voles (*Microtus agrestis*) and the larger longer-lived Orkney vole (*Microtus orcadensis*) are both tractable and easily handled (Ranson, 1941; Leslie *et al.*, 1955; Chitty, 1967). Bank voles (*Clethrionomys glareobus britannicus*) on the other hand, are agile and jump more readily (Steven, 1967). They should be grasped by the base of the tail and scruff of the neck as described for mice.

Ether and pentobarbitone were each used for anaesthesia of voles (*Microtus ochrogaster*) by Richmond & Conoway (1969). They preferred pentobarbitone (60 mg/kg ip), claiming that it produced 3 h of anaesthesia. Lee (1969) gave pentobarbitone (60–90 mg/kg) by the im route to achieve 15–20 min of surgical anaesthesia. Penicillin and streptomycin should not be used in voles post-operatively (Lumb & Jones, 1973).

Recommendations
(i) *Methoxyflurane* with O_2 is the safest method of anaesthetizing voles.
(ii) *Pentobarbitone* at 60 mg/kg ip is well tolerated.

Rat (*Rattus norvegicus*)

Healthy rats which are free of chronic respiratory disease (CRD) are excellent subjects for anaesthesia. Few aberrant reactions to the drugs commonly used in anaesthetic management have been recorded. Conversely, rats with the gross pulmonary lesions associated with CRD are poor risks, and mortality may occur during anaesthesia or in the post-operative period. Pathological changes which may influence the outcome of anaesthesia include damage to tracheal epithelium resulting from ammonia accumulation in holding boxes (Gamble & Clough, 1976), and lymphocyte cuffing, narrowing of the airway, as well as frank pneumonitis (Lamb, 1975). The advantages to the anaesthetist of using specified-pathogen-free (SPF) or gnotobiotic animals is well recognized (Stevenson, 1964), and has been quantified in comparisons between conventional and barrier-maintained animals (Davey, 1962; Paterson & Rowe, 1972). The high incidence of low-grade changes in the respiratory tract of rats was revealed in the histological screening of several breeding colonies by Lamb (1975). The ubiquitous distribution of CRD with frank symptoms and macroscopic lung lesions was considered likely to invalidate many experimental findings (Newberne *et al.*, 1961).

Other sources of variation affecting the outcome of anaesthesia are associated with age, sex, strain, husbandry and nutritional status of the rat. The limited ability of the liver in young animals to metabolize drugs to glucuronides was demonstrated by both Lathe & Walker (1957) and Brown *et al.* (1958). It is perhaps not surprising, therefore, that young rats are more sensitive than adults to pentobarbitone and ether (Weatherall, 1960), and to hexobarbitone (Griffith & Farris, 1942).

According to Moir (1937) and Crevier *et al.* (1950), female rats are more sensitive to pentobarbitone and to hexobarbitone than males, although this sex difference does not develop until the 4–5th week of life (Quinn *et al.*, 1958). Collins & Lott (1968) noted that female Wistar and Long-Evans rats were less likely to recover from pentobarbitone (72 mg/kg ip) than males. In addition, female rats are much more sensitive than males to the neuromuscular blockade induced by d-tubocurarine (Wolf *et al.*, 1964). Strain sensitivity to N_2O was demonstrated by Green (1968), who found that those rats with the highest leukocyte count before anaesthesia had the most significant depression in cell numbers afterwards.

154

The influence of husbandry practices on anaesthetic responses was discussed by Keplinger et al. (1959). Pentobarbitone was demonstrably more toxic to rats when the ambient temperature was lowered from 30 to 15°C (Setnikar & Temelco, 1962). Rather surprisingly, rats which had been fed a low-calorie diet were relatively resistant to pentobarbitone (Peters & Boyd, 1965).

Although most laboratory rats are best handled without gloves, there are occasions in dealing with particularly vicious animals when it is prudent to wear protective boning gloves as suggested by Cisar (1973) or prevent bite wounds by techniques suggested by Davies & Grice (1962), Evans et al. (1968) or Redfern (1971). The animal can be physically restrained in the 'hammock' designed by Danscher (1971), rolled in a towel or suitable cloth (Griffith & Farris (1942), secured in clamps (Hill et al., 1960), or in devices described by Keighley (1966), Lawson et al. (1966), Sholkoff et al. (1969), or Wilson (1969). A similar apparatus was described for restraint of rats undergoing long periods of ECG monitoring (Osborne, 1973).

A number of ataractic and neuroleptanalgesic combinations have been assessed in rats. Fentanyl–droperidol (0·2 ml/kg im) was recommended by Jones & Simmons (1968) for intraabdominal surgery. The righting reflex was lost in about 8 min, the rats were completely immobilized for 30–60 min and had recovered in 1–2 h. Similar results were reported by Lewis & Jennings (1972) who used a dose of 0·13 ml/kg im for dental procedures. Garcia et al. (1975) diluted fentanyl–droperidol 1 in 10 (2 mg droperidol and 0·04 mg fentanyl per ml) and mixed this with atropine at 0·004 mg/ml to reduce secretions and the vagal inhibitory effects of fentanyl. They then gave this mixture at 4·5 ml/kg ip followed 15 min later by pentobarbitone (1·25% solution) at 15 mg/kg ip. Deep surgical anaesthesia was achieved with a mortality of 7%. Females were significantly more sensitive to this combination of agents than males, and both sexes were more responsive to the agents after midday compared with injections made between 0900 and 1000. When deep anaesthesia of 2 h or greater duration was required, a further dose of 15 mg/kg of pentobarbitone was given ip. Experience in this laboratory over a period of 9 years (CRC) with fentanyl–fluanisone has been favourable. At a dose of 1·0 ml/kg im, many surgical procedures can be safely achieved and, where better muscle relaxation is required, an ip injection of diazepam at 2·5 mg/kg is an effective supplement (Green, 1975).

The influence of atropine on the heart rate of rats has been studied (Tipton & Taylor, 1965; Secord et al., 1973), whilst the effect of training on cardiovascular dynamics was discussed by Tipton (1965).

Experience with ketamine in rats has been very variable. Weisbroth & Fudens (1972) claimed that 44 mg/kg im was suitable for surgery including laparotomy but McCarthy et al. (1965) recommended doses of 80–160 mg/kg. Youth et al. (1973) suggested that the best results were obtained in rats if ketamine was given at 60 mg/kg im followed 5 min later by pentobarbitone at 21 mg/kg ip. Deep surgical anaesthesia lasted at least 60 min and mortality was low. Ketamine at 100–120 mg/kg ip together with atropine at 0·8 mg/ml to reduce salivation was claimed to be effective for minor surgical procedures in rats by Markovsky & Orentreich (1976). The cardiovascular system of rats was shown to be depressed by ketamine (Chang et al., 1969). Halothane was shown to prolong its duration of activity (White et al., 1975). Ketamine at 60 mg/kg im is an effective immobilizing agent, but the lack of muscle relaxation and variable degree of analgesia attained fails to provide surgical conditions (Green, 1975).

Tribromoethanol was recommended for rats by Payne & Chamings (1964) in spite of the intraperitoneal fibrous adhesions noted at autopsy and the high volume (10 ml) needed for ip injection. We assessed this agent as a 2·5% solution in rats and gained a favourable impression of its anaesthetic properties at 300 mg/kg (surgical anaesthesia for 45 min). However, autopsy revealed extensive adhesions and a fragile intestinal muscularis which could be easily stripped from dissected viscera (Green, 1975).

The variability in response of rats to barbiturates has already been emphasized. Payne & Chamings (1964) claimed that pentobarbitone at 20 mg/kg ip was a safe dose for albino Wistar rats in their colony, but caused an unacceptably high mortality in their hooded Norwegian strain. This is a very low dose for rats, since most commentators recommend dose rates of 30–40 mg/kg ip for light surgical anaesthesia and up to 50 mg/kg ip for deep surgical levels (Lumb & Jones, 1973; Routtenberg, 1968; Paterson & Rowe, 1972). Chloral hydrate has been suggested (Valenstein, 1961) to supplement pentobarbitone and reduce the dosage of the latter to 35 mg/kg ip, but this combination may lead to pulmonary oedema. Chlorprothixene was suggested by Rye & Elder (1966) as a suitable agent for use with pentobarbitone, but the barbiturate dosage needed is still 40 mg/kg ip and the postoperative recovery time is unduly prolonged. Shearer et al. (1973) studied the cumulative median LD_{50} of pentobarbitone after administration of progressively increasing doses to 7 different strains of male rats and found that albino rats has a significantly lower LD_{50} than pigmented strains, and were generally more sensitive in their responses. The LD_{50} averaged 60–70 mg/kg when the results were pooled, emphasizing the narrow therapeutic index.

Methohexitone iv into a caudal vein was used by Medd & Heywood (1970) to induce anaesthesia for intubation and repeated administration of gases to rats. They concluded that the best technique was to inject an induction dose of about 7 mg/kg iv followed 5–10 s later by a further 0·3–0·5 of the original induction dose. Recovery was smooth and the animals resumed normal eating habits very quickly. However, the authors warned that metho-hexitone-induced apnoea is rarely transient as in cats or dogs, but is quickly followed by cardiac failure unless immediately resuscitative measures are taken.

Hexobarbitone has been used for short periods of anaesthesia at 100 mg/kg ip but the drug is poorly tolerated by young rats and is accompanied by high mortality (Griffith & Farris, 1942).

It has been proposed that a 20% solution of ethanol in saline can be injected at 20 ml/kg ip to produce about 1 h of complete relaxation, with phenoxybenzamine (3 mg/kg) added to minimize bleeding (Florsheim, 1968).

The value of alphaxolone–alphadolone in rats was established in the early pharmacological studies of Child et al. (1971) but it has been little used subsequently. At a dose level of 6 mg/kg iv a 'sleep time' of 12 min was recorded with no sex variation noted. Experience in this laboratory where dosages ranging from 12–30 mg/kg have been given im or ip suggests that the response is too variable to recommend by these routes, although a mean dosage of 20 mg/kg ip is safe. However, this is an excellent agent if given iv at 10–12 mg/kg. Medium depth surgical anaesthesia of 5–12 min duration is safely achieved and this can be prolonged by incremental administration of 3–4 mg/kg at 20–25 min intervals (Green et al., 1978).

Of the inhalational agents, halothane, methoxy-flurane and ether are commonly used. Paterson & Rowe (1972) described a method of anaesthetizing germ-free rats within their cages in an isolator. Halothane (3%) with O_2 at 5–6 litres/min was necessary for induction, but the concentration was reduced to 1·5% for maintenance. They commented on the smooth induction and complete recovery in 20–40 min, and concluded that it was an ideal agent for rats. Payne & Chamings (1964) were less enthusiastic about halothane, and preferred ether for induction followed by maintenance with tri-chloroethylene, emphasizing that the latter agent is exceedingly safe. Methoxyflurane is popular in the anaesthesia of rats for the reasons described earlier for mice (Molello & Hawkins, 1968). However, much of the investigational work to examine the nephrotoxicity of methoxyflurane was carried out in rats (Mazze et al., 1973; Cousins et al., 1974;

Cook et al., 1975), and exposure to low con-centrations was shown to produce marked polyuria and morphologic lesions typical of fluoride-induced nephrotoxicity (Cook et al., 1975). We have recently used enflurane in rats at concentrations ranging from 0·5–2% in $N_2O:O_2$ (1:1), and found that anaesthesia was rapidly and smoothly induced, and the animals recovered within 5 min of ceasing administration (40–50 min anaesthetic period).

The equipment described for administration of inhalational agents to mice can be adapted for rats. Larger face masks are used, or the animals can be intubated. Simple methods of administering ether to rats were described by Griffith & Farris (1942).

Really precise control of inhalational anaes-thesia can be achieved only after endotracheal intu-bation. Griffith & Farris (1942) performed tracheo-stomy and insufflation with ether via a glass catheter of about 1 mm outside diameter. They paralysed respiration with d-tubocurarine (1 mg/kg im) during open-chest surgery. Kluge & Tveten (1968) also described endotracheal intubation for intrathoracic surgery in rats. Duke et al. (1971) connected the halothane vaporizer designed by Sebesteny (1971) to a stiff polyethylene tube inserted through a tracheostomy, and successfully maintained anaesthesia for hypophysectomy. Jaffe & Free (1973) passed an endotracheal tube through the larynx after first inducing deep anaes-thesia with halothane administered by a nose cone. The tube was constructed from a 80 × 2·10 mm (14 gauge) stainless-steel cannula. These authors emphasized the importance of minimizing the total airway dead space. They also quoted Adolph (1949) as calculating tidal volume (ml) as 0·0062 times the bodyweight in g (approximate estimation). Medd & Heywood (1970) constructed endotracheal tubes for laryngeal passage from polyethylene tubes of 1–1·5 mm outside diameter.

Hypothermia as a means of anaesthetizing newly born rats was described by Weisner (1934). The pups are cooled to 2°C, when they will fail to react to sensory stimuli, and surgery (e.g. thymectomy) can be performed during the next 3–10 min. Gradual rewarming is allowed at ambient tem-perature for 10–30 min before they are warmed in the palm of the hand for 20 min.

Physiological measurements relating to cardio-pulmonary function have been reported. Denckla (1970) published useful information on the minimal metabolic O_2 requirements of rats, and the anaesthetic requirements were discussed by White et al. (1974). ECGs have been recorded for a number of experimental purposes but the anaesthetics themselves may interfere with in-terpretation (Hafkesbring & MacCalmont, 1937; Kohn & Lederer, 1938). ECGs from rats suffering from nutritional deficiencies have been recorded by

Fig. 10.12. Picking up rats by gentle but firm hand encircling neck and thorax.

Hundley *et al.* (1945), Ensor (1946) and Hill *et al.* (1960). More recently, Osborne (1973) described a technique for obtaining ECGs from restrained but conscious rats. Systolic blood pressure was measured by plethysmographic and microphonic methods in the early studies of Byrom & Wilson (1938) and Williams *et al.* (1939) and, more recently, a technique using a Doppler ultrasonic flowmeter was described (Newman & Looker, 1972).

Recommended anaesthetic techniques
Preanaesthetic management
The need for healthy rats free from CRD, preferably used in experiments as soon as they are obtained from a barrier-maintained colony and before they have contact with other rats, is as important in this species as in mice. It is our experience that SPF animals present minimal anaesthetic risk, whilst rats which have been

Fig. 10.13. Lifting rats from cage by base of tail.

housed with others under conventional conditions are often unable to withstand more than 1–2 h of anaesthesia however much care is taken (CRC).

Time spent in frequent handling before experiment is also an investment, as rats are easily tamed and enjoy gentle stroking. They are then much easier to anaesthetize with minimal stress to animal and operator.

Food, but not water, should be withheld for 6 h prior to anaesthesia if intraabdominal surgery is to be performed.

Physical restraint and handling
Rats should be approached quietly and without hesitation, since they are easily frightened by tentative and jerky movements of the hands. Most laboratory rats are docile creatures, especially if adapted to handling as suggested above. They should be handled without gloves to avoid grasping them too firmly. Ideally, they should not be picked up by the tail. The hand is placed palm downward high up over the animal's back with the thumb round the neck and under the mouth so that it is virtually impossible for the animal to bite (Fig. 10.12). However, it is permissible to lift them out of their cage or box by the base of the tail (Fig. 10.13) and immediately transfer them to a surface which they can grip. Another good technique is to place them head down on the handler's thigh and, as they pull away, grasp them firmly by the scruff of the neck between finger and thumb. If it is turned on its back quickly, and a hold is retained on its tail, a rat will usually lie still without struggling (Fig. 10.14). It must not be carried by the tail as this is strongly resented and the rat can easily climb its own tail to bite the handler. Vicious, wild, or

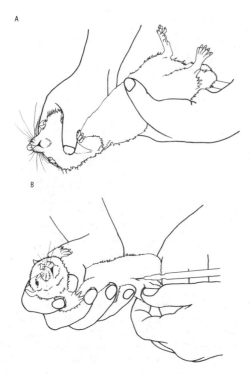

A

B

Fig. 10.14. Holding rats on back for ip injection.

needle if the tail is warmed under a lamp, and gentle pressure is applied to the base of the tail to impede venous return of blood. The dorsal metatarsal vein can be seen after clipping and swabbing with alcohol, and entered using a 10×0.40 mm (27 gauge) needle. The lingual vein can be entered with a 10×0.40 mm (27 gauge) needle but is fragile and easily transfixed. Finally, in male rats, the dorsal penile vein is large and a 0.80 mm (21 gauge) butterfly needle can be taped in for sequential injections (but it is essential to administer a neuroleptanalgesic agent im before attempting entry by this route). When intermittent administration of accurately measured volumes of agent is required, then cannulation of the tail vein or the jugular vein after surgical exposure under anaesthesia is essential (Green *et al.*, 1978).

Chemical restraint and preanaesthetic therapy
Atropine (0.05 mg/kg im or sc) about 30 min before other agents are given is helpful in minimizing salivary and bronchial secretions.

Neuroleptanalgesia is particularly effective in rats using either fentanyl–fluanisone or fentanyl–droperidol. The former is in routine use at this centre (CRC). Fentanyl–fluanisone at 0.3 ml/kg im of the undiluted commercial solution provides profound analgesia and sedation which develops in 5–7 min and lasts for 20–30 min. Full recovery takes up to 60 min but can be accelerated by injecting nalorphine at 1 mg/kg im. Neuroleptanalgesia alone is suitable for most superficial operations, but diazepam at 2.5 mg/kg im or ip is necessary to provide enough muscle relaxation for intraabdominal surgery, and the fentanyl–fluanisone dose should then be reduced to 0.2 ml/kg im (Green, 1975). Respiration is depressed and this may present problems in diseased rats. However, if the usual precautions regarding a patent airway and supplying O_2 are followed, fatalities should be avoided. Depression is rapidly reversed by the antagonist nalorphine, and artificial respiration by digital compression over the sternum at 50–100 presses/minute can be instituted until it takes effect.

Chloral hydrate (see p. 80).

Surgical anaesthesia
General notes. The same strict attention to conservation of body heat, hydration and maintenance of a patent airway described for mice (p. 151) should be followed in rats.

Assessment of anaesthetic depth is based on the respiratory rate, tail pinch, pedal and ear pinch reflexes. We find the latter the most sensitive in assessing surgical depths of anaesthesia prior to making an incision. Cyanosis of mucous mem-

infected rats which present a hazard if they do bite the operator, can be handled with industrial or flexible metal-link butcher's boning gloves (Cisar, 1973). Alternatively, they can be enclosed in a dark bag or covered in a drape, and are usually sufficiently subdued by such blindfolding to allow injection to be made.

Prolonged restraint of the conscious untreated rat can be achieved most simply by rolling it in a drape or piece of towel secured with safety pins leaving the tail outside for iv injections. Alternatively, broad webbing straps can be passed over the animal's back and secured to a board or bench top by drawing pins, or a sling can be fashioned out of broad strips of adhesive tape. The nylon mesh 'hammock' described by Danscher (1971) and the plastic restraining tubes described for mice (p. 151) are useful purpose-built devices which appear to cause the rats no distress.

Intraperitoneal injections are made with the animal on its back and slightly head down, a 16×0.50 mm (25 gauge) needle being inserted about 3 mm lateral to the umbilicus. Intramuscular injections should be made with a 10×0.45 mm (26 gauge) needle into the posterior aspect of the thigh. 4 useful vessels are available for percutaneous venepuncture. The lateral caudal vein is easily seen and entered with a 16×0.50 mm (25 gauge) branes, ears and the interdigital webs should be regarded as indicating severe respiratory depression, and emergency action should be instituted immediately. Rats are unable to tolerate apnoea for more than a few minutes, and cardiac failure follows respiratory failure in quick succession. Artificial respiration, gentle blowing into the mouth via a polyethylene catheter, or insufflation with O_2 are each valuable resuscitative measures. If all else fails, it is sometimes possible to restart respiration by swinging the rat back and forth head down in a gentle arc.

Injectable anaesthetic techniques. The neuroleptanalgesic technique using fentanyl–fluanisone and diazepam is the simplest to administer and is both effective and safe. If these drugs are contraindicated, barbiturates, alphaxolone–alphadolone, propanidid or ketamine may be used, preferably given to effect by iv injection. We prefer these agents in the following order.

Fentanyl–fluanisone (0·3 mk/kg im) with diazepam (2·5 mg/kg ip) produces profound analgesia, relaxation and narcosis suitable for intra-abdominal and intrathoracic surgery. The peak effect is maintained for 45–90 min, 'sleep time' is 130–150 min and time to full recovery may be up to 8 h. Narcosis can be reversed with nalorphine but the effects of diazepam are persistent and return of appetite may be delayed.

Alphaxolone–alphadolone does not produce reliable dose responses in rats if given ip or im, but is an excellent anaesthetic agent when injected iv. At 10–12 mg/kg iv, medium surgical anaesthesia lasting 5–12 min is achieved within 20 s and the rats are fully recovered in 60 min. The agent is also valuable for prolonged periods of anaesthesia given iv (caudal or penile vein) at 3–4 mg/kg every 15–20 min. Cardiopulmonary function is very stable (Green *et al.*, 1978); the wide therapeutic index is an important consideration if the assistance of an anaesthetist is not available during surgery.

Propanidid (20 mg/kg iv) is a useful agent for induction of anaesthesia and intubation. Deep surgical anaesthesia lasts for 2–3 min and the rats recover completely in about 10 min.

Methohexitone (1% solution) is a valuable induction agent injected iv at 7–10 mg/kg. Half the computed dose should be injected rapidly followed by slow injection over 30 s of the remainder to effect. Light surgical anaesthesia with sufficient relaxation for endotracheal intubation is achieved within 10–20 s and lasts for 5–8 min. The animals recover fully within 2 h. Further increments can be given to extend the effective period, but a cumulative effect will become evident in time (cf. alphaxolone–alphadolone).

Pentobarbitone is best freshly prepared from powder as a 3% solution. The animals should be carefully weighed and an assessment of their health and nutritional status made before computing the dose. To achieve surgical anaesthesia, 40 mg/kg ip is a fair approximation. Narcosis will develop in 5–10 min and last for 25–40 min. Further increments can be given iv to effect to prolong or deepen anaesthesia. Respiratory depression and hypothermia are the main hazards associated with this drug, so that it is essential to maintain a patent airway, fluid and thermal homeostasis both during surgery and during the post-operative recovery period.

Inhalational anaesthetic techniques. Inhalational agents can be vaporized as described for mice using simple methods (e.g. induction chambers or face cones) or in properly designed vaporizers. As an alternative to insufflation catheters or tracheostomy intubation, an endotracheal tube can be passed via the larynx (Medd & Heywood, 1970) whenever repeated or prolonged administration of gases, or artificial respiration by IPPV, are indicated. Their technique is simple and strongly recommended. After induction of anaesthesia with alphaxolone–alphadolone, propanidid or methohexitone, the rat is taped out on a cork board with adhesive tape across each limb and across the abdomen. The upper jaw is fixed to the board by elastic bands around the upper incisors. The whole platform is then tilted vertically so that the rat's head is raised. The rat's tongue is withdrawn and the larynx located using an illuminated oral spectrum ('Twinlite') for passage of the endotracheal tube. The tubes are constructed from polyethylene tubing with an endotracheal portion of 1–1·5 mm outside diameter, 2 cm long cemented into a pharyngeal tube of appropriate internal diameter. 2 precautions should be taken. If there is any delay in passing the tube, the animal should be returned to the horizontal position, since the airway is easily occluded when vertical. Care should also be taken that the tongue is not impaled on the lower incisors (Medd & Heywood, 1970).

Conventional inhalational techniques may be employed using halothane, enflurane, methoxyflurane or ether with O_2 or $N_2O : O_2$ (1:1) as selected for the experiment.

Premixed $CO_2 : O_2$ (1:1) is useful for rapid induction within seconds in a chamber, and is suitable for inoculations or cardiac puncture, but is unsafe for periods beyond 2 min.

Methoxyflurane with O_2 is safe and can be used at 0·5–1% to maintain long periods of stable anaesthesia. Gas flow is maintained at about 500 ml/min. Methoxyflurane is vaporized in a suitable apparatus (e.g. the modified Sebesteny or Parbrook vaporizers) and can be delivered to face cones, close-fitting masks with overflows, 1 mm catheters in the trachea, 1·25 mm (18 gauge) 'Medicut' tubes reaching to the larynx, or to the endotracheal tubes described above. Recovery is smooth but may be prolonged up to 24 h. Doubts about the nephrotoxicity of this agent suggest that it should not be used for renal experiments.

Halothane with O_2 or halothane with $N_2O:O_2$ is less safe in inexperienced hands but is an excellent agent if used with properly calibrated vaporizers. Induction is rapid (1–2 min) and smooth recovery takes only 3–4 min. Nitrous oxide:O_2 (1:1) are delivered at a total flow of 500 ml/min, and halothane is adjusted to effect from 1–2%. This is the combination of choice for many experiments but particularly those involving renal transplantation or those designed to study renal failure.

Enflurane with O_2 or with $N_2O:O_2$ is also an excellent inhalational agent in rats, and can be used in the same way as halothane.

Ether with O_2 can be used as a last resort or for simple procedures where its advantages outweigh the risks of respiratory tract irritation and subsequent infections.

Hypothermia. Refrigeration of neonates to obtain safe anaesthesia is recommended exactly as for mice. It is ideal for thymectomy or castration within the 1st 24 h of life. Good management is important if the recently operated pups are to be accepted by the dam without being cannibalized. The dam should be removed from the nest before the pups and retained in a separate unlit container. A single pup should be left in the nest when the others are removed for surgery. All blood should be washed from the pup skin at the end of the operation (using plain water and avoiding disinfectants or antiseptics) and the pups should be gently

Table 10.5. Rat: physiological data

Measurement	Values
Respiratory frequency (breaths/min)	90 (70–150)
Tidal volume (ml)	1·6 (1·5–1·8)
Minute volume (l/min)	0·22 (0·16–0·24)
Mean heart rate (beats/min)	350 (260–450)
Arterial blood pressure (mmHg)	116/90
Arterial blood pH	7·35
PaO_2 (mmHg)	—
$PaCO_2$ (mmHg)	42
Haematocrit (%)	40 (35–45)
Haemoglobin (g/100 ml)	15 (12–18)
Erythrocytes ($10^6/mm^3$)	9 (7–10)
*Blood volumes (ml/kg bodyweight)	
Total	50
Expected terminal exsanguination	20
Safe maximum single sample	5
Mean rectal temperature (°C)	38·0 (36·0–39·5)

*Archer (1965).

but thoroughly rubbed in their soiled bedding when returned to the nest. The dam can be returned to them within 15 min. They should then be left in a darkened room undisturbed by sudden changes in noise or light intensity.

Recovery and post-operative management
The precautions described for mice should also be followed in rats. Antibiotics may be injected into rats without complications arising, or tetracyclines can be administered in drinking water (80 μg/ml). Hydration is ensured by a final injection of 5 ml of 0·9% (normal) saline solution sc at the end of surgery.

European hedgehog (*Erinaceus europaeus*)

Hedgehogs have been used in experiments designed to study immune responses, embryology and physiological responses in the hibernating animal (Suomalainen & Suvanto, 1953; Morris, 1967).

Morris (1967) used ether routinely in adult animals for short and long periods without observing adverse respiratory effects. It was also used for short periods in young animals to obtain blood samples. Pentobarbitone (40 mg/kg ip) was used to produce deep anaesthesia for 1–1·5 h in young hedgehogs (32–65 days old).

Recommendations
The simplest means of restraining hedgehogs for blood sampling or access to the abdomen is to induce narcosis in a chamber with a volatile agent on gauze sponges. The animal can then be unrolled for ip or im injection with other agents, or anaesthesia can be deepened and maintained for surgery by cone administration of mixtures of methoxyflurane or halothane and O_2 or $N_2O:O_2$ (1:1). Otherwise, the hedgehog is unrolled by placing it on a flat surface, and gently prodding it over the rump or back of the neck. As it begins to uncurl, the anterior spines on the crown of the head are grasped with a strong pair of artery forceps. It is then lifted clear of the table, gently rocked up and down until it uncurls and gradually lowered until the hind legs just touch the table. A pencil can then be placed across them to hold them in position. The head and body may now be lowered until the animal is lying on its back, and it cannot roll itself up again whilst the hind legs are pinioned.

Surgical conditions can be obtained by inhalational anaesthesia as above, by neuroleptanalgesia with fentanyl–fluanisone and diazepam (0·2 ml/kg + 2·5 mg/kg ip respectively) or with pentobarbitone (40 mg/kg ip).

The bat wing is an excellent preparation for direct observation of skin microvasculature responses to drug administration (Seldon & Lundy, 1942) and, as such, is commonly employed as an assay in the development of new anaesthetic agents (Nicoll, 1964; Harris *et al.*, 1970; Harris *et al.*, 1971; Baez, 1971).

They should be handled with leather gloves to prevent bites (Church & Noronha, 1965). Inhalation anaesthesia was administered via face cone after pretreating bats with chlorpromazine (25 mg/kg im) by Ladhani & Thies (1968). Pentobarbitone (50 mg/kg ip) was used in a number of genera to achieve surgical anaesthesia by Henson (1969), whilst smaller doses (30–45 mg/kg ip) were recommended by Grinnell (1963) and Suga (1964). Ketamine was given im into the right pectoralis muscle of *Myotis lucifugus* and *M. sodalis* by Longnecker *et al.* (1974), who found that 120 mg/kg was necessary to produce consistent surgical anaesthesia lasting 20–30 min. Hime (1967) suggested that 5% halothane with O_2 at 400–800 ml/min is sufficient to induce anaesthesia in a chamber, and maintenance could be continued with a loose fitting nose-cone using 2% halothane with O_2.

Recommendations

After catching in nets, the bats should be handled with gloves to avoid being bitten, and injected with ketamine at 80–120 mg/kg im. This allows 15–30 min of deep sedation or light surgical anaesthesia which can be continued with 1% methoxyflurane in O_2 supplied by nose cone.

CHAPTER ELEVEN

SUPERORDER: UNGULATA
ORDERS: PERISSODACTYLA, ARTIODACTYLA, PROBOSCIDEA

ORDER PERISSODACTYLA: FAMILY EQUIDAE

Domestic horse (*Equus caballus*)

The development of agents for effective sedation and chemical restraint of horses and ponies has so improved their anaesthetic management that these animals are becoming increasingly considered for inclusion in physiological experiments. The most recent and complete account of preanaesthetic and anaesthetic management in this species is contained in Hall (1971).

Atropine was recommended for horses in doses up to 60 mg per animal to depress secretions if irritant agents such as ether were used as the main anaesthetic (Hall, 1971).

The phenothiazine derivatives have been widely accepted for quietening intractable horses and ponies and for routine preanaesthetic treatment in all Equidae (Carey & Sanford, 1963; Pugh, 1964; Jones, 1972). Chlorpromazine was recommended at doses not exceeding 0·4 mg/kg im since higher doses may produce panic and violent struggling (Hall, 1971). Earlier work suggested that 2 mg/kg im or 1 mg/kg iv was necessary to produce a noticeable tranquillizing effect (Owen & Neal, 1960), although again it was found that transient excitement and a tendency to plunge forward or rear up were occasionally encountered. Promazine has similar disadvantages according to Hall (1971) who suggested a dose of 1·0 mg/kg im. Acepromazine was recommended by the same author as the most useful phenothiazine at a dose of 0·03 mg–0·1 mg/kg im and this has since become widely regarded as the ataractic of choice for this species either alone or in combinations with the potent sedative–analgesics. Gabel *et al.* (1964) recorded decreases in arterial blood pressure following the im administration of promazine, whilst similar hypotension was reported by Kerr *et al.* (1972a) and Glen (1972) after im administration of acepromazine. In addition, promazine and acepromazine may occasionally cause hyperexcitability (Carey & Sanford, 1963).

The sedative xylazine was assessed by Clarke & Hall (1969) for its effects on the cardiovascular and respiratory systems of horses. After im injection of 2–3 mg/kg, deep sedation developed in 10–15 min and lasted for 15–20 min, with negligible effects on physiological functions. However, after slow iv injection of 0·5 mg/kg an almost immediate effect was produced with deep sedation again lasting 15–20 min, but accompanied by an immediate transient rise in arterial blood pressure followed by hypotension, bradycardia and a fall in cardiac output (Clarke & Hall, 1969). Similar studies by Kerr et al. (1972b) also demonstrated the wide safety margin (LD$_{50}$: ED$_{50}$ = 10:1) but gave evidence of a partial A–V block after iv administration. This could be effectively abolished by the prior iv administration of 0·011 mg/kg of atropine. After noting that induction of anaesthesia with thiopentone (10 mg/kg iv) was markedly slower following preanaesthetic medication with xylazine than with acepromazine, Frankland & Camburn (1977) concluded that blood circulation is slowed for at least 15 min after xylazine administration. Nevertheless, several groups have concluded that xylazine is the best sedative agent currently available for horses because of its consistency of effect, speed of onset, short duration and analgesic properties (Hall, 1971; McCashen & Gabel, 1971; Kerr et al., 1972b; Hoffman, 1974).

More recently, the butyrophenone tranquillizer azaperone has been used in the horse (Roztočil et al., 1971; Aitken & Sanford, 1972; Ehmke, 1972; de Leglise, 1973). In a study designed to establish specific pharmacological data when azaperone was administered to horses, Serrano & Lees (1976) concluded that an excellent sedative effect was obtained at 0·4–0·8 mg/kg im within 10 min of administration. However, hypotension was more marked than that generated by acepromazine and persisted for 4 h (Lees & Serrano, 1976). A moderate tachycardia was observed for 1–2 h after injection, in contrast to Roztočil et al. (1971) who found that 1 mg/kg azaperone had no appreciable effect on heart rate in the horse. In a recent study, MacKenzie & Snow (1977) compared azaperone (0·7–0·9 mg/kg im), xylazine (2 mg/kg im), and acepromazine (0·5 mg/kg im) and concluded that azaperone was superior to the other agents. A mild transient tachycardia and reduction in packed-cell volume were encountered with both acepromazine and azaperone.

Several sedative–analgesic drugs have been used alone and in combination with neuroleptics. Morphine itself was suggested at a total dose of 60 mg for a large horse by Hall (1971), whilst pethidine was recommended at total doses up to 1000 mg im. Schauffler (1968) used pethidine with acepromazine to produce neuroleptanalgesia. Thiambutene may provoke muscle spasms and nervous excitement (Hall, 1971), although Harbison et al. (1974) claimed that analgesia and sedation were induced by doses of 0·33 mg/kg iv, and that significant excitement was not detected until doses of 0·83–0·93 mg/kg were injected iv.

The same authors claimed that these symptoms were not provoked even at the high doses levels if acepromazine (0·05 mg/kg) was injected iv beforehand, and recovery was then smooth and uneventful. Thiopentone doses were reduced by 50% after preanaesthetic injection with this combination, and nalorphine was effective in speeding the recovery period. Pentazocine was evaluated as an analgesic in horses by Lowe (1969) who found that it had about half the potency of morphine, and was effective at doses ranging between 0·5–4·0 mg/kg im.

The more potent analgesic etorphine was used in combination with acepromazine in producing reversible immobilization of domestic and wild Equidae (Harthoorne, 1967) before receiving wide acceptance for clinical use. Hall (1971) emphasized the need for care in using such a potent agent in practice with the twin dangers of induction and recovery excitement in intractable horses. The marked stimulatory effects of etorphine on the cardiovascular system of horses has been reported by many workers (Hillidge & Lees, 1971; Daniel & Ling, 1972; Jenkins et al., 1972; Schlarmann et al., 1973; Lees & Hillidge, 1975). The depressant effects on respiratory function were reported by Schlarmann et al. (1973) who described symptoms of hypoxic hypoxia developing after administration of this drug. In a later study, Hillidge & Lees (1975a) made blood gas and acid–base measurements at intervals after injection of etorphine–acepromazine, and recorded marked respiratory depression and hypoxia. Etorphine should be used with particular care in donkeys (Dobbs & Ling, 1972; Van Laun, 1977). Similarly, excitement (Rafferty, 1972) and even deaths may be encountered in ponies after reversal of etorphine–acepromazine with diprenorphine (Hillidge & Lees, 1974b; Lane, 1974).

Of the barbiturates, only thiopentone, thiamylal and methohexitone have been widely accepted for inducing anaesthesia in equines. Pentobarbitone is unacceptable because of the long recovery period and associated excitement and struggling (Hall, 1971). However, Fowler (1946) recommended its use in foals up to a few months of age, provided it was given slowly iv to effect. He found that the animals remained recumbent for 2·5–3 h, and that struggling during recovery was easily controlled.

Anaesthesia with thiopentone alone (Longley, 1950; Ford, 1951) has similar severe disadvantages of excitement and struggling during induction and recovery (Hall, 1971; 1976) but has gained in popularity when administered rapidly at 6–9 mg/kg iv after prior tranquillization with promazine (Jones et al., 1960), acepromazine (Hall, 1971), thiambutene and acepromazine (Harbison et al., 1974), or together with the relaxant suxamethonium at 0·15 mg/kg iv (Hall, 1971). Provided the dangers of perivascular or intra-arterial injection are avoided, the rapid injection technique is very safe indeed when combined with these agents. Anaesthesia will only be produced if a sufficient dose is injected within one neck-to-brain circulation time, so that the total computed dose must in practice be included in 50 ml or less (Hall, 1971). The effect of thiopentone on several physiological parameters has been investigated by Tyagi et al. (1964) and Tavernor & Lees (1970), who concluded that iv administration of thiopentone (10 mg/kg) resulted in a moderate tachycardia, a slight reduction in mean arterial pressure and a short period of respiratory depression. The danger of prolonged recovery in foals was emphasised by Hall (1971, 1976) who concluded that this agent should not be used in subjects under 8 weeks of age.

Thiamylal is used in a similar manner to thiopentone in horses, i.e. at a dose of 7–10 mg/kg by rapid iv injection after suitable tranquillization (Lumb & Jones, 1973). According to these authors it may be used in young, aged or poor-risk subjects with complete safety.

Methohexitone was recommended for induction of anaesthesia by Tavernor (1962) and Monahan (1964), although the characteristic muscle tremors and paddling movements observed during recovery (Grono, 1966) suggest that it is only suitable if followed by inhalational anaesthesia. However, Hall (1971) reported that it gave very similar results to thiopentone if administered rapidly iv at 5–6 mg/kg after previous treatment with acepromazine (0·4 mg/kg im) and with the relaxant suxamethonium (0·1 mg/kg iv).

A similar degree of light surgical anaesthesia may be obtained if azaperone at 0·2–0·8 mg/kg im is followed by iv injection of the hypnotic metomidate at 3·5 mg/kg (Roztočil et al., 1972; Hillidge et al., 1973). In further studies to investigate the effect of this combination on physiological function, Hillidge et al. (1974) and Hillidge et al. (1975) concluded that it produced excellent induction of anaesthesia comparable with acepromazine–thiopentone, and significant changes in cardiovascular and respiratory function were avoided. The favourable findings were offset to some extent by struggling observed during recovery although this would be masked if the combination was used for induction followed by inhalational maintenance anaesthesia.

Alphaxolone–alphadolone (1·9 mg/kg iv) has also been evaluated in horses for the induction of anaesthesia. The first half of the computed dose was given rapidly iv, and the remainder combined with suxamethonium (0·1 mg/kg) injected in the next 10 s. Anaesthesia lasting for 5–8 min was induced but was associated with excitement, poor muscle relaxation and marked tactile and auditory hyperaesthesia. It was concluded that this steroid combination had no place in equine anaesthesia (Eales, 1976).

Muscle relaxants have been used as chemical casting agents as well as aids to surgery in equine anaesthesia. Suxamethonium was administered iv to conscious horses to produce recumbency (Larsen, 1958; Neal & Wright, 1959; Schleiter & Schneider, 1964). This procedure was discussed by Hall (1971) who concluded from the accumulated evidence that it was unsafe and inhumane, principally because of the marked tachycardia and cardiac arrhythmias as well as deaths due to primary cardiac arrest encountered (Stowe, 1955; Larsen et al., 1959; Tavernor, 1959, 1960; Hofmeyer, 1960; Dietz et al., 1961). The combined effect of thiopentone and suxamethonium administration was studied by Tavernor & Lees (1970), who concluded that pronounced increases in heart rate and blood pressure, marked cardiac arrhythmias and periods of apnoea invariably occurred with this technique. D-tubocurarine at 0·22–0·25 mg/kg iv produces good relaxation according to Hall (1971). The same author suggested that gallamine was effective at 0·5–1·0 mg/kg iv, but concluded from the work of Massey (1970) that pancuronium at 0·06 mg/kg was probably superior to other competitive blocking agents in horses (Hall, 1971).

Because of the high cost of supplying inhalational agents to adult horses, they are usually used for maintenance of anaesthesia after induction with injectable agents, and are administered in closed or semi-closed to-and-fro or circle systems (Hall, 1971). This authority concluded that ether and halothane (with or without N_2O) are both valuable agents for maintenance of anaesthesia, and cyclopropane was considered unlikely to displace them in popularity owing to the explosive risk, the difficulty in assessing depth by the normal clinical criteria and the severe respiratory depression which could be induced by this agent. Following 2 h of surgical anaesthesia with halothane in horses, slight centrilobular necrosis and glycogen depletion was observed in livers 2 days afterwards (Wolff et al., 1967). The immediate effects of halothane on ventilation rate, plasma pH and pCO_2 in horses were described by Fisher (1961). Large differences in alveolar-arterial pO_2 tensions were attributed to posture and restricted ventilation of dependent lung lobes when horses were retained in one position for long periods (Hall et al., 1968; Littlejohn & Mitchell, 1972). The heart rates of horses anaesthetized either with halothane or ether were compared by Tavernor & Lees (1969), and the effectiveness of propranolol in treating catecholamine-induced cardiac arrhythmias was demonstrated. Cardiac output was compared in conscious and anaesthetized horses by Hillidge & Lees (1975b), and another report from the same laboratory described experiments to measure tissue oxygenation in conscious and anaesthetized horses (Hillidge & Lees, 1974a).

Recommended anaesthetic techniques

Preanaesthetic management
The equine stomach is small in relation to body-weight and is easily ruptured if the animal is inadvertently allowed to fall heavily on its side during induction of anaesthesia. The risk is probably reduced if the stomach is empty and this is sufficient reason for fasting the subjects for 24 h prior to anaesthesia. Access to water should be allowed until immediately before preanaesthetic medication is given.

Physical restraint and handling
The animal must be furnished with a strong head-collar, halter or bridle, and held by an experienced assistant. It should then be backed into a corner and placed against a wall to prevent sideways movement. It is essential to ensure that the ground gives a good foothold to prevent slipping and panic struggling, whilst overhead projections, hayracks and beams must be given a wide berth in case the animal rears up during injection. Further restraint depends on the nature of the animal. A blindfold almost invariably quietens an intractable individual and a foreleg lifted by an assistant is a useful restraint if the anaesthetist is working around the hindquarters e.g. injecting local analgesics into a hind leg. A rope twitch may be applied to the nose or to an ear in particularly resistant individuals, but this is rarely necessary if the other recommendations are tried first. Modern methods of chemical restraint have considerably eased the dangers of handling equines and eliminated the need for casting with ropes. However, the anaesthetist should still be able to apply hobbles in case they are needed to prevent self-inflicted injury during recovery. Furthermore, an experienced assistant should be stationed at the head with strict instructions to keep the head up whilst the animal sinks to the ground during induction of anaesthesia.

Chemical restraint and preanaesthetic therapy
Atropine is valuable in diminishing secretions and for protecting the heart from vagal inhibition. It can be given iv, im or sc at 0·01 mg/kg, but 20–30 min should be allowed for maximum effect to develop if the im or sc routes are used.

Xylazine is an excellent sedative for horses and is effective by the iv or im route. Deep sedation develops in 10–15 min after im injection of 2–3 mg/kg, is maintained for 15–20 min and recovery is complete within 1–2 h. If given by slow iv injection at 0·5 mg/kg, xylazine produces an almost immediate sedative effect lasting 15–20 min, but recovery is complete within 30 min. Increasing dosages further serves only to prolong recovery and makes little difference to the depth of CNS depression. Sedation develops smoothly without excitement or struggling, and is characterized by the animal standing firmly on all 4 legs and a refusal to move in any direction. The head is gradually lowered, the eyelids droop until almost closed, the lower lip droops and the penis protrudes from the prepuce. Horses can be aroused but rapidly sink back into a sleep-like state. Excitement never occurs either during induction or recovery, although sharp movements of the head and neck are commonly encountered in response to loud metallic noises. Most subjects sweat around the ears and the upper neck during sedation with xylazine. The induction dose of barbiturate should be reduced by 40% after preanaesthetic sedation with this drug. The experimentalist should be aware of the cardiovascular effects of xylazine, particularly the partial A-V block which is commonly experienced (especially after iv administration), and note that this can be prevented by the prior administration of atropine at 0·1 mg/kg as recommended.

Azaperone (0·4–0·8 mg/kg) produces a more consistent and profound response than acepromazine, good sedation developing within 10 min of im injection. The maximal effect is maintained for 20–60 min whilst complete recovery may take 2–6 h. The subjects are particularly sensitive to noise during recovery so the ears should be plugged with cotton wool and the animal allowed to recover in quiet surroundings. It is particularly important to reduce the barbiturate dosage (by 40%) after sedation with azaperone, otherwise prolonged apnoea may occur.

Acepromazine (0·03–0·1 mg/kg) by im injection is an excellent ataractic with a wide safety margin and is recommended as an alternative agent to xylazine or azaperone for horses. It is important to allow the drug to take effect with the animal in a quiet environment free of stimuli, yet closely observed in case it becomes excited. The subject will then allow considerable manipulation so long as suitable local analgesia is employed and it is handled gently and quietly. Barbiturate dosages are not affected by preanaesthetic treatment with acepromazine in horses.

Etorphine–acepromazine (0·5 ml/50 kg im or 0·25 ml/50 kg iv) is probably the most widely used injectable combination in horses in spite of its known disadvantages (p. 164). After im injection, excitation is occasionally encountered and the animal is best walked in a circle controlled by a strong rope and halter. The gait becomes stiff in 2–3 min and the animal usually lies down in 3–5 min. Head, neck and foreleg hypertonus and tremors are often experienced, while initial tachycardia and shallow respiration may lead on to hypoxia and acidosis.

Administration by iv injection results in a much more predictable response, and the excitation and muscle tremors are unlikely to occur. The animal usually lies down quietly 30–45 s after rapid injection. Profound analgesia develops and is accompanied by central nervous depression. Muscle tone is often accentuated—hence the agent is only suitable for superficial surgery or for induction of anaesthesia. Analgesia is maintained for about 30 min if the antagonist is not given earlier. However, *equal* volumes of dipremorphine solution should *always* be given iv at the end of the procedure to ensure that the animal recovers without struggling—it will then stand up in 1–4 min after injection, but may appear mildly tranquillized for about 4 h afterwards. Occasionally a further small dose (half initial volume) of diprenorphine is needed 2–4 h after initial recovery if the horse becomes restless or appears likely to relapse into sedation.

Local analgesia
Apart from local infiltration techniques used in conjunction with xylazine sedation and pethidine analgesia, local analgesia is of limited value in experimental work. The techniques for spinal and conduction analgesia in equines are detailed by Hall (1971).

Surgical anaesthesia
The options open for surgical anaesthesia in equines are limited by cost of agents, the apparatus available and the need to induce without passing through voluntary or involuntary excitement phases. In practice, injectable agents are always used for induction of adults although mask and inhalational agents may be used in foals. Anaesthesia can then be maintained by inhalational and balanced techniques. The administration of preanaesthetic agent and barbiturate for induction in the standing position eliminates the dangerous and stressful need to cast the conscious animal with hobbles and ropes. The general management during anaesthesia is standard as described earlier (p. 97). Particular attention must be paid to cardiovascular and respiratory deficiencies developing if the animals are retained in dorsal or lateral recumbency for long periods, since poor venous return and pulmonary oedema may eventually result in acidosis and acute cardiovascular failure.

Injectable anaesthetic techniques. Venepuncture is made into the jugular vein half way down the neck. The horse should be held at the front by a stout head collar and a blindfold fitted. The use of a twitch should be avoided since it frequently makes the animal tense its neck muscles and this prevents easy dilation of the vein. It is preferable to give particularly intractable individuals a low dose of xylazine or azaperone im and allow time for this to take effect before attempting iv injections. Local infiltration with 1% lignocaine should always be carried out to desensitize an area over the jugular furrow before venepuncture is attempted.

A needle, 60–70 × 2–2·5 mm and fitted with a stilette, is suitable for horses and ponies. It is first directed through the skin and patency is assured before the stilette is removed. It is then inserted into the dilated jugular vein for 4–5 cm towards the head to minimize the risk of dislodgement and perivascular leaks. A further precaution is to introduce a suitable plastic catheter through the needle for a distance of 15–20 cm to ensure that the infusion is entirely within the vein.

The weight of a horse is usually estimated for computing the anaesthetic dosage. The formula suggested by Hall (1971) provides a reasonably accurate estimate:

$$\text{weight (kg)} = \frac{\text{girth (inches)}^2 \times \text{length (inches)}}{660}$$

where the girth (circumference around the chest) is measured just behind the elbow, and the length is from the point of shoulder to the line of the ischial tuberosity.

Alternatively, where the height is measured at the highest point of the back (the 'withers'), the following gives a rough guide:

Height (cm)	Weight (kg)
110	150–180
130	250–300
140	300–350
150	400–450
160	450–600

The depth of anaesthesia is assessed with some difficulty as many of the muscle relaxation reflexes are lost after treatment with xylazine, phenothiazine derivatives or azaperone. Clinical observations are based on: (a) the eye (b) the pulse rate (c) depth of respiration (d) analgesia and (e) muscle relaxation.

(a) The eyeball commences to rotate laterally, and slow horizontal nystagmus develops during basal narcosis, but accelerates as light and medium surgical anaesthesia are achieved. Horizontal movements persist almost to the point of death. The corneal reflex remains brisk during basal narcosis but progressively slower during surgical anaesthesia, and it persists until just before the point of death. Pupillary responses to light are weak until deep surgical anaesthesia is achieved, when there is marked constriction.

(b) The pulse rate accelerates to 60–65 beats/min during surgical anaesthesia using ether, but usually remains within the normal range (35–45 beats/min) with halothane.

(c) Respiration is depressed during induction, and apnoea for a period of 15–70 s is often encountered. After 1–2 deep breaths, spontaneous respiration should recommence and remain steady at a normal rate and amplitude until medium to deep surgical anaesthesia is attained. Once the horse is deeply anaesthetized, the respiratory rate increases while the depth decreases, and a pause between inspiration and expiration may become apparent.

(d) As basal narcosis is reached, the withdrawn tongue will cease to respond to vigorous pinching. The anal sphincter reflex will not be lost until medium surgical anaesthesia has been attained.

(e) Loss of muscle tone is indicated by failure to retract the tongue if this is grasped and withdrawn through the interdental space (a reflex which is lost during basal narcosis), the response if the tail is deliberately and suddenly raised is lost as narcosis progresses to light surgical anaesthesia, and the penis, vulval lips and anus relax with the onset of surgical anaesthesia.

In practice, anaesthesia is induced with the barbiturates thiopentone, thiamylal or methohexitone after pretreatment as described, or with the combination of azaperone and metomidate.

Thiopentone (10% solution) should be given by rapid (5–10 s) iv injection at 6–10 mg/kg. The lower dose is used after preanaesthetic treatment with xylazine or azaperone and the upper limit after acepromazine. The animal sinks quietly to the ground within 20–30 s and surgical anaesthesia lasting 5–15 min is produced. Apnoea is almost invariably caused by such rapid administration and lasts 15–70 s (mean 40 s). The recovery time varies with the neuroleptic or ataractic used, but the effect of thiopentone alone is usually indiscernible in 35–40 min. Success with this technique depends on injecting a sufficient dose intravascularly at a speed sufficient to attain high blood and hence brain levels, and in practice this entails making up the thiopentone in a 50 ml volume or less. If the drug is accidentally injected outside the vessel, the region

should be immediately infiltrated with 0·5–1·0 litre of 0·9% saline solution containing hyaluronidase to minimize the risk of necrosis caused by the highly irritant alkaline solution. The rapid iv injection technique is safe in healthy subjects but should not be used in foals less than 6 weeks of age. In these cases methohexitone should be used instead of thiopentone.

Thiamylal is used as an alternative at 7–10 mg/kg after previous sedation and is given by rapid iv injection as above.

Methohexitone (5–7 mg/kg) again given by rapid iv injection after preanaesthetic treatment, is an excellent induction agent for experimental surgery in this species since recovery is even quicker than with thiopentone, and physiological responses rapidly return to normal (20–35 min). Foals under 8 weeks of age can be induced with even lower doses at 1–2 mg/kg if the iv injection is given rapidly.

Azaperone (0·4–0·8 mg/kg im) followed 20 min later by iv injection of *metomidate* (3·5 mg/kg), provides smooth induction of anaesthesia which is ideal if followed by inhalational maintenance anaesthesia. Light surgical anaesthesia lasting 5–10 min is produced by the azaperone–metomidate combination and full recovery may take up to 120 min. The subjects are fully conscious or mildly sedated 2–3 h after administration. Physiological measurements are minimally disturbed, and this technique is recommended for pharmacological preparations in which it is important to maintain cardiovascular and respiratory function near normal.

Inhalational anaesthetic techniques. As soon as anaesthesia has been induced, a cuffed endotracheal tube should be passed.

Relaxation of the jaws and larynx is facilitated by the iv injection of suxamethonium at 0·1–0·15 mg/kg, a dose low enough to avoid significant apnoea. Tubes ranging from 16·0 mm (ponies up to 150 kg) to 30 mm outside diameter (small thoroughbred horses) are used. The head and neck should be extended with the animal laid on its side. The mouth is then opened and a 'gag' inserted between the molars to prevent chewing, and the tongue is pulled forward. The tube is passed into the mouth with the concavity facing toward the hard palate and is rotated through 180° as the tip passes over the epiglottis. It is guided into the trachea at the next inspiration and the cuff is inflated.

Inhalational gas mixtures of $N_2O : O_2$ and either halothane or ether, alternatively O_2 and cyclopropane, are then administered in circle or to-and-fro, closed or semi-closed systems. A reservoir bag of 12–15 litre capacity is necessary for adult equines, and a soda-lime canister capable of holding 4–5 kg of granules is necessary for reasonable CO_2 absorption from expired gases. Foals under 100 kg can be maintained on a standard Boyle's-type apparatus. The reservoir bag should be half-filled with O_2 and connected to the endotracheal tube. With the expiratory valve open, a flow of O_2 (5 litres/min) is passed into the circuit, and halothane (4–6%) or ether (8–10%) administered to the animal. The soda-lime canister is not introduced into the circuit until surgical anaesthesia is fully established. Thereafter, the expiratory valve is closed and an O_2 flow rate sufficient to replenish the animal's metabolic needs is supplied (in practice 500–2000 ml/min depending on the size of the animal).

Alternatively, the expiratory valve may be kept open and $N_2O : O_2$ (1 : 1) with 2–3% halothane or 6–10% ether supplied for maintenance. Recovery takes 30–40 min before the horse is capable of standing safely from the time inhalation of halothane is terminated, while it takes 50–60 min to recover from ether.

Cyclopropane is administered in a closed system. After connecting the circuit to the endotracheal tube, the rebreathing bag is filled with a mixture of O_2 and cyclopropane (1 : 1). A similar mixture is run into the circuit with expiratory valve open and no soda-lime absorption until surgical anaesthesia is induced. Thereafter the expiratory valve is closed, the absorber introduced and the cyclopropane flow turned off. Oxygen is run into the circuit at low flow rates to keep the rebreathing bag $\frac{3}{4}$ full at the end of each expiration. Recovery takes 30–50 min and is usually free of excitement or struggling.

Table 11.1. Horse: physiological data (resting values)

Measurement	Values
Respiratory frequency (breaths/min)	8–12
Tidal volume (1)	9 (8·5–9·5)
Minute volume (l/min)	100–110
Mean heart rate (beats/min)	40 (35–50)
Arterial blood pressure (mmHg)	90/60
Arterial blood pH	7·2–7·5
PaO_2 (mmHg)	95
$Pa\,CO_2$ (mmHg)	47
Haematocrit (%)	33 (28–42)
Haemoglobin (g/100 ml)	11 (8–14)
Erythrocytes (10^6 mm³)	9 (8–10)
*Blood volumes (ml/kg bodyweight)	
Total	75
Expected terminal exsanguination	40
Safe maximum single sample	8
Mean rectal temperature (°C)	38·1 (37·5–39·0)

* Archer (1965).

Recovery and post-surgical therapy
In the absence of a padded recovery-box, the animal should be allowed to recover surrounded by straw bales and a thick straw bed underfoot. We attempt to exclude sensory stimuli by leaving the animal blindfolded, plugging the ears with cotton-wool and by restraining the horses with hobbles until they are clearly able to stand safely. Since the introduction of xylazine as a sedative agent for horses, problems of violent recovery have been virtually eliminated.

Chemical restraint and capture: exotic species

The etorphine–acepromazine combination is highly effective Equidae (King, 1965; King & Klingel, 1965; Ebedes, 1966).

The domestic horse (*Equus caballus*) and Przewalski horse (*Equus przewalski*) require dosages of 0·02 mg/kg : 0·1 mg/kg im, but this is halved in the former case if administered iv (Jones, 1973; Manton, 1966).

The common zebra (*Equus burchelli*) (King & Klingel, 1965; Ebedes, 1966; Jones, 1973), onagar (*Equus hemionus*) (Manton, 1966; Jones, 1973), Brazilian tapir (*Tapirus terrestris*) and Malayan tapir (*Tapirus indicus*) (Hime, 1973; Jones, 1973) can be successfully immobilized with etorphine–acepromazine (0·01 mg/kg : 0·1 mg/kg im).

Recommendations
Etorphine-acepromazine (0·25 ml/50 kg im 'Immobilon LA') gives very good results. The etorphine is readily antagonized and reversed by an equal dose rate of diprenorphine and this should always be given since hypothermia may cause problems in the post-surgical period. For surgery, thiopentone at low dosages (5 mg/kg iv) is then ideal for induction of anaesthesia (Hime, 1973).

FAMILY RHINOCEROTIDAE

The etorphine–acepromazine combination has proved highly successful in these animals. They are rendered ataxic and sufficiently tractable to allow guidance into a crate. If they lie down, they should be supported in the prone position.

White rhinoceros (*Ceratotherium simum*) (Harthoorn, 1962; Player, 1967; Jones, 1973), black rhinoceros (*Diceros bicornis*) (King & Carter, 1965; King, 1969; Denney, 1969), and Indian rhinoceros (*Rhinoceros unicornis*) (Jones, 1973) have all been immobilized with etorphine–acepromazine at approximate dosages of 0·15 mg/100 kg and 0·01–0·02 mg/kg im respectively.

Recommendations
Etorphine–acepromazine (0·15 mg/100 kg : 0·01

mg/kg im) is very effective. Crating of free-ranging specimens is facilitated by the inclusion of hyoscine (0·1 mg/kg) in the drug mixture (Keep, 1970) as this interferes with the animal's visual acuity. Xylazine (0·25–0·50 mg/kg im) is an excellent sedative for zoo specimens or animals already restrained in crates or pens (Harthoorn, 1975). An excellent alternative is etorphine–ketamine (1·0 mg/500 kg:0·5 mg/kg im). Etorphine is best reversed with nalorphine in these animals (Hime, 1973).

ORDER PROBOSCIDEA: FAMILY ELEPHANTIDAE

Wild African elephants (*Loxodonta africana*) (Pienaar, 1966b; Wallach & Anderson, 1968) and wild Asiatic elephants (*Elephas maximus*) (Jones, 1975) have been successfully captured with etorphine–acepromazine (about 1 mg/500 kg:0·01–0·02 mg/kg im). Xylazine (0·08–0·14 mg/kg im) may also be used to sedate these animals (Schmidt, 1975). Etorphine alone is also effective at dosages of 1·2 mg/500 kg for Asiatic and 0·7 mg/500 kg im for African elephants (Hime, 1973).

Recommendations
Etorphine–acepromazine gives excellent results. The antagonists diprenorphine or cyprenorphine (1·0 mg/100 kg) should be given iv into an ear vein to reverse narcosis. Immobilized elephants should not be allowed to lie in sternal recumbency as the pressure of abdominal viscera on the diaphragm causes respiratory depression and they should always be pulled over onto their side (Jones, 1973).

ORDER ARTIODACTYLA: FAMILY BOVIDAE: GENUS BOS

European domestic ox (*Bos taurus*)
Adult cattle are often required for experimental surgery involved in studies of rumenal or uterine physiology, while calves are commonly used for open heart surgery, heart-lung preparations and studies involving synthetic vascular prostheses. General anaesthesia of adults is often complicated by rumenal tympany with accompanying respiratory and cardiovascular embarrassment arising from compression by the viscera; by passive regurgitation of rumen contents and the danger of aspiration into the lungs; and by the continual copious production of saliva. These 'mechanical' problems are less dangerous in calves but the low levels of liver enzymes capable of biodegrading injectable agents make other demands of the anaesthetist in the young animal. For these reasons, local and regional analgesic techniques have been widely

adopted in the past, and surgery has been performed on the restrained, standing animal. These techniques are still commended to the reader for consideration when planning any experimental protocol in this species. Anaesthesia in cattle has been usefully reviewed recently by Reynolds (1975). General descriptions of local and regional analgesia were given by Westhues & Fritsch (1964), Horney (1966), Hall (1971), Soma (1971), and Lumb & Jones (1973).

Regional blocks of the limbs have caused problems in cattle (Jennings, 1961), although it has been claimed by several groups (Manohar et al., 1971; Weaver, 1972; Tyagi et al., 1973) that application of a tourniquet to a limb with intravenous retrograde injection of a local analgesic distal to the tourniquet provides efficient regional blockade. However, the sudden release of agent into the general circulation when the tourniquet is released may render the technique unsuitable for certain purposes. We prefer to produce ring blocks by infiltrating relatively large volumes of dilute solutions (0·5–1%) of lignocaine around the limb or digit. Ring infiltration is also useful for surgery on the teats, whilst blockade of the pudendal nerve is valuable in examination and manipulation of the penis (Larson, 1953; Habel, 1956).

Anterior epidural spinal analgesia was described by Hall (1971) for surgery of the hindquarters, udder, uterus, scrotum, penis and abdomen. Caudal epidural analgesia was recommended for manipulation of the vulva and vagina (Hall, 1971).

Flank operations for access to the alimentary tract and uterus are usually carried out under infiltration (L-block) analgesia or paravertebral analgesia (Hall, 1971), with the clear advantage that overdosage and hypotension is unlikely to occur (cf. anterior spinal analgesia). Paravertebral analgesia is the method chosen by most workers for flank laparotomy, but we have had more consistent results with local infiltration with dilute solutions (1%) of lignocaine, and believe that the animal is more likely to suffer pain and discomfort whilst needles are inserted through the back muscles during paravertebral injections.

Several sedatives and tranquillizers have been described for controlling intractable individuals or for restraint to accompany local analgesia. Results with phenothiazine derivatives, phencyclidine and etorphine were described by Kidd et al. (1971). Etorphine by itself or with acepromazine is contraindicated in cattle as insufficient sedation is produced, and regurgitation, struggling and dyspnoea result (Jones, 1973). Xylazine is, by common consent, the sedative of choice in Bovidae whether farm (Hall, 1971), laboratory (Hopkins, 1972), or zoological specimens (Jones, 1971, 1973). It can be used to achieve variable degrees of CNS depression extending to basal narcosis. Provided an im injection can be made, it has superseded chloral hydrate for basal narcosis, although the latter may still be given orally in the drinking water as a 1·25% solution (Jennings, 1971). Etorphine and xylazine provide good restraint (Jones, 1971) and ensure excellent surgical conditions if supplemented with local analgesics.

The use of barbiturates is usually limited to induction of anaesthesia prior to intubation and maintenance with inhalation agents, since attempts at prolonging anaesthesia with intravenous agents are invariably attended by prolonged recovery and its associated problems in ruminants (Jennings, 1971). In adult cattle, thiopentone, thiamylal, methohexitone and pentobarbitone have been used successfully for induction. Rapid iv injection of 10% thiopentone (10 mg/kg) was used by Hall (1971) and Jennings (1971) to produce 3–4 min of light surgical anaesthesia. Recovery, which is complete within 45 min, is usually quiet and free from excitement. The authors commented on the remarkable safety of thiopentone in this species but Hall (1976) has indicated that hypocalcaemia may be induced in heavily-lactating cows after recovery. Hall (1971, 1976) has emphasized the danger of prolonged recovery in young calves and, in the later report, suggested that thiopentone should not be used in calves less than 8 weeks old. Methohexitone (4–5 mg/kg iv) was given to adult cows to produce sufficient anaesthesia for endotracheal intubation (Hall, 1971), and recovery was reported to be smooth and uneventful. This was considered to be the agent of choice in young calves, and was administered at 1 mg/kg by rapid iv injection by Tavernor (1962). Similarly, it was recommended at the same dose rate for calves between 6 weeks and 10 months of age by Robertshaw (1964). Pentobarbitone (25–30 mg/kg) was given by slow iv injection over 4 min by Hall (1971) to induce anaesthesia lasting about 30 min, but recovery was delayed for 3 h. The same authority stated that pentobarbitone is definitely contraindicated in calves less than 4 weeks old as recovery may take up to 48 h. Jennings (1971) stated that pentobarbitone could be given by rapid iv injection at 10 mg/kg to produce anaesthesia of about twice the duration of thiopentone. The dosage of thiopentone and methohexitone is significantly reduced by pretreatment with xylazine (0·18 mg/kg im) according to Reynolds (1975), who quotes the anaesthetic doses necessary as 5 mg/kg and 2 mg/kg iv respectively.

Ketamine has been used successfully in adult cows (Fuentez & Tellez, 1974, 1976). It was given at 2 mg/kg iv 20 min after xylazine (0·1 mg/kg iv) to produce surgical anaesthesia suitable for midline laparotomy, and anaesthesia was maintained by iv infusion of ketamine in a normal saline solution (2 mg ketamine in 1 ml saline). The cow stood up within 45 min of stopping administration.

Atropine is considered to be contraindicated in ruminants as it renders secretions more viscid and less easily removed from the oropharynx (Hall, 1971). However, atropine is useful in calves under 3 months of age if used at the high dose rate of 0·2 mg/kg. Secretions are significantly reduced and the heart is protected from vagal inhibition during thoracic and cardiac surgery (CRC).

Muscle relaxants have been little used in adult cattle because of difficulties in providing controlled ventilation, but these animals are very sensitive to them and are paralysed by very small dosages (Hansson, 1958; Reynolds, 1975). For example, the minimal blocking iv dose of suxamethonium is 0·04 mg/kg in cows, compared with 0·6 mg/kg in horses and 0·4 mg/kg in pigs (Hansson, 1958). Hall (1966) reported that gallamine effectively paralysed young calves and lambs at 0·4 mg/kg but produced prolonged apnoea, whilst d-tubocurarine was effective at 0·03 mg/kg iv. Harthoorn (1962) reported on im administration of 1·1–2·2 mg/kg gallamine to adult cattle, and noted that doses of 1·5 mg/kg or more produced respiratory paralysis and relaxation for approximately 30 min. We have used pancuronium at 0·01 mg/kg iv to produce relaxation for 40–60 min in 8–10-week-old calves. Anaesthesia was induced first with methohexitone (1 mg/kg iv), maintained with $N_2O:O_2$ (1:1), and analgesia was supplemented with fentanyl (0·02 mg/kg iv).

Hall (1971) gives a full account of inhalational anaesthesia in cattle, including the use of halothane, methoxyflurane, ether, cyclopropane and N_2O. Halothane in closed or semiclosed circuits was suggested for maintenance after induction with thiopentone, and the rapid recovery within 6–7 min was noted favourably. Methoxyflurane was evaluated by Douglas et al. (1964) for use in adult cattle, and it was considered a satisfactory agent for use in a rebreathing circuit with 'in-circle' vaporization. However, the slow induction and recovery were considered to be serious disadvantages by Hall (1971) and Jennings (1971). The explosive properties of cyclopropane have limited its use under laboratory conditions (Reynolds, 1975), but it was considered an excellent anaesthetic for cattle by Hall (1971) provided that closed rebreathing to-and-fro or circle systems are available for administration. Nitrous oxide can be used either as the main agent together with O_2 or as a 2nd carrier gas with volatile agents such as halothane or ether (Hall, 1971). However, it was pointed out that denitrogenation is essential. In addition, the use of N_2O precludes administration of the gas mixture in a completely closed circuit, since N_2O rapidly

171

saturates the system and its concentration may build up if it is continuously administered (Short, 1970).

Ether has been used for open heart surgery in calves (Larson et al., 1963; Wright & Holmes, 1964), whilst different anaesthetic techniques available for cardiovascular surgery in calves have been compared and evaluated (Donawick et al., 1969; Short et al., 1969). For calves under 8 weeks old scheduled for intrathoracic and intracardiac surgery with cardiopulmonary bypass and cooling, we routinely induce anaesthesia with $N_2O:O_2$ (7:3) delivered via a plastic-beaker mask. Halothane is then added as necessary for endotracheal intubation. The calves receive no treatment other than atropine 30 min beforehand, and cardiac arrhythmias which were encountered when xylazine and barbiturate induction was used in earlier experiments have since been avoided (CRC).

Recommended anaesthetic techniques

Preanaesthetic management
Adult cattle may be fasted for 24 h and denied access to water for 10 h prior to initiation of anaesthesia if intraabdominal and rumenal surgery are involved. Calves under 6 weeks of age may be fasted for 6 h but should be allowed access to water until anaesthetized. However, it is doubtful if these measures significantly alter the danger of rumenal tympany, and we prefer to pass a stomach tube at the earliest opportunity. Fasted animals must be rehydrated with dextrose–saline solution iv as soon as practicable.

Physical restraint and handling
Physical restraint of bulls must be undertaken with the greatest care for reasons of personnel safety; as a general rule, chemical restraint with xylazine is always advisable. Adult cows are held by an assistant by gripping the septum between the nostrils either manually or with metal 'bulldog' grips (Fig. 11.1). The head of the animal can be

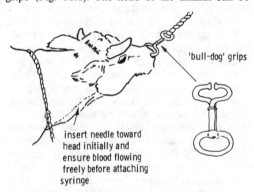

insert needle toward head initially and ensure blood flowing freely before attaching syringe

'bull-dog' grips

Fig. 11.1. Physical restraint and jugular venepuncture in the ox.

well restrained for iv jugular injection with a rope taken up and over a rigid bar as shown. We prefer to handle cows in a loose milking standing or against one wall in a loose box, rather than making injections in yokes or holding 'crushes'.

Young animals of 3–12 months are best haltered and tethered to a firm ring or bar, whilst an assistant positions the head and neck for injection by gripping the nostrils. The initial catching can be achieved by trapping the animal between a hinged gate and wall.

Younger calves are held by an assistant with one arm around the neck while the other hand positions the head by gripping the lower jaw. Thumb pressure exerted between the maxillae on the inside of the mouth will immediately restrain a strong animal whereas gripping of the nostrils is strongly resented as the calf struggles to breathe.

Chemical restraint and preanaesthetic therapy
Xylazine. Adult bulls and cows are best injected with xylazine (0·10–0·18 mg/kg im) in their normal holding pen. They can then be walked in a tranquillized state into the operating theatre within 5–7 min. Most animals are well sedated and lying in sternal recumbency within 10–25 min. The peak effect of xylazine lasts about 30 min and recovery is complete within 3 h. A state of basal narcosis bordering on general anaesthesia can be induced if a dose of 0·10 mg/kg is given iv, and a degree of analgesia as well as muscle relaxation is produced in adult cattle (Hopkins, 1972).

For tranquillization of a fractious cow, lower doses (0·05 mg/kg im) of xylazine or 0·1 mg/kg im of acepromazine are equally effective. The agents of choice vary with age in younger animals. We prefer acepromazine (0·1 mg/kg im) for preanaesthetic treatment of calves under 3 months of age, but give xylazine (0·2 mg/kg im) to animals of 3–12 months. Both agents allow adequate restraint for local analgesic techniques to be used for surgery.

Pethidine (2 mg/kg im) is a useful analgesic and does not produce significant respiratory depression in calves. It should be given some 30 min before anaesthesia is induced and its effects last about 4 h.

Atropine is valuable in calves under 8 weeks of age, and should be given im or sc 30 min before other agents. It is not indicated in adult cattle.

Local analgesia
It is proposed to describe only those local analgesic techniques which are of particular value to the experimental surgeon. Clearly, these will principally involve blocks of the flank for laparotomy for rumenal, uterine or foetal surgery, and blocks to the udder and teats for surgical preparations in the lactating animal.

Lignocaine (as a 2% solution with adrenaline 1:100 000) is the agent of choice for infiltration and spinal analgesia. It is diluted as necessary to a 0·5–1% solution. It is dangerous to administer more than 600 mg of lignocaine in an adult cow.

Local field infiltration blocks. After clipping, cleansing and preparing the surgical field as usual, a 75 × 1·65 mm (16 gauge) needle is inserted directly into the subcutaneous tissue and run parallel to the skin surface injecting 1% lignocaine at a rate of 1·0 ml/cm traversed. The pattern of infiltration depends on the length of the surgical incision and the innervation of the area.

(a) The cone pattern (Fig. 5.1) is suitable for superficial surgery.

(b) An inverted-L pattern (Fig. 5.2) provides excellent analgesia for flank laparotomy so long as proper care is taken in infiltrating each muscle layer and the peritoneum. The horizontal line of injection should be made just beneath the transverse lumbar processes, while the vertical is infiltrated just caudal to the last rib. The area should be ready for surgery within 10 min.

Lignocaine does not come into contact with tissue surrounding the surgical incision in either cone or L-blocking. In spite of the occasional failure to desensitize peritoneum, the inverted-L field block is as effective as paravertebral analgesia in our experience and is suitable for flank laparotomy, rumenal and uterine interventions (including caesarian section). Furthermore, we believe it causes less pain whilst injecting the analgesic than the paravertebral technique.

Conduction analgesia (nerve blocks). Paravertebral block is the only example of conduction analgesia which is commonly used in cattle for experimental surgery. Spinal nerves, thoracic 13 and lumbar 1 and 2, are blocked by surrounding them with 2% lignocaine as the dorsal and ventral branches pass above and below the transverse processes of lumbar vertebrae 1, 2 and 3 respectively.

After palpation of the transverse processes of L_1, L_2 and L_3, injection sites can be marked directly over the anterior border of the processes and approximately 5, 6, and 8 cm from the midline. A 100 × 1·25 mm (18 gauge) needle is inserted vertically at each site until the anterior border is detected, and 5 ml of 2% lignocaine is injected. The needle is then further advanced to pass anterior to the border and to increase depth by some 0·5 cm when a further 5 ml should be injected. This process should be repeated at points 1 cm on either side of the original injection (Fig. 11.2). Hence 3 separate injections are made above each transverse process and 3 ventral to it, involving infiltration with a total of 30 ml lignocaine (2%) around the appropriate nerve trunks.

If the paravertebral technique is properly carried out, the flank musculature should be well relaxed and the peritoneum rendered insensitive to incision. Although it is fairly simple to carry out in small Channel Island breeds, efficient location of individual transverse processes in really heavy subjects is difficult, and we prefer the field block in these cases.

Spinal analgesia. Caudal epidural analgesia is a useful technique in cattle and the extent of hind areas desensitized will depend on the quantity of lignocaine 2% injected.

The site of injection is the 1st intercoccygeal space. This is easily palpated by raising the tail vertically and lowering it again as illustrated (Fig. 11.3). The site should be clipped, scrubbed and disinfected. A 75 × 1·25 mm (18 gauge) needle is inserted. As a guide, 5 ml of 2% lignocaine will produce posterior block in a small adult up to 350 kg

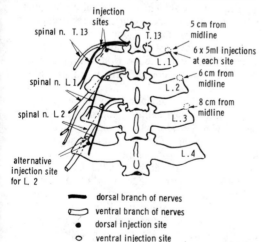

injection sites
spinal n. T. 13 — T. 13 — 5 cm from midline
6 × 5ml injections at each site
6 cm from midline
spinal n. L 1 — L.1 — L.2
8 cm from midline
spinal n. L 2 — L.3
L.4
alternative injection site for L. 2

▬ dorsal branch of nerves
▭ ventral branch of nerves
● dorsal injection site
○ ventral injection site

Fig. 11.2. Paravertebral nerve blocks in the ox. If T13, L1 and L2 are blocked, the flank from the last rib to just anterior to the pelvic girdle is desensitized.

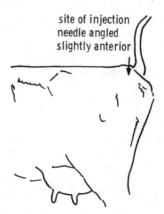

site of injection
needle angled
slightly anterior

Fig. 11.3. Caudal epidural analgesia in the ox: 1st intercoccygeal space located by raising tail vertically.

bodyweight, while large cows may need 10 ml. This will provide analgesia of the tail, anus, vulva and vagina. Onset can be detected by tail flaccidity within 2 min, but 10–20 min should be allowed before maximum analgesia develops. This should persist for 60–90 min.

Anterior block involves the injection of 60 ml of 2% lignocaine in small adults and up to 120 ml in very large beasts. As the motor innervation to hind limbs will be paralysed, the animal will be unable to stand and plenty of bedding should be supplied to avoid damage. Once the animal is lying down, it is advisable to hobble the hind legs loosely and remove the ties only when the tail has regained motor function. The chest should be slightly elevated to minimize movement of the drug anteriorly along the epidural space.

Spinal analgesia is attended by several potential complications. Severe hypotension may develop with signs of collapse, rapid, shallow respiration and tachycardia, especially if complete anterior blockade is attempted. This is particularly the case in ruminants as sympathetic vascoconstrictor nerves innervating viscera become blocked. Therapy with metaraminol (4 mg/100 kg iv) should be instituted immediately. Improvement is obtained within seconds and the pulse should regain a normal 'bounce' on palpation as compared with the weak thready pulse associated with hypotension. Another possible hazard is accidental injection of local analgesic into the subarachnoid space. Severe respiratory depression may occur and the animal will need assisted ventilation as well as treatment with metaraminol. Finally, particular attention should be paid to aseptic techniques in the preparation of the injection site, as infection within the canal is always a potential danger when spinal analgesia is used.

Surgical anaesthesia

General notes. If general anaesthesia is preferred to restraint and local analgesia, the following precautions will minimize the dangers inherent in ruminant physiology.

Always pass a cuffed endotracheal tube immediately anaesthesia is induced.

Always pass a stomach tube to allow continuous release of gas from the rumen, and keep a trochar and cannula available for emergency in case tympany develops.

Place the animal on a sloping table so that the hind quarters are lower than the neck, and viscera will then tend to fall away from the diaphragm.

Conversely, incline the head downward with respect to the pharynx so that saliva and rumenal fluid drains from the mouth.

Avoid retaining the animal on its back for long periods, as dependent portions of lung tend to become oedematous and poorly perfused.

Institute iv fluid therapy with Hartmann's solution at 1 litre/h and sodium bicarbonate at 200 mg/kg/h to balance loss of bicarbonate ions in saliva and prevent the possible development of an acidosis.

Injectable anaesthetic techniques. The most useful vessels for venepuncture in adult cattle are the ear veins and the jugular veins.

The marginal or central ear veins are easily identified if the ear is clipped and swabbed with alcohol. Venous return should be obstructed by thumb pressure at the base of the ear and venepuncture made with a 1·65 or 1·25 mm (16 or 18 gauge) butterfly needle which can then be taped in position for continuous infusion of drugs or fluids.

The jugular vein is easily seen after clipping and swabbing. Venous return may be obstructed by thumb pressure in the jugular furrow or by means of a nylon neck tourniquet which is easily released after insertion of the needle. The technique is simple in unsedated animals so long as proper physical restraint is applied and the head and neck are extended slightly away and up from the anaesthetist (Fig. 11.1). 1·65 mm (16 gauge) polyethylene cannulae of the 'Medicut' or 'Intracath' variety (p. 74) should be taped in position for further administration of drugs or withdrawal of blood samples.

In calves under 3 months of age both these sites may be used for venepuncture, but 0·80 mm (21 gauge) butterfly needles are used in the ear veins, and 1·25 mm (18 gauge) 'Medicut' needles are inserted into the jugular vein. In addition, the cephalic and the recurrent tarsal veins are useful. The cephalic vein is identified on the anteromedial aspect of the forelimb above the carpus, and after clipping and swabbing, may be raised by rubber tubing tourniquet for puncture. The recurrent tarsal vein is visible running diagonally across the lateral aspect just above the tarsal joint. A 0·80 mm (21 gauge) butterfly needle or 0·90 mm (20 gauge) 'Medicut' can be conveniently taped in place in each of these veins.

Endotracheal intubation presents no particular problem. In adult animals, tubes of 24–28 mm outside diameter are suitable, whilst a range of 12–16 mm tubes are used in calves. They should be lubricated, but preparations containing local analgesic drugs should be avoided. Calves are laid on their side after induction by rapid iv methohexitone injection. An assistant stabilizes the upper jaw with a tape around the dental pad and holds the tongue out as far as possible. The anaesthetist can then see the larynx after depressing the epiglottis with the tip of a laryngoscope blade, and the tube is passed under direct vision.

The most useful indicators of anaesthetic depth

are loss of muscle tone, variations in respiratory rate and ocular changes (Thurman et al., 1968). As anaesthesia is induced, the eyeball usually rotates downward until the pupil is hidden, but a strong palpebral reflex can be elicited by tapping the inner canthus. The eyeball assumes a fixed position with the pupil visible and partially closed as light surgical anaesthesia is attained, and slight movement of the iris will be detected if a strong light is shone directly into the eye. At this depth, slow, regular thoracic respiration should be present. Deep surgical anaesthesia is indicated by a widely dilated pupil, loss of reaction to light, loss of palpebral reflex and complete loss of response when the anal sphincter is pinched.

The barbiturates are recommended for induction of anaesthesia in cattle, but care must be taken in calves.

Thiopentone is best given to adults as a rapid iv injection at 12 mg/kg of a 10% solution. The wide safety margin allows a computed dose to be given as a single bolus. The animal will gently subside within 20 s and light surgical anaesthesia lasting 3–5 min is attained. Full recovery usually takes 45 min. This barbiturate should not be given to calves of less than 6 weeks of age as recovery may be dangerously prolonged. In young animals, 6 weeks to 12 months old, thiopentone should be used as a 2·5% solution, and a computed dose of 15 mg/kg given in stages; half the volume is injected rapidly and the remainder given slowly to effect over 60–90 s, observing the animal closely for loss of muscle tone, quickening respiration and loss of eye movements until apnoea occurs. The apnoeic period lasting 15–60 s is an ideal time to intubate the animal. The larynx is frequently closed when first visualized by laryngoscope, but compression of the thorax by an assistant will usually provoke gasping respirations and the tube may be passed without difficulty. A stomach tube should also be passed at this stage if anaesthesia is to be maintained for more than 15 min.

Methohexitone may be used as an alternative to thiopentone for induction in adult animals and it is the agent of choice in calves under 6 weeks of age.

It should be given to adult cattle at a dose of 5 mg/kg iv slowly to effect to allow 2–3 min of light surgical anaesthesia sufficient for endotracheal intubation. Recovery is usually complete within 20 min. In young animals 2–6 months of age, the drug can be given slowly to effect at 6 mg/kg over a period of 60–90 s to produce anaesthesia lasting 8–10 min with recovery to the standing position in about 15 min. Methohexitone can be given to calves under 8 weeks of age by rapid injection at 1 mg/kg iv, when anaesthesia is induced in 15–20 s and 2–3 min are available for endotracheal intubation, or it may be given at 4 mg/kg iv slowly

to effect over 45–60 s, when the duration of anaesthesia will be extended to about 7 min. The animal should be allowed to recover quietly in deep straw bedding and surrounded by straw bales, as muscle tremors and limb movements are commonly encountered after methohexitone.

Pentobarbitone is useful for basal narcosis and induction of light surgical anaesthesia in animals 2–6 months of age. It should be given at 25 mg/kg iv slowly to effect over 3–5 min, its peak effect lasting for 40 min. Recovery is usually quiet but it may take up to 4 h. Under no circumstances should pentobarbitone be used in calves under 8 weeks of age, since recovery may extend beyond 8 h and be associated with pulmonary oedema and respiratory embarrassment.

Inhalational anaesthetic techniques. Standard techniques are used and are complicated only by the large volumes of gas needed.

Halothane (1–2%) with O_2 is a suitable mixture for closed circuit administration with soda-lime reabsorption. Conventional Boyle's type apparatus can be used for animals up to 6 months of age, but specially developed machines such as those described by Hall (1971) are necessary for larger subjects. A flow rate of 4 litres/min with the expiratory valve open is suitable for calves up to 6 months, and rates of 5–6 litres/min are used for adults. This can be reduced to 1–2 litres/min once the animal is stabilized and the expiratory valve closed. Closed circuit administration is safe as long as the soda-lime absorption is efficient. For long operations, it is good practice to change the soda-lime every 2 h, regardless of colour indicator changes. Furthermore, the whole circuit should be washed out with fresh O_2 every 30 min with the valves open, and the rebreathing bag can then be refilled with fresh O_2 and halothane.

Halothane 1–2% with $N_2O:O_2$ (1:1) may be used in the same circle system semi-closed—i.e. with the expiratory valve open and a high flow rate of 4 litres/min maintained throughout the anaesthetic period. This technique is safer for extended periods of anaesthesia than closed circuit administration but greater amounts of anaesthetic agents are used. Deep anaesthesia with halothane should be avoided as the direct cardiovascular depression associated with this agent together with the poor venous return commonly encountered in recumbent ruminants may cause severe hypotension. Even if administered with care, halothane anaesthesia may result in a progressive fall in blood pressure to such levels as 70/40 mmHg when administered for more than 4 h. In our experience this hypotension is rarely fatal but is difficult to correct whilst halothane administration is continued.

Cyclopropane has the advantage that long periods of anaesthesia can be maintained without producing severe deviations in physiological functions. Although respiratory rate is depressed, hypotension and acidosis are avoided since the cardiac output is somewhat enhanced. In the event of emergency, the gas can be excluded and anaesthesia rapidly reversed by assisted respiration with O_2. It is particularly valuable for extended periods of anaesthesia in calves, as long as the explosive risk can be avoided by taking the necessary precautions.

The animals are intubated after induction of anaesthesia with thiopentone and maintained for 10 min on an anaesthetic mixture of cyclopropane and O_2. This is supplied at a rate of 300 ml cyclopropane: 1000 ml O_2 per min via a semi-closed circuit with the expiratory valve open and the soda-lime absorber bypassed. Thereafter, a closed circuit is established. As a guide and depending on leakages in the circuit, a flow of approximately 40 ml cyclopropane: 400 ml O_2/min is sufficient to maintain a calf of 80 kg but the anaesthetist will in practice have to adjust flows to fill the rebreathing bag without overdistension.

Balanced anaesthesia, involving CNS depression with $N_2O:O_2$ (1:1) supplied by IPPV, analgesia with pethidine (5 mg/kg iv) or fentanyl (0·02 mg/kg iv), and muscle relaxation with pancuronium (0·1 mg/kg iv), is satisfactory for extended periods of anaesthesia and for intrathoracic surgery. Alternatively, where the demands of the surgeon are less exacting, calves may be maintained for long periods on $N_2O:O_2$ (1:1) supplied by IPPV (after intubating under methohexitone anaesthesia) and supplemented by slow iv injection of α-chloralose at 80 mg/kg.

Recovery and post-surgical therapy
It is essential to retain the endotracheal and stomach tubes in position until the animal has fully recovered swallowing and eructative reflexes. The subjects should be returned to a warm pen with a dry non-slip flooring and positioned upright in sternal recumbency well supported by bales of straw. They should be observed to ensure that tympany does not develop. Fluid therapy with dextrose–saline and sodium bicarbonate solutions should be maintained for 24 h.

Sheep (*Ovis* spp) and goats (*Capra* spp)

Domestic sheep (*Ovis aries*) and goats (*Capra hircus*) are placid animals of manageable size and are the animals of choice in several areas of biomedical research. They tolerate implanted electrodes and indwelling catheters in blood vessels and lymphatics better than most other species, and make little effort to remove them. Hence they are often used for chronic experimental preparations to investigate pregnancy and foetal physiology, for studies of endocrine function, and for immunological or isotope research involving chronic collection of lymph draining different anatomical areas. An excellent account of the use of these animals in biomedical research is given by Hecker (1974).

Most surgical procedures can be performed under local analgesics given either by field infiltration, or by regional or spinal epidural blocks, and the docile temperament of these species allows a minimum of physical or chemical restraint. General anaesthetics are avoided whenever possible to minimize the risks of regurgitation and tympany. Local analgesia for abdominal surgery has been described by several authorities. The inverted-L field infiltration block described by Hall (1971) for cattle is equally useful in sheep and goats, but regional analgesia by the paravertebral technique (Hall, 1971) is often preferred. A technique for bilaterally blocking the pudendal nerves was described by McFarlane (1963), and is useful for relaxing and exposing the penis, and for manipulations involving the vagina. Caudal epidural analgesia (Bradley, 1966; Hall, 1971) is useful for intravaginal obstetrical procedures. Lumbar segmental epidural analgesia was produced in standing goats for surgery on the mammary gland and pregnant uterus by Linzell (1964), while Hopcraft (1967) and Hall (1971) restrained sheep on their left side for injection into the epidural space. Grono (1966) recommended restraining sheep in ventral recumbency with their hind legs over one edge of a table when injecting the local analgesic. He commented on the danger of unilateral or bilateral paralysis and lameness developing after epidural analgesia. Since this problem has also been experienced by Brook (1958), it was concluded that spinal anaesthesia had no great advantage over

Table 11.2. Ox: physiological data (resting values)

Measurement	Values
Respiratory frequency (breaths/min)	23–30
Tidal volume (l)	3–4·5
Minute volume (l/min)	90–120
Mean heart rate (beats/min)	60–70
Arterial blood pressure (mmHg)	130/90
Arterial blood pH	7·38
Pa O_2 (mmHg)	—
$PaCO_2$ (mmHg)	50
Haematocrit (%)	37 (33–48)
Haemoglobin (g/100 ml)	11 (8–14)
Erythrocytes (10^6/mm³)	8 (6–11)
*Blood volumes (ml/kg bodyweight)	
Total	60
Expected terminal exsanguination	30
Safe maximum single sample	7
Mean rectal temperature (°C)	38·5 (38–39)

general anaesthesia in sheep or goats for most procedures, but that it is the method of choice for delivery of lambs by caesarian section because foetal respiration is not depressed (Hecker, 1974). We have combined chemical restraint using xylazine (1 mg/kg), acepromazine (0·05 mg/kg) or diazepam (2 mg/kg) with local infiltration field blocks using 0·5% lignocaine for caesarian section and consider it to be safer than spinal analgesia. Sheep were recently used as a model for evaluating spinal subarachnoid and epidural analgesia with 0·25% tetracaine and 0·25% bupivicaine, and it was concluded that the regional analgesia produced was similar to that experienced in human work (Lebeaux, 1975).

The value of atropine in all ruminants has been questioned by Hall (1971), who feels that it serves only to render secretions more viscid and hence more difficult to drain from the oropharynx. However, Bryant (1969) suggested that salivation in sheep could be prevented by using high doses of atropine (0·2 mg/kg im repeated every 15 min iv), while Collan (1970) recommended scopolamine (0·03 mg/kg im) as superior to atropine. Lumb & Jones (1973) quoting Booth (1963) recommended even higher doses of atropine (approximately 0·8 mg/kg) given 15 min before induction, with maintenance doses of 0·15 mg/kg given iv every 15 min. We have used atropine in sheep during thoracic surgery to protect the heart from vagal inhibition, administering 0·5 mg/kg iv 15 min prior to induction with iv barbiturates and have not encountered problems with saliva accumulating.

Phenothiazine tranquillizers have been used as preanaesthetic agents (Irwin & Briel, 1966; Reitmeyer et al., 1967), and their ability to delay recovery from barbiturate anaesthesia was reported in goats (Linzell, 1964). Triflumeprazine (0·5 mg/kg iv) was recommended in conjunction with local analgesia or general anaesthesia by Jha et al. (1961) and Tyagi & Lumb (1961). Acepromazine was recommended as an adjunct to chemical immobilization of bighorn sheep (Ovis canadensis) with etorphine (Logsdon, 1969). We have found it satisfactory in sheep at 0·05 mg/kg in conjunction with local analgesia, and consider it the agent of choice in goats at 0·1 mg/kg im (CRC).

Logsdon (1969) reported the use of diazepam mixed in bait at approximately 13 mg/kg to facilitate handling of bighorn sheep. We sometimes use diazepam (2 mg/kg im) for sedation of sheep. This produces good muscle relaxation but no analgesia (CRC).

Chloral hydrate has been used alone to produce basal narcosis in sheep and goats (De Koch & Quinlan, 1926; Dukes & Sampson, 1937), and with magnesium sulphate in goats (Gadgil et al., 1969), but it has little to commend it. A similar degree of

sedation can be achieved more safely in sheep with xylazine at 1 mg/kg im (Straub, 1971). We have found goats to be very sensitive to xylazine and encountered marked cardiac arrhythmias at doses of 0·05 mg/kg im. However, it has been recommended for these animals by Hime & Jones (1970).

The dissociative agents have been used to produce varying degrees of CNS depression. Phencyclidine (1·0 mg/kg) was recommended (Wilkins, 1961) for short procedures in goats, and in conjunction with promazine for immobilization (Seal & Erickson, 1969). Ketamine was reportedly successful for sheep in the hands of Thurman et al. (1973) and was the anaesthetic agent of choice (2 mg/kg iv), for intrauterine surgery according to Taylor et al. (1972). At 20 mg/kg im, ketamine was found to be a satisfactory sedative for sheep, and physiological variables were not affected (Britton et al., 1974). Tiletamine–zolazepam (10–20 mg/kg iv) produced surgical anaesthesia in sheep which was immediate in onset and lasted for a mean time of 40 min, whilst recovery took up to 140 min (Ward et al., 1974). This group commented on the wide safety margin, and noted particularly that rumenal bloat did not occur since the animals continued to eructate throughout anaesthesia and recovery. Gray et al. (1974) claimed that it sucessfully immobilized various types of zoological sheep and goats at doses ranging from 5–15 mg/kg. We had very poor experience with ketamine at 2 mg/kg iv when attempting to mimic the surgery and anaesthesia reported by Taylor et al. (1972), and considered that analgesia and muscle relaxation were wholly inadequate for abdominal surgery. However, simultaneous iv injection of diazepam (1·0 mg/kg) or xylazine (0·05 mg/kg) with ketamine provided reasonable surgical conditions (CRC).

Neuroleptanalgesic combinations have had only limited acceptance in these species. Etorphine was successfully used in domestic sheep by Ducker & Body (1972), while etorphine–acepromazine was used to capture bighorn sheep (Logsdon, 1969) and is often useful in experimental situations (Mitchell, 1978). When thiambutane with and without acepromazine was assessed in sheep, it was found that the toxic signs which developed with thiambutane (2·0 mg/kg iv) alone were suppressed if acepromazine (0·1 mg/kg) was given iv 3 min before the analgesic (Harbison et al., 1974). Furthermore, this combination markedly reduced the dose of thiopentone required for induction.

Although Logsdon (1969) reported the value of muscle relaxants for immobilization of bighorn sheep and used suxamethonium at 0·7 mg/kg im, they do not appear to have been widely used for experimental work. We have found pancuronium (0·05 mg/kg iv) to be a good relaxant during anaesthesia for thoracic surgery, but have not evaluated the drug in sufficient animals to establish optimum dosages or observe toxicity (CRC).

The barbiturates have been used extensively for achieving various depths of narcosis. Thiamylal was evaluated in sheep by Ivascu & Cociu (1970), thialbarbitone by Titchen *et al.* (1949) and methitural by Ivascu (1971). Methohexitone (Stewart, 1965; Robertshaw, 1966; Hall, 1971) was recommended for sheep and goats at 4 mg/kg iv to produce 5–7 min of anaesthesia, with recovery complete in 10–14 min. According to Robertshaw (1966), anaesthesia may be prolonged by slow infusion of methohexitone at 1–2 mg/kg/min. We have found it ideal as an induction agent in lambs and adults prior to intubation and maintenance with inhalational anaesthesia. However, we always pretreat the animals with acepromazine or diazepam to prevent recovery excitement if methohexitone is used alone for short procedures, and reduce the dose to 2 mg/kg iv (CRC).

Thiopentone was given iv slowly to effect by Titchen *et al.* (1949) as a 5% solution. This group commented favourably on the smooth and rapid induction, but adversely on the frequent occurrence of rumenal regurgitation. Rae (1962) concluded that recovery from thiopentone was considerably quicker than from pentobarbitone, although the time to recovery of rumenoreticular activity was not significantly different in the study of Iggo (1956). Incremental doses were shown to accumulate and cause prolonged anaesthesia (Rae, 1962; Sharma *et al.*, 1970). According to Orsag (1969), recovery from thiopentone anaesthesia can be halved by injecting bemegride (5 mg/kg iv). An initial dose of 15–25 mg/kg of a 2·5% thiopentone solution given as a single rapid injection is ideal for rapid induction, and allows sufficient relaxation during the 30–60 s period of apnoea for easy endotracheal intubation (Hecker, 1974). Thiopentone should not be given to young sheep or goats below 3 months of age Hall (1976).

Pentobarbitone was used in adult sheep and lambs by Phillipson & Barnett (1939), who found wide variations in dosage and duration of effect, but that a mean of 30 mg/kg iv produced surgical anaesthesia lasting 15–30 min in adults, and surgical anaesthesia of longer duration in lambs. They also noted that castrated males were more sensitive to pentobarbitone than ewes or entire males. Anaesthesia with pentobarbitone was first produced in goats by Hill *et al.* (1935) and Lukens (1938). Allam & Churchill (1946) claimed that iv injection of about 10–15 mg/kg produced surgical anaesthesia, but Linzell (1964) recommended a dose rate of 30 mg/kg. Further extensive experience with this drug has accumulated since those early reports. The variability in response has been confirmed (Irwin & Briel, 1966), and a range

of 10·0–54·0 mg/kg iv reported (Harrison, 1964). Apnoea is commonly encountered at doses above 54 mg/kg, and the value of bemegride (22·5 mg/kg iv) in reversing this reported (Turner & Hodgetts, 1956). Relatively rapid recovery in healthy sheep is due to the rapid degradation in the liver (Rae, 1962). It is now accepted that pentobarbitone is satisfactory only for induction of anaesthesia (Hall, 1971; Hecker, 1974), as struggling may occur suddenly during surgery and in recovery unless other agents are also administered. Haemolysis of red cells in sheep (Potter, 1958) and goats (Linzell, 1964) has been attributed to propylene glycol in commercial preparations of pentobarbitone, and Hecker (1974) recommended that fresh solutions should be made up in sterile saline and used within 4 days.

An excellent account of inhalational anaesthesia in sheep and goats is given by Hall (1971). Halothane was strongly recommended either alone or with a $N_2O : O_2$ mixture. It can be used to induce anaesthesia at 3–4% using a close-fitting face mask or following induction with injectable agents and endotracheal intubation. Dhindsa *et al.* (1970) reported the use of halothane in semiclosed circuits in goats, and Hull & Reilly (1968) anaesthetized sheep repeatedly with this agent. Disturbance in respiratory function during inhalation of halothane was evaluated by Fisher (1961), and the depression of respiratory and cardiovascular function was blamed for the failure of foetal surgery in sheep (Comline & Silver, 1970). Methoxyflurane was reported as a satisfactory anaesthetic for sheep by Perper & Najarian (1967) but the agent has no obvious advantage over halothane in these animals. Ether has been used for maintenance of anaesthesia in sheep, although Hecker (1974) commented on the very slow recovery because these animals pass directly into a deep sleep. He also found that salivation was greater with ether than with other drugs. Cyclopropane was recommended as an anaesthetic agent for sheep or goats by Gregory (1947), Linzell (1964) and Hall (1971), who commented favourably on the speed of mask induction, the stability of anaesthetic depth over many hours of administration, and the rapid recovery within 15 min when administration was terminated. Both ether and cyclopropane are explosive in air or O_2, so cautery during surgery is excluded and closed circuits must be employed. Nitrous oxide and trichloroethylene were both recommended for use in sheep and goats following induction with other agents, although it must be remembered that trichloroethylene must not be administered in rebreathing (soda-lime CO_2 absorption) circuits.

Protection of the CNS (brain and spinal cord) from anoxic damage when the heart is stopped or aorta clamped can be achieved by cardiopulmonary bypass or by whole-body cooling. A technique for achieving hypothermia by whole-body cooling has been described (Borrie & Woodruff, 1955; Borrie & Mitchell, 1960). In brief, it consisted of placing the anaesthetized animal in a bath of iced water and preventing shivering by muscle relaxation with suxamethomium. Sheep weighing 45 kg could be cooled from 38 to 29°C in less than 1 h. Rewarming after surgery was achieved by replacing the ice-slush with water at 47°C and removing the animal when its core temperature had reached 35°C.

Positive–pressure ventilation was described in some detail by Borrie & Mitchell (1960) in their valuable contribution to experimental surgery in sheep. They recommended mechanical ventilation and provided data indicating the relationship between tidal volume and bodyweight.

Endotracheal intubation was described by Gregory (1947) and Hall (1971), and a relationship between age, dentition and the required size of endotracheal tube was plotted for goats by Linzell (1964). A rigid plastic or wooden bite-block ('gag') was recommended by Bryant (1969), and a length of metal tube by Borrie & Mitchell (1960) and Irwin & Briel (1966) for preventing the tube being chewed as anaesthesia lightens. Intubation without a laryngoscope ('blind') was well described by Hecker (1974).

Electrocardiographic measurement using 2 electrodes has been described (Brockway & McEwan, 1969) in experiments correlating cardiac performance with O_2 uptake. One electrode was passed down the jugular vein to the atrium and the other was placed in the vagina. Webster (1967) implanted 3 electrodes to obtain satisfactory records in unrestrained sheep. One was placed subperiosteally on the 5th rib adjacent to the cardiac apex, and the other two were implanted on to the 3rd and 5th thoracic vertebrae. Arterial pressure was measured by infant sphygmomanometer on a carotid loop by Denton (1957), and by sphygamomanometer around a hind limb by Romagnoli (1956) and Glen (1970). We normally make direct measurements using a pressure transducer after inserting cannulae into the femoral artery or carotid artery. Respiratory function was studied by Hales & Webster (1967) and Hoover et al. (1970). Electroencephalographic recordings have been made from electrodes inserted through the skull to touch the dura (Mullenax & Dougherty, 1964) and these were essentially similar to the traces obtained when needles were inserted into soft tissues overlying the skull.

Recommended anaesthetic techniques

Preanaesthetic management
Sheep brought in from pasture should be allowed

several days to adjust to laboratory diet before commencing experiments.

Many workers consider it essential to fast animals for 24 h before surgery (Hecker, 1974). Similarly, it has been suggested that they should be denied access to water for 10 h before anaesthesia is scheduled, thus reducing the risk of rumenal tympany during anaesthesia. However, we believe that rumenal tympany should be prevented by passing a stomach tube as soon as the animals are sedated and that in most circumstances it is better to allow access to hay and water before anaesthesia (CRC). Certainly, care must be taken in fasting heavily pregnant ewes, as they readily develop an irreversible metabolic syndrome (pregnancy toxaemia) which results in hypoglycaemia and CNS damage. It is advisable to give pregnant animals glucose solution by mouth ('drench') or stomach tube 6 h before anaesthesia and 500 ml of dextrose–saline solution iv 1 h before induction, with corticosteroid therapy im.

The operative sites are preferably clipped well before anaesthesia is induced.

Physical restraint and handling
Goats are easily restrained by holding the horns in the right hand and encircling the head and neck with the left arm (Fig. 11.4) or as in Fig. 11.5. The animal can then be backed into a corner and the neck presented to the anaesthetist for easy access to the jugular vein. Sheep should not be grasped by the wool but the head should be held and the neck encircled in one arm of an assistant. Intravenous injection into the jugular vein can be made in the standing animal, although we prefer to turn the sheep up until it is sitting on its haunches (Fig.

Fig. 11.4. Holding horned goats for jugular venepuncture.

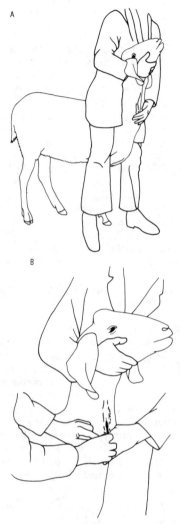

Fig. 11.5. Venepuncture in hornless goats.

11.6), when it will stay absolutely still for venepuncture.

Chemical restraint and preanaesthetic therapy

Preanaesthetic agents are useful when operations are to be performed under local infiltration or regional analgesia, and to improve the surgical conditions when barbiturates or ketamine are the chosen anaesthetics.

Atropine (0·5 mg/kg iv) 15 min prior to other agents and at 15 min intervals iv, or 0·8 mg/kg sc and at 30 min intervals sc, will significantly reduce secretions and protect the heart from inhibition when the viscera are handled.

The following drugs are recommended in order of slight preference, but each is effective in sedating or tranquillizing sheep.

Xylazine (1 mg/kg im) produces deep sedation in sheep within 10–15 min, the peak effect is maintained for 30–35 min and recovery is complete in 2–3 h. In goats a dose of 0·05 mg/kg im should not be exceeded.

Diazepam (2 mg/kg im or 1 mg/kg iv) is a safe and effective tranquillizer in sheep and goats. It is particularly effective as a supplement to iv ketamine.

Acepromazine (0·05–0·1 mg/kg im) is an effective ataractic in sheep and goats. The peak effect is reached in 15–20 min.

Local analgesia

Sheep and goats can be easily handled on a table if suitably premedicated with xylazine, diazepam or acepromazine. They will remain in the supine position or in lateral recumbancy if the limbs are taped out to operating table cleats, the head is covered, the ears are plugged with cottonwool and loud noises in the vicinity are avoided. If tympany develops, the animal should be placed in sternal recumbancy when it will usually eructate. In general the techniques described for the adult ox can be applied to sheep and goats and are recommended in order of preference.

Infiltration. 0·5–1% lignocaine should be used. Cone and inverted-L field blocks are useful, and the latter is suitable for analgesia of the flank for caesarian section, laparotomy and rumenal surgery.

Paravertebral block is simple to perform in sheep and goats and cannot result in posterior paralysis as unwanted sequelae. Using 2% lignocaine, spinal nerves T_{13} and L_1, L_2 and L_3 are infiltrated. The 1st lumbar process is palpated and the needle inserted about 3 cm from the midline, angled anteriorly and pushed in until it passes through the intertransverse ligament. A volume of 5 ml of lignocaine is injected at this site, the needle is then withdrawn until the point is judged to be above the level of the ligament and a further 2 ml is injected. The needle is then partially withdrawn and inserted caudally to repeat the process, i.e. one skin insertion site has been used to infiltrate nerves T_{13} and L_1. The other nerves are infiltrated by injecting over the transverse process of L_2 and L_3 and directing the needle to pass across the posterior border of each. Analgesia should be evident in 5 min (tested by pricking the flank skin and observing obvious hyperaemia) and should persist for 45–60 min.

Spinal analgesia. Lignocaine (2% with 1 : 100 000 adrenaline) is injected into either (a) the sacrococcygeal space or (b) the lumbosacral space. Injection can be made either with the animal standing or lying on one side with the back arched by an assistant holding all 4 limbs together. Alternatively, the animal can be laid on its sternum on a table but with the hind legs hanging over one edge so that again the back is arched. Stringent aseptic technique must be observed.

(a) Injection of 2 ml of 2% lignocaine into the sacrococcygeal space provides analgesia to the perineum, vulva and anal area.

(b) Lumbosacral injection: the whole of the hindquarters can be desensitized by injecting 8–10 ml of 2% lignocaine into the epidural space at this site. Motor paralysis is usually incomplete so that although the hindlimbs may move during an operation, they are unable to support the weight of the animal during recovery if standing is attempted. Analgesia is usually complete in 10 min, generally lasts for at least 2 h, and will be effective to about the level of the 1st lumbar vertebra. Mild convulsions may occur within 2 min of injection but these wear off rapidly and do not appear to be important.

Procedure: an area 20 cm square is carefully clipped over the lumbosacral space, which is located midway between the anterior borders of the ileum. The site should be scrubbed at least twice with an iodine preparation and finally sprayed with alcohol. The sheep is then restrained and the spine flexed as described earlier. The space is at a depth of 3–4 cm so a $50-60 \times 1.5$ mm (16 gauge) needle (with stilette) is necessary. The needle is inserted immediately behind the spinous process of the last lumbar vertebra and directed slightly caudally. Marked resistance will be felt as the tough ligamentum flavum is encountered, and the stilette should be removed at this stage.

After attaching a 20 ml syringe containing air up to the 5 ml mark, the needle is advanced gently through the ligamentum until sudden loss of resistance is detected by easy movement of the syringe piston. The epidural space has been entered. It is now essential to aspirate the syringe to ensure that no blood or cerebrospinal fluid is present. If the latter is seen, it indicates that the dura has been punctured and the procedure should be abandoned. Otherwise, the lignocaine can now be injected. The table should be tilted with the sheep's head down at 10°. If bilateral flank analgesia is required, the animal should be held on its back, but if one side only then that side should be dependent with the beast lying in lateral recumbancy.

Surgical anaesthesia
General notes. Whichever anaesthetic method is employed there are several management rules which should be adhered to.

Always pass an endotracheal tube and inflate the cuff. Sheep and goats are both prone to passive regurgitation of rumenal fluid during induction of anaesthesia and even small quantities of fluid inhaled may provoke intense bronchospasm. The airway must be protected as soon as the animal is sufficiently relaxed to pass a tube without provoking laryngospasm.

Always pass a stomach tube as soon as the endotracheal tube has been inserted. Sheep in particular are prone to rumenal tympany, with resultant obstruction of the surgical field, respiratory embarrassment due to pressure exerted on the diaphragm, and decreased venous return of blood. If gas still accumulates despite the stomach tube, a 75×2.10 mm (14-gauge) needle should be inserted into the swollen rumen before it becomes tense.

If possible the animal should be positioned on a jointed table, which is tilted so that the hindquarters are about 15 cm lower than the neck to allow the viscera to fall away from the diaphragm, and the head is inclined downward to allow saliva and rumenal fluid to drain away from the mouth.

The animals should not be retained on their backs for long periods, as dependent portions of lungs tend to become oedematous and poorly perfused. Sheep in particular deteriorate in such abnormal postures. In an extensive series of adult ewes anaesthetized for 4–6 h for thoracic and cardiac surgery in this laboratory (CRC), a progressive decrease in arterial and central venous pressure accompanied by low pH was monitored whilst the animals were retained on their back, but each measurement rapidly returned to normal if the subject was turned onto one side or the other.

Excessive loss of saliva (100–500 ml/h) may lead to a progressive acidosis, and hypovolaemia may develop as further fluid is lost by evaporation from the respiratory tract. Fluid therapy with Hartmann's solution given iv at 500 ml/h should be instituted and sodium bicarbonate should be injected at a rate of 100 mg/kg/h.

Body temperature should be monitored continuously and heat loss conserved where necessary. Hypothermia can be a problem in sheep in spite of their thick woolly insulation.

Injectable anaesthetic techniques. Venepuncture in sheep and goats is a simple procedure and a choice of site can be made depending on experimental requirements. The marginal and central ear veins are easily located after the ear has been clipped and swabbed with alcohol. We insert a 0.8 or 0.63 mm (21 or 23 gauge) butterfly needle and tape this to the ear for sequential injections as required. Goats and sheep can then be injected whilst standing with a minimum of restraint. This route of anaesthetic administration is clear of the neck which is often required for surgical cannulation of the jugular vein or carotid artery. The anterior cephalic and recurrent tarsal veins in the front and hind limbs respectively are also convenient vessels. Butterfly

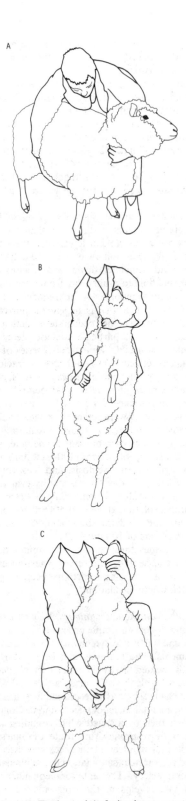

Fig. 11.6. Turning up sheep for jugular venepuncture.

needles 0·8 or 0·63 mm are taped to the leg for injection as required.

The jugular vein is easily punctured in sheep and goats provided the site is properly clipped. Goats can be injected whilst standing, with an assistant holding the head and neck extended slightly upward and away from the anaesthetist (Figs. 11.4 and 11.5). Sheep are more conveniently held in the sitting position with the head turned away from the anaesthetist (Fig. 11.6). A 1·10 mm (19–gauge) 'Medicut' needle is ideal for adults and the poly-ethylene cannula can then be left in place for further injections.

The depth of anaesthesia during induction can be assessed by several reflexes and observations:

(i) Thoracic respiration becomes rapid and shallow immediately following the period of apnoea and is frequently initiated by 2 deep gasps. As anaesthesia deepens, the rate increases still further but the character becomes more diaphragmatic. If the nostrils twitch spontaneously with each ex-piratory movement, the animal is still 'light'. If the animal is allowed to recover from a single dose of barbiturate, respirations usually become deeper and slower as the animal lightens. However, if anaesthesia is maintained with inhalational agents, slow thoracic respiratory movements are usually observed. The presence of diaphragmatic or ab-dominal movements indicates respiratory embarrassment.

(ii) As induction proceeds, there is a progressive loss of muscle tone until the jaw can be opened easily without evoking swallowing or chewing movements. At this point, a state of surgical anaes-thesia is approached. If this lightens, spontaneous chewing and swallowing movements may com-mence, together with uncoordinated limb move-ments.

(iii) The pedal reflex is less useful in sheep and goats than in dogs and cats. A hind limb is extended and the 2 digits squeezed together firmly. A lightly anaesthetized animal will flex the limb sharply.

(iv) The eye gives some indication of anaesthetic depth. In general, the pupil dilates initially and this may be accompanied by nystagmus (oscillating movements of the eyeball). As anaesthesia deepens, the eyeball may rotate downward but will usually return to a normal position. The pupil constricts as surgical anaesthesia develops. However, if the animal deepens to dangerous levels, the pupil will dilate completely and will not react to a strong light shone into the eye (photomotor reflex). A palpebral (eye-blink) reflex is retained until the sheep is deeply anaesthetized.

Barbiturates are recommended only for the induction of anaesthesia and are listed in order of personal preference. We give diazepam or acepromazine as preanaesthetic treatment in each case to ensure smooth induction and recovery. Dose levels of barbiturates should be reduced by 30% after diazepam administration.

Thiopentone (2% solution) renders a sheep or goat sufficiently unconscious for easy intubation within 20 s of a single iv rapid injection of 15 mg/kg. A period of apnoea lasting 30–60 s is usually encountered if the rapid injection technique is used but pressure applied to the thorax will usually trigger a return to spontaneous respiration. During this period of apnoea the mouth can be opened easily, the larynx sprayed with lignocaine and an endotracheal tube passed. The duration of anaesthesia is from 10–15 min.

Alternatively, the first half of the computed dose can be injected rapidly, followed by the rest to effect over about 2 min. The depth of anaesthesia is assessed by the onset of muscular relaxation as assessed by ease of opening the jaw, by the onset of shallow breathing and by the loss of the interdigital pinch reflex. The duration of light surgical anaesthesia is extremely variable after injecting by this technique but is approximately 10–25 min. A 2nd maintenance dose can be given iv about 20 min after the initial injection at a dose of 9–12 mg/kg. An endotracheal and stomach tube should be passed as early as possible after induction.

Lambs less than 3 months old should not be anaesthetized with thiopentone.

Methohexitone (4 mg/kg) given iv over 60 s to effect, produces anaesthesia of 5–7 min duration with full recovery in 15–20 min. If it is given 30 min after pretreatment with diazepam or acepromazine, it can be administered as a rapid iv injection at 2–3 mg/kg to produce immediate anaesthesia lasting for a similar period. Recovery is not then accompanied by limb movements or struggling, but the return to normal feeding is delayed. Diazepam and methohexitone can be given to lambs of any age but the methohexitone should always be given slowly to effect at 1–2 mg/kg.

Pentobarbitone may also be used to induce anaesthesia, and is rapidly metabolized in sheep and goats unless the liver is severely damaged e.g. by fascioliasis. Commercially available solutions containing propylene glycol should not be used in either species but fresh 6·0% solutions should be made up from powdered pentobarbitone in sterile saline and used within 4 days.

A dose of 30 mg/kg should be injected in 2 stages: half the volume is injected rapidly and the remainder is given slowly to effect over 3–5 min. An actual dose of 17–25 mg/kg is often sufficient to permit endotracheal intubation. The duration of light surgical anaesthesia after a single injection is 15–20 min and this can be extended by giving further doses of 12–15 mg/kg iv at about 20 min intervals as required. Pentobarbitone can be given to lambs and kids under 8 weeks of age at a computed dosage of 20 mg/kg but it is advisable to inject the whole volume slowly to effect. The duration of light surgical anaesthesia will be 30–45 min and full recovery will be delayed.

Severe respiratory depression and apnoea are encountered if the injection rate is too rapid and this may necessitate assistance with IPPV. An endotracheal and stomach tube should be passed as soon as possible. Analgesia is poor and pentobarbitone is not recommended for maintenance of anaesthesia in sheep. Violent struggling is often encountered during recovery from this barbiturate, but this can be avoided if it is given in reduced doses after pretreatment with xylazine or diazepam in sheep, or diazepam or acepromazine in goats.

Ketamine can be used for induction of anaesthesia if it is important that barbiturates should not be used, e.g. studies of the foetal circulation. We always pretreat the animals 15 min beforehand with diazepam (2 mg/kg iv) and then give an initial dose of ketamine (4 mg/kg iv). Further increments of ketamine may be infused iv to effect, but in our experience the animal must be intubated, and $N_2O:O_2$ (1:1) administered before good surgical conditions are produced. Alternatively, ketamine and diazepam may be used to restrain the animal whilst local infiltration analgesia is used for the surgical incision.

The main advantages of ketamine given alone to sheep and goats are that swallowing and eructative reflexes are preserved, the subjects return to normal posture within 15 min, and they are eating normally within 30 min. Respiration is not depressed but there is usually slightly raised arterial blood pressure. Foetal circulation is not affected (cf. halothane or barbiturates). However, muscle tone and reflex activity are insufficiently suppressed unless the agent is supplemented with diazepam or N_2O.

Etorphine–acepromazine (0·5 ml/50 kg im) is occasionally useful e.g. when sheep have to be manipulated within a sterile chamber and when conventional anaesthetics would be inconvenient. According to Mitchell (1978) who has used etorphine–acepromazine in a large series of sheep and experienced a very low mortality (less than 1%), the animals become stiff and arch their backs in 1–2 min after im injection, and then lie down on their side in 2–3 min. For animals less than about 30 kg bodyweight, it is more convenient to use etorphine–methotrimeprazine. As in other species, analgesia and central nervous depression are well developed but muscle tone is often exaggerated, and the limbs and thorax appear markedly rigid (Mitchell, 1978). Perhaps due to poor mechanical ventilation and to marked bradycardia, the animals may become hypoxic and a respiratory acidosis may develop. The effects are reversed within 2 min of iv injection of the antagonist diprenorphine (0·5 ml/50 kg).

Inhalational anaesthetic techniques. Anaesthesia may be induced directly in both species with a gas mixture of 2% halothane in $N_2O:O_2$ (7:3) if injectable agents are for any reason contra-indicated. The animals generally stand quietly while a rubber face mask or converted plastic beaker is fitted, and gradually increasing concentrations of halothane are administered via a Magill system with a flow rate of 4–6 litres/min. An endotracheal tube is passed as soon as the subject is adequately relaxed, usually after a period of 3–4 min inhalation. Alternatively, anaesthesia is induced with one of the injectable agents as described above, and the subject is transferred to an inhalation technique after endotracheal and stomach intubation.

Endotracheal intubation presents no particular problems, although laryngospasm is easily provoked in sheep and goats, particularly in young animals. We lay the animals on their left side immediately after induction with thiopentone. A tape is then passed around the dental pad and held in an assistant's left hand, whilst the tongue is fully extended with the other. The anaesthetist can then see the larynx after depressing the epiglottis with the laryngoscope tip. The larynx should be sprayed with 2% lignocaine and an endotracheal tube passed. The cuff must be inflated immediately and tested for leaks. If laryngospasm does occur, it may lead to complete airway obstruction. It may even be necessary to perform an emergency tracheostomy, pass an endotracheal tube between the tracheal rings and institute O_2 therapy.

Halothane (2%) with O_2: closed-circuit administration with soda-lime absorption and 3–5 litre rebreathing bags may be used with or without IPPV. A flow rate of 4–6 litres/min with the expiratory valve fully open should be used initially but, after the animal has equilibrated with halothane (taking 5–10 min), the expiratory valve can be closed and the gas flow reduced to 1 litre/min. The normal precautions already emphasized for the use of soda-lime and closed circuits should be observed.

Halothane (1–2%) and $N_2O:O_2$ (1:1): using the same circuit semiclosed with the expiratory valve partially open and a flow rate adjusted to 3–4 litres/min, inhalational anaesthesia can be safely maintained for prolonged surgery. However, halothane will produce respiratory and cardiovascular depression. We have measured a fall in spontaneous respiratory rate to 12–15/min from a normal 30–40/min, with an accompanying de-

crease in arterial pressure from 120/80 mmHg to 80/50 mmHg over a period of 2 h, even though the halothane concentration was only 1%. Whenever anaesthesia is scheduled for more than 1 h, we use IPPV with tidal volume set at 350–500 ml (depending on the size of animal), and at a rate of 15–20/min.

As we routinely employ diathermy during experimental surgery, we always use halothane and N_2O mixtures for inhalational anaesthesia. For acute preparations of long duration and for thoracic surgery, we use a balanced technique combining inhalation of $N_2O:O_2$ (1:1) and halothane (0·5%) with pancuronium (0·05 mg/ml) relaxation, and fentanyl (0·02 mg/kg iv) or pethidine (2 mg/kg iv) analgesia after induction and intubation with methohexitone (4 mg/kg iv).

Cyclopropane has the major disadvantage of explosive risk but is otherwise an excellent agent for inhalational anaesthesia in sheep and goats. Although respiration is depressed, the arterial blood pressure, heart rate and cardiac output are slightly elevated. To effect the most economic use of an expensive agent, anaesthesia is first induced with thiopentone and the animal is intubated. The subject is then connected to a circle system with the expiratory valve open and soda-lime absorber switched out of the system, and a 20% mixture of cyclopropane in O_2 (200 ml cyclopropane: 1000 ml O_2/min) is supplied for 10 min. A closed circuit including CO_2 absorption and rebreathing is then established, and a mixture of 40 ml cyclopropane: 40 ml O_2/min is administered to replace metabolized O_2 and to balance leaks in the circuit. Depth of anaesthesia can be altered rapidly by varying the cyclopropane in the mixture. A very stable experimental preparation can be maintained over many hours with cyclopropane and the animals will recover within 15–20 min of terminating the anaesthetic supply.

Hypothermia

Sheep and goats have large hearts relative to whole body size, and so are often chosen for experimental cardiac surgery and aortic clamping. Whole-body cooling is essential for any procedure involving circulatory arrest to the brain or spinal cord, remembering that neurones at all levels are damaged by anoxia of only a few minutes at normal body temperature. Conventional inhalational anaesthesia is employed during cooling by cardiopulmonary bypass machine but is modified during surface-induced hypothermia.

The sheep is prepared for surface cooling by clipping and, after anaesthesia is induced with thiopentone, it is intubated and immersed on its back in a bath containing ice-slush. Shivering is prevented by injecting suxamethonium (0·02

184

mg/kg iv). A sheep can be cooled from 38 to 28°C in about 60 min by this technique, and 25°C is about the lowest limit which can be attained with a reasonable chance of survival. Anaesthesia should be maintained with $N_2O:O_2$ (1:1) administered by IPPV until the temperature falls to 30°C, and small doses (3–5 mg/kg) of thiopentone are also given iv as required. The animal can be removed from the bath at this stage since the core temperature will continue to fall whilst it is anaesthetized and during surgery. Rewarming is achieved by immersing the sheep in water at 47°C until the body temperature has risen to 35°C. The animal is then dried, covered with blankets and artificially ventilated until it is clearly capable of spontaneous respiration. The endotracheal tube should be retained in situ until the animal has regained swallowing and cough reflexes.

The approximate 'safe' periods of circulatory arrest are 6 min at 30°C, 8 min at 28°C and 12 min at 25°C in adult sheep and goats. Calves and lambs under 2 months of age are usually more resistant to anoxic damage so these periods can be extended slightly.

Recovery and post-surgical therapy
Sheep should be returned to a warm pen with a dry non-slip floor (we prefer thick rubber mattresses). Endotracheal and stomach tubes, together with bite-blocks to prevent chewing, should be retained as long as the animal will allow. As with all ruminants, the subject should be positioned upright in the prone position supported on either side by bales of straw or hay, and carefully observed to ensure that tympany does not develop. If the animal is dry and has not been shorn, heat conservation does not demand particular attention at this stage, but an

Table 11.3. Sheep: physiological data (resting values)

Measurement	Values
Respiratory frequency (breaths/min)	20 (12–30)
Tidal volume (ml)	280–330
Minute volume (l/min)	5–6
Mean heart rate (beats/min)	75 (70–80)
Arterial blood pressure (mmHg)	114/90
Arterial blood pH	7·44
Pa O_2 (mmHg)	100
Pa CO_2 (mmHg)	38
Haematocrit (%)	34 (29–38)
Haemoglobin (g/100 ml)	11 (10–12)
Erythrocytes (10^6/mm³)	11 (8–14)
*Blood volumes (ml/kg bodyweight)	
Total	60
Expected terminal exsanguination	25
Safe maximum single sample	6
Mean rectal temperature (°C)	39·1 (38·2–40·0)

*Archer (1965).

Table 11.4. Goat: physiological data (resting values)

Measurement	Values
Respiratory frequency (breaths/min)	20
Tidal volume (ml)	300–350
Minute volume (l/min)	5·7–6·2
Mean heart rate (beats/min)	80 (70–125)
Arterial blood pressure (mmHg)	120/84
Arterial blood pH	7·4
Pa O_2 (mmHg)	—
Pa CO_2 (mmHg)	38
Haematocrit (%)	34 (29–38)
Haemoglobin (g/100 ml)	11 (8–14)
Erythrocytes (10^6/mm³)	15 (13–18)
*Blood volumes (ml/kg bodyweight)	
Total	70
Expected terminal exsanguination	30
Safe maximum single sample	7
Mean rectal temperature	39·4 (38·5–40·0)

*Archer (1965).

intravenous cannula or indwelling butterfly needle should be retained to allow fluid therapy with dextrose–saline and sodium bicarbonate solutions. The infusion of dextrose solution is mandatory (100 ml of a 5% solution) on completion of uterine or foetal surgery in heavily pregnant ewes, and we always give a corticosteroid–dexamethasone (0·08 mg/kg im) or betamethasone (0·04 mg/kg im) to these subjects for the following 4 days.

Chemical restraint and capture: exotic species

Etorphine has been used extensively in captive ruminants (Alford *et al.*, 1974). The value of xylazine has also been reviewed (Bauditz, 1972). Large numbers of roan antelope (*Hippotragus equinus equinus*) were successfully sedated for transportation with fentanyl–azaperone (Hofmeyr, 1974). Etorphine–xylazine (0·01–0·02 mg/kg:0·2–0·6 mg/kg im) has proved highly successful in mainly zoological specimens (Presnell *et al.*, 1973; Harrington & Wilson, 1974; Manton & Jones, 1974; Jones & Manton, 1976), but has also been recommended for field immobilization (Young, 1973; Drevemo & Karstad, 1974; Harthoorn, 1975).

African buffalo (*Syncernus caffer*): recommendations

Etorphine–xylazine (0·01 mg/kg:0·5 mg/kg im) provides complete immobilization (Jones, 1971), and is more consistent than etorphine–acepromazine, etorphine–fluanisone–acepromazine (Pienaar *et al.*, 1966) or fentanyl–azaperone (0·1 mg/kg:0·5 mg/kg im) (Pienaar, 1968). Captive specimens can be restrained with xylazine alone (0·3–0·5 mg/kg im) (Hime, 1973).

185

European bison (*Bison bonasus*) and American bison (*Bison bison*): recommendations
Etorphine–xylazine (0·01 mg/kg : 0·5 mg/kg im) is most effective for field immobilization (Jones, 1973). Captive specimens can be sedated with xylazine alone (0·3–0·5 mg/kg im) (Hime, 1973).

Musk ox (*Ovibos moschatus*): recommendations
Morphine-type drugs should not be used as severe excitation results. Xylazine alone (0·5–1·0 mg/kg im) is the best agent for restraint (Jones, 1973).

Hartebeestes (*Alcelaphus*) and wildebeestes (*Connochaetes*): recommendations
Etorphine–acepromazine (0·015 mg/kg : 0·1 mg/kg im) is the combination of choice in both these groups of antelope. No excitement is shown during induction (Jones, 1971, 1977c).

Kobs and waterbuck (*Kobus*): recommendations
These antelope all show some degree of excitation during etorphine–acepromazine induction. Etorphine–xylazine (0·01 mg/kg : 0·5 mg/kg im) is the best combination (Jones, 1977c).

Roan and sable antelope (*Hippotragus*), oryx (*Oryx*), and kudus, eland, nyala and bongo (*Tragelaphus*): recommendations
These animals show marked excitement and dyspnoea during etorphine–acepromazine induction, and etorphine–xylazine (0·01 mg/kg : 0·5 mg/kg im) is much the best combination (Jones, 1977c). Alternatively, fentanyl–azaperone (0·1 mg/kg : 1·2 mg/kg) can be used. Captive specimens may be calmed with xylazine alone (1·0–3·0 mg/kg im).

FAMILY CERVIDAE

Xylazine alone at doses ranging from 0·5–8·0 mg/kg has proved successful in different species of captive deer (Lindau & Gorgas, 1969). However, etorphine–xylazine is the safest way of capturing free-ranging deer of most species (Presnell *et al.*, 1973; Harrington & Wilson, 1974; Jones, 1977a). Fallow deer (*Dama dama*) are particularly difficult to capture safely, and it has been found necessary to reduce the standard dose rate of acepromazine by half to avoid a high mortality (Low, 1973). Perhaps the safest combination yet assessed in this species (Haigh, 1977) is fentanyl–xylazine (0·3–0·66 mg/kg : 0·46–1·3 mg/kg im) or fentanyl–azaperone (0·31–0·57 mg/kg : 0·8–1·3 mg/kg im). Tiletamine–zolazepam (CI744) is also claimed to be satisfactory in Cervidae (Gray *et al.*, 1974).

Recommendations
Free-ranging animals: etorphine–xylazine (0·01 mg/kg : 0·5 mg/kg im) is first choice for all species except fallow deer in which fentanyl–xylazine (0·5 mg/kg : 0·5 mg/kg im) is recommended.

Captive animals: xylazine is the sedative of choice in all Cervidae at the following dosages:

Mule deer (*Odocoileus hemionus*), white-tailed sika (*Cervus nippon*), red deer (*Cervus elaphus*)and spotted deer (*Axis axis*) 2–4 mg/kg im
Fallow deer (*Dama dama*) 4–8 mg/kg im
Elk (*Cervus canadensis*) 0·5 mg/kg im
Moose (*Alces alces*) 2·0 mg/kg im

In each species, a good degree of analgesia is obtained and the animals neither develop rumenal tympany nor regurgitate rumenal content. The onset of activity occurs within 10 min and the effect lasts 1–2 h. Surgery is then best done under local infiltration or regional analgesia (Hime, 1973).

FAMILY CAMELIDAE

Sedative-analgesics should not be used in any of this family since they provoke excitement, dyspnoea and convulsions. Phencyclidine (1·0–1·4 mg/kg im) and ketamine (7·5–15·0 mg/kg im) have been used (Beck, 1972), but xylazine (0·25–0·35 mg/kg) is very much better (Lindau & Gorgas, 1969; Hime & Jones, 1970).

Recommendations
Arabian (*Camelus dromedarius*) and Bactrian camels (*Camelus bactrianus*) are very sensitive to xylazine (0·5–1·0 mg/kg im) whereas llamas (*Lama glama*) and gaunaco (*Lama guanicoe*) need higher dosages (1·0–1·5 mg/kg im). The onset of effect occurs in 10 min and lasts 45 min to several hours, depending on the dosage used (Jones, 1973).

FAMILY GIRAFFIDAE

Whatever chemical is used for restraint, the animal should be prevented from falling or lying down whenever possible. Low doses of drug and physical support in the standing position in padded crates are essential (Hirst, 1966; Hime, 1973). Etorphine–acepromazine–hyoscine (1·0–1·5 mg total : 0·1 mg/kg : 0·1 mg/kg) has been recommended (Hirst, 1966) as has fentanyl–azaperone–hyoscine (0·1 mg/kg : 1·0 mg/kg : 0·1 mg/kg) (Pienaar, 1968).

Recommendations
Etorphine–xylazine (1·0 mg total : 0·5 mg/kg im) allows sedated subjects to walk into padded crates. Xylazine alone (0·2–0·8 mg/kg im) provides adequate sedation for superficial surgery if supplemented with local infiltration analgesia (Hime, 1973).

186

Domestic pig (*Sus scrofa*)

Domestic pigs (*Sus scrofa*) are suitable for many investigations in biomedical research as they have certain anatomical and physiological characteristics similar to man, yet they are often excluded from consideration partly because of their rapid growth rate during an experiment but also because of difficulties encountered in restraint and anaesthesia. Immobilizing agents and handling techniques therefore assume particular importance in this species.

The phenothiazine derivatives, chlorpromazine, promazine, acepromazine and trimeprazine have all been used in pigs, although there is some disagreement about their effectiveness. According to Perry (1964) and Hall (1971), pigs are easily restrained 45–60 min after the im injection of chlorpromazine (1·0 mg/kg), but Ritchie (1957) and Vaughan (1961) reported that sedation was always inadequate in a proportion of subjects. Other dose rates which have been recommended include 2·0–4·4 mg/kg (Ritchie, 1957), 2·0–2·5 mg/kg (Hill & Perry, 1959) and 4 mg/kg (Vaughan, 1961). Several authors agree that iv administration produces a more consistent response to phenothiazine drugs but this presents problems of restraint (Ritchie, 1957; Hibbs, 1958; Tavernor, 1960a; Vaughan, 1961). Furthermore, venous thrombosis is a common problem unless very dilute solutions are used. Doses of chlorpromazine recommended by the iv route ranged from 0·5–3·3 mg/kg, depending on the degree of sedation required, and peak effect was reached in 10–20 min.

Promazine has been used at 2 mg/kg by iv, and 4 mg/kg by im injection (Vaughan, 1961). Other accounts (Johnson, 1961; Sinclair, 1961) emphasize the usefulness of promazine in adult sows. Booth (1963) recommended preanaesthetic treatment with promazine (2 mg/kg im), pethidine (2 mg/kg) and atropine (0·06 mg/kg im) to be given 45–60 min prior to general anaesthesia. According to Hall (1971), trimeprazine is more effective and produces less hypotension than chlorpromazine, but Tavernor (1960) found that it was an unreliable tranquillizer in pigs unless given by iv injection at 2·2 mg/kg. Acepromazine was recommended at dose rates of 0·03–0·1 mg/kg (Hall, 1971), and the drug gave more predictable responses in miniature swine than either promazine or perphenazine (Ragan & Gillis, 1975). Several of these commentators suggest that phenothiazine drugs are valuable because they do not potentiate barbiturates in pigs, but this seems a questionable proposition based, as it is, on one report in the literature (Vaughan, 1961).

The dissociative agents phencyclidine, ketamine and tiletamine have each been used in Suidae. Phencyclidine was first evaluated in domestic pigs by Tavernor (1963), who concluded that it was a most useful agent for this species. At 2 mg/kg im the subjects became recumbent within 5 min, and analgesia was sufficient for superficial surgery. Perry (1964) found that 4·0–6·0 mg/kg im was needed to avoid excitement and ataxic movements in young pigs. Since these early reports, phencyclidine has been used extensively in pigs of all sizes including pregnant sows, and has proved invaluable (Gillman, 1965; Mount & Ingram, 1971; Vaughan, 1977). However, when used in miniature swine by Ragan & Gillis (1975), it rapidly produced what they described as 'persistent ataxic hysteria', and it was concluded that the agent was contraindicated. They also found that barbiturate dosage was greatly reduced, recovery from halothane anaesthesia was considerably prolonged and cardiac arrhythmias were common after its use as a preanaesthetic agent. House *et al.* (1971) found that phencyclidine alone rapidly produced sedation, but that paddling movements of limbs frequently occurred; they recommended that phencyclidine should be given at 2 mg/kg im together with chlorpromazine at 1 mg/kg im after atropine pretreatment to prevent salivation. A similar regimen was recommended in zoo pigs (Suidae) and peccaries (Tayassuidae) by Manton (1966) and Manton & Jones (1972). Phencyclidine (1·0–1·5 mg/kg im) combined with promazine (1·0 mg/kg im) or acepromazine (0·1 mg/kg im) produced sedation in 8–10 min, recumbency in 15–20 min and the animals recovered in 4–5 h. Jones (1973) reported that mild clonic spasms of the neck and mandibular muscles encountered in a collared peccary (*Tayassu tajacu*), were counteracted by giving a further 0·1 mg/kg acepromazine. Cases of fatal ulcerative gastritis in collared peccaries 24–48 h after phencyclidine sedation were reported from the same centre, but were never definitely attributed to the drugs (Jones, 1973).

Ketamine has been evaluated in this species (Roberts, 1971; Thurman *et al.*, 1972) but not in miniature pigs. According to these authors, pigs were rapidly immobilized by ketamine at doses of 20 mg/kg im, and analgesia was adequate for minor surgical procedures. However, in our experience, ketamine alone is not always satisfactory in pigs. A few animals pass through an excited, ataxic phase, with markedly accelerated respiration and cardiac rate so we now give ketamine at 10–20 mg/kg im about 3 min after diazepam at 1–2 mg/kg im.

Tiletamine–zolazepam was reported to produce surgical anaesthesia at doses in excess of 19 mg/kg im in collared peccaries, and at 4·0–8·8 mg/kg im in domestic pigs by Gray *et al.* (1974).

From the evidence in the literature, it may be concluded that the dissociative agents have a definite place in pig sedation and restraint, but are best given with ataractics such as acepromazine or diazepam.

Other ataractics have been assessed in miniature swine by Ragan & Gillis (1975). Chlordiazepoxide (5–10 mg/kg im) produced unpredictable sedation after about 60 min. Chlorprothixene (3·3 mg/kg im) was an effective tranquillizer but the peak effect was not reached until 60 min after injection, and severe pain was caused at the injection site. Diazepam (5·5 mg/kg im) was effective as a tranquillizer, and at 8·5 mg/kg im produced excellent sedation within 30 min, potentiated barbiturates by about 50% and enhanced muscle relaxation when used together with these drugs. The authors concluded that diazepam was the ataractic of choice in miniature swine.

Droperidol and azaperone, neuroleptic agents of the butyrophenone group, have both been used in pigs. Mitchell (1966) found that droperidol (0·1–0·4 mg/kg im) produced good sedation in 5–15 min, but recovery took 2–5 h depending on the dose used. These results were partially confirmed by Lamberth (1968), who gave weaner pigs 0·4 mg/kg of droperidol im and claimed that good sedation was induced in an average time of 4 min. Recovery, however, averaged only 28 min. Similarly, azaperone was recommended for tranquillization and sedation in domestic pigs (Marsboom & Symoens, 1968); after im injection of 4–8 mg/kg, deep sedation developed in 15–30 min and persisted for 30–120 min. Several reports followed in quick succession. Clarke (1969) reported that a small fall in blood pressure invariably followed im injection of azaperone (0·3–3·5 mg/kg). Low doses of 0·5–3·0 mg/kg were recommended to prevent transport stress and aggressive behaviour (Symoens & Van den Brande, 1969; Casteels et al., 1969; Symoens, 1970). Extensive clinical trials were reported by Lang (1970), and by Callear & Van Gestal (1971). However, Jones (1972) found that azaperone alone at doses up to 4 mg/kg im was ineffective in collared peccaries. In our experience over 5 years it has proved (at dose rates up to 8 mg/kg im) little better than acepromazine (0·2 mg/kg im) and less reliable than diazepam (2–8 mg/kg im) in domestic pigs. We have concluded that it is an effective tranquillizer for animals under 20 kg but it is unreliable in large boars or sows (CRC).

Combinations of azaperone and droperidol with sedative–analgesics or hypnotics have also been used in pigs. Mitchell (1966) concluded that there was no advantage in using droperidol combined with fentanyl (or haloanisone with fentanyl) over using the neuroleptic alone. Ragan & Gillis (1975)

assessed droperidol (2 mg/kg) with fentanyl (at 0·04 mg) in miniature swine, and found that the animals became excited rather than sedated. Lamberth (1968) found that droperidol (0·4 mg/kg) given to standard weaner pigs together with pethidine (5 mg/kg) provided effective sedation but the response was not significantly better than with the neuroleptic alone. Pethidine at 5 mg/kg im alone was ineffective. Conversely, Piermattei & Swan (1970) reported that droperidol (1·6 mg/kg) and fentanyl (0·03 mg/kg) were highly effective in sedating miniature swine prior to halothane anaesthesia. Azaperone combined with fentanyl has also been used in immobilizing wild warthog, Phacochoerus aethiopicus (Pienaar, 1968; Janssen, 1969).

Azaperone has also been used in combination with the hypnotic agent, metomidate. This drug, if used alone, induces sleep in pigs accompanied by very good muscle relaxation but little or no analgesia. Dimigen & Reetz (1970) concluded that azaperone (2 mg/kg im) and metomidate (15 mg/kg ip) provided a state of light surgical anaesthesia within 10–15 min in pigs up to 50 kg in weight. Clinical evaluation of the combination has since confirmed its value in pig anaesthesia, although it has become standard practice to inject the metomidate iv in larger subjects (Prasse, 1970; Roztočil et al., 1971a; Jones, 1972; Callear & Van Gestal, 1973; Cox, 1973). The effects of these drugs on cardiovascular and respiratory functions were assessed by Jageneau et al. (1974), who found that heart rate, respiratory rate and tidal volume decreased to 80% of control values within 10 min after injection and gradually recovered within 60 min. More recently Orr et al. (1976) found that, although administration of the drugs led to decreases in cardiac and pulmonary function, this was insignificant as compared with barbiturate or inhalational anaesthesia. They concluded that azaperone–metomidate was the drug combination of choice for setting up physiological preparations. Our experience with azaperone and metomidate over 5 years indicates that the combination is valuable for induction of anaesthesia in pigs under 50 kg since administration is simple and there is a wide therapeutic index. However, we prefer phencyclidine with acepromazine or diazepam as recommended above for large boars and sows (CRC).

Morphine and related sedative-analgesic compounds have a variable effect in pigs. Jones (1957) found that morphine stimulated rather than depressed the CNS and this was confirmed by others (Vaughan, 1961; Wright & Ball, 1961). However, Booth et al. (1965) reported that morphine was a satisfactory sedative in pigs at a dose of 0·1–0·9 mg/kg. Vaughan (1961) found that thiambutene also produced excitement and convulsions in some pigs. Similarly, pethidine was mildly depressant in some pigs but contributed nothing to restraint, although it was useful as a post-operative analgesic at 10 mg/kg sc. Hastings *et al.* (1965) used pethidine (1·0 mg/kg sc) in pigs as a prelude to administering muscle relaxants and general anaesthetics, but they did not comment on its effects. Lamberth (1968) evaluated pethidine at 5 mg/kg im in weaner pigs and found that it had no sedative effect, nor did he encounter any cases of excitement directly attributable to the drug. Fentanyl has been used in combination with droperidol or fluanisone in the sedation of pigs (Mitchell, 1966), and with azaperone in the immobilization of warthog (Pienaar, 1968; Janssen, 1969) but with no obvious advantage over the neuroleptic agents alone. Lumb & Jones (1973) used fentanyl–droperidol at 0·1 ml/kg im as preanaesthetic medication for pigs but did not comment on its value. On the other hand, Ragan & Gillis (1975) had no doubt that the drugs (0·1 ml/kg im) were contraindicated in miniature swine since they caused CNS stimulation within 5 min and severe ataxia resulted. Their results were at variance with those reported by Piermattei & Swan (1970) who allegedly found fentanyl–droperidol useful at 0·12 ml/kg im in miniature swine prior to halothane anaesthesia. Etorphine in combination with acepromazine has been recommended in the past at a dose of 0·01 ml/kg of the mixture (Leach, 1972) but has not been widely accepted for pig work.

In preliminary studies, alphaxolone–alphadolone (6–8 mg/kg im) was reported to produce excellent sedation in pigs (Cox *et al.*, 1975). This could be deepened to surgical anaesthesia within 20 s if injected iv at 2·0–3·0 mg/kg. The authors concluded that the agent was superior to etorphine–acepromazine in that excellet muscle relaxation was produced with minimal impairment of respiration, and that recovery was free from the struggling often encountered during recovery from metomidate. Similar results have been reported in pigs being prepared for liver transplantation (Baker & Reitter, 1976). Irritation at the site of im injection was not encountered as was reported in earlier attempts to sedate pigs with similar steroids (Huhn & Schulz, 1961). However, as in other species, the large volume needed for im administration is a big disadvantage, and precludes its widespread clinical use in pigs. We consider it to be the agent of choice for neonates and pigs under 10 kg, both for sedation and intravenous anaesthesia.

The use of anticholinergic agents in miniature swine was considered mandatory by Ragan & Gillis (1975) whatever method of narcosis was subsequently followed, in order to reduce secretions and lessen susceptibility to cardiac arrhythmias. They recommended atropine sulphate (0·05 mg/kg sc) 30 min prior to anaesthesia, or atropine methyl nitrate (0·10–0·15 mg/kg iv) immediately after induction with short-acting barbiturates. We use atropine sulphate routinely at 0·05 mg/kg sc prior to all forms of chemical restraint or anaesthesia in pigs (CRC).

Neuromuscular blocking agents have been recommended for facilitating endotracheal intubation and for increasing muscle relaxation during general anaesthesia. Hastings *et al.* (1968) recommended suxamethonium (2·2 mg/kg iv) for intubation, whilst De Young *et al.* (1970) found 0·88–1·1 mg/kg sufficient for restraining swine long enough for intubation and induction with halothane anaesthesia. However, we believe that light anaesthesia should be induced before neuromuscular blocking agents are given iv. Ragan & Gillis (1975) injected even lower doses of suxamethonium (0·6 mg/kg iv) after first inducing light anaesthesia with short-acting barbiturates iv. The latter group used this agent with halothane anaesthesia in miniature swine without eliciting the malignant hyperthermia reported by Jones *et al.* (1972). We have used suxamethonium (2 mg/kg iv), gallamine (2 mg/kg iv) and pancuronium (0·05 mg/kg iv) in Landrace × Large White pigs during prolonged halothane anaesthesia (4–5 h) without encountering hyperthermia (CRC).

The barbiturates have long been used for inducing anaesthesia in pigs. Thiopentone, thiamylal and methohexitone are necessarily given by the iv route as their duration of activity is so short, but this is inconvenient in pigs unless they have been previously sedated. Pentobarbitone has been given by the ip or intratesticular route as an alternative to iv injection, but the margin of safety is then dangerously narrow (CRC).

Thiopentone was used as a 5% solution by Muhrer (1950) to induce anaesthesia in pigs. He found that the required dose varied considerably. At dose rates between 8–10 mg/kg, anaesthesia lasted 5–10 min and recovery occurred in 30–60 min if half the computed dose was given rapidly into the ear vein, followed by the remainder over 2–3 min. Mount & Ingram (1971) suggested doses of 10–15 mg/kg given iv very slowly to produce anaesthesia lasting 10–20 min. However, Hall (1971) found that low doses (5 mg/kg) could be given iv as a single injection for immediate induction of anaesthesia, and the dose could be reduced still further if the subject had been treated with azaperone (2 mg/kg im) some 20 min beforehand. This authority (Hall, 1971; Hall, 1976) recommends that solutions should be 2·5% or less to avoid perivascular necrosis, and that it is unwise to administer the drug via the anterior vena cava by the technique of Carle & Dewhirst (1942) as peri-vascular leakage is likely to occur. Pigs below 6 weeks of age should not be given thiopentone as they are deficient in the liver enzyme responsible for biodegradation of the drug (Hall, 1976).

Thiamylal was used as a 10% solution by Miller & Gudmundson (1964). An initial dose of 3–4 mg/kg iv was used to induce anaesthesia, and further increments were given for prolonging the duration. Sawyer et al. (1971) maintained thiamylal anaesthesia in pigs for 3 h reporting that cardiac output was depressed and recovery was slow as compared with halothane or methoxy-flurane anaesthesia. Ragan & Gillis (1975) found that doses of 12–15 mg/kg iv provided safe anaes-thesia for short periods, and that sequential incre-ments could be given by indwelling catheter to extend the anaesthetic period.

Methohexitone can also be used to induce anaes-thesia in pigs with safety (Emberton, 1966). According to Noakes (1966), a single dose of 11–12 mg/kg iv is sufficient for short periods of anaes-thesia and recovery is complete in 10–15 min.

Pentobarbitone (25 mg/kg) was recommended for iv injection in small weaner pigs (Jones, 1957). It was noted that violent reflex activity in response to surgical stimuli returned within 15–20 min of injection although full recovery took from 3–8 h (i.e. surgical anaesthesia was considerably briefer in pigs than dogs after a single injection). Vaughan (1961) suggested doses of 24 mg/kg for pigs up to 50 kg, 20 mg/kg for subjects 50–100 kg and 10 mg/kg for larger animals. Sawyer et al. (1971) reported a prolonged recovery time in miniature pigs after 3 h of pentobarbitone anaesthesia, and noted depressed cardiac output with increased peri-pheral vascular resistance. Ragan & Gillis (1975) reporting on their experience with pentobarbitone in minature swine, suggest a basic computed dose of 20 mg/kg iv to be increased by 10–15% for lean animals and reduced by an equivalent amount in obese subjects. They commented favourably on the lack of excitatory phase either during induction or recovery but also noted the short duration (10–30 min) of surgical anaesthesia. Wesolowski (1962) gave pentobarbitone ip to pigs destined for experi-mental thoracic surgery, but Hall (1971) and Ragan & Gillis (1975) emphasize the variability in narcosis which is inevitably produced by this route using doses between 20–24 mg/kg. The intra-testicular route suggested by Henry (1968), em-ploying doses of 45 mg/kg, has little to commend it. Ragan & Gillis (1975) recommended the iv injection of the analeptic bemigride at 3 mg/kg in miniature swine for reversing emergency respiratory failure during barbiturate anaesthesia.

α-chloralose was used in experiments to study baroreceptor reflex mechanisms in pigs (Booth et al., 1960). Hypnosis was induced with 55–86 mg/kg iv after administration of morphine (0·3–0·9 mg/kg), but limb paddling movements were encountered necessitating iv administration of small doses of pentobarbitone to effect.

Epidural analgesia has been described by Hopcroft (1965), Getty (1966), Booth (1969) and Hall (1971) for abdominal surgery and obstetrical procedures. The method of Hall (1971) will be described later in this section (p. 195).

Inhalational anaesthesia presents no particular problems once pigs have been adequately restrained. Weaners may be held under the arm of an assistant and anaesthesia induced direct with gas mixtures delivered to rubber face masks, plastic beakers, or buckets equipped with a rubber gasket to fit close over the pig snout (Routledge et al., 1968; Mount & Ingram, 1971). However, it is now accepted that pigs should be intubated as soon as convenient either following light anaesthesia and muscle relaxation with 2 mg/kg iv of suxa-methonium (Hastings et al., 1965), or after pre-anaesthetic sedation and induction of anaesthesia with a short-acting agent iv (Ragan & Gillis, 1975). We have induced anaesthesia in pigs up to 25 kg in weight with 4% halothane and $N_2O:O_2$ (1:1) administered by mask, and intubated them when they were sufficiently deep, but this is recommen-ded only when muscle relaxants or injectable agents are contraindicated for the experiment (CRC). Several accounts of intubation have in-dicated the problems in this species (Hill & Perry, 1959; Fowler et al., 1963; Rowson, 1965; Hall, 1966). Briefly, difficulties are caused by anatomical features such as the small lumen of the trachea relative to the size of animal, the larynx set at an angle to the trachea so that passage may be obstructed at the cricoid cartilage, vocal chords which tend to obstruct the passage of the tube and laryngospasm which is easily provoked. In ad-dition, difficulties in locating the larynx may be encountered due to excess salivation and secre-tions, and to the long face of larger pigs.

Ether and chloroform have been used in the past and trichlorethylene administration via a simple open drop method was described by Booth (1963). Cyclopropane administered in closed circuits to intubated pigs was found satisfactory by Hall (1966), but the disadvantages of flammability and tendency to vomiting during recovery have limited its use. Halothane, methoxyflurane and N_2O, are the agents now most widely accepted in pig anaes-thesia and we have recently found enflurane an excellent alternative to halothane in these animals (CRC).

Halothane has been recommended by several workers (Vaughan, 1961; Dawson, 1963; Dziuk et al., 1964; Hall, 1966; Terblanche et al., 1968;

Mazzoni et al., 1971). The significant reduction in cardiac output and work was emphasized by Sawyer et al. (1971). Halothane in a gas mixture of equal parts of $N_2O:O_2$ was considered to be the anaesthetic method of choice in heart-lung by-pass experiments by Piermattei & Swan (1970), whilst $N_2O:O_2$ (70:30) was used with halothane for thoracic surgery in swine by Hastings et al. (1965). However, Ragan & Gillis (1975) abandoned this mixture for miniature pigs and returned to maintenance with halothane (0·5–1·5%) and O_2 because they considered that the depth of anaesthesia could be more easily controlled.

Methoxyflurane may also be used for maintenance of anaesthesia, but has a significantly longer recovery period than halothane and also reduces cardiac output (Sawyer et al., 1971).

Electroanaesthesia was assessed in pigs by Short (1964), who found that it was particularly difficult to maintain a uniform level of narcosis in this species. Electrodes were placed on the head and a current of 100 mA was passed at a frequency of 700 cycles/s. Ragan & Gillis (1975) also recorded difficulties in controlling the anaesthetic plane in miniature pigs, but Michwitz & Reinhard (1966) reported successful electroanaesthesia including anaesthesia for abdominal surgery in pigs.

Valuable data can be obtained from the fairly extensive literature on cardiovascular research involving pigs but unfortunately there is relatively little information available on respiratory function. An excellent review of cardiovascular and respiratory function is presented in Mount & Ingram (1971), and Smith et al. (1964) and Johnson (1966) described methods of restraint and altered cardiovascular function in pigs subjected to starvation and refeeding stress.

Cardiopulmonary mechanics in anaesthetized pigs have been described by Attinger & Cahill (1960). Values for blood gases are given in tables published by Bartels & Harms (1959). Figures for tidal volume were given by Morrison et al. (1967) and Ingram & Legge (1970), and the respiratory rate by Ingram (1964a, b).

Recommended anaesthetic techniques
Preanaesthetic management
Pigs should be fasted for 24–36 h but have access to water until the first preanaesthetic agents are administered. During the fasting period they should be kept without bedding to ensure that nothing is ingested. Attention to the alimentary tract is important in pigs, especially if prolonged abdominal surgery is to be undertaken. There are several reasons for these precautions. Firstly, swine readily vomit under anaesthesia if food is present in the stomach. They are also prone to develop severe gaseous gastrointestinal distension which not only

makes intra-abdominal surgery difficult but interferes with ventilation and with venous return; capillary stasis, oedema of the gut wall and pooling in the mesenteric veins may result from this distension, and predispose to acute cardiovascular failure. Furthermore, handling of the distended bowel and packing off from the operative field increases the risk of apnoea and severe shock due to tension on the mesenteric root. Emphasis is laid on the need for watering because swine are prone to sodium chloride toxicity if deprived of water, particularly in high ambient temperatures.

Evacuation of the alimentary tract can be ensured by the administration of magnesium sulphate (25g) or sodium sulphate (25–125 g) orally, or castor oil at about 3 ml/kg by gastric

A

B

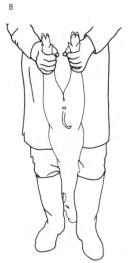

Fig. 11.7. Pig up to 25 kg held for simple procedures.

intubation some 12–18 h before surgery. Where surgery or radiography of the descending colon is to be performed, a soapy enema is advisable (Ragan & Gillis, 1975).

Physical restraint and handling

Pigs are particularly uncooperative animals and resist physical coercion with violent struggling and noisy protest. Any attempt at handling therefore requires gentle but forceful application of proper techniques with an adequate number of assistants. Animals up to 25 kg can be picked up by both hind limbs, held with the neck and head trapped between an assistant's knees and presented for injection or minor procedures (Fig. 11.7). Subjects 25–60 kg can be laid on their backs and restrained in a V-shaped trough, or held up by the hind legs and suspended head down in a waste bin.

Intramuscular injections can be given into the rump with the pig restrained as described above. Larger subjects may be trapped behind a gate pushed against a wall or can be tempted into a weighing cage, trolley or crate. A pig will stand more quietly if its back is scratched during injection, and if the site of injection is tapped 3–4 times before inserting the needle.

Intraperitoneal injection is best made with the pig held up by its hind legs and belly presented to the anaesthetist (Fig. 11·8). The needle should be inserted about 2 cm to one side of the mid-line midway between diaphragm and navel, and directed toward the head at a shallow angle. A 50 × 1·10 mm (19 gauge) needle is suitable for pigs under 50 kg.

Restraint of adult animals presents greater problems. They may be manoeuvred into cages or crates of the kind described by Baker & Andresen (1964), Pugh & Penny (1966) and Pekas (1968).

Fig. 11.8. Pig up to 25 kg held for ip injection.

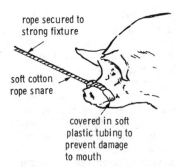

rope secured to strong fixture

soft cotton rope snare

covered in soft plastic tubing to prevent damage to mouth

Fig. 11.9. Running noose used to snare large pig for physical restraint. Snare is slipped over upper jaw and behind the tusks.

Alternatively, pigs may be restrained in the standing position by placing a snare around the upper jaw just behind the canine teeth; they will always back away from the handler, thus tightening the loop (Fig. 11.9), and the rope can then be secured to a firm support. The cord of the snare should be covered with heavy plastic tubing to prevent damage to the soft tissues in the mouth (Ragan & Gillis, 1975). Injections can then be made into the rump or into the soft tissue immediately behind the ear.

Mount & Ingram (1971) make 3 other suggestions which are particularly valuable in handling larger pigs. They are more tractable if removed from their peers and conditioned to their new quarters a few days before experiments. They can be trained to enter restraining crates by the attendant that feeds them regularly, since they are easily tempted by the sight of a food bucket. Finally, a suitable low-level trolley or stretcher should be readily available to take the weight of the subject as it falls unconscious after injection.

Chemical restraint and preanaesthetic therapy

Atropine should be given routinely at a dosage of 0·05 mg/kg im 40 min before further treatments.

Pigs of 15 kg and smaller are well sedated by im injection of the following drugs, listed in order of preference.

Ketamine (10 mg/kg im) with *diazepam* (2·0 mg/kg im) provides rapid and effective sedation. The peak effect is reached in 10 min, although posterior ataxia develops in 2 min and pigs are usually recumbent in 5 min. Pigs are deeply sedated, are not easily aroused by noise or other sensory stimuli, good muscle relaxation is usually produced, and subsequent narcosis with barbiturates is enhanced and prolonged (e.g. pentobarbitone dosage can be reduced by about 50%). The subjects are readily handled for intravenous injections or cannulation. The only problem with diazepam is the relatively large volume (6 ml) which has to be injected even at this low dose rate.

Diazepam (8 mg/kg im) alone produces deep

sedation but this entails injecting a volume of 24 ml to a 15 kg pig.

Alphaxolone–alphadolone (6 mg/kg im) provides excellent sedation in pigs with a peak effect within 10 min, maintained for up to 80 min and with complete recovery within 180 min. Some analgesia and muscle relaxation develops at this dose rate, and allows venepuncture or iv cannulation for administration of anaesthetic doses of the same agent. Barbiturates should not be used for induction or maintenance of anaesthesia after alphaxolone–alphadolone but conventional inhalational techniques are compatible with the steroids. The disadvantage of this formulation lies with the relatively large volume which has to be injected im.

Azaperone (5 mg/kg im) produces a state of sedation in pigs without analgesia within 20 min. Although there is only a small fall in blood pressure and respiration is unaffected, there is a profound fall in body temperature unless the necessary precautions are taken (in our experience a fall of 4°C occurs within 15 min at an ambient temperature of 26°C). Salivation is excessive unless atropine is previously administered, and the pig must be allowed to fall asleep away from other animals, undisturbed by noise or other sensory stimuli. The animal remains sensitive to noise, and any approach (e.g. for venepuncture) must be made quietly and gently.

Metomidate may be given ip at 10 mg/kg after azaperone injection to produce a state of hypnosis with fair analgesia. Alternatively, it can be given iv at 4 mg/kg to deepen narcosis within 3–5 min of injection and lasting about 40 min. A good degree of analgesia and fair muscle relaxation is attained. The addition of metomidate to azaperone usually eliminates all responses to sensory stimuli, but tremors and paddling movements may be observed during the recovery period. The wide safety margin allows a computed dose to be used without first weighing the subject.

Acepromazine (0·2 mg/kg im) provides sufficient tranquillization within 15 min to allow handling of the ears and venepuncture for induction of anaesthesia. Subsequent doses of barbiturate should be reduced by about 50% as their effect will be enhanced and prolonged.

Pigs between 15 and 80 kg are best sedated with the azaperone im and metomidate iv technique, or acepromazine im followed by induction with iv methohexitone, thiopentone or thiamylal.

Phencyclidine (2 mg/kg im) is the agent of choice for large boars and sows. A 50 × 1·10 mm (19 gauge) needle should be used to inject into rump or shoulder muscles. A state of deep sedation accompanied by profound analgesia is produced within 10 min and lasts 1–3 h. It is longer lasting but otherwise comparable with the azaperone–metomidate combination and is much more easily injected. It is ideal for the initiation of anaesthesia as it does not cause respiratory depression. Muscle relaxation can be enhanced, and the tremors or limbs movements commonly encountered during recovery can be eliminated, by iv administration of 1 mg/kg of diazepam. Dose levels of barbiturates subsequently used for induction of anaesthesia should be reduced by 60–70%. Phencyclidine always provokes excessive salivation so atropine (0·05 mg/kg iv) should be injected first. The pigs should be allowed to fall asleep by themselves on a dry, non-slip surface such as a thick rubber mat, and large subjects should be encouraged to go down on a stretcher or low trolley which can be used to transport them to the operating facilities.

Etorphine-acepromazine (0·5–1·0 ml/50 kg im) has, like phencyclidine, the advantage of high potency so that small and rapidly injected volumes can be given to large adults. Pigs become ataxic in 2–3 min after im injection and lie on their sides in 4–5 min. Good analgesia develops, but central nervous depression is very variable, and muscular rigidity and hindleg tremors are commonly encountered. As in other species, cardiopulmonary depression is usually produced but is unlikely to prove fatal if the anaesthetist is watchful and ready to administer diprenorphine iv in an emergency. Piglets delivered from sows immobilized with this agent will also suffer from respiratory depression but this can be readily reversed by injecting the antagonist diprenorphine iv into the umbilical vessels. Now that phencyclidine is becoming increasingly difficult to obtain from the US, etorphine–acepromazine is likely to become more widely accepted for the immobilization of large pigs.

Maintenance of body temperature is of prime importance from the time of initial injection throughout the surgical and postoperative period. The newborn pig is particularly susceptible to hypothermia because of its small mass : surface area ratio and low thermal insulation (Mount, 1959, 1963), and young animals remain relatively susceptible to cold until they are about 50 kg in weight. Weaners are adapted to conserve heat by huddling as a group, and are prone to hypothermia if separated and chemically restrained. It has already been noted that phencyclidine and azaperone have a profound depressant effect on body temperature. It is therefore essential that the pigs should be sedated in an area free of draughts, on an insulated, dry floor surface, and radiant heat lamps should be switched on in advance to heat the local environment to a temperature of 35°C.

Surgical anaesthesia

Injectable anaesthetic techniques. Once the pig is

sedated, subsequent doses of anaesthetic agents should be given iv to effect.

The most convenient vessels for injection are the central and marginal ear veins. The vessels are often dilated after sedation with azaperone or phencyclidine, especially if the pigs have been sedated under radiant heat lamps. However, if they are contracted the circulation may be increased by massaging the ear with a hot wet flannel or rubbing a little xylene into the tip of the ear. Venous dilation can be achieved by manual occlusion of the vessels or by placing an elastic band round the base of the ear. Topical analgesia is a valuable aid to ear venepuncture using either an ethyl chloride spray or 2% tetracaine solution. Injections should be given slowly as the thin-walled vessels will otherwise 'balloon'. In larger pigs, it is possible to pass a catheter through a 14 gauge needle and, once the tip has negotiated the angle between ear flap and head, pass it down into the large veins. The catheter can be filled with heparinized saline, the Luer fitting stoppered with a rubber injection teat (Braunula closure stopper) and then used for continuous or periodic sequential injections over a period of several weeks. The central is better than the marginal ear vein for this technique, and the central artery is preferable to both for catheterization of large pigs (Anderson & Elsley, 1969). However, in most cases we prefer to insert a 0·8 or 0·63 mm (21 or 23 gauge) butterfly needle taped to the ear flap for the duration of surgery and use this for injection of anaesthetics and fluids. Alternative vessels for percutaneous venepuncture are the anterior cephalic and the saphenous veins but, since the skin is so thick and tough, venous distension must be palpated rather than visualized, and the technique is only really practicable in subjects under 10 kg in weight.

For experimental surgery involving multiple sequential infusions or when frequent blood samples are to be taken, it is best to catheterize a jugular vein after surgical exposure or, alternatively, catheterize the anterior vena cava (AVC) by the 'blind' procedure described by Carle & Dewhirst (1942). The latter is the preferred technique of Ragan & Gillis (1975) for all iv infusions. Animals up to 30 kg are restrained on their backs in a V-shaped trough with neck fully extended and head hanging down. A 50–70 × 1·65 mm (16 gauge) needle is then inserted into the depression palpated just lateral to the anterior limit of the sternum and formed by the angle between 1st ribs and trachea, and is directed posteriorly, medially and dorsally toward an imaginary point midway between the scapulae. Penetration of the AVC will be indicated by return of blood into the syringe if slight suction is maintained. It is important to keep the neck extended without lateral deviation of the head to ensure longitudinal tension on the vessel during venepuncture. Care must be taken to avoid the carotid artery, the thoracic duct, the trachea and the vessels at the base of the heart. A suitable polyethylene catheter is then threaded through the needle into the AVC and, after patency has been ensured by aspiration of blood, the needle can be withdrawn and the catheter strapped to the body with adhesive tape. In larger pigs, the AVC is entered and cannulated with the animal snared and standing. Again, great care must be taken to ensure extension of the neck, and a 70 × 1·8 mm (15 gauge) needle is used. Wider bore needles should not be used as extensive haematoma formation adjacent to vital thoracic structures may then occur.

The depth of narcosis may be assessed in several ways. The carpo-pedal reflex is elicited by pushing the thumb between the digits and squeezing (the limb will be withdrawn in lightly-anaesthetized subjects). The loss of the palpebral reflex and the position of the eye are particularly valuable indices in pigs. As anaesthesia develops the eyes roll downward to expose the whites, until deep surgical anaesthesia is reached, when they return to their normal position. Analgesia can be assessed by pinching the ears or the tip of the snout. A medium depth of surgical anaesthesia suitable for most procedures is indicated by the loss of palpebral reflex, loss of response to pain, regular steady ventilation, and the eyes rolled downward to expose the whites.

It is safer to use inhalational agents for anaesthesia of pigs for other than induction and short periods of maintenance. The following injectable agents are recommended in order of preference.

Metomidate is injected iv at 4 mg/kg 20 min after the pig has received atropine (0·08 mg/kg) and azaperone at (5 mg/kg im). Light surgical anaesthesia with good analgesia and muscle relaxation develops without significant side effects, and the peak effect lasts 20–30 min. Recovery may take up to 6 h during which the animal must be kept warm. Further increments of metomidate can be given iv at about 20 min intervals to prolong anaesthesia.

Alphaxolone–alphadolone can be given iv at 2·0 mg/kg after previous treatment with atropine (0·08 mg/kg) and ketamine–diazepam, alphaxolone–alphadolone, azaperone or acepromazine by im injection at sedating doses. Medium depth surgical anaesthesia is induced within 10–20 s, with very good muscle relaxation, good analgesia and minimal respiratory depression. The peak effect is maintained for 4–10 min and recovery is smooth. Further increments can be given at about 10 min intervals to prolong anaesthesia.

Methohexitone can be injected iv slowly to effect at about 5 mg/kg after ketamine–diazepam, azaperone, acepromazine or phencyclidine (with atropine 0·05 mg/kg) have been allowed sufficient time to attain their maximum sedative effect. Medium depth surgical anaesthesia with good muscle relaxation and analgesia develops within seconds and is of sufficient duration (10–15 min) for endotracheal intubation and minor procedures.

Thiopentone (1% solution) can be similarly given iv slowly to effect after previous administration with sedatives and atropine. Doses of about 6–9 mg/kg are usually sufficient for intubation and minor procedures, and further increments can be given to prolong anaesthesia if required.

Surgical conditions can be improved by means of local analgesic infiltration along incision lines, by inhalational administration of $N_2O:O_2$ (3:2) or by regional analgesia using lumbar epidural injection.

Epidural analgesia is obtained by injecting 2% lignocaine (0·15 mg/kg up to a maximum of 20 ml) into the lumbosacral space. The technique is best described by Hall (1971). The sedated pig is restrained on its side with the back arched. The site for injection is located by identifying the anterior iliac border and the spinous process of the last lumbar vertebra; the lumbosacral space is in the midline immediately behind the spine. The needle is inserted in the midline and directed downwards and posteriorly at an angle of 20° to the vertical. For pigs weighing 30–50 kg, an $80 \times 1\cdot25$ mm (18 gauge) needle should be inserted 50–60 mm until the epidural space is detected by decreased resistance. In larger subjects, $120 \times 1\cdot20$ mm needles should be used and they may require insertion to about 90–100 mm before the space is reached. As soon as the injection has been made, the pig should be turned on to its front so that the effect of the analgesic will be evenly distributed.

Inhalational anaesthetic techniques. Endotracheal intubation should be performed routinely following chemical restraint, administration of atropine and induction of anaesthesia as described above. If the laryngeal reflex is still too pronounced after spraying with 2% lignocaine, and laryngospasm still prevents passage of the tube, anaesthesia can be deepened with 2% halothane and $N_2O:O_2$ (1:1) administered by mask until the pig is sufficiently relaxed. Alternatively, the pig should be hyperoxygenated via a mask immediately before injecting suxamethonium (1·0 mg/kg iv) to obtain adequate relaxation for intubation. Provision must then be made for controlled ventilation until spontaneous respiration is re-established. The possibility of malignant hyperpyrexia (Sybesma & Eikelenboom, 1969; Jones *et al.*, 1972) must always be borne in mind if suxamethonium is used. In pigs weighing less than 30 kg, anaesthesia can be induced by mask with 4% halothane in $N_2O:O_2$

(1:1) at 4 litres/min without previous medication, and they can then be intubated for maintenance of anaesthesia.

Various techniques to facilitate the passage of an endotracheal tube have been described (Hill & Perry, 1959; Rowson, 1965; Mount & Ingram, 1971). The first essential is to select a tube which is not too large in diameter (remembering that the pig's trachea is disproportionately small in relation to the animal's size) but long enough to traverse the distance from front to back of the mouth and the trachea. For example, pigs of 15–20 kg require tubes of 7–7·5 mm outside diameter; 25–35 kg animals need 8 mm, and for 50 kg pigs, a 10 mm tube is used. It must be well lubricated and a malleable rubber-shod stiffener aids the initial passage past the cricoid cartilage. The pig must be deeply anaesthetized or well relaxed with suxamethonium. Some workers recommend that the pig be laid on its back with the head well extended over the end of a table but we prefer to lie the animal on its side. The mouth should be opened by an assistant using two lengths of tape, and a gag or rubber bite blocks should be inserted between the molars to prevent the mouth closing. The tongue is then depressed with a laryngoscope and the latter is advanced until the epiglottis is visible. The epiglottis is reflected ventrally with the blade tip to reveal the arytenoid cartilages and vocal cords. The tube, complete with its stiffener is now passed between the vocal cords. It is often useful at this stage to flex the head downward toward the feet and to withdraw the stiffening rod before passing the tube into the trachea. If the tip of the tube lodges in the middle ventricle of the larynx, it should be slightly withdrawn, rotated about 180°, pushed on if it moves freely, and then rotated again to its original alignment. After inflating the cuff, the tube should be checked to ensure that it has not been pushed on into one bronchi by compressing the rebreathing bag to be certain that bilateral expansion of the thorax occurs.

Conventional inhalational anaesthesia can then be used to provide the required depth for surgery. Gases may be supplied via a Magill non-rebreathing system or a semiclosed system with CO_2 absorption and rebreathing. Halothane (or enflurane) is administered initially at 1·5–2% with O_2, but once the required surgical depth is attained, the concentration of volatile agents can be reduced to 0·5–1·5% for maintenance. Alternatively, a mixture of 0·5% halothane in $N_2O:O_2$ (1:1) can be used for maintenance. Although there is no reason why methoxyflurane should not be used, we have had such good results with halothane and enflurane for surgery lasting up to 6 h that they are recommended.

Long periods of anaesthesia require particular

195

attention to the management suggestions repeatedly emphasized in this text. Pulmonary ventilation becomes progressively more inefficient in pigs and this may pass undetected as the thoracic excursions are so small (cf. dogs). Assisted respiration with IPPV is strongly recommended for extended periods of anaesthesia, suitable ventilator settings being 15 cycles/min and tidal volume 300 ml for a 12 kg pig, and at 1000 ml for a 40 kg subject. Fluid balance must be continually maintained by continuous infusion of Hartmann's solution at 5–10 ml/kg/h and plasma expanders (such as 'Haemaccel') infused whenever haemorrhage has occurred. Body temperature should be continually monitored, and heat loss prevented by means of heated blanket and drapes. An oesophageal stethoscope is particularly valuable in pigs for auscultation of the heart beat.

Inhalational methods may be combined in a balanced regimen with analgesics and muscle relaxants. For long periods of abdominal surgery we have administered iv pancuronium at 0·05 mg/kg, fentanyl at 0·05 mg/kg or pethidine at 2 mg/kg, whilst $N_2O:O_2$ (3:2) was supplied by IPPV. Minimal metabolic disturbance was encountered provided that due attention was paid to management.

Recovery and post-surgical therapy
Endotracheal tubes should be left in situ until the pig is well recovered since laryngeal oedema and salivary accumulation may otherwise combine to obstruct the airway. Pigs are best left to recover by themselves in a heated box or pen (30–32°C) preferably on a thick rubber mattress without sawdust or litter to contaminate surgical wounds. Baby pigs should be returned to the mother or maintained in special humidified oxygenated incubators at 40°C.

Indwelling catheters can be retained in the jugular vein for weeks with the outside connection brought out on to the back between the scapulae. A rubber teat in the Luer fitting can then be used for injecting therapeutic substances or for taking blood samples. After use, the catheter should be filled with heparinized saline (500 iu heparin/100 ml) together with a wide-spectrum antibiotic such as neomycin.

Pethidine at 2 mg/kg im is effective as a post-surgical analgesic, but care should be taken to ensure that it does not contribute to respiratory depression early in recovery. Similarly, if antibiotics are given, administration should be delayed to ensure that they do not cause CNS depression and a relapse in anaesthetic recovery.

Chemical restraint and capture: exotic species

Warthog (*Phacochoerus aethiopicus*) have been effectively immobilized with etorphine–acepromazine–hyoscine mixtures (Pienaar *et al.*, 1966) and fentanyl–azaperone (Pienaar, 1968). Phencyclidine has been used in several species (Beck, 1972).

Recommendations
Phencyclidine-acepromazine (1·0–1·5 mg/kg:0·1 mg/kg im) produces recumbency in 15–20 min (Jones, 1973).

FAMILY HIPPOPOTAMIDAE

Owing to their aggressive temperament, difficulties in preventing dehydration and hyperthermia if immobilized on land, and difficulties in preventing drowning if these animals are given drugs whilst swimming, Hippopotomidae present severe problems of restraint. Phencyclidine–acepromazine (0·5

Table 11.5. Pig: physiological data

Measurement	Adult (200 kg)	Young (20–40 kg)
Respiratory frequency (breaths/min)	12 (8–18)	14 (12–18)
Tidal volume (ml)	3800	420
Minute volume (l/min)	36	6·0
Mean heart rate (beats/min)	60–70	70–85
Arterial blood pressure (mmHg)	170/108	170/108
Arterial blood pH	7·35	7·35
Pa O_2 (mmHg)	—	—
Pa CO_2 (mmHg)	—	—
Haematocrit (%)	40 (30–50)	40 (30–50)
Haemoglobin (g/100 ml)	13 (10–16)	11 (10–13)
Erythrocytes (10^6/mm³)	7 (5–9)	7 (5–9)
*Blood volumes (ml/kg bodyweight)		
Total		65
Expected terminal exsanguination		25
Safe maximum single sample		6
Mean rectal temperature (°C)		39·0 (38·6–39·5)

*Archer (1965).

mg/kg:0·2 mg/kg im) or xylazine alone at 1·3 mg/kg (York & Quinn, 1973) are considered to be the safest agents if the animals are in or near water (Pienaar, 1968; Harthoorn, 1975), while etorphine (4–5 mg/300 kg) has been recommended for restraint on land (Harthoorn, 1975).

Recommendations

No combination is ideal. Phencyclidine–acepromazine (0·5 mg/kg:0·2 mg/kg im) is probably the safest for field immobilization. Phencyclidine–xylazine (0·5 mg/kg:0·5 mg/kg im) would also probably be effective.

ORDER CARNIVORA

FAMILY CANIDAE

Domestic dog (*Canis familiaris*)

Dogs are the most commonly used animal for experimental surgery, and are excellent subjects for anaesthesia. The full accounts contained in the texts of Hall (1971) and Lumb & Jones (1973) will not be repeated in detail here but attention will be directed towards special experimental requirements.

Atropine (0·05 mg/kg sc) was recommended as an anticholinergic for dogs by Jones (1957). Toxic symptoms of excitement are not produced until dose levels of 0·5 mg/kg are given iv (Hatch, 1967). Atropine disappears very rapidly from the dog circulation, part being excreted unchanged in urine and part excreted in urine as tropine, the fate of the remainder being unknown.

The phenothiazine ataractics have been used extensively in dogs. Chlorpromazine can be given by the im, iv or sc routes at doses up to 1 mg/kg. The full effects develop in 10–15 min after iv and in 60–90 min after im injection (Hall, 1971). The safety margin is wide. In one study dogs survived 50 mg/kg sc and 100 mg/kg orally (Courvoisier *et al.*, 1953), and in another no ill effects were observed in foetuses or pregnant bitches after therapeutic doses had been administered (Macko *et al.*, 1958). Rapid iv injection of 14 mg/kg produced collapse from which a dog recovered within 30 min (Estrada, 1956). Intravenous administration of chlorpromazine has since been shown to cause hypotension which may result in acute cardiovascular failure since it antagonizes and can reverse the pressor and vasoconstrictor effects of endogenous sympathomimetic amines (Lumb & Jones, 1973). Hypotension probably results from loss of vasomotor tone and atrioventricular block (Lees, 1978). According to Bourgeois-Gavardin *et al.* (1955), iv injection of chlorpromazine (2–5 mg/kg) reduced respiratory rate, increased tidal volume and decreased O_2 consumption.

Promazine has been reported as a safe and effective preanaesthetic agent for dogs (Krawitz, 1957; Weberlein *et al.*, 1959) at doses up to 1 mg/kg im (Hall, 1971). Doses as high as 2–6 mg/kg iv were recommended by Lumb & Jones (1973), who claimed that barbiturate dosage could then be reduced by 30–50%. Similar high doses produced no respiratory depression in pups delivered to tranquillized bitches by caesarian section, after local infiltration analgesia had been used along the line of surgical incision (Gupta et al., 1970).

Acepromazine is effective in dogs at doses of 0·1–0·2 mg/kg im and 1–3 mg/kg by the oral route (Hall, 1971). At the higher doses (0·5–1·0 mg/kg iv) recommended by Lumb & Jones (1973), the onset of action is more rapid and the duration is extended, but the degree of CNS depression is little different. The amount of barbiturate required for anaesthesia is decreased by 30–50% after acepromazine administration.

Morphine was the first of the potent sedative analgesics to be used in dogs. An associated fall in blood pressure may be due to the marked brady-cardia and peripheral capillary dilatation (Krantz & Carr, 1951). These authors also concluded that morphine is 85% excreted in urine over several days, and the remainder is either excreted in faeces or is destroyed in the liver (Krantz & Carr, 1951). The toxicity of morphine in dogs was studied by Jones (1957) who reported that the lethal dose could be 100–200 mg/kg im depending on the condition of the animal. However, Booth (1961) found that doses as high as 400–500 mg/kg im were not necessarily lethal if pentobarbitone was given iv to counteract the resultant spinal convulsions. Morphine must not be injected rapidly iv as convulsions may be produced. In poor-risk cases such as dogs in a shocked condition, morphine is contraindicated (Powers et al., 1947). A dose of 5 mg/kg im given at least 30 min before induction of anaesthesia was recommended by Booth (1961) who stated that doses of barbiturates should subsequently be reduced by 33%.

Pethidine has been used as an alternative analgesic to morphine at doses ranging from 10–20 mg/kg im or sc for both preanaesthetic treatment and post-operative analgesia after barbiturate anaesthesia (Hall, 1971; Lumb & Jones, 1973). There is a fall in blood pressure if it is given iv, probably due to peripheral dilatation (Gruber et al., 1941), and some degree of respiratory depression is usually encountered whatever the mode of injection. It may cause convulsions if given too rapidly iv, and histamine may be released. It is rapidly destroyed in the liver and therapeutic doses disappear from the plasma within 4 h.

Thiambutene was assessed for clinical use in dogs by Owen (1955) using doses of 4·4 mg/kg by slow iv injection or 22 mg/kg sc. Narcosis and analgesia lasted up to 2·5 h. The onset of effect occurred in 5–10 min and maximal effect was reached about 30 min later. Narcosis was readily reversed by injection of 2 mg/kg of nalorphine. However, Hall (1971) emphasized the undesirable features of this agent in dogs including vocalization, defaecation, and CNS excitement, particularly if it is given too rapidly iv.

After etorphine was assessed in dogs by Blane et al. (1967) and found to produce analgesia and immobilization without excitement, vomiting or defaecation, it was used in combination with the phenothiazine tranquillizer, methotrimeprazine at 7·5 μg/kg and 6·0 mg/kg of etorphine and methotrimeprazine respectively (Blane et al., 1968; Alford & Wosnick, 1970). Reversible neuroleptanalgesia with this combination was later evaluated in clinical work by Crooks et al. (1970) after it was shown that nalorphine or cyprenorphine were effective in antagonizing the effects of etorphine (Burkhart, 1967). Yet another antagonist to etorphine has since been developed—diprenorphine—and this is now recommended as the drug of choice for reversing neuroleptanalgesia.

Neuroleptanalgesia has also been obtained with fentanyl either in combination with droperidol (Soma & Shields, 1964; Franklin & Reid, 1965) or with fluanisone, and has been used extensively in dogs for clinical work (Marsboom et al., 1964). Fentanyl–droperidol iv followed by pentobarbitone (6 mg/kg iv) led to minimal effects on cardiovascular function, and post-operative diarrhoea in 25% of the animals was the only undesirable feature noted (Hamlin et al., 1968). The combination is more widely accepted for dog anaesthesia than pethidine–acepromazine (Warner, 1968) or methadone–acepromazine (Schauffler, 1970). In pharmacological experiments, Lin et al. (1976) concluded that large doses of fentanyl or fentanyl plus N_2O do alter cardiovascular function but less so than equianalgesic doses of morphine. In other studies, it was found to be more difficult to induce ventricular tachycardia in dogs anaesthetized with ketamine or fentanyl–droperidol than in those animals anaesthetized with pentobarbitone (Ivankovich et al., 1975). In a study comparing the effects of fentanyl and pethidine on cardiovascular function in dogs, Freye (1974) concluded that high dosages of fentanyl did not depress the cardiovascular system or induce any hyperactivity of the autonomic nervous system.

Neither phencyclidine nor ketamine have been widely accepted for anaesthesia in the dog, although there are reports in the literature of their use in wild and zoological subjects. At a dose of 3·0 mg/kg im, phencyclidine produces either cataleptoid narcosis or convulsions, but 2·0 mg/kg iv produces surgical anaesthesia (Stoliker, 1965). Seal et al. (1970) used doses of 0·8–1·2 mg/kg im in combination with promazine (1·0 mg/kg im), and this regimen was recommended by Jones (1973) for zoological specimens of Canidae.

Ketamine was evaluated in studies involving several species including dogs (Chen et al., 1966; Kaump et al., 1969). Premedication with promazine (1·0 mg/kg im) or acepromazine (0·2 mg/kg im) was considered necessary to prevent confusional states (Jones, 1973). Several authors have recommended ketamine for clinical use in dogs (Humphrey, 1971; Akusawa et al., 1972; Kaplan, 1972; De Young et al., 1972). The effects of ketamine on the circulation and O_2 uptake by dog brain was studied by Kreuscher & Grote (1967), whilst Lennartz et al. (1970) compared ketamine with propanidid for their effects on cardiovascular dynamics. The effects of ketamine on the coronary circulation of dogs already sedated with chloralose were described by Constantin et al. (1971).

Barbiturates have been used extensively in dogs both for clinical and experimental work. The reviews in Hall (1971), Lumb & Jones (1973) and Soma (1972) need extension only where physiological and pharmacological variables of interest to the laboratory worker need to be emphasized. A significant decrease in circulating leukocytes was recorded in normal and splenectomized dogs following anaesthesia with pentobarbitone, thiopentone, thiamylal and methohexitone (Usenik & Cronkite, 1965). When Shanker (1963) compared the rates of distribution from blood to cerebrospinal fluid of thiopentone and pentobarbitone, he showed that the former is taken up more quickly. A return to basal narcosis if adrenaline, sodium lactate or glucose were administered during recovery from barbiturates (the 'glucose effect') has been demonstrated (Lamson et al., 1951; Hatch, 1966; Heavner & Brown, 1968). The danger of prolonging pentobarbitone anaesthesia in dogs and cats if chloramphenicol was administered concurrently was emphasized by Adams & Dixit (1970).

The cardiovascular responses of dogs to pentobarbitone anaesthesia were examined by Priano et al. (1969), who concluded that the drug significantly depressed the cardiovascular system. Decreases in regional blood flow were observed after iv administration of pentobarbitone (MacConnell, 1969), while respiration was significantly depressed and 25% of dogs given 30 mg/kg iv developed side-effects resembling acute cardiovascular failure in the hands of Mylon et al. (1942). According to Carson et al. (1966), respiratory and metabolic acidoses develop in dogs under pentobarbitone anaesthesia, and the dangers of hypothermia were emphasized by Dale et al. (1968). A marked leukopaenia reaching a peak in 90 min was observed in dogs after iv injection of pentobarbitone (Graca & Garst, 1957).

Since the use of thiopentone by iv injection was first recorded in dogs (Sweebe, 1936), it has been widely accepted for induction of anaesthesia prior to inhalation of gas mixtures. Oral and rectal administration of thiopentone have also been described (Corley et al., 1969). Uptake and distribution was studied in dogs by Brodie et al. (1952) who concluded that the short duration of effect was due to rapid redistribution to fat depots. However, Saidman & Eger (1966) demonstrated that an appreciable amount was metabolized in dog's liver. The cumulative effects were demonstrated in a study in dogs by Wyngaarden et al. (1947). Walton et al. (1950) found that thiopentone was mildly hepatotoxic in the presence of reduced pO_2, but large dosages are thought to be hepatotoxic anyway (Dundee, 1956). The slow degradation of thiopentone by neonatal livers prolongs recovery unduly and the agent should not be used in puppies below 3 months of age (Hall, 1976).

Thiamylal was found to be 1·5 times more potent than thiopentone by Wyngaarden et al. (1947), and was less cumulative when given to dogs repeatedly. No tolerance developed to thiamylal after repeated administration over 4 weeks (Swanson, 1952), and it was considered to be less cardiotoxic by Woods et al. (1947). Thiamylal administration with fentanyl–droperidol was described for use in dogs by Lee (1973).

Methohexitone has also been used for induction of anaesthesia in dogs (Fowler & Stevenson, 1961; Fowler, 1964; Hall, 1971; Lumb & Jones, 1973). Studies of the excretion of C_{14}-labelled methohexitone in dogs showed that 21·7% is excreted in bile and urine in the first hour and over 50% in 8 h (Welles et al., 1963). The undesirable features include muscle tremors and occasional convulsions during recovery if the subjects are stimulated (Fowler & Stevenson, 1961).

α-chloralose (1% solution prepared at 60°C) was commended for use in studies on baroreceptor reflexes since a higher blood pressure and more active reflexes are maintained than with other agents (Brown & Hilton, 1956). The dose rate for dogs is approximately 100 mg/kg iv (King & Unna, 1954).

Inhalational agents have been similarly reviewed (Hall, 1971; Lumb & Jones, 1973; Massey, 1973). Much of the experimental work to study the pharmacology of commonly used drugs has been performed in dogs. The metabolic pathways for ether were described by Chenoweth (1965), and the concentration of ether in various tissues of dogs after 2·5 h of anaesthesia was measured (Chenoweth et al., 1962). Minimal hepatotoxic changes were reported by Stephen et al. (1958) after repeated administration, but reversible nephrotoxicity and anuria was demonstrated by MacNider (1920). Although cardiac arrhythmias associated with stimulated catecholamine release are common, the impressive lack of cardiovascular depression was emphasized by Blalock (1928). According to Brewster et al. (1952), ether administration causes a metabolic acidosis in dogs.

The potency of halothane as some 4 times that of ether was established in dog experiments (Raventos, 1956), and was compared with other agents on a MAC basis by Eger et al. (1965). The effects on ventilation, plasma pH and pCO_2 in animals including dogs was explored by Fisher (1961), and it was concluded that respiratory failure precedes cardiac failure by a considerable margin. Minimal pathological changes were found in livers and kidneys after repeated administration but their function was within normal limits (Stephen et al., 1958).

Methoxyflurane has achieved popularity in canine anaesthesia since it is safe and provides good muscle relaxation and analgesia. Its toxicity in man suggests that it should be used at low concentrations in dogs (Pezzi et al., 1966; Crandell & Macdonald, 1968), although neither Bergeron et al. (1966) nor Cale et al. (1962) could detect nephrotoxic symptoms in dogs after methoxyflurane anaesthesia, and hepatotoxicity seemed restricted to reversible watery vacuolation of cord cells. Jaundice has been encountered in a dog after 4 h of methoxyflurane anaesthesia (Soma, 1965).

Enflurane has similar anaesthetic properties to halothane in dogs. Induction and recovery from anaesthesia are smooth and rapid, and nephrotoxicity could not be demonstrated in the early studies of Virtue et al. (1966). Higher concentrations of enflurane are required for equivalent analgesia (MAC 2·2 in dogs compared with halothane MAC 0·8 and methoxyflurane MAC 0·23). More recently, it was concluded that the rapid recovery, good muscle relaxation and apparent absence of side effects make it a useful alternative to halothane and methoxyflurane for canine anaesthesia (Cribb et al., 1977). However, enflurane has been shown capable of producing seizures similar to those produced by known convulsants and this may limit its acceptance as an 'ideal' agent (Michenfelder & Cucchiara, 1974).

$N_2O:O_2$ mixtures have been used as the carrier gas for all of the above volatile agents (Carter, 1964; Hall, 1971). The latter author emphasized the need for effective denitrogenation of the subject using high gas-flows and a supply of sufficient O_2 during semi-closed administration. The anaesthetic potency (MAC) of N_2O was compared in dogs, cat and stump-tailed monkey by Steffey et al. (1974).

Although general or balanced anaesthetic techniques are usually selected in experimental dogs, local analgesia is occasionally indicated. Epidural anaesthesia was described in a large number of dogs for caesarian section by Evers (1968), and further experience was reported by Kumar & Singh (1970) and Redderson et al. (1974).

The use of muscle relaxants in small-animal anaesthesia was reviewed by Lumb (1972). Suxamethonium, d-tubocurarine, gallamine and pancuronium have all been used in dogs to produce muscle relaxation. Muscle relaxants cross the placenta in pregnant bitches (Pittinger & Morris, 1953). Suxamethonium was evaluated in dogs and other animals by Hansson (1958). Relaxation is accompanied by increased plasma concentration of potassium (Stevenson, 1960). Prolonged apnoea may follow administration of 3 or more doses (Hall, 1959).

D-tubocurarine has been used alone and together with intravenous barbiturates (Pickett, 1951; Brinker, 1951). A fall in blood pressure and histamine release has been demonstrated following iv administration of 0·4 mg/kg (Wright & Hall, 1961), and Booth (1963) suggested that a low dose (33% of normal) should be used if ether was the anaesthetic agent since this itself has a curariform action.

Gallamine was recommended as the non-depolarizing relaxant of choice in dogs as it does not promote the release of histamine and in clinical doses has no obvious effect on the CNS, liver or kidneys (Lumb & Jones, 1973). It is not detoxified in the body and is excreted unchanged in urine so is probably best avoided in animals suffering from renal failure or during experiments involving depressed renal function. It was found that 84% of tritium-labelled gallamine was excreted in urine in 24 h (Feldman et al., 1969).

Pancuronium was assessed in dogs, cats and horses by Massey (1970), who showed that there was no change in heart rate, central venous pressure or electrocardiogram after iv injection of normal doses. The drug did not provoke histamine release. We consider it the drug of choice in dogs (CRC).

Electronarcosis has been achieved in dogs by passing alternating current of 700 cycles, 35–50 mA at 40 V (Hardy et al., 1961). Alternatively, combined DC/AC producing a rectangular wave of 1·0–1·4 ms duration at 100 waves/s can be used to maintain anaesthesia after first inducing narcosis with direct current (Smith et al., 1961a). Problems have been encountered including hyperthermia, salivation, brain lesions (Herin, 1968) and skin burns (Smith et al., 1961b). Furthermore, muscle relaxation is variably developed and it is difficult to assess the degree of analgesia. High levels of catecholamines and corticosteroids are found in the plasma which may indicate severe stress and an uninhibited response of the adrenal glands (McNeil & Hardy, 1959; Hardy et al., 1961).

Hypothermia has been deliberately induced in dogs by whole-body surface cooling or by extracorporeal cardiopulmonary bypass techniques. Local cooling has also been used to protect the spinal cord during short periods of ischaemia. Bigelow et al. (1950) found that O_2 uptake in dogs was reduced by 50% at 30°C and 65% at 25°C. With the circulation maintained on a pump-oxygenator, dogs have survived cooling to 1·5°C (Gollan et al., 1955). The effect of hypothermia in lowering the concentration of inhalational anaesthetics needed for a given effect in dogs was described by Regan & Eger (1967). A method for cooling the brain to 14°C whilst retaining body temperature at 31–32°C by cannulating the carotid artery and passing the blood through a cooling loop was developed by Kimoto et al. (1956). Severe damage to vital organs was demonstrated in dogs after prolonged periods of hypothermia at 25°C (Knocker, 1955). Induction of hypothermia for surgery in dogs was described by Lumb & Jones (1973), and involves administration of promazine (2·2 mg/kg iv), thiamylal for induction of anaesthesia and intubation, gallamine as a relaxant to abolish shivering, IPPV and immersion in iced water until the core temperature has fallen to 30°C.

Lumb & Jones (1973) also described in some detail the basic techniques for cardiopulmonary bypass. According to Wesolowski et al. (1952), the upper limit of normothermic ischaemia tolerated by the dog's heart is 20 min but the animal can withstand 30–60 min with bypass and moderate hypothermia (28°C).

Albin et al. (1966, 1967, 1968) found that the dog spinal cord could tolerate 3 h of ischaemia if cooled locally, and the hypothermia prevented an otherwise irreversible paraplegia. Similarly Lumb & Brasmer (1970) used whole-body cooling to 30°C, and local cooling of exposed spinal cord with iced Ringer's solution to prevent permanent damage to the cord during extensive local surgery.

Electronic measurement in animals including dogs was recently reviewed by Klemm (1976) and this contained descriptions of flow pressure, strain, ECG and EEG measuring techniques. These included ultrasonic techniques (Franklin et al., 1964; Rushmer et al., 1966), thermocouple techniques for measuring cardiac output (Felger, 1953), radio telemetry in unrestrained animals (Franklin et al., 1966), ECG recordings (Hamlin & Smith, 1960; Hamlin et al., 1966; Hamlin, 1968; Hill, 1968) and EEG recordings (Croft, 1962, 1964; Pampiglione, 1963; Herin et al., 1968; Klemm, 1968; Klemm & Hall, 1974).

The relative value of different anaesthetic agents in a canine haemorrhagic shock model was compared by Furneaux (1968). Cardiovascular data in anaesthetized dogs was compiled by Giles & Burch (1970). Anaesthetic requirements during thoracic surgery of dogs and cats was described by Mitchell (1968).

Recommended anaesthetic techniques
Preanaesthetic management
Dogs should be purchased well before the surgical procedure and given time to settle to strange surroundings, and to the handlers and experimentalists. Any dog which is obviously vicious despite gentle and kindly handling should be excluded from any recovery experiment. Only animals which have been vaccinated against canine distemper, hepatitis and leptospirosis, with a minimum of 2 weeks allowed for immunity to develop, should be allowed in to laboratory kennels. They should be given a thorough examination for health on entry to the laboratory, paying particular attention to the respiratory and cardiovascular systems as well as noting the general condition of the skin and coat, and they should be routinely dosed against round and tapeworms.

The animal should be starved for 12–24 h prior to anaesthesia but access to water should be allowed. This is important not only to reduce the risk of vomiting, but also the risk of intussusception. The latter may otherwise present problems after extensive intraabdominal surgery e.g. liver or kidney transplantation, when the intestines and mesentery have necessarily been handled or retracted for long periods.

Physical restraint and handling
A minimum of physical restraint should be necessary in laboratory dogs if they have been properly selected as suggested. Commonly-used breeds such as beagles, greyhounds and retrievers are usually good tempered and respond well to gentle handling. A nervous or suspicious dog should always be approached from directly in front, talked to constantly in a quiet voice and the back of a clenched fist held out towards it. Every effort should be made by the experimentalist to overcome unpleasant associations between himself and repeated procedures such as venepuncture by rewarding the dog with food and approval.

Methods of physical restraint are shown in Figs 12.1 and 12.2. The dog should always be fitted with a strong leather collar and, if there is any doubt about its temperament, a tape should be applied as in Fig. 12.2.

Chemical restraint and preanaesthetic therapy
Atropine (0·05 mg/kg sc) should be given 30–40 min before other agents.

The choice of ataractic or sedative will depend very much on the nature of the surgery to be performed and a consideration of unwanted side effects associated with the agents. These treatments are best given in the holding pens by personnel known to the dog.

Ataractics or sedatives are used in dogs for reduction of apprehension and elimination of

Fig. 12.1. Method of holding dog for examination.

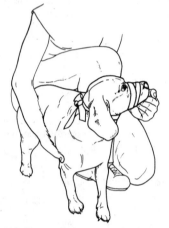

Fig. 12.2. Tape applied to muzzle of unfriendly dog.

excitement or struggling during induction or recovery:

Acepromazine (0·5 mg/kg im) takes 5–10 min for onset of effect, reaches peak effect in dogs within 20 min and lasts 2–4 h.

Diazepam (1·0 mg/kg im) takes 5 min for onset of effect, reaches its peak effect within 15 min and this lasts for 2–6 h.

Xylazine (2·0 mg/kg im) reaches peak effect within 15 min and lasts for 1–1·5 h. Dogs are particularly sensitive to sharp metallic noises whilst sedated with this agent and some vomit once within 15 min of im administration. Cardiac arrhythmias (bradycardia and partial A-V block) are encountered in the absence of atropine pre-treatment, but we have never encountered fatalities with xylazine. In other respects xylazine is a good sedative in dogs, conferring a degree of analgesia and producing good skeletal muscle relaxation without undue respiratory depression (CRC). Barbiturate dosages should be reduced by 50–70% for the induction of general anaesthesia.

Chlorpromazine (2 mg/kg im) takes 45–50 min to reach peak effect and this lasts 4–6 h.

Sedative–analgesics are valuable for the reduction of pain with modest CNS depression.

Pethidine (10 mg/kg sc or im) produces analgesia within 15 min and this lasts for 1–2 h. Some degree of respiratory depression is usually encountered but otherwise the dog is fairly alert if disturbed.

Pentazocine (2–4 mg/kg im) produces similar levels of analgesia to pethidine in dogs within 15 min, but the duration of effect is shorter—30–60 min in our experience (CRC). The dogs are slightly sedated at this dosage and respiration is also somewhat depressed.

Thiambutene (15–20 mg/kg im) is a more potent analgesic and is useful if given with ataractic drugs.

Neuroleptanalgesia using combinations of potent sedative–analgesics with neuroleptics is valuable both for preparing dogs for full surgical anaesthesia and by itself for superficial surgery.

Fentanyl–fluanisone (or fentanyl–droperidol) (0·1–0·2 ml/kg im) produces profound analgesia with some sedation within 10 min, and analgesia is maintained for 20–40 min. The dogs usually defaecate soon after administration, and respiration is depressed. Cardiovascular function is only mildly affected if the dog is first treated with atropine to protect the heart from vagal inhibition. The administration of diazepam (1·0 mg/kg im) prolongs sedation to 1 h and enhances muscle relaxation.

Pethidine–xylazine (10 mg/kg and 2 mg/kg im respectively) produces a more prolonged neuroleptanalgesia lasting up to 2 h. The degree of analgesia is significantly less than fentanyl–fluanisone and respiration is similarly depressed, but muscle relaxation is greater.

Thiambutene–diazepam (10 mg/kg and 1·0 mg/kg im respectively) produces prolonged neuroleptanalgesia of 2–3 h in dogs with good analgesia, and some sedation and muscular relaxation. Respiration is depressed, but the undesirable side-effects such as salivation and occasional excitement during recovery associated with the administration of thiambutene alone are prevented by atropine and diazepam. Acepromazine may be used instead of diazepam, but muscular relaxation is not then produced.

Neuroleptanalgesia with each of these combinations can be rapidly reversed within 60 s by slow iv injection of nalorphine (2·0 mg/kg) or within 2–5 min if it is given im.

Etorphine–methotrimeprazine (0·5 ml/4 kg im or 0·25 ml/4 kg iv) has a more profound analgesic and sedative effect than any of the above neuroleptanalgesic combinations. After deep im injection, the onset of effect is seen after about 1 min, when the dogs lie down in the prone position and start panting. Deep sedation develops and the peak effect is reached in 3–10 min. Unless the antagonist diprenorphine is given, the effects of the agent may last from 2 up to 4 h. Once the diprenorphine has been injected iv, signs of decreasing narcosis are observed within 10 s; breathing and cardiac rates increase noticeably, and eye and head movements commence. Most dogs can walk reasonably steadily within 10 min. If etorphine–methotrimeprazine is injected iv initially, neuroleptanalgesia develops smoothly within 20 s.

The adverse side-effects are seldom serious. The dogs rarely vomit but some defaecate and urinate either after im injection or during recovery. They still react to sudden noise (particularly metallic sounds) even though in other respects they appear completely insensible. Cardiopulmonary depression is marked in the majority of cases but particularly if high dosages are used to obtain profound neuroleplanalgesia—and this may be important in translating physiological data during experiments.

Local analgesia

Local analgesic techniques should always be considered for experimental dogs because they provide surgical conditions without altering physiological responses. Local infiltration is commonly employed using low concentrations of lignocaine—0·5–1·0% with 1:200 000 adrenaline to delay absorption.

Lumbar epidural analgesia is a simple and safe procedure in dogs. Injection is made into the lumbosacral space in the midline immediately behind the spinous process of the last lumbar vertebra. After suitable sedation or neuroleptanalgesia, the dog should be restrained on its right side. A needle 40–50 × 0·80 mm (21 gauge) is introduced into the midline and directed slightly caudally. The space should be entered at a depth of 2–4 cm from the skin, and a distinct decrease in resistance is felt as the interarcual ligament is penetrated. Lignocaine (1% with 1:200 000 adrenaline) should then be injected slowly over 15–20 s, after ensuring that the needle is in the epidural space. A dose of approximately 0·3 ml/kg produces anterior block for abdominal operations. The usual aseptic precautions should be taken to avoid contamination of the spinal canal.

Surgical anaesthesia
General notes. There are no particular problems associated with healthy dogs provided they have been carefully selected. Short-nosed breeds should be avoided to minimize the risk of ventilation problems, and the possibility of chronic renal failure should always be borne in mind if using aged ex-racing greyhounds for surgery.

Injectable anaesthetic techniques. The cephalic vein on the anterior face of a forelimb is the most convenient vessel for injection. It is easily seen if the area is carefully clipped and swabbed with

Fig. 12.3. Intravenous injection in cephalic vein of dog.

alcohol, and is dilated by gripping the limb above the elbow so that it is extended as shown (Fig. 12.3). The anaesthetist stabilizes the vein with the thumb of his left hand and penetrates the vessels from the antero-medial aspect (Fig. 12.3). Butterfly needles 25 × 0·80 mm (21 gauge) or 0·80–0·65 mm (21–23 gauge) 'Medicut' indwelling catheters can be strapped in place and connected directly to a syringe or to a 3-way tap for sequential injections or for withdrawal of blood.

The recurrent tarsal vein is less easily stabilized for puncture but is a useful alternative to the cephalic veins (Fig. 12.4).

The jugular vein is accessible in dogs for percutaneous puncture and is another alternative. It is often used in experimental work for tying in indwelling catheters, in which case a 3-way tap may be attached for administration of fluids and anaesthetic agents over long periods of anaesthesia.

Since neither the steroids alphaxolone–alphadolone nor propanidid can be given to dogs because of the excessive histamine release caused by the cremaphor vehicle, the use of injectable agents is in practice restricted to the barbiturates, thiopentone, thiamylal, methohexitone and pentobarbitone. The indicators of anaesthetic depth are particularly important when inducing anaesthesia with these agents because safety margins are

Fig. 12.4. Method of extending limb of dogs, cats and monkeys for iv injection of recurrent tarsal vein.

narrow. Analgesia is poor until the dogs are deeply anaesthetized. Respiration is usually depressed, so the anaesthetist must pay close attention to the rate, depth and nature of breathing. Other responses will be modified by preanaesthetic treatment, particularly if neuroleptanalgesic combinations have been employed. However, as an approximate guide to deepening narcosis as barbiturates are given to effect, the following signs are useful:

(a) Basal narcosis is indicated by loss of ability to raise the head when disturbed, but a yawn and curling of the tongue is still provoked if the jaws are deliberately opened.

(b) As light surgical anaesthesia is reached, the jaw and tongue fail to respond and are completely relaxed, but the pinch (pedal) reflex remains brisk, the corneal and photomotor reflexes are still present, and breathing is deep and regular.

(c) Medium and deep anaesthesia are judged by gradual loss of the pedal reflex, loss of corneal and photomotor reflexes, and slow shallow but regular respiration. The injectable agents (so-called 'intravenous anaesthetics') which are commonly used in dogs, are described in personal order of preference.

Thiopentone (1·25–2·5% solution) is generally used for induction and short periods of general anaesthesia. When the dogs have been pretreated by any of the described methods, the following doses should be decreased depending on the agents used.

At a dose of 10–20 mg/kg iv, a period of anaesthesia lasting 5–10 min is induced if 0·6 of the computed dose is administered rapidly and the remainder is given within 30 s to effect. The anaesthetic depth obtained is sufficient for endotracheal intubation, but analgesia is poor and surgical stimulation may provoke limb movements.

At a dose of 20–30 mg/kg iv, a longer period of light anaesthesia lasting 10–20 min is induced if the drug is given slowly to effect over 2–3 min. Because thiopentone accumulates in the body, it is poor technique to prolong anaesthesia by repeated sequential injections. A total of 30 mg/kg iv should not be exceeded.

Thiopentone should not be used in puppies less than 10 weeks of age or in greyhounds, whippets or dalmatians since recovery is often dangerously prolonged.

Thiamylal (2–4% solution) may be used as an alternative to thiopentone. At doses between 15–20 mg/kg, medium surgical anaesthesia lasting 10–15 min can be produced by injecting 0·3 of the computed dose rapidly and the remainder slowly to effect. Dogs are usually able to regain their feet within 45 min and recover without excitement.

Methohexitone (1% solution) is an excellent agent for induction and endotracheal intubation if used correctly. At a dose of 4–8 mg/kg given by rapid iv injection, anaesthesia is induced smoothly without excitement, but violent convulsions are often evoked if given slowly without pretreatment. Anaesthesia is achieved in one limb to brain circulation time and lasts 3–5 min with full recovery occurring in 30 min. Further doses can be given at 2–4 mg/kg iv to prolong the period of anaesthesia but full recovery will then be protracted. Methohexitone is also useful if administered iv at 2–4 mg/kg to deepen narcosis in dogs which have been treated with neuroleptanalgesic combinations (e.g. fentanyl–fluanisone), and its effects are then extended to 10–20 min. In the absence of any ataractics, recovery from methohexitone may be accompanied by muscle tremors and high pitched barking, and it is essential that the subjects are allowed to recover in quiet, dark surroundings.

Methohexitone is the agent of choice for inducing anaesthesia in greyhounds, whippets and dalmatians and in puppies under 10 weeks of age.

Pentobarbitone is still the most commonly used agent for experimental work in dogs in spite of its disadvantages. At a dose of 20–30 mg/kg given by slow iv injection, basal narcosis–light surgical anaesthesia lasting 45–60 min is induced. The first half of the computed dose should be given rapidly to avoid induction excitement and the remainder should be given very slowly over at least 5 min to effect, since pentobarbitone takes 3–5 min to equilibrate across the blood–brain barrier. If it is used alone to produce surgical anaesthesia, the dog should be intubated and placed on IPPV to ensure that respiration, pO_2, PCO_2 and plasma pH are maintained within normal limits. Alternatively, a balanced regimen can be adopted using pethidine (5 mg/kg im), diazepam (1·0 mg/kg im) and low doses of pentobarbitone (5 mg/kg iv to effect) after the other drugs have been allowed time to produce their peak effect. Respiratory depression must be closely monitored nevertheless and provision made for O_2 therapy in case of emergency. Similar combinations, e.g. acepromazine–pentobarbitone, xylazine–pentobarbitone, fentanyl–fluanisone–pentobarbitone, are effective in reducing the dangers inherent in the barbiturate used alone, reducing the dosage by 30–70% and preventing the excitatory phases during recovery.

The anaesthetist must ensure a clear airway until the animal is fully recovered and pay particular attention to the maintenance of body temperature. Fluid therapy should be provided, but infusions containing glucose or sodium lactate are contraindicated.

Pentobarbitone is also useful for long periods of anaesthesia and acute experimental preparations. Low doses of 5 mg/kg administered at 60 min intervals to effect in conjunction with a muscle relaxant, e.g. pancuronium (0·05 mg/kg iv) every 30–40 min, and an analgesic, e.g. pethidine (5 mg/kg iv) or fentanyl (0·02 mg/kg iv or im), are effective in providing basal narcosis. The animals should be intubated and respired by IPPV with $N_2O:O_2(1:1)$. Remarkably stable preparations can be maintained in this way for 6–10 h with minimal physiological disturbance. Alternatively, pentobarbitone can be diluted in a 0·9% saline solution (200 mg/100 ml) and, once anaesthesia is induced and stabilized, can be delivered by continuous infusion at a rate e.g. of 100 ml/h to a 20 kg dog. Respiration should again be artificially maintained with $N_2O:O_2$ (1:1) delivered by IPPV.

α-chloralose (freshly prepared as a 1% solution in 0·9% saline solution) is also valuable in maintaining acute near-physiological preparations. Anaesthesia is induced with methohexitone (4 mg/kg iv), the dog is intubated and immediately supplied with a $N_2O:O_2$ (1:1) gas mixture. α-chloralose is then injected slowly iv at a rate of 40–80 mg/kg to produce basal narcosis which is maintained for 6–10 h. This combined technique avoids the movements of head and limbs which are associated with narcosis with α-chloralose alone. There is little or no direct myocardial depression, respiratory depression is minimal even if maintained on spontaneous respiration, and blood pressure is slightly raised. However, hyperpyrexia is commonly encountered and core temperature should be constantly monitored.

Inhalational anaesthetic techniques. Anaesthesia of sufficient depth for intubation is best achieved with thiopentone, thiamyl or methohexitone given rapidly iv at low dose. Alternatively, if these barbiturates are specifically contraindicated for the experiment, gas mixtures can be supplied via a suitable close-fitting face-mask and Magill circuit at total flow rates of 3–4 litre/min. Most dogs will breathe a mixture of $N_2O:O_2$ (7:3) without struggling, and halothane can gradually be introduced until concentrations of 2% are reached. The animal should be intubated as soon as it is sufficiently relaxed.

Cuffed endotracheal tubes of 6–10 mm outside diameter are suitable for dogs. The subject is laid on one side, the jaws are opened wide and the tongue pulled out to the maximum extent by an assistant. The larynx is then easily seen with a laryngoscope and, after depressing the epiglottis with the blade tip, the lubricated tube is passed and the cuff inflated. Having adjusted the tube to ensure that it is within the trachea and has not passed into a bronchus, it should be secured in place with tape tied around the upper jaw.

Halothane (1–2%) in O_2 may be used in closed circuits with soda-lime absorption, with 2–3 litre rebreathing bags and with or without IPPV. A flow rate of 3–4 litres/min with the expiratory valve wide open should be used whilst the subject is adjusting to inhalational anaesthesia. After 5–10 min, the expiratory valve is closed and the gas flow reduced to 100–300 ml/min (i.e. sufficient to make up for leaks in the system and supply the metabolic O_2 requirements of the animals). At this low flow rate, the efficiency of most halothane vaporizers falls dramatically so that it may be necessary to set it at a higher concentration to prevent concentrations in the rebreathing bag falling. Nitrous oxide must not be used in a completely closed system.

Halothane (0·5–1·5%) or methoxyflurane (0·5–

Table 12.1. **Dog: physiological data (resting values)**

Measurement	Large (30–40 kg)	Small (10–15 kg)
Respiratory frequency (breaths/min)	15–18	30
Tidal volume (ml)	350–450	200–250
Minute volume (l/min)	5–7	3·5–4·5
Mean heart rate (beats/min)	70–100	100–200
Arterial blood pressure (mmHg)	112/56	112/56
Arterial blood pH	7·36	7·36
Pa O_2 (mmHg)	90	90
Pa CO_2 (mmHg)	38	38
Haematocrit (%)	45 (38–53)	45 (38–53)
Haemoglobin (g/100 ml)	15 (11–18)	15 (11–18)
Erythrocytes (10^6/mm³)	6 (4–8)	6 (4–8)
*Blood volumes (ml/kg bodyweight)		
Total	90	
Expected terminal exsanguination	45	
Safe maximum single sample	9	
Mean rectal temperature (°C)		38·3 (38·1–38·9)

*Archer (1965).

1·5%) in $N_2O:O_2$ (*1:1*) are excellent gas mixtures for dogs if used in the same circuit as above but with the expiratory valve partially open (i.e. a semi-closed system). The gases should be supplied at 3–4 litres/min. A ratio of $3:2$ $N_2O:O_2$ is permissible for short periods of anaesthesia up to 20 min, but should be no greater than $1:1$ for more prolonged maintenance.

Nitrous oxide/O_2 (*1:1*) provides excellent 'background' narcosis for extensive periods of anaesthesia, particularly if supplied by IPPV. Low doses of muscle relaxants, neuroleptanalgesics and barbiturates can then be injected iv to provide a balanced regimen to satisfy the experimental requirements.

Recovery and post-surgical therapy
The endotracheal tube with a suitable wooden bite-block should be retained until swallowing and chewing reflexes have clearly returned. Dogs should be returned to special recovery boxes or pens with external sources of heat to maintain body temperature until fully recovered. We employ warm air blowers or infrared lamps, as well as blankets to keep the animal warm. Although it should be observed at frequent intervals, the dog should be allowed to recover undisturbed in a quiet, dimly-lit pen.

Chemical restraint and capture: exotic species

Phencyclidine–promazine (1–2 mg/kg : 1–2 mg/kg) was effective in a range of Canidae including wild dogs (*Lycaon pictus lupinus*), foxes (*Vulpes vulpes*), timber wolves (*Canis lupus*) and jackal (*Canis aureus*), but hypertonicity, hyperthermia and salivation caused problems (Seal et al., 1970). Tiletamine–zolazepam is also satisfactory (Gray et al., 1974). Ketamine (7 mg/kg) proved satisfactory in Cape hunting dogs (*Lycaon pictus*) (Ebedes & Grobler, 1973), but up to 10% of dogs show excitement and even convulsions (Hime, 1973). Xylazine (6–8 mg/kg im) is useful in animals which are already physically restrained (Goltenboth & Klös, 1970) but the large volumes necessary make it impracticable to give in projectile syringes (Jones, 1973).

Etorphine–methotrimeprazine is also useful with the advantage that narcosis can be reversed with diprenorphine (Jones, 1973).

Recommendations
Foxes may be picked up by the tail and held at arm's length whilst given im injections. Other dogs need to be immobilized by projectile or in a crush cage.

Ketamine (6–10 mg/kg im) or ketamine-xylazine (6 mg/kg : 2 mg/kg) are relatively safe for chemical restraint. Conventional anaesthetic techniques can then be used, but the dosage requirements for other agents, e.g. thiopentone, are reduced by up to 60%.

Domestic cat (*Felis domesticus*)
Although cats have been little used for experimental surgery, they are frequently selected for experimental physiological and pharmacological preparations. Anaesthetic management for surgery is standard and similar to that described for dogs. Local analgesia, apart from infiltration techniques, has limited applications.

Atropine in doses as high as 1·0 mg/kg was recommended by Stoliker (1969), after Cloetta (1908) reported a minimum lethal dose for cats of 30·0 mg/kg. Tolerance to such high levels of atropine in cats is due to the presence of liver atropine esterase which rapidly breaks down the agent (Godeaux & Tonneson, 1949; Stormont & Suzuki, 1970).

The phenothiazine derivatives have been widely employed in cats. Hall (1971) recommended doses up to 1·0 mg/kg im of chlorpromazine, whilst doses of 4·4 mg/kg im produced over 8 h of tranquillization without analgesia in the hands of Davis & Donnelly (1968). Promazine has been used at similar doses in cats, both alone and in combination with other agents. Clifford (1957) obtained good results with promazine (4·4 mg/kg sc) and pethidine (10 mg/kg sc) as preanaesthetic treatment 1 h before administering low doses of pentobarbitone iv to effect. Acepromazine is effective in cats at 0·1–0·2 mg/kg im (Hall, 1971) and at 1·0–2·0 mg/kg according to Lumb & Jones (1973). We have used 0·25–0·5 mg/kg im or sc and observed no ill effects (CRC).

Morphine and other powerful sedative–analgesics have long been considered contra-indicated for cats since they frequently produce mania and convulsions which may be fatal (Alexander, 1960). However, this supposition was questioned by Davis & Donnelly (1968), who suggested that low doses could be used. They found that morphine (0·1 mg/kg sc) provided 4 h of effective analgesia without unwanted side-effects. Nevertheless, since morphine at 0·5 mg/kg im or sc had previously been shown to produce excitement (Krueger et al., 1941), it is perhaps best avoided in this species.

The analgesic activity of pethidine in cats is also in doubt. According to Booth & Rankin (1954), doses of 5–19 mg/kg sc rendered cats more tractable, and not until doses of 30–50 mg/kg were administered did muscular spasms and other excitatory behaviour occur. However, they were unable to demonstrate consistent analgesia. Similar inconsistency was observed by Davis & Donnelly (1968) who found that pethidine was rapidly metabolized in this species and any effect observed 2 h after injection was no longer apparent 2 h later. We have given doses of 3–5 mg/kg im or sc without observing excitation, and were able to use lower doses of barbiturate iv to effect for anaesthesia.

Although phencyclidine (Stoliker, 1965; Bordet et al., 1967) and tiletamine (Bennett, 1969; Garmer, 1969) have been evaluated in domestic cats, the disadvantages of long recovery and poor muscle relaxation have precluded clinical acceptance. Ketamine on the other hand, has proved useful in wild and domestic cats (Commons, 1970; Hoeppner & Short, 1971; Beck et al., 1971; Reid & Frank, 1972; Eads, 1972; Glen, 1973; Hatch, 1973; Hime, 1974) at doses ranging from 10–44 mg/kg. However, Glen (1973) and Stock (1973) considered that ketamine was only really satisfactory for chemical immobilization of intractable subjects, and they emphasized the lack of relaxation, frequent occurrence of myoclonic jerking and the long time to complete recovery (6–8 h). The activity of ketamine on the CNS was studied in acute cat preparations by Corssen & Domino (1966), and changes in EEG and evoked potentials during ketamine anaesthesia in unrestrained cats was studied by Kayama & Iwama (1972) and Wong & Jenkins (1974).

Xylazine was considered to be a useful sedative for cats by Sagner et al. (1968). Doses of 1–2 mg/kg im or sc were recommended and the wide safety margin was emphasized (Lumb & Jones, 1973). Cats usually vomit soon after administration and remain sensitive to sharp auditory stimuli. Xylazine should be given at least 20 min before induction of anaesthesia and dosages of barbiturate should be reduced by 60–75%. It is also valuable as an adjunct to ketamine (Amend et al., 1972). We have given xylazine (1 mg/kg im) 10 min before ketamine (30 mg/kg im) to produce complete immobilization, with good muscle relaxation, analgesia and suppression of myoclonic movements. Peak effect was maintained for 40–60 min but full recovery took up to 8 h (CRC).

Much of the early pharmacological testing of steroid anaesthetics was performed in cats and, after the preliminary communication of Child et al. (1971) reporting the value of alphaxolone–alphadolone, extensive clinical trials of the combination were performed and reported (Evans et al., 1972; Baxter & Evans, 1973; Dodds & Twissell, 1973; Evans, 1973; Gregory, 1973). These steroids have since met with widespread approval for feline anaesthesia. They can be given im to produce safe sedation or iv to induce surgical anaesthesia comparable to thiopentone and with a similar duration of effect (Stock, 1973). However, occasional failure to induce sedation or anaesthesia may be encountered after im administration and this is thought to be due to deposition into intramuscular fascia instead of muscle itself (Baxter & Evans, 1973). These authors recommend injection into the quadriceps group of muscles, while Stock (1973) claimed better results if it was injected into the triceps humeri muscles. From the studies of Child et al. (1971), alphaxolone–alphadolone appears to be compatible with commonly used ataractics, analgesics, muscle relaxants and inhalational anaesthetics, but not with barbiturates, and accumulation has not been observed (cf. thiopentone). It has also been suggested that alphaxolone–alphadolone may significantly prolong the effects of pancuronium by Smith (1977), who experienced a case of prolonged muscle relaxation lasting nearly 8 h.

The induction of anaesthesia with barbiturates is fully described by Hall (1971) and Lumb & Jones (1973). A 3% solution of pentobarbitone, 1·25% solution of thiopentone, 2% solution of thiamylal and 1% solution of methohexitone are recommended concentrations for cats, but otherwise the dosages and precautions already described for dogs are applicable in this species. Hall (1976) has concluded that pentobarbitone and thiobarbiturates should not be used in kittens under 10 weeks of age because of prolonged recovery.

Induction and maintenance with inhalational agents has been described (Lumb, 1963; Clifford & Soma, 1969; Hall, 1971; Lumb & Jones, 1973) using conventional gas mixtures of halothane, ether or methoxyflurane with O_2 or N_2O and O_2. The respiratory effects of inhalational agents in cats was examined by Ngai et al. (1965) and, in a study comparing pentobarbitone, thiamylal, ether and methoxyflurane for use in newborn kittens, Sis & Herron (1972) concluded that methoxyflurane was the agent of choice for safe induction and maintenance of anaesthesia.

The effects of muscle relaxants are similar in cats to those described in dogs, except that cats are more resistant to suxamethonium (Hall, 1971). Very large doses were found to depress the respiratory centre (Ellis et al., 1952), but otherwise this agent appears to have no significant effect on the CNS. Lincoff et al. (1957) found that suxamethonium increased intraocular pressure in cats due to contracture of extraocular muscles. D-tubocurarine causes severe arterial hypotension if given iv and is contraindicated in this species (Hall, 1971). A transient fall in blood pressure was also noted after iv administration of gallamine, but this was not considered dangerous at therapeutic doses (1·0 mg/kg iv) by Hall (1971). According to Mushin *et al.* (1949), 30–100% of a total dose of gallamine can be recovered from the urine of cats within 2 h of administration. Pancuronium (0·06 mg/kg iv) was found to be effective in cats by Massey (1970) and, as the effects can be completely reversed with neostigmine (with atropine), this was suggested as the drug of choice for long periods of relaxation. Pharmacological studies involving muscle relaxants in cats are numerous and several are of interest to the experimentalist (Paton & Zanis, 1951; Rack & Westbury, 1966; Savarese *et al.*, 1975).

Recommended anaesthetic techniques
Preanaesthetic management
Cats should be procured from specified-pathogen-free breeding colonies if possible, and vaccinated against feline enteritis at least 2 weeks before introduction to the laboratory. They should be examined for health, paying particular attention to watery discharges from the eyes and nose, since these animals are subject to viral infections of the upper respiratory tract (feline influenza). They should also be routinely dosed against round and tapeworms.

Food should be withheld for 12 h prior to anaesthesia, but cats should be allowed access to water until anaesthesia is induced.

Physical restraint and handling
Cats are often intractable and resent physical restraint. Equipped with sharp teeth and claws, they can be more difficult to handle than dogs, and care must be taken that inexperienced laboratory staff are not exposed to danger unnecessarily. All doors and windows must be closed before attempts are made to handle the animal. The anaesthetist should always attempt to restrain the subject by gentle persuasion first, holding the animal for venepuncture as illustrated (Fig. 12.5). If, however, the animal indicates resentment by snarling and hissing, a decision must be made whether to increase the physical restraint, resort to injectable chemical restraint, or induce anaesthesia by inhalation of agents piped into a chamber. If further physical

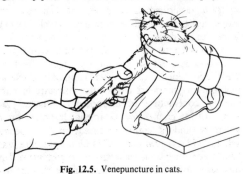

Fig. 12.5. Venepuncture in cats.

control is chosen, the handler must grasp the skin at the back of the neck in one hand and over the loins with the other and then press the cat firmly down to the table so that the legs are flexed and it is resting on its chest in the prone position. The anaesthetist may then induce anaesthesia by iv injection or, if this proves impossible, an im injection of sedative can be made. Further physical control of a difficult subject is afforded by wrapping it in a towel or a suitable plastic sleeve, or in specially constructed rigid plastic cylinders.

Chemical restraint and preanaesthetic therapy
Atropine (0·05 mg/kg sc) should be administered 30–40 min before other agents.

For deep sedation the following agents are recommended in order of preference.

Alphaxolone–alphadolone (9 mg/kg im) given deeply into the triceps humori muscle or into the anterior aspect of a hind limb into the quadriceps femoris muscle group, sedates the cats for a period of 5–7 min, the effect developing 6–7 min after injection. An im dose of 12 mg/kg produces deep sedation to light surgical anaesthesia in 7–8 min, and this is maintained for about 15 min. Further doses may be given by im or iv injection to extend the duration of effect as required but barbiturates must not be used after alphaxolone–alphadolone.

Ketamine (10–20 mg/kg im) produces a state of cataleptoid sedation lasting 30–45 min with recovery complete in 4–5 h. This period can be extended by further im or iv injections of 4 mg/kg doses at 60 min intervals. The cats become ataxic within 5 min, the eyes remain open with dilated pupils, and analgesia accompanied by enhanced muscle tone gradually develops within 10 min.

Salivation is profuse in spite of previous atropine administration, respiration is mildly depressed but there is usually mild cardiovascular stimulation. Ketamine is valuable as an immobilizing agent for intractable subjects or for large zoo cats, as the small volume can be injected rapidly and deposition within muscle is not crucial to success (cf. alphaxolone–alphadolone).

Xylazine (1–2 mg/kg im) provides effective sedation in cats, the peak effect developing in 7–10 min, and lasting for 30–40 min. The animals usually vomit within 10 min of administration, but salivation and cardiac arrhythmias are prevented by the prior administration of atropine. We have found it an excellent agent administered prior to induction of anaesthesia with barbiturates iv (reducing dosage by approximately 75%). If given im 10 min prior to ketamine (20 mg/kg im), analgesia and muscle relaxation are enhanced to produce a state similar to surgical anaesthesia.

Xylazine (1–2 mg/kg im) with pethidine (2·0 mg/kg im) produces sufficient sedation and analgesia within 30 min to allow superficial surgery and manipulation to be carried out in cats, and this can be further improved by local infiltration with an 0·5% solution of lignocaine.

Acepromazine (0·5 mg/kg im) takes 5–10 min for onset of effect and lasts 2–4 h. It is useful in tranquillizing cats for induction and for eliminating excitement during recovery from barbiturates or ketamine.

Surgical anaesthesia

General notes. There are no special comments to make regarding surgical anaesthesia in cats. Choice lies between the excellent injectable steroid combination alphaxolone–alphadolone which can be used for short or long operations, and inhalational agents. Neonates and kittens under 10–12 weeks of age are best anaesthetized with inhalational techniques.

Injectable anaesthetic techniques. Three vessels are commonly used for venepuncture:

The cephalic vein on the anterior face of a forelimb is the most convenient vessel for injection. It is located and dilated by compression above the elbow after clipping and swabbing with alcohol (Fig. 12.5). Injection is best made either with a 16 × 0·65 mm (23 gauge) needle or with a 0·65 mm (23 gauge) butterfly needle which can be taped in place for sequential injections and fluid therapy.

The jugular vein is convenient for percutaneous placement of indwelling catheters and is easily entered once the cat is suitably sedated.

The femoral vein is also convenient for placement of indwelling catheters as long as the animal is deeply sedated. It is possible to pass an 'Intracath' (p. 74) percutaneously, but we prefer to make a small surgical incision under local infiltration analgesia to expose the vessel and pass the catheter by direct vision.

The criteria for estimating depth of anaesthesia are similar to those described for the dog, i.e. loss of consciousness, muscle relaxation, pupillary (photomotor) reflexes, and the protective pain, palpebral, corneal, laryngeal and pharyngeal reflexes. However, these are so modified by preanaesthetic treatment, especially with xylazine or ketamine, that the anaesthetist must often make an assessment on depth of respiration and the degree of analgesia attained.

Induction of anaesthesia can be achieved with the following agents in order of preference.

Alphaxolone–alphadolone: half of a computed dose of 9–12 mg/kg is injected rapidly iv and the remainder slowly to effect. The subject relaxes within 10 s, light-to-medium surgical anaesthesia develops within 25–35 s depending on the speed of injection, and lasts for 8–12 min. Recovery is uneventful unless the cat is disturbed, in which case limb paddling and twitching may be provoked. The advantages of alphaxolone–alphadolone over barbiturates are that the therapeutic index is higher, narcosis is accompanied by good analgesia and muscle relaxation, and anaesthesia can be prolonged by sequential injections without cumulative effects or tolerance developing. Furthermore, the cats rapidly return to normal eating and behavioural patterns on recovery even after extended periods of steroid anaesthesia (cf. pentobarbitone and thiopentone). Cats can be intubated under alphaxolone–alphadolone anaesthesia for maintenance with inhalational agents.

Methohexitone (1% solution) is also useful for induction and intubation of cats. It should be given at 4–8 mg/kg by rapid iv injection to achieve smooth induction of light surgical anaesthesia within 5–10 s; the peak effect lasts 3–5 min and full recovery takes 20–30 min. Further doses can be given at 2–4 mg/kg iv to prolong anaesthesia but some accumulation does occur and recovery may then be unduly protracted. The cats should be allowed to recover without disturbance if methohexitone is the only agent which has been used since tremors and paddling movements may be provoked by noise or other stimuli.

Thiopentone (1·25% solution) may be used for induction by giving half of a computed dose (10–15 mg/kg) rapidly iv, and the remainder within 20 s to effect. A period of light surgical anaesthesia lasting 5–10 min is produced but full recovery may be prolonged up to 24 h and, unless the animals are pretreated with ataractics such as acepromazine, may be accompanied by excitement.

Thiamylal (2% solution) is used as an alternative to thiopentone at doses of 15–20 mg/kg iv, injecting 33% rapidly and the remainder slowly to effect.

Ketamine–xylazine by im injection is useful in inducing a state of narcosis bordering on surgical anaesthesia. The xylazine is given at 1 mg/kg im 10 min prior to ketamine at 20 mg/kg im. The maximal effect develops within 20 min of ketamine administration, and lasts 30–40 min. Further increments of ketamine can then be given at 2 mg/kg iv every 30 min for maintenance. A maximum total dose of 30 mg/kg of ketamine should not be exceeded. Full recovery may take 8–12 h depending on the dosage used.

Maintenance of anaesthesia in recovery experiments can be achieved by increments of injectable agents (not thiobarbiturates) or with inhalational techniques.

Alphaxolone–alphadolone can be used to maintain anaesthesia over long periods by intermittent iv injection of 4 mg/kg increments at 15–20 min intervals via an indwelling catheter or 0·65 mm

(23-gauge) butterfly needle. We have maintained cats for up to 6 h and encountered minimal respiratory depression and minimal deviation in cardiovascular dynamics so long as the subjects were intubated and normal management procedures adopted. Periods of light surgical anaesthesia can be maintained up to 24 h with minimal cardiopulmonary disturbance (Smith, 1977), but oedema of the paws and ears may be encountered.

Alternatively, balanced combinations of ketamine–pentobarbitone, ketamine–xylazine, or xylazine–pethidine–pentobarbitone can be used iv. In each case, it is important to use minimal doses of pentobarbitone (5–8 mg/kg) to avoid the prolonged recovery which accompanies anaesthetic doses of this barbiturate if it is used alone in cats.

For non-recovery experiments, α-chloralose may be used for long periods of maintenance with minimal physiological disturbance. After inducing anaesthesia with alphaxolone–alphadolone or methohexitone and passing an endotracheal tube, $N_2O:O_2$ (1:1) should be administered via an Ayres T-piece at a flow rate of 3 litres/min. α-chloralose (1% solution) is then given by slow iv injection at 40–80 mg/kg to produce basal narcosis or light surgical anaesthesia for 6–10 h. The methohexitone and N_2O are usually sufficient to suppress the paddling and twitching movements invariably encountered in cats if α-chloralose is used alone.

Inhalational anaesthetic techniques. Anaesthesia can be induced by piping gas mixtures directly into a suitable box or via a malleable rubber Hall's cat mask and Magill circuit. The latter system is convenient for periods of anaesthesia up to 30 min but, as in other species, it is much preferable to pass an endotracheal tube, and present the gas via a Rees-modified Ayres T-piece to minimize dead space and expiratory resistance.

Cuffed endotracheal tubes of 3–5·5 mm outside diameter are suitable for cats. Laryngospasm is easily provoked so it is essential to minimize secretions by giving atropine, and then anaesthetize the cat sufficiently deeply by mask and inhalational agent (e.g. halothane) or iv alphaxolone–alphadolone and spray the larynx with 2% lignocaine before attempting to pass the tube. Intubation is achieved under direct vision using a laryngoscope fitted with a paediatric blade, and is facilitated if a rubber-shod stiffener is retained in the tube until the tip passes the vocal cords. If laryngeal spasm occurs in spite of these precautions, suxamethonium (0·3 mg/kg) should be injected iv and artificial respiration provided for a short period.

Cats rarely object to breathing a $N_2O:O_2$ (3:2)

gas mixture via a face mask and Magill system, to which gradually increasing concentrations of halothane are added. This technique avoids the prolonged and deliberate apnoea which can arise if the cat is suddenly introduced to induction concentrations of halothane, and the stressful, voluntary excitement encountered if anaesthesia is induced with ether alone. Smooth induction can be anticipated with halothane in $N_2O:O_2$ or methoxyflurane in $N_2O:O_2$, but even if ether is introduced to $N_2O:O_2$ by stages, it will still provoke coughing and sneezing.

Once anaesthesia is induced, the subject should be intubated as described, and humidified gases supplied to a Rees modified T-piece at a flow rate of 2–3 litres/min. Under no circumstances should cats be maintained on rebreathing circuits. Anaesthesia is well maintained with $N_2O:O_2$ (1:1) supplemented with 0·2–1·5% halothane or 0·5–1% methoxyflurane.

Body temperature must be constantly monitored and warm solutions (Hartmann's) infused iv to balance the insensible fluid loss associated with the T-piece and high gas flow.

Recovery and post-surgical therapy
Cats should be allowed to recover in a warm, humidified environment, with the endotracheal tube and bite-blocks retained until reflex activity is regained. After long periods (4–6 h) of anaesthesia, we return the cat to an infant incubator maintained at 35°C, into which we pass a humidified 95% O_2 with 5% CO_2 gas mixture.

Table 12.2. Cat: physiological data (resting values)

Measurement	Values
Respiratory rate (breaths/min)	26 (20–30)
Tidal volume (ml)	12–18
Minute volume (l/min)	0·3–0·4
Mean heart rate (beats/min)	150 (110–240)
Arterial blood pressure (mmHg)	120/75
Arterial blood pH	7·35
Pa O_2 (mmHg)	120
Pa CO_2 (mmHg)	36
Haematocrit (%)	40 (30–50)
Haemoglobin (g/100 ml)	11 (8–14)
Erythrocytes (10^6/mm^3)	8 (6–10)
*Blood volumes (ml/kg bodyweight)	
Total	75
Expected terminal exsanguination	35
Safe maximum single sample	7
Mean rectal temperature (°C)	38·6

*Archer (1965).

Chemical restraint and capture: exotic species

Many exotic and zoo species have been immobilized with phencyclidine (0·6–2·0 mg/kg im),

212

but clonic spasms are often a problem particularly in tigers (*Panthera tigris*) unless promazine is given concurrently (Seal *et al.*, 1970). Even when the tranquillizer is given, convulsions may still occur (Baily, 1971; Beck, 1972; Hornocker & Wiles, 1972). More recently, tiletamine–zolazepam (Cl 744) at 4–5 mg/kg tiletamine was used to capture wild leopards (*Panthera pardus*) and tigers (Seidensticker *et al.*, 1974).

Ketamine alone (8·0–15·2 mg/kg im) (Dolensek, 1971; Mathews, 1971) was effective in wild cheetah (*Acinonyx jubatus*) and leopard (Smuts *et al.*, 1973)—the lower dosage being sufficient in cheetahs. Similarly, ketamine (5–25 mg/kg im) was considered highly effective in captive non-domesticated cats (Hime, 1974) although convulsions are seen in a few cases (Hime, 1977).

Xylazine has also been reported as effective at about 6 mg/kg im (Schmidt, 1974). Alphaxolone–alphadolone (12–18 mg/kg im) works well in zoo specimens already held in restraining cages but has the severe disadvantage that a large volume has to be injected deep im and this is impossible by projectile syringe.

Recommendations

Ketamine–xylazine (12 mg/kg : 1 mg/kg im) is probably best. Once the cat is sedated, the lateral caudal vein can be exposed and catheterized. Surgical anaesthesia can then be achieved by iv injection of a low dose of thiopentone (1 mg/kg) or alphaxolone–alphadolone (10 mg/kg) followed by intubation and conventional inhalational techniques.

FAMILY MUSTELIDAE

Ferrets (*Mustela putorius furo*)

This species presents no particular anaesthetic problems. The existing references consist of recommendations on the value of pentobarbitone in ferrets at 50 mg/kg ip (Wright, 1957) and 36 mg/kg ip (Donovan, 1964), and the inhalation of either for intraabdominal operations (Hill & Parkes, 1933).

Recommended anaesthetic techniques
Preanaesthetic management
Animals destined for experiment should be handled frequently. They are usually easily tamed. Those ferrets which remain intractable can often be tamed by giving diazepam (2 mg/kg im) for 2–3 consecutive days, and handling them frequently and gently whilst they are tranquillized.

Ferrets readily vomit when anaesthetized so they should be fasted for at least 6 h before induction.

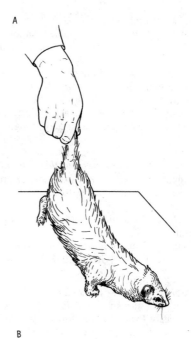

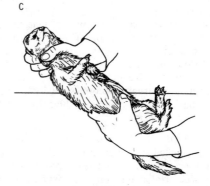

Fig. 12.6. Physical restraint of ferrets.

213

Physical restraint and handling

Ferrets once tamed can be handled without fear of bites or scratches. Otherwise, they should be handled with thick leather gloves, grasped firmly by encircling the neck and chest, and supported with the other hand under the belly. If gloves are not available, it is permissible to pick the ferret out of its cage by its tail, and then grasp it firmly about its neck after placing it on a grid or rough surface (Fig. 12. 6).

Chemical restraint and preanaesthetic therapy

Atropine should be given at 0·05 mg/kg im or sc. We have used acepromazine (0·05 mg/kg im) and diazepam (2 mg/kg im) to tranquillize, and alphaxolone–alphadolone (6–8 mg/kg im), ketamine (10–20 mg/kg im) and fentanyl–fluanisone (0·3 ml/kg im) to sedate ferrets with no untoward responses. (Green, 1978b).

Surgical anaesthesia

Injectable anaesthetic techniques. The simplest injection routes are im or ip. However, the cephalic vein is easily located if the foreleg is clipped and swabbed, and venepuncture is achieved with a 16 × 0·50 mm (25 gauge) needle. Alternatively the recurrent tarsal vein can be used.

Alphaxolone–alphadolone injected at 12–15 mg/kg im into the shoulder muscles (triceps humori) produces light surgical anaesthesia in 10–12 min and this lasts 15–30 min. A further dose of 6–8 mg/kg im or small increments to effect iv may be given to extend the period of anaesthesia. Full recovery takes 60–90 min and the animals then appear normal and eat if offered food.

Ketamine (20–30 mg/kg im) produces deep cataleptoid stupor or light surgical anaesthesia within 10 min of administration and this lasts about 40–60 min.

Fentanyl–fluanisone (0·5 ml/kg im) produces profound neuroleptanalgesia suitable for many surgical procedures and is rapidly reversed with nalorphine im. However, tremors and excitability may be encountered occasionally 2–3 min after administration.

Pentobarbitone is a reasonable anaesthetic in ferrets. After administration of 36 mg/kg ip, light surgical anaesthesia develops in 6–10 min and lasts for 50–120 min. Full recovery takes many hours and, in the absence of ataractic or sedative premedication, is usually accompanied by excitatory behaviour including twitching, shivering and limb paddling movements.

Inhalational anaesthetic techniques. Conventional methods including induction in specially constructed boxes, or by mask and semi-open circuits may be used. Halothane or methoxyflurane with $N_2O:O_2$ (1:1) are used at 1–2 litre/min flow rates.

Stoats (*Mustela erminae*) and weasels (*Mustela nivalis*)

Both species are vicious if handled and will bite through thick leather gloves. In addition, it is possible to grip them so tightly that they are asphyxiated. It is generally preferable, therefore, to induce anaesthesia without handling whenever possible.

Recommendations

They should be coaxed into a clear plastic induction box as described by Healey (1967), or transferred from traps into a box (Lockie & Day, 1964) where they can be anaesthetized within 60 s with halothane sprayed on to gauze taped to the inside wall. Thereafter, anaesthesia can be maintained with 1–2% halothane or 1–1·5% methoxyflurane delivered by face mask in O_2 at a flow of 1 litre/min.

Mink (*Mustela vison*)

Mink are extremely vicious and should if possible be tempted into an induction box without handling. A handling tube constructed of metal was described by Hummon (1945). Reserpine given orally in feed at 0·05 mg has been reported as a useful tranquillizer (Lafortune & Rheault, 1960). Phencyclidine (1·0 mg/kg im) with promazine (2·0 mg/kg im) rendered mink tractable and easily handled (Seal & Erickson, 1969). Propiopromazine followed by pentobarbitone (6 mg/kg ip) produced 5–6 h of anaesthesia according to Padgett (1964). This is somewhat surprising since pentobarbitone alone at 40 mg/kg produced surgical anaesthesia in only 75% of test animals (Graham et al., 1967). A useful outline of general management was contributed by Rice (1967).

Recommendations

Mink should be fasted for 12 h before anaesthesia. Physical restraint should be avoided since they are excitable and vicious animals. They should be persuaded to enter a clear plastic induction box from their cage door either by blowing in their face so that they back away and into it, or by covering the clear plastic with a dark cloth and scratching on one side of the box until the animal feels impelled to investigate to satisfy its curiosity. Anaesthesia can then be induced painlessly either using a $CO_2:O_2$ (1:1) or a $N_2O:O_2$ (3:2) gas mixture piped into the box prior to handling. They can be injected with a range of anaesthetic agents as described above for ferrets, i.e. alphaxolone–alphadolone im, ketamine im, fentanyl–fluanisone im, or pentobarbitone (36–40 mg/kg iv to effect or ip). The cephalic or recurrent tarsal veins are convenient for injection and a 16 × 0·50 mm (25 gauge) needle should be used. Alternatively, inhalation anaesthesia with halothane, enflurane or methoxyflurane in $N_2O:O_2$ (1:1) delivered by mask and Magill system can be used for maintenance.

Skunks (*Mephitis mephitis*)

Recommendations
Similar problems are associated with the restraint and anaesthesia of skunks (McCune, 1973), with the additional hazard that the anaesthetist may be sprayed with musk unless precautions are taken. Anaesthesia is best induced with a volatile agent in a box or heavy-duty clear plastic bag which can be thrown away after use. The scent glands can be deliberately expressed by holding the skunk with its hindquarters away from the operator and pulling the tail up and forward towards its head.

Badgers (*Taxidea taxus*)

Recommendations
Badgers resist handling by biting and scratching. The safest procedure is to immobilize them with ketamine (10–20 mg/kg im) prior to maintenance anaesthesia with conventional techniques.

FAMILY URSIDAE

Etorphine (0·02 mg/kg im) was effective in polar bears (*Thalarctos maritimus*) (Larsen, 1967; Flyger *et al.*, 1967; Flyger & Townsend, 1968). Etorphine–methotrimeprazine was recommended for the brown bear (*Ursus arctos*) (Jones, 1973). Phencyclidine (about 1·0 mg/kg im) was used successfully in a large number of specimens (Seal *et al.*, 1970) and has the advantage over etorphine that bears are able to swim without drowning. Induction time varies from 3–13 min, and recovery time 30 min to 3 h (Lentfer, 1968).

Recommendations
Small bears: Etorphine–methotrimeprazine (0·1 ml/kg 'Immobilon SA') is the best combination.

Large bears: etorphine–acepromazine (0·25 ml/50 kg 'Immobilon LA') is recommended.

Polar bears: phencyclidine (0·5 mg/kg im) by projectile followed by roping and injection of etorphine (0·01 mg/kg im) is the least likely to cause death by drowning.

FAMILY HYAENIDAE

Phencyclidine has proved useful in captive Hyaenidae at about 1·0 mg/kg im, while ketamine (14·0 mg/kg im) was used in wild spotted hyaena (*Crocuta crocuta*) by Smuts (1973). Xylazine (3·7–4·5 mg/kg im) immobilized captive hyaena of different species (Goltenboth & Klös, 1970). Etorphine–methotrimeprazine at conventional dosages (0·1 ml/kg 'Immobilon SA') is considered best by Hime (1973).

Recommendations
Etorphine–methotrimeprazine (0·1 ml/kg 'Immobilon SA' im) is first choice followed by ketamine–xylazine (10·0 mg/kg:2·0 mg/kg im).

FAMILY VIVERRIDAE

Phencyclidine (1·0 mg/kg im) was used to immobilize a wide variety of these animals (Seal *et al.*, 1970). Similarly, tiletamine–zolazepam (CI744) was found effective at 4 mg/kg im (Gray *et al.*, 1974).

Recommendations
Unless CI744 becomes readily available, ketamine–xylazine (10 mg/kg:1·0 mg/kg im) is suggested.

FAMILY PROCYONIDAE

Recommendations
As a better alternative to phencyclidine (1·0 mg/kg im) suggested by Seal *et al.* (1970), ketamine which has already been found effective in wild racoons (*Procyon lotor*) at 20 mg/kg (Bigler & Hoff, 1974; Gregg & Olson, 1975) is recommended.

CHAPTER THIRTEEN

ORDERS: PRIMATA, MARSUPIALIA, EDENTATA, TUBULIDENTATA

ORDER PRIMATA (NONHUMAN)

It is always undesirable to handle conscious monkeys if this can be avoided. Not only can they inflict bite and scratches, they are also potential carriers of viruses highly pathogenic to man, as well as tuberculosis, salmonellosis and shigellosis. The first requirement of any method of chemical restraint must be that it eliminates the bite reflex whilst causing minimal stress to the animal. Since in our experience (CRC), oral administration of drugs is virtually impossible they must be given by rapid im injection while the monkey is physically restrained in a crush-back cage or in nets. A number of particular properties are required of an injectable agent in addition to those which are desirable for other species. The drug should be soluble in a small volume which can be rapidly injected and rapidly absorbed from accessible intramuscular sites. The therapeutic index should be wide enough to allow dosage to be calculated on an estimated weight. Finally, normal appetite and behaviour should be re-established quickly after recovery.

In a trial designed to compare a number of narcotic and tranquillizing agents in baboons (*Papio hamadryas*), Newsome & Robinson (1957) provided some valuable data. They assessed the barbiturates, pentobarbitone, hexobarbitone and amylbarbitone and the inhalational anaesthetics, ether, nitrous oxide and chloroform, as well as other CNS depressants including chlorpromazine, paraldehyde, α-chloralose, chloral hydrate and morphine. The authors concluded that the barbiturates were unsuitable for administration by im or oral routes. Nitrous oxide was supplied to a specially-constructed induction box (Graham-Jones, 1964) until the baboons were sedated, and was followed by inhalational anaesthesia with ether. These findings were later confirmed by Robinson (1964), who stated that the response to im pentobarbitone was unpredictable. Of the other agents assessed by Newsome & Robinson (1957), paraldehyde was of some value in reducing the dose of pentobarbitone when given im concurrently with the latter, but the response was still unpredictable. Chloral hydrate was not accepted orally whereas α-chloralose produced heavy sedation at a dose of 200 mg/kg if taken in bait, but clonic movements of the limbs and head were noted. Morphine was ineffective whether administered orally or im. Chlorpromazine was considered valuable at dose rates up to 3·5 mg/kg im, although the slow attainment of peak effect (2–6 h) was a disadvantage.

The intraperitoneal route was favoured by earlier commentators for the administration of barbiturates. Thus, Weidman (1930) claimed that ip injection of amylobarbitone at 50–65 mg/kg produced deep narcosis in rhesus monkeys (*Macaca mulatta*). In experiments designed to study the action of anaesthetic agents on the primate motor cortex, Keller & Fulton (1931) compared the activity of amylobarbitone, pentobarbitone, phenobarbitone, chloral hydrate and tribromoethanol given ip, and concluded that surgical anaesthesia was achieved with pentobarbitone at 35–40 mg/kg with complete recovery in 4–5 h. Similar conclusions were reached by Kennard et al. (1946), who found that pentobarbitone at 35–45 mg/kg ip produced surgical anaesthesia for 2–3 h, while varying degrees of CNS depression were achieved with amylobarbitone at 50–65 mg/kg ip.

Not surprisingly, the administration of agents per rectum has met with little popularity, although it is of interest that Elder (1937) trained adult chimpanzees (*Pan troglodytes verus*) to accept rectal administration of pentobarbitone at 25–30 mg/kg. It was claimed that narcosis was effected in 6–15 min while recovery took 6–9 h.

However, barbiturates have produced more predictable responses in subhuman primates when given by iv injection. Mills (1950) gave injections into the recurrent tarsal vein at a point traversing the gastrocnemius muscle on the posterior aspect of the leg. He considered this to be a simple technique if the animal was properly restrained, and suggested doses of barbiturate ranging from 25–40 mg/kg. However, in our experience (CRC) the strength of chimpanzees, baboons and even large male macaques renders iv injection difficult unless they are sedated, although it is relatively simple in monkeys weighing less than 10 kg. Bywater & Rutty (1964) reported their experience with barbiturates administered iv to a large number of *Macaca* and *Cercopithecus* monkeys. They were impressed by the overall safety and lack of pre- and post-anaesthetic excitement associated with pentobarbitone anaesthesia. Medium surgical anaesthesia was produced by approximately 30 mg/kg injected over 30 s, with a duration of 40–60 min and time to recovery of 1–5 h. Thiopentone, at doses ranging from 17–50 mg/kg iv, produced basal narcosis for 10–20 min. Methohexitone was also assessed at doses of 6, 10, 30 and 40 mg/kg by rapid iv injection, and it was concluded that 10 mg/kg was sufficient to produce light surgical anaesthesia lasting 10 min. They warned, however, that periods of excitement sometimes occurred. Conversely, the animals might pass directly from anaesthesia into sleep and were then easily aroused if handled by unwary staff.

The use of methohexitone in monkeys was first reported by Gibson *et al.* (1955), but thereafter attracted little attention until recently when it was assessed as an im injection by several groups. It was considered more suitable than other agents for repeated daily administration in *Macaca irus* (Cohen, 1970; Wallace *et al.*, 1972). A 2·5% solution was injected im at 12–15 mg/kg and produced light surgical anaesthesia with abolition of the bite reflex in 5–15 min. Anaesthesia lasted for 20–25 min. A 5% solution injected into shoulder muscles at 16–17 mg/kg was considered superior in *Macaca speciosa* monkeys by Reed & Staple (1976). In our experience methohexitone is certainly effective in *M. irus* and *M. mulatta*, as well as in *Cercopithecus* and *Papio* spp., but the large volumes of solution required (2–10 ml depending on the degree of narcosis required) is a significant disadvantage.

Phencyclidine was the first of the dissociative anaesthetic agents to be used extensively in subhuman primates (Chen *et al.*, 1959; Chen & Weston, 1960). They found that CNS depression was dose–dependent, ranging from sedation with

Table 13.1. Clinical signs after intramuscular administration of phencyclidine to subhuman primates (after Bywater & Rutty, 1964)

Dose mg/kg im	Observations
0·1	Face normally alert, but eye blink slows, monkey repeatedly licks lips, bite reflex decreased. Animal backs into corner of cage if approached.
0·3	Face appears slightly anxious, eye blink noticeably slow and, although tone in the jaw muscles retained, the biting reflex is lost completely. The monkey becomes increasingly ataxic, sits in a corner and rocks to-and-fro on haunches. Movements of the eyeball (nystagmus) may be observed.
0·5	Facial expression appears sad, eyelids partially close (ptosis). The animal can be safely picked up and handled e.g. for venepuncture.
1·0	The animal is usually immobilized yet apparently conscious. Attempts to 'mould' the limbs resisted and muscle tone strong. Analgesia usually well developed at this stage. Vertical and horizontal nystagmus commonly exhibited.
3·0	A state of cataleptoid stupor develops in which there is no response to pain or other stimuli, eyelids are partially closed and respiratory and cardiovascular function are near normal. Animals may be handled in less than 10 min.
5·0	A state resembling light surgical anaesthesia develops within 6 min, the tongue protrudes and profuse salivation is exhibited unless atropine is previously administered. The eyelids often blink, nystagmus is common and the pupil may dilate and contract in rapid succession. Analgesia well developed but muscle tone still marked.
10·0	Tetanic spasms of limbs progress to clonic extensor spasms.

early loss of the bite reflex through ataxia to cataleptoid narcosis and profound analgesia. At 3 times the dose needed to induce cataleptic narcosis, the CNS was stimulated to produce convulsions and finally respiratory failure. The clinical signs reported by Bywater & Rutty (1964) are shown in Table 13.1 and correspond to our own experience with phencyclidine (CRC). The im injection of 3 mg/kg allowed monkeys to be handled within 10 min (Spalding & Heymann, 1962), while iv injection of 5 mg/kg produced light surgical anaesthesia within 60 s and lasting for 60 min (Rutty & Thurley, 1962). According to Bywater & Rutty (1964), phencyclidine could be given im or orally, but the period of induction after ip injection was unacceptably long. The use of phencyclidine by the im or oral routes was extended in several different species of primate by Graham-Jones (1964), Melby & Baker (1965) and Stoliker (1965), to include baboons (*Papio* spp.), the chimpanzee (*Pan troglodytes verus*), *Macaca* spp., squirrel monkey (*Saimiri sciureus*), bonobo (*Pan paniscus*), black mangabey (*Cercocebus aterrimus*), gibbon (*Hylobates lars*), gorilla (*Gorilla gorilla gorilla*), lemur (*Lemur catta*), lion-tailed mandrill (*Mandrillus sphinx*), orang-utan (*Pongo pygmaeus*), siamuang (*Symphalangus syndactylus*) and talapoin monkeys (*Miopithecus talapoin*). The data summarized by Parke-Davis & Co. (1967) indicated that catalepis was induced in 6–20 min with doses ranging from 0·8–3 mg/kg im. Our experience with baboons, cynomolgus, rhesus and vervet monkeys confirmed the value of phencyclidine as an agent which could be given repeatedly for prolonged immobilization, provided particular care was taken to maintain body temperature. However, results with marmosets (*Callithrix jacchus*) using dose rates ranging from 0·5–2 mg/kg im have been less predictable, and the animals were only tranquillized (CRC).

Although phencyclidine has proved to be a valuable immobilizing agent, surgical conditions are less than ideal for all except minor procedures. Muscular relaxation is poor, and the limbs, digits and neck may undergo slow clasping and flexing movements. Several agents have been given concurrently with phencyclidine in an effort to overcome these unwanted side effects. Promazine at 1 mg/kg im was recommended by Graham-Jones (1964) and by Seal & Erickson (1969). Acepromazine (0·1 mg/kg im) was used in chimpanzees by Jones (1973). Pentobarbitone (2·4–5 mg/kg iv) was recommended by Lumb & Jones (1973) after initial restraint with phencyclidine. We have assessed xylazine at 0·5 mg/kg im given together with phencyclidine at 1·5 mg/kg in *M. irus*. The combination produced deep sedation with profound muscle relaxation (CRC). Phencyclidine has also been given in low doses (sufficient to overcome the bite reflex) before administering halothane in O_2 by mask (Graham-Jones, 1964; Hime, 1972). This technique had the advantage that recovery was rapid since the dosage of phencyclidine was low (0·2–0·4 mg/kg).

Phencyclidine has now been superseded by ketamine for use in primates. Bree *et al.* (1967) investigated the safety and tolerance of repeated ketamine anaesthesia in rhesus monkeys. They concluded that doses of 10–25 mg/kg im produced anaesthesia of varying duration and that tolerance, as indicated by decreasing duration of effect for a given dose rate, developed after repeated administration. The clinical effectiveness of ketamine in macaque monkeys was described in a separate

communication (Bree, 1967). This has since been confirmed in a wide variety of simian species (Beck & Dresner, 1972), in patas monkeys (*Erythrocebus patas*) by Britton *et al.* (1974), and in squirrel monkeys at 25 mg/kg (Greenstein, 1975).

Physiological responses to ketamine administration have been measured in detail in rhesus monkeys (Massopust *et al.*, 1972). It was concluded that ketamine blocks the nonspecific thalamocortical system with deactivation of the cerebral cortex except for the frontal lobes, and enhances electrical activity in the limbic and extrapyramidal system. Hence the corneal, palpebral and certain spinal reflexes remain intact. Salivation increases but swallowing and cough reflexes are preserved. The neural mechanisms involved were explored in further experiments in *M. mulatta* (Sparks *et al.*, 1973, 1975). They suggested that the profound analgesia attained was due to functional disorganization of pathways to non-specific midbrain and thalamic nuclei, as well as to blockade of spinal-cord reflexes. The effects of ketamine on muscle tone was compared with phencyclidine by Kuroda & McNamara (1972), who concluded that ketamine was less likely to interfere with experiments on neuromuscular activity.

From our own experience (CRC), ketamine is considered to be the agent of choice for chemical restraint of most subhuman primates. It has many advantages over other agents. Firstly, at dose rates of 10–25 mg/kg, small volumes of the 10% solution can be injected rapidly into the thigh muscles of a struggling monkey. The rapid onset and attainment of peak effect after im injection (5–10 min) and the relatively short period of sedation (30–60 min) are convenient for many experimental procedures. The complete recovery in 1–5 h (depending on species and dose) allows for a period of normal behaviour and for taking food between experiments. In addition, cardiovascular function is slightly stimulated, respiratory depression is produced only if high doses are given iv, profound analgesia develops and protective pharyngeal–laryngeal reflexes are well maintained (although the airway may still become obstructed). The therapeutic index is high and the drug can be given repeatedly (although tolerance may develop).

The 3rd dissociative agent, tiletamine, has been assessed for clinical use alone in subhuman primates (Bree, 1972), and in combination with zolazepam in dogs and primates (Bree, *et al.*, 1972). This combination has since been used in a wide range of primates to provide chemical restraint at doses ranging from 2–6 mg/kg im and 6–17 mg/kg orally in orange juice (Gray *et al.*, 1974). However, an analysis of their results suggests that the combination has no major advantage over ketamine especially if the latter is given together with ataractics such as xylazine or diazepam.

Neuroleptanalgesia with a combination of fentanyl and droperidol has been relatively successful in a wide range of primates (Marsboom et al., 1962; Marsboom et al., 1963; Field et al., 1966; Mortelmans, 1969). Dose rates of 0·02 mg/kg fentanyl with 2·0 mg/kg droperidol im in apes, and 0·04 mg/kg fentanyl with 3·0 mg/kg droperidol im in monkeys, produced sufficient analgesia for 30–60 min of surgery. Marsboom et al. (1963) claimed that the mixture was readily accepted in milk or fruit juice to achieve effective narcosis, but this has certainly not been our experience in M. irus or M. mulatta (CRC).

Etorphine was also effective in immobilizing several primates including spider monkeys and orang-utan (Wallach et al., 1967) at a dosage of approximately 0·005 mg/kg. Pethidine (10 mg/kg) was recommended by Lumb & Jones (1973). We have used thiambutene at 10 mg/kg im and this produced light sedation and analgesia. The peak effect was attained in 15 min and lasted for 60–120 min (CRC).

After extensive clinical use in feline anaesthesia, the steroid combination alphaxolone–alphadolone was recommended for use in cynomolgus monkeys (Box & Ellis, 1973). An im dose of 12 mg/kg sedated monkeys, and higher doses (up to 60 mg/kg im) produced light surgical anaesthesia for up to 3 h. The recommended technique for full surgical anaesthesia was to give 18 mg/kg im, wait 5–7 min for sedation to develop and then give a further 6–12 mg/kg iv to effect. This combination has since been evaluated in many species of primate and several desirable features noted. It has a wide safety margin, it can be given im or iv, induction is smooth and rapid, and good muscular relaxation develops. Respiration is not significantly depressed except at unnecessarily high dose levels administered iv. The recovery period is short and uncomplicated, and the animals rapidly regain their full appetite. Tolerance has not been encountered after repeated sequential administration nor have behavioural changes been observed. Unfortunately, these steroids are relatively insoluble and the volume is inconvenient for rapid im injection in large primates (cf. ketamine). Furthermore, alphaxolone–alphadolone must not be used after barbiturates. Nevertheless, this is a valuable injectable short-acting anaesthetic in subhuman primates (CRC). It was recommended as the agent of choice for marmosets at doses up to 18 mg/kg im by Phillips & Grist (1975) and we prefer it to ketamine for marmosets and squirrel monkeys (CRC).

The use of muscle relaxants in primates has not been widely reported. Suxamethonium 1·5–2·0 mg/kg iv was recommended by Aronson et al.

(1965) for the intubation of baboons (Papio spp.), although only 30–60 s of relaxation was produced. We have used gallamine at 1 mg/kg iv and pancuronium at 0·01 mg/kg iv in macaques and baboons to produce reversible muscle relaxation of about 20 and 50 min respectively (CRC).

Unfortunately, all these methods of chemical restraint entail handling for injection and are bound to produce physiological changes. It has recently been shown that the plasma cortisol levels in M. mulatta sampled after chemical immobilization are over 10 times higher than in subjects trained to move into a box and allow venepuncture for reward (Setchel et al., 1975). Such conditioning is difficult and it might be simpler to avoid sympathetic stimulation by giving tranquillizers disguised in food or drink. According to Wallace et al. (1960), perphenazine was accepted by chimpanzees at dose levels of 2·4–4·4 mg/kg in pineapple juice, maple syrup or peanut butter. The authors claimed that the animals were tranquillized within 3 h for a period of 6–7 h. However, most workers have been unsuccessful in persuading primates to accept drugs by the oral route. It is occasionally possible to squirt ketamine or phencyclidine into the mouth of a monkey, but this must also be frightening for the animal.

Inhalational anaesthesia without previous chemical immobilization can be achieved by enticing the primate into an induction box into which anaesthetic gases may be piped. Induction boxes have been designed and described by Graham-Jones (1964), Newsome & Robinson (1957), Robinson (1964) and Cohen (1964).

Nitrous oxide was piped into a box to initiate anaesthesia of baboons by Newsome & Robinson (1957). When the animal was unconscious the N_2O supply was discontinued, the animal was removed to the operating table and anaesthesia was continued with an ether–air mixture. Halothane in O_2 has since been widely used in subhuman primates (Graham-Jones, 1964; Day, 1965; Aronson et al., 1965) whilst a halothane in $N_2O:O_2$ mixture was recommended by Cohen (1964), Day (1965) and Martin et al. (1972). A halothane and ether in O_2 mixture was used by Hime (1972). In the valuable communication of Cohen (1964), cynomolgus monkeys were persuaded to enter a clear plastic catching box through the front door of their cage, and $N_2O:O_2$ (4:1) was piped in to induce a light plane of anaesthesia. Anaesthesia was then deepened by adding 1–4% halothane to the $N_2O:O_2$ until it was possible to pass an endotracheal tube. Methoxyflurane has also been used in a number of different primate species (Sawyer, 1965; Bennett, 1969).

In our experience, the most acceptable method combines sedation with ketamine to permit safe handling, followed by maintenance with $N_2O:O_2$ (1:1) and 0·5–1% halothane or enflurane delivered by mask or preferably a modified Ayres T-piece.

Some mention should be made of previous experience in measuring physiological responses in subhuman primates. Many experiments have required restraint without sedation or anaesthesia, and various restraining devices have been described (Sledjeski, 1964; Ferron, 1966; Adair, 1969; Glassman *et al.*, 1969; Howard *et al.*, 1971; Withrow & Devine, 1972). Electrocardiographs were recorded by Osborne (1973) in macaques strapped to a restraining board for periods up to 10 min. Osborne & Roberts (1972) provided valuable data on the ECG of restrained but unsedated baboons, and compared these with previous reports where the animals had received drugs (Cheetham 1934; Kaminer, 1958; Groover *et al.*, 1963; Van Citters & Lasry, 1965; Hermann & Williams, 1965). ECGs of anaesthetized slender lorises (*Loris tardigradus*) and bonnet monkeys (*Macaca radiata*) were described by Rahmann *et al.* (1975).

The published information available on respiratory function in primates is scanty (Stahl & Malinow, 1967). Ventilation requirements have been measured in anaesthetized rhesus monkeys by Crosfill & Widdicombe (1961), and in restrained, unanaesthetized rhesus monkeys by Binns *et al.* (1972). Blood gas characteristics have also been measured in unanaesthetized, restrained rhesus monkeys (Forsyth *et al.*, 1968; Munson *et al.*, 1970; Binns & Clark, 1972), but each group differed somewhat in the acid–base data presented. Gas tension measurements in cynomolgus monkeys were presented by Banerjee *et al.* (1968).

The effects of many drugs on the CNS of subhuman primates has been reviewed by Reynolds (1969) and EEG measurements have been recorded by Massopust *et al.* (1968).

Recommended anaesthetic techniques
Preanaesthetic management
Primates should undergo a period of quarantine for at least 8 weeks before being included in experiments. During this period they should be weighed, tested for tuberculosis, salmonellosis and shigellosis, and closely observed for any other symptoms of disease (particularly herpes virus B) or behavioural changes. This also allows time for conditioning to their environment and adaptation to the many stressors which may otherwise affect the experiment.

Small species such as marmosets and squirrel monkeys should be fasted for 6 h prior to anaesthesia, whilst adult macaques and larger animals should have no food for 24 h. All animals should be allowed free access to water until the first drugs are administered.

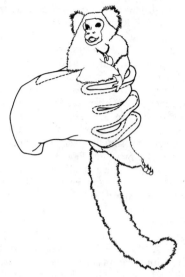

Fig. 13.1. Marmosets (and similar small species) can be caught by hand in their cage.

Physical restraint and handling
Marmosets and squirrel monkeys can be caught in their cage by an operator wearing thick leather gauntlets, a gown and protective face mask or vizor (Fig. 13.1). Marmosets are best grasped between forefinger and thumb around the thorax. Alternatively, all handling can be avoided by persuading the marmosets to enter a small clear plastic induction box into which is piped $N_2O:O_2$ (70:30) and adding volatile agents to attain surgical depths of anaesthesia. Squirrel monkeys are best grasped by their arms held behind their back and then

Fig. 13.2. Correct way to hold monkeys.

injected or introduced to inhalational anaesthetics by face mask. Removal from their cage is facilitated by catching them in standard fishermen's landing nets of 2 cm mesh.

Larger species should be held in squeeze-back cages to facilitate im injection of drugs. Alternatively, they can be netted as described by Graham-Jones (1964) or persuaded to enter induction boxes of suitable size and construction. After netting the monkey, the net is placed flat on the floor. The operator should cover the subject's head with a blindfold, press its whole body to the floor and then draw both the animal's elbows up behind its back. The monkey can then be safely lifted and presented for injection (Fig. 13.2). If it is decided to induce anaesthesia directly with inhalational agents, primates up to 10 kg in weight can be persuaded to enter a box attached to the front door of the cage. A box 45 × 38 × 38 cm constructed of fibreglass with clear plastic viewing panels, inlet and outlet attachments for 12 mm rubber tubing, and a sliding panel for transfer of the animal is suitable for this size of animal. Chimpanzees, large baboons, and bigger animals will need special induction cages as described by Newsome & Robinson (1957), Graham-Jones (1964) and Lumb & Jones (1973).

Chemical restraint and preanaesthetic therapy
Intramuscular injection is best made either into the belly or the deltoid muscle over the shoulder (Fig. 13.3), the lateral aspect of the anterior thigh (quadriceps group of muscles) or the lateral aspect

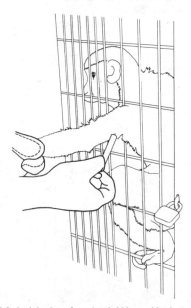

Fig. 13.3. Im injection of monkey held in crushback cage—into deltoid muscle.

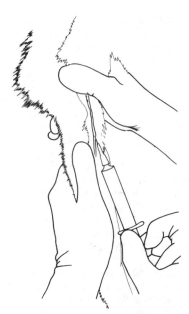

Fig. 13.4. Iv injection into brachial vein of the monkey forearm.

of the posterior thigh (gastrocnemius muscle). In small species, 12 × 0·40 mm (27 gauge) and in larger animals 16 × 0·65 or 0·50 mm (23–25 gauge) needles are suitable. Ip injections should be made in the midline, approximately one third of the distance from pubis to sternum. The animal should be held on its back, slightly head down, and the injection made through the tented abdominal muscles with the needle directed cranially to minimize risk of injury to viscera. Iv injections can be made into the brachial (radial) vein in the forearm (Fig. 13.4), the recurrent tarsal vein on the posterolateral aspect of the hind limb or the femoral vein, taking care in the latter instance not to puncture the adjacent artery. A 16 × 0·65 mm (23-gauge) needle is suitable in macaques and a 40 × 0·80 mm (21 gauge) needle is ideal for baboons.

Atropine at 0·05 mg/kg sc or im should be routinely administered as early as possible in the anaesthetic sequence.

The following agents are recommended for restraint in personal order of preference.

Ketamine is the agent of choice for the restraint of all primates except marmosets and squirrel monkeys. At dose levels ranging from 5 mg–25 mg/kg im, loss of bite reflex and sedation are produced at the lower end of the range and cataleptic stupor at the high dosage. Although further increments can be given, a total of 40 mg/kg should not be exceeded. Species variations in dose response have been reported, but are not, in our experience, significant. The time to onset of effect varies from 2–6 min, the duration of action is dose related and ranges from 20–60 min, and recovery time varies from 40–140 min. The advantages of ketamine were described earlier (p. 219). A few responses are less desirable. Tongue protrusion and excess salivation may contribute to airway obstruction unless the monkey has been given atropine. Significant heat loss occurs from the time that CNS depression is first noted until the animals are fully recovered. Muscle tone is enhanced at all dose rates, and hand and limb movements are frequently encountered in an otherwise deeply sedated animal. The pharyngeal and laryngeal reflexes are only partially preserved and protection of the airway is incomplete. However, they may interfere with endotracheal intubation, hence, anaesthesia has to be deepened or muscle relaxants administered before a tube can be passed.

The sequence of behavioural changes during induction with ketamine is as follows. Within 1–2 min of injection, the monkey starts to lick its lips and looks around slowly with a sad, slightly apprehensive expression. It often retreates to a corner, sits on its haunches and sways back and forth, starts salivating and becomes progressively ataxic in 4–5 min. Vertical nystagmus is commonly noted at this stage. As the monkey passes into a cataleptic stupor it usually lies face down on the bottom of its cage, eye movements cease, the eyelids droop but remain slightly open, the tongue protrudes and excess saliva drips from the lips. Profound analgesia develops within 5–7 min. It can usually be safely picked up by the arms within 4–5 min of injection since the bite reflex is lost early in the development of CNS depression.

Alphaxolone–alphadolone is the agent of choice in marmosets and squirrel monkeys, and is valuable in other species. The best site for injection is into the muscles on the anterior aspect of a hind limb just above the knee joint (quadriceps and triceps femoris muscles). The drug is poorly absorbed if it is deposited sc or into the intermuscular fascia.

At a dosage of 12–18 mg/kg im, a state of deep sedation to light surgical anaesthesia is produced in macaques and baboons within 10 min, but the monkeys can be safely handled in about 7 min. The peak effect is maintained for 10 min, recovery is complete within 45 min and appetite returns within 2 h. In marmosets and squirrel monkeys a dose of 18 mg/kg im produces light surgical anaesthesia in 2–6 min and this lasts for 40–60 min. Recovery to full consciousness and the desire to drink takes between 1 and 3 h.

Anaesthesia may be deepened by giving increments of alphaxolone–alphadolone iv to effect. Medium depths of surgical anaesthesia can be achieved with safety. The animals can then be intubated and maintained on inhalational agents if desired. The steroid combination has several qualities which are useful in anaesthesia. It can be given im or iv to produce good muscle relaxation and analgesia. It has a wide safety margin and respiratory depression is insignificant at working dose rates. Perhaps of most significance to the experimentalist, tolerance does not develop and the drug does not accumulate to dangerous levels, so that sequential incremental doses can be given over many hours to maintain anaesthesia. The disadvantage of this agent is the large volume which is inconvenient when making im injections.

Methohexitone may be administered by im injection. A 2·5–5% solution is well tolerated at the local site with minimal tissue reaction. Light surgical anaesthesia can be produced within 2–10 min and this lasts for approximately 20 min at a dosage of 20 mg/kg im. This technique has a few advantages over ketamine. It produces moderate muscle relaxation and the monkeys may be intubated without administering other drugs. Excess salivation is not a problem and the fall in body temperature is less pronounced than with ketamine. Recovery is complete within 60 min and appetite returns rapidly, allowing daily treatments to be given without loss of weight. The main disadvantage is the relatively large volume (2–4 ml in an average rhesus monkey) to be injected.

Neuroleptanalgesic combinations are also useful for the restraint of primates. The main advantages of each of these combinations are the profound analgesia produced and the ability to reverse CNS depression with morphine antagonists. Against this, respiratory depression and bradycardia of varying intensity usually develop. Muscle relaxation is poorly developed unless the sedative–analgesics are given concurrently with xylazine or diazepam. In the latter instances, endotracheal intubation is possible provided the larynx is first sprayed with 2% lignocaine.

Fentanyl–fluanisone (0·3 ml/kg im) produces deep sedation and profound analgesia in 6–10 min, and this lasts for 30–60 min. Full recovery takes 120–160 min but can be accelerated by administration of nalorphine iv or sc.

Fentanyl–droperidol (0·3 ml/kg im) has very similar activity in primates.

Pethidine–xylazine (10 mg/kg:2 mg/kg im) produces analgesia with some muscular relaxation in 10–15 min and this lasts for 45–90 min. Full recovery takes 100–150 min.

Thiambutene–xylazine (10 mg/kg:2 mg/kg im) produces analgesia with some muscular relaxation in 5–10 min and this lasts for 45–90 min. Full recovery takes 100–200 min.

Phencyclidine is still used at some centres in preference to ketamine. It is administered im at doses of 1–3 mg/kg, takes 5–20 min to reach peak effect and has a mean duration of 100 min (but there is very wide variation in recovery times). Muscle tone is retained, and slow deliberate limb movements may be encountered during apparently deep sedation. Although the drug can be given repeatedly, tolerance does develop until doses up to 10 mg/kg may be needed for an equivalent degree of sedation. A profound fall in body temperature always occurs unless steps are taken to conserve body heat, and hypothermia induced by phencyclidine may last for 4–6 h.

Surgical anaesthesia
General notes. Any method of inducing anaesthesia involves some degree of stress and probably results in elevated levels of circulating catecholamines, corticosteroids and blood glucose. For example, primates induced directly by inhalational agents, even with the non-irritant $N_2O:O_2$ at high concentrations (4:1), often pass through an involuntary excitement period and defaecate in the box. However, alterations in ECG appear to subside once the animal accepts restraint and is securely strapped in a chair or to a board (Osborne, 1973).

The responses observed during induction of anaesthesia depend very much on the agent used. As a general rule, induction with inhalational gas mixtures follows a similar pattern to that described by Guedel (1951) in man. There are usually periods of voluntary and involuntary excitement if ether or halothane are used, and a period of involuntary excitement occurs with N_2O and methoxyflurane. Excitement will be eliminated if preanaesthetic drugs (e.g. ketamine) are given. As anaesthesia deepens, there is a progressive loss of pedal and palpebral reflexes, and gradual loss of muscle tone. When barbiturates are administered iv the subject rapidly reaches a deep level of narcosis without passing through any excitatory phase. Depth of anaesthesia is monitored by pedal and palpebral reflexes, loss of muscle tone gauged by resistance to jaw opening, and by the quality of respiration. The behavioural responses observed after injection of ketamine or phencyclidine have been described earlier (p. 223).

An intravenous infusion should be started as soon as the monkey is sedated. Indwelling 0·65 mm (23 gauge) butterfly needles or 0·65 mm (23 gauge) catheters of the 'Medicut' or 'Intracath' variety (p. 74) can be conveniently taped into the brachial vein for the duration of anaesthesia. It is important to maintain fluid balance by injecting warm (36°C) Hartmann's (Ringer's lactate) or dextrose–saline solution via this 'drip'. As an approximate guide we inject 10 ml/kg/h in a paediatric disposable infusion set (p. 74). Body temperature should be monitored constantly, preferably by rectal or oesophageal thermistor probes.

Every attempt should be made to conserve body heat, since thermoregulatory centres are depressed by all CNS depressants. In our experience, the rectal temperature of rhesus monkeys falls to 35°C within 10 min of injecting ketamine at sedative doses (ambient temperature 30°C). We restore this to normal by laying the anaesthetized animal on a hot-water circulating pad (37°C) and covering it with an aluminium-lined reflective blanket.

Intubation presents no particular problem in macaques since the larynx is easily seen using a paediatric laryngoscope fitted with a neonatal blade. Cuffed endotracheal tubes (4 mm outside diameter) are ideal for *M. irus* and *M. mulatta* adults. Baboons and mandrills with their longer face are slightly more difficult to intubate and a longer laryngoscope blade is required. Cuffed 5–8 mm outside diameter tubes are suitable depending on the subject's size. The sedated animals are prepared for intubation by deepening anaesthesia until the cough reflex is lost either by injectable anaesthetic agents, mask inhalation or muscle relaxation with suxamethonium (1·0–2·0 mg/kg iv). Excess saliva and fluid accumulations should be removed from the oropharynx by suction and swabbing, and the larynx should be sprayed with 2% lignocaine before attempting intubation. The tube should be passed with care to ensure that it does not extend beyond the tracheal bifurcation and then secured in place by tapes passing around the upper jaw and behind the neck to ensure that it cannot be dislodged. Alternatively, macaques can be intubated by the method of Cohen (1964). The author recommended passing the tube through the nose, since it could not then be dislodged during operations. Endotracheal tubes (4 mm outside diameter) were deliberately cut to a shallow bevel and smeared with lubricant; having passed them through the nose, the tip was grasped with McGill forceps and passed into the trachea under direct vision with a paediatric laryngoscope.

Surgical anaesthesia can now be provided in several ways. Injectable agents can be administered by iv injection into the infusion set. Alternatively, inhalational gas mixtures can be delivered to the endotracheal tube in conventional circuits e.g. Magill or Rees modified Ayres T-piece or by IPPV. In addition, an injectable agent e.g. barbiturate or sedative–analgesic, inhalational gas mixtures, and muscle relaxants may be selected in a balanced anaesthesia regimen. Light surgical anaesthesia may be enhanced with local infiltration analgesia. The choice will be dictated by the experimental requirements.

Injectable anaesthetic techniques. The following agents are recommended in personal order of preference.

Alphaxolone–alphadolone (10–12 mg/kg iv) administered via the 'drip' (p. 224) at 20–30 min intervals provides good surgical conditions. Inhalation of $N_2O:O_2$ (1:1) delivered at 4 litres/min via endotracheal tube and Rees modified T-piece can then be superimposed to further enhance analgesia and muscle relaxation. Experience with this regimen has been favourable in macaques and baboons, and serious metabolic disturbance have not been encountered in periods up to 4 h (CRC).

Acute preparations can be safely anaesthetized for long periods with alphaxolone–alphadolone (6–9 mg/kg) administered every 20 min. At the same time, the monkey should be given atropine, intubated and supplied with $N_2O:O_2$ (1:1) by IPPV. Provided total body fluid and core temperature are kept within physiological limits, a remarkably stable preparation can be maintained for 8–10 h.

Pentobarbitone (25–35 mg/kg iv) administered slowly to effect to animals which have had no other medication provides light surgical anaesthesia within 3 min of injection. As in other species, respiration is depressed. The drug should not therefore be used alone for intraabdominal or intrathoracic surgery unless the monkey is well ventilated on IPPV. Peak effect is maintained for 40–60 min after a single injection but full recovery may take 2–6 h.

If pentobarbitone is used to deepen CNS depression to anaesthetic levels after other drugs have been used for chemical restraint, it should be injected very slowly to effect and the dose rates should be markedly reduced (5–15 mg/kg iv depending on the other agents used). Under no circumstances must pentobarbitone be administered after alphaxolone–alphadolone.

It is always preferable to maintain prolonged anaesthesia with $N_2O:O_2$ (1:1) and reduced doses of pentobarbitone thus minimizing the risk of respiratory depression.

Inhalational anaesthetic techniques. The inhalational equipment selected depends on the nature of the experiment and the estimated duration of anaesthesia. Semi-open Magill systems, Rees-modified T-pieces and to-and-fro systems are the 3 which are most useful. To-and-fro systems are currently out of favour in human anaesthetic practice, although *M. mulatta* have been intubated and maintained on halothane with O_2 via a Water's paediatric to-and-fro system for 2 h periods without altering acid–base balance (Medd, 1974). We have maintained *M. irus* and *M. mulatta* on gas mixtures administered via a rubber face mask (Hall's cat mask) and Magill system, or mask and modified T-piece for periods up to 3 h and encountered few problems (CRC). However, intubation is so simple that it is strongly recommen-

ded as routine practice in the anaesthesia of primates. Gas mixtures should be humidified and warmed as described earlier (p. 220).

Inhalation of $N_2O:O_2$ (1:1) after chemical restraint with ketamine is usually adequate for surgical anaesthesia for up to 45 min. Gas flows of 4 litres/min are preferably delivered to a Rees-modified T-piece and endotracheal tube. Enflurane, halothane or methoxyflurane may then be administered at low concentrations (0·5–1%) to maintain anaesthesia for periods up to 6 h.

Recovery and post-surgical therapy
Attention to heat conservation, airway patency and fluid balance are of prime importance during the post-operative recovery period. The subjects should be allowed to recover in an ambient temperature of 30°C, preferably in an oxygenated, humidified infant incubator. The endotracheal tube and intravenous catheter are retained until the subject has regained laryngeal and swallowing reflexes, but removed before it becomes dangerous to handle the

Table 13.1. Rhesus monkey: physiological data

Measurement	Values
Respiratory frequency (breaths/min)	38 (30–50)
Tidal volume (ml)	39
Minute volume (l/mm)	1·4
Mean heart rate (beats/min)	192 (165–240)
Arterial blood pressure (mmHg)	160/127
Arterial blood pH	7·34
Pa O_2 (mmHg)	96
Pa CO_2 (mmHg)	43
Haematocrit (%)	42
Haemoglobin (g/100 ml)	12
Erythrocytes (10^6/mm^3)	5
Blood volumes (ml/kg bodyweight)	
Total	75
Expected terminal exsanguination	32
Safe maximum single sample	5
Mean rectal temperaure (°C)	38·9 (38·4–39·6)

Table 13.2. Baboon: physiological data

Measurement	Values
Respiratory frequency (breaths/min)	35
Tidal volume (ml)	48
Minute volume (l/min)	1·6
Mean heart rate (beats/min)	150
Arterial blood pressure (mmHg)	148/100
Arterial blood pH	7·36
Pa O_2	—
Pa CO_2	—
Haematocrit (%)	35·6
Haemoglobin (g/100 ml)	12
Erythrocytes (10^6/mm^3)	5
Blood volumes (mg/kg bodyweight)	
Total	60
Expected terminal exsanguination	25
Safe maximum single sample	5
Mean rectal temperature (°C)	39·0

animal. Post-surgical therapy with analgesics or antibiotics should be delayed until the subjects are completely recovered to avoid the possibility of re-induction of anaesthesia (p. 201).

ORDER MARSUPIALIA: FAMILY MACROPODIDAE (KANGAROOS AND WALLABIES)

The difficulties of physical restraint in Macro-podidae have been described, and the strength and well-developed claws on the hind limbs of a fully-grown adult which may weigh up to 70 kg, and the possibility of biting or clawing with the fore-limbs emphasized (Denny, 1973). The unique responses of marsupials to sedatives and anaes-thetic agents were described by Jones (1973) who reported that both phencyclidine and xylazine produce very variable responses, and phenothiazine derivatives are ineffective. Similarly, 2–3 times the conventional doses of thiopentone may be needed to induce anaesthesia (Hime, 1967; Watson & Way, 1972). Etorphine alone is unreliable as a sedative–analgesic for the Bennett's wallaby, *Protemnodon rufozrisia frutica* (Jones, 1973), but etorphine–acepromazine (0·04 mg/kg:0·16 mg/kg im) was effective in red kangaroos (Wilson, 1974). Attempts to induce anaesthesia with halothane by mask met with little success (Hime, 1972; Jones, 1973), but Henschel (1958) described intubation and inhalation with ether in $N_2O:O_2$. Phen-cyclidine with promazine was used in kangaroos by Seal & Erickson (1969). Intravenous injection of thiopentone via the recurrent tarsal vein was described by Larsen (1963), while Denny (1973) reported that pentobarbitone at 37 mg/kg injected into a tail vein gave unreliable results. This barbi-turate had earlier been reported as valuable in acute experiments (Maxwell *et al.*, 1964). According to Cisar (1969), the rat kangaroo (*Potorous tri-dactylus*) has a low tolerance to pentobarbitone, thiopentone and ether. Ketamine at 15–20 mg/kg im seems to be the most reliable agent so far assessed in kangaroos (Denny, 1973) and in wallabies (Jones & Manton, 1976). Surgical anaes-thesia was effectively and safely induced within 4 min, lasted about 20 min and the animals were immobilized for over 60 min. Field capture of the agile wallaby (*Macropus agil*) has also been reported (Keep, 1973).

In a description of the scrub wallaby (*Wallabia rufogrisea*) as a laboratory animal, Redshaw (1971) provided valuable information on their handling and anaesthesia. They were caught by the tail and lifted so that the powerful hindlegs were off the ground, and a large sack was drawn over the head to envelop the forelimbs and chest. Anaes-thesia was induced with pentobarbitone at 30–40

mg/kg ip. It was observed that if a solution of freshly mixed crystalline salt in saline was used instead of a commercial preparation, induction time was reduced from 30 to 10 min. D-tubocurarine was then injected via the jugular vein to provide sufficient relaxation for endotracheal intubation, and halothane in $N_2O:O_2$ was supplied by IPPV for maintenance of anaesthesia.

Recommendations

After physical restraint in nets or hessian bags, atropine (0·1 mg/kg) is first given im, and ketamine (15–20 mg/kg im) is injected into the gluteal muscles (Denny, 1973). A lower dose rate (9 mg/kg im) is effective in grey kangaroos (Hime, 1973). The animals sway from side to side within 2 min of the injection and become progressively ataxic until they fall over after 3–3·5 min. Ocular, laryngeal and pharyngeal reflexes persist as in other species. Respiratory rate remains normal at 20–40/min. Surgical anaesthesia is maintained for at least 20 min, and, although the animals are able to stand 50–65 min after the injection, they are ataxic for another 60 min. Muscle relaxation is poor. The jugular and tail veins are easily cathe-terized after surgical exposure of the vessels, and increments of 2–4 mg/kg ketamine may be given iv to extend the duration of surgical anaesthesia.

FAMILY DIDELPHIDAE

American opossum (*Didelphis virginiana*)

As a marsupial, the opossum has been used for studies in early development of the foetus and neonate, particularly in investigating the develop-ment of immune mechanisms and the production of lymphocytes from an undifferentiated lymphoid system at birth, and exploring the role of the thymus in this period (Millican & Millican, 1964). A review of husbandry, experimental techniques and routine health measures was supplied by Krupp & Quillin (1964).

α-chloralose at 12 mg/kg iv every 2 h success-fully maintained prolonged anaesthesia in opossums with a wide margin of safety, but induction of anaesthesia with thiopentone iv was necessary first (Krupp & Quillin, 1964; Lumb & Jones, 1973). Tribromoethanol administered orally to the opossum resulted in prolonged anaesthesia exceeding 10 h with persistent drowsiness for 14 h.

According to Lumb & Jones (1973) pento-barbitone produces satisfactory anaesthesia if given iv to effect but is unreliable and unsafe in these animals if given ip.

Ether has also been used to induce and maintain prolonged anaesthesia in this species (Krupp &

Quillin, 1964). After administering atropine and induction in a chamber, anaesthesia can be maintained with ether in O_2 by mask and a closed system or, alternatively, the animal can be intubated after iv thiopentone induction for more controlled maintenance. Halothane was administered in a similar way by Luschei & Mehaffey (1967).

In a valuable contribution, Feldman & Self (1971) evaluated 5 drugs for use in these animals. 4 were selected for im injection, and the results were compared with inhalation of methoxyflurane for induction and maintenance. Ketamine (20–25 mg/kg im) and fentanyl–droperidol (0·75–1·0 ml/kg im) were considered to be successful, phencyclidine (5–6 mg/kg im) was relatively ineffective, and promazine had no effect even at very high dose levels (10 mg/kg im). Ketamine at 25 mg/kg im produced immobilization for 35–50 min and, surprisingly, muscular relaxation was pronounced, although analgesia was poor and the animals remained conscious. Fentanyl–droperidol (1·0 ml/kg im) produced profound analgesia, good muscle relaxation and 50–80 min of recumbency, although consciousness was not lost. Methoxyflurane induced anaesthesia in 5–12 min, endotracheal intubation was performed without difficulty and recovery was rapid, taking only 5–8 min.

Recommended anaesthetic techniques
Physical restraint and handling
Detailed examination of these animals requires the presence of 2 persons since they are difficult to hold safely. The opossum turns and faces handlers if cornered, snarls, bares its teeth and makes darting movements with its head. It should be approached with caution as it has sharp, grasping claws which grip and slash human skin quite easily.

The animal should be caught by the tail and, as it tends to pull away, grasped with the other hand behind the neck. It must not be picked up from a wire grid or rough surface because it is likely to hold on so firmly that the claws are torn out. Opossums can be safely carried by the tail but the handler must beware the possibility of the animal climbing up its own tail to attack him.

Chemical restraint and surgical anaesthesia
Inhalational anaesthesia is best induced in a chamber containing gauze sponges saturated with methoxyflurane to give high (3%) concentrations of vapour. It can then be intubated with a non-cuffed endotracheal catheter (4·5 mm outside diameter) and maintained on a Magill or an Ayres T-piece system with methoxyflurane (0.5%) and $N_2O:O_2$

(1:1). Recovery is surprisingly rapid in opossums, e.g. about 10 min after 2 h of anaesthesia.

Neuroleptanalgesia with fentanyl–fluanisone (0·5–1·0 ml/kg im) induces recumbency, good muscle relaxation and profound analgesia in 8–12 min to last about 1 h. Recovery may be accelerated by administration of nalorphine at 1·0 mg/kg iv or im.

ORDERS EDENTATA (SLOTHS, ARMADILLOS, ANTEATERS) AND TUBULIDENTATA (AARDVARKS)

Attention has been drawn to the ease with which hypothermia develops in these animals after administration of CNS depressant drugs (Seal et al., 1970; Jones, 1973). These authors recommended low doses of phencyclidine (0·5 mg/kg im) and phenothiazine derivatives e.g. 0·2 mg/kg im of promazine for restraint. For induction of anaesthesia, theiopentone injected iv is effective at conventional dosages (Jones, 1973). Aardvarks (Orycteropus afer) respond well to phencyclidine, a dose rate of 0·7–0·8 mg/kg im being sufficient to induce light surgical anaesthesia (Seal et al., 1970), while ketamine was used at 10–20 mg/kg im) to achieve chemical restraint by Beck (1972). Sloths (Choloepus hoffmani) were effectively sedated with tiletamine–zolazepam at tiletamine dose rates of 2·2–4·4 mg/kg im (Gray et al., 1974).

Anaesthesia of armadillos (Dasypus novemcinctus) was described in some detail by Lumb & Jones (1973). Of particular interest were their comments on handling and management. They emphasized that armadillos should be caught close to the tail to avoid the hind claws, and noted that they are capable of incurring a large oxygen debt and are able to lie completely still without breathing for long periods. Intramuscular injections should be made slightly to one side of the midline between carapal bands, and the site should be thoroughly cleansed and disinfected to avoid abscess formation.

The hazards of inhalational anaesthesia in armadillos were emphasized by Anderson & Benirschke (1966) who recommended pretreatment with atropine im and endotracheal intubation with 3–5 mm outside diameter soft polyethylene tubing. The same authors recommended slow iv infusion of thiopentone using 5 ml of a 0·5% solution over a period of 1 h (5–6 mg/kg/h). Wampler (1969) injected pentobarbitone at 25 mg/kg iv into the superficial femoral vein, half rapidly and the remainder to effect. The superficial femoral veins are the only vessels readily accessible for injection or blood sampling but these are easily catheterized (Lumb & Jones, 1973). Fentanyl–droperidol (0·20–0·25 ml/kg im) produced sufficient neuroleptanalgesia for surgery according to Szabuniewisz & McCrady (1969).

Recommendations

It is important to pay particular attention to body temperature and fluid balance. Injectable anaesthetic agents are the simplest to use.

Fentanyl–fluanisone (0·25 ml/kg im) can be followed by methohexitone (4–6 mg/kg iv) as required.

Ketamine (20 mg/kg im) can be followed by methohexitone (6 mg/kg iv) or further ketamine at 4 mg/kg as required to extend or deepen anaesthesia.

AQUATIC ANIMALS

CLASS CRUSTACEA

After netting, crustaceans are best kept in polyethylene tubs containing sea water into which O_2 is continuously bubbled. Sand to a depth of 8–10 cm should be supplied on the bottom to allow the animals to burrow. The tubs may be used for transporting them long distances without tranquillization and are also convenient for inducing anaesthesia when required.

Crabs and lobsters have been anaesthetized by immersion in solutions of isobutyl alcohol and of ether, but tricaine has not proved effective (Oswald, 1977). Foley et al. (1966) reported the use of isobutyl alcohol in lobsters (Homarus americanus) in concentrations of 0·5–14·4 ml/l aerated sea water at 10°C. They noted that, after a brief period of agitation the lobsters gradually became ataxic until their limbs eventually fixed in an upright position. The lobsters remained anaesthetized for 10 min after removal from the solution and returning them to sea water.

After comparing a number of agents which were administered to restrained crabs intravascularly by 0·50 mm (25 gauge) needle inserted through the coxal-arthrodial membrane of a posterior pereiopod, Oswald (1977) concluded that alphaxolone–alphadolone (30 mg/kg) and procaine (25 mg/kg) were the most effective. Procaine induced anaesthesia within 30 s of injection and the crabs remained asleep for 2–3 h. The crabs went through a short period of excitement lasting up to 10 s immediately after injection, but no other disadvantages were reported.

Recommended anaesthetic techniques

On the basis of the studies quoted above, intravascular injection of procaine at 25 mg/kg appears to be the best anaesthetic in decapod crustaceans.

CLASS OSTEICHTHYES (BONY FISHES) AND CLASS CHONDRICHTHYES (CARTILAGENOUS FISHES)

Physical restraint of fish without the aid of drugs is always attended by some degree of risk. Not only are they water-breathing poikilotherms dependent on gas exchange across the gill lamellae, and therefore liable to rapid suffocation when removed from their proper environment, but trauma induced by intense muscular activity and loss of the protective mucilaginous covering renders them susceptible to bacterial and fungal invasion (Jolly et al., 1972). Short periods of immobilization may be required for taking measurements, fin clipping, tagging and local treatment of skin lesions. Sedation for many hours may be required for live transportation without fatal stress, while relatively deep anaesthesia may be required for experimental surgery.

Early attempts to reduce handling stress involved deliberate hypothermia, or immersion in water which either contained soluble anaesthetic agents or into which narcotic gases could be introduced. It was appreciated that suitable molecules would be taken up by the circulation from water perfusing the gill lamellae, and to a limited extent, through the intact skin.

Parker (1939) claimed that immersion of teleosts in crushed ice for 10–15 min allowed handling for minor procedures. Similarly, use of this technique in the elasmobranch Mustelus canis, in goldfish (Carassius auratus) and in catfish (Amiurus melas) has been reported by Abramowitz et al. (1940), Castrejon & Flores (1953) and Osborn (1941) respectively. However, its limitations were exposed when severe depletion of spleen lymphoid tissue was demonstrated after deliberate cooling. This suggested that the fish had been severely stressed

(Rasquin, 1951; Pickford & Atz, 1957; Ball & Slicher, 1962).

Immersion in an aqueous solution of urethane was one of the earliest methods of inducing chemical narcosis. A 0·5% solution has been used to anaesthetize a minnow, *Phoximum phoximus* (von Frisch & Stetter, 1932). Similarly a 2–4% solution was used for lampreys, *Lampetra* spp. (Young, 1935) and a 1–5% solution for trout, *Salmo trutti* (Savage, 1935). Urethane is no longer an acceptable anaesthetic agent because of its potent carcinogenic properties (p. 82).

Ether in air was bubbled through water to anaesthetize the elasmobranch *Scyliorhinus caniculus* and the teleost *Gobius paganellus* (Vivien, 1941), and an ether-in-water solution was used for the eel *Anguilla anguilla* by Callamand *et al.* (1951), and for trout by Eschmeyer (1953).

Carbon dioxide was recommended by Fish (1942) for short periods of anaesthesia up to 20 min. The optimum concentrations suggested were 200 ppm for salmon (*Onchorhynchus nerka*) and trout, and this was produced by the addition of sodium bicarbonate and sulphuric acid to water at 7–16°C. The fish turned over after losing consciousness and sank to the bottom of the container within 90 s of exposure to CO_2. The solution was restored to its normal CO_2 concentration by neutralization with sodium carbonate. It was concluded that fish could be exposed to anaesthetic concentrations of CO_2 for a maximum of 5 min and remained anaesthetized for a further 5–10 min after the solution was restored to normal.

Methods involving the injection of narcotics into fish have been little used. Pentobarbitone was injected im at a dose of 20 mg/kg into tench (*Tinca tinca*), eel and roach (*Rutilus rutilus*) by Shelton & Randall (1962), who claimed that light anaesthesia was achieved.

Procaine (0·25–1·00 ml of a 5% solution) was injected intracranially at a midline site just behind eye-level by Kish (1947). General anaesthesia lasting for 0·5–1 h was safely maintained provided the head was covered in water to allow normal respiration to continue.

The advantage of avoiding handling until after induction of narcosis has been amply confirmed, and immersion remains the method of choice. Many chemicals, including some of those used for mammalian anaesthesia, have been described in recent years (McFarlane, 1959; Klontz, 1964; Healey, 1964; Bell, 1967; Thienpont & Niemegeers, 1965; Smith & Bell, 1967; McErlean & Kennedy, 1968; Klontz & Smith, 1968; McFarlane & Klontz, 1969; Jolly *et al.*, 1972; Laird & Oswald, 1975; Dick, 1975). Several authors emphasize the variation between species in response to a given agent, and the need to carry out an anaesthetic trial before starting experiments. From the excellent comparative review of McFarlane & Klontz (1969), it is worth describing briefly a few agents which were the most successful in their hands. All these agents can be dissolved in the water perfusing the gill lamellae, thus avoiding injections.

Ether is used at dilutions of 10–50 ml/litre water. According to Jolly *et al.* (1972), deep anaesthesia is induced in 3–5 min in gold fish (*Carassius auratus*), and recovery takes 5–15 min after removal from the solution.

Methyl pentynol, at dilutions of 0·5–0·9 ml/litre of water can induce deep anaesthesia in 2–3 min. Maintenance may be complicated by respiratory arrest, and recovery takes 5–20 min.

2-Phenoxyethanol is an oily liquid with anaesthetic and bactericidal properties (Reichenbach-Klinke & Elkan, 1965). It was used at a dilution of 0·1–0·5 ml/litre of water to anaesthetize salmon (*O. nerka*) by Klontz & Smith (1968), who found that induction took 10–30 min, anaesthesia was well maintained while the fish were exposed to the solution, and recovery was complete in 5–15 min after removal. Jolly *et al.* (1972) described its use in goldfish, and found that induction took only 2–4 min and recovery 3–6 min after removal.

4-Styrylpyridine is a white powder freely soluble in water, and is one of the few agents commonly used for fish anaesthesia which is considered safe for handling by personnel. It is used at a concentration of 20–50 mg/litre of water. Induction takes 1–5 min, maintenance is uncomplicated, and fish recover in 20–30 min.

Quinaldine, although insoluble in water, is readily dissolved in acetone (1:1). The mixture is then added to water at a dilution of 0·01–0·03 ml/litre. It can be used over a wide range of temperatures, but is a poor analgesic. Induction takes 1–3 min, maintenance is fairly good and recovery occurs in 5–20 min.

Tricaine methanesulphonate (*MS222*) is a crystalline powder best used as a freshly prepared solution in salt fresh water. It has been used for fish sedation and anaesthesia since 1920 and is still the most popular in current use. Its use in teleosts was first reported by Strzyzowski (1920) who found that a 1:10 000 solution anaesthetized goldfish within 5–10 min. Baudin (1932*a*, *b*, *c*) described the effects of tricaine on goldfish respiration and how this varied with water temperature. Of particular interest was the depressed O_2 uptake to about 25% of normal when fish were immersed in a 1:20 000 solution of tricaine at 16°C; if the temperature was raised to 20°C, O_2 uptake increased and double the concentration of tricaine (i.e. 1:10 000) was needed for an equivalent degree of narcosis. This may partially explain the marked species differences in response which have been noted. For example, lake trout (*Salmo namaycush*) and some strains of rainbow trout (*Salmo gairdneri*) have been shown to be very sensitive to tricaine (Marking, 1967), and this may be related to the high O_2, and the high rate of gill perfusion required by these species. When Hunn (1971) measured blood concentrations of tricaine 60 s after exposure to the solution, he found them to be 8 times as high in rainbow trout (*S. gairdneri*) as in the shortnose gar (*Lepidosteus platostonius*). Recent reports in the literature give more up-to-date information on changes in physiological measurements during anaesthesia with tricaine (Chavin & Young, 1970; Wedemayer, 1970; Houston *et al.*, 1971; Houston & Woods, 1972; Houston *et al.*, 1973; Luhning, 1973; Soivio *et al.*, 1974a, b; Soivio & Oikari, 1976; Soivio *et al.*, 1977).

Tricaine has also been used to anaesthetize large species. Sharks and rays were anaesthetized by spraying the internal opening of the gills with 100 to 1000 ml of a 1:1000 concentration solution (Gilbert & Wood, 1957). The head of large specimens was held above the water by means of a gaff or hook whilst the solution was administered. It was found that even large sharks were anaesthetized within 60 s and that recovery could be accelerated by towing the fish through water on a hook or spraying the gills with fresh seawater.

Various species of fish have been transported safely whilst sedated with low concentrations of tricaine, either immersed in a solution in suitable containers or in ice. According to Steinbrecht (1957), teleosts anaesthetized with this agent could be kept alive in ice in contrast to untreated subjects which rapidly succumbed to hypothermia. Lightly sedated trout were packed in water in plastic containers surrounded by ice (Thompson, 1959), whilst Gossington (1957) pointed out the value of tranquillizing aggressive species such as pirhana (*Betta* spp.) before transportation, reporting that concentrations of 1:12 000 to 1:24000 provided safe tranquillization for up to 48 h depending on the species, temperature and oxygenation of surrounding media. Martin & Scott (1959) used a dilution of 60 mg/l in water at 5°C to immobilize fish to the stage where they turned over, and then transferred them to layers of moss and ice chips for transportation without water. The mortality was 10% after 4 h.

Several conclusions can be drawn from the literature. Firstly, there is a direct relationship between the concentration of tricaine needed to produce a given degree of CNS depression and the size of the fish—larger fish requiring higher concentrations. At temperatures below those to which the fish are adapted, lower concentrations are needed to produce a given response. However, sudden temperature rises may also lower the concentration of tricaine needed. Mortality has been reported when the agent has been used in salt water in direct sunlight but this can be avoided if anaesthesia is conducted in shaded light (Klontz & Smith, 1968). Concentrations of 50–100 mg/l are needed for anaesthesia, whilst for light sedation 20–50 mg/l are adequate. The induction time is 1–3 min, the required level of depression is well maintained and recovery occurs in 3–15 min of removal from the solution. It is claimed that tricaine is not toxic to personnel handling the fish.

Propoxate (*R7464*) is a crystalline ester of carboxylic acid which is highly soluble in fresh and salt water, and claimed to be some 100 times more potent than tricaine (Thienpont & Niemegeers, 1965). In preliminary trials with goldfish, they described 4 levels of narcosis which depended on concentrations and duration of immersion. Initially, respiratory rate increased but this was soon followed by a fall in rate and generally depressed activity. Further exposure led to loss of equilibrium, and respiration was markedly depressed. As CNS depression increased, the righting reflex was lost, and fish tended to lie on the container bottom. Overdosage resulted in respiratory arrest which was fatal in 2–3 min.

According to Klontz & Smith (1968), the dosage for anaesthetizing adult salmon is 2–4 ppm. Induction takes 2–3 min, maintenance is good, and uncomplicated recovery occurs within 5–9 min.

Jolly *et al.* (1972) recommended propoxate at 1 ppm for anaesthetizing rainbow trout and 2–4 ppm for fish ranging from large pike (*Esox lucius*) to small cyprinids. They suggested that anaesthetic solution should be freshly mixed before use. Anaesthesia was induced in 30–60 s and the fish recovered within 10 min.

Benzocaine: the advantages of benzocaine over tricaine have been discussed by McErlean & Kennedy (1968), Wedemayer (1970), and Laird & Oswald (1975). In fact when tricaine is buffered to pH 7 it exists in its free base form (ethyl *m*-aminobenzoate) which is almost identical to benzocaine (ethyl *p*-aminobenzoate). Benzocaine is relatively insoluble in water and must be disolved in acetone before use (200 mg benzocaine in 5 ml acetone). If this is then added to 8 litres of water, a benzocaine concentration of 25 ppm is produced.

Probably because of its neutral pH, benzocaine does not produce the initial excitement seen when fish are immersed in unbuffered tricaine (pH 3·8). In other respects it has similar CNS depressant effects to tricaine. Fish are rapidly sedated after immersion and recover within 3 min of returning them to untreated water following anaesthesia for 60 min. Concentrations of 25–50 ppm are used depending on the level of depression required. The cost of benzocaine is very much less than tricaine (Laird & Oswald, 1975).

Recommended anaesthetic techniques

It is generally accepted that it is safer to transfer fish from their resident tank to a special anaesthetizing container in which the chemicals can be adequately mixed beforehand. However, since fish are sensitive to abrupt change in water temperature, pH and dissolved minerals, Jolly *et al.* (1972) recommend that some of the resident tank water should be included in the anaesthetic solution. The container should be constructed of chemically inert substances such as polyethylene, and metal fixtures, particularly copper and zinc, should be avoided.

Fish should be fasted for 24–48 h since they otherwise vomit, and gill lamellae may become blocked by solids. Small species can be netted and transferred to the anaesthetic container, while larger fish can be netted and anaesthetized by immersion of head and gills, or alternatively by spraying the gills with anaesthetic solution.

After an initial phase of excitement lasting only a few seconds followed by rather erratic swimming, a fairly standard pattern of narcosis is observed when fish are allowed to swim freely in an anaesthetic solution. The behavioural changes associated with 6 levels of narcosis have been described by McFarlane & Klontz (1969)—Table 9.1. The initial agitation is followed by gradual loss of equilibrium, swimming movements become less frequent, the fish turns upside down and then usually swims to the bottom to rest on its back. The total time to reach this stage depends on the agent and concentration used, but with tricaine, at 100 mg/litre, it takes only 60–90 s. Level 4 is adequate for most surgical procedures. It is indicated by dispersal of pigment within innervated chromatophores so that the overall colour of the fish is intensified; by increased respiratory rate with opercular movements so shallow that they may be difficult to detect; by complete muscle relaxation and a diminished, but not necessarily abolished, reaction if the tail-base muscle is squeezed. The fish can now be removed from the solution for maintenance during manipulative procedures. If muscle spasms are observed when handled or during short procedures, it can simply be returned to the anaesthetic solution for a few seconds to deepen narcosis.

A relatively steady level of narcosis can be maintained for prolonged periods provided the fish is kept moist by wrapping it in damp cloths, or laying it in a V-shaped trough constructed from sponges in a shallow tray. The head and gills can be totally immersed in anaesthetic solution, or they may be intermittently sprayed or continuously irrigated by gravity drip feed over the buccal surface. If surgical anaesthesia is required for many hours it is necessary to control water temperature, provide aeration and remove waste products (Klontz & Smith, 1968). These authors claimed that salmonids were particularly easy to maintain for long periods in this way. Clearly, continuous irrigation with fresh anaesthetic solution draining from the tray is a simple way of satisfying these requirements. Alternatively, the solution may be recycled after filtration and oxygenation in a continuous perfusion circuit.

Overexposure to anaesthetic and imminent medullary collapse are signalled by cessation of regular opercular movements, with the occasional exaggerated respiratory flaring of the operculae eventually becoming weaker until they cease altogether. Cardiac arrest is then likely to occur within 60–90 s unless emergency action is taken. Anaesthesia can be rapidly reversed by irrigating the buccal cavity with fresh water, by immersing the fish and moving it backwards and forwards with its mouth open, or by working the mouth open and shut in a beaker of fresh water. Water must not be pumped through the opercular opening to flow over the gills in an anterior direction and thence out of the mouth, since very little O_2 will be taken up into the lamellar circulation and the fish will rapidly die from hypoxia.

Table 14.1. Behavioural changes at various levels of narcosis (after McFarlane & Klontz, 1969)

		Level
Normal		Reactive to external stimuli: muscle tone normal.
Light sedation	1	Equilibrium normal; slight loss of reactivity to external visual and tactile stimuli.
Deep sedation	2	Equilibrium normal; total loss of reactivity to external stimuli *except* strong pressure; slight decrease in opercular rate.
Partial loss of equilibrium	3	Partial loss of muscle tone; swimming erratic; increased opercular rate; reactive only to strong tactile and vibrational stimuli.
Total loss of equilibrium	4	Total loss of muscle tone and equilibrium; rapid opercular rate (slow with some agents); reactive only to deep pressure stimuli.
Loss of reflex reactivity	5	Total loss of reactivity; opercular movements very shallow; heart rate very slow.
Medullary collapse	6	Opercular movements cease immediately after gasping, followed by cardiac arrest.

Recovery is complete in 5–30 min after fish are removed from the anaesthetic solution and returned to clean water. Jolly *et al.* (1972) recommend washing the fish in an intermediate container before returning it to the resident tank to avoid contamination of the latter and possibly delaying recovery. Food should be withheld for 24–48 h after prolonged anaesthesia, but this is not necessary after short periods of narcosis (Klontz & Smith, 1968).

Benzocaine, tricaine and propoxate are the agents of choice but unfortunately, the latter is not easily obtained commercially. In the absence of any specialized agents, ether can be used with reasonably safety. The following methods are recommended in order of preference.

(i) Make up a fresh solution of 200 mg *benzocaine* in 5 ml acetone and use it the same day. When this is added to 8 litres of water, the benzocaine concentration is 25 ppm. This should be thoroughly stirred before use. A concentration of 20–30 ppm provides sufficient sedation for tagging, marking and measuring fish, but 50 ppm is required for surgical anaesthesia. The peak effect is reached in 1–2 min and recovery is complete within 3 min of removal from the solution.

(ii) Make up a fresh solution of *tricaine* immediately before use at concentrations of 25–300 mg/l depending on the required level of narcosis. A concentration of 25 mg/l (1:40 000) is safe for sedation for periods up to 48 h, and 50–100 mg/l is suitable for deep narcosis of most small teleosts. Large species may need up to 300 mg/l. The water temperature should be between 5 and 16°C. Level 4 of narcosis is reached within 1–2 min of immersion and recovery is complete within 5 min of removal from the anaesthetic solution. Management should follow the general pattern described above.

Large fish such as sharks or rays should be anaesthetized with a freshly mixed solution of tricaine in sea water at 1 g/l. It may only be practicable to spray this directly into the mouth, or over the gill exits in the pharynx after first hooking the subject. Up to 1 litre of this solution may be needed to induce anaesthesia within 2 min in a large shark. Recovery may take 5–30 min from the time the fish is re-introduced to untreated sea-water, but may be hastened by retaining the hook for a period and towing the shark through the water.

(iii) Prepare a fresh solution of *propoxate* in fresh or sea-water at 1 to 4 ppm depending on species. 1 ppm anaesthetizes rainbow trout to level 4, while 2–4 ppm are needed for larger fish such as pike. Induction occurs in 30–60 s and recovery some 10 min after removal from anaesthetic solution.

(iv) Use *ether* at a concentration of 10–50 ml/l

of water. Induction to level 4 takes between 3–5 min, and recovery takes some 5–10 min after removal from the anaesthetic.

MARINE MAMMALS

Order Pinnipedia (seals, sea-lions)

Marine biologists increasingly require effective means of chemical restraint and anaesthesia for pinnipeds under field and laboratory conditions. Such restraint has met with only limited success.

Several important modifications from the 'normal' mammalian respiratory and cardiovascular systems are associated with their adaptation to a marine environment and ability to dive to considerable depths. These are of particular interest to the anaesthetist. The external nares are equipped with sphincters which close to prevent water entering the respiratory tract during deep diving. Both seals and sea-lions commonly take several deep breaths within a min, and may then hold their breath for 3–5 min before another ventilatory phase. This pattern is normal during sleep and may also be observed under deep anaesthesia.

The cardiovascular system is also adapted so that when the animal dives or when it is frightened, blood is held back in a series of venous sinuses until a breath is taken. It then returns to the heart and, if it contains anaesthetic agents, a high concentration may suddenly be pumped to the CNS (Backhouse, 1964).

Inhalational techniques have been described by several groups of workers. Seals were anaesthetized with $N_2O:O_2$ and ether delivered to an induction box, and were then intubated and maintained on $N_2O:O_2$ and lower concentrations of ether to effect (Finer, 1954). This technique has been superseded by inhalation anaesthesia with halothane Ridgway & Simpson (1969), who recommended that the animals should first be strapped to a board or restrained within a crush cage manufactured to their design. After injection with 1–2 mg of atropine sc, anaesthesia was induced with 10% halothane vapour delivered by mask or glass hood. Thereafter, the subjects were well maintained on 0·75–1·5% halothane in O_2, and recovered rapidly when the halothane was withdrawn. Eiseman *et al.* (1965) restrained sea-lions in a crush cage, injected thiamylal at 2 mg/kg iv into a vein on the ventral aspect of a flipper and administered methoxyflurane by face mask or endotracheal tube to maintain anaesthesia.

Immobilization of pinnipeds in the wild has proved difficult. Sedgwick & Acosta (1969) reported that etorphine was ineffective in sea-lions but that phencyclidine (2 mg/kg im) with propiopromazine (4 mg/kg im) was effective within 20 min.

Hubbard & Poulter (1968) stated that phenothiazine-derived ataractics are ineffective in seals and sea-lions, but that chordiazepoxide and diazepam are of some value. However, Peterson (1965) and Seal *et al.* (1970) claimed that promazine and acepromazine were of value in combination with phencyclidine. Ling *et al.* (1967) found that suxamethonium (2·5 mg/kg im) effectively immobilized elephant seals (*Miroungar leonina*) confirming the earlier findings of Jewell & Smith (1963) in common seals (*Phoca vitulina*). More recently, ketamine (4·5–11·0 mg/kg im) with 0·3–0·6 mm atropine was allegedly successful in immobilizing several wild and captive species (Geraci, 1973). Ringed seals (*Pusa hispida*) were netted and injected im in the dorsal right hip area for immobilization and capture during the initial trials. The drug was later assessed in captive harp seals (*Phoca groenlandica*), common seals (*Phoca vitulina*), California sea-lions (*Zalophus californianus*), and a northern fur seal (*Horhinus ursinus*). Using 4·5–6·5 mg/kg im, seals were immobilized for about 30 min after an induction period of 2–16 min. At 6·5–11 mg/kg im they were totally immobilized, with narcosis varying from analgesia to complete anaesthesia lasting 38–118 min. Body temperature stayed within the normal range, and the main drawback to the technique appears to have been enhanced muscle tone, with tremors or even convulsive movements occurring in several cases. It was concluded that ketamine was a reasonably safe agent for use in pinnipeds, but that there would always be some risk attached to their immobilization. The respiratory and cardiovascular depression inherent in the drugs might be compounded by the heavy lungworm and heartworm burdens commonly carried by these animals. Other workers have reported poor results with ketamine used alone, and consider that more consistent results are obtained if low doses of ketamine (1–2 mg/kg im) are given concurrently with diazepam at 0·2 mg/kg im (Greenwood, 1976). In fact, diazepam alone at 0·2 mg/kg iv was recently used in a grey seal. Excellent sedation lasting 30 min was obtained with no significant deterioration in physiological measurements, and it was concluded that diazepam is the ataractic of choice in pinnipeds (Greenwood, 1976).

Tiletamine–zolazepam at 1·0–2.0 mg/kg was said to be successful in elephant seals (*Mirounga angustirostris*), providing good immobilization at the lower and surgical anaesthesia at the higher dose level (Gray *et al.*, 1974).

Recommended anaesthetic techniques
The available evidence suggests that ketamine (1–2 mg/kg im) with diazepam (0·2 mg/kg im) are the drugs of choice for immobilizing seals and sea-lions. They should be injected im using a 100 × 1·65 mm (16 gauge) needle to ensure blubber penetration. Seals are best caught in nets first, whilst sea-lions can be injected on land by projectile syringe at close range. After immobilization with the above combination or with a ketamine alone at 4·0–6·0 mg/kg, anaesthesia can be completed with halothane delivered by mask or by endotracheal intubation for prolonged surgery.

Order Cetacea (dolphins, whales)
Of all the cetaceans, the bottlenosed dolphin (*Tursiops truncatus*) has attracted the most interest in biomedical research. Dolphins pose complex problems for the anaesthetist, and it is only recently that attempts at anaesthesia have been successful (Ridgeway, 1965; Ridgway & McCormick, 1967; Ridgway, 1968). Several factors have been responsible. The respiratory system is quite unique and the thermoregulatory mechanisms necessary to maintain a body temperature of 36°C in a cold environment are highly specialized. Drugs commonly used in other species are poorly tolerated or do not work at all. Finally, dolphins are very susceptible to handling stress unless they have been conditioned to the personnel looking after them.

Dolphins breathe through a single nostril on the forhead surface, known as the blowhole. This is normally held closed by a combination of muscular nasal plug and muscular sphincter around the orifice but it can be opened rapidly whilst the dolphin is swimming at full speed to allow a complete respiratory cycle in 0·3 s (Lawrence & Schevill, 1956). This alone presents a challenge to the anaesthetist since passages must be anatomically capable of allowing very rapid flow rates to satisfy a tidal volume of 5–10 litres of air. However, adult *Tursiops* normally breathe 2–3 times/min, inflating their lungs to about 80% of their capacity (5–10 litres), and holding an apneustic plateau for 20–30 s before a rapid exhalation. They usually hyperventilate with 4–5 rapid breaths before diving. The larynx is specialized to allow a direct passage between the internal nares and the lungs. The trachea is short, of wide bore and rigidly constructed of semifused cartilaginous rings, and the bronchi and bronchioles are also strongly supported by cartilage. An elaborate system of membranes, air sacs and tubes open into the nasal passage (Lawrence & Schevill, 1956) but are unlikely to affect anaesthetic management.

Dolphins maintain a stable body temperature in their cold and highly conductive aquatic environment by several evolutionary adaptations. Firstly, their high metabolic rate may be up to 3 times higher in some species than terrestrial mammals of similar weight. Furthermore, they are equipped with a countercurrent heat exchange system in peripheral blood vessels (Scholander & Schevill, 1955) and with a thick insulating layer of blubber.

Loss of respiratory control was held to be the cause of death when pentobarbitone was given ip at 10–30 mg/kg, suggesting that respiratory centres in the CNS were depressed before other symptoms of narcosis developed (Lilly, 1962). Similarly, failure of spontaneous respiration and paralysis of the muscular blowhole resulted when thiopentone at 6 mg/kg was administered iv to Pacific white-striped porpoises (*Lazenorhynchus obliquidens*) (Ridgway, 1965). Deep anaesthesia was achieved with further administration of thiopentone to effect (15–20 mg/kg iv), but the animals died within 10 min. Barbiturates were again used when Nagel *et al.* (1964) attempted to support a dolphin on artificial ventilation which mimicked the normal cycle of deep inspiration, apneustic plateau and rapid expiration. Although the animal died after induction with a mixture of thiopentone (13 mg/kg iv) and methohexitone (5 mg/kg iv), the technique was to prove a significant improvement on previous attempts at anaesthesia. The same group reported mechanically ventilating *T. truncata* with a $N_2O:O_2$ mixture after injecting suxamethonium (1 mg/kg im) and claimed that muscle relaxation lasted 30–60 min (Nagel *et al.*, 1966). However, Ridgway (1965, 1968) considers that N_2O provides inadequate analgesia for surgery in dolphins if used in this way.

It was clear from the early failures that mechanical ventilation with a specially modified respirator was essential whatever agent was used for anaesthesia, and this necessitated endotracheal intubation. Although Rieu & Gautheron (1968) described as a method for intubating common dolphins (*Delphinus delphis*) and spotted dolphins (*Stenella styx*) directly through the blowhole, the technique described by Ridgway & McCormick (1967) is the most widely accepted. After taking the dolphin from the water it is firmly belted onto a specially constructed stretcher. Anaesthesia is induced with thiopentone (10 mg/kg) injected into the central veins of the flukes. As the jaws relax, they are held apart by an attendant, and after the glottis has been dislocated from its position within the internal nares, a 24–30 mm cuffed endotracheal tube is introduced directly into the glottis and the cuff is inflated. Positive pressure ventilation with a suitably modified respirator delivers 2% halothane in air initially, and anaesthesia can be maintained thereafter on 0·5–1·0% halothane in air or in an air and O_2 (60:40) gas mixture. When delivery of halothane is stopped, air and O_2 (60:40) is supplied throughout recovery until the blowhole reflex returns (some 15–45 min after the dolphin has regained consciousness). The endotracheal tube can then be withdrawn, the glottis relocated within the nares and the dolphin returned to water as soon as spontaneous respiration is well established.

Recommended anaesthetic techniques

Tursiops truncata is more adaptable to captivity than other cetaceans, but even so is particularly susceptible to disease during the first 3 months after capture. As pointed out by Backhouse (1964), post-mortem examination of freshly captured dolphins has often revealed evidence of adrenal exhaustion and he concluded that they were particularly susceptible to 'stress'. It is therefore most important that they should be allowed at least 3 months for conditioning before being used in experiments. Dolphins may be lightly tranquillized with 0·2 mg/kg diazepam given either orally in fish or im after netting (Greenwood, 1976), but must be carefully observed for respiratory depression. They should then be strapped to a board or canvas stretcher, and water at 25–30°C sprayed or sponged over their surface to keep them moist. After intubation and induction with the thiopentone–halothane technique of Ridgeway & McCormick (1967), controlled ventilation must be instituted with a gas mixture humidified through a suitable in-line water vaporizer.

Ridgway (1968) described 9 reflexes as useful in assessing the depth of narcosis, 3 of which are particularly valuable during induction. Once the palpebral reflex (blink when the inner canthus is touched), corneal reflex (blink when the cornea is touched) and swimming movements of the free tail flukes each disappear, the depth of anaesthesia is adequate for surgery.

Anaesthesia may be maintained for several hours with low concentrations (0·5–1·0%) of halothane (Ridgway, 1968) provided the subject is efficiently ventilated. The lightest level of anaesthesia sufficient to inhibit movement of the tail flukes should be maintained.

Mechanical ventilation with 60% air:40% O_2 must be maintained until spontaneous ventilation is fully established and the dolphin has clearly regained muscular control of the blowhole and thorax.

There have been no recent developments in the anaesthetic management of dolphins which are superior to the above thiopentone–halothane technique.

Order Sirenia (dugong, manatees)

There are no published reports of effective anaesthesia in these animals. It is proposed that the recommendations for pinnipeds are likely to apply.

EUTHANASIA

Euthenasia involves by definition the killing of an animal with a minimum of physical and mental suffering. The animal may be killed instantly or it may pass quietly into an unconscious state and then die without regaining consciousness. In selecting a method, the experimentalist must first aim to avoid frightening the animal and avoid transmission of apprehension amongst any group of animals to be killed. Secondly he should consider the safety of personnel and avoid using aesthetically unpleasant methods which add to the strong emotional distaste felt by those involved. Finally, he must avoid damage which could interfere with post-mortem investigation and analysis.

Whatever method is used, therefore, the animals should be handled gently, taking care not to frighten or antagonize them unnecessarily. They should always be removed from the holding room and never killed in the presence of another live animal. Any blood which escapes from one animal during euthensia should be cleaned up and the area washed with disinfectant before another animal is brought in.

Physical methods

These mostly involve breaking the continuity of the spinal cord in the neck or damaging the cerebrum by stunning or penetrating blows. They may be distasteful to the operator but are, if applied properly, the least distressing to the animal since it is rendered instantly unconscious.

Dislocation of the neck is a quick and painless technique which is useful for mice, young rats, guinea-pigs, rabbits, young kittens, young puppies and birds. However, excessive bruising and local haemorrhage of the neck and upper respiratory tract caused by this method may interfere with subsequent fixation of the lungs and interpretation of histological sections.

Rapid freezing is used when it is important to minimize enzyme activity for subsequent bio-chemical estimations of tissues. The animal is plunged head first into a beaker of liquid air, held for about a minute until frozen solid, and then decapitated. The method is only suitable for small animals such as mice.

Stunning followed by exsanguination is the method of choice where collection of blood uncontaminated by anaesthetic agents is required. A blow on the head should only be used to stun animals which have relatively thin skulls e.g. rabbits or young kittens. Blood is then collected by severing the neck (jugular veins and carotid arteries). Larger animals may be stunned by electrical methods (Croft, 1952; Hickman, 1954; Croft & Hume, 1956) or by commercially available captive-bolt pistols, compressed-air guns, humane stunning cartridges or 'knocker-stunners'. The animals are rendered unconscious for long enough to bleed them out.

Electrocution is effective for dogs if performed properly but is unsuitable for cats (perhaps owing to the high conductivity of their coats). It is essential to anaesthetise the animal first with a low voltage AC shock between 2 head electrodes before applying a much higher voltage shock between one head and a hind-leg electrode.

Induction of hypoxia by rapid decompression in a special chamber or by supplying the animals in a chamber with pure nitrogen has been used and recommended for humane euthanasia (Lumb & Jones, 1973). Decompression requires specialist equipment and staff to use it, whilst asphyxiation without initial anaesthesia is an inhumane procedure in which the animals are clearly distressed.

Chemical methods

Euthanasia using chemical methods is simply an extension of anaesthesia to irreversible cardiac arrest. It follows that inhalational or injectable agents may be used.

Inhalational agents

Ether is commonly used in a chamber to kill numbers of rodents, but it has several disadvantages. It is doubtful whether this can be regarded as a humane method since the irritant nature of this agent to skin and mucous membranes at high concentrations is stressful to the animals. The explosive risk presents a particular laboratory hazard since bags full of dead animals may build up a high concentration of ether which can easily be fired by sparking connections in refrigerator or deep-freeze cabinets. The respiratory tract is severely affected (bronchial secretions and pulmonary oedema) and this will inevitably interfere with interpretation of histological sections. Finally, it cannot be used if lipoid estimations of tissues are to be made.

Carbon monoxide inhalation causes rapid death by combining with erythrocyte haemoglobin to produce a fatal anoxic anoxemia. The onset is so rapid that loss of consciousness occurs before the animal is stressed. The animals are killed in a chamber to which either household (coal) gas is supplied; cooled, filtered, exhaust fumes from a 4-stroke petrol engine are piped; or carbon monoxide is formed from the chemical interaction between crystals of sodium formate and sulphuric acid. Carbon monoxide concentrations of 0·5–14% have been used. Animals collapse and are unconscious within 40 s, failure of the respiratory centre occurs in about 2 min, and cardiac arrest follows in 5–7 min. If normal haemoglobin is necessary for the study, then clearly this method cannot be used.

Carbon dioxide at concentrations above 60% in air causes loss of consciousness, paralysis of the respiratory centre and cardiac arrest. As it is non-irritant, it is undoubtedly the inhalational agent of choice for euthanasia of small animals, including all rodent species, rabbits, birds, ferrets, mink, cats and small pigs. It can be piped into a killing chamber, clear polyethylene bags, or into the animals' holding cages enveloped in suitable bags, where the gas will rapidly fall by gravity to build up concentrations around the animals. Unconsciousness is induced quickly, peacefully and painlessly within 10–20 s of exposure, but it is wise to leave the animal in the gas for a further 20 min to ensure that it is dead. Neonates are particularly tolerant of carbon dioxide and can survive up to 30 min exposure to the gas (90–100% concentrations). They should therefore be placed in disposal bags into which carbon dioxide has been piped before they are sealed.

It has been assumed in the past that carbon dioxide euthanasia would produce minimal changes to organs. However, Fawell *et al.* (1972) showed that oedema of perivascular connective tissue and extravasation of blood into interstitial spaces was an artefact in lung sections after carbon dioxide euthanasia. Similar lesions have been noted in lungs from mice and rats anaesthetized with $CO_2:O_2$ (1:1) for periods longer than 2 min and we have suggested a loss of endothelial integrity resulting from a rapid fall in plasma pH (CRC).

Chloroform should not be used in laboratories since it is dangerously hepatotoxic to personnel and animals. Trace concentrations carried to breeding rooms in the ventilation system have been shown to interfere seriously with the breeding programme in rodent colonies.

Injectable agents

Although lethal doses of drugs such as barbiturates or tribromoethanol can be given orally or by rectal suppository, animals are in practice killed by intravenous (or intracardiac), intraperitoneal or intrathoracic injections of drugs. When intravenous or intracardiac injection is feasible, a saturated solution (80 g/100 ml) of magnesium sulphate (80 mg/kg) can be used with or without small doses of pentobarbitone (10 mg/kg) to kill animals quickly and cheaply. However, large volumes of solution must be injected, and the animals may exhibit muscle spasms, convulsive seizures, vocalization, gasping breaths and involuntary defaecation before death. There is also some doubt about the degree of cortical depression and analgesia produced before ventricular fibrillation occurs.

Pentobarbitone (18% concentration), preferably by rapid intravenous or intracardiac injection at 60 mg/kg, is the most satisfactory injectable agent for most animals. The intraperitoneal or intrathoracic routes are reasonable alternatives for intractable subjects or where intravascular injection is difficult, but higher doses (80–150 mg/kg depending on species) should be used, and the animals must be carefully observed afterwards to ensure that they are dead. It is important to auscultate the heart to ensure irreversible arrest, since some animals (particularly cats) may appear to be dead but, after a short time or after a stimulus such as being dropped into a disposal bag, the heart may start beating normally again.

Recommendations

Horses and donkeys

A captive-bolt stunner is fired into a site immediately below the roots of the forelock and along a line parallel with the crest of the neck (Fig. 15.1). The animal must be restrained with a strong halter, and in addition, can be blindfolded to minimize apprehension. Horses usually slump forward when stunned so the handler and operator of the bolt should stand to one side of the head.

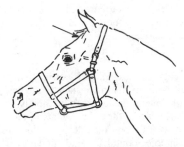

Fig. 15.1. Horse: direction of captive-bolt parallel with crest of neck.

They can then be killed by 'pithing' with a 10 mm diameter rod passed into the hole in the head and pushing this down into the mid-brain, or by bleeding out via the jugular and carotid vessels.

Cattle

The captive-bolt stunner is suitable for adult bulls, cows and calves, but the site of penetration is slightly different in each (Fig. 15.2 and 15.3). A site offset from the midline by 1 cm is selected to avoid the thick bony ridge in bulls. Alternatively, calves may be stunned by electrical methods using a commercial apparatus at about 90 V AC (fluctuating 200–240 mA) (Croft & Hume, 1956). The animals are then pithed and exsanguinated whilst stunned. Young calves may also be killed by injection of pentobarbitone (20 mg/kg) and magnesium sulphate (150 mg/kg) into a suitable vein.

Fig. 15.2. Site of captive-bolt penetration in bulls—1 cm to one side of bony ridge in mid-line.

Fig. 15.3. Calf: site of captive-bolt penetration.

Fig. 15.4. Sheep: captive-bolt fired toward larynx.

Fig. 15.5. Horned sheep: captive-bolt penetration in position just behind horns in midline.

Sheep

Electrical or captive-bolt stunning is normally used. In hornless breeds, the captive bolt is fired in a line directed towards the larynx (Fig. 15.4) but in horned animals it is placed behind the ridge joining the horns (Fig. 15.5) and directed forwards.

Lambs are killed with barbiturate (80 mg/kg) injected by iv, ip or intracardiac routes.

Goats

Electric or captive-bolt stunning is used. The muzzle of the captive bolt should be directed toward the mouth of the animal whether young or adult (Fig. 15.6). Kids may be killed with pentobarbitone (80 mg/kg iv) or with pentobarbitone (20 mg/kg) and magnesium sulphate (80 mg/kg) injected iv, ip, intracardiac or intrathoracic.

Pigs

Small pigs can be injected with lethal dose of pentobarbitone (70 mg/kg iv) after sedation with

Fig. 15.6. Goat: captive-bolt fired just behind line drawn between horns.

Fig. 15.7. Pig: captive-bolt fired horizontally parallel with crest of neck.

acepromazine (0·1 mg/kg) or diazepam (2 mg/kg). Alternatively, they can be bled out after stunning by electrical or captive bolt methods, or after narcosis has been induced with a $CO_2:O_2$ (1:1) gas mixture. Large animals must be suitably restrained, either physically by snare or chemically by phencyclidine (2 mg/kg im) and stunned by captive bolt before pithing and bleeding out (Fig. 15.7).

Primates
After monkeys have been physically restrained, they can be given sedative doses of ketamine (20 mg/kg im) before injecting lethal doses of pentobarbitone (50 mg/kg) by the intracardiac route. The handler is thus exposed to minimum hazard, a consideration which may be particularly important if the animals are being destroyed because of disease.

Ferrets (and other Mustelidae)
The simplest way to kill these animals is in a chamber or thick polyethylene bag supplied with commercial carbon dioxide. To ensure that they are dead, the neck can be broken by striking it on a hard narrow surface such as the rim of a dustbin. Alternatively, a lethal dose of pentobarbitone (70 mg/kg) can be injected ip to ensure a peaceful death.

Hedgehogs
These animals can be killed in a lethal chamber with carbon dioxide or carbon monoxide, or by pentobarbitone (80 mg/kg ip) after they have been unrolled to expose the ventral surface.

Dogs
The simplest and most humane way of killing dogs is by rapid iv injection of a concentrated solution (180 mg/ml) of pentobarbitone at 40 mg/kg. Respiratory paralysis and cardiac arrest are produced within seconds with no untoward vocalization or struggling. Dangerous animals must be adequately restrained either physically, or chemically with e.g. ketamine (40 mg/kg im), before attempting euthanasia. The intracardiac route is then often the most convenient for injecting

lethal doses of pentobarbitone (40 mg/kg) or a mixture of pentobarbitone and magnesium sulphate (10 mg/kg : 80 mg/kg).

Cats
Young cats are best killed by striking the base of the skull on a hard surface such as the bench edge or rim of a metal dustbin; this method is quick and least distressing to the animal. Cats of all ages can be killed with carbon dioxide or carbon monoxide in a suitable container and undergo minimal discomfort. Alternatively, pentobarbitone (180 mg/ml) can be given by the iv, ip or intrathoracic routes at a dose rate of 50 mg/kg. If the animals are considered to be dangerous to handle, they can be covered in thick towelling and injected with ketamine (40 mg/kg im) prior to removal from their box for injection with pentobarbitone (30 mg/kg ic).

Rabbits
These may be killed by a sharp blow at the back of the neck with a short stout length of wood if other more aesthetically satisfactory methods are contraindicated. Alternatively, the neck may be dislocated if the head is bent sharply backward at the same time as the legs and body are jerked sharply downward with the other hand—but this must never be attempted on live animals until practice has been gained on dead rabbits. Both methods provide instant and painless death if carried out properly but can be barbaric in the hands of the novice.

The most satisfactory method is injection of pentobarbitone (60 mg/kg) into an ear vein, after ensuring proper physical restraint. Rabbits struggle if exposed to volatile agents in euthanasia chambers, and even appear apprehensive if exposed to carbon dioxide or carbon monoxide.

Guinea-pigs
Dislocation of the neck is the simplest and the most humane method in guinea-pigs. The right hand is placed over the front of the animal's head and the neck is gripped between finger and thumb. The arm is swung downward vertically to one side and the weight of the animals dislocates the neck at the bottom of the drop. Alternatively they can be killed with carbon dioxide or carbon monoxide in a chamber, or with pentobarbitone (90 mg/kg ip).

Coypu
These are best killed by a blow over the neck with a stout length of wood followed by intracardiac injection of pentobarbitone (90 mg/kg).

Hamsters
These are best killed with carbon dioxide or carbon

monoxide in a killing chamber or with pento-barbitone (150 mg/kg ip).

Rats

Young rats may be stunned on the edge of the bench or be killed by neck disarticulation. Adults are best killed in a killing chamber with carbon dioxide or carbon monoxide, or by ip injection of pentobarbitone (100 mg/kg).

Mice

Mice may be killed humanely by dislocation of the neck. The mouse is placed on a flat surface, a pencil or pair of forceps is placed across the back of the neck and dislocation is effected by sharp backward jerk on the base of the tail.

Alternatively, mice can be killed in chambers or bags with carbon dioxide or carbon monoxide, taking care to ensure the pups are dead as well as adults, or by ip injection or pentobarbitone (150 mg/kg).

Birds

Small species or chicks can be killed physically by pressing the neck against a sharp bench edge to dis-articulate the vertebrae. Alternatively, they may be killed in a chamber with carbon dioxide, carbon monoxide, methoxyflurane or ether. Adult fowl, pigeons and quail are best killed physically by neck dislocation. The legs are taken in the left hand, and the head held between the first 2 fingers of the right hand with the thumb under the beak. A sharp jerk with each hand, pulling the head backward over the neck will break the spinal cord. Exposure to carbon dioxide may also be used for these birds. Large species such as turkeys or geese are stunned with a blow to the base of the skull, before bleeding out through the severed neck vessels.

Reptiles

The chosen method will depend on the species, size and any hazard presented by physical restraint for injection. Since induction with inhalational anaes-thetic agents can present difficulties in these animals, they are best killed by injectable agents or by physical methods. Tortoises, terrapins, lizards and salamanders are best injected with lethal doses of ketamine (100 mg/kg im) or pentobarbitone (150 mg/kg ip) followed by decapitation with a strong pair of kitchen scissors. Snakes can be killed by a sharp blow just behind the head or by high doses of ketamine (100 mg/kg im).

Amphibians

These are best anaesthetized in a chamber with methoxyflurane followed by decapitation or pithing as described by Scott (1967).

Fish

Small fish under 200 g in weight are killed by dislocation of the neck. The fish is held in the left hand, the right thumb is pushed into the mouth with the forefinger squeezing the junction of head and neck, and the head is bent sharply back until a 'crack' is felt. Alternatively, the head can be struck against a sharp edge.

Larger fish are killed by striking the back of the head a sharp blow with a suitable length of wood, whilst eels may be decapitated with a sharp knife.

Crustaceans

The CNS of crabs is concentrated into anterior and posterior centres and it has been suggested that these should be pierced with a pointed awl before boiling (Baker, 1955; UFAW, 1963). The CNS of lobsters is more diffusely organized and this technique is not possible. It is alleged that they die within 15 s if put into vigorously boiling water. Since Oswald (1977) has demonstrated anaes-thetic activity of xylazine (70 mg/kg) and pento-barbitone (250 mg/kg) in edible crabs, it is tenta-tively suggested that narcosis should be induced in laboratory specimens either by injecting one of these agents or by immersion in ethanol, mag-nesium chloride (7%) or saturated carbon dioxide solutions before the animal is killed in boiling water.

Molluscs (and other aquatic invertebrates)

These creatures may be narcotized with pento-barbitone, amylocaine or tricaine. Alternatively, most land and freshwater species are narcotized by keeping them overnight in cooled boiled water from which air has been excluded or into which carbon dioxide has been bubbled. Freshwater snails, marine worms and sea-anemones can be killed by leaving them overnight in a covered container in which menthol crystals have been scattered on the water surface. Marine molluscs are best treated with a 7% solution of magnesium chloride in sea-water or a 1% solution of propylene phenoxetol (Wright, 1967; Runham et al., 1965). It is suggested that molluscs should be narcotized before they are killed and fixed for experimentation.

Sources for drugs*

Generic name	Trade name	Manufacturer or supplier
Acepromazine maleate	*Acetylpromazine*	13
Acepromazine maleate + etorphine hydrochloride	*Immobilon Large Animal* (*LA*)	5,53
Adrenaline (also epinephrine hydrochloride)	*Adrenaline BP*	41, 52
Alpha-chloralose	—	10, 29
Alphaxolone + alphadolone acetate	*Saffan; Althesin*	30
Amethocaine	*Pontocaine*	68
Amphetamine sulphate	*Amfetasul; Benzedrine*	14, 41
Atropine sulphate	—	7, 31
Azaperone	*Suicalm; Stresnil*	36, 52
Bemegride sodium	*Megimide; Mikedimide*	45, 49
Betamethasone	*Betsolan*	30
Calcium chloride 20% w/v solution		40
Calcium gluconate 10% w/v solution		27
Chloral hydrate		42
Chlordiazepoxide	*Librium*	54, 55
Chlorobutanol	*Chloretone*	47, 48
Chlorpromazine hydrochloride	*Largactil; Megaphen*	41, 52
Chlorprothixen	*Taractan*	54, 55
Cyprenorphine hydrochloride	*M-285*	53
Dexamethasone	*Dexadreson; Dexone*	35, 60
Dextran 70	*Macrodex*	50, 51
Dextran 40	*Rheomacrodex*	50, 51
Diazepam	*Valium*	54, 55
Diethylthiambutene hydrochloride	*Themalon*	14, 15
Dihydromorphine	*Dilaudid*	38, 39
Diprenorphine hydrochloride	*Revivon*	5, 53
Di-triazine diaceturate	*Berenil*	6, 32
Doxapram hydrochloride	*Dopram*	3, 4
Droperidol (dehydrobenzperidol)	*Droperidol; Droleptan R4749; Inapsin*	36, 52
Droperidol-fentanyl	*Innovar-Vet; Thalamanol*	36, 52
D-tubocurarine chloride	*Tubarine*	14, 15
Edrophonium chloride	*Tensilon*	54, 55
Enflurane	*Ethrane*	1, 2
Etamiphylline camsylate	*Millophyline V*	19
Ether (diethyl ether)	—	41, 52
Ethyl chloride	—	27
Ethylisobutrazine	*Diquel*	37
Etorphine hydrochloride	*M99*	5, 53
Etorphine hydrochloride + acepromazine maleate	*Immobilon Large Animal* (*LA*)	5, 53
Etorphine hydrochloride + methotrimeprazine	*Immobilon Small Animal* (*SA*)	5, 53
Fentanyl citrate	*Sublimaze; Fentanyl Vet*	36, 52
Fentanyl citrate + droperidol	*Innovar-Vet; Thalamonal*	36, 52
Fentanyl citrate + fluanisone	*Hypnorm*	36
Fluanisone	*Haloanisone; R2028*	36, 52
Fluphenazine hydrochloride	*Prolixin*	25, 26
Frusemide	*Lasix*	6, 32
Gallamine triethiodide	*Flaxedil*	41, 52
Gelatin polypeptides solution	*Haemaccel*	6, 32
Halothane	*Fluothane*	33, 34
Heparin sodium	—	62, 64
Hexobarbitone sodium	*Evipal*	68, 69
Hyaluronidase	*Hyalase; Wyalase*	11, 70
Hydrocortisone	*Solucortef*	62, 64
Isoprenaline hydrochloride	*Isuprel*	61, 68

* European, Australian and USA suppliers are given where possible—numbers refer to list of manufacturers.

243

Generic name	Trade name	Manufacturer or supplier
Ketamine hydrochloride	*Vetalar; Ketalar*	47, 48
Levallorphan tartrate	*Lorfan*	54, 55
Levarteranol bitartrate	*Levophed*	20, 28, 69
Lignocaine hydrochloride (lidocaine hydrochloride)	*Xylocaine; Xylotox*	8, 67
Mepazine	*Pacatal; Paxital*	65, 66
Meperidine hydrochloride (pethidine hydrochloride)	*Demerol*	54, 55
Mephenesin	*Myanesin; Tolserol*	25
Mephentermine sulphate	*Wyamine*	11, 70
Meprobamate	*Anthisan; Equanil*	41, 70
Metaraminol bitartrate	*Aramine*	42, 43
Methadone hydrochloride	*Amidone; Dolophine*	1, 14, 21
Methamphetamine hydrochloride	*Desoxyn; Methedrine*	1, 14
Methetharimide sodium	*Megimide; Mikedimide*	45, 49
Methohexitone sodium	*Brevane; Brietal Sodium*	21, 22
Methotrimeprazine hydrochloride	*Levoprome*	5, 18
Methotrimeprazine hydrochloride + etorphine hydrochloride	*Immobilon Small Animal (SA)*	5, 53
Methoxamine hydrochloride	*Vasoxyl*	14, 15
Methoxyflurane	*Metofane; Penthrane*	1, 2
Methyl dihydromorphine	*Metopon*	54, 55
Metomidate (methoxymol)	*Hypnodil; R7315*	36
Nalorphine hydrochloride	*Lethidrone*	14, 15
Naloxone hydrochloride	*Narcan*	23, 24
Neostigmine methylsulphate	*Prostigmine*	54, 55
Nikethamide	*Coramine*	16, 17
Noradrenaline acid tartrate	*Levorphed*	20, 28
Pancuronium bromide	*Pavulon*	46
Paraldehyde	—	42, 43
Pentazocine lactate	*Talwin*	68, 69
Pentobarbitone sodium	*Sagatal; Euthatal*	41, 52
Pentobarbitone sodium + chloral hydrate + magnesium	*Equithesin; Sedax*	37
Pentobarbitone sodium + thiopentone sodium	*Combuthal*	20
Pentomethylene tetrazol	*Metrazol; Leptazol*	38, 39
Perphenazine	*Trilafon*	58, 63
Phencyclidine hydrochloride	*Sernylan*	12
Phenoxybenzamine hydrochloride	*Dibenzyline*	59
Phentolamine mesylate	*Regitine*	16, 17
Procaine hydrochloride	*Novocaine; Planocaine*	61, 68
Promazine hydrochloride	*Sparine*	11, 70
Promethazine hydrochloride	*Phenergan*	41, 52
Propanidid	*Epontol*	28
Propoxate	*R7464*	36
Propranolol hydrochloride	*Inderal*	33, 34
Propriopromazine hydrochloride	*Tranvet*	20
Protamine sulphate	—	13
Reserpine	*Serpasil*	16, 17
Suxamethonium chloride (succinylcholine chloride)	*Anectin; Sucostrin*	15, 25
Suxamethonium bromide	*Brevedil M*	41
Tetracaine hydrochloride	*Pontocaine; Cetacaine*	31
Theophylline ethylene diamine	*Aminophylline*	3, 4
Thiamylal sodium	*Surital*	47
Thiopentone sodium	*Intraval sodium*	41
	Pentothal	1
Tiletamine hydrochloride	*CI-634*	47
Tiletamine hydrochloride + zolazepam	*CI-744*	47
Tribromoethanol solution	*Avertin*	68, 69
Tricaine methane sulphonate	*MS-222*	56, 57
Trichloroethylene	*Trilene*	33, 34
Triflupromazine hydrochloride	*Vetame*	25, 26

Generic name	Trade name	Manufacturer or supplier
Trimeprazine tartrate	*Vallergan*	41, 52
Tromethamine	*THAM*	1, 2
Xylazine hydrochloride	*Rompun*	20, 28

List of drug manufacturers and suppliers

1. Abbott Laboratories,
    North Chicago,
    Illinois 60064,
    USA.

2. Abbott Laboratories Ltd.,
    Queenborough,
    Kent,
    England.

3. A. H. Robins,
    1407, Cummings Drive,
    Richmond,
    Virginia 23220,
    USA.

4. A. H. Robins Co. Ltd.,
    Redkiln Way,
    Horsham,
    Sussex, RH13 5QP,
    England.

5. American Cyanamid Co.,
    PO Box 400,
    Princeton,
    New Jersey 08540,
    USA.

6. American Hoechst Corp.,
    Route 202-206 North,
    Somerville,
    New Jersey 08876,
    USA.

7. Antigen Ltd.,
    Roscrea,
    Ireland.

8. Astra Pharmaceutical Products,
    Worcester,
    Massachusetts 01600,
    USA.

9. Ayerst Laboratories,
    685, 3rd Avenue,
    New York,
    New York 10017,
    USA.

10. BDH Ltd.,
    Poole,
    Dorset,
    England.

11. Benger Laboratories Ltd.,
    Holmes Chapel,
    Cheshire,
    England.

12. Bio-Ceutic Laboratories Inc.,
    PO Box 999,
    St Joseph,
    Missouri 64502,
    USA.

13. Boots Pure Drugs Co.,
    Station Street,
    Nottingham,
    England.

14. Burroughs Wellcome & Co.,
    183–193 Euston Road,
    London, NW1,
    England.

15. Burroughs Wellcome & Co. Inc.,
    Tuckahoe,
    New York 10707,
    USA.

16. Ciba-Geigy Ltd.,
    Basle,
    Switzerland.

17. Ciba Pharmaceutical Co.,
    Summit,
    NJ 07901,
    USA.

18. Cyanamid of Great Britain Ltd.,
    Fareham Road, Gosport,
    Hampshire, PO13 0AS,
    U.K.

19. Dale Pharmaceuticals Ltd.,
    Steeton,
    Keighley,
    Yorks,
    England.

20. Diamond Laboratories Inc.,
    2538 South East 43rd Street,
    Des Moines,
    Iowa 50304,
    USA.

21. Elanco Products Co.,
    Eli, Lilly & Co.,
    Indianapolis,
    Indiana 46206,
    USA.

22. Eli, Lilly & Co. Ltd.,
    Kingsclere Road, Basingstoke,
    Hampshire, RG21 2XA,
    UK.

23. Endo Laboratories,
    Australia (Pty) Ltd.,
    448, Pacific Highway,
    Artarmon,
    New South Wales,
    Australia.

24. Endo Laboratories Inc.,
    1000 Stewart Avenue,
    Garden City,
    New York 11530,
    USA.

25. E. R. Squibb & Sons,
    745, 5th Avenue,
    New York,
       New York 10022,
          USA.

26. E. R. Squibb & Sons Ltd.,
    Regal House,
       Twickenham,
          Middlesex, TW1 3QT,
          England.

27. Evans Medical Ltd.,
    Speke,
       Liverpool,
          Lancashire,
             UK.

28. Farbenfabriken Bayer AG.,
    Leverkussen,
       Germany.

29. Fisher Scientific Co.,
    711, Forbes Avenue,
       Pittsburgh,
          Pennsylvania 15219,
             USA.

30. Glaxo Laboratories Ltd.,
    Greenford,
       Middlesex, UB6 0HE,
          England.

31. Haver-Lockhart Laboratories,
    Kansas City,
       Missouri 64100,
          USA.

32. Hoechst Pharmaceuticals,
    Veterinary Division,
       Hoechst House,
          Salisbury Road,
             Hounslow,
                Middlesex,
                   England.

33. ICI American Inc.,
    Atlas International Div.,
       Wilmington,
          Delaware 19899,
             USA.

34. ICI Pharmaceuticals,
    Alderley House,
       Alderley Park,
          Macclesfield,
             Cheshire, SK10 4TF,
                England.

35. Intervet Laboratories Ltd.,
    Viking House,
       Viking Way,
          Bar Hill,
             Cambridge,
                UK.

36. Janssen Pharmaceutica,
    Research Laboratories,
       Beerse,
          Belgium.

37. Jensen-Salsbery Laboratories Inc.,
    520, West 21st Street,
       Kansas City,
          Missouri, 64141,
             USA.

38. Knoll AG,
    67, Ludwighshafen am Rhein,
       Postfach 210805,
          Germany.

39. Knoll Pharmaceutical Co.,
    Orange,
       New Jersey 07000,
          USA.

40. Macarthys Ltd.,
    Chesham House,
       Chesham Close,
          Romford,
             Essex,
                England.

41. May and Baker Ltd.,
    Dagenham,
       Essex,
          England.

42. Merck & Co.,
    Rahway,
       NJ 07065,
          USA.

43. Merck, Sharp & Dohme,
    Hertford Road,
       Hoddesdon,
          Hertfordshire, EN11 9BU,
             UK.

44. Moore Kirk Laboratories Inc.,
    Worcester,
       Massachusetts 01600,
          USA.

45. Nicholas Laboratories Ltd.,
    225 Bath Road,
       Slough,
          Berkshire, SL1 4AU,
             UK.

46. Organon Laboratories Ltd,
    Crown House,
       London Road, Marden,
          Surrey, SM4 5DZ,
             UK.

47. Parke Davis & Co.,
    Joseph Campau Avenue-at-the-River,
       Detroit,
          Michigan 48232,
             USA.

48. Parke, Davis & Co. Ltd,
    Usk Road,
       Pontypool,
          Gwent, NP4 8YH,
             UK.

49. Parlam Division,
    Ormont Drug and Chemical Co.
    South Dean Street,
    Englewood,
    New Jersey 07631,
    USA.

50. Pharmacia (Great Britain) Ltd.,
    Paramount House,
    75 Uxbridge Road,
    Ealing,
    London, W5,
    UK.

51. Pharmacia Laboratories, Inc.,
    800, Centennial Avenue,
    Piscataway,
    New Jersey 08854,
    USA.

52. Pitman-Moore Co.,
    PO Box 344,
    Washington Crossing,
    NJ 08560,
    USA.

53. Reckitt and Colman,
    Dansom Lane,
    Hull, HU8 7DS,
    England.

54. Roche Laboratories,
    Hoffman-La Roche Inc.,
    Nutley,
    NJ 97110,
    USA.

55. Roche Products,
    Welwyn Garden City,
    Herts,
    England.

56. Sandoz Ltd.,
    Sandoz House,
    98, The Centre,
    Feltham,
    Middlesex, TW13 4EP,
    England.

57. Sandoz Pharmaceuticals,
    Hanover,
    New Jersey 07936,
    USA.

58. Schering Corporation,
    PO Box 500,
    Kenilworth,
    New Jersey 07033,
    USA.

59. Smith, Kline & French,
    1500, Spring Garden Street,
    Philadelphia,
    Pennsylvania 19101,
    USA.

60. Sterivet Laboratories Ltd.,
    PO Box 209,
    Bolton,
    Ontario,
    Canada.

61. Sterling Drugs International,
    Sterling House,
    14, Hewlett Street,
    London, EC2 A3NJ,
    England.

62. The Upjohn Co.,
    301, Henrietta Street,
    Kalamazoo,
    Michigan 49006,
    USA.

63. Unilabo Cetrane,
    92, Rue Baudin,
    Levallois 92307,
    France.

64. Upjohn Ltd.,
    Fleming Way,
    Crawley,
    West Sussex,
    RH10 2NJ,
    UK.

65. Warner-Chilcott,
    Morris Plains,
    New Jersey 07950,
    USA.

66. Warner-Lambert,
    Woodthorp Road,
    Middlesex,
    England.

67. Willows Francis,
    Westhoughton,
    Epsom,
    Surrey,
    England.

68. Winthrop Laboratories,
    1450 Broadway,
    New York,
    New York 10012,
    USA.

69. Winthrop Laboratories,
    Surbiton-on-Thames,
    Surrey,
    England.

70. Wyeth Laboratories,
    PO Box 8299,
    Philadelphia,
    Pennsylvania 19101,
    USA.

List of manufacturers of equipment

Product	Manufacturer or supplier
Air Shield 10 000 Respirator	Cory Bros. (Hospital Contracts Co.) Ltd., 4, Dollis Park, London, N3 1HG, England.
Anaesthetic units, various vaporizers, Waters to-and-fro absorbers, Ayres T-piece	British Oxygen Co. Ltd., Pinnacles, Harlow, Essex, England.
Atlas nylon syringes	Chas F. Thackray Ltd., Park Street, Leeds 1, England.
Bard 'I-Catheter' inside needle iv placement unit	C. R. Bard International Ltd., Clacton-on-Sea, Essex, England.
Blease 'Minor Anaesthesia Trolley' (circle, Waters to-and-fro vaporizers and other items available)	Blease Medical Equipment Ltd., Deansway, Chesham, Bucks, England.
'Braunula Closure Stopper'	Armour Pharmaceutical Co. Ltd., Eastbourne, Sussex, England.
'Brunswick' syringes and needles	Southern Syringe Services Ltd., New Universal House, 303, Chase Road, London, N14 6JB, England.
'Buretrol' burette infusion set	Travenol Laboratories Ltd., Thetford, Norfolk, England.
'Butterfly' infusion set	Abbott Laboratories Ltd., Queenborough, Kent, England.
'Cap-Chur' equipment	Palmer Chemical & Equipment Co. Inc., Box 867, Douglasville, Georgia 30134, USA.
Cavendish 'Junior' Anaesthetic Apparatus (circle absorbers, vaporizers and other items available), or MIE 'Casualty and Out-Patients Anaesthetic Unit'	Medical and Industrial Equipment Ltd., 26–40, Broadwick Street, London, W1A 2AD, England.
'Dist-Inject' syringes and projectors + 'Miniject' blowpipe	Peter Ott & Co., Oetlingerstrasse 81, Postfach CH-4007, Basle, Switzerland.
East 'Automatic Vent' miniature ventilator	H. G. East & Co. Ltd., Sandy Lane West, Littlemore, Oxford, OX4 5JT, England.

Product	Manufacturer or supplier
Gillette syringes and needles	Gillette Surgical, Gillette Industries Ltd., Great West Road, Isleworth, Middlesex, England.
Harvard Animal Ventilators	TEM Sales Ltd., Gatwick Road, Crawley, Sussex, England.
Hook and Tucker Halothane Meter	Hook and Tucker Instruments Ltd., Vulcan Way, New Addington, Croydon, Surrey, CR0 9UG, England.
Jack-the-Yeoman crossbow projector and 'Hypodart' syringes	Jack-the-Yeoman Ltd., Lysander Grove, London, England.
'Medicut' iv cannula	Sherwood Medical Industries Ltd., Crawley, Sussex, England. or Sherwood Medical Industries Inc., 1831, Olive Street, St Louis, Missouri 63103, USA.
Palmer Animal Ventilator	C. F. Palmer (London) Ltd., Lane End Road, High Wycombe, Bucks, PH12 4HL, England.
Paxarms syringes and projectors	Paxarms Ltd., PO Box 317, Timaru, New Zealand.
Penlon 'SAM Anaesthetic Apparatus'	Penlon Ltd., Abingdon, Oxford, OX14 3PH, England.
Platon 'Flowbits' flowmeters Wade 'All Plastic' needle valves	Flowbits, Wella Road, Basingstoke, Hants, RG22 4AQ, England.
'Portex' plastic catheters, tubing and connectors	Portex Ltd., Hythe, Kent, England.
'Small Animal Anaesthetic Unit' and temperature compensated vaporizers e.g. 'Fluotec'	Cyprane Ltd., Scott Strut, Keighley, Yorkshire, England.

Product	Manufacturer or supplier
'Speedframe' (product of Dexion Ltd.,)	Construction and Industrial Supplies Ltd., Apex House, Fulton Road, Wembley, Middlesex, HA9 0DD, England.
'Telinject' blowpipe	W. Kullman, 6700 Ludwigshafen/Rhein, Hohenzollerstrasse 99, West Germany.
'Universal Veterinary Unit' (Magill, Waters to-and-fro circuits and other items available)	Air-Med Ltd., Edinburgh Way, Harlow, Essex, England.
'Viaflex' disposable infusion bags	Baxter Division, Travenol Laboratories Ltd., Thetford, Norfolk, England.

APPENDIX B

Standard weights and equivalents

Metric weights

1 gram (1g) = weight of 1 cc water at 4°C
1000 g = 1 kilogram (kg)
0·1 g = 1 decigram (dg)
0·01 g = 1 centigram (cg)
0·001 g = 1 milligram (mg)
0·001 mg = 1 microgram (µg)

Useful equivalents

Metric : Avoirdupois

28·35 g = 1 oz
453·60 g = 1 lb
1·00 kg = 2·2 lb

Metric volumes

1000 ml or cc = 1 litre (l)
100 ml = 1 decilitre (dl)

Useful equivalents

Metric : Imperial

28·4 ml = 1 fluid oz
568·2 ml = 1 pint = 20 fluid oz
1000 ml = 1·75 pint = 3·28 fluid oz
4·5 l = 8·00 pint = 1 gallon

Solution equivalents

To calculate the number of mg of solute to include in 1 ml of solvent to make up a solution of given % strength simply move the decimal point one place to the right e.g. to make a 10·0% solution, mix 100 mg solute in 1 ml solvent.

1 part in 10 = 10.00% (1 ml contains 100 mg)
1 part in 50 = 2.00% (1 ml contains 20 mg)
1 part in 100 = 1.00% (1 ml contains 10 mg)
1 part in 500 = 0.20% (1 ml contains 2 mg)
1 part in 1000 = 0.10% (1 ml contains 1 mg)
1 part in 5000 = 0.02% (1 ml contains 0.20 mg)

Thermometer scales—equivalents centigrade:fahrenheit

To convert °C to °F, multiply by $\frac{9}{5}$ and add 32*

e.g. 10°C = 50°F

to convert °F to °C, subtract 32 from °F and multiply by $\frac{5}{9}$. * For temperatures in the physiological range.

°C	°F	°C	°F
0	32	21	69·8
+1	33·8	22	71·6
2	35·6	23	73·4
3	37·4	24	75·2
4	39·2	25	77·0
5	41·0	26	78·8
6	42·8	27	80·6
7	44·6	28	82·4
8	46·4	29	84·2
9	48·2	30	86·0
10	50·0	31	87·8
11	51·8	32	89·6
12	53·6	33	91·4
13	55·4	34	93·2
14	57·2	35	95·0
15	59·0	36	96·8
16	60·8	37	98·6
17	62·6	38	100·4
18	64·4	39	102·2
19	66·2	40	104·0
20	68·0	41	105·8
		42	107·6

External diameter

Metric gauge (mm)	Standard wire gauge
0·25	30
0·35	28
0·40	27
0·45	26
0·50	25
0·55	24
0·65	23
0·70	22
0·80	21
0·90	20
1·10	19
1·25	18
1·45	17
1·65	16
1·80	15
2·10	14
2·40	13
2·80	12

GLOSSARY

Common terms, abbreviations, symbols and conventions

Abbreviations—see specific examples and symbols.

Anaesthesia—a state of controllable, reversible insensibility in which sensory reception and motor response are both markedly reduced.

Analgesia—the temporary abolition or diminution of pain perception.

Anoxia—complete deprivation of oxygen for tissue respiration.

Apnoea—temporary cessation of breathing.

BMR—basal metabolic rate.

Bradycardia—a significant slowing of heart rate.

Catheter sizes—all are given as outside diameter metric measurements.

CNS—central nervous system.

CNS depressant—*any* agent which modifies function by depressing sensory or motor responses in the CNS.

Compliance—defined as the change in volume of a distensible bag, lung or alveolus in response to unit change in pressure of gas enclosed within it and is usually expressed in litres/cmH$_2$O. In a sense then it is an index of 'distensibility'.

CRD—chronic respiratory disease.

CTZ—chemoreceptor trigger zone in the brain stem.

Cyanosis—the colour change from pink to blue or purple observed in skin and visible membranes as a symptom of hypoxia. It is caused by reduced haemoglobin in capillary blood.

Dead space—that space where no gas exchange takes place, lying between the source of fresh gases and the lung capillaries.

Dosages—all drugs (except the fentanyl–fluanisone and etorphine–acepromazine combinations) are expressed as mg of solid administered per kg of animal's bodyweight and written mg/kg. The exceptions are expressed as ml of solution per kg of bodyweight and written ml/kg.

Drug descriptions—the shortest generic name available is used throughout the text, and the salts commonly available, together with their trade names, are listed in Appendix A.

Dyspnoea—laboured breathing.

Endotracheal tube (catheter) sizes—all are given as outside diameter metric measurements.

Exotic animals—an imprecise term but by common usage refers to animals which have not been domesticated or used in laboratories.

Hyperpnoea—fast or deep breathing.

Hypopnoea—slow or shallow breathing.

Hypothermia—a lowering of body temperature either by default or done deliberately to protect organs during anoxia.

Hypovolaemia—a fall in fluid volume in the extracellular compartment.

Injections—routes of administration are abbreviated:

> iv = intravenous
> im = intramuscular
> ip = intraperitoneal
> ic = intracardiac
> sc = subcutaneous

Large animal—this may appear self-evident but refers in this text to the common domesticated species, horse, ox, sheep, goat and pig.

Local analgesia—synonymous with local anaesthesia and is the term used in this text.

Minute volume—the product of tidal volume and rate of breathing (i.e. $V_T \times f$).

Narcosis—a state of insensibility or stupor from which it is difficult to arouse the animal.

Narcotic agents—*any* drugs capable of producing narcosis and the term is not restricted in this text to morphine-like drugs or sedative-analgesics.

Needle sizes—given in metric sizes (length × outside diameter) with standard wire gauge (swg) in parenthesis.

Perfusion—the circulation of blood through a tissue or organ via the vascular bed.

pH—an expression of hydrogen ion concentration in any solution providing an index of acid–base balance—the higher the hydrogen ion concentration the lower the pH and vice versa.

Polypnoea—rapid, panting breathing.

Pulmonary ventilation—the mechanical expansion and contraction of the lungs in order to renew alveolar air with fresh atmospheric air.

251

RAS—reticular activating system.

Shock—in common usage but is being replaced by the more precise term 'acute cardiovascular failure' abbreviated to CVF.

Symbols—a dash above any symbol indicates a mean value, whereas a dot indicates a unit of time—primary symbols are in large capital letters, secondary in small (e.g. V = gas volume, A = alveolar gas, hence $\dot{V}_A$ = volume of alveolar gas/unit time).

Gases:

V = gas volume
$\dot{V}$ = gas volume/min
P = gas pressure
$\bar{P}$ = mean gas pressure
f = respiratory frequency (breaths/min)
A = alveolar gas
T = tidal gas

Blood:

a = arterial blood, e.g. PaO_2 = partial pressure of O_2 in arterial blood

v = venous blood
c = capillary blood

Tachycardia—a significant increase in heart rate.

Therapeutic index— $LD_{50}:AD_{50}$ or $LD_{50}:ED_{50}$— an indication of the safety margin in drug dosage—the bigger the ratio, the safer the drug. The following abbreviations are used in this text as indices of drug response:

AD_{50}—dosage of drug which anaesthetises 50% of a group of animals.
ED_{50}—dosage of drug which is effective in 50% of a group of animals.
AD_{95}—dosage of drug which anaesthetises 95% of a group.
LD_{50}—dosage of drug which kills 50% of a group of animals.

Tidal volume (V_T)—the volume of air inspired or expired in one breath.

Tympany—accumulation of gas in the alimentary tract.

REFERENCES

Abramowitz, A. A., Hisaw, F. W., Bettiger, F. & Papandrea, D. N. (1940). The origin of the diabetogenic hormone in the dogfish. *Biological Bulletin Marine Biological Laboratory, Woods Hole, Mass.* **78,** 189-201.

Adair, E. R. (1969). An effective restraining chair for small primates. *Laboratory Primate Newsletter* **8** (1), 3-6.

Adams, A. P., Morgan-Hughes, J. O. & Sykes, M. K. (1968). pH and blood-gas analysis II. Anaesthesia. *Anaesthesia* **23,** 47-64.

Adams, H. R. (1970). Prolongation of barbiturate anesthesia by chloramphenicol in laboratory animals. *Journal of the American Veterinary Medical Association* **157,** 1908-1913.

Adams, H. R. & Dixit, B. N. (1970) Prolongation of pentobarbital anesthesia by chloramphenicol in dogs and cats. *Journal of the American Veterinary Medical Association* **156,** 902-905.

Adams, H. R., Teske, R. H. & Mercer, H. D. (1976). Anesthetic-antibiotic interrelationships. *Journal of the American Veterinary Medical Association* **168,** 409-412.

Adolph, E. F. (1949). Quantitative relations in the physiological constitutions of mammals. *Science, New York* **109,** 579–585.

Adolph, E. F. (1957). Ontogeny of physiological regulation in the rat. *Quarterly Review of Biology* **32,** 89-137.

Aitken, M. M. & Sanford, J. (1972). Comparative assessment of tranquillizers in the horse. *Proceedings of the Association of Veterinary Anaesthetists of Great Britain and Ireland* **3,** 20-28.

Akusawa, M., Matsumura, K. & Yamanouchi, S. (1972). The efficacy of Ketalar as a short-acting anesthetic for dogs and cats. *Kurume Medical Journal* **19,** 39–41.

Albin, M. S., White, R. J., Donald, D. E., MacCarty, C. S. & Faulconer, A. J. (1966). Spinal cord hypothermia by localized perfusion cooling. *Nature, London* **210,** 1059–1060.

Albin, M. S., White, R. J., Locke, G. S., Massopust, L. C. & Kretchmer, H. E. (1967). Localized spinal cord hypothermia. *Anesthesia and Analgesia: Current Researches* **46,** 8-16.

Albin, M. S., White, R. J., Acosta-Rua, G. & Yashon, D. (1968). Study of functional recovery produced by delayed localized cooling after spinal cord injury in primates. *Journal of Neurosurgery* **29,** 113-120.

Aldrete, J. A., Le Vine, D. S. & Gingrich, T. F. (1969). Experience in anaesthesia for liver transplantation. *Anesthesia and Analgesia: Current Researches* **48,** 802–814.

Alexander, F. (1960). *An introduction to veterinary pharmacology.* Edinburgh: Livingstone.

Alford, B. T. & Wozniak, L. A. (1970). Neurolept-analgesia in the dog and reversal by an antagonist. *Journal of the American Veterinary Medical Association* **156,** 208-212.

Alford, B. T., Burkhard, R. L. & Johnson, W. P. (1974). Etorphine and diprenorphine as immobilizing and reversing agents in captive and free-ranging mammals. *Journal of the American Veterinary Medical Association* **165,** 702-705.

Allam, M. W. & Churchill, E. A. (1946). Pentobarbital sodium anaesthesia in swine and goats. *Journal of the American Veterinary Medical Association* **109,** 355-361.

Allison, A. C. (1972). Analogies between triggering mechanisms in immune and other cellular reactions. In *Cell interactions* (ed. L. G. Silvestri), pp. 156-161. Amsterdam: North Holland.

Allison, A. C. & Nunn, J. F. (1968). Effects of general anaesthetics on microtubules. *Lancet* 1968 **2,** 1326–1329.

Altman, P. L. & Dittmer, D. S. (1961). *Blood and other body fluids,* Federation of American Societies for Experimental Biology, Washington, D.C.

Altman, P. L. & Dittmer, D. S. (1964). *Biology data book,* Federation of American Societies for Experimental Biology, Washington, D.C.

Altman, P. L. & Dittmer, D. S. (1974). *Biology data book—2nd Edition,* Federation of American Societies for Experimental Biology, Washington, D.C.

Amend, J. F., Klavano, P. A. & Stone, E. C. (1972). Premedication with xylazine (Rompun) to eliminate muscular hypertonicity in cats during ketamine anesthesia. *Veterinary Medicine—Small Animal Clinician* **67,** 1305-1307.

Anderson, J. C. (1967). A simple method of anaesthesia in the fowl. *Veterinary Record* **81,** 130-131.

Anderson, D. M. & Elsley, F. W. H. (1969). A note on the use of indwelling catheters in conscious adult pig. *Journal of Agricultural Science, Cambridge* **72,** 415-477.

Anderson, J. M. & Benirschke, K. (1966). The armadillo, *Dasypus novemcinctus* in experimental biology. *Laboratory Animal Care* **16,** 202-216.

Arbon, D. H. & Theye, R. A. (1972). Lactic acidaemia during hemorrhagic hypotension and cyclopropane anesthesia. *Anesthesiology* **37,** 634-640.

Archer, R. K. (1965). *Haematological techniques for use on animals,* p. 11. Oxford: Blackwell.

Arnall, L. (1964). Aspects of anaesthesia in cagebirds. In *Small animal anaesthesia* (ed. O. Graham-Jones), pp. 137-146. Oxford: Pergamon.

Aronson, H. B., Robin, G. C., Weinberg, G. & Nathan, H. (1965). Some observations on general anesthesia in the baboon. *Anesthesia and Analgesia: Current Researches* **44,** 289.

Askrog, V. & Harvard, B. (1970). Teratogen effekt af inhalationsanaestetika. *Nordisk Medicin* **83,** 498-500.

Attinger, E. O. & Cahill, J. M. (1960). Cardiopulmonary mechanics in anesthetised pigs and dogs. *American Journal of Physiology* **198,** 346-348.

Auerbach, C. (1967). The chemical production of mutations. *Science, New York* **158,** 1141–1146.

Ayre, P. (1956). The T-piece technique. *British Journal of Anaesthesia* **28,** 520-523.

Azzoli, S. G., Shahinian, T. K. & Ghing, J. (1972). Correlation among mean central venous pressure, mean pulmonary wedge pressure and cardiac output after acute hemorrhage and replacement with Ringer's lactate sodium in the dog. *American Journal of Surgery* **123,** 385-392.

Bachrach, A. (1954). Strictly for the birds. *Veterinary Excerpts, New York* **14,** 99.

Backhouse, K. M. (1964). Anaesthesia of marine mammals. In *Small animal anaesthesia* (ed. O. Graham-Jones), pp. 79-86. Oxford: Pergamon.

Baer, H. (1971). Long-term isolation stress and its effects on drug response in rodents. *Laboratory Animal Science* **21,** 341-349.

Baez, S. (1971). Anesthesia and the microcirculation. *Anesthesiology* **35,** 333-334.

Bailey, R. E. (1953). Surgery for sexing and observing gonad conditions in birds. *Auk* **70,** 497-499.

Baily, T. N. (1971). Immobilization of bobcats, coyotes and badgers with phencyclidine hydrochloride. *Journal of Wildlife Management* **35,** 847-849.

Baker, J. B. (1955). Experiments on the humane killing of crabs. *Journal of the Marine Biology Association of the United Kingdom* **34,** 15-24.

Baker, L. N. & Andresen, E. (1964). Restraining rack and blood collecting technique for large pigs. *American Journal of Veterinary Research* **25,** 1559-1560.

Baker, P. G. & Reitter, F. H. (1976). An evaluation of alphaxolone and alphadolone ('Saffan') for sedation of pigs. *International Research Communication Systems*.

Ball, D. J. (1974). Handling and restraint of reptiles. *International Zoo Yearbook 14,* 138-140.

Ball, J. N. & Slicher, A. M. (1962). Influence of hypophysectomy and of an adreno-cortical inhibitor (SU-4885) on the stress response of the white blood cells in the teleost fish *Mollienesia catipinna*. *Nature, London* **196,** 1331-1332.

Banerjee, C. J., Alarie, Y. & Woolard, M. (1968). Gas tension in conscious monkeys. *Proceedings of the Society for Experimental Biology and Medicine* **128,** 1183-1185.

Bannister, W. K., Sattilaro, A. J. & Otis, R. D. (1961). Therapeutic aspects of aspiration pneumonitis in experimental animals. *Anesthesiology* **22,** 440-443.

Barger, E. H., Card, L. E. & Pomeroy, B. S. (1958). In *Diseases and parasites of poultry*, 5th ed., p. 56. Philadelphia: Lea & Febiger.

Bartels, H. & Harms, H. (1959). Oxygen dissociation curves in the blood of man, rabbit, guinea-pig, dog, cat, pigs, ox and sheep. *Pflügers Archiv für die Gesamte Physiologie des Menschen und der Tiere* **268,** 334-365.

Bastron, R. D. & Deutsch, S. (1976). *Anesthesia and the kidney*, p. 29. New York: Grune & Stratton.

Baudin, L. (1932*a*). Action de la tricaine sur la consommation d'oxygène de *Carassius auratus*. *Comptes rendus des séances de la Société de biologie* **109,** 731-733.

Baudin, L. (1932*b*). Action de la tricaine sur le quotient respiratoire de *Carassius auratus*. *Comptes rendus des séances de la Société de biologie* **109,** 1081-1083.

Baudin, L. (1932*c*). Perte de la sensibilité à la dépression chez les poissons anesthésiés à la tricaine. *Comptes rendus des séances de la Société de biologie* **110,** 151-153.

Bauditz, R. (1972). Sedation, immobilisation and anaesthesia of zoo and wild animals with xylazine. *Veterinary Medicine Review* **3,** 204-206.

Baxter, J. S. & Evans, J. M. (1973). Intramuscular injection in the cat. *Journal of Small Animal Practice* **14,** 297-302.

Beaton, J. M. & Gilbert, R. M. (1968). Injection controls for drug studies. *Nature, London* **218,** 391-392.

Beck, C. C. (1972). Chemical restraint of exotic species. *Journal of Zoo Animal Medicine* **3,** 3-66.

Beck, C. C., Coppock, R. W. & Ott, B. S. (1971). Evaluation of Vetalar (ketamine HCl) a unique feline anesthetic. *Veterinary Medicine—Small Animal Clinician* **66,** 993-996.

Beck, C. C. & Dresner, A. J. (1972). Vetalar (ketamine HCl) a cataleptoid anesthetic agent for primate species. *Veterinary Medicine—Small Animal Clinician* **67,** 1082-1084.

Becker, R. F., Flannagan, E. & King, J. E. (1958). The fate of offspring from mothers receiving sodium pentobarbital before delivery: a study in the guinea-pig. *Neurology, Minneapolis* **8,** 776-782.

Becker, M. J. & Koppe, J. G. (1969). Pulmonary structural changes in neonatal hyaline membrane disease treated with high pressure artificial respiration. *Thorax* **24,** 689-694.

Beks, J. W. F., Doorenbos, H. & Walstra, G. J. M. (1972). In *Steroids and brain edema* (ed. H. J. Reulen & K. Schurmann). Berlin: Springer.

Bell, G. R. (1967). A guide to the properties, characteristics and uses of some general anaesthetics for fish. *Bulletin of the Fisheries Research Board Canada* No. 148.

Bennett, E. J., Daughety, M. J. & Jenkins, M. T. (1970). Some controversial aspects of fluids for the anesthetised neonate. *Anesthesia and Analgesia: Current Researches*. **49,** 478-486.

Bennett, R. R. (1968). The use of metofane in experimental laboratory birds. *Practising Veterinarian* **40,** 184-187.

Bennett, R. R. (1969). Methoxyflurane anesthesia in the sub-human primate. *Practising Veterinarian* **41,** 20-22.

Bennett, R. R. (1969). The clinical use of 2-(ethylamino)-2-(2-enenyl)cyclohexanone-HCl (CI-634) as an anesthetic for the cat. *American Journal of Veterinary Research* **30,** 1469-1470.

Bergeron, J. L., Shinaberger, J. H., Frederickson, E. L., Martinez, F. J. & Buckalew, V. M. (1966). The effect of methoxyflurane (M) anesthesia on renal tubular handling of water. Paper presented at the *Southern Anesthesia Society Meeting, 1966*.

Bernard, G. R. (1961). Experimental trichinosis in the golden hamster. IV. Some observations on the leukocytic response. *Journal of Parasitology* **47,** 721-726.

Betteridge, K. J. (1973). A simple and inexpensive apparatus for halothane anaesthesia in rabbits and other small animals. *Veterinary Record* **93,** 398-399.

Betz, T. W. (1962). Surgical anesthesia in reptiles with special reference to the water snake (*Natrix rhombifera*). *Copeia* 284-287.

Bevan, J. C. & Burn, M. C. (1973). Acid base and blood glucose levels of paediatric cases at induction of anaesthesia: the effects of pre-operative starvation and feeding. *British Journal of Anaesthesia* **45**, 115.

Beyer, K. H., Stutzman, J. W. & Hafford, B. (1944). The relation of vitamin C to anesthesia. *Surgery, Gynecology and Obstetrics* **79**, 49-56.

Biester, H. E. & Schwarte, L. H. (1962). *Disease of poultry*, 4th ed., p. 931. Ames: Iowa State College Press.

Bieter, R. N., Harvey, A. M. & Burgess, W. E. (1932). Spinal anaesthesia in summer frogs. *Journal of Pharmacology and Experimental Therapeutics* **45**, 291-298.

Bigelow, W. G., Lindsay, W. K., Harrison, R. C., Gordon, R. A. & Greenwood, W. F. (1950). Oxygen transport and utilization in dogs at low body temperatures. *American Journal of Physiology* **160**, 125-129.

Bigler, W. J. & Hoff, G. L. (1974). Anesthesia of raccoons with ketamine hydrochloride. *Journal of Wildlife Management* **38**, 364-366.

Binns, R. & Clark, G. C. (1972). Lung function in cynomolgus monkeys and baboons. *Folia primatologica* **17**, 209-217.

Binns, R., Clark, G. C. & Simpson, C. R. (1972). Lung function and blood gas characteristics in the rhesus monkey. *Laboratory Animals* **6**, 189-198.

Biver, A., Jacquet, N., Moor, M. C. & Lamy, M. (1975). Combined azaperone and metomidate anaesthesia in liver transplantation in the pig. *European Surgical Research* **8**, 81-88.

Blalock, A. (1928). The effects of ether, chloroform and ethyl chloride anaesthetics on the minute cardiac output and blood pressure. *Surgery, Gynecology and Obstetrics* **46**, 72-78.

Blane, G. F., Boura, A. L. A. & Dobbs, H. E. (1968). Neuroleptanalgesia in the dog caused by the interaction of etorphine with methotrimeprazine. *Journal of Physiology, London* **196**, 26–27.

Blane, G. F., Boura, A. L. A., Fitzgerald, A. E. & Lister, R. E. (1967). Actions of etorphine hydrochloride (M-99). A potent morphine-like agent. *British Journal of Pharmacology and Chemotherapy* **30**, 11-22.

Bloom, R. F., Costa, E. & Salmoiraghi, G. C. (1965). Anesthesia and the responsiveness of individual neurons of the caudate nucleus of the cat to acetylcholine, norephinephrine, and dopamine administered by electrophoresis. *Journal of Pharmacology and Experimental Therapeutics* **150**, 244-252.

Blume, W. & Sroka, K. (1943). Comparative studies on the action of paraldehyde and methaldehyde on frogs, fishes and leeches. *Naunyn-Schmiedebergs Archives für experimentelle Pathologie und Pharmakologie* **202**, 1-20.

Blythe, W. B., D'Avila, D., Gitelman, H. J. & Welt, L. G. (1971). Further evidence for a humoral natriuretic hormone. *Circulation Research* **29**, Suppl. II, 21-31.

Boelaert, R. (1941). Sur la physiologie de la respiration des lacertiens. *Archives internationales de physiologie et de biochimie* **51**, 379–437.

Boelaert, R. (1942). Sur la physiologie de la respiration de l'alligator mississippiensis. *Archives internationales de physiologie et de biochimie* **52**, 57–72.

Boever, W. J. & Wright, W. (1975). Use of ketamine for restraint and anesthesia of birds. *Veterinary Medicine—Small Animal Clinician* **70**, 86-88.

Booth, N. H. (1961). Cited by Lumb, W. V. & Jones, E. W. (1973) in *Veterinary anesthesia*, Philadelphia: Lea & Febiger.

Booth, N. H. (1963). Cited by Lumb, W. V. & Jones, E. W. (1973). in *Veterinary anesthesia*, p. 474. Philadelphia: Lea & Febiger.

Booth, N. H. (1965). Local anesthetics. In *Veterinary pharmacology and therapeutics*, 3rd ed. (ed. L. M. Jones), Ch. 20. Ames, Iowa State University Press.

Booth, N. H. (1969). Anesthesia in the pig. *Federation Proceedings* **28**, 1547-1552.

Booth, N. H., Bredeck, H. E. & Herin, R. A. (1965). Baroreceptor and chemoreceptor reflex mechanism in swine. In *Swine in medical research* (ed. L. K. Bustad & R. O. McClellan), pp. 331–346. Seattle: Frayn.

Booth, N. H. & Rankin, A. D. (1954). Evaluation of meperidine hydrochloride in the cat. *Veterinary Medicine* **49**, 249-252.

Boothe, H. W. (1953). Diseases of the chinchilla. *Proceedings of the American Veterinary Medical Association 19th Annual Meeting*, 1953.

Bordet, R., Boivin, R., Piquereau, M. & Sevestre, J. (1967). General anesthesia with phencyclidine in cats and monkeys. *Recueil de Médecine Vétérinaire de L'Ecole d'Alfort* **143**, 399-409.

Borrie, J. & Mitchell, R. M. (1960). The sheep as an experimental animal in surgical science. *British Journal of Surgery* **47**, 435-445.

Borrie, J. & Woodruff, M. F. A. (1955). A technique for hypothermia in sheep. *Proceedings of the University of Otago Medical School* **33**, 33-34.

Borzio, F. (1973). Ketamine hydrochloride as an anesthetic for wildfowl. *Veterinary Medicine—Small Animal Clinician* **68**, 1364-1367.

Bourgeois-Gavardin, M., Nowill, W. K., Margolis, G. & Stephen, C. R. (1955). Chlorpromazine: A laboratory and clinical investigation. *Anesthesiology* **16**, 829-847.

Boutelle, J. L. & Rich, S. T. (1969). An anesthetic chamber for prolonged immobilization of mice during tumour transplantation and radiation procedures. *Laboratory Animal Care* **19**, 666-667.

Bowman, W. C. Rand, M. J. & West, G. B. (1968). *Textbook of pharmacology*, p. 559. Oxford: Blackwell.

Boyd, D. R., Folk, F. A., Condon, R. F., Nyhus, L. M. & Baker, R. J. (1970). Predictive value of serum osmolality in shock following major trauma. *Surgical Forum* **21**, 32-33.

Boyes, J. E. & Howells, T. H. (1972). Humidification in anaesthesia. *British Journal of Anaesthesia* **44**, 879-886.

Box, P. G. & Ellis, K. R. (1973). Use of CT1341 anaesthetic ('Saffan') in monkeys *Laboratory Animals* **7**, 161-170.

255

Brackenbury, J. H. (1972). Physical determinants of airflow pattern within the avian lung. *Respiratory Physiology* **15**, 384-397.

Bradley, E. C. (1965). Results with phentolamine (Regitine) in the treatment of selected patients with shock. *California Medicine* **103**, 314-315.

Bradley, W. A. (1966). Epidural analgesia for tail docking in lambs. *Veterinary Record* **79**, 787-788.

Bree, M. M. (1967). Clinical use of the short acting anesthetic 2-(O-chlorophenyl)-2-methylamino cyclohexanone hydrochloride (CI-581) in *Macaca mulatta*, *Macaca irus*, and *Macaca nemastrina* monkeys. *Laboratory Animal Care* **17**, 547-550.

Bree, M. M. (1972). Clinical evaluation of tiletamine as an anesthetic in six non-human primate species. *Journal of the American Veterinary Medical Association*, **161**, 693-695.

Bree, M. M. & Cohen, B. J. (1965). Effects of urethane anaesthesia on blood and blood vessels in rabbits. *Laboratory Animal Care* **15**, 254-259.

Bree, M. M., Cohen, B. H. & Abrams, G. D. (1971). Injection lesions following intramuscular administration of chlorpromazine in rabbits. *Journal of the American Veterinary Medical Association* **159**, 1598-1602.

Bree, M. M., Cohen, B. J. & Rowe, S. E. (1972). Dissociative anesthesia in dogs and primates, clinical evaluation of C1744. *Laboratory Animal Science* **22**, 878-881.

Bree, M. M., Feller, I. & Corssen, G. (1967). Safety and tolerance of repeated anesthesia with CI-581 (Ketamine) in monkeys. *Anesthesia and Analgesia: Current Researches* **46**, 596–600.

Bree, M. M. & Gross, N. B. (1969). Anesthesia of pigeons with CI581 (Ketamine) and Pentobarbital. *Laboratory Animal Care* **19**, 500-502.

Brewis, R. A. L. (1969). Clinical measurements relevant to the assessment of hypoxia. *British Journal of Anaesthesia* **41**, 742-750.

Brewster, W. R., Bunker, J. P. & Beecher, H. E. (1952). Metabolic effects of anesthesia VI. Mechanism of metabolic acidosis and hyperglycemia during ether anesthesia in the dog. *American Journal of Physiology* **171**, 37-47.

Brinker, W. O. (1951). Use of surital sodium and curare in small-animal surgery. *North American Veterinarian* **32**, 832–834.

Brisbin, I. L. J. (1966). Reactions of the American alligator to several immobilising drugs. *Copeia* 129-130.

Britton, B. J., Wood, W. G. & Irving, M. N. (1974). Sedation of sheep and patas monkeys with ketamine. *Laboratory Animals* **8**, 41-44.

Brockway, J. M. & McEwan, E. H. (1969). Oxygen uptake and cardiac performance in the sheep. *Journal of Physiology, London* **202**, 661–669.

Brodie, B. B., Bernstein, E. & Mark, L. C. (1952). The role of body fat in limiting the duration of action of thiopental. *Journal of Pharmacology and Experimental Therapeutics* **105**, 421-426.

Brody, S. (1945). *Bioenergetics and growth*, New York: Rheinhold.

Brook, G. B. (1958). Accidents associated with anaesthesia. *Veterinary Record* **70**, 944.

Brown, A. M. (1959). The investigation of specific responses in laboratory animals. *Laboratory Animals Centre Collected Papers* **8**, 9-16.

Brown, A. M. & Dinsley, M. (1967). Skin grafting and the homogeneity of inbred mouse strains. *Laboratory Animals* **1**, 81-89.

Brown, A. K. & Zuelzer, W. W. (1958). Studies on the neonatal development of glucuronide conjugating system. *Journal of Clinical Investigation* **37**, 332-340.

Brown, R. V. & Hilton, J. G. (1956). The effectiveness of the baroreceptor reflexes under different anesthetics. *Journal of Pharmacology and Experimental Therapeutics* **118**, 198-203.

Bruce, D. L., Eide, K. A., Linde, H. W. & Eckenhoff, J. E. (1968). Causes of death among anaesthesiologists: a 20-year survey. *Anesthesiology* **29**, 565-569.

Bryant, S. H. (1969). General anaesthesia in the goat. *Federation Proceedings* **28**, 1553-1556.

Buchanan, J. W. (1965). Spontaneous arrhythmias and conduction disturbances in domestic animals. *Annals of the New York Academy of Science* **127**, 224-238.

Buchsbaum, M. & Buchsbaum, R. (1962). Age and ether anaesthesia in mice. *Proceedings of the Society for Experimental Biology and Medicine* **109**, 68-70.

Burger, R. E. & Lorenz, F. W. (1960). Artificial respiration in birds by unidirectional air flow. *Poultry Science* **39**, 236-237.

Burke, T. J. & Wall, B. E. (1970). Anesthetic deaths in cobras (*Naja naja* and *Ophiagus hannah*) with methoxyflurane. *Journal of the American Veterinary Medical Association* **157**, 620-621.

Burkhart, R. L. (1967). Evaluation of M-99 (etorphine) and antagonists, nalorphine and M-285 (cyprenorphine) in wild animals. *Research and Development Agricultural Division*. Princeton, N.J.: American Cyanamid Co.

Burns, J. J., Cucinell, S. A., Koster, R. & Conney, A. H. (1965). Application of drug metabolism to drug toxicity studies. *Annals of the New York Academy of Science* **123**, 273-286.

Burton, G. W. (1969). Measurement of inspired and expired oxygen and carbon dioxide. *British Journal of Anaesthesia* **41**, 723-730.

Butterworth, K. R., Shillito, E. E., Spencer, K. E. V. & Stewart, H. C. (1962). The laboratory use of *Myocastor coypus* (the coypu). *Journal of Physiology, London* **162**, 36–37.

Byles, P. H. (1960). Observations on some continuously-acting spirometers. *British Journal of Anaesthesia* **32**, 470-475.

Byrom, F. B. & Wilson, C. (1938). A plethysmographic method for measuring systolic blood pressure in the intact rat. *Journal of Physiology, London* **93**, 301–306.

Bywater, J. E. C. & Rutty, D. A. (1964). Simple techniques for simian anaesthesia. In *Small animal anaesthesia* (ed. O. Graham-Jones), pp. 9-18. Oxford: Pergamon.

Cairy, C. F., Leash, A. & Sisodia, C. S. (1961). Comparison of several drugs in treating acute barbiturate depression in the dog. II. Pairs of drugs. *Journal of the American Veterinary Medical Association* **138**, 132-135.

Calderwood, H. W. (1971). Anesthesia for reptiles. *Journal of the American Veterinary Medical Association* **159**, 1618-1625.

Calderwood, H. W., Klide, A. M. & Cohn, B. B. (1971). Cardiorespiratory effects of tiletamine in cats. *American Journal of Veterinary Research* **32,** 1511-1515.

Cale, J. O., Parks, C. R. & Jenkins, M. T. (1962). Hepatic and renal effects of methoxyflurane in dogs. *Anesthesiology* **23,** 248-250.

Callamand, O., Fontaine, M., Olivereau, M. & Raffy, A. (1951). Hypophyse et osmorégulation chez les poissons. *Bulletin de l'Institut Oceanographique de Monaco* **984,** 1-7.

Callear, J. F. F. (1971). Use of the hypnotic agent methoxymol (R7315) in birds of prey. *Veterinary Record* **88,** 242.

Callear, J. F. F. & Van Gestal, J. F. E. (1973). An analysis of the results of field experiments in pigs in the U.K. and Eire with the combination anaesthetic azaperone and metomidate. *Veterinary Record* **92,** 284-287.

Cannell, H. (1972). Pentobarbitone sodium anaesthesia for oral and immunological procedures in the guinea-pig. *Laboratory Animals* **6,** 55-60.

Cannell, H. (1973). Personal communication.

Cannon, W. B. (1929). *Bodily changes in pain, hunger, fear and rage,* 2nd ed. New York: Appleton.

Capel-Edward, S. M. (1967). Management of the coypu. *Journal of the Animal Technicians Association* **18,** 60-65.

Carey, F. M. & Sanford, J. (1963). Tranquillisers in equine practice. *Proceedings of the 2nd Annual Congress of the British Equine Veterinary Association,* pp. 18-25.

Caridis, D. T. Reinhold, R. B., Woodruff, P. W. M. & Fine, J. (1972). Endotoxaemia in man. *Lancet* 1972 **1,** 1381–1385.

Carle, B. N. & Dewhirst, W. H. (1942). A method for bleeding swine. *Journal of the American Veterinary Medical Association* **101,** 495-498.

Carmalt, T. M. & Whitehead, T. B. (1966). Alkalaemia following surgery. *British Journal of Surgery* **53,** 987–988.

Carmichael, E. B. & Posey, L. C. (1937). Nembutal anaesthesia. I. Toxicity of Nembutal (pentobarbitone sodium) for guinea pigs. *Anaesthesia and Analgesia: Current Researches* **16,** 156-162.

Carson, S. A. A., Chorley, G. E., Hamilton, F. N., Lee, D. C. & Morris, L. E. (1966). Variations in cardiac output with acid-base changes in the anesthetized dog. *Journal of Applied Physiology* **20,** 948-953.

Carter, H. E. (1964). Induction of anaesthesia in dogs by the inhalation of nitrous oxide, halothane and oxygen. *Veterinary Record* **76,** 147-148.

Carvell, J. E. & Stoward, P. J. (1975). Halothane anaesthesia of normal and dystrophic hamsters. *Laboratory Animals* **9,** 345-352.

Casteel, D. A. & Edwards, W. R. (1965). Surgical anaesthesia for cottontails. *Journal of Wildlife Management* **29,** 196-198.

Casteels, M., Van Hoof, J. & Eeckhout, W. (1969). The influence of azaperone on the meat quality of fattening pigs. *Tijdschrift voor Diergeneeskunde* **94,** 883-895.

Castrejon, B. B. & Flores, I. S. (1953). Estudio de los factores que determinan los alteraciones cromaticas en *Carassius auratus.* 1. Tecnica de hipofisectomia. *Revista de la Sociedad mexicana de historia natural* **14,** 59-61.

Chalstrey, L. J. & Edwards, G. B. (1972). Fatal hyperpyrexia following the use of pancuronium bromide in the pig. *British Journal of Anaesthesia* **44,** 91-92.

Chance, M. R. A. (1947). Factors influencing the toxicity of sympathomimetic amines to solitary mice. *Journal of Pharmacology and Experimental Therapeutics* **89,** 289-296.

Chang, P., Chan, K. E. & Ganendran, A. (1969). Cardiovascular effects of 2-(O-chlorophenyl)-2-methylaminocyclohexanone (CI-581) in rats. *British Journal of Anaesthesia* **41,** 391-395.

Chapman, R. L., Modell, J. H., Ruiz, B. C., Calderwood, H. W., Hood, C. I. & Graves, S. A. (1974). Effect of continuous positive-pressure ventilation and steroids on aspiration of hydrochloric acid (ph 1.8) in dogs. *Anesthesia and Analgesia: Current Researches* **53,** 556–562.

Chaudrey, I. H., Sayeed, M. M. & Baue, A. E. (1974). Effect of adenosine triphosphate-magnesium chloride administration in shock. *Surgery* **75,** 220–227.

Chavin, W. & Young, J. E. (1970). Factors in the determination of normal serum glucose levels of goldfish (*Carassius auratus*). *Comparative Biochemistry and Physiology* **33,** 629-653.

Cheetham, R. W. S. (1934). Premature artificial systoles in the baboon. *South African Medical Journal* **8,** 739-740.

Chen, G. & Bohner, B. (1968). Surgical anesthesia in the rabbit with 2-(Ethylamino)-2-(2-Thienyl) Cyclohexanone HCl (CI 634) and chloral hydrate. *American Journal of Veterinary Research* **29,** 869-875.

Chen, G., Ensor, C. R. & Bohner, B. (1966). The neuropharmacology of 2-(O-Chlorophenyl)-2-methylaminocyclohexanone hydrochloride. *Journal of Pharmacology and Experimental Therapeutics* **152,** 332-339.

Chen, G. M., Ensor, C. R., Russell, D. & Bohner, B. (1959). The pharmacology of 1-(1-phenyl-cyclohexyl)pyserdine HCl. *Journal of Pharmacology and Experimental Therapeutics* **127,** 241-250.

Chen, G. M. & Weston, J. K. (1960). The analgesic and anesthetic effect of 1-(1-phenylcyclohexyl) piperidine HCl on the monkey. *Anesthesia and Analgesia: Current Researches* **39,** 132-137.

Chenoweth, M. B. (1965). Physiologic and biochemical responses to methoxyflurane anesthesia. In *Experimental animal anesthesiology* (ed. D. C. Sawyer), Brooks Air Force Base, Texas: U.S.A.F. School of Aerospace Medicine.

Chenoweth, M. B., Robertson, D. N., Erley, D. S. & Gohlke, R. (1962). Blood and tissue levels of ether, chloroform, halothane and methoxyflurane in dogs. *Anesthesiology* **23,** 101-106.

Child, K. J., Currie, J. P., Davis, B., Dodds, M. G., Pearce, D. R. & Twissell, D. J. (1971). The pharmacological properties in animals of CT1341—a new steroid anaesthetic agent. *British Journal of Anaesthesia* **43,** 2-13.

Chitty, D. (1967). In *The UFAW handbook on the care and management of laboratory animals,* p. 321. Edinburgh: Livingstone.

257

Church, J. C. T. & Noronha, R. F. X. (1965). The use of the fruit bat in surgical research. *East African Medical Journal* **42**, 348-355.

Church, L. E. (1957). Combuthal as an anaesthetic for baby chicks. *Poultry Science* **36**, 788-791.

Cisar, C. F. (1969). The rat kangaroo (*Potorous tridactylus*). Handling and husbandry practices in a research facility. *Laboratory Animal Care* **19**, 55-59.

Cisar, C. F. (1973). The use of a butcher's boning glove for handling small laboratory animals. *Laboratory Animals* **7**, 139-140.

Clarke, K. (1969). Effect of azaperone on the blood pressure and pulmonary ventilation of pigs. *Veterinary Record* **85**, 649-651.

Clarke, K. & Hall, L. W. (1969). Xylazine, a new sedative for horses and cattle. *Veterinary Record* **85**, 512-517.

Clarke, R. S. J. & Dundee, J. W. (1966). Survey of experimental and clinical pharmacology of propanidid. *Anesthesia and Analgesia: Current Researches* **45**, 250-276.

Clements, J. A. & Wilson, K. M. (1962). The affinity of narcotic agents for interfacial films. *Proceedings of the National Academy of Sciences, U.S.A.* **48**, 1008-1014.

Clifford, D. H. (1957). Effect of preanesthetic medication with chlorpromazine, meperidine and promazine on pentobarbital anesthesia in the cat. *Journal of the American Veterinary Medical Association* **131**, 415-419.

Clifford, D. H. & Soma, L. R. (1969). Feline anesthesia. *Federation Proceedings. Federation of American Societies for Experimental Biology* **28**, 1479-1499.

Cline, D. R. & Greenwood, R. J. (1972). Effect of certain anesthetic agents on mallard ducks. *Journal of the American Veterinary Medical Association* **161**, 624-633.

Cloetta, M. (1908). On the behavior of atropine in animal species with different sensitivities. *Archiv für experimentelle Pathologie und Pharmakologie* **23**, 119-125.

Clutton Brock, J. (1960). Some pain threshold studies with particular reference to thiopentone. *Anaesthesia* **15**, 71-72.

Cohen, B. (1964). An anaesthetic method for oral surgery on monkeys. In *Small animal anaesthesia* (ed. O. Graham-Jones), pp. 19-25. Oxford: Pergamon.

Cohen, B. (1970). Personal communication.

Collan, R. (1970). Anaesthetic and paraoperative management of sheep for total heart replacement. *Anesthesia and Analgesia* **49**, 336-343.

Collins, T. B. & Lott, D. F. (1965). Stock and sex specificity in the response of rats to pentobarbital sodium. *Laboratory Animal Care* **18**, 192-194.

Colman, R. W., Robboy, S. J. & Minna, J. D. (1972). Disseminated intravascular coagulation: an approach. *Journal of the American Medical Assocation* **52**, 679-681.

Comline, R. S. & Silver, M. (1970). Daily changes in foetal and maternal blood of conscious pregnant ewes, with catheters in umbilical and uterine vessels. *Journal of Physiology, London* **209**, 567-586.

Commons, M. (1970). Clinical experiences with ketamine hydrochloride as an intramuscular general anesthetic in the cat. *Veterinary Medicine—Small Animal Clinician* **65**, 1151-1152.

Comroe, J. H. (1965). *Physiology of respiration: an introductory text.* Chicago: Year Book Medical Publishers.

Conner, G. H., Coppock, R. W. & Beck, C. C. (1974). Laboratory use of CI-744, a cataleptoid anesthetic, in sheep. *Veterinary Medicine—Small Animal Clinician*, 479-482.

Conney, A. H. & Burns, J. J. (1962). Factors influencing drug metabolism. *Advances in Pharmacology* **1**, 31-58.

Constantin, B., Condat, P., Jourde, M., Condat, M. & Lapalus, P. (1971). Some effects of ketamine on cardiac circulation in chloralosed dog. *Comptes rendus des séances de la Société de biologie* **165**, 299-300.

Conway, C. M. & Ellis, D. B. (1970). Propanidid. *British Journal of Anaesthesia* **42**, 249-254.

Cook, R. & Dorman, R. G. (1969). Anaesthesia of germ-free rabbits and rats with halothane. *Laboratory Animals* **3**, 101-106.

Cook, T. L., Beppu, W. J., Hitt, B. A., Kosek, J. C. & Mazze, R. I. (1975). Renal effects and metabolism of sevoflurane in Fischer 344 rats: and *in vivo* and *in vitro* comparison with methoxyflurane. *Anesthesiology* **43**, 70–77.

Cooley, D. A., Beall, A. C. & Grondin, R. (1962). Open heart surgery by a simplified technique: using disposable oxygenators, 5 per cent dextrose solution prime, and normothermia. *Presented at Foundation Cardiologique Princesse Liliane International Cardiology Symposium.* Belgium: Brussels.

Cooper, E. A. (1969). The measurement of ventilation. *British Journal of Anaesthesia* **41**, 718-722.

Cooper, J. E. (1968). The trained falcon in health and disease. *Journal of Small Animal Practice* **9**, 559-566.

Cooper, J. E. (1970). Use of the hypnotic agent methoxymol in birds of prey. *Veterinary Record* **87**, 751-752.

Cooper, J. E. (1974a). Metomidate anaesthesia of some birds of prey for laparotomy and sexing. *Veterinary Record* **94**, 437-440.

Cooper, J. E. (1974b). Ketamine hydrochloride as an anaesthetic for East African reptiles. *Veterinary Record* **95**, 37-41.

Cooper, J. E. (1976). Anaesthesia and surgery in reptiles. *Report of the Cotswold Herpetological Society Symposium 1976*, pp. 16-20.

Cooper, J. E. (1977). Personal communication.

Cooper, J. E. & Frank, L. (1973). Use of the steroid anaesthetic CT1341 in birds. *Veterinary Record* **92**, 474-479.

Cooper, J. E., Needham, J. R. & Hetherington, C. M. (1977). The use of a simple barrier system to exclude murine pathogens. *Laboratory Animals* **11**, 47-48.

Cooper, J. E. & Redig, P. T. (1975). Unexpected reactions to the use of CT1341 by red-tailed hawks. *Veterinary Record* **97**, 352.

Copenhaver, W. M. (1939). Initiation of beat and intrinsic contraction rates in the different parts of the amblyostoma heart. *Journal of Experimental Zoology* **80,** 193-224.

Coran, A. G. (1973). The long-term total intravenous feeding of infants using peripheral veins. *Journal of Paediatric Surgery* **8,** 801-807.

Corley, W. D., Versteeg, J. D., Mulligan, R. M. & Virtue, R. M. (1969). Oral and rectal administration of thiopental to dogs. *Anesthesia and Analgesia: Current Researches* **48,** 438-442.

Corssen, G. & Domino, E. F. (1966). Dissociative anesthesia: further pharmacologic studies and first clinical experience with the phencyclidine derivative CI-581. *Anesthesia and Analgesia: Current Researches* **45,** 29-40.

Corssen, G., Miyasaka, M. & Domino, E. G. (1968). Changing concepts in pain control during surgery: dissociative, anesthesia with CI581. *Anesthesia and Analgesia: Current Researches* **47,** 746-759.

Corssen, G., Sweet, R. B. & Chenoweth, M. B. (1966). Effects of chloroform, halothane and methoxyflurane on human liver cells *in vitro. Anaesthesiology* **27,** 155-162.

Coultas, R. J., Strunin, L., Walder, W. D., Strunin, J. M., Reynard, A. & Simpson, B. R. (1969). A comparison of the effects of halothane and methoxyflurane on the isolated perfused canine liver. *British Journal of Anaesthesia* **41,** 790-791.

Courtin, R. F., Bickford, R. G. & Faulconer, A. (1950). Classification and significance of electro-encephalographic patterns produced by nitrous oxide-ether anesthesia during surgical operations. *Proceedings of Staff Meetings, Mayo Clinic* **25,** 197-206.

Courvoisier, S., Fournel, J., Ducrot, R., Kolsky, M. & Koetschet, P. (1953). Pharmacodynamic properties of 3 - chloro - 10(3 - dimethylaminopropyl) - phenothiazine hydrochloride. *Archives Internationales de Pharmacodynamie et de Therapie* **92,** 305-361.

Cousins, M. J., Mazze, R. I., Kosek, J. C., Hitt, B. A. & Love, F. V. (1974). The etiology of methoxyflurane nephrotoxicity. *Journal of Pharmacology and Experimental Therapy* **190,** 530-541.

Cox, J. E. (1973). Immobilization and anaesthesia of the pig. *Veterinary Record* **92,** 143-147.

Cox, J. E., Done, S. E., Lees, P. & Walton, J. R. (1975). Preliminary studies of the actions of alphaxolone and alphadolone in the pig. *Veterinary Record* **97,** 497-498.

Crandell, W. B. & MacDonald, A. (1968). Nephropathy associated with methoxyflurane anesthesia. *Journal of the American Medical Association* **205,** 789-799.

Crawford, J. M. & Curtis, O. R. (1966). Pharmacological studies of feline Betz cells. *Journal of Physiology* **186,** 121-138.

Crevier, M., D'Lorio, A. & Robillard, S. (1950). Influence of the sexual glands on detoxification of pentobarbital by the liver. *Revue canadienne de Biologie* **9,** 336-343.

Cribb, P. H. & Haigh, J. C. (1977). Anaesthetic for avian species. *Veterinary Record* **100,** 472-473.

Cribb, P. H., Hird, J. F. R. & Hall, L. W. (1977). Clinical evaluation of enflurane in the dog. *Veterinary Record* **101,** 50-54.

Crider, E. D. & McDaniel, J. C. (1967). Alpha-chlora-lose used to capture Canada Geese. *Journal of Wildlife Management* **31,** 258-264.

Croft, P. G. (1952). The effect of electrical stimulation of the brain on perception of pain. *Journal of Mental Science* **98,** 421-426.

Croft, P. G. (1960). *An introduction to the anaesthesia of laboratory animals.* London: Universities Federation for Animal Welfare.

Croft, P. G. (1962). The EEG as an aid to diagnosis of nervous diseases in the dog and cat. *Journal of Small Animal Practice* **3,** 205-213.

Croft, P. G. (1964a). Recording of the electro encephalogram from the conscious dog. *Journal of Small Animal Practice* **5,** 540.

Croft, P. G. (1964b). Problems of anaesthesia in the rabbit. In *Small animal anaesthesia* (ed. O. Graham-Jones), pp. 99-102. Oxford: Pergamon.

Croft, P. G. & Hume, C. W. (1956). Electric stunning of sheep. *Veterinary Record* **68,** 318-321.

Crooks, J. L., Whiteley, H., Jenkins, J. T. & Blane, G. F. (1970). The use of a new analgesic-tranquilliser mixture in dogs. *Veterinary Record* **87,** 498-502.

Crosbie, W. A., Snowden, S. & Parsons, V. (1972). Changes in lung capillary permeability in renal failure. *British Medical Journal* **4,** 388-390.

Crosfill, M. L. & Widdicombe, J. G. (1961). Physical characteristics of the chest and lungs and the work of breathing in different mammalian species. *Journal of Physiology, London* **158,** 1-14.

Czajkowski, J., Deszkiewicz, A., Polanski, J., Ruka, M. & Olszewski, W. (1976). Anaesthesia for orthotopic allogenic liver transplantation in pigs. *Anaesthesia, Resuscitation and Intensive Therapy, Warsaw* **4,** 149-158.

Dale, H. E., Elefson, E. E. & Niemeyer, K. H. (1968). Influence of environmental temperature on recovery of dogs from pentobarbital anesthesia . *American Journal of Veterinary Research* **29,** 1339-1347.

Dallman, D. E., Lang, J., Larson, S. J., Reigel, D. H. & Sances, A. (1970). Electroanesthesia currents: a comparison. *Medical Research Engineering* **9,** 22-25.

Daniel, M. & Ling, C. M. (1972). The effect of an etorphine-acepromazine mixture on the heart rate and blood pressure of the horse. *Veterinary Record* **90,** 336-339.

Danowski, T. S., Fergus, E. B. & Mateer, F. M. (1955). The low salt syndrome. *Annals of Internal Medicine* **43,** 643-657.

Danscher, G. (1972). An instrument for immobilization of small experimental animals. *Zeitschrift für Versuchstierkunde* **14,** 69-71.

Darbinjan, T. M., Golovchinsky, V. B. & Plehotkina, S. I. (1971). Effects of anesthetics on reticular and cortical activity. *Anesthesiology* **34,** 219-229.

Davey, D. G. (1962). The use of pathogen free animals. *Proceedings of the Royal Society of Medicine* **55,** 256-259.

Davies, L. & Grice, H. C. (1962). A device for restricting the movements of rats suitable for a variety of procedures. *Canadian Journal of Comparative Medicine and Veterinary Science* **26,** 62-63.

Davis, H. S., Collins, W. F., Randt, C. T. & Dillon, W. H. (1957). Effect of anesthetic agents on evoked central nervous system responses: gaseous agents. *Anesthesiology* **18,** 634-642.

Davis, L. E. & Donnelly, E. J. (1968). Analgesic drugs in the cat. *Journal of the American Veterinary Medical Association* **153,** 1161-1167.

Davis, N. L. & Malinin, T. I. (1974). Rabbit intubation and halothane anesthesia. *Laboratory Animal Science* **24,** 617-621.

Davis, R. A. & Shillito, E. (1967). The coypu or nutria. In *The UFAW handbook on the care and management of laboratory animals.* pp. 457-467. Edinburgh: Livingstone.

Cambridge, G. W. (1962). Anaesthetic procedures suitable for the coypu. *Journal of Physiology* **162,** 48.

Davis, W. M. (1962). Day-night periodicity in pentobarbital response of mice and the influence of sociopsychological conditions. *Experientia* **18,** 235-237.

Dawson, B., Michenfelder, J. D. & Theye, R. A. (1971). Effects of ketamine on canine cerebral blood flow and metabolism: modification by prior administration of thiopental. *Anesthesia and Analgesia: Current Researches* **50,** 443-447.

Dawson, J. B. (1963). Anaesthesia for the experimental pig. *British Journal of Anaesthesia* **35,** 736-746.

Day, P. W. (1965). Anesthetic techniques for the chimpanzee. In *Experimental animal anesthesiology* (ed. D. C. Sawyer). Brooks Air Force Base, Texas: U.S.A.F. School of Aerospace Medicine.

De Boer, A. (1969). Body fluid compartment changes following large volume hemodilution. *Archives of Surgery* **98,** 602-606.

De Boer, B. (1947). Factors affecting pentothal anesthesia in dogs. *Anesthesiology* **8,** 375-381.

Deetjen, P., Boylan, J. W. & Kramer, K. (1975). *Physiology of the kidney and of water balance.* Berlin: Springer.

De Koch, G. & Quinlan, J. (1926). Department of Agriculture, Union of South Africa, 11th and 12th reports, part i, p. 361.

Delay, J. (1959). *Psychopharmacology frontiers.* Boston: Little & Brown.

Delius, J. D. (1966). Pentobarbitone anesthesia in the herring and lesser blackheaded gull. *Journal of Small Animal Practice* **7,** 605–609.

Denckla, W. D. (1970). Minimal oxygen consumption in the female rat, some new definitions and measurements. *Journal of Applied Physiology* **29,** 263-274.

Denney, R. N. (1969). Black rhinoceros immobilisation utilising a new tranquillising agent. *East African Wildlife Journal* **7,** 159-165.

Denny, M. J. S. (1973). The use of ketamine hydrochloride as a safe short duration anaesthetic in kangaroos. *British Veterinary Journal* **129,** 362-365.

Denton, D. A. (1957). The effect of variations in blood supply on the secretion rate and compositon of parotid saliva in Na^+ depleted sheep. *Journal of Physiology, London* **135,** 227–244.

Desforges, M. F. & Scott, H. A. (1971). Use of anaesthetics in the Aylesbury domestic duck. *Research in Veterinary Science* **12,** 596-598.

Desmedt, J. E. & Delwaide, P. J. (1966). Physiological experimentation on the pigeon. *Laboratory Animal Care* **16,** 191-197.

Detweiler, D. K. & Patterson, D. F. (1972). *Equine medicine and surgery.* Wheaton: American Veterinary Publications.

De Young, D. W., Lumb, W. V. & Chase, P. A. (1970). Succinylcholine chloride dosage in miniature swine for the purpose of endotracheal intubation. *Laboratory Animal Science* **20,** 998-1001.

De Young, D. W., Paddleford, R. R. & Short, C. E. (1972). Dissociative anesthetics in the cat and dog. *Journal of the American Veterinary Medical Association* **161,** 1442-1445.

Dhindsa, D. S., Hoversland, A. S. & Kluempke, R. (1970). Halothane semi-closed circuit anesthesia in pygmy and large goats. *American Journal of Veterinary Research* **31,** 1897-1899.

Dick, G. L. (1975). Some observations on the use of MS222 Sandoz with grey mullet (*Mugil chelo*). *Journal of Fish Biology* **7,** 263-268.

Dietz, O., Schmidt, V. & Werner, E. (1961). Vergleichende electrokardio-graphische untersuchungen an pferd und Rind bei Anwend von perpher und zentral angreifenden muskel relaxantien zum zweeke des sogenannten medikamentosen Niederlegens. *Monatscheffe für Veterinarmedizin* **16,** 794-798.

Dilbone, R. P. (1965). Thiamylal anesthesia in a penguin. *Journal of the American Veterinary Medical Association* **147,** 1076.

Dimigen, J. & Reetz, I. (1970). Trials with the neuroleptic azaperone and the hypnotic metomidate for anaesthesia in pigs. *Deutsche tierärztliche Wochenschrift* **77,** 470-473.

Djojosugito, A. M., Folkow, B. & Kovach, G. B. (1968). The mechanism behind the rapid blood volume restoration after haemorrhage in birds. *Acta physiologica scandinavica* **74,** 114-122.

Dobbs, H. E. & Ling, C. M. (1972). The use of etorphine-acepromazine in the horse and donkey. *Veterinary Record* **91,** 40-41.

Dodds, M. G. & Twissell, D. J. (1973). CT.1341 and thiopentone compared in feline anaesthesia by an intermittent injection technique. *Journal of Small Animal Practice* **14,** 487-492.

Dodge, A. B. (1963). Cited by Lumb, W. V. & Jones, E. W. (1973). In *Veterinary anesthesia.* p. 444. Philadelphia: Lea & Febiger.

Dolensek, E. P. (1971). Anaesthesia of exotic feline with ketamine HCl. *Journal of Zoo Animal Medicine* **2,** 16-19.

Dolowy, W. C. & Hesse, A. L. (1959). Chlorpromazine premedication with pentobarbital anaesthesia in the rabbit. *Journal of the American Veterinary Medical Association* **134,** 183-184.

Dolowy, W. C., Mombelloni, P. & Hesse, A. L. (1960). Chlorpromazine premedication with pentobarbital anaesthesia in a mouse. *American Journal of Veterinary Research* **21,** 156-157.

Donawick, W. J., Hiremath, I. & Baue, A. E. (1969). Anesthesia, ventilation and experimental thoracotomy in the calf. *American Journal of Veterinary Research* **30,** 533-541.

Donovan, B. T. (1964). Anaesthesia of the ferret. In *Small animal anaesthesia* (ed. O. Graham-Jones), p. 185. Oxford: Pergamon.

Donovan, E. W. & Boone, M. A. (1965). A method of anaesthetising the chicken with diethyl ether. *Avian Diseases* **9**, 227-231.

Douglas, T. A., Jennings, S., Longstreath, J. & Weaver, A. D. (1964). Methoxyflurane anaesthesia in horses and cattle. *Veterinary Record* **76**, 615-623.

Dowd, D. A. & Jones, D. R. (1968). A method for recording baby rat systolic blood pressures. *Journal of Applied Physiology* **25**, 772-774.

Dowd, J. & Jenkins, L. C. (1972). The lung in shock: a review. *Canadian Anaesthetists' Society Journal* **19** (3), 309-318.

Drevemo, S. & Karstad, L. (1974). The effect of xylazine and xylazine-etorphine-acepromazine combinations on some clinical and haematological parameters in impala and eland. *Journal of Wildlife Diseases* **10**, 377-383.

Ducker, M. J. & Boyd, J. S. (1972). The successful use of etorphine hydrochloride-diprenorphine hydrochloride in sheep. *Veterinary Record* **91**, 458-459.

Dudley, W. R. & Marshall, B. E. (1974). Steroid treatment for acid-aspiration pneumonitis. *Anesthesiology* **40**, 136-141.

Duke, D. I., Clark, B. F. & Askill, S. (1971). A small-animal operating table for use with halothane anaesthetic administered by intubation or inhalation. *Laboratory Animals* **5**, 233-237.

Dukes, H. H. (1947). *The physiology of domestic animals*, 6th ed, p. 454. New York: Comstock.

Dukes, H. H. & Sampson, J. (1937). Gastrointestinal motility in the ruminant. *Cornell Veterinarian* **27**, 139-149.

Duncker, H. R. (1971). The lung air sac system of birds. *Ergebnisse der Anatomie und Entwicklungsgeschichte* **45**, 1-171.

Duncker, H. R. (1972). Structure of avian lungs. *Respiratory Physiology* **14**, 44-63.

Dundee, J. W. (1956). *Thiopentone and other barbiturates*. Edinburgh: Livingstone.

Dundee, J. W. & Wyant, G. M. (1974). *Intravenous anaesthesia*. Edinburgh: Churchill Livingstone.

Durant, A. J. (1953). Removing the vocal cords of the fowl. *Journal of the American Veterinary Medical Assocation* **122**, 14-17.

Dziuk, P. J., Phillips, T. N. & Graber, J. W. (1964). Halothane closed-circuit anesthesia in the pig. *American Journal of Veterinary Research* **109**, 1773-1775.

Eads, F. E. (1972). Vetalar: an intramuscular feline anesthetic and analgesic. *Feline Practice* **2**, 17-19.

Eales, F. A. (1976). Effects of Saffan administered intravenously in the horse. *Veterinary Record* **99**, 270-272.

Ebedes, H. (1966). Notes on the immobilisation and biology of Zebra (*Equus burchelli antiquorum*) in Etosha Game Park, South West Africa. *Journal of the South African Veterinary Medical Association* **37**, 299-303.

Ebedes, H. (1973). The capture of free living vultures in the Etosha National Park with phencyclidine. *Journal of the South African Wildlife Management Association* **3**, 105-106.

Edmonds-Seal, J. & Prys-Roberts, C. (1970). Pharmacology of drugs used in neuroleptanalgesia. *British Journal of Anaesthesia* **42**, 207-216.

Eger, E. I. (1974). *Anesthetic uptake and action*. Baltimore: Williams & Wilkins.

Eger, E. I. & Ethans, C. T. (1968). The effects of inflow, overflow and valve placement on economy of the circle system. *Anesthesiology* **29**, 93-100.

Eger, E. I., Saidman, L. J. & Brandstater, B. (1965). Minimum alveolar anesthetic concentration: a standard of anesthetic potency. *Anesthesiology* **26**, 756-763.

Ehmke, J. (1972). Stresnil in kombination mit polamivet zur sedation und narkose-pramedikation beim pferd. *Deutsche tierärztliche Wochenschrift* **79**, 539-543.

Eiseman, B., Dilbone, R. & Slater, J. (1965). Devocalising sea lions. *Journal of the American Veterinary Medical Association* **147**, 1086-1089.

Elder, J. H. (1937). Methods of anesthetizing chimpanzees. *Journal of Pharmcology and Experimental Therapeutics* **60**, 347-357.

Elkins, R. C., McCurdy, J. R., Brown, P. P. & Greenfield, L. J. (1973). Effects of coronary perfusion pressure on myocardial performance during endotoxin shock. *Surgery, Gynecology and Obstetrics* **137**, 991-996.

Ellis, C. H., Morgan, W. V. & De Beer, E. J. (1952). Central depressant activity of certain myoneural blocking agents. *Journal of Pharmacology and Experimental Therapeutics* **106**, 353-363.

Emberton, G. A. (1966). Methohexitone sodium anaesthesia in pigs. *Veterinary Record* **78**, 541-542.

Ensor, C. R. (1946). The electrocardiogram of rats on vitamin E deficiency. *American Journal of Physiology* **147**, 477-480.

Eschmeyer, P. H. (1953). The effect of ether anaesthesia on fin-clipping rate. *Progessive Fish Culturist* **15**, 80.

Estrada, E. (1956). Clinical uses of chlorpromazine in veterinary medicine. *Journal of American Veterinary Medical Assocation* **128**, 292-294.

Evans, C. S., Smart, J. L. & Stoddart, R. C. (1968). Handling methods for wild house mice and wild rats. *Laboratory Animals* **2**, 29-34.

Evans, J. M. (1973). CT1341 and feline anesthesia. *Veterinary Record* **92**, 381.

Evans, J. M., Aspinall, K. W. & Hendy, P. G. (1972). Clinical evaluation in cats of a new anaesthetic CT 1341. *Journal of Small Animal Practice* **13**, 479-486.

Evers, W. H. (1968). Epidural anesthesia in the dog: a review of 224 cases with emphasis on cesarian section. *Veterinary Medicine—Small Animal Clinician* **63**, 1121-1124.

Fankhauser, G. (1945). The effects of changes in chromosome number on amphibian development. *Quarterly Review of Biology* **20**, 20-78.

Farman, J. V., Lines, J. G., Williams, R. S., Evans, D. B., Samuel, J. R., Mason, S. A., Ashby, B. S. & Calne, R. Y. (1974). Liver transplantation in man. Anaesthetic and biochemical management. *Anaesthesia* **29**, 17-32.

Faulconer, A. & Bickford, R. G. (1960). *Electroencephalography in anesthesia*. Springfield, Illinois: Thomas.

Fawell, J. K., Thomson, C. & Cooke, L. (1972). Respiratory artefact produced by carbon dioxide and pentobarbitone sodium euthanasia in rats. *Laboratory Animals* **6**, 321-326.

Fedde, M. R., Burger, R. E. & Kitchell, R. L. (1961). Anatomic and electromyographic studies of the costopulmonary muscles in the cock. *Poultry Science* **43,** 1177-1184.

Feldman, D.B. & Self, J. L. (1971). Sedation and anesthesia of the Virginia opossum, *Didelphis virginiana. Laboratory Animal Science* **21,** 717-720.

Feldman, S. A., Cohen, E. N. & Golling, R. C. (1969). The excretion of gallamine in the dog. *Anesthesiology* **30,** 593-598.

Felger, G. (1953). A thermocouple method of determination of heart output in anesthetized dogs. *XIX International Physiological Congress, Montreal.* Abstract p. 341.

Ferguson, B. R. (1961). Cited by Lumb, W. V. & Jones, E. W. (1973). In *Veterinary anaesthesia*, p. 438. Philadelphia: Lea & Febiger.

Ferron, R. R. (1966). Restraining boards for radiography of small primates. *Laboratory Animal Care* **16,** 459-464.

Field, E. J. (1957). Anaesthesia in rabbits. *Journal of the Animal Technicians Association* **8,** 47-48.

Field, W. E., Yelnosky, J., Mundy, J. & Mitchell, J. (1966). Use of droperidol and fentanyl for analgesia and sedation in primates. *Journal of the American Veterinary Medical Association* **149,** 896-901.

Fine, J. (1973). Cause of respiratory distress syndrome. *Lancet* **ii,** 797.

Fine, L. G. & Eliahou, H. E. (1969). Acute oliguric renal failure: diagnostic criteria and clinical features in 61 patients. *Israel Journal of Medical Sciences* **5,** 1024-1031.

Finer, B. L. (1954). Anaesthesia of the common seal. *Anaesthesia* **9,** 34.

Fish, F. F. (1942). The anesthesia of fish by high carbon dioxide concentration. *Transactions of the American Fisheries Society* **72,** 25-27.

Fisher, E. W. (1961). Observations on the disturbance of respiration of cattle, horses, sheep and dogs caused by halothane anaesthesia and the changes taking place in plasma pH and plasma CO_2 content. *American Journal of Veterinary Research* **22,** 279-286.

Flack, M. B. (1964). Some aspects of husbandry of the coypu (*Myocastor coypus*) in the laboratory. *Journal of the Animal Technicians Association* **14,** 145-156.

Flear, C. T. G. & Clark, R. (1955). The influence of blood loss and blood transfusion upon changes in the metabolism of water, electrolytes and nitrogen following civilian trauma. *Clinical Science* **14,** 575-599.

Flear, C. T. G. & Greener, J. S. (1970). Active transport of sodium from frog heart muscle; the effect of various factors on this. *2nd Annual Meeting, International Study Group for Research in Cardiac Metabolism* p. 396, Gargnano, Milan.

Flear, C. T. G. & Singh, C. M. (1973). Hyponatraemia and sick cells. *British Journal of Anaesthesia* **45,** 976-994.

Florsheim, W. J. (1968). Cited by Lumb, W. V. & Jones, E. W. (1973). In *Veterinary anaesthesia*, p. 451. Philadelphia: Lea & Febiger.

Flyger, C. & Townsend, M. R. (1968). The migration of Polar bears. *Scientific American*, 108.

Flyger, V., Schein, M. W., Erickson, A. W. & Larsen, T. (1967). Capturing and handling Polar bears. A progress report on Polar bear ecological research. *Transactions of the North American Wildlife Conference*, p. 107.

Foley, D. M., Stewart, J. E. & Holley, R. A. (1966). Isobutyl alcohol and methyl pentynol as general anaesthetics for the lobster (*Homarus americanus*). *Canadian Journal of Zoology* **44,** 141-143.

Forbes, A. R. (1974). Temperature, humidity and mucus flow in the intubated trachea. *British Journal of Anaesthesia* **46,** 29-34.

Ford, E. J. H. (1951). Some observations on the use of thiopentone in large animals. *Veterinary Record* **63,** 636-638.

Forrester, J. S., Diamond, G. & Swan, H. J. C. (1971). Filling pressures in right and left sides of heart in acute myocardial infarction. *New England Journal of Medicine* **285,** 190-192.

Forsyth, R. P., Nies, A. S., Wyler, F., Neutze, J. & Melmon, K. (1968). Normal distribution of cardiac output in the unanesthetized, restrained rhesus monkey. *Journal of Applied Physiology* **25,** 736-741.

Foster, P. A., Groenewald, J. H., Schoonees, R., Wivanzyl, J. J. & Van Zyl, J. A. (1968). Anaesthesia for baboons during major surgical procedures—observation during renal allotransplantation. *South African Medical Journal Supplement* 1-3.

Fouts, J. R. & Adamson, R. H. (1959). Drug metabolism in the newborn rabbit. *Science, New York* **129,** 897-898.

Fowler, G. R. (1940). General anesthesia in large animals. *Journal of the American Veterinary Medical Association* **96,** 210-219.

Fowler, M. E. (1974). Restraint and anesthesia in zoo animal practice. *Journal of the American Veterinary Medical Association* **164,** 706-711.

Fowler, M. E., Parker, E. E., McLaughlin, E. F. & Tyler, W. S. (1963). An inhalation anesthetic apparatus for large animals. *Journal of the American Veterinary Medical Association* **143,** 272-276.

Fowler, N. G. (1964). Methohexitone sodium anaesthesia in the dog and cat. In *Small animal anaesthesia* (ed. O. Graham-Jones), p. 195. Oxford: Pergamon.

Fowler, N. G. & Stevenson, D. E. (1961). The use of methohexital sodium in small-animal anaesthesia. *Veterinary Record* **73,** 917-919.

Fowler, N. O. & Holmes, J. C. (1969). Hemodynamic effects of isoproterenol and norepinephrine in acute cardiac tamponade. *Journal of Clinical Investigation* **48,** 502-507.

Frank, L. G. & Cooper, J. E. (1974). Further notes on the usje of CT1341 in birds of prey. *Raptor Research* **8,** 29-32.

Frankland, A. L. & Camburn, M. A. (1977). Induction of anaesthesia using thiopentone sodium in the horse. *Veterinary Record* **100,** 472.

Franklin, I. & Reid, J. S. (1965). Clinical use of a combination of fentanyl and droperidol in dogs. *Veterinary Medicine—Small Animal Clinician* **60,** 927-930.

Franklin, D. E., Watson, N. W. & Van Citters, R. L. (1964). Blood velocity telemetered from untethered animals. *Nature, London* **203,** 528-530.

Franklin, D. E., Watson, N. W., Pierson, K. E. & Van Citters, R. L. (1966). Technique for radio telemetry of blood-flow velocity from unrestrained animals. *American Journal of Medical Electronics* 5, 24-28.

Freeman, B. M. (1976). Physiological responses to stress with reference to the domestic fowl. *Laboratory Animals* 10, 385-388.

Freeman, B. M. & Manning, A. C. C. (1976). Mediation of glucagon in the response of the domestic fowl to stress. *Comparative Biochemistry and Physiology* 53A, 169-171.

Freeman, M. J. & Bailey, S. P. (1965). Premedication, tracheal intubation and methoxyflurane anaesthesia in the rabbit. *Laboratory Animal Science* 15, 254-259.

Freeman, M. J., Bailey, S. P. & Hodesson, S. (1972). Premedication, tracheal intubation and methoxyflurane anesthesia in the rabbit. *Laboratory Animal Science* 22, 576-580.

French, J. D., Verzeano, M & Magoun, H. W. (1953). Neural basis of anesthetic state. *Archives of Neurology and Psychiatry* 69, 519-529.

Fretz, V. C. (1932). Anaesthetising poultry. *Veterinary Medicine* 27, 109-112.

Freund, F. G., Martin, W. E. & Hornbein, T. F. (1969). The H-reflex as a measure of anesthetic potency in man. *Anesthesiology* 30, 642-647.

Freundlich, J. J., Detweiler, D. K. & Hance, H. E. (1972). Indirect blood pressure determination by the ultrasonic doppler technique in dogs. *Current Therapeutic Research* 14, 73-80.

Freye, E. (1974). Cardiovascular effects of high dosages of fentanyl, meperedine and naloxone in dogs. *Anesthesia and Analgesia: Current Researches* 53, 40-47.

Friedburg, K. M. (1961). Problems encountered in pet bird practice. *Veterinary Medicine* 56, 157-159.

Friedburg, K. M. (1962). Anesthesia of parakeets and canaries. *Journal of the American Veterinary Medical Association* 141, 1157-1160.

Friedman, M. & Freed, S. C. (1949). Microphonic manometer for indirect determination of systolic blood pressures in the rat. *Proceedings of the Society for Experimental Biology and Medicine* 70, 670-672.

Frye, F. L. & Dutra, F. (1973). Fibrosarcoma in a boa constrictor. *Veterinary Medicine—Small Animal Clinician* 68, 245-246.

Fuentes, V. O. & Tellez, E. (1974). Ketamine dissociative analgesia in the cow. *Veterinary Record* 94, 482.

Fuentes, V. O. & Tellez, E. (1976). Mid-line caesarian section in a cow using ketamine anaesthesia. *Veterinary Record* 99, 338.

Furneaux, R. W. (1968). Anesthesia in canine hemorrhagic shock model: relative value of different anesthetic agents and combinations. *American Journal of Veterinary Research* 29, 1631-1636.

Gabel, A. A., Hamlin, R. & Smith, C. R. (1964). Effects of promazine and chloral hydrate on the cardiovascular system of the horse. *American Journal of Veterinary Research* 25, 1151-1158.

Gadgil, B. A., Janakiraman, K. & Zala, P. M. (1969). Chloral hydrate and magnesium sulphate as general anaesthetic for goats. *Indian Veterinary Journal* 46, 231-233.

Galicich, J. H. & French, L. A. (1961). Use of dexamethasone in treatment of cerebral edema associated with brain tumours. *American Practitioner* 12, 169-174.

Galindo, A. (1969). Effects of procaine, pentobarbital and halothane on synaptic transmission in the central nervous system. *Journal of Pharmacology and Experimental Therapeutics* 169, 185-195.

Galla, S. J. (1969). Techniques of anesthesia. *Federation Proceedings. Federation of American Societies for Experimental Biology* 28, 1404-1409.

Gamble, M. R. & Clough, G. (1976). Ammonia build-up in animal boxes and its effect on rat tracheal epithelium. *Laboratory Animals* 10, 93-104.

Gandal, C. P. (1956). Satisfactory general anaesthesia in birds. *Journal of the American Veterinary Medical Association* 128, 332-334.

Gandal, C. P. (1967). Synopsis-avian anesthesia and surgery. *Proceedings of American Animal Hospitals Association*, p.22.

Gandal, C. P. (1968). A practical anesthetic technique in snakes utilizing methoxyflurane. *Journal of the American Animal Hospital Association*, 4, 258-260.

Gandal, C. P. (1969). Avian anesthesia. *Federation Proceedings* 28, 1533-1534.

Garcia, D. A., Wrenn, C. E., Jansons, D. & Maire, K. E. (1975). Deep anesthesia in the rat with the combined action of droperidol-fentanyl and pentobarbital. *Laboratory Animal Science* 25, 585-587.

Gardner, A. F. (1964). The development of general anesthesia in the albino rabbit for surgical procedures. *Laboratory Animal Care* 14, 214-225.

Garmer, L. N. (1969). Effects of 2-ethylamino-2-(2-thienyl) cyclohexanone HCl. *Research in Veterinary Science* 10, 382-388.

Garner, H. E. (1973). New simplified equine blood pressure measurement. *Journal of the American Veterinary Medical Association* 162, 345.

Garner, H. E., Coffman, J. R., Hahn, A. W. & Hartley, J. (1972). Indirect blood pressure measurement in the horse. *American Association of Equine Practitioners Proceedings* 18, 343-349.

Geraci, J. R. (1973). An appraisal of ketamine as an immobilizing agent in wild and captive pinnipeds. *Journal of the American Veterinary Medical Association* 163, 574-577.

Gerlach, H. (1969). Surgical conditions in wild and pet birds. *Veterinary Record* 84, 342.

Getty, R. (1963). Epidural anesthesia in the hog. Its technique and application. In *Proceedings of 100th Annual Meeting, A.V.M.A.*, pp. 88-98.

Gibson, W. R., Doran, W. J., Wood, W. C. & Swanson, E. E. (1959). Pharmacology of stereo-isomers of 1-methyl-5-(1-methyl-2-pentynyl)-allyl-barbituric acid. *Journal of Pharmacology and Experimental Therapeutics* 125, 23-27.

Gilbert, P. N. & Wood, F. G. (1957). Method of anaesthetising large sharks and rays safely and rapidly. *Science, New York* 126, 212–213.

Gilbertson, A. A. (1974). Pulmonary artery catheterisation and wedge pressure measurement in the general intensive therapy unit. *British Journal of Anaesthesia* 46, 97-104.

Giles, T. D. & Burch, G. E. (1970). Anesthesia, dogs and cardiovascular data. *American Heart Journal* 79, 141-142.

Gillman, T. (1965). Discussion session. In *Swine in biomedical research*. (ed. L. K. Bustad & R. O. McClellan), p. 678. Seattle: Frayn.

Glassman, R. B., Negrao, N. & Doty, R. W. (1969). A safe and reliable method for temporary restraint of monkeys. *Physiology and Behavior* 4, 431-432.

Glen, J. B. (1970). Indirect blood measurement in anaesthetised animals. *Veterinary Record* 87, 349-354.

Glen, J. B. (1972). Indirect blood pressure measurements in conscious horses. *Equine Veterinary Journal* 4, 204-208.

Glen, J. B. (1973). The use of ketamine (CI-581) in feline anaesthetic practice. *Veterinary Record* 92, 65-68.

Glenn, J. L., Straight, R. & Snyder, C. C. (1972). Clinical use of ketamine hydrochloride as an anaesthetic agent for snakes. *American Journal of Veterinary Research* 33 (9), 1901-1903.

Glenn, T. M. & Lefer, A. M. (1970). Role of lysosomes in pathogenesis of splanchnic ischaemic shock. *Circulation Research* 27, 783-797.

Godeaux, J. & Tonnesen, M. (1949). Investigations into atropine metabolism in the animal organism. *Acta Pharmacologica et Toxicologica* 5, 95-109.

Goldberg, L. I. (1968). Use of sympathomimetic amines in heart failure. *American Journal of Cardiology* 22, 177-182.

Gollan, F., Tysinger, D. S., Grace, J. T., Kory, R. C. & Meneely, G. R. (1955). Hypothermia of 1.5°C in dogs followed by survival. *American Journal of Physiology* 181, 297-302.

Goltenboth, R. & Klös, H. G. (1970). Application of Rompun (Bayer) for the immobilisation of zoo animals. *Berliner und Münchener Tierärztliche Wochenschrift* 83, 147-151.

Gossington, R. (1957). An aid to fish handling—tricaine. *Aquarium Journal* 28, 318-321.

Graca, J. G. & Garst, E. L. (1957). Early blood changes in dogs following intravenous pentobarbital anesthesia. *Anesthesiology* 18, 461-465.

Graham, D. L., Dunlop, R. H. & Travis, H. F. (1967). Barbiturate anesthesia in ranch mink (*Mustela vison*). *American Journal of Veterinary Research* 28, 293-296.

Graham-Jones, O. (1960). Discussion—the opener. *Veterinary Record* 72, 890-892.

Graham-Jones, O. (1964). Restraint and anaesthesia of some captive wild mammals. *82nd Annual Congress of the British Veterinary Association, 1964*.

Graham-Jones, O. (1966). The clinical approach to tumours in cage birds. III. Restraint and anaesthesia of small cage birds. *Journal of Small Animal Practice* 7, 231-239.

Grängsjö, G. & Persson, E. (1971). Influence of some vaso-active substances on regional blood flow in the dog kidney. *Acta Anaesthesiologica Scandinavica* 15, 71-95.

Gray, C. W., Bush, M. & Deck, C. C. (1974). Clinical experience using CI 744 in chemical restraint and anesthesia of exotic specimens. *Journal of Zoo Animal Medicine* 5 (4), 12-21.

Green, C. D. (1968). Strain sensitivity of rats to nitrous oxide. *Anesthesia and Analgesia* 47, 509-513.

Green, C. J. (1975). Neuroleptanalgesic drug combinations in the anaesthetic management of small laboratory animals. *Laboratory Animals* 9, 161-178.

Green, C. J. (1978a). Reptilian anaesthesia. *Veterinary Record* 102, 110.

Green, C. J. (1978b). Anaesthetising ferrets. *Veterinary Record* 102, 269.

Green, C. J., Halsey, M. J., Precious, S. & Wardley-Smith, B. (1978). Alphaxolone-alphadolone anaesthesia in laboratory animals. *Laboratory Animals* 13, 85-89.

Greenstein, E. T. (1975). Ketamine HCl, a dissociative anesthetic for squirrel monkeys (*Saimiri sciurens*). *Laboratory Animal Science* 25, 774-777.

Greenwood, A. G. (1978). Personal communication.

Gregg, D. A. & Olson, L. D. (1975). The use of ketamine hydrochloride as an anesthetic for raccoons. *Journal of Wildlife Diseases* 11, 335-337.

Gregory, R. A. (1947). A technique of general anaesthesia in ruminants. *Veterinary Record* 59, 377-378.

Gregory, P. A. (1973). CT1341 and feline anaesthesia. *Veterinary Record* 92, 350.

Griffith, J. Q. & Farris, E. J. (1942). *The rat in laboratory investigation*. Philadelphia: Lippincott.

Grinnell, A. D. (1963). The neurophysiology of audition in bats: intensity and frequency parameters. *Journal of Physiology* 167, 38-66.

Grogono, A. W. & Lee, P. (1970). Danger lists for the anaesthetist. A revised version. *Anaesthesia* 25, 518-524.

Grono, L. R. (1961). Anaesthesia of budgerigars. *Australian Veterinary Journal* 37, 463-464.

Grono, L. R. (1966). Spinal anaesthesia in the sheep. *Australian Veterinary Journal* 42, 58-59.

Grono, L. R. (1966). Methohexital sodium anaesthesia in the horse. *Australian Veterinary Journal* 42, 398-400.

Groover, M. E., Seljeskog, E. L., Haglin, J. J. & Hitchcock, C. R. (1963). Myocardial infarction in the Kenya baboon without demonstrable atherosclerosis *Angiology* 14, 409-416.

Gruber, C. M., Hart, E. R. & Gruber, C. M. Jr. (1941). The pharmacology and toxicology of the ethyl ester of 1-methyl-4-phenyl-piperidine-4-carboxylic acid (Demerol). *Journal of Pharmacology and Experimental Therapeutics* 73, 319-334.

Guedel, A. E. (1951). *Inhalation anaesthesia*, 2nd ed. New York: Macmillan.

Gupta, B. N., Moore, J. A. & Conner, G. H. (1970). The use of promazine hydrochloride in cesarean section in the dog. *Laboratory Animal Care* 20, 474-476.

Guthy, E. (1975). The sleeping-machine: a simple device for prolonged anesthesia in small laboratory animals. *European Surgical Research* 7, 375-376.

Haahen, C., Holdrimet, A. & Wijdeveld, P. (1971). Intravascular clotting and acute renal failure. *Scandinavian Journal of Haematology Suppl.* 13, 337-343.

Habel, R. E. (1956). A source of error in the bovine pudendal nerve block. *Journal of the American Veterinary Medical Association* 128, 16-17.

Hackenbrock, C. R. & Finster, M. (1963). Fluothane: a rapid and safe inhalation anaesthetic for poisonous snakes. *Copeia* 440-441.

Hafkesbring, R. & MacCalmont, W. (1937). Effect of barbital derivatives on the electrocardiogram. *American Journal of Physiology* 119, 322-323.

264

Hagen, E. O. & Hagen, J. M. (1964). A method of inhalation anesthesia for laboratory mice. *Laboratory Animal Care* **14,** 13-15.

Hahn, A. W., Garner, H. E., Coffman, J. R. & Sanders, C. W. (1973). Indirect measurement of arterial blood pressure in the laboratory pony. *Laboratory Animal Science* **23,** 889-893.

Haigh, J. C. (1977). Fallow deer immobilisation with fentanyl and a neuroleptic. *Veterinary Record* **100,** 386-387.

Hales, J. R. S. & Webster, M. E. D. (1967). Respiratory function during thermal tachypnoea in sheep. *Journal of Physiology, London* **190,** 241-260.

Hall, L. W. (1959). Accidents and emergencies in anesthesia. *Modern Veterinary Practice* **40** (15), 28-35.

Hall, L. W. (1966). *Wright's veterinary anaesthesia and analgesia,* 6th ed., London: Baillière, Tindall & Cox.

Hall, L. W. (1971). Local analgesia. In *Wright's veterinary anaesthesia and analgesia*, p. 50. London: Baillière Tindall.

Hall, L. W. (1971). Regional analgesia about the trunk. In *Wright's veterinary anaesthesia and analgesia*, p. 95. London: Baillière Tindall.

Hall, L. W. (1971). Caudal epidural analgesia. In *Wright's veterinary anaesthesia and analgesia*, p. 127. London: Baillière Tindall.

Hall, L. W. (1972a). Althesin in the large animal. *Post-graduate Medical Journal* **48,** 55-58.

Hall, L. W. (1972b). The anaesthesia and euthanasia of neonatal and juvenile dogs and cats. *Veterinary Record* **90,** 303-306.

Hall, L. W. (1976a). The clinical use of thiopentone sodium. *Veterinary Review* **24** (3), 52-55.

Hall, L. W. (1976b). Prolonged anaesthesia. *Journal of Small Animal Practice* **17,** 661-668.

Hall, L. W., Gillespie, J. R. & Tyler, W. S. (1968). Alveolar-arterial oxygen tension differences in anaesthetized horses. *British Journal of Anaesthesia* **40,** 560-568.

Hall, L. W. & Massey, G. M. (1969). Three miniature lung ventilators. *Veterinary Record* **85,** 432-437.

Hallen, B., Ehrner-Samuel, H. & Thomason, M. (1970). Measurements of halothane in the atmosphere of an operating theatre and in expired air and blood of the personnel during routine anaesthetic work. *Acta anaesthesiologica scandinavica* **14,** 17-27.

Halmagyi, D. F. J., Colebatch, H. J. H., Starzecki, B. & Horner, G. J. (1964). Pulmonary alveolar-vascular reflex. *Journal of Applied Physiology* **19,** 105-112.

Halsey, M. J. (1974). Mechanisms of general anaesthesia. In *Anesthetic uptake and action* (E. I. Eger), p. 45-76, Baltimore: Williams & Wilkins.

Hamlin, R. L. (1968). Electrocardiographic detection of ventricular enlargement in the dog. *Journal of the American Veterinary Medical Association* **153,** 1461-1469.

Hamlin, R. L. (1976). Electrocardiography. In: *Applied electronics for veterinary medicine and animal physiology* (ed. W. R. Klemm). Springfield, Illinois: Thomas.

Hamlin, R. L. & Smith, C. R. (1960). Anatomical and physiological basis for interpretation of the electro-cardiogram. *American Journal of Veterinary Research* **21,** 701-708.

Hamlin, R. L., Ginaven, S. M. & Smith, C. R. (1968). Fentanyl citrate-droperidol and pentobarbital for intravenous anesthesia in dogs. *Journal of the American Veterinary Medical Association* **152,** 360-364.

Hamlin, R. L., Redding, R. W., Reiger, J. E., Smith, R. C. & Prynn, R. E. (1965). Insignificance of the 'glucose effect' in dogs anesthetized with pento-barbitol. *Journal of the American Veterinary Medical Association* **146,** 238-241.

Hamlin, R. L., Smith, C. R. & Smetzer, D. L. (1966). Sinus arrhythmia in the dog. *American Journal of Physiology* **210,** 321-328.

Handler, A. H. (1958). Chemotherapy studies on transplantable human and animal tumors in Syrian hamsters. *Annals of the New York Academy of Sciences* **76,** 775-788.

Hansson, C. H. (1958). Studies on the effect of succinyl-choline in domestic animals. *Nordisk Veterinaer-medicin Dansk Udgave* **10,** 201-216.

Harbison, W. D., Slocombe, R. F., Watts, S. J & Stewart, G. A. (1974). Thiambutene and acepromazine as analgesic and preanaesthetic agents in horses and sheep. *Australian Veterinary Journal* **50,** 543-546.

Hardaway, R. M. (1961). Disseminated intravascular coagulation syndromes. *Archives of Surgery* **83,** 842-850.

Hardaway, R. M. (1973). Disseminated intravascular coagulation as a possible cause of acute respiratory failure. *Surgery, Gynecology and Obstetrics* **137,** 419-423.

Hardaway, R. M., McKay, D. G. & Wahle, G. H. (1956). Pathological study of intravascular coagulation following incompatible blood transfusion in dogs. *American Journal of Surgery* **91,** 24-31.

Harding, K. A. (1977). The use of ketamine anaesthesia to milk two tropical rattlesnakes (*Crotalus durissus terrificus*). *Veterinary Record* **100,** 289-290.

Hardy, J. D., Turner, M. D. & McNeil, C. D. (1961). Electrical anesthesia. III. Development of a method and laboratory observations. *Journal of Surgical Research* **1,** 152-158.

Harrington, R. & Wilson, P. (1974). Immobilon-Rompun in deer. *Veterinary Record* **94,** 362-363.

Harris, P. D., Greenwald, E. K. & Nicoll, P. A. (1970). Neural mechanisms in small vessel response to hemorrhage in the unanesthetised bat. *American Journal of Physiology* **281,** 560-565.

Harris, P. D., Hodoval, L. F. & Longnecker, D. E. (1971). Quantitative analysis of microvascular diameters during pentobarbital and thiopental anesthesia in the bat. *Anesthesiology* **35,** 337-342.

Harris, R. (1972). *Paediatric fluid therapy*. Oxford: Blackwell.

Harrison, F. A. (1964). The anaesthesia of sheep using pentobarbitone sodium and cyclopropane. In *Small animal anaesthesia* (ed. O. Graham-Jones), p. 149. Oxford: Pergamon.

Harrison, G. G. (1971). Anaesthetic-induced malignant hyperpyrexia—a suggested method of treatment. *British Medical Journal* 1971 **3,** 454-456.

Harthoorn, A. M. (1962). Capture of the White (Square Lipped) Rhinoceros *Ceratotherium simum(Burchell)* with the use of drug immobilisation techniques. *Canadian Journal of Comparative Medicine* 26, 203-208.

Harthoorn, A. M. (1962). The use of a neuromuscular blocking agent on domestic cattle. *Veterinary Record* 74, 395-398.

Harthoorn, A. M. (1965). The use of a new oripavine derivative for restraint of domestic hoofed animals. *Journal of the South African Veterinary Medical Association* 36, 45-50.

Harthoorn, A. M. (1966). Restraint of undomesticated animals. *Journal of the American Veterinary Medical Association* 149, 875-880.

Harthoorn, A. M. (1967). Comparative pharmacological reactions of certain wild and domestic mammals to thebaine derivatives in the M-series of compounds. *Federation Proceedings* 26, 1251-1261.

Harthoorn, A. M. (1975). *The chemical capture of animals*. London: Baillière Tindall.

Harthoorn, A. M. & Bligh, J. (1965). The use of a new oripavine derivative with potent morphine-like activity for the restraint of hoofed wild animals. *Research in Veterinary Science* 6, 290-299.

Hassan, A. (1973). Gram-negative bacteremic shock. *Medical Clinics of North America* 57, 1403-1415.

Hastings, S. G., Booth, N. H. & Hopwood, M. L. (1965). General anesthesia for thoracic surgical procedures in swine. In *Swine in medical research* (ed. L. K. Bustad & R. O. McClellan), p. 679. Seattle: Frayn.

Hatch, D. J., Cogswell, J. J., Taylor, B. W., Battersby, E. F., Glover, W. J. & Kerr, A. A. (1973). Continuous positive airway pressure after open heart operations in infancy. *Lancet* 1973 2, 469-471.

Hatch, R. C. (1966). The effect of glucose, sodium lactate and epinephrine on thiopental anesthesia in dogs. *Journal of the American Veterinary Medical Association* 148, 135-140.

Hatch, R. C. (1967). Restraint, preanesthetic medication and postanesthetic medication of dogs with chlorpromazine and atropine. *Journal of the American Veterinary Medical Association* 150, 27-32.

Hatch, R. C. (1973). Effects of ketamine when used in conjunction with meperidine or morphine in cats. *Journal of the American Veterinary Medical Association* 162, 964-966.

Hatch, R. C., Currie, R. B., & Grieve, G. A. (1970). Feline electroencephalograms and plasma thiopental concentrations associated with clinical states of anesthesia. *American Journal of Veterinary Research* 31, 291-306.

Hayes, F. A. (1955). Modifications for caesarian section in chinchillas. *Veterinary Medicine* 50, 367-368.

Hazelhoff, E. H. (1951). Structure and function of the lung of birds. *Poultry Science* 30, 3-10.

Healey, E. G. (1964). Anaesthesia of fishes. In *Small animal anaesthesia*, (ed. O. Graham-Jones), p. 59-70. Oxford: Pergamon.

Healey, P. (1967). A simple method for anaesthetising and handling small carnivores. *Journal of the Institute of Animal Technicians* 18, 37-38.

Healy, T. E. J., Robinson, J. S. & Vickers, M. D. (1970). Physiological responses to intravenous diazepam as a sedative for conservative dentistry. *British Medical Journal* 1970 3, 10-13.

Heavner, J. A. & Bowen, J. M. (1968). Influence of adrenergic agents on recovery of dogs from anesthesia. *American Journal of Veterinary Research Association* 29, 2133-2139.

Hecker, J. F. (1974). *Experimental surgery on small ruminants*, London: Butterworth.

Henry, D. P. (1968). Anaesthesia of boars by intratesticular injection. *Australian Veterinary Journal* 44, 418-419.

Henschel, V. E. (1958). Intubations—narkose biem kanguruh. *Berliner und münchener tierärztliche Wochenschrift* 71, 225-227.

Henson, O. W. (1969). Cited by Lumb, W. V. & Jones, E. W. (1973). In *Veterinary anesthesia*. Philadelphia: Lea & Febiger.

Herbert, W. I., Scott, E. B. & Lewis, G. B. (1971). Fluid management of the paediatric surgical patient. *Anesthesia and Analgesia: Current Researches* 50, 376-380.

Herin, R. A. (1963). Electrical anesthesia in the dog. *Journal of the American Veterinary Medical Association* 142, 865-871.

Herin, R. A. (1969). Electroanesthesia in the dog. *Federation Proceedings. Federation of American Societies for Experimental Biology* 28, 1469.

Herin, R. A., Purinton, P. T. & Flectcher, T. F. (1968). Electroencephalography in the unanesthetized dog. *American Journal of Veterinary Research* 29, 329-336.

Hermreck, A. S. & Thal, A. P. (1968). The adrenergic drugs and their use in shock therapy. In: *Current problems in surgery*, Chicago: Year Book Medical Publishers.

Herrmann, G. R. & Williams de H., A. H. (1965). The electrocardiographic patterns in 170 baboons in the domestic and African colonies at the primate centre of the Southwest Foundation for Research and Education. *Proceedings of the 1st International Symposium on the Baboon and its Use as an Experimental Animal*, p. 251. Austin: University of Texas Press.

Herzog, P. & Norlander, O. P. (1968). Distribution of alveolar volumes with different types of positive pressure gas flow patterns. *Opuscula Medica* 13, 3-18.

Heuschele, W. (1960). Castration of a squirrel. *Modern Veterinary Practice* 41, 59.

Hewitt, O. H. (1959). The use of Serpasil in the rearing and handling of pheasants. *Conference on the Use of the Tranquillising and Antihypertensive Agent Serpasil in Animal and Poultry Production, New Brunswick, 1959.*

Heykants, J., Pardoel, L. & Janssen, P. A. J. (1971). On the distribution and metabolism of azaperone (R1929) in the rat and pig. I. Excretions and metabolism of azaperone in the Wistar rat. *Arzneimittel Forschung* 21, 1263-1269.

Hibbs, C. M. (1958). Use of chlorpromazine in swine. *Veterinary Medicine* 53, 571-572.

Hickman, J. (1954). The electrical stunning of animals for slaughter. *Veterinary Record* 66, 498-501.

Hill, J. D. (1968). The significance of the foreleg positions in the interpretation of electrocardiograms and vectorcardiograms from research animals. *American Heart Journal* **75**, 518-527.

Hill, K. J. & Noakes, D. E. (1964). Cyclopropane anaesthesia in the fowl. In *Small animal anaesthesia*. (ed. O. Graham-Jones), pp. 123-126. Oxford: Pergamon.

Hill, K. J. & Perry, J. S. (1959). A method for closed circuit anaesthesia in the pig. *Veterinary Record* **71**, 296-299.

Hill, M. & Parkes, A. S. (1933). Studies on the hypophysectomised ferret. I. Technique. *Proceedings of the Royal Society of Biology* **112**, 138-146.

Hill, R., Howard, A. N. & Gresham, G. A. (1960). The electrocardiographic appearance of myocardial infarction in the rat. *British Journal of Experimental Pathology* **41**, 633-637.

Hill, R. T., Turner, C. W., Uren, A. E. & Gomez, E. T. (1935). *Research Bulletin of the University of Missouri Agricultural Experimental Station* No. 230.

Hillidge, C. J. & Lees, P. (1971). Preliminary investigations of the actions of Immobilon in the horse. *Veterinary Record* **89**, 280-281.

Hillidge, C. J. & Lees, P. (1974a). Studies of whole body oxygenation in conscious and anaesthetised horses. *Archives internationales pharmacodynamie et de thérapie* **210**, 333-346.

Hillidge, C. J. & Lees, P. (1974b). Fatality after Revivon *Veterinary Record* **94**, 476.

Hillidge, C. J. & Lees, P. (1975a). Influence of the neuroleptanalgesic combination of etorphine and acepromazine on the horse: blood gases and acid-base balance. *Equine Veterinary Journal* **7**, 148-154.

Hillidge, C. J. & Lees, P. (1975b). Cardiac output in the conscious and anaesthetised horse. *Equine Veterinary Journal* **7**, 16-21.

Hillidge, C. J., Lees, P., Mullen, P. A. & Serrano, L. (1974). Influence of acepromazine/etorphine and azaperone/metomidate on serum enzyme activities in the horse. *Research in Veterinary Science* **17**, 395-397.

Hillidge, C. J., Lees, P. & Serrano, L. (1973). Investigations of azaperone-metomidate anaesthesia in the horse. *Veterinary Record* **93**, 307-311.

Hillidge, C. J. Lees, P. & Serrano, L. (1975). Influence of azaperone and metomidate on cardiovascular and respiratory functions in the pony. *British Veterinary Journal* **131**, 50-64.

Hilwig, R. (1976). Equine electrocardiography. In *Applied electronics for veterinary medicine and animal physiology* (ed. W. R. Klemm). Springfield, Illinois: Thomas.

Hime, J. M. (1967). Scientific Report, Zoological Society of London.

Hime, J. M. (1972). Personal communication.

Hime, J. M. (1972). Cited by Jones, D. M. (1973). In *The veterinary annual*, 13th issue (ed. C. S. G. Grunsell & W. G. Hill), p. 320-352. Bristol: Wright.

Hime, J. M. (1973). Personal communication.

Hime, J. M. (1974). The use of ketamine hydrochloride in non-domesticated cats. *Veterinary Record* **95**, 193-195.

Hime, J. M. (1977). Personal communication.

Hime, J. M. & Jones, D. M. (1970). The use of xylazine in captive wild animals. *12th International Symposium of Zoo Animal Diseases*, p. 143.

Hirst, S. M. (1966). Immobilisation of the Transvaal giraffe (*Giraffa camelopardalis giraffa*) using an oripavine derivative. *Journal of the South African Veterinary Medical Association* **37**, 85-89.

Hoar, R. M. (1964). The use of Metofane (methoxyflurane) anaesthetic in guinea-pigs. *Allied Veterinarian* **36**, 131-134.

Hoar, R. M. (1969). Anaesthesia in the guinea-pig. *Federation Proceedings* **28**, 1517-1521.

Hobson, B. M. & Townsend, B. G. (1964). The anaesthetic action of di-ethyl ether, ethyl carbamate and tricaine methanesulfonate upon *Xenopus laevis*. In *Small animal anaesthesia* (ed. O. Graham-Jones), pp. 47-58. Oxford: Pergamon.

Hodesson, S., Rich, S. T., Washington, J. O. & Apt, L. (1965). Anesthesia of the rabbit with 'Equithesin' following the administration of preanesthetics. *Laboratory Animal Care* **15**, 336-344.

Hoeppner, G. L. & Short, C. E. (1971). Ketamine anesthesia. *Southwestern Veterinarian* **24**, 175-182.

Hoffman, P. E. (1974). Clinical evaluation of xylazine as a chemical restraining agent, sedative and analgesic in horses. *Journal of the American Veterinary Medical Association* **164**, 42-45.

Hofmeyr, C. F. B. (1960). Some observations on the use of succinyl choline chloride (suxamethonium) in horses with particular reference to the effect on the heart. *Journal of the South African Veterinary Medical Association* **31**, 251-259.

Hofmeyr, J. M. (1974). Developments in the capture and airlift of Roan antelope *Hippotragus equinus equinus* under narcosis to the Etosha National Park. *Madoqua* **2**, 37-39.

Hoge, R. J. (1966). Anesthesia and surgery for egg bound parakeets. *Animal Hospital* **2**, 46-48.

Hoge, R. S., Hodesson, S., Snow, I. B. & Wood, A. I. (1969). Intubation technique and methoxyflurane administration in rabbits. *Laboratory Animal Care* **19**, 593-595.

Holland, A. J. (1973). Laboratory animal anaesthesia. *Canadian Anaesthetists' Society Journal* **20**, 693-705.

Hollingsworth, H. & Howes, J. R. (1965). A comparison of some new anaesthetics for avian surgery. *Poultry Science* **44**, 1380-1383.

Hoover, W. H., Young, P. J., Sawyer, M. S. & Apgar, W. P. (1970). Ovine physiological responses to elevated ambient carbon dioxide. *Journal of Applied Physiology* **29**, 32-35.

Hopcroft, S. C. (1965). Extradural anaesthesia in the pig. *British Journal of Anaesthesia* **37**, 982-986.

Hopcroft, S. C. (1966). A technique for the simultaneous bilateral removal of the adrenal glands in guinea-pigs, using a new type of safe anaesthetic. *Experimental Medicine and Surgery* **24**, 12-19.

Hopcroft, S. C. (1967). Technique of epidural anaesthesia in experimental sheep. *Australian Veterinary Journal* **43**, 213-214.

Hopkins, T. J. (1972). Clinical pharmacology of xylazine in cattle. *Australian Veterinary Journal* **48**, 109-112.

Horney, F. D. (1966). Anaesthesia in the bovine. *Canadian Veterinary Journal* **7**, 224-230.

Hornocker, M. G. & Wiles, W. V. (1972). Immobilizing pumas (*Felis concolor*) with phencyclidine hydrochloride. *International Zoo Yearbook* **12**, 220-223.

267

House, W. H., Van Pelt, L. F. & Winchester, W. J. (1971). Swine for surgical research. *Practising Veterinarians* **43**, 42-44.

Houston, A. H., Czerwinski, C. L. & Woods, R. J. (1973). Cardiovascular-respiratory activity during recovery from anaesthesia and surgery in brook trout (*Salvelinus fontinalis*) and carp (*Cyprinus carpio*). *Journal of the Fisheries Research Board of Canada* **30**, 1705-1712.

Houston, A. H., Madden, J. A., Woods, R. J. & Miles, H. M. (1971). Some physiological effects of handling and tricaine methanesulphonate anaesthetization upon the brook trout (*Salvelinus fontinalis*). *Journal of the Fisheries Research Board of Canada* **28**, 625-633.

Houston, A. H. & Woods, R. J. (1972). Blood concentrations of tricaine methane sulphonate in brook trout, *Salvelinus fontinalis*, during anaesthetization branchial irrigation and recovery. *Journal of the Fisheries Research Board of Canada* **29**, 1344-1345.

Houston, D. C. & Cooper, J. E. (1973). Use of the drug metomidate to facilitate the handling of vultures. *International Zoo Yearbook* **13**, 269-270.

Howard, W. H., Parcher, J. W. & Young, D. R. (1971). Primate restraint system for studies of metabolic responses during recumbency. *Laboratory Animal Science* **21**, 112-117.

Hubbard, R. C. & Poulter, T. C. (1968). Seals and sea lions as models for studies in comparative biology. *Laboratory Animal Care* **18**, 249.

Hubbard, T. F. & Goldbaum, L. R. (1949). The mechanism of tolerance to thiopental in mice. *Journal of Pharmacology and Experimental Therapeutics* **97**, 488-491.

Huckabee, W. E. (1961). Abnormal resting blood lactate. 2. Lactate acidosis. *American Journal of Medicine* **30**, 840-848.

Hughes, G. M. (1973). Comparative vertebrate ventilation and heterogeneity. In *Comparative physiology*, (ed. L. Bolis, K. Schmidt-Nielsen & S. H. P. Maddrell), pp. 187-220. North-Holland.

Huhn, J. E. & Schulz, H. U. (1961). Steroid anaesthesia in young pigs. *Berliner und munchener tierärztliche Wochenschrift* **74**, 369-374.

Hull, M. W. & Reilly, M. G. (1968). Effect of repeated halothane anaesthesia on sheep. *American Journal of Veterinary Research* **29**, 1161-1165.

Hummon, O. J. (1945). A device for the restraint of mink during certain experimental procedures. *Journal of the American Veterinary Medical Association* **106**, 104-106.

Humphrey, W. J. (1971). Ketamine HCl as a general anesthetic in dogs. *Modern Veterinary Practice*, **52** (6), 38-39.

Hundley, J. M., Ashburn, L. L. & Sebrell, W. H. (1945). The electrocardiogram in chronic thiamine deficiency in rats. *American Journal of Physiology* **144**, 404-414.

Hunn, J. B. (1971). Investigations in fish control 42. *U.S. Bureau of Sport, Fisheries and Wildlife Research Publication* **42**, 10-16.

Hunt, T. J. (1964). Anaesthesia of the tortoise. In *Small animal anaesthesia* (ed. O. Graham-Jones), pp. 71-76. Oxford: Pergamon.

Hyde, J. L. (1962). The use of solid carbon dioxide for producing short periods of anesthesia in guinea pigs. *American Journal of Veterinary Research* **23**, 684-685.

Iggo, A. (1956). Central nervous control of gastric movements in sheep and goats. *Journal of Physiology, London* **131**, 248-256.

Illman, O. (1961). The coypu (*Myocastor coypus molina*) as a laboratory animal. *Journal of the Animal Technicians Association* **12**, 8-10.

Ingram, D. L. (1964a). The effect of environmental temperature on body temperatures, respiratory frequency and pulse rate in the young pig. *Research in Veterinary Science* **5**, 348-356.

Ingram, D. L. (1964b). The effect of environmental temperature on heat loss and thermal insulation in the young pig. *Research in Veterinary Science* **5**, 357-364.

Ingram, D. L. & Legge, K. F. (1970). The effect of environmental temperature on respiratory ventilation in the pig. *Respiration Physiology* **8**, 1-12.

Inkster, J. S. (1973). Respiratory assistance for neonates and infants. *Anaesthesia* **28**, 653-661.

Inkster, J. S. (1975). In *Modern trends in anaesthesia* (ed. T. C. Gray & G. J. Rees). London: Butterworth.

Irvin, T. T., Modgill, V. K., Hayter, C. J. & Goligher, J. C. (1972). Clinical assessment of postoperative blood volume. *Lancet* 1972 **2**, 446-448.

Irwin, D. H. G. & Briel, B. J. (1966). Some aspects of anaesthesia in Merino sheep with particular reference to dose and effect of pentobarbitone sodium ('Sagatal', May & Baker). *Journal of the South African Veterinary Medical Association* **37**, 444-447.

Iturrian, W. B. & Fink, G. B. (1968). Effect of noise in the animal house on seizure susceptibility and growth in mice. *Laboratory Animal Care* **18**, 557-560.

Ivankovich, A. D., El-Etr, A. A., Janeczko, G. F. & Maronic, J. P. (1975). The effects of ketamine and of Innovar(R) anesthesia on digitalis tolerance in dogs. *Anesthesia and Analgesia: Current Researches* **54**, 106-111.

Ivascu, I. (1971). Intrathoracic narcosis with Thiogenal (methitural) in sheep, cats and rabbits. *Veterinary Bulletin, Weybridge* **41**, 697.

Ivascu, I. & Cociu, A. (1970). Trials with Surital (Thiamylal) sodium as an anaesthetic agent for sheep. *Ceylon Veterinary Journal* **18**, 43-45.

Jackson, O. F. (1970). Snake anaesthesia. *British Journal of Herpetology* **4**, 172-175.

Jacobs, A. G. (1967). An anesthetic machine for small mammals. *Anesthesiology* **28**, 217-219.

Jaffe, R. A. & Free, M. J. (1973). A simple endotracheal intubation technique for inhalation anesthesia of the rat. *Laboratory Animal Science* **23**, 266-269.

Jageneau, A. H. M., Bergen, A. & Symoens, J. (1974). The effect of azaperone-metomidate anaesthesia on respiratory and cardiac functions in the pig. In: *Proceedings International Pig Veterinary Society (I.P.V.S. 3rd Int. Cong.)*.

Janssen Pharmaceuticals (1969). *Immobilization and restraint of large wild mammals with azaperone and fentanyl*. Beerse, Belgium: Janssen Pharmaceutica.

Jay, G. E. (1955). Variation in response of various mouse strains to hexobarbital (Evipal). *Proceedings of the Society for Experimental Biology and Medicine* **90,** 378-380.

Jeffries, L. & Price, S. A. (1964) The evaluation and modification of a technique for comparing the efficiency of antiseptics against subcutaneously deposited bacteria in mice. *Journal of Clinical Pathology* **17,** 504-510.

Jenkins, J. T., Crooks, J. L., Charlesworth, C., Blane, G. F. & Ling, C. M. (1972). The use of etorphine-acepromazine (analgesic tranquilliser) mixtures in horses. *Veterinary Record* **90,** 207-210.

Jennings, S. (1971). In *Textbook of veterinary anaesthesia* (ed. L. R. Soma). Baltimore: Williams & Wilkins.

Jensen, E. C. & Klemm, W. R. (1967). Clinical evaluation of the analeptic doxapram, in dogs and cats. *Journal of the American Veterinary Medical Association* **150,** 516-525.

Jewell, P. & Smith, E. A. (1963). Cited in *Small animal anaesthesia* (ed. O. Graham-Jones), p. 81. Oxford: Pergamon.

Jha, S. K., Lumb, W. V. & Johnston, R. F. (1961). Some effects of triflupromazine hydrochloride on goats. *American Journal of Veterinary Research* **22,** 915-920.

Johnson, B. C. (1966). Some enzymatic and cardiovascular effects of starvation–refeeding stress. In *Swine in biomedical research* (ed. L. K. Bustad & R. O. McClellan), pp. 193-211. Seattle: Frayn.

Johnson, R. F. (1961). Promazine hydrochloride as a tranquilliser for sows. *Veterinary Record* **73,** 588.

Johnson, V. L., Klavano, P. A., Wright, R & Sax, D. (1958). Some effects of trichlorethylene on the electrocardiogram of the cat. *Veterinary Medicine* **53,** 375-377.

Jolly, D. W., Mawdesley-Thomas, L. E. & Bucke, D. (1972). Anaesthesia of fish. *Veterinary Record* **91,** 424-426.

Jones, D. M. (1971). The immobilization of cattle and related species. *Veterinary Record* **80,** 173-174.

Jones, D. M. (1973). The use of drugs for immobilization, capture and translocation of non-domestic animals. *Veterinary Annual* **13,** 320-352.

Jones, D. M. (1975). Elephant rescue in Sri Lanka. *Oryx* **13,** 185-196.

Jones, D. M. (1976). An assessment of weapons and projectile syringes used for capturing mammals. *Veterinary Record* **99,** 250-253.

Jones, D. M. (1977a). Recent advances in the use of drugs for immobilization, capture and translocation of non-domestic animals. *Veterinary Annual* **17,** 280-285.

Jones, D. M. (1977b). The sedation and anaesthesia of birds and reptiles. *Veterinary Record* **101,** 340-342.

Jones, D. M. (1977c). Immobilising exotic animals. *Veterinary Record* **101,** 352-353.

Jones, D. M. (1978). Personal communication.

Jones, D. M. & Manton, V. J. A. (1976). Biennial report for Whipsnade Park in the Scientific Report of the Zoological Society of London 1973-1975. *Journal of Zoology* **178,** 494-507.

Jones, E. C. & Krohn, P. L. (1960). Orthotopic ovarian transplantation in mice. *Journal of Endocrinology* **20,** 135-146.

Jones, E. W. (1949). Cited by Lumb, W. V. & Jones, E. W. (1973). In *Veterinary anaesthesia*. Philadelphia: Lea & Febiger.

Jones, E. W., Johnson, L. & Heinze, C. D. (1960). Thiopental sodium anaesthesia in the horse: a rapid induction technique. *Journal of the American Veterinary Medical Association* **137,** 119–124.

Jones, E. W., Nelson, T. E., Anderson, I. L., Kerr, D. D. & Burnap, T. K. (1972). Malignant hyperthermia of swine. *Anesthesiology* **36,** 42-51.

Jones, J. B. & Simmons, M. L. (1968). Innovar-Vet as an intramuscular anesthetic for rats. *Laboratory Animal Care* **18,** 642-643.

Jones, L. M. (1957). *Veterinary pharmacology and therapeutics*, 2nd ed. Ames, Iowa: Iowa State College Press.

Jones, N. O. (1972). Methoxyflurane nephrotoxicity—a review and a case report. *Canadian Anaesthetists' Society Journal* **19,** 152-159.

Jones, R. S. (1966). Halothane anaesthesia in turkeys. *British Journal of Anaesthesia* **36,** 656-658.

Jones, R. S. (1972). A review of tranquillisation and sedation in large animals. *Veterinary Record* **90,** 613-617.

Jordan, F. T. W., Sanford, J. & Wright, A. (1960). Anaesthesia in the fowl. *Journal of Comparative Pathology* **70,** 437-449.

Kain, M. L. & Nunn, J. F. (1967). Fresh gas flow and rebreathing in the Magill circuit with spontaneous respiration. *Proceedings of the Royal Society of Medicine* **60,** 749-750.

Kallos, T. & Smith, T. C. (1968). Naloxone reversal of pentazocine-induced respiratory depression. *Journal of the American Medical Association* **204,** 932.

Kalow, W. (1962). *Pharmacogenetics*. Philadelphia: Saunders.

Kaminer, B. (1958). The electrocardiogram of the baboon (*Papio ursinus*). *South African Journal of Medical Sciences* **23,** 231-240.

Kaplan, B. (1972). Ketamine HCl anesthesia in dogs: observation of 327 cases. *Veterinary Medicine—Small Animal Practice* **67,** 631-634.

Kaplan, H. M. (1969). Anesthesia in amphibians and reptiles. *Federation Proceedings. Federation of American Societies for Experimental Biology* **28,** 1541-1546.

Kaplan, H. M., Brewer, N. R. & Kaplan, M. (1962). Comparative value of some barbiturates for anaesthesia in the frog. *Proceedings of the Animal Care Panel* **12,** 141-148.

Kaplan, H. M. & Kaplan, M. (1961). Anesthesia in frogs with ethyl alcohol. *Proceedings of the Animal Care Panel* **11,** 31-36.

Kaplan, H. M. & Taylor, R. (1957) Anesthesia in turtles. *Herpetologica* **13,** 43-45.

Karkstrom, E. L. & Cook, S. F. (1955). Notes on snake anesthesia. *Copeia* **1,** 57-58.

Kato, R. & Takanaka, A. (1968). Metabolism of drugs in old rats. I. Activities of NADPH-linked electron transport and drug-metabolizing enzyme systems in liver microsomes of old rats. *Japanese Journal of Pharmacology* **18,** 381-388.

Katz, R. L. & Bigger, J. T. (1970).Cardiac arrhythmias during anesthesia and operation. *Anesthesiology* **33,** 193-213.

Kaufman, L. & Hahnenberger, R. (1975). CI-744 anesthesia for ophthalmological examination and surgery in monkeys. *Investigative Ophthalmology* **14,** 788-792.

Kaump, D. H., Kurtz, S. M., Fisken, R. A., Schardein, J. L., Roll, D. E. & Reutner, T. F. (1969). Toxicology of ketamine. *Proceedings of the International Symposium on Ketamine.* Berlin: Springer.

Kay, B. (1976). A clinical assessment of the use of etomidate in children. *British Journal of Anaesthesia* **48,** 207-211.

Kayama, Y. & Iwama, K. (1972). The EEG, evoked potentials, and single-unit activity during ketamine anaesthesia in cats. *Anesthesiology* **36,** 316–328.

Keep, J. M. (1973). Notes on the field capture of the Agile Wallaby (*Macropus agil*). *Australian Veterinary Journal* **49,** 385-387.

Keep, M. E. (1970). Cited by Jones, D. M. (1973). *Veterinary Annual* **13,** 320-352.

Keighley, G. (1966). A device for intravenous injection of mice and rats. *Laboratory Animal Care* **16,** 185-187.

Keller, A. D. & Fulton, J. F. (1931). The action of anesthetic drugs on the motor cortex of monkeys. *American Journal of Physiology* **97,** 537.

Kelman, G. R. & Kennedy, B. R. (1971). Cardiovascular effects of pancuronium in man. *British Journal of Anaesthesia* **43,** 335-339.

Kennard, M. A., Ruch, T. C. & Fulton, J. F. (1946). Housing, care and surgical handling of laboratory primates. *Yale Journal of Biology and Medicine* **18,** 443-471.

Kennedy, W. P. (1934). Sodium salt of C-C-cyclohexenylmethyl-N-methyl barbituric acid (Evipan) anaesthesia in laboratory animals. *Journal of Pharmacology and Experimental Therapeutics* **50,** 347-353.

Kent, G. M. (1971). General anesthesia in rabbits using methoxyflurane, nitrous oxide and oxygen. *Laboratory Animal Science* **21,** 256-257.

Keplinger, M. L., Lanvier, G. E. & Deichmann, W. B. (1959). Effects of environmental temperature on the acute toxicity of a number of compounds in rats. *Toxicology and Applied Pharmacology* **1,** 156-161.

Kerlin, R. E. (1964). Venepuncture of small birds. *Journal of the American Veterinary Medical Association* **144,** 870-874.

Kerr, D. D., Jones, E. W. Holbert, D. & Huggins, K. (1972*a*). Comparison of the effects of xylazine and acetylpromazine maleate in the horse. *American Journal of Veterinary Research* **33,** 777-784.

Kerr, D. D., Jones, E. W., Huggins, K. & Edwards, W. C. (1972*b*). Sedative and other effects of xylazine given intravenously to horses. *American Journal of Veterinary Research* **33,** 525-532.

Kidd, A. R. M. Broughton, E. & Done, J. T. (1971). Sedation and immobilisation of cattle in the field. *Veterinary Record* **88,** 679-687.

Kimoto, S., Sugie, S. & Asano, K. (1956). Open heart surgery under direct vision with the aid of brain-cooling by irrigation. *Surgery* **39,** 592-597.

King, E. E. & Unna, K. R. (1954). The action of mephenesin and other interneuron depressants on the brain stem. *Journal of Pharmacology and Experimental Therapeutics* **111,** 293-301.

King, J. M. (1965). A field guide to the reproduction of the Grants Zebra and Grevys Zebra. *East African Wildlife Journal* **3,** 99-108.

King, J. M. (1969). The capture and translocation of the Black Rhinoceros. *East African Wildlife Journal* **7,** 115-130.

King, J. M. & Carter, B. H. (1965). The use of the Oripavine derivative M.99 for the immobilisation of the Black Rhinoceros (*Diceros bicornis*) and its antagonism with the related compound M.285 or Nalorphine. *East African Wildlife Journal* **3,** 99-108.

King, J. M. & Klingel, H. (1965). The use of the Oripavine derivative M.99 for the restraint of Equine animals and its antagonism with the related compound M.285. *Research in Veterinary Science* **6,** 447-455.

Kinsey, V. E. (1940). The use of sodium pentobarbitone for repeated anaesthesia in the guinea pig. *Journal of the American Pharmaceutical Association* (Scientific Edition) **29,** 387-390.

Kisch, B. (1947). A method to immobilise fish for cardiac and other experiments with procaine. *Biological Bulletin. Marine Biological Laboratory, Woods Hole, Mass.* **93,** 208.

Kittle, E. L. (1971). Ketamine HCl as an anesthetic for birds. *Modern Veterinary Practice* **52,** 40-41.

Kleinman, L. I. & Radford, E. P. (1964). Ventilation standards for small mammals. *Journal of Applied Physiology* **19,** 360-362.

Klemm, W. R. (1966). Evaluation of effectiveness of doxapram and various analeptic combinations in dogs. *Journal of the American Veterinary Medical Association* **148,** 894-899.

Klemm, W. R. (1968*a*). Subjective and quantitative analyses of the electroencephalogram of anesthetized normal dogs: control data for clinical diagnosis. *American Journal of Veterinary Research* **29,** 1267-1277.

Klemm, W. R. (1968*b*). Attempts to standardize veterinary electroencephalographic techniques. *American Journal of Veterinary Research* **29,** 1895-1900.

Klemm, W. R. (1969). *Animal electroencephalography.* New York: Academic Press.

Klemm, W. R. (1976). Electroencephalography. In *Appled electronics for veterinary medicine and animal physiology* (ed. W. R. Klemm). Springfield, Illinois: Thomas.

Klemm, W. R. & Hall, C. L. (1974). Current status and trends in veterinary electroencephalography. *Journal of the American Veterinary Medical Association* **164,** 529-532.

Klide, A. M. (1973). Avian anesthesia. *Veterinary Clinics of North America* **3,** 175-186.

Klontz, G. W. (1964). Anesthesia of fish. *Proceedings: Symposium of the Anesthesiology of Laboratory Animals,* pp. 1-7. Brooks Air Force Base, Texas.

Klontz, G. W. & Smith, L. S. (1968). Methods of using fish as biological research subjects. In *Methods of animal experimentation* (ed. W. I. Gay), pp. 323-385. New York: Academic Press.

Kluge, T. & Tveten, L. (1968). Endotracheal anesthesia for intrathoracic surgery in rats. *Acta Pathologica et microbiologica scandinavica* **72**, 103-108.

Knocker, P. (1955). Effects of experimental hypothermia on vital organs. *Lancet* 1955 **2**, 837-839.

Kohn, R. & Lederer, L. (1938). Pentothal studies with special reference to the electrocardiogram. *Journal of Laboratory and Clinical Medicine* **23**, 717.

Kolff, J., Webb, J. A. & Loop, F. D. (1972). Electrical analogues of methods for continuous positive pressure ventilation. *Journal of Thoracic and Cardiovascular Surgery* **64**, 586-591.

Koppanyi, T. & Karczmar, A. G. (1948). Comparison of anaesthetic action of acetanilid, tricaine (MS-222) and aliphatic depressants. *Federation Proceedings* **7**, 234.

Kovach, A. G. B. (1972). The function of the central nervous system after haemorrhage. *Journal of Clinical Pathology* **23**, Suppl. 4, 202-212.

Krahwinkel, D. J. & Evans, A. T. (1972). Anesthetic equipment for small animals. *Journal of the American Veterinary Medical Association* **161**, 1430-1434.

Kraner, K. L., Silverstein, A. M. & Parshall, C. J. (1965). Surgical anesthesia in snakes. In *Experimental animal anesthesiology* (ed. D. C. Sawyer). Brooks Air Force Base, Texas: U.S.A.F. School of Aerospace Medicine.

Krantz, J. C. & Carr, C. J. (1951). *The pharmacologic principles of medical practice*, 2nd ed. Baltimore: Williams & Wilkins.

Krawitz, L. (1957). A safer technique for the induction of general anesthesia in small animals. *Veterinary Medicine* **52**, 442-444.

Kreuscher, H. & Grote, J. (1967). Effect of phencyclidine derivative ketamine (CI-581) on circulation and oxygen uptake in dog's brain. *Anaesthesist* **16**, 304-308.

Kroll, W. R. (1962). Experience with sernylan in zoo animals. *International Zoo Yearbook* **4**, 131-141.

Krueger, H., Eddy, N. B. & Sumwalt, M. (1941). *The pharmacology of the opium alkaloids*, Part 1. U.S. Public Health Service.

Krupp, J. H. & Quillin, R. (1964). A review of the use of the opossum for research: husbandry, experimental techniques and routine health measures. *Laboratory Animal Care* **14**, 189-194.

Kumar, A. & Singh, M. (1970). Studies in epidural anesthesia in canine surgery. *Indian Veterinary Journal* **47**, 1110-1115.

Kuroda, T. & McNamara, J. A. (1972). The effect of ketamine and phencyclidine on muscle activity in nonhuman primates. *Anesthesia and Analgesia: Current Researches* **51**, 710-716.

Kursajimia, K., Wax, S. D. & Webb, W. R. (1974). Effects of methyl prednisolone on the pulmonary microcirculation. *Surgery, Gynecology and Obstetrics* **139**, 1-5.

Ladhani, F. M. & Thies, R. E. (1968). Fiber lengths and end-plate locations in fruit bat web muscles. *Proceedings of the Society for Experimental Biology and Medicine* **127**, 787-789.

Lafortune, J. G. & Rheault, J. P. E. (1960). Essai d'evaluation clinique de la reserpine (Serpasil) chez le vision. *Canadian Journal of Comparative Medicine and Veterinary Science* **24**, 243-251.

Laird, L. M. & Oswald, R. L. (1975). A note on the use of benzocaine (ethyl p-aminobenzoate) as a fish anaesthetic. *Journal of the Institute of Fish Management* **6**, 92-94.

Lamb, D. (1975). Rat lung pathology and quality of laboratory animals: the user's view. *Laboratory Animals* **9**, 1-8.

Lamberth, J. L. (1968). Droperidol, ethyl isobutrazine and pethidine as premedicants for weaner pigs. *Australian Veterinary Journal* **44**, 333-334.

Lamson, P. D., Greig, M. E. & Hobdy, C. J. (1951). Modification of barbiturate anesthesia by glucose, intermediary metabolites, and certain other substances. *Journal of Pharmacology and Experimental Therapeutics* **103**, 460-470.

Lane, J. G. (1974). Fatality after Revivon. *Veterinary Record* **94**, 427.

Lang, E. (1970). The use of azaperone for pigs. *Berliner und munchener tieraerztliche Wochenschrift* **83**, 141-143.

Larrabee, M. G. & Posternak, J. M. (1952). Selective action of anesthetics on synapses and axons in mammalian sympathetic ganglia. *Journal of Neurophysiology* **15**, 91-114.

Larsen, L. H. (1958). Recent developments in anaesthetics and muscular relaxants. *New Zealand Veterinary Journal* **6**, 61-75.

Larsen, L. H. (1963). Restraint of wild animals in captivity. *Australian Veterinary Journal* **39**, 73-80.

Larsen, L. H., Loomis, L. N. & Steel, J. D. (1959). Muscular relaxants and cardiovascular damage: with special reference to succinyl choline chloride. *Australian Veterinary Journal* **35**, 269-275.

Larsen, T. (1967). The trapping and study of polar bears, Spitzbergen. *Polar Record* **13**, 589-593.

Larson, L. L. (1953). The internal pudendal (pubic) nerve block for anesthesia of the penis and relaxation of the retractor penis muscle. *Journal of the American Veterinary Medical Association*, 18-27.

Larson, R. E., Moffit, E. A. & McGoon, D. C. (1963). Experimental cardiac surgery in calves. *Journal of Surgical Research* **3**, 101-103.

Lathe, G. H. & Walker, M. (1957). An enzyme defect in human neonatal jaundice and in Gunn's strain of jaundiced rats. *Biochemical Journal* **67**, 9 P.

Lawrence, B. & Schevill, W. E. (1956). The functional anatomy of the delphinoid nose. *Bulletin of the Museum of Comparative Zoology at Harvard College* **114**, 103-152.

Lawson, D. W., Defalco, A. J., Phelps, J. A., Bradley, B. E. & MacLanathan, J. E. (1966). Corticosteroids as treatment for aspiration of gastric contents: an experimental study. *Surgery* **59**, 845-852.

Lawson, R. L., Barranco, S. & Sorenson, A. M. (1966). A device to restrain the mouse, rat, hamster and chinchilla to facilitate semen collection and other reproductive studies. *Laboratory Animal Care* **16**, 72-79.

Leach, T. N. (1972). The use of Immobilon in pigs. *Veterinary Record* **91**, 495-496.

Leash, A. M., Beyer, R. D. & Wilbur, R. C. (1973). Self-mutilation following Innovar-Vet[R] injection in the guinea pig. *Laboratory Animal Science* **23**, 720-721.

Lebeaux, M. (1975). Sheep: a model for testing spinal and epidural anaesthetic agents. *Laboratory Animal Science* **25,** 629-633.

Lechleitner, R. J. (1967). Cited by Lumb, W. V. and Jones, E. W. (1973). In *Veterinary anaesthesia*, p. 461. Philadelphia: Lea & Febiger.

Lee, C. C. (1953). Experimental studies on the actions of several anaesthetics in domestic fowls. *Poultry Science* **32,** 624-627.

Lee, C. (1969). Cited by Lumb, W. V. and Jones, E. W. (1973). In *Veterinary anaesthesia*, p. 465. Philadelphia: Lea & Febiger.

Lee, J. A. & Atkinson, R. S. (1968). *A synopsis of anaesthesia*, 6th ed. Baltimore: Williams & Wilkins.

Lee, J. B. (1973). Clinical observations on the use of thiamylal sodium with fentanyl-droperidol as an anaesthetic in dogs. *Journal of Veterinary Medicine—Small Animal Clinician* **68,** 738-739.

Lees, P. (1977). Personal communication.

Lees, P. (1978). Personal communication.

Lees, P. & Hillidge, C. J. (1975). Neuroleptanalgesia and cardiovascular function in the horse. *Equine Veterinary Journal* **7** (4), 1-8.

Lees, P. & Serrano, L. (1976). Effects of azaperone on cardiovascular and respiratory functions in the horse. *British Journal of Pharmacology* **56,** 263-269.

Lefer, A. M. & Martin, J. (1969). Mechanism of the protective effect of corticosteroids in hemorrhagic shock. *American Journal of Physiology* **216,** 314-320.

de Leglise, J. (1973). Contribution à l'etude de l'anèsthesie générale. Emploi de l'azaperone (R1929) en premedication chez le cheval. *These. Ecole National d'Alfort*.

Leininger, F. G. (1965). Clinical use of methoxyflurane anesthetic in small animal practice. *Veterinary Medicine—Small Animal Clinician* **60,** 401-405.

Leloup, P. (1970). Trials with MS-222 SANDOZ on Rattlesnakes. *Report to Seminar SANDOZ/WANDER, Zurich*.

Lennartz, H., Zindler, M. & Herpfer, G. (1970). Comparative study of cardiovascular dynamics of ketamine, propanidid and Baytinal in animal experiments. *Anaesthesist* **19,** 252-257.

Lentfer, J. W. (1968). A technique for immobilising and marking polar bears. *Journal of Wildlife Management* **32,** 317-321.

Leonard, R. H. (1960). Parakeet and canary practice. *Journal of the American Veterinary Medical Association* **136,** 378-380.

Leslie, P. H., Thener, J. S., Vizoso, M. & Chitty, H. (1955). The longevity and fertility of the Orkney vole, *Microtus orcadensis*, as observed in the laboratory. *Proceedings of the Zoological Society of London* **125,** 115-125.

Levinger, I. M., Kedem, J. & Abram, M. (1973). A new anaesthetic-sedative agent for birds *British Veterinary Journal* **129,** 296-300.

Levy, C. J. & Owen, G. (1964). Thiopentone transmission through the placenta. *Anaesthesia* **19,** 511-513.

Lewis, D. G. & Mackenzie, A. (1972). Cooling during major vascular surgery. *British Journal of Anaesthesia* **44,** 859-864.

Lewis, G. E. & Jennings, P. B. (1972). Effective sedation of laboratory animals using Innovar-Vet[R]. *Laboratory Animal Science* **22,** 430-432.

Lewis, J. J. (1970). *Lewis's pharmacology*, 4th ed. Edinburgh: Linvingstone.

Lillehei, R. C., Lillehei, C. W., Grismer, J. T. & Levy, M. J. (1963). Plasma catecholamines in open heart surgery. *Surgical Forum* **14,** 269-271.

Lilly, J. C. (1962). *Man and dolphin*, pp. 46-57. London: Gollancz.

Lincoff, H. A., Breinin, G. M. & De Voe, A. G. (1957). The effect of succinylcholine on the extraocular muscles. *American Journal of Ophthalmology* **43,** 440-444.

Liu, W. S., Bidwai, A. V., Stanley, T. H. & Isern-Amaral, J. (1976). Cardiovascular dynamics after large doses of fentanyl and fentanyl plus N_2O in the dog. *Anesthesia and Analgesia: Current Researches* **55,** 168-172.

Lindau, K. H. & Gorgas, M. (1969). Versuche mit Bayer Va 1470. *11th International Symposium of Zoo Animal Diseases, Zagreb*, p. 135.

Linde, H. W., Lamb, V. E., Quimby, C. W., Homi, J. & Eckenhoff, J. E. (1970). The search for better anesthetic agents: clinical investigation of ethrane. *Anesthesiology* **32,** 555-559.

Lindsay, H. A. & Kullman, V. S. (1966). Pentobarbital sodium: variation in toxicity. *Science, New York* **151,** 576-677.

Ling, J. K., Nicholls, D. G. & Thomas, C. D. B. (1967). Immobilization of Southern Elephant Seals with succinylcholine chloride. *Journal of Wildlife Management* **31,** 468-479.

Linzell, J. L. (1964). In: *Small animal anaesthesia* (ed. O. Graham-Jones), p. 102. Oxford: Pergamon.

Linzell, J. L. (1964). Some observations on general and regional anaesthesia in goats. In *Small animal anaesthesia* (ed. O. Graham-Jones), pp. 163-175. Oxford: Pergamon.

Lindquist, P. A. (1972). Induction of methoxyflurane anesthesia in the rabbit after ketamine hydrochloride and endotracheal intubation. *Laboratory Animal Science* **22,** 898-899.

Littlejohn, A. & Mitchell, B. (1972). The effects of changes of posture and anaesthesia on cardiopulmonary function in man and horses. *Proceedings of the Association of Veterinary Anaesthetists* **3,** 47-55.

Livezey, R. L. (1957). Procaine hydrochloride as a killing agent for reptiles and amphibians. *Herpetologica* **13,** 280.

Lockie, J. D. & Day, M. G. (1964). The use of anaesthesia in the handling of stoats and weasels. In *Small animal anaesthesia* (ed. O. Graham-Jones), p. 187. Oxford: Pergamon.

Loeb, H. S., Winslow, E. B. J., Rahimtoola, J. H., Rosen, K. M. & Gunnar, R. A. (1971). Acute hemodynamic effects of dopamine in patients with shock. *Circulation* **44,** 163-173.

Logsdon, H. S. (1969). Use of drugs as a capture technique for desert bighorn sheep. Thesis. Colorado: Colorado State University, Fort Collins.

Longley, E. O. (1950). Thiopentone (Pentothal Sodium) as a general anaesthetic in the horse. *Veterinary Record* **62,** 17-20.

Longnecker, D. E., Miller, F. N. & Harris, P. D. (1974).

Small artery and vein response to ketamine HCl in the bat wing. *Anesthesia and Analgesia: Current Researches* **53**, 64-68.

Low, R. J. (1973). Immobilon in deer. *Veterinary Record* **93**, 86-87.

Lowe, J. E. (1969). Cited in *Wright's veterinary anaesthesia and analgesia*, p. 156. London: Baillière Tindall.

Løyning, Y., Oshima, T. & Yokota, T. (1964). Site of action of thiamylal sodium on the monosynaptic spinal reflex pathways in cats. *Journal of Neurophysiology* **27**, 408-428.

Luhning, C. W. (1973). Residues of MS-222, benzocaine and their metabolites in striped bass following anaesthesia. *U.S. Bureau of Sport, Fisheries and Wildlife: Investigations in Fish Control* **52**, 3-11.

Lukens, F. D. W. (1938). Pancreatectomy in the goat. *American Journal of Physiology* **122**, 729-733.

Lumb, W. V. (1963). In *Small animal anaesthesia* p. 112-198. Philadelphia: Lea & Febiger.

Lumb, W. V. (1972). Muscle relaxants in small animal anesthesia. *Journal of the American Veterinary Medical Association* **161**, 1436-1441.

Lumb, W. V. & Brasmer, T. H. (1970). Improved spinal plates and hypothermia as adjuncts to spinal surgery. *Journal of the American Veterinary Medical Association* **157**, 338-342.

Lumb, W. V. & Jones, E. W. (1973). *Veterinary anaesthesia*. Philadelphia: Lea & Febiger.

Luschei, E. S. & Mehaffey, J. J. (1967). Small animal anesthesia with halothane. *Journal of Applied Physiology* **22**, 595-597.

MacCannell, H. L. (1969). The effect of barbiturates on regional blood flows. *Canadian Anaesthetists' Society Journal* **16**, 1-6.

MacCannell, K. L., McNay, J. L., Meyer, M. B. & Goldberg, L. I. (1966). Dopamine in the treatment of hypotension and shock. *New England Journal of Medicine* **275**, 1389-1398.

MacDonald, R. H., Goldberg, L. I., McNay, S. L. & Tuttle, E. P. (1964). Effects of dopamine in man, augmentation of sodium excretion, glomerular filtration rate and renal plasma flow. *Journal of Clinical Investigation* **43**, 1116-1124.

Mackenzie, G. & Snow, D. H. (1977). An evaluation of chemical restraining agents in the horse. *Veterinary Record* **101**, 30-33.

Mackintosh, J. H. (1962). Effect of strain and group size in the response of mice to 'Seconal' anaesthesia. *Nature, London* **194**, 1304.

Macko, E., Scheidy, S. F. & Tucker, R. G. (1958). Chlorpromazine in the dog. *Veterinary Medicine* **53**, 378-381.

MacNider, W. de B. (1920). A study of the anurias occurring in normal animals during the use of general anesthetics. *Journal of Pharmacology and Experimental Therapeutics* **15**, 249-259.

Magalhaes, H. (1967). In *The UFAW handbook on the care and management of laboratory animals*. Edinburgh: Livingstone.

Mandelker, L. (1970). Anesthesia for parakeets and other birds. *Journal of the American Veterinary Medical Association* **157**, 1081-1083.

Mandelker, L. (1972). Ketamine hydrochloride as an anesthetic for parakeets. *Veterinary Medicine—Small Animal Clinician* **67**, 55-56.

Mandelker, L. (1973). A toxicity study of ketamine HCl in parakeets. *Veterinary Medicine—Small Animal Clinician* **68**, 487-489.

Mann, D. E. (1965). Biological ageing and its modification of drug activity. *Journal of Pharmaceutical Sciences* **123**, 499-510.

Manohar, M., Kumar, R. & Tyagi, R. P. S. (1971). Studies on intravenous retrograde regional anaesthesia of the forelimb in buffalo calves. *British Veterinary Journal* **127**, 401-407.

Manton, V. J. A. (1966). *Scientific Report, Zoological Society of London, 1966*.

Manton, V. J. A. & Jones, D. M. (1972). Scientific Report, Zoological Society of London. *Journal of Zoology* **166**, 541-558.

Manton, V. J. A. & Jones, D. M. (1974). Whipsnade Park, 1971 and 1972. In: The Zoological Society of London Scientific Report 1971-1973. *Journal of Zoology* **173**, 84-103.

Mapletoft, R. J. & Futter, G. J. (1969). Repeated halothane anaesthesia in an American Bald Eagle. *Canadian Veterinary Journal* **10**, 274-277.

Marking, L. L. (1967). Tricaine methanesulfonate anesthesia in fish. *U.S. Bureau of Sport, Fisheries and Wildlife Research Publication* **21**, 3-6.

Markofsky, J. & Orentreich, N. (1976). An improved method for repeated plasmapheresis in the rat. *Laboratory Animal Science* **26**, 93-95.

Marley, E. & Payne, J. P. (1962). Anaesthesia for young animals. *Journal of Physiology* **162**, 35-36.

Marley, E. & Payne, J. P. (1962). A method of anaesthesia with halothane suitable for newborn animals. *British Journal of Anaesthesia* **34**, 776-783.

Marley, E. & Payne, J. P. (1964). Halothane anaesthesia in the fowl. In *Small animal anaesthesia* (ed. O. Graham-Jones), pp. 127-136, Oxford: Pergamon.

Marsboom, R. & Mortelmans, J. (1964). Some pharmacological aspects of analgesics and neuroleptics and their use for neuroleptanalgesia in primates and lower monkeys. In *Small animal anaesthesia* (ed. O. Graham-Jones), p. 31. Oxford: Pergamon.

Marsboom, R. & Symoens, J. (1968). Azaperone as a sedative for pigs. *Netherlands Journal of Veterinary Science* **1**, 124-131.

Marsboom, R. & Symoens, J. (1968). Experience with azaperone (R1929) as a sedative for pigs. *Tijdschrift voor Diergeneeskunde* **93**, 3-15.

Marsboom, R., Mortelmans, J. & Vercruysse, J. (1963). Neuroleptanalgesia in monkeys. *Veterinary Record* **75**, 132-133.

Marsboom, R., Mortelmans, J. & Vercruysse, J. (1965). Methoxymol (R7315) Janssen: a new hypnotic agent in birds. *International Zoo Yearbook* **5**, 200-201.

Marsboom, R., Mortelmans, J., Vercruysse, J. & Thienpont, D. (1962). Effective sedation and anaesthesia in gorillas and chimpanzees. *Nordisk Veterinaermedicin* **14**, 95-101.

Marsboom, R., Verstraete, A., Thienpont, D. & Mattheeuws, D. (1964). The use of haloanisone and phentanyl for neuroleptanalgesia in dogs. *British Veterinary Journal* **120**, 466-468.

Marston, J. H. & Chang, M. C. (1965). The breeding management and reproductive physiology of the Mongolian gerbil (*Meriones unguiculatus*). *Laboratory Animal Care* **15**, 34-48.

Martin, A. R. (1959). A technique for studying the action of antiseptics on bacteria in subcutaneous tissues with special reference to chlorhexidine. *Journal of Clinical Pathology* **12**, 48-51.

Martin, D. P., Darrow, C. C., Valerio, D. A. (1972). Methods of anesthesia in nonhuman primates. *Laboratory Animal Science* **22**, 837-843.

Martin, J. T., Faulconer, A. & Bickford, R. G. (1959). Electroencephalography in anesthesiology. *Anesthesiology* **20**, 359-376.

Martin, L. L. (1967). Comparison of methoxymol, alpha-chloralose and two barbiturates for capturing doves. *Proceedings of 21st Annual Conference, S.E. Association of Game and Fish Commissioners, New Orleans, 1967.*

Martin, N. V. & Scott, D. C. (1959). Use of tricaine methanesulfonate (MS222) in the transport of live fish without water. *Progressive Fish Culturist* **21**, 183-184.

Massey, G. N. (1970). Cited by Hall, L. W. (1971). In *Wright's veterinary anaesthesia and analgesia*, p. 405. London: Baillière Tindall.

Massey, G. N. (1973). Anaesthesia in the dog and cat. *Australian Veterinary Journal* **49**, 207-210.

Massion, W. H. (1965). Value of high energy compounds in treatment of shock. *American Journal of Surgery* **110**, 342-347.

Massopust, L. C., White, R. J., Wolin, L. R., Albin, M. S., Yashon, D. & Taslitz, N. (1968). Electrical activity of the isolated macaque brain. *Experimental Neurology* **22**, 303-325.

Massopust, L. C., Wolin, L. R., & Albin, M. S. (1972). Electrophysiologic and behavioural responses to ketamine hydrochloride in the rhesus monkey, *Anesthesia and Analgesia: Current Researches* **51**, 329-341.

Mathews, M. (1971). The use of ketamine to immobilize a black leopard. *Journal of Zoo Animal Medicine* **2**, 25-27.

Mattila, M. A. K. & Suutarinan, T. (1971). Clinical and experimental evaluation of the Loosco baby respirator. *Acta anaesthesiologica scandinavica* **15**, 229-237.

Mattingly, B. E. (1972). Injectable anaesthetic for raptors. *Raptor Research* **6**, 51-52.

Mauderly, J. L. (1975). An anesthetic system for small laboratory animals. *Laboratory Animal Science* **25**, 331-333.

Maxwell, G. M., Elliott, R. B. & Kneebone, G. M. (1964). Hemodynamics of kangaroos and wallabies. *American Journal of Physiology* **206**, 967-970.

Maxwell, R. E., Long, D. M. & French, L. A. (1972). In *Steroids and brain edema* (ed. H. J. Reulen & K. Schurmann). Berlin: Springer.

Maykut, M. D. (1958). The combined action of pentobarbitone and meperidine and of procaine and meperidine in guinea-pigs. *Canadian Anaesthetists' Society Journal* **5**, 161-169.

Maykut, M. D. & Kalow, W. (1955). Experiments with animals on the combined action of procaine and barbiturates. *Canadian Anaesthetists' Society Journal* **2**, 109-115.

Mazze, R. I., Cousins, M. J. & Kosek, J. C. (1973). Strain differences in metabolism and susceptibility to the nephrotoxic effects of methoxyflurane in rats. *Journal of Pharmacology and Experimental Therapeutics* **184**, 481-488.

Mazzoni, G., Partino, C., Melis, M., Demofonti, A., Valli, A., Francesconi, M. & Pelligrini, S. (1971). Organ transplantation in pigs with different portal and caval venous drainage. *European Surgical Research* **3**, 62-71.

McCaffrey, F. W. & Mate, M. J. (1963). Methoxyflurane ('Penthrane'): a report on 1200 cases. *Canadian Anaesthetists' Society Journal* **10**, 103-113.

McCarthy, D. A., Chen, G., Kaump, D. H. & Ensor, C. (1965). General anesthetic and other pharmacological properties of 2-(O-chlorphenyl)-2-methylamino cyclohexanone HCl (CI-581). *Journal of New Drugs* **5**, 21-33.

McCashen, F. B. & Gabel, A. A. (1971). In *Proceedings 17th Annual Convention American Association, Equine Practitioners, Chicago, 1971*, p. 111.

McCormick, M. J. & Ashworth, M. A. (1971). Acepromazine and methoxyflurane anesthesia of immature New Zealand White rabbits. *Laboratory Animal Science* **21**, 220-223,

McCune, P. (1973). Striped skunk-pet or threat. *Iowa State University Veterinarian* **35**, 52-54.

McDonald, H. S. (1976). Methods for the physiological study of reptiles. In *Biology of the reptilia, vol. V. physiology A* (ed. C. Gans & W. R. Dawson), pp. 19-126. New York: Academic Press.

McDowall, D. G. (1976). Neurosurgical anesthesia and intensive care. In *Recent advances in anaesthesia and analgesia* (ed. C. Langton Hewer & R. S. Atkinson), p. 31. Edinburgh: Churchill Livingstone.

McErlean, A. J. & Kennedy, V. S. (1968). Comparison of some anesthetic properties of benzocaine and MS222. *Transactions of the American Fisheries Society* **97**, 496-498.

McFarlane, L. S. (1963). The lateral approach to pudendal nerve block in the bovine and ovine. *Journal of the South African Veterinary Medical Association* **34**, 73-76.

McFarlane, W. N. (1959). A study of the effects of anaesthetics on the behaviour and physiology of fishes. *Publications of the Institute of Marine Science* **6**, 24-29.

McFarlane, W. N. & Klontz, G. W. (1969). Anesthesia in fish. *Federation Proceedings* **28**, 1535-1540.

McGovern, S. H. & Rugh, H. (1944). Efficacy of M-amine ethyl benzoate as an anaesthetic for amphibian embryos. *Proceedings of the Society for Experimental Biology and Medicine* **57**, 127-130.

McGrath, C. J., Nichols, M. F. & Hartley, J. W. (1974). *Proceedings of the 24th Annual Gaines Veterinary Symposium*, **29**.

McInnes, I. C. & Goldwater, H. L. (1972). Gas removal systems for commonly used circuits. *Anaesthesia* **27**, 340-347.

McIntyre, B. W., Laws, A. K. & Ramachandran, P. R. (1969). Positive expiratory pressure plateau: improved gas exchange during mechanical ventilation. *Canadian Anaesthetists' Society Journal* **16**, 477-486.

McIntyre, J. W. R. (1971). An introduction to general anaesthesia of experimental animals. *Laboratory Animals* **5**, 99-114.

McLaren, A. & Michie, D. (1956). Variability of response in experimental animals. A comparison of the reactions of inbred F_1 hybrid and random bred mice to a narcotic drug. *Journal of Genetics* **54**, 440-455.

McLeish, I. (1977). Doppler ultrasonic arterial pressure measurement in the cat. *Veterinary Record* **100**, 290-291.

McNeil, C. D. & Hardy, J. D. (1959). Electrical anesthesia: some metabolic observations and comparisons. *Surgical Forum* **9**, 394-398.

McShay, W. H., Potter, V. R., Goldman, A., Shipley, E. G. & Meyer, R. V. (1945). Biological energy transformation during shock as shown by blood chemistry. *American Journal of Physiology* **145**, 93-106.

Medd, R. (1974). Personal communication.

Medd, R. (1975). Personal communication.

Medd, R. K. & Heywood, R. (1970). A technique for intubation and repeated short-duration anaesthesia in the rat. *Laboratory Animals* **4**, 75-78.

Meier, R., Yonkman, F. F., Craver, B. N. & Gross, F. (1949). 17083P, a new imidazoline derivative with marked adrenolytic properties. *Proceedings of the Society for Experimental Biology and Medicine* **71**, 70-72.

Melby, E. C. & Baker, H. J. (1965). Phencyclidine for analgesia and anesthesia in simian primates. *Journal of the American Veterinary Medical Association* **147**, 1068-1072.

Michenfelder, J. D. & Cucchiara, R. F. (1974). Canine cerebral oxygen consumption during enflurane anesthesia and its modification during induced seizures. *Anesthesiology* **40**, 575-580.

Michwitz, G. V. & Reinhard, H. J. (1966). Experiments on electric anaesthesia in swine. *Deutsche tierärztliche Wochenschrift* **73**, 49-56.

Millenbruck, E. W. & Wallinga, M. H. (1946). A newly developed anesthetic for horses. *Journal of the American Veterinary Medical Association* **108**, 148-151.

Miller, A. E. & Gudmundson, J. (1964). Use of thiamylal in mature swine. *Canadian Veterinary Journal* **5**, 217-220.

Miller, E. V., Ben, M. & Cass, J. S. (1969). Comparative anaesthesia in laboratory animals. *Federation Proceedings. Federation of American Societies for Experimental Biology* **28**, 1373.

Miller, S. L. (1961). A theory of gaseous anesthetics. *Proceedings of the National Academy of Sciences, U.S.A.* **47**, 1515-1524.

Millican, K. G. & Millican, D. (1964). Some observations on the American opossum (*Didelphis virginiana*) as a laboratory animal. *Journal of the Animal Technicians Association* **14**, 141-144.

Millichamp, N. J. (1974). Anaesthesia in snakes—a review of past literature. *Herptile* **4**, 39-41.

Mills, H. D. (1950). Obstructed cheek-pouch in a monkey. *Veterinary Record* **62**, 356.

Mills, M., McFee, A. S. & Blaisch, B. F. (1967). The post resuscitation wet lung syndrome. *Annals of Thoracic Surgery* **3**, 182.

Mitchell, B. (1966). Sedation of the pig: clinical use of neuroleptic agents. *Veterinary Record* **78**, 651-656.

Mitchell, B. (1968). Thoracic surgery in the dog and cat. II. Anaesthetic requirements for thoracic surgery. *Journal of Small Animal Practice* **9**, 399-407.

Mitchell, B. (1978). Personal communication.

Miyasaka, M. & Domino, E. F. (1968). Neuronal mechanisms of ketamine-induced anesthesia. *International Journal of Neuropharmacology* **7**, 557-573.

Moir, W. M. (1937). The influence of age and sex on the repeated administration of sodium pentobarbital to albino rats. *Journal of Pharmacology and Experimental Therapeutics* **59**, 68-85.

Molello, J. A. & Hawkins, K. (1968). Methoxyflurane anesthesia of laboratory rats. *Laboratory Animal Care* **18**, 581-583.

Monahan, C. M. (1964). The use of methohexitone for induction of anaesthesia in large animals. *Veterinary Record* **76**, 1333.

Monks, P. S. (1972). The reversal of non-depolarising relaxants. A comparison of tubocurarine, gallamine and pancuronium. *Anaesthesia* **27**, 313-318.

Moore, F. D. (1959). *Metabolic care of the surgical patient.* Philadelphia: Saunders.

Moran, N. C. & Perkins, M. E. (1961). An evaluation of adrenergic blockade of the mammalian heart. *Journal of Pharmacology and Experimental Therapeutics* **133**, 192-201.

Morris, B. (1967). The European hedgehog. In *The UFAW handbook on the care and management of laboratory animals*, p. 478. Edinburgh: Livingstone.

Morrison, S. R., Bond, T. E. & Heitman, H. (1967). Skin and lung moisture loss from swine. *Transactions of the American Society of Agricultural Engineering* **10**, 691-696.

Mortelmans, J. (1969). Tranquillization and anaesthesia. *Primates in Medicine* **2**, 113-122.

Mosby, H. S. & Cantner, D. E. (1955). The use of avertin in capturing wild turkeys and as an oral-based anaesthetic for other wild animals. *Southwestern Veterinarian* **9**, 132-135.

Moss, G. (1969). Fluid distribution in prevention of hypovolemic shock. *Archives of Surgery* **98**, 281-286.

Mostert, J. W., Evers, J. L., Hobika, G. H., Moore, R. H., Kenny, G. M. & Murphy, G. P. (1970). The haemodynamic response to chronic renal failure as studied in the azotaemic state. *British Journal of Anaesthesia* **42**, 501-513.

Motulsky, A. G. (1965). The genetics of abnormal drug responses. *Annals of the New York Academy of Sciences* **123**, 167-177.

Moult, P. J. A. & Sherlock, S. (1975). Halothane-related hepatitis. *Quarterly Journal of Medicine* **173**, 99-114.

Mount, L. E. (1959). The metabolic rate of the new-born pig in relation to environmental temperature and to age. *Journal of Physiology, London* **147**, 333-345.

Mount, L. E. (1963). The environmental temperature preferred by the young pig. *Nature, London* **199**, 122-123.

Mount, L. E. & Ingram, D. L. (1971). *The pig as a laboratory animal*, p. 81. London: Academic Press.

Mueller, H., Ayres, S. M., Gregory, J. J., Giannelli, S. & Grace, W. J. (1970). Hemo-dynamics, coronary bloodflow and myocardial metabolism in coronary shock response to L-norepinephrine and isoproterenol. *Journal of Clinical Investigation* **49**, 1885-1902.

Muhrer, M. E. (1950). Restraint of swine with pentothal sodium. *Journal of the American Veterinary Medical Association* **117**, 293-296.

Mulder, J. B. (1973). A unit for inhalation anesthesia of small laboratory animals. *Anesthesia and Analgesia: Current Researches* **52**, 369-371.

Mulder, J. B. & Brown, R. V. (1972). An anesthetic unit for small laboratory animals. *Laboratory Animal Science* **22**, 422-423.

Mullenax, C. H. & Dougherty, R. W. (1964). Systemic responses of sheep to high concentrations of inhaled carbon dioxide. *American Journal of Veterinary Research* **25**, 424-440.

Mullins, L. J. (1972). Anaesthetics. In *Handbook of neurochemistry* (ed. A. Lajtha). New York: Plenum Press.

Munson, E. S. (1970). Effect of hypothermia on anesthetic requirement in rats. *Laboratory Animal Science* **20**, 1109-1113.

Munson, E. S., Gillespie, J. R., & Wagman, I. H. (1970). Respiratory blood gases and pH in two species of unanesthetized monkeys. *Journal of Applied Physiology* **28**, 108-109.

Munson, E. S., Martucci, R. W. & Smith, R. E. (1970). Circadian variations in anesthetic requirement and toxicity in rats. *Anesthesiology* **32**, 507-514.

Murdock, H. R. (1969). Anesthesia in the rabbit. *Federation Proceedings* **28**, 1510-1516.

Mushin, W. W., Rendell-Baker, L., Thompson, P. W. & Mapleson, W. W. (1969). *Automatic ventilation of the lungs*, 2nd ed. Philadelphia: Davis.

Mushin, W. W., Wien, R., Mason, D. F. J. & Langston, G. T. (1949). Curare-like actions of tri(diethylaminoethoxy)-benzene triethyliodide. *Lancet* 1949 **1**, 726-729.

Myers, R. E. & Stettner, L. J. (1969). Safe and reliable general anaesthesia in birds. *Physiology and Behaviour* **4**, 227-278.

Mylon, E., Winternitz, M. C. & De Suto-Nagy, G. J. (1942). Studies on therapy in traumatic shock. *American Journal of Physiology* **139**, 313-324.

Nagel, E. L., Morgane, P. J. & McFarland, W. L. (1964). Anaesthesia for the bottlenose dolphin, *Tursiops truncatus*. *Science, New York* **146**, 1591-1593.

Nagel, E. L., Morgane, P. J. & McFarland, W. L. (1966). Anaesthesia for the bottlenose dolphin, *Tursiops truncatus*. *Veterinary Medicine—Small Animal Clinician* **61**, 233-236.

Nair, V. (1969). An ontogenic study of the effects of exposure to X-irradiation on the pharmacology of barbiturates. *Chicago Medical School Quarterly* **28**, 9-25.

Neal, P. A. & Wright, J. G. (1959). The use of succinylcholine chloride as a casting agent in the horse prior to the induction of general anaesthesia. *Veterinary Record* **71**, 731-735.

Newberne, P. M., Salmon, W. D. & Hare, W. V. (1961). Chronic murine pneumonia in an experimental laboratory. *Archives of Pathology* **72**, 224-233.

Newsome, J. & Robinson, D. L. H. (1957). Sedatives and anaesthetics for baboons. *British Veterinary Journal* **113**, 163-166.

Newman, D. L. & Looker, T. (1972). Simultaneous measurement of the systolic blood pressure and heart rate in the rat by a transcutaneous method. *Laboratory Animals* **5**, 207-211.

Ngai, S. H., Katy, R. L. & Farhie, S. E. (1965). Respiratory effects of ether, trichlorethylene, halothane and methoxyflurane. *Journal of Pharmacology and Experimental Therapeutics* **148**, 123-130.

Ngai, S. G. & Papper, E. M. (1962). *Metabolic effects of anesthesia*. Springfield, Illinois: Thomas.

Nicholas, J. S. & Barron, D. H. (1932). The use of sodium amytal in the production of anesthesia in the rat. *Journal of Pharmacology and Experimental Therapeutics* **46**, 125-129.

Nickerson, M. (1963). Sympathetic blockade in the theory of shock. *American Journal of Cardiology* **12**, 919-923.

Nicoll, P. A. (1964). Structure and function of minute vessels in autoregulation. *Circulation Research* **15** (1), 245-253.

Nightingdale, D. A., Richards, C. C. & Glass, A. (1965). An evaluation of rebreathing in a modified T-piece system during controlled ventilation of anaesthetised children. *British Journal of Anaesthesia* **37**, 762-771.

Noakes, D. E. (1966). Methohexitone sodium anaesthesia in pigs. *Veterinary Record* **78**, 669-670.

Noordhoek, J. & Rümke, C. L. (1969). Sex differences in the rate of drug metabolism in mice. *Archives internationales de pharmacodynamie et de thérapie* **182**, 401-402.

Northfield, T. C. & Smith, T. (1970). Central venous pressure in clinical management of acute gastro-intestinal bleeding. *Lancet* 1970 **2**, 584-586.

Northway, R. B. (1969). Electro anaesthesia of green iguanas (*Iguana iguana*). *Journal of the American Veterinary Medical Association* **155**, 1034.

Noyes, D. H. & Siekierski, D. M. (1975). Anesthesia of marmots with sodium pentobarbital, ketamine hydrochloride and a combination of droperidol and fentanyl. *Laboratory Animal Science* **25**, 557-562.

Nunn, J. F. & Bergman, N. A. (1964). The effect of atropine on pulmonary gas exchange. *British Journal of Anaesthesia* **36**, 68-73.

Orland, F. J. & Orland, P. M. (1946). Pentobarbital sodium anaesthesia in the Syrian hamster. *Journal of American Pharmaceutical Association* **35**, 263-265.

Orr, J. A., Manohar, M. & Will, J. A. (1976). Cardiopulmonary effects of the combination of neuroleptic azaperone and hypnotic metomidate in swine. *American Journal of Veterinary Research* **37**, 1305-1308.

Orsag, A. (1969). Effect of bemegride in interrupting thiopental anaesthesia in sheep. *Veterinary Bulletin, Weybridge* **40**, 585.

Osborne, B. E. (1973). A restraining device facilitating electrocardiogram recording in rats. *Laboratory Animals* **7**, 185-188.

276

Osborne, B. E. (1973). A restraining device for use when recording electrocardiograms in monkeys. *Laboratory Animals* **7**, 289-292.

Osborne, B. E. & Roberts, C. N. (1972). The electrocardiogram (ECG) of the baboon (*Papio* spp.). *Laboratory Animals* **6**, 127-133.

Osborn, C. M. (1941). The effect of hypophysectomy upon the growth of melanophores in the catfish (*Amuras melas*). *Anatomical Record* **81** (Suppl.), 59-60.

Oswald, R. L. (1977). Immobilization of decapod crustacea for experimental procedures. *Journal of the Marine Biological Association of the United Kingdom* **57**, 715-721.

Owen, L. N. (1955). The narcotic effects of thiambutene in the dog and its antagonism by nalorphine. *Veterinary Record* **67**, 561-566.

Owen, L. N. & Neal, P. A. (1957). Sedation with chlorpromazine in the horse. *Veterinary Record* **69**, 413-417.

Padgett, G. A. (1964). Cited by Lumb, W. V. & Jones, E. W. (1973). In *Veterinary anesthesia*. Philadelphia: Lea & Febiger.

Palminteri, A. (1966). Clinical appraisal of the narcotic antagonist n-allylnoroxymorphone. *Journal of the American Veterinary Medical Association* **148**, 1396-1399.

Pampiglione, G. (1963). *Development of cerebral function in the dog*. London: Butterworth.

Pandeya, N. K. & Lemon, H. M. (1965). Paraldehyde: An anesthesia for recovery experiments in albino rabbits. *Laboratory Animal Care* **15**, 304-306.

Pansky, B., Jacobs, M., House, E. L. & Tassoni, J. P. (1961). The orbital region as a source of blood sample in the golden hamster. *Anatomical Record* **139**, 409-412.

Parbrook, G. D. (1966). A halothane vaporiser for small animal anaesthesia. *Anaesthesia* **21**, 403-405.

Parker, G. H. (1939). General anaesthesia by cooling. *Proceedings of the Society for Experimental Biology and Medicine* **42**, 186-187.

Paterson, R. C., & Rowe, A. H. R. (1972). Surgical anaesthesia in conventional and gnotobiotic rats. *Laboratory Animals* **6**, 147-154.

Paton, W. D. M. & Zaimis, E. J. (1951). The action of d-tubocurarine and of decamethonium on respiratory and other muscles in the cat. *Journal of Physiology, London* **112**, 311-331.

Pauling, L. (1961). A molecular theory of general anaesthesia. *Science, New York* **134**, 15-21.

Payne, J. M. & Chamings, J. (1964). The anaesthesia of laboratory rodents. In *Small animal anaesthesia* (ed. O. Graham-Jones), pp. 103-108. Oxford: Pergamon.

Pearson, D. T. (1972). The use of isoprenaline and alpha adrenergic blockers in open heart surgery. *Resuscitation* **1**, 149-161.

Pekas, J. C. (1968). Versatile swine laboratory apparatus for physiologic and metabolic studies. *Journal of Animal Science* **27**, 1303-1306.

Perper, R. J. & Najarian, J. S. (1967). Anesthesia in large experimental animals. *Surgery* **61**, 824-826.

Perry, J. S. (1964). Anaesthesia of the adult sow. In *Small animal anaesthesia* (ed. O. Graham-Jones), pp. 155-156. Oxford: Pergamon.

Peters, J. M. & Boyd, E. M. (1965). Resistance to pentobarbital in rats fed a cachexigenic diet. *Toxicology and Applied Pharmacology* **8**, 464-471.

Peterson, R. S. (1965). Drugs for handling fur seals. *Journal of Wildlife Management* **29**, 688-693.

Petter, F. (1967). In *The UFAW handbook on the care and management of laboratory animals*, p. 449. Edinburgh: Livingstone.

Pezzi, P. J., Frobese, A. S. & Greenberg, S. R. (1966). Methoxyflurane and renal toxicity. *Lancet* 1966 **1**, 823.

Pfaff, J. (1974). Noise as an environmental problem in the animal house. *Laboratory Animals* **8**, 347-354.

Phillips, I. R. & Grist, S. M. (1975). Clinical use of CT1341 anaesthetic ('Saffan') in marmosets (*Callithrix jacchus*). *Laboratory Animals* **9**, 57-60.

Phillipson, A. T. & Barnett, S. F. (1939). Anaesthesia in sheep. *Veterinary Record* **51**, 869-876.

Pickett, D. (1951). Curare in canine surgery. *Journal of the American Veterinary Medical Association* **119**, 346-353.

Pickford, G. E. & Atz, J. W. (1957). *The physiology of the pituitary gland of fishes*. New York: New York Zoological Society.

Pienaar, U. de V. (1966). The use of oripavine hydrochloride (M.99) in the drug immobilisation and marking of wild African elephant (*Loxodonta africana Blumenbach*) in the Kruger National Park. *Koedoe* **9**, 108-123.

Pienaar, U. de V. (1968). Recent advances in the field immobilization and restraint of wild ungulates in South African National Parks. *Acta Zoologica et Pathologica Antverpiensia* **46**, 17-38.

Pienaar, U. de V., Niekerk, J. W. van, Young, E., Wyk, P. van & Fairall, N. (1966) Neuroleptic narcosis of large wild herbivores in South African National Parks with the new potent morphine analgesics, M.99 and M.183. *Journal of the South African Veterinary Medical Association* **37**, 277-290.

Piermattei, D. L. & Swan, H. (1970). Techniques for general anaesthesia in miniature pigs. *Journal of Surgical Research* **10**, 587-592.

Piiper, J. & Scheid, P. (1973). Gas exchange in avian lungs: models and experimental evidence. In *Comparative physiology* (ed. L. Bolis, K. Schmidt-Nielsen & S. H. P. Maddrell), pp. 616-618. Amsterdam: North Holland.

Pindak, F. F. & Kendrick, J. Z. (1969). Simple method for anaesthetising small animals for intranasal inoculations. *Applied Microbiology* **17**, 920.

Pittinger, C. B. & Morris, L. E. (1953). Placental transmission of d-tubocurarine chloride from maternal to fetal circulation in dogs. *Anesthesiology* **14**, 238-244.

Platts, M. M. (1966). Electrolyte excretion in uraemia. *Clinical Science* **30**, 453-471.

Player, I. (1967). Translocation of the White Rhinoceros in South Africa. *Oryx* **9**, 137-150.

Pleuger, C. A. (1950). Gastrotomy in a crocodile: a case report. *Journal of the American Veterinary Medical Association* **117**, 297-298.

Polak, A. & Plum, F. (1964). Comparison of new analeptics in barbiturate-poisoned animals. *Journal of Pharmacology and Experimental Therapeutics* **145**, 27-33.

Potter, B. J. (1958). Haemoglobinuria caused by propylene glycol in sheep. *British Journal of Pharmacology and Chemotherapy* **13**, 385-389.

Powers, S., Reed, C. & Gregersen, M. I. (1947). The effects of morphine on dogs in hemorrhagic and traumatic shock. *American Journal of Physiology* **148**, 269-274.

del Pozo, R. & Armas, M. C. (1973). The use of diazepam as premedication in pentobarbital anaesthesia in guinea-pigs. *Experientia* **29**, 635-636.

Prasse, R. (1970). Die anwendung von stresnil in der schweinepraxis. *Der praktische Tieraratz* **51**, 278.

Prescott, L. F. (1969). Pharmacokinetic drug interactions. *Lancet* 1962 **2**, 1239-1243.

Presnell, K. R., Presidente, P. J. A. & Rapley, W. A. (1973). Combination of etorphine and xylazine in captive white-tailed deer. 1. Sedative and immobilisation properties. *Journal of Wildlife Diseases* **9**, 336-341.

Priano, L. L., Traber, D. L. & Wilson, R. D. (1969). Barbiturate anesthesia: an abnormal physiologic situation. *Journal of Pharmacology and Experimental Therapeutics* **165**, 126-135.

Price, H. L. (1961). Circulatory actions of general anesthetic agents and the homeostatic roles of epinephrine and norepinephrine in man. *Clinical Pharmacology and Therapeutics* **2**, 163-176.

Prys-Roberts, C. (1969). The measurement of cardiac output. *British Journal of Anaesthesia* **41**, 751-760.

Pugh, D. M. (1964). Acepromazine in veterinary use. *Veterinary Record* **76**, 439-442.

Pugh, O. L. & Penny, R. H. C. (1966). A crate for the restraint of large pigs. *Veterinary Record* **79**, 390-392.

Purdie, W. L. (1972). Anaesthesia and intensive care. *New Zealand Veterinary Journal* **20**, 153-155.

Quinn, G. P., Axelrod, J. & Brodie, B. B. (1958). Species, strain and sex differences in metabolism of hexobarbitone, on amidopyrine, antipyrine and aniline. *Biochemical Pharmacology* **1**, 152-159.

Rack, P. M. H. & Westbury, D. R. (1966). The effects of suxamethonium and acetylcholine on the behavior of cat muscle spindles during dynamic stretching and during fusimotor stimulation. *Journal of Physiology, London* **186**, 698-713.

Rae, J. H. (1962). The fate of pentobarbitone and thiopentone in the sheep. *Research in Veterinary Science* **3**, 399-407.

Rafferty, G. C. (1972). Hazards of immobilization. *Veterinary Record* **90**, 430.

Ragan, H. A. & Gillis, M. F. (1975). Restraint, venepuncture, endotracheal intubation and anesthesia of miniature swine. *Laboratory Animal Science* **25**, 409-419.

Rahmann, H., Srihari, K. & Krishnamoorthy, R. V. (1975). Comparative haematology, haemachemistry and electrocardiography of the slender loris and bonnet monkey. *Laboratory Animals* **9**, 69-78.

Rammazzotto, L. J., Carlin, R. & Engstrom, R. (1973). Serum acid phosphatase activity during haemorrhagic shock. *Life Sciences* **12**, 563-573.

Ranson, R. M. (1941). Pre-natal and infant mortality in a laboratory population of voles (*Microtus agrestis*). *Proceedings of the Zoological Society of London* **111**, 45-47.

Rapson, W. S. & Jones, T. C. (1964). Restraint of rabbits by hypnosis. *Laboratory Animal Care* **14**, 131-133.

Rashad, K. F. & Benson, D. W. (1967). Role of humidity in prevention of hypothermia in infants and children. *Anesthesia and Analgesia: Current Researches* **46**, 712-718.

Rasquin, P. (1951). Effects of carp pituitary and mammalian ACTH on the endocrine and lymphoid systems of the teleost *Astyanax mexicanus. Journal of Experimental Zoology* **117**, 317-357.

Raventos, J. (1956). The action of fluothane—a new volatile anaesthetic. *British Journal of Pharmacology and Chemotherapy* **11**, 394-409.

Rea, W. J., Ecker, R. R., Watson, S. T. & Sugg, W. L. (1973). Long term membrane oxygenation in respiratory failure. *Annals of Thoracic Surgery* **15**, 170-178.

Redderson, C. L., Uy, D. & Anton, A. H. (1974). New techniques for spinal anesthesia in the dog. *Anesthesiology* **40**, 187-188.

Redfern, R. (1971). Technique for oral intubation of wild rats. *Laboratory Animals* **5**, 169-172.

Redshaw, N. R. (1971). The Australian scrub wallaby (*Wallabia rufogrisea*) as a laboratory animal. *Laboratory Animals* **5**, 15-23.

Reed, M. J. & Staple, P. H. (1976). Improved technique for anaesthesia of *Macaca speciosa* with methohexitone sodium. *Laboratory Animals* **10**, 65-67.

Rees, G. J. (1950). Anaesthesia in the newborn. *British Medical Journal* **2**, 1419-1422.

Rees, G. J. (1965). In *General anaesthesia*, Vol. 2. (ed. F. T. Evans & T. C. Gray), p. 191. London: Butterworth.

Reese, A. J. H., & Nunn, J. F. (1961). An apparatus for administering known concentrations of volatile anaesthetics to small laboratory animals. *British Journal of Anaesthesia* **33**, 54-57.

Regan, M. J. & Eger, E. I. (1967). Effect of hypothermia in dogs on anesthetizing and apneic doses of inhalation agents. *Anesthesiology* **23**, 689-694.

Reichenbach-Klinke, H. & Elkan, E. (1965). *The principal diseases of lower vertebrates*, p. 202. London: Baillière, Tindall & Cassell.

Reid, J. S. & Frank, R. J. (1972). Prevention of undesirable side reactions of ketamine anesthesia in cats. *Journal of the American Animal Hospital Association* **8**, 115-119.

Reitmeyer, J. C., Vail, L. A., Hill, W. A., Crookshank, H. R. & Davis, W. D. (1967). Use of tranquillizers for restraint of sheep during radiography. *Laboratory Animal Care* **17**, 397-399.

Reves, J. G. & McCracken, L. E. (1976). Failure to induce hepatic pathology in animals sensitized to a halothane metabolite and subsequently challenged with halothane. *Anesthesia and Analgesia: Current Researches* **55**, 235-242.

Reynolds, H. H. (1969). Nonhuman primates in the study of toxicological effects on the central nervous system: a review. *Annals of the New York Academy of Sciences* **162**, 617-629.

Reynolds, W. T. (1975). Anaesthesia in cattle. *Australian Veterinary Journal* **51**, 270-272.

Rice, R. P. (1967). The mink: a short outline of general

management. *Journal of the Institute of Animal Technicians* **18**, 66-79.

Richmond, M. & Conoway, C. H. (1969). Management, breeding and reproductive performance of vole, *Microtus ochrogaster*, in a laboratory colony. *Laboratory Animal Care* **14**, 80-87.

Ricketts, C. R. (1973). Blood substitutes. *British Journal of Anaesthesia.* **45** (9), 958-962.

Riddell, W. K. (1952). Caudal anaesthesia in canine surgery. *Journal of Small Animal Medicine* **1**, 159-161.

Ridgway, S. H. (1965). Medical care of marine mammals. *Journal of the American Veterinary Medical Association* **147**, 1077-1085.

Ridgway, S. H. (1968). The bottlenosed dolphin in biomedical research. In *Methods of animal experimentation*, Vol. 3 (ed. W. I. Gay), pp. 387-446. New York: Academic Press.

Ridgway, S. H. & McCormick, J. G. (1967). Anesthetization of porpoises for major surgery. *Science, New York* **158**, 510-512.

Ridgway, S. H. & Simpson, J. G. (1969). Anesthesia and restraint for the Californian Sea Lion *Zalophus californianus*. *Journal of the American Veterinary Medical Association* **155**, 1059-1063.

Rieu, M. & Gautheron, B. (1968): Preliminary observations concerning a method for introduction of a tube for anaesthesia in small delphinids. *Life Sciences* **7**, 1141-1150.

Riordan, J. F. & Walters, G. (1968). Pulmonary oedema in bacterial shock. *Lancet* 1968 **1**, 719-721.

Ritchie, H. E. (1957). Chlorpromazine sedation in the pig. *Veterinary Record* **69**, 895-900.

Roberts, F. W. (1971). Anaesthesia in pigs: intramuscular ketamine as an induction agent. *Anaesthesia* **26**, 445-449.

Robertshaw, D. (1964). Methohexital sodium anaesthesia in calves. *Veterinary Record* **76**, 357-358.

Robertshaw, D. (1966). Methohexital anaesthesia in sheep and goats. *Veterinary Record* **78**, 433.

Robinson, D. L. H. (1964). Sedatives and anaesthetics for baboons. In *Small animal anaesthesia* (ed. O. Graham-Jones), pp. 27-29. Oxford: Pergamon.

Robinson, P. T. & Fairfield, J. (1974). Immobilisation of an ostrich with ketamine. *Journal of Zoo Animal Medicine* **5**, 11-14.

Romagnoli, A. (1956). Indirect blood pressure measurement in sheep and goats employing the electronic plethysmograph: validation against the capacitance manometer. *British Veterinary Journal* **112**, 247-252.

Root, W. S., Allison, J. B., Cole, W. H., Holmes, J. H., Walcott, W. W. & Gregerson, M. I. (1947). Disturbances in the chemistry and in the acid base balance in hemorrhagic and traumatic shock. *American Journal of Physiology* **149**, 52-63.

Rosenbaum, D. K., Frank, E. D., Ruttenberg, I. M. & Frank, H. A. (1957). High energy phosphate content of liver tissue in experimental hemorrhagic shock. *American Journal of Physiology* **188**, 86-90.

Rosenbaum, R. W., Hayes, M. F., Marello, D. C. & Matsumoto, T. (1973). The importance of pulmonary artery pressure monitoring. *Surgery, Gynecology and Obstetrics* **136**, 261-264.

Rosenblum, R., Tai, A. R. & Lawson, D. (1972).

Dopamine in man; cardiorenal hemodynamics in normotensive patients with heart disease. *Journal of Pharmacology and Experimental Therapeutics* **183**, 256-263.

Routledge, F. G., Topliff, E. D. L. & Livingstone, S. D. (1968). Animal respiratory mask. *Canadian Journal of Physiology and Pharmacology* **46**, 700-701.

Routtenberg, A. (1968). Pentobarbital anesthesia of albino rats. *Journal of Experimental Analysis of Behavior* **11**, 52.

Rowson, L. E. A. (1965). Endotracheal intubation in the pig. *Veterinary Record* **77**, 1465.

Roztočil, V., Němeček, L. & Pavlica, J. (1971). Stresnil as a sedative in horses. *Veterinarni Medicina, Praha* **16**, 613-619.

Roztočil, V., Němeček, L. & Pavlica, J. (1971a). The use of the sedative Stresnil and the hypnotic Hypnodil for surgical operations in pigs. *Veterinarni Medicina, Praha* **16**, 591-602.

Roztočil, V., Němeček, L. Pavlica, J., Bouda, J. & Mišič, B. (1972). Effects of the combination of Stresnil and Hypnodil in the horse. *Acta Veterinaria Brno* **41**, 271-280.

Rubin, G. J. (1968). Applications of electrocardiology in canine medicine. *Journal of the American Veterinary Medical Association* **153**, 17-39.

Rubright, W. C. & Thayer, C. B. (1970). The use of Innovar-Vet[R] as a surgical anaesthetic for the guinea-pig. *Laboratory Animal Care* **20**, 989-991.

Rümke, C. L. & Noordhoek, J. (1969). Sex differences in the duration of hexobarbital narcosis and in serum MUP content in mice. *Archives internationales de pharmacodynamie et de thérapie* **182**, 399-400.

Runham, N. W., Isarankura, K. & Smith, B. J. (1965). Methods for narcotising and anaesthetising gastropods. *Malacologia* **2**, 231-238.

Rush, B. F., Richardson, J. D., Bosomworth, P. & Eiseman, B. (1969). Limitations of blood replacement with electrolyte solutions. *Archives of Surgery* **98**, 49-52.

Rushmer, R. F., Baker, D. W. & Stegall, H. F. (1966). Transcutaneous Doppler flow detection as a nondestructive technique. *Journal of Applied Physiology* **21**, 554-566.

Rutty, D. A. & Thurley, D. C. (1962). Further observations on the use of phencyclidine in monkeys. *Veterinary Record* **74**, 883.

Ryder-Davis, P. (1973). The use of metomidate, an intramuscular narcotic for birds. *Veterinary Record* **92**, 507-509.

Rye, M. M. & Elder, S. T. (1966). A suggestion concerning the anesthetization of the rat. *Journal of Experimental Analysis of Behavior* **9**, 243-244.

Sabawala, P. B. & Keats, A. S. (1972). Anaesthesia for transplantation of heart, lungs, heart and lungs. In *Anaesthesia in organ transplantation* (ed. T. H. Howells & A. W. Grogono). Basel: Karger.

Sable-Amplis, R., Agid, R. & Abadie, D. (1974). Reversal of the action of morphine on the secretory activity of the adrenal cortex. *Biochemical Pharmacology* **23**, 2111-2118.

Sagner, F., Hoffmeister, F. & Kroneberg, G. (1968). Fundamentals of a new type of preparation for analgesia, sedation and relaxation in veterinary medicine, (Bay VA 1470). *Deutsche tierärztliche Wochenschrift* **75**, 565-572.

Saidman, L. J., & Eger, E. I. (1966). The effect of thiopental metabolism on duration of anesthesia. *Anesthesiology* **27**, 118-126.

Saksonov, P. O. & Kozlov, V. A. (1968). Features of the pharmacological action of some anaesthetic drugs in radiation injury. *Voenno-meditsinskii Zhurna* **10**, 40-44.

Sandoz (1959). MS222 Sandoz, the anaesthetic of choice in work with cold-blooded animals. New Jersey: Sandoz Pharmaceuticals.

Sanford, J. (1971). Avian anesthesia. In *Veterinary anaesthesia*. Baltimore: Williams & Wilkins.

Sanger, V. L. & Smith, H. R. (1957). General anaesthesia in birds. *Journal of the American Veterinary Medical Association* **131**, 52-55.

Sauberman, A. J., Gallagher, M. L. & Hedley-Whyte, J. (1974). Uptake, distribution and anaesthetic effect of pentobarbital -2-14C after intravenous injection into mice. *Anesthesiology* **40**, 41-51.

Savage, J. (1935). Copepod infection of speckled trout. *Transactions of the American Fisheries Society* **65**, 339-343.

Savarese, J. J., Antonio, R. P. & Ginsburg, S. (1975). Potential clinical uses of short-acting nondepolarising neuromuscular-blocking agents as predicted from animal experiments. *Anesthesia and Analgesia: Current Researches* **54**, 669-677.

Sawyer, D. C. (1965). Anesthetic techniques of the *Macaca mulatta*. In *Experimental animal anesthesiology* (ed. D. C. Sawyer). Texas: U.S.A.F. School of Aerospace Medicine, Brooks Air Force Base.

Sawyer, D. C. (1965). Anesthetic techniques of rabbits and mice. In *Experimental animal anesthesiology* (ed. D. C. Sawyer). Texas: U.S.A.F. School of Aerospace Medicine, Brooks Air Force Base.

Sawyer, D. C., Lumb, W. V. & Stone, H. L. (1971). Cardiovascular effects of halothane, methoxyflurane, pentobarbital and thiamylal. *Journal of Applied Physiology* **30**, 36-43.

Schaffer, A. (1965). Anaesthesia and sedation. In *Methods of animal experimentation*, Vol. 1 (ed. W. I. Gay), p. 94. New York: Academic Press.

Schaffer, A. (1965). Open forum. In *Experimental animal anesthesiology* (ed. D. C. Sawyer). Texas: U.S.A.F. School of Aerospace Medicine, Brooks Air Force Base.

Schanker, L. S. (1963). Passage of drugs across body membranes. *Pharmacology Revues* **14**, 501-530.

Schauffler, A. F. (1968). Acepromazine and meperidine: new drug combination aids in equine restraint. *Modern Veterinary Practice* **49**, 43-45.

Schauffler, A. F. (1970). Use of acetylpromazine-methadone in dogs. *Modern Veterinary Practice* **51** (2), 72-74.

Scheid, P. & Piiper, J. (1972). Experimental evidence for cross-current gas exchange in avian lungs. *The Physiologist* **15**, 258.

Schleiter, H. & Schneider, J. (1964). Effect of intramuscular injection of succinyl chloride and hyaluronidase in horses. *Wiener tierartzliche Monatsschrift* **51**, 381-391.

Schlarmann, B., Görlitz, B. D., Wintzer, H. J. & Frey, H. H. (1973). Clinical pharmacology of an etorphine-acepromazine preparation: experiments in dogs and horses. *American Journal of Veterinary Research* **34**, 411-415.

Schmidl, J. A. (1974). Experimental use of Rompun in the exotic species. *Journal of Zoo Animal Medicine* **5**, (4), 8-11.

Schmidt, M. J. (1975). A preliminary report on the use of Rompun in captive Asian elephants. *Journal of Zoo Animal Medicine* **6**, 13-21.

Schmidt, R. F. (1963). Pharmacological studies on the primary afferent depolarization of the toad spinal cord. *Pflügers Archiv für die gesamte Physiologie des Menschen und der Tiere* **227**, 325-346.

Scholander, P. F. & Schevill, W. W. (1955). Counter-current vascular heat exchange in the fins of whales. *Journal of Applied Physiology* **8**, 279-282.

Schulz, T. A. & Fowler, M. E. (1974). The clinical effects of CI744 in chinchillas, *Chinchilla villidera* (*Laniger*). *Laboratory Animal Science* **24**, 810-812.

Scott, W. N. (1967). Some additional notes on anaesthesia and euthanasia. In *The UFAW handbook on the care and management of laboratory animals*, pp. 996-997. Edinburgh: Livingstone.

Seal, U.S. & Erickson, A. W. (1969). Immobilisation of carnivora and other mammals with phencyclidine and promazine. *Federation Proceedings* **28**, 1410-1419.

Seal, U.S., Erickson, A. W. & Mayo, J.G. (1970). Drug immobilization of the carnivora. *International Zoo Yearbook* **10**, 157-170.

Sealy, W. C., Young, W. G., Lesage, A. M. & Brown, I. W. (1961). Observations on heart action during hypothermia induced and controlled by a pump oxygenator. *Annals of Surgery* **153**, 797-814.

Sears, B. E. (1971). Complications of ketamine. *Anesthesiology* **35**, 231.

Sebesteny, A. (1971). Fire-risk-free anaesthesia of rodents with halothane. *Laboratory Animals* **5**, 225-231.

Secord, D. C., Taylor, A. W. & Fielding, W. (1973). Effect of anaesthetic agents on exercised atropinised rats. *Laboratory Animal Science* **23**, 397-400.

Sedgwick, C. J. & Acosta, A. L. (1969). Capture drugs. *Modern Veterinary Practice* **50**, 32-36.

Seidensticker, J., Kirti Man Tamang & Gray, C. W. (1974). The use of CI 744 to immobilise free ranging tigers and leopards. *Journal of Zoo Animal Medicine* **5**, 22-25.

Seidenstricker, J. C. & Reynolds, H. V. (1969). Preliminary studies on the use of a general anesthetic in falconiform birds. *Journal of the American Veterinary Medical Association* **155**, 1044-1045.

Seldon, T. H. & Lundy, J. S. (1942). Effect of certain general anesthetic agents on the small blood vessels in the ear of the rabbit. *Anesthesiology* **3**, 146-158.

Selye, H. (1937). Studies in adaptation. *Endocrinology* **21**, 169-188.

Selye, H. (1950). *The physiology and pathology of exposure to stress*. Montreal: Acta.

Serrano, L. & Lees, P. (1976). The applied pharmacology of azaperone in ponies. *Research in Veterinary Science* **20**, 316-323.

Setchell, K. D. R., Shackleton, C. H. L. & Himsworth, R. L. (1975). Studies on plasma corticosteroids in the rhesus monkey (*Macaca mulatta*). *Journal of Endocrinology* **67**, 241-250.

Setnikar, I. & Temelcou, O. (1962). Effect of temperature on toxicity and distribution of pentobarbital and barbital in rats and dogs. *Journal of Pharmacology and Experimental Therapeutics* **135**, 213-222.

Sharma, R. P., Stowe, C. M. & Good, A. L. (1970). Studies on the distribution and metabolism of thiopental in cattle, sheep, goats and swine. *Journal of Pharmacology and Experimental Therapeutics* **172**, 128-137.

Sharpe, J. J., Nelson, S. W. & Lumb, W. V. (1969). Estimation of arterial acid-base values from toenail blood of the anesthetized dog. *American Journal of Veterinary Research* **29**, 2365-2369.

Sharpstone, P., Medley, D. R. K. & Williams, R. (1971). Halothane hepatitis—a preventable disease? *British Medical Journal* 1971 **1**, 448-450.

Shearer, D., Creel, D. & Wilson, C. E. (1973). Strain differences in the response of rats to repeated injections of pentobarbital sodium. *Laboratory Animal Science* **23**, 662-664.

Shelton, G. & Randall, D. J. (1962). The relationship between heart beat and respiration in teleost fish. *Comparative Biochemistry and Physiology* **7**, 237-250.

Sherrard, E. (1966). Anaesthesia of rabbits. *Veterinary Record* **78**, 253-254.

Shoemaker, W. C. & Brown, R. S. (1971). Vasopressors and vasodilators in therapy of shock. *Surgery, Gynecology and Obstetrics* **132**, 51-57.

Sholkoff, S. D., Glickman, M. G. & Powell, M. R. (1969). Restraint of small animals for radiopharmaceutical studies. *Laboratory Animal Care* **19**, 662-663.

Short, C. D. (1964). The application of electroanesthesia in large animals. *Journal of the American Veterinary Medical Association* **145**, 1104-1106.

Short, C. E. (1970a). Advances in small animal anesthesiology. *Journal of the American Veterinary Medical Association* **157**, 1719-1721.

Short, C. E. (1970b). Considerations in anesthetic management for animal experimentation. *Anesthesia and Analgesia: Current Researches* **49**, 125-131.

Short, C. E. (1970c). Bovine inhalation anesthesia. *Journal of the American Veterinary Medical Association* **157**, 1571-1573.

Short, C. E., Keats, A. S., Liotta, D. & Hall, C. W. (1969). Anesthesia for cardiac surgery in calves. *American Journal of Veterinary Research* **29**, 2287-2294.

Short, C. E., Cloyd, G. D. & Ward, J. W. (1970). The use of doxapram hydrochloride with intravenous anesthetics in horses. *Veterinary Medicine—Small Animal Clinician* **65**, 157-160.

Simmons, M. L. & Smith, L. H. (1968). An anesthetic unit for small laboratory animals. *Journal of Applied Physiology* **25**, 324-325.

Simpson, B. R., Strunin, L. & Walton, B. (1971). The halothane dilemma: a case for the defence. *British Medical Journal* 1971 **4**, 96-100.

Sinclair, D. V. (1961). Promazine hydrochloride as a tranquillizer for sows. *Veterinary Record* **73**, 561.

Sis, R. F. & Herron, M. A. (1972). Anesthesia of the newborn kitten. *Laboratory Animal Science* **22**, 746-747.

Skartvedt, S. M. & Lyon, N. C. (1972). A simple apparatus for inducing and maintaining halothane anesthesia of the rabbit. *Laboratory Animal Science* **22**, 922-924.

Slawson, K. B. (1972). Anaesthesia for the patient in renal failure. *British Journal of Anaesthesia* **44**, 277-282.

Sledjeski, M. (1969). A monkey chair for temporary restraint with minimal human contact. *Physiology and Behavior* **4**, 273-276.

Smith, A. C. & Hahn, C. E. W. (1969). Electrodes for the measurement of oxygen and carbon dioxide tensions. *British Journal of Anaesthesia* **41**, 731-741.

Smith, D. M., Goddard, K. M., Wilson, R. B. & Newberne, P. M. (1973). An apparatus for anesthetizing small laboratory rodents. *Laboratory Animal Science* **23**, 869-871.

Smith, G. S., Smith, J. L., Mameesh, M. S., Simon, J. & Johnson, B. C. (1964). Hypertension and cardiovascular abnormalities in starved-refed swine. *Journal of Nutrition* **82**, 173-182.

Smith, J. B. & Hill, H. H. (1972). Correspondence on ketamine HCl in North American Golden Eagle. *Veterinary Medicine—Small Animal Clinician* **67**, 353.

Smith, L. S. & Bell, G. R. (1967). Anaesthetic and surgical technique for Pacific salmon. *Journal of the Fisheries Research Board of Canada* **24**, 1579-1588.

Smith, K. (1977). Personal communication.

Smith, R. H., Goodwin, C., Fowler, E., Smith, G. W. & Volpitto, P. P. (1961a). Electronarcosis produced by a combination of direct and alternating current. A preliminary study. I. Apparatus and electrodes. *Anesthesiology* **22**, 163-168.

Smith, R. H., Gramling, Z. W., Smith, G. W. & Volpitto, P. P. (1961b). Electronarcosis by combination of direct and alternating current. 2. Effects on dog brain, as shown by EEG and microscopic study. *Anesthesiology* **22**, 970-975.

Smith, S. M. & Kaplan, H. M. (1974). Ketamine-methoxyflurane anaesthesia for the Mongolian gerbil, *Meriones unguiculatus*. *Laboratory Animals* **8**, 213-216.

Smuts, G. L. (1973). Ketamine hydrochloride: a useful drug for the field immobilisation of the spotted hyaena, *Crocuta crocuta*. *Koedoe* **16**, 175-180.

Smuts, G. L., Bryden, B. R., de Vos, V. & Young, E. (1973). Some practical advantages of CI 581 (ketamine) for the field immobilisation of larger wild felines, with comparative notes on baboons and impala. *Lammergeyer* **18**, 1-14.

Snyder, S. H., Axelrod, J. & Zweig, M. (1967). Circadian rhythm in the serotonin content of the rat pineal gland: regulating factors. *Journal of Pharmacology and Experimental Therapeutics* **158**, 206-213.

Sodi-Pallares, D., Testelli, M. R., Fishleder, B. L., Bisteni, A., Medrano, G. A., Friedland, C. & de Micheli, A. (1962). Effects of an intravenous infusion of a potassium-glucose-insulin solution on the electrocardiographic signs of myocardial infarction. *American Journal of Cardiology* **9**, 166-181.

Soifer, F. K. (1968). Surgery successful on 500-lb. tortoise. *Journal of the American Veterinary Medical Association* **152**, 418.

Soivio, A. & Oikari, A. (1976). Haematological effects of experimental stress on a teleost, *Esox lucius*. *Journal of Fish Biology* **8**, 397-411.

Soivio, A., Nyholm, K. & Huhti, M. (1977). Effects of anaesthesia with MS222, neutralised MS222 and benzocaine on the blood constituents of rainbow trout, *Salmo gairdneri*. *Journal of Fish Biology* **10**, 91-101.

Soivio, A., Westman, K. & Nyholm, K. (1974*a*). The influence of changes in oxygen tension on the haematocrit value of blood samples from asphyxic rainbow trout (*Salmo gairdneri*). *Aquaculture* **3**, 395-401.

Soivio, A., Westman, K. & Nyholm, K. (1974*b*). Changes in haematocrit values in blood samples treated with and without oxygen: a comparative study with four Salmonid species. *Journal of Fish Biology* **6**, 763-769.

Soma, L. R. (1965). Cited by Lumb, W. V. & Jones, E. W. (1973). In *Veterinary anesthesia*, p. 237. Philadelphia: Lea & Febiger.

Soma, L. R. (1971). In *Textbook of veterinary anesthesia* (ed. L. R. Soma). Baltimore: Williams & Wilkins.

Soma, L. R. & Kenny, R. (1967). Respiratory, cardiovascular, metabolic and electroencephalographic effects of doxapram hydrochloride in the dog. *American Journal of Veterinary Research* **28**, 191-198.

Soma, L. R. & Shields, D. R. (1964). Neuroleptanalgesia produced by fentanyl and droperidol. *Journal of the American Veterinary Medical Association* **145**, 897-902.

Spalding, V. T. & Heymann, C. S. (1962). The value of phencyclidine in the anaesthesia of monkeys. *Veterinary Record* **74**, 158.

Sparks, D. L., Corssen, G., Aizenman, B. & Black, J. (1975). Further studies of the neural mechanisms of ketamine-induced anesthesia in the rhesus monkey. *Anesthesia and Analgesia: Current Researches* **54**, 189-195.

Sparks, D. L., Corssen, G., Sides, J., Black, J. & Kholeif, A. (1973). Ketamine-induced anesthesia: Neural mechanisms in the rhesus monkey. *Anesthesia and Analgesis: Current Researches* **52**, 288-297.

Spath, J. A., Gorczinski, R. S. & Lefer, A. M. (1973). Possible mechanism of the beneficial actions of glucocorticosteroids in circulatory shock. *Surgery, Gynecology and Obstetrics* **137**, 597-607.

Spellerberg, I. F. (1969). Capturing and immobilising McCormick skuas. *Journal of the American Veterinary Medical Association* **155**, 1034-1040.

Stahl, W. R. (1967). Scaling of respiratory variables in mammals. *Journal of Applied Physiology* **22**, 453-460.

Stahl, W. R. & Malinow, M. R. (1967). A survey of physiological measurements in *Macaca mulatta*. *Folia primatologica* **7**, 12-33.

Starzecki, B., Reddin, J. L. & Spink, W. E. (1968). Effect of isoproterenol on survival in canine endotoxin shock. *Annals of Surgery* **167**, 35-40.

Stefanova-Mazakova, Z., Puchta, V. & Romonovsky, A. (1964). The use of MS222 in amphibians. In *Small animal anaesthesia* (ed. O. Graham-Jones), p. 77. Oxford: Pergamon.

Steffey, E. P., Gillespie, J. R., Berry, J. D., Eger, E. I. II & Munson, E. S. (1974). Anesthetic potency (MAC) of nitrous oxide in the dog, cat and stump-tail monkey. *Journal of Applied Physiology* **36**, 530-532.

Steinbrecht, K. (1957) Narkose von fischen. *Aquarien und Terrarien Zeitschrift Stuttgart* **10**, 305-306.

Stephen, C. R., Margolis, G., Fabian, L. W. & Bourgeois-Gavardin, M. (1958). Laboratory observations with fluothane. *Anesthesiology* **19**, 770-781.

Steven, D. M. (1967). In *The UFAW handbook on the care and management of laboratory animals*. Edinburgh: Livingstone.

Stevenson, D. E. (1960). A review of some side-effects of muscle relaxants in small animals. *Journal of Small Animal Practice* **1**, 77-83.

Stevenson, D. E. (1964). General aspects of rodent anaesthesia. In *Small animal anaesthesia* (ed. O. Graham-Jones), pp. 89-98. Oxford: Pergamon.

Steward, A. (1973). A simple and inexpensive method for anaesthetising small animals. *Veterinary Record* **93**, 640.

Steward, A., Mapleson, W. W. & Allott, P. R. (1972). A comparison of in vivo and in vitro partition coefficients for halothane in the rabbit. *British Journal of Anaesthesia* **44**, 650-655.

Stewart, W. E. (1965). Methohexital sodium, brevane, anaesthesia for calves and sheep. *Journal of Dairy Science* **48**, 251.

Stewart, S., Edmunds, L. H., Kirklin, J. W. & Allarde, R. R. (1973). Spontaneous breathing with continuous positive airway pressure after open intracardiac operations in infants. *Journal of Thoracic and Cardiovascular Surgery* **65**, 37-44.

Stock, J. E. (1973). Advances in small animal anaesthesia. *Veterinary Record*, **92**, 351-354.

Stockmann, U., Liepe, B., Baer, P., Wallner, F. (1974) A device for long-term respirating and anesthetising rats. *Journal of Surgical Research* **16**, 183-184.

Stoddart, J. C. & Wardle, E. N. (1974). Post-traumatic respiratory distress due to endotoxinaemia and intravascular coagulation. *British Journal of Anaesthesia* **46**, 892-896.

Stoliker, H. E. (1965). The physiologic and pharmacologic effects of Sernylan: a review. In *Experimental animal anesthesiology* (ed. D. C. Sawyer). Brooks Air Force Base, Texas: U.S.A.F. School of Aerospace Medicine.

Stormont, C. & Suzuki, Y. (1970). Atropinesterase and cocainesterase of rabbit serum: localization of the enzyme activity in isozymes. *Science, New York* **167**, 200-202.

Stowe, C. M. (1955). Intravascular injection ot succinyl dicholine chloride. *Veterinary Record* **67**, 174-175.

Strack, L. E. & Kaplan, H. M. (1968). Fentanyl and droperidol for surgical anesthesis of rabbits. *Journal of the American Veterinary Medical Association* **153**, 822-827.

Straub, O. C. (1971). Anaesthesie beim Schaf durch Rompun. *Deutsche tierärztliche Wochenschrift* **78**, 537-538.

Strittmatter, J. von. (1972). Anaesthesie beim Gold-hamster mit Ketamine und Methoxyflurane. *Zeitschrift für Versuchtierkunde* **14,** 129-133.

Strobel, G. E. & Wollman, H. (1969). Pharmacology of anesthetic agents. *Federation Proceedings: Federation of American Societies for Experimental Biology* **28,** 1386-1403.

Stromberg, B. & Story, E. (1972). *Acta radiologica,* Supplementum 319, Progress in Veterinary Radiology, Proceedings of the 2nd International Conference of Veterinary Radiologists, Stockholm, 1970.

Strzyzowski, C. (1920). Préparations et propriétés physiologiques de la tricaine. *Bulletin de la Société vaudoise des sciences naturelle* **53,** 199-205.

Stunkard, J. A. & Miller, J. C. (1974). An outline guide to general anaesthesia in exotic species. *Veterinary Medicine—Small animal Clinician* **69,** 1181-1186.

Suga, N. (1964). Single unit activity in cochlear nucleus and inferior colliculus of echolocating bats. *Journal of Physiology, London* **172,** 449-474.

Sulyok, E., Jequier, E. & Prod'hom, L. S. (1973). Respiratory contribution to the thermal balance of the newborn infant under various ambient conditions. *Pediatrics* **51,** 641-650.

Suomalainen, P. & Suvanto, I. (1953). Studies on the physiology of the hibernating hedgehog. I. The body temperature. *Annales Acadamie Scientarum Fennicae, series A, section IV (Biologica)* **20,** 1-20.

Swan, H. J. C., Ganz, W., Forrester, J. & Chonette, D. (1970). Catheterisation of the heart in man with use of a flow-directed catheter. *New England Journal of Medicine* **283,** 447-451.

Swanson, E. E. (1952). Sodium 5-allyl-5-(1-methylbutyl)-2-thiobarbiturate, a short-acting anesthetic. *Journal of Pharmacy and Pharmacology* **3,** 112-116.

Swanson, E. E. & Fry, W. E. (1957). A comparative study of short acting barbituric acid derivatives. *Journal of the American Association* **26,** 1248-1250.

Sweebe, E. E. (1936). Anesthesia. *Veterinary Medicine* **31,** 158-162.

Sybesma, W. & Eikelenboom, G. (1969). Malignant hyperthermia syndrome in pigs. *Netherlands Journal of Veterinary Science* **2** (2), 155-160.

Sykes, A. H. (1964). Some aspects of anaesthesia in the adult fowl. In *Small animal anaesthesia* (ed. O. Graham-Jones), pp. 117-121. Oxford: Pergamon.

Sykes, M. K. (1963). Venous pressure as a clinical indication of the adequacy of transfusion. *Annals of the Royal College of Surgeons of England* **33,** 185-197.

Symoens, J. (1970). Prevention and cure of aggressiveness in pigs using the sedative azaperone. *Deutsche tierärztliche Wochenschrift* **77,** 144-148.

Symoens, J. & Van den Brande, M. (1969). Prevention and cure of aggressiveness in pigs using the sedative azaperone. *Veterinary Record* **85,** 64-67.

Szabuniewicz, M. & McCrady, J. D. (1969). Some aspects of the anatomy and physiology of the armadillo. *Laboratory Animal Care* **19,** 843-848.

Taber, R. & Irwin, S. (1969). Anesthesia in the mouse. *Federation Proceedings* **28,** 1528-1532.

Taggart, P., Carruthers, M. & Somerville, W. (1973). Electrocardiogram, plasma catecholamines and lipids, and their modification by oxprenolol when speaking before an audience. *Lancet* 1973 **2,** 341-388.

Talaat, S. M., Massion, W. H. & Schilling, J. A. (1964). Effects of adenosine triphosphate administration in irreversible hemorrhagic shock. *Surgery* **55,** 813-819.

Tan, E. S. & Snow, H. D. (1968). Continuous epidural anaesthesia in the guinea-pig. *American Journal of Veterinary Research* **29,** 487-490.

Tarin, D. & Sturdee, A. (1972). Surgical anaesthesia of mice: evaluation of tribromo-ethanol, ether, halothane and methoxyflurane, and development of a reliable technique. *Laboratory Animals* **6,** 79-84.

Tavernor, W. D. (1959). The use of succinyl choline chloride as a casting agent in the horse. *Veterinary Record* **71,** 774.

Tavernor, W. D. (1960*a*). Clinical observation on the use of trimeprazine tartrate as a sedative and premedicant in horses, pigs and dogs. *Veterinary Record* **72,** 317-321.

Tavernor, W. D. (1960*b*). The effect of succinyl choline chloride on the heart of the horse: clinical and pathological aspect. *Veterinary Record* **72,** 569-572.

Tavernor, W. D. (1962). Recent trends in equine anaesthesia. *Veterinary Record* **74,** 595-598.

Tavernor, W. D. (1963). A study of the effect of phencyclidine in the pig. *Veterinary Record* **75,** 1377-1383.

Tavernor, W. D. & Lees, P. (1969). The influence of propanolol on cardiovascular function in conscious and anaesthetised horses. *Archives internationales pharmacodynamie et de thérapie* **180,** 89-99.

Tavernor, W. D. & Lees, P. (1970). The influence of thiopentone and suxamethonium on cardiovascular and respiratory function in the horse. *Research in Veterinary Science* **11,** 45-53.

Taylor, P., Hopkins, L., Young, M. & McFadyen, I. R. (1972). Ketamine anaesthesia in the pregnant sheep. *Veterinary Record* **90,** 35-36.

Terblanche, J., Peacock, J. H., Bowes, J. & Hobbs, K. E. F. (1968). The technique of orthotopic liver homotransplantation in the pig. *Journal of Surgical Research* **8,** 151-160.

Teske, R. H. & Carter, G. G. (1971). Effect of chloramphenicol on pentobarbital-induced anesthesia in dogs. *Journal of the American Veterinary Medical Association* **159,** 777-780.

Thal, A. P., Brown, E. B., Hermreck, A. S. & Bell, H. H. (1971). *Shock, a physiological basis for treatment.* Chicago: Year Book Medical Publishers.

Thienpont, D. & Niemegeers, C. J. E. (1965). Propoxate (R7464): a new potent anaesthetic agent in cold-blooded vertebrates. *Nature, London* **205,** 1018-1019.

Thomasson, B., Ruuskanen, O. & Merikanto, J. (1974). Spinal anaesthesia in the guinea-pig. *Laboratory Animals* **8,** 241-244.

Thompson, R. B. (1959). Tricaine methanesulfonate (MS-222) in transport of cutthroat trout. *Progressive Fish Culturist* **21,** 96-98.

Thurman, J. C., Kumar, A. & Link, R. P. (1973). Evaluation of ketamine hydrochloride as an anaesthetic in sheep. *Journal of the American Veterinary Medical Association* **162,** 293-297.

Thurman, J. C., Nelson, D. R. & Christie, C. J. (1972). Ketamine anesthesia in swine. *Journal of the American Veterinary Medical Association* **160,** 1325-1330.

283

Thurman, J. C., Romack, F. E. & Garner, H. E. (1968). Excursions of the bovine eyeball during gaseous anesthesia. *Veterinary Medicine* **63**, 967-970.

Tipton, C. M. (1965). Training and bradycardia in rats. *American Journal of Physiology* **209**, 1089-1099.

Tipton, C. M. & Taylor, B. (1965). Influence of atropine on heart rate of rats. *American Journal of Physiology* **208**, 408-484.

Titchen, D. A., Steel, J. D. & Hamilton, F. J. (1949). Clinical observations on thiobarbiturate anaesthesia in sheep. *Australian Veterinary Journal* **25**, 257-261.

Trinkle, J., Helton, N., Wood, R. & Bryant, L. (1969). Metabolic comparison of a new pulsatile pump and a roller pump for cardiopulmonary bypass. *Journal of Thoracic and Cardiovascular Surgery* **58**, 562-569.

Tuffery, A. A. (1967). In *The UFAW handbook on the care and management of laboratory animals.* Edinburgh: Livingstone.

Turbyfill, C. L., Peterson, R. P. & Soderwall, A. L. (1962). The cardiac puncture in adult, fetal and young golden hamsters. *Turtox News* **40**, 162-163.

Turner, A. W. & Hodgetts, V. E. (1956). Barbiturate antagonism: the use of 'megimide' and of 'daptazole' in curtailing 'nembutal' anaesthesia and in treating apnoeic 'nembutal' intoxication in sheep. *Australian Veterinary Journal* **32**, 49-52.

Tyagi, R. P. S. & Lumb, W. V. (1961). Uterine healing after caesarotomy in goats. *American Journal of Veterinary Research* **22**, 1097-1105.

Tyagi, R. P. S., Arnold, J. P., Usenik, E. A. & Fletcher, T. F. (1964). Effects of thiopental sodium (pentothal sodium) anaesthesia on the horse. *Cornell Veterinarian* **54**, 584-692.

Tyagi, R. P. S., Kumar, R. & Manohar, M. (1973). Studies on intravenous retrograde regional anaesthesia for the forelimbs of ruminants. *Australian Veterinary Journal* **49**, 321-324.

U.F.A.W. (1963). *The humane killing of crabs and lobsters.* London: UFAW.

Usenik, E. A. & Cronkite, E. P. (1965). Effects of barbiturate anesthetics on leukocytes in normal and splenectomised dogs. *Anesthesia and Analgesia: Current Researches* **44**, 167-170.

Vale, R. J. (1973). Normothermia: its place in operative and post-operative care. *Anaesthesia* **28**, 241-245.

Valenstein, E. S. (1961). A note on anaesthetising rats and guinea-pigs. *Journal of the Experimental Analysis of Behaviour* **4**, 6-9.

van Citters, R. L. & Lasry, J. E. (1965). Cardiovascular function in adult baboons as indicated by standard diagnostic tests. *Folioa primatologica* **3**, 13–21.

Van Laun, T. (1977). Anaesthetising donkeys. *Veterinary Record* **100**, 391.

Van Nimwegen, C., Van Eijnsbergen, B., Boter, J. & Mullink, J. W. M. A. (1973). A simple device for indirect measurement of blood pressure in mice. *Laboratory Animals* **7**, 73-84.

Van Proosdij-Hartzema, E. G. (1954). Indirect measurement of the blood pressure in the rat. *Acta physiologica et pharmacologica neerlandica* **3**, 472-474.

Van Tyne, J. & Berger, A. J. (1959). *Fundamentals of ornithology.* New York: Wiley.

Vaughan, R. S., Mapleson, W. W. & Mushin, W. W. (1973). Prevention of pollution of operating theatres with halothane vapour by adsorption with activated charcoal. *British Medical Journal* 1973 **1**, 727-729.

Vaughan, L. C. (1961). Anaesthesia in the pig. *British Veterinary Journal* **117**, 383-391.

Vaughan, L. C. (1977). Personal communication.

Vick, J. A. (1964). Endotoxin shock in the primate. Treatment with phenoxybenzamine. *Journal of Clinical Investigation* **43**, 279-284.

Virtue, R. W., Lund, L. O., Phelps, M. K., Vogel, J. H. K., Beckwith, H. & Heron, M. (1966). Difluoromethyl 1,1,2-trifluoro-2-chloroethyl ether as an anaesthetic agent; results with dogs. *Canadian Anaesthetists' Society Journal* **13**, 233-241.

Vivien, J. H. (1941). Contribution à l'étude de la physiologie hypophysaire dans ses relations avec l'appareil génital, la thyroide et les corps suprarenaux chez les poissons sélaciens et téléostéens. *Bulletin biologique de la France et de la Belgique* **75**, 257-309.

von Frisch, K. & Stetter, H. (1932). Untersuchungen über den sitz des gehörsinnes bei der elritze. *Zeitschrift für vergleichende Physiologie* **17**, 686-801.

Vos-Maas, M. G. & Zwart, P. (1976). A technique for intravenous injection in the red-eared turtle (*Pseudemys scripta elegans*). *Laboratory Animals* **10**, 399-401.

Waldhausen, J. A., Kilman, J. W. & Abel, F. L. (1965). Effects of catecholamines on the heart. *Archives of Surgery* **91**, 86-91.

Wallace, G. D., Fodor, A. R. & Barton, L. H. (1960). Restraint of chimpanzees with perphenazine. *Journal of the American Veterinary Medical Association* **136**, 222-224.

Wallace, J., Johnson, N. W. & Kenney, E. B. (1972). Repeated general anaesthesia in Macaques by intramuscular methohexitone sodium. *Laboratory Animals* **6**, 61-66.

Wallach, J. D. (1969). Medical care of reptiles. *Journal of the American Veterinary Medical Association* **153**, 1017-1034.

Wallach, J. D. & Anderson, J. L. (1968). Oripavine (M.99) combinations and solvents for immobilisation of the African elephant. *Journal of the American Veterinary Medical Association* **153**, 793-797.

Wallach, J. D. & Hoessle, C. (1970). M.99 as an immobilising agent in poikilothermes. *Veterinary Medicine—Small Animal Clinician* **65**, 161-162.

Wallach, J. D., Frueh, R. & Lentz, M. (1967). The use of M.99 as an immobilising and analgesic agent in captive wild animals. *Journal of the American Veterinary Medical Association* **151**, 870-876.

Walton, C. H., Uhl, J. W., Egner, W. M. & Livingstone, H. H. (1950). Use of thiopental sodium intravenously in the presence of hepatic damage; an experimental study. *Archives of Surgery* **60**, 986-994.

Wampler, S. N. (1969). Husbandry and health problems of armadillos *Dasypus novemcinctus. Laboratory Animal Care* **19**, 391-393.

Ward, G. S., Johnsen, D. O. & Roberts, C. R. (1974). The use of CI-744 as an anesthetic for laboratory animals. *Laboratory Animal Science* **24**, 737-742.

Warner, H. E. (1968). New drug combination for small animal restraint. *Modern Veterinary Practice* **49**, 20.

Warren, A. G. (1964). In *Small animal anaesthesia* (ed. O. Graham-Jones), p. 239. Oxford: Pergamon.

Wass, J. A. & Kaplan, H. M. (1974). Methoxyflurane anesthesia for *Rana pipiens*. *Laboratory Animal Science* 24, 669-671.

Wass, J. A., Keene, J. R. & Kaplan, H. M. (1974). Ketamine-methoxyflurane anesthesia for rabbits. *American Journal of Veterinary Research* 35, 317-318.

Watson, C. R. R. & Way, J. S. (1972). Unusual tolerance of Marsupials to barbiturate anaesthesia. *International Zoo Yearbook* 12, 208-211.

Watson, S. C. & Cowie, A. T. (1966). A simple closed-circuit apparatus for cyclopropane and halothane anaesthesia of the rabbit. *Laboratory Animal Care* 10, 515-519.

Weatherall, J. A. C. (1960). Anaesthesia in new-born animals. *British Journal of Pharmacology and Chemotherapy* 15, 454-457.

Weaver, A. D. (1972). Intravenous local anaesthesia of the lower limb in cattle. *Journal of the American Veterinary Medical Association* 160. 55-57.

Webb, W. R., Lemmer, R. A. & Elman, R. (1950). Absorption rates, electrolyte and volume changes following subcutaneous and intraperitoneal injections of solutions containing salt, glucose and amino acids. *Surgery, Gynecology and Obstetrics* 91, 265-270.

Weberlein, M. K., McClumpha, C. A., Brengle, L. A., Lickfeldt, W. E. & Dawson, H. A. (1959). Promazine in ' canine medicine. *Journal of the American Veterinary Medical Association* 134, 518-519.

Webster, A. J. F. (1967). Continuous measurement of heart rate as an indicator of the energy expenditure of sheep. *British Journal of Nutrition* 21, 769-785.

Wedemeyer, G. (1970). Stress of anaesthesia with MS222 and benzocaine in rainbow trout (*Salmo gairdneri*). *Journal of the Fisheries Research Board of Canada* 27, 909-914.

Weeks, J. R. & Jones, J. A. (1960). Routine direct measurement of arterial pressure in unanaesthetised rats. *Proceedings of the Society for Experimental Biology and Medicine* 104, 646-648.

Weidman, F. D. (1930). Alopecia in a woodchuck. *Report: Laboratory and Museum of Comparative Pathology of the Zoological Society of Philadelphia: 58th Annual Report*, pp. 54-55.

Weil, M. H., Shubin, N. & Biddle, M. (1964). Shock caused by Gram-negative micro-organisms. *Annals of Internal Medicine* 60, 384-400.

Weinreb, H. L., Naftchi, N. & Mendlowitz, M. (1960). The measurement of digital arterial blood pressure. *Archives of Surgery* 80, 131-134.

Weisbroth, S. H. & Fudens, J. H. (1972). Use of ketamine hydrochloride as an anesthetic in laboratory rabbits, rats, mice and guinea pigs. *Laboratory Animal Science* 22, 904-906.

Weisner, B. P. (1934). The post-natal development of the genital organs of the albino rat. *Journal of Obstetrics and Gynaecology of the British Empire* 41, 867-922.

Welles, J. S., McMahon, R. E. & Doran, W. J. (1963). The metabolism and excretion of methohexital in the rat and dog. *Journal of Pharmacology and Experimental Therapeutics* 139, 166-171.

Wentges, H. (1975). Medicine administration by blow-pipe. *Veterinary Record* 97, 281.

Wesolowski, S. A. (1962). *Evaluation of tissue and prosthetic vascular crafts*. Springfield, Illinois: Thomas.

Wesolowski, S. A., Fisher, J. H., Fennessey, J. F., Cubiles, R. & Welch, C. S. (1952). Recovery of the dog's heart after varying periods of acute ischemia. *Surgical Forum* 3, 270-277.

Westhues, M. & Fritsch, R. (1964). *Animal anaesthesia I. Local anaesthesia* Edinburgh: Oliver & Boyd.

White, J. J., Andrews, H. G., Risemberg, H., Mazur, D. & Haller, J. A. (1971). Prolonged respiratory support in newborn infants with a membrane oxygenator. *Surgery* 70, 288-296.

White, P. F., Johnston, R. R. & Eger, E. I. (1974). Determination of anesthetic requirements in rats. *Anesthesiology* 40, 52-57.

White, P. F., Johnston, R. R. & Pudwill, C. R. (1975). Interaction of ketamine and halothane in rats. *Anesthesiology* 42, 179-186.

Whitney, R. (1963). In *Animals for research*, pp. 365-392. New York: Academic Press.

Whittow, G. C. & Ossorio, N. (1961). A new technique for anaesthetising birds. *Veterinary Record* 73, 134-142.

Whittow, G. C. & Ossorio, N. (1970). A new technique for anesthetising birds. *Laboratory Animal Care* 20, 651-656.

Wiedeman, M. P. (1963). Dimensions of blood vessels from distributing artery to collecting vein. *Circulation Research* 12, 375-378.

Wilgus, H. S. (1960). Reserpine for tranquillising geese. *The 2nd Conference on the Use of Reserpine in Poultry Production. The Institute of Agriculture, Minnesota, 1960.*

Wilkins, J. H. (1961). The effect of a new analgesic induction agent on goats. *Veterinary Record* 73, 767-768.

Willey, G. L. (1962). Effect of antisympathomimetic drugs on plasma concentrates of catacholamines. *British Journal of Pharmacology* 19, 365-374.

Williams, J. R., Harrison, T. R. & Grollmann, A. (1939). A simple method for determining the systolic blood pressure of the unanaesthetised rat. *Journal of Clinical Investigation* 18, 373-376.

Williams, L. E. (1965). *Proceedings of the Annual Conference of the S.E. Association of Game Fisheries Commission*, p. 1.

Williams, L. E. (1967). Preliminary report of Methoxy-mol to capture turkeys. *Proceedings, 21st Annual Conference, S.E. Association of Game and Fish Commissioners.*

Wilson, G. R. (1974). The restraint of Red kangaroos using etorphine-acepromazine and etorphine-methotrimeprazine mixtures. *Australian Veterinary Journal* 50, 454-458.

Wilson, J. T. (1969). A simple restraining apparatus for rats. *Laboratory Animal Care* 19, 533-534.

Wilson, J. W. (1972). Treatment or prevention of pulmonary cellular damage with pharmacological doses of corticosteroid. *Surgery, Gynecology and Obstetrics* 134, 675-681.

Wilson, R. F., Jablonski, D. V. & Thal, A. P. (1964). Use of dibenzylline in human shock. *Surgery* 56, 172-183.

Winter, C. A. & Flataker, L. (1962). Cage design as a factor influencing acute toxicity of respiratory depressant drugs in rats. *Toxicology and Applied Pharmacology* **4,** 650-655.

Withrow, G. & Devine, M. C. (1972). A new restraining device for testing anti-radiation drugs in monkeys. *Laboratory Animal Science* **22,** 419-423.

Witschi, E. (1927). Testis grafting in tadpoles of *Rana temporaria* and its bearing on the hormone theory of sex determination. *Journal of Experimental Zoology* **47,** 269-274.

Woldring, S., Owens, G. & Woolford, D. C. (1966). Blood gases: continuous *in vivo* recordings of partial pressures by mass spectrography. *Science, New York* **153,** 885-887.

Wolf, S. M., Simmons, R. L. & Nastok, W. L. (1964). Effect of age and sex on sensitivity to d-tubocurarine in the rat. *Proceedings of the Society for Experimental Biology and Medicine* **117,** 1-3.

Wolff, W. A., Lumb, W. V. & Ramsey, K. (1967). Effects of halothane and chloroform anaesthesia on the equine liver. *American Journal of Veterinary Research* **28,** 1363-1372.

Wong, D. H. W. & Jenkins, L. C. (1974). An experimental study of the mechanism of action of ketamine on the central nervous system. *Canadian Anaesthetists' Society Journal* **21,** 57-67.

Wood, E. M. (1956). Urethane as a carcinogen. *Progressive Fish Culturist* **18,** 135-136.

Woods, L. A., Wyngaarden, J. B., Rennick, B. & Seevers, M. H. (1967). The cardiovascular effects of sodium pentothal and sodium 5-allyl-5(1-methylbutyl)-2-thiobarbiturate in the dog. *Federation Proceedings. Federation of American Societies for Experimental Biology* **6,** 387.

Wood-Smith, F. G., Vickers, M. D. & Stewart, H. C. (1973). *Drugs in anaesthetic practice*, 4th ed. London: Butterworth.

Wright, C. A. (1967). In *The UFAW handbook on the care and management of laboratory animals*, p. 987. Edinburgh: Livingstone.

Wright, J. G. (1957). *Veterinary anaesthesia*, 4th ed. London: Baillière, Tindall & Cox.

Wright, J. G. & Hall, L. W. (1961). *Veterinary anaesthesia & analgesia* 5th ed. London: Baillière, Tindall & Cox.

Wright, M. P. & Holmes, C. M. (1964). In *Small animal anaesthesia* (ed. O. Graham-Jones), pp. 199-203. Oxford: Pergamon.

Wyke, B. D. (1957). Electrographic monitoring of anaesthesia. *Anaesthesia* **12,** 157-173.

Wyler, F. & Weisser, K. (1972). Effect of halothane anaesthesia on distribution of cardiac output and organ blood flow in the rabbit. *British Journal of Anaesthesia* **44,** 551-556.

Wyler, F., Rutishauser, M. & Weisser, K. (1972). Endotoxin induced regional circulatory reactions in the rabbit with and without halothane anesthesia. *Journal of Surgical Research* **13,** 13-19.

Wyngaarden, J. B., Woods, L. A. & Seevers, M. H. (1947). The cumulative action of certain thiobarbiturates in dogs. *Federation Proceedings. Federation of American Societies for Experimental Biology* **6,** 388-389.

Yankow, M. (1962). An unusual case of limb regeneration. *Turtox News* **40,** 146.

Yerganian, G. (1967). In *The UFAW handbook on the care and management of laboratory animals*. Edinburgh: Livingstone.

York, W. F. & Quinn, W. C. (1973). Restraint of wild animals by pharmacological methods. Privately circulated.

Young, D. G. (1973). Fluid balance in paediatric surgery. *British Journal of Anaesthesia* **45,** 953-957.

Young, E. (1973). *The capture and care of wild animals.* Cape Town: Human & Rousseau.

Young, J. Z. (1935). The photoreceptors of lampreys. II. The functions of the pineal complex. *Journal of Experimental Biology* **12,** 254-270.

Young, R. & Kaplan, M. (1960). Anesthesia of turtles with chlorpromazine and sodium pentobarbital. *Proceedings of the Animal Care Panel* **10,** 57-61.

Young, W. A. (1948). Wing amputation of birds in lieu of pinioning. *Journal of the American Veterinary Medical Association* **122,** 224-226.

Youth, R. A., Simmerman, S. J., Newell, R. & King, R. A. (1973). Ketamine anesthesia for rats. *Physiology and Behavior* **10,** 633-636.

Zeuthen, E. (1942). The ventilation of the respiratory tract in birds. *Kongelige Danske Videnskabernes Selskabs Biologiske Meddelelser* **17,** 1-51.

Zimmerman, J. E. (1971). Respiratory failure complicating traumatic acute renal failure: clinical features and management. *Annals of Surgery* **174,** 12-18.

INDEX